THE HOMEMAKER/HOME HEALTH AIDE

Grace Odiase

THE HOMEMAKER/ HOME HEALTH AIDE

Julie K. Wernig, R.N., B.S.N., M.H.A.

Sheila A. Sorrentino, R.N., B.S.N., M.A.
Assistant Dean, Academic Programs and Services
Kankakee Community College
Kankakee, Illinois

with 495 illustrations

The C. V. Mosby Company
St. Louis ● Baltimore ● Toronto ● 1989

A TRADITION OF PUBLISHING EXCELLENCE

Editor in chief: David T. Culverwell
Editorial Project Manager: Lisa G. Cunninghis
Project Management: Editing, Design and Production, Inc.
Book design: Liz Fett
Cover design: Rick Brady/Brady Photographic

Printed in the United States of America

The C. V. Mosby Company

11830 Westline Industrial Drive, St. Louis, Missouri 63146

Library of Congress Cataloging in Publication Data

Wernig, Julie K.
  The homemaker/home health aide / Julie K. Wernig, & Sheila A.
Sorrentino.
      p.   cm.
  An adaptation of: Mosby's textbook for nursing assistants / Sheila
A. Sorrentino. 2nd ed. 1987.
  Includes index.
  ISBN 0-8016-5390-8
  1. Home health aides.   2. Home care services.   I. Sorrentino,
Sheila A.   II. Sorrentino, Sheila A. Mosby's textbook for nursing
assistants.   III. Title.
  [DNLM: 1. Home Care Services—organization & administration.
2. Nurses's Aides. 3. Nursing Care.   WY 115 W496h]
RA645.3.W47   1989
649'.8—dc19
DNLM/DLC
for Library of Congress   88-8267
                                                                CIP

CL/VH/VH 9 8 7 6 5

To the memory of Fred and Hilda Lund, special
people in the lives of the Sorrentino kids

—S. A. S.

To Mom and Dad for their unlimited love, support and
encouragement

—J.K.W.

Acknowledgment

Writing this book has been a challenging and educational experience. The continued support, encouragement, and technical expertise of friends and colleagues throughout the various phases of this project have made its completion possible.

I would like to extend a special thanks to the following individuals:

- Ron, who was always willing to listen and support my involvement in this project
- David Culverwell, who provided the opportunity and continually maintained positive enthusiasm for the project
- Ann Moy, who listened and understood
- The reviewers, who provided invaluable suggestions
- Pat Bruce, who contributed the chapter "Communicating Effectively"
- My colleagues at Enloe Hospital (Chico, California) and Peninsula Hospitals (Burlingame, California), who were supportive throughout this project
- Hank, Barb, Kim, Beth and the many friends and associates, whose support and friendship contributed greatly to the development of this book
- Glenn Davidson (my father), who provided countless hours of computer and technical support
- Joan Davidson (my mother), who always had encouraged me towards completion of the project

Julie K. Wernig

Preface

The *Homemaker/Home Health Aide* is designed for individuals preparing to be homemakers/home health aides in today's society. Intended for use in any educational program for homemakers/home health aides, the book focuses on safe and effective functioning when giving client care. An adaptation of *Mosby's Textbook for Nursing Assistants* (second edition), the book emphasizes caring, understanding, and respect for the client as an individual.

The book is divided into 23 chapters. Basic needs, the total person, and essential nursing concepts and skills are the basis for the book's organizational pattern. Where appropriate throughout the text, home care adaptations are identified for the homemaker/home health aide. For example, in Chapter 14, "Personal Care," adaptive devices for bathing and showering are described and/or illustrated.

Another organizational feature is that content areas are fully developed within each chapter. Chapter 15, "Elimination," includes assisting clients with bedpans, urinals, and commodes; care of clients with catheters; giving a commercial enema; and care of clients with colostomies and ileostomies. This is considered preferable to scattering related content throughout two or more chapters. Similarly, collecting urine specimens and testing urine are contained in the same chapter. Other key features of this book are:

- The reading level is appropriate and the book is easy to read.
- The book covers the life span. Growth and development, changes due to aging, care of the newborn, and safety precautions for infants, children, and the elderly are included throughout the text.
- The basic needs, as identified by Abraham Maslow, are emphasized.
- The client is presented as an individual with physical, pyschological, social, and spiritual needs. Cultural and religious considerations are presented when appropriate.
- Procedures provide specific step-by-step instructions and are well illustrated.
- Key terms, with definitions, are provided at the beginning of each chapter.
- True/false and multiple-choice study questions, with answers, are provided at the end of each chapter. Discussion questions are also included.

- Adaptations for the home environment are integrated throughout.
- Emphasis is placed on wearing gloves when in contact with the client's blood or body fluids.

The *Homemaker/Home Health Aide* is a comprehensive book. In addition to being used in educational programs, it is intended to be a reference for homemakers and home health aides as they expand their skills and knowledge. Along with basic nursing skills, the following content areas are presented:

- An extensive section on ethics and legalities
- Verbal and nonverbal communication
- Growth and development section
- Body structure and function including the changes due to aging
- Isolation techniques in the home
- Homemaking and home maintenance considerations
- Client safety and personnel safety for the homemaker/home health aide
- Sexuality
- Care of the postoperative client
- Common health problems, including Alzheimer's disease, AIDS, and sexually transmitted diseases
- Care of the mother and her newborn

Any effort such as writing a textbook requires the assistance and support of many individuals. Those deserving acknowledgment include:
- Dr. Larry D. Huffman, Dr. Dorothy Buchan, Pat Walters, Elva Ruth Alexander, the LRC staff, and my other colleagues and friends at Kankakee Community College, who were supportive and helpful
- Linda Thompsen and Jacque Rehmer of Quality Care in Kankakee and Merle Wiens and Annette Zanto of St. Mary's Home Health Care, also in Kankakee, Illinois, for their advice, consultative services, and support during this project
- Mary Heath, for doing the workbook and instructor's manual
- David Culverwell, Lisa Cunninghis, Richard Weimer, Patty Mahaffey, Ann Moy, and others associated with the Lanham, Maryland office of C. V. Mosby, who were involved in the development and production of this book

And finally, a thank-you to my family and friends who understood the time-consuming nature of this project.

Contents

x   **Contents**

THE HOMEMAKER/HOME HEALTH AIDE

1 Introduction to Home Care

Chapter Highlights	What you will learn to do
Purpose of home care	■ Explain why home care is popular
Home care providers	■ Explain the purposes of home care
Home care services	■ Describe clients who need home care
Arranging for home care	■ Describe five types of home care services
Paying for home care	■ Explain how a client can arrange for home care
Organization of home care agencies	■ Describe how clients can pay for home care
The home care team	■ Follow an organizational chart
	■ Describe the contents of a policy and procedure manual
	■ List the members of the home care team
	■ Identify the responsibilities of the home care team

Diagnostic related group (DRG) A method of paying hospitals for Medicare and Medicaid clients

Health maintenance organization (HMO) A prepaid group insurance plan that provides a wide range of services to meet a client's total health care needs

Homebound Confined to the home

Home health aide (HHA) A health worker who provides personal care, comfort, and housekeeping services; certification or completion of a course is required in some states

Homemaker A health care worker who provides homemaker services

Homemaker services A program that helps the client and family maintain the home

Hospice A program for dying persons

Medicaid A health insurance plan for the poor, elderly, blind, and disabled, and for families with dependent children; sponsored by the federal and state governments

Medicare A federally funded health insurance program for the elderly

Plan of treatment A written plan that describes the client's home care; the plan must be signed by the doctor

Policy and procedure manual A manual that describes how the agency operates and how procedures are to be done

People often need the help of others to stay well and prevent illness. They need care when sick or disabled. Many services meet the health care needs of children, adults, and the aged. At some time most people will use one or more of these services:

- Physicians
- Hospitals
- Clinics
- Nursing homes
- Pharmacies
- Medical equipment companies
- Emergency services
- Home care

A single illness can involve several health care services. Each service offers a different type of health care. Yet each is important in helping the client. For example, an 85-year-old woman falls and breaks her hip. An ambulance takes her to a hospital. At the hospital a doctor examines her and admits her to the hospital. There she has laboratory tests, x-rays, medications, and surgery to repair her hip. After the hospital stay she needs nursing home care for a while. When she goes home, she needs nursing care and physical therapy in her home. She gets her medicine from a pharmacy and special equipment from a medical equipment company.

Purpose of Home Care

Home care is not new. For centuries family members have cared for the sick and injured in their homes. Hospitals have been preferred during most of this century. However, home care is becoming popular again. Sick, disabled, and frail people can receive needed care in their own familiar surroundings (Fig. 1-1). Home care is popular for several reasons:

- People are happier in their own homes.
- Home care is usually less expensive than hospital care.
- Home care helps maintain a stable home and family life.
- Home care promotes self-care, independence, and dignity.
- Insurance programs now pay for home care services.

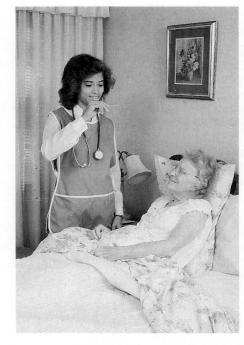

Fig. 1-1 This client is being cared for in her own home.

Purposes

People of all ages and income levels can benefit from home care. Consider the following situations:

- An 80-year-old widow is discharged from the hospital. She lives alone and needs her dressings changed daily for two weeks. She wants to live in her own home where she can enjoy her cat and rose garden.
- An 8-year-old has brain damage from a serious illness. The family does not want to place the child in an institution. However, it is hard to care for the other children, work, and maintain the home with a sick child.
- A 45-year-old husband is dying of cancer. He wants to spend his remaining time at home with his family.

Although each circumstance is different, all need home care. Home care has three main purposes:

- To maintain or restore health
- To promote independence
- To minimize the effects of disability or illness

Home Care Clients

You will care for clients of all ages. However, most home care clients are elderly. Because people are living longer, there are more and more elderly people. They have more health problems than younger people. Many are released from the hospital sooner than in the past. Some may need home care while recovering from illness or injury. Besides the elderly, home care clients include:

1. Clients discharged from the hospital or nursing home who can recover at home with the help of aides, nurses, or therapists.
2. Clients who have chronic diseases. A *chronic disease* lasts a long time. Clients need weekly or monthly supervision.
3. Clients with terminal illnesses. A *terminal illness* is one from which the person is not expected to recover. Many want to die in the secure, familiar surroundings of their own homes.
4. Clients who are frail, ill, or disabled and who need help to live alone at home.
5. Families who need instructions on how to care for their loved ones at home.

Home Care Providers

Family and friends provide home care more than any other group. This involves emotional strain, time, and physical demands. Caring for a loved one can be very hard. When it is, families often hire others to help with care. Home care services are provided by:

- Government agencies
- Hospitals and nursing homes
- Private companies
- Community organizations

Government agencies are supported by taxes. They are operated by the state or county. These agencies provide home health services to people with limited incomes. To be eligible clients have to meet certain age, income, social, and health requirements. One kind of government agency is the public health department.

Some *hospitals* offer home care services to clients who have been discharged. The home care department is part of the hospital.

Private companies own and operate home health agencies. The company is owned by individuals. Home care is their business from which they expect to earn a profit.

Community organizations are supported by the community, churches, and donations. Some have special government funding. They are not owned by private individuals. Clients may have to meet certain age, income, or health requirements.

There are state and federal laws for home health care. Agencies must follow these laws. The agency may be fined, be denied payment, or be closed for not following the law.

Home Care Services

A number of home care services are available. An agency may offer one or all of the following programs.

Home health services are provided to clients who have specific health care needs. The care must be medically necessary and ordered by a doctor. Most clients are *homebound* or confined to their homes. Nurses, therapists, or home health aides give care on a part-time basis or periodically. Care may be needed once a month or every day.

Homemaker services help the client or family maintain the home. Services may include basic housekeeping, fixing meals, shopping, laundry, and personal care. Child care services are also available. The services are provided by a homemaker (see Chapter 9). A doctor's order is not needed.

Hospice services are for the terminally ill. Social, emotional, spiritual, and physical care are provided to the client and family. Hospice care helps the dying client maintain quality of life and dignity. Hospice care can also be provided in hospitals and nursing homes.

Medical equipment services help the client obtain sickroom equipment. Items include hospital beds, walkers, wheelchairs, oxygen, and respiratory equipment. Equipment can be bought or rented.

Private duty nursing services can provide home care 24 hours a day, 7 days a week. Some clients need a lot of nursing care. Others need help with personal care and home maintenance.

Arranging for Home Care

Anyone can contact a home health agency to arrange for home care. Besides families, friends, and physicians, organizations can refer clients to home health agencies. These organizations include hospitals, nursing homes, social service agencies, churches, and other health care agencies.

Hospitals help clients plan for care after the hospital. The *discharge planner* arranges for needed services. Services may include home care, medical supplies, meals, counseling, and transportation.

Once the referral is made, agencies find out if the client is eligible for home care. Agencies have policies and procedures that outline specific requirements. Requirements are often based on need, where the person lives, age, the type of illness, income, and payment source. A nurse or other professional will talk with the client, family, and doctor to determine the type and amount of services needed.

When the client is eligible for home care, a *plan of treatment* is developed. This written plan must be signed by the doctor. The plan describes:
1. The client's health problems
2. The type of home care services needed
3. The frequency of visits
4. Special instructions
5. The length of treatment
6. The improvement expected over a specific period of time
7. A care plan for the staff to follow

Paying for Home Care

Home health care is less costly than hospital care, but it is not cheap. Most people have some kind of insurance. The insurance pays part of the medical bills, including home care.

Medicare is a health insurance plan administered by the Social Security Administration of the federal government. Persons 65 years of age and older are eligible. Younger people who are disabled may also be eligible. People with this insurance pay monthly premiums.

Medicare has two parts. Part A pays for some hospital costs up to certain amounts during a specified time period. (See diagnostic related groups.) Nursing home and home care are included if certain regulations are met.

Part B pays for some medical expenses such as doctor office visits, tests, and treatments. If they are ordered by the doctor, Part B may cover such things as physical therapy and rental of hospital equipment for home care. The benefits and regulations for Medicare are complex and change often. Your local Social Security office can provide information and answer questions.

Medicaid is a health insurance program sponsored by the federal and state governments. The benefits, regulations, and eligibility requirements vary from state to state. People over 65, the blind, the disabled, and low-income families are usually eligible. Besides home care, Medicaid usually pays for hospital services, doctor fees, x-ray and laboratory tests, family planning, dental and eye care, immunization and well-child clinics, and rehabilitation. There is no insurance premium to pay.

Diagnostic related groups (DRGs) were created by Congress in 1983. Their purpose is to reduce Medicare and Medicaid costs. Before DRGs, Medicare and Medicaid paid for a certain percentage of actual hospital costs. The amount was determined *after* the hospital stay. Under the DRG system, Medicare and Medicaid payments have been determined *before* hospitalization.

A diagnostic related group consists of specific diagnoses. For a DRG, the length of stay and the cost of treating illnesses in a specific category have been determined. The hospital is paid the predetermined amount for Medicare and Medicaid clients. If the hospital's costs for treating the client are less than the DRG payment, the hospital keeps the extra money. If the hospital costs are higher than the DRG amount, the hospital takes the loss.

DRGs have had a great effect on health care. Hospitals want to avoid financial loss from lengthy client stays. Therefore, clients are being discharged earlier than in the past. These clients are often still quite ill. Care in a nursing home or home care is often required.

Private insurance is bought by individuals and families. Depending on the plan, some or all health care costs are paid by the insurance company.

Group insurance covers members of a group. Often employers offer group health insurance to employees. The insurance premium is paid by the employee or by the employer as a fringe benefit. Premiums are lower with group plans than with private insurance plans.

A *health maintenance organization* (HMO) provides health care services for a prepaid fee. The set fee is paid every month, every 3 months, or every year. For this fee individuals receive all needed services offered by the organization. Some may only need a yearly physical exam. Others may need hospital care. Regardless of the services used, the cost is covered by the prepaid fee. HMOs emphasize disease prevention and maintaining health. The costs of keeping someone healthy are far less than illness care.

A *preferred provider organization* (PPO) is a group of doctors or a hospital that provides health care at reduced rates. Usually the arrangement is made between the PPO and a company. The company's employees are given reduced rates for the services used.

Other payment sources include veteran's services, special insurance, and worker's compensation. The Older Americans Act and Title XX of the Social Security Act provide for homemaker services.

Clients or families may pay for home care. This usually happens when a client has no insurance or when the insurance policy does not cover all services. For example, Medicare and most insurance companies will not pay for 24-hour care. Homemaker services may

not be covered. If not, the client or family has to pay for these services.

Someone from the agency discusses payment with the client or family. Most agencies bill the insurance company, Medicare, or Medicaid. A client's questions about payment should be referred to your supervisor.

Organization of Home Care Agencies

There are state and federal laws that home health agencies must follow. For example, agencies must be certified by Medicare to receive payment for

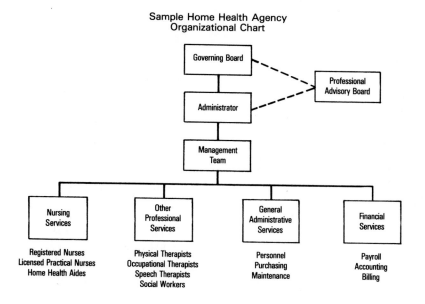

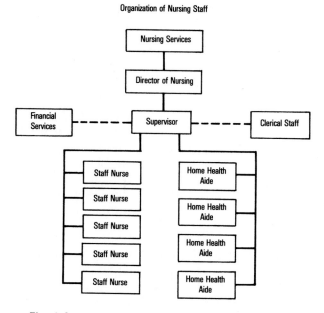

Fig. 1-2 Organizational chart of a home care agency.

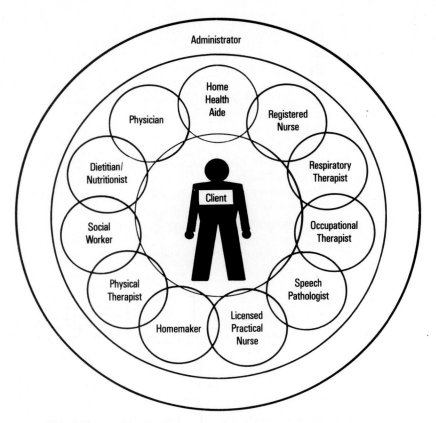

Fig. 1-3 Team members work together to help the client. The client is the focus of care.

Medicare clients. Some states require that agencies have a state license. Agencies must follow specific rules about organization and the services provided. These rules are designed so that clients receive quality care.

Each home health agency has an organizational chart. See Fig. 1-2 on page 5. The chart shows lines of authority and responsibility. The chart also shows who to report to with problems, concerns, and questions. You need to know who you report to and how your position fits into the whole organization. Organizational charts vary with each agency. You will be shown the structure for your agency when you begin working.

An agency's *policy and procedure* manual describes how the organization operates. It describes the agency's philosophy about client care. Expectations of employees are also described. The policy and procedure manual includes the following.

1. *Administrative policies* explain how agency activities are to be structured and controlled. They describe each person's role within the organization.
2. *Personnel policies* explain such issues as hiring, firing, and benefits.
3. *Operational policies* explain how each department functions.
4. *Nursing policies and procedures* describe specific standards for client care. These tell how procedures are to be done and special situations handled. They also

state what home health aides and homemakers can and cannot do.
5. *Job descriptions* explain required education and work experience and the responsibilities of each position in the agency.

The Home Care Team

Home health care is a team effort. All members of the team work together to help the client (Fig. 1-3). This may mean helping the client return to the same level of functioning as before the illness or accident. Some clients may need to learn how to transfer from the bed to a wheelchair. For others it may be dying pain-free and comfortable at home. Each team member has specific functions and responsibilities. All are important and essential in the delivery of quality client care. Table 1-1 describes members of the home care team.

Several team members may work together to provide home health care to a client. Consider the following case:

Mrs. Jones is 82 years old. She has returned home from the hospital following a stroke (see chapter 21). Her right side is weak, which limits her ability to move about. She has trouble with normal activities such as cooking, bathing,

Table 1-1   Members of the Home Care Team

MEMBER	RESPONSIBILITIES
Dietician/nutritionist	Counsels and instructs in nutrition, food preparation, and special diets Requires a college degree with a major in nutrition or food science
Director or administrator	Directs and organizes the agency's activities Responsible for all activities and employees Usually requires a college degree: a masters degree is preferred
Doctor	A person licensed to practice medicine Diagnoses, prescribes, and treats clients Develops a treatment plan for client care Monitors the client's progress Changes the treatment plan as needed
Home health aide (HHA)	Works under the supervision of a registered nurse Gives personal care, performs simple nursing procedures, gives emotional comfort, provides housekeeping services, reports changes in the client's condition, and completes necessary records Must have a certificate or complete a course in some states
Homemaker	Does basic housekeeping tasks: dusting, vacuuming, changing beds, washing dishes, mopping floors, laundry, ironing, mending, shopping, and fixing meals Child care may be provided Some states require completion of a course
Licensed practical nurse (LPN)	An individual who has completed a 1-year nursing program and has passed a licensing exam Must be licensed in the state in which he or she is working Works under the supervision of a registered nurse
Occupational therapist (OT)	Teaches clients how to manage daily living tasks Helps the client use special devices for eating, dressing, and other daily activities A college degree in occupational therapy is required A state license or certification is usually required
Physical therapist (RPT)	Provides treatments and exercises that help restore function or prevent disability following an illness, injury, or loss of a body part Must be a college graduate with a degree in physical therapy A state license or certification is usually required
Registered nurse (RN)	Assesses, plans, implements, and evaluates care Carries out doctors' orders; may assign them to LPNs or aides A graduate of a 2-, 3-, or 4-year nursing program who has passed a licensing exam Must be licensed by the state in which he or she is working
Respiratory therapist	Gives breathing treatments, evaluates breathing, and checks respiratory equipment Completion of a respiratory therapy program is required A license or state certification may be required

Continued

Table 1-1—cont'd.   Members of the Home Care Team

MEMBER	RESPONSIBILITIES
Social worker	Counsels clients, families, and groups with social or psychological problems Helps find other community services or organizations that may meet the client's and family's needs (Meals-on-Wheels, Easter Seal Society, American Cancer Society) A master's degree is usually required
Speech pathologist	Provides treatments to clients with speech, language, or swallowing disorders A master's degree, work experience, and passing a national exam are required
Supervisor	An RN who assigns and supervises the activities of other RNs, LPNs, home health aides, and homemakers

and personal care. Her speech is slurred making it hard to communicate. She has a history of heart disease and breathing problems. Her husband died one month ago. She has no family in the area. Mrs. Jones lives alone.

A *nurse* will assess Mrs. Jones and develop a plan of care. The plan will also be based on the doctor's orders. The nurse will share information with other team members and the doctor so services are coordinated. The *supervisor* will work with the team members to coordinate Mrs. Jones's care. This includes scheduling and supervising the home health aide.

A *home health aide* will visit Mrs. Jones several times a week. Mrs. Jones will be helped with bathing, personal grooming, and home maintenance.

A *physical therapist* will help Mrs. Jones strengthen her weak side. This involves an exercise program. She may be taught how to walk with a walker. The home health aide may be taught how to assist the client with the exercises. A *speech therapist* will help Mrs. Jones relearn how to speak clearly. An *occupational therapist* will help Mrs. Jones change her home so she can do her normal activities. This may involve placing bars in the shower and hand rails in the halls. A ramp may be needed over the entrance steps.

A *nutritionist* may plan a low-salt diet for Mrs. Jones because of her heart problems. A *respiratory therapist* may give her breathing treatments.

A *social worker* may help Mrs. Jones cope with her husband's death and living alone. The social worker can give counseling and support to help Mrs. Jones live a happy life.

Team members are responsible to the client and the team. Team responsibilities include the following:

1. Providing care as described in the treatment plan
2. Observing the client's progress and changes in condition
3. Reporting changes in a client's condition
4. Recording all observations and care provided accurately
5. Working together
6. Communicating frequently and clearly with the team

You play an important role in home care. As a home health aide you are the eyes and ears of the home care team. You spend more time with the client than any other team member. You often see changes in the client's condition before anyone else. For example, when giving a bath you see a reddened area on Mrs. Jones' back. She tells you she has been too weak to get up all day. Your prompt reporting of these concerns can prevent other problems. (The roles and responsibilities of home health aides are discussed in Chapter 2).

Summary

Home care is not a new idea. It has been an important part of health care for hundreds of years. Home care today allows people to recover from illnesses, injuries, or disabilities in the comfort of their own homes. Usually home care is much cheaper than hospital care. Home care services include home health services, homemaker services, hospice care, medical equipment, and private duty nursing.

Many different agencies provide these services. Home care is paid for by federal and state programs, private insurance, group plans, the client, or the family. Home health aides are important members of the home care team. The team works together to provide care.

Study Questions

1. Explain why home care has become so popular.
2. Describe the agencies that employ home health aides.
3. Describe your experiences in caring for an ill family member or friend at home.
4. Describe the clients you might care for as a home health aide.
5. Identify the services available in your community to help ill clients remain in their homes.
6. Explain how members of the home care team work together to provide quality client care.

Circle the *best* answer.

7. Which is *not* a purpose of home care?
   a. To maintain or restore health
   b. To promote independence
   c. To replace hospital care
   d. To minimize the effects of disability or illness

8. The following agencies provide home care. Which expect to earn a profit?
   a. Government agencies
   b. Hospitals
   c. Private companies
   d. Community organizations

9. Homemaker services provide
   a. Basic housekeeping services
   b. Nursing care
   c. Hospice care
   d. All of the above

10. A program for dying clients is called
    a. A hospice
    b. A nursing home
    c. Private duty nursing
    d. A hospital

11. The plan of treatment must be signed by
    a. The client
    b. The doctor
    c. Your supervisor
    d. Both you and your supervisor

12. The following statements are about insurance programs. Which is *false*?
    a. Preferred provider organizations (PPOs) provide health care at reduced rates.
    b. Health maintenance organizations (HMOs) provide health care for a prepaid fee.
    c. Medicare and Medicaid are government programs for anyone in need.
    d. Diagnostic related groups (DRGs) affect Medicare and Medicaid payments.

13. Where will you find personnel policies?
    a. The plan of treatment
    b. The policy and procedure manual
    c. Nursing policy and procedure guides
    d. The agency's advertising and pamphlets

14. The home care team includes
    a. Registered nurses and licensed practical nurses
    b. Doctors
    c. Home health aides and homemakers
    d. All of the above

Answers

7. c	9. a	11. b	13. b
8. c	10. a	12. c	14. d

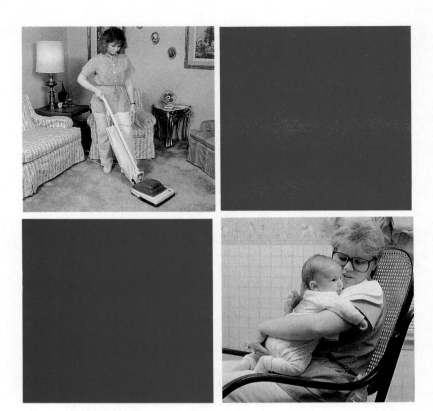

2

The Home Health Aide

Chapter Highlights	**What you will learn to do**

- List personal care, nutrition, and home maintenance functions
- Explain what a home health aide can and cannot do
- Describe the qualities, characteristics, and personal habits of a good home health aide
- Give examples of confidential information
- Give examples of ethical and unethical behavior
- Describe assault, battery, and false imprisonment
- Explain how to prevent negligent acts
- Explain why incidents should be reported
- Explain the guidelines for witnessing a will

Key Terms

Assault Threatening or attempting to touch a person's body without his or her consent

Battery Touching a person without his or her consent

Confidentiality Keeping information about a client private

Ethics Standards for behavior; deals with right or wrong

False imprisonment Restricting a person's movements without consent

Incident An accident or unusual occurrence

Negligence The unintentional harming of another person or his or her property

Will A legal document that states what should be done with money and property after a person's death

Roles and Responsibilities

Home health aides play a special role in home care. They give personal care, help with nutrition, and maintain the home (Fig. 2-1). Their major roles include:

Personal care to promote hygiene and health (Fig. 2-2)
- Assist with mouth care
- Assist with bathing
- Provide skin care
- Assist with grooming
- Assist with dressing
- Assist with exercise and activity
- Assist with transfers
- Measure vital signs
- Measure intake and output
- Collect specimens
- Record activities and observations
- Perform special procedures

Nutritional tasks to promote good nutrition (Fig. 2-3)
- Shop for groceries
- Plan meals
- Prepare meals
- Store food

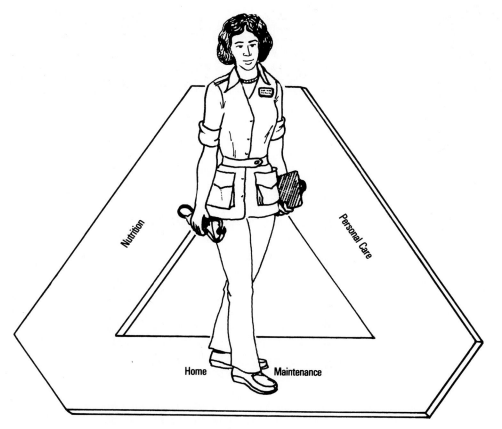

Fig. 2-1 Roles of home health aides.

11

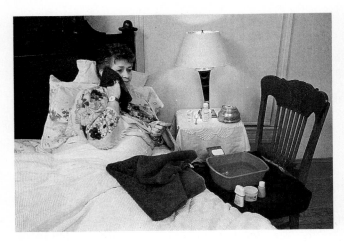

Fig. 2-2 Aide promotes hygiene and health by assisting with bathing.

Fig. 2-3 Aide promotes nutrition by fixing meals.

Fig. 2-4 Aide promotes a safe, clean home by doing light housekeeping.

Home maintenance to maintain a safe, clean home (Fig. 2-4)

- Do light housekeeping: dusting, vacuuming, washing dishes, cleaning the bathroom, and keeping the home neat
- Do laundry
- Make beds

You are a member of the home health care team. The client, family, and agency depend on you. *Clients* may see you as both a companion and caregiver. You provide comfort through personal care, conversation, and household tasks. This means a great deal to clients. They look forward to your visits. You help make their lives more comfortable and meaningful.

Families depend on you to give competent and safe care to their loved ones. They may expect a great deal from you. They may not be home or able to help with the required care. Families expect you to be trustworthy. They want you to perform your duties with skill and compassion. You need to understand the family's expectations and feelings.

The *agency* depends on you to do your job well. How well you do your job affects the agency's reputation in the community.

You must understand what is expected of you. You will have certain responsibilities in caring for the client and family. There are also things that you cannot do as a home health aide. This book has some advanced procedures that your agency *may not* allow you to do. Your supervisor will assign only those tasks you can do. You must follow your assignment and agency rules. You must also perform each task to the best of your ability. Failure to do so could injure the client or you. The following guidelines will help you to do your job well.

GENERAL GUIDELINES

1. Be on time for assignments. Some clients cannot be left alone. Being late could harm the client or inconvenience the family or other caregiver. If your replacement is late, do not leave the client unattended. Notify your supervisor.
2. Perform your duties as directed by your supervisor. The client or family may ask you to do something else. Or they may want to change your schedule or duties. Contact your supervisor at these times.
3. Perform only what you have been trained to do. If your supervisor asks you to do an unfamiliar task, ask for more training.
4. Call your supervisor if you are unclear about your assignment or a procedure. Also, call if you have questions about the client.
5. Do not give opinions about the client's diagnosis or treatment plan.

6. Do not accept gifts or money from clients or families.
7. Do not talk about your personal problems with the client or family.
8. Discuss clients or their families *only* with your supervisor or in staff meetings. Do not talk about their problems with anyone else.
9. Accept help and advice from your supervisor when it is offered. You should also accept help from other team members.
10. Attend educational workshops to learn more about home care.
11. Report and record your observations accurately. Changes in the client's physical or emotional condition must be reported and recorded.
12. Treat the client, family, and their belongings with respect. You are a guest in their home.
13. Present yourself in a professional manner. Clients and their families look to you as an example.

There are certain functions, procedures, and tasks that home health aides should never do. It is extremely important that you understand what you *cannot* do as a home health aide.

Never give medications. This includes medications given orally, rectally, by injection, or directly into the bloodstream through an intravenous line. You can assist with medications only if they are set up by a nurse or a family member. Assisting with medications is discussed in Chapter 18, Special Procedures.

Never insert tubes or objects into a client's body openings or remove them from the body. You must not insert tubes into the client's bladder, esophagus, trachea, nose, ears, or bloodstream. Do not insert tubes into body openings that have been surgically created. Exceptions to this rule are those procedures in this textbook that you will learn with your instructor's supervision.

Never take oral or telephone orders from a doctor. The doctor may call or visit while you are with a client. The doctor may want to give a treatment or prescription order. You should politely give your name and title. Offer to notify your supervisor to call the doctor. Or ask the doctor if he or she wants to call the supervisor.

Never perform procedures that require sterile technique. With sterile technique objects that will be in contact with the client's body are free of all microorganisms. Sterile technique requires skills and judgment beyond the training received by home health aides. You may be asked to assist a nurse during a sterile procedure. However, you will not perform the procedure yourself.

Never tell the client or family the client's diagnosis or treatment plans. The doctor is responsible for telling the client and family about the diagnosis and treatment. Nurses may further explain what the doctor has told the client and family.

Never diagnose or prescribe treatments or medications for clients or anyone else. Only doctors can diagnose and prescribe.

Never supervise the work of other home health aides. Nurses are responsible for supervising home health aides. You will not be trained or paid to supervise the work of others. Supervising others could have serious legal effects.

Never just ignore an order or request to do something that you cannot do or that is beyond the scope of home health aides. Promptly explain to your supervisor why you cannot carry out the order or request. Your supervisor will assume you are doing what you were told unless you explain otherwise. Client care cannot be neglected.

Never move or rearrange the client's belongings without permission. Home health aides have been accused of stealing when clients could not find their possessions.

Personal Qualities and Characteristics

Working in home health care is different from working in a hospital or nursing home. In hospitals and nursing homes there are RNs, LPNs, and other aides working in the same area. They can help each other with many care activities. A nurse is right there if aides have questions or problems. In home care you work alone. Sometimes your supervisor will visit the home with you. But usually you will be by yourself. Your supervisor will be available by phone. Therefore you must be able to work alone without supervision. This involves

- Performing procedures properly
- Understanding your assignment and the needs of the client and family
- Recognizing changes in the client's condition
- Recognizing harmful situations
- Knowing when to call for help or advice

The work of a home health aide can be demanding. Not everyone can do it. Besides being able to work alone, successful home health aides *care* about others. They have a sincere *desire to help* those in need. They should also have these other qualities and characteristics (Fig. 2-5):

Flexibility—The ability to adjust to changes. Sometimes changes must be made in a client's routine. The aide will need to adjust calmly.

Empathy—The ability to see things from another's point of view. Feeling what another is feeling.

Cheerfulness—The ability to be pleasant and warm.

Sensitivity—Being aware of the needs, feelings, likes, and dislikes of others.

Dependability—Being reliable. Performing duties correctly at the right time.

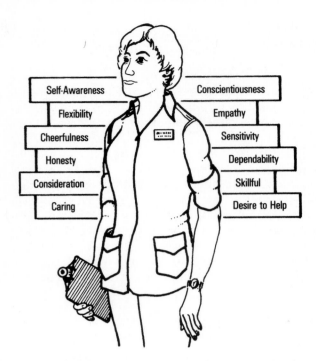

Fig. 2-5 Qualities and characteristics of a home health aide.

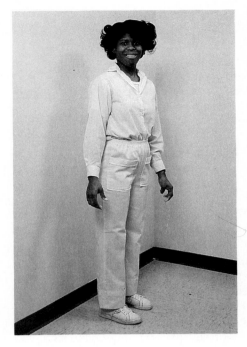

Fig. 2-6 A well-groomed home health aide.

Honesty—Being truthful and accurate.
Consideration—Being able to show a genuine concern for others. Being kind.
Conscientiousness—Performing duties to the best of your ability; trying to do the right thing.
Skillful—Performing tasks properly and communicating clearly.
Self-awareness—Knowing your own strengths and weaknesses.

Personal Habits

How you look and act affects how people feel about you. You set an example for your clients and their families (Fig. 2-6). They can learn by observing Therefore you need to have good personal hygiene. The following guidelines will help you look and act professional. They will also help protect you and the client.

GENERAL GUIDELINES

1. Bathe daily to prevent odors and promote cleanliness.
2. Brush your teeth after meals. This prevents cavities, gum disease, and breath odors.
3. Keep your hair neat and clean. Make sure your hair is off of your collar and does not fall in your face (see Fig. 2-6).
4. Use makeup only in small amounts.
5. Keep nails clean and short.
6. Avoid perfume and cologne. They can nauseate the client.
7. Wear the uniform required by your agency. Some agencies require smocks or uniforms. Others allow regular clothing.
8. Do not wear jewelry while on duty. Most agencies allow employees to wear a wedding ring. Large rings and bracelets can scratch clients. Necklaces, bracelets, and earrings can easily be pulled off by confused clients.
9. Keep your uniform neat, clean, pressed, and mended.
10. Wear clean underclothes and a clean uniform every day.
11. Wear low-heeled, nonskid shoes. They should be comfortable, clean, and polished.
12. Wear your name tag to identify yourself and your agency.
13. Take drugs only if prescribed by a doctor.
14. Do not care for clients while you are under the influence of drugs or alcohol.
15. Do not smoke in the client's home.
16. Maintain a healthy body weight.
17. Stay healthy. Eat well-balanced meals, exercise daily, and get enough sleep.

Confidentiality

People naturally tend to talk about their work with their friends and family. If you worked as a clerk or a salesperson, talking about your job might be all right. A home health aide is in an entirely different situation. You will be involved in the private lives of others. You must never discuss your clients or their problems with your friends or family. You must keep information confidential.

Confidentiality is keeping all information about a client private. There are laws to protect the client's right to privacy. Right to privacy means the right not to have confidential information revealed. Certain personal things about the client or family are confidential. Examples include:

- The client's health problems; what is wrong with the client
- Marital, family, or money problems
- If the client is not expected to recover
- Information about the client's treatment
- Thoughts or feelings the client shares with you

As a home health aide you must keep all confidential information to yourself. However, sometimes others need to have the information. For example, a client tells you about "occasional chest pains." She asks you not to tell her daughter. She does not want her daughter to worry. "It's only indigestion," she says. The chest pains could mean she has a serious problem. You must tell your supervisor. On the other hand, you overhear a husband and wife having an argument. You should not report what you have heard.

You must decide what information your supervisor needs to know. The supervisor needs to know if:

- The information affects the client's care
- The client may be injured
- The information will help others plan or give better care

As clients get to know you, they may tell you very personal things. They will trust you to respect their privacy. A client may tell you something that could be harmful. If so, you must report the information. Explain to the client why you must share this privileged information with your supervisor.

GENERAL GUIDELINES

1. Do not talk about one client to another client.
2. Do not discuss confidential client information with the client's family or friends.
3. Do not talk about your clients in public places (Fig. 2-7). Client information should be shared only in appropriate places, such as your agency's office.
4. Discuss clients only with other team members.
5. Do not gossip about your clients.

Ethical and Legal Considerations

As a home health aide, you must know how to act in different situations. You must decide what you should or should not do ethically and legally. Ethics are standards that guide behavior. Legal considerations relate to laws. Laws are established by the government

Fig. 2-7 These home health aides could easily be overheard by others sitting nearby.

to protect all individuals. Both ethics and laws give you important guidelines to follow when caring for clients.

Ethics

Ethics are a set of standards for behavior. They are generally accepted by society. The standards are moral judgments about right and wrong. The nursing and medical professions each have a code of ethics. Nurses or doctors who act unethically can lose their licenses to practice. Home health aides are also expected to behave ethically. The following are examples of ethical and unethical behavior.

Ethical Behavior

- Being kind, considerate, and accepting
- Showing respect for others and their property
- Doing the best job possible
- Being honest
- Being responsible and reliable
- Keeping information confidential

Unethical Behavior

- Refusing to care for a client because of race, religion, age, or moral beliefs
- Being rude or short-tempered with the client or the family
- Being unreliable
- Lying to the client, family, or employer
- Stealing
- Making fun of a client
- Gossiping about clients or their families
- Sexual contact with a client
- Sharing confidential information

You may have to decide if an action is ethical or unethical. If so, ask yourself the following questions:

1. How will my behavior affect the *client*?
2. How will my behavior affect the *family*?
3. How will my behavior affect my *employer*?
4. How will my behavior affect *me*?

Your answers will help you choose the right action. Behaving ethically protects the client, the family, the employer, and you from harm.

Legal Considerations

As a home health aide and a private citizen, you must follow the laws of your community, state, and nation. If you break a law, you have committed a crime. Crimes are punished by fines or imprisonment.

Examples of Crimes

- Stealing from a client, family member, employer, or employee
- Striking or roughly handling a client
- Harming a client on purpose
- Sexually abusing a client or family member
- Restraining a client without permission

You need to be aware of the following crimes.

Assault is threatening or attempting to touch a client without his or her consent. Trying to touch a client without his or her consent may cause the fear of being harmed. For example, a home health aide threatens to tie down Mr. Smith unless he stays at the table to finish eating. Do not threaten clients. This could be considered assault.

Battery is touching a client without his or her consent. Clients must give permission for you to touch them. They must give permission for such things as bathing, assisting with exercise, and taking a pulse. Consent can be given orally, or with a nod or other gesture. If a client tells you "No" or pushes you away, you do not have consent. Therefore, you must stop your action. If this happens, talk with the client. Find out why care is being refused. If a client refuses to allow care to be given, you must respect the decision. Report the situation to your supervisor immediately. Never force a client to receive care.

False imprisonment is restricting a client's movement without consent. Do not force a client to stay in bed or in a chair by applying restraints. *Restraints* are cloth or leather devices. They are used to secure hands, legs, or a client's chest to another object such as a chair or bed. Restraints are often used to prevent a client from wandering off, pulling out tubes, or getting up without help. There must be a doctor's order to use restraints.

There are laws governing the practice of home health aides. The laws vary in each state. You may be able to do certain procedures in one state but not in another state. What you can do depends on your training. Many states require training for home health aides. These laws say what home health aides can do and what training they need. Some states require as little as 60 hours of training. Others require 120 to 180 hours of training. In some states home health aides must have prior work experience in a hospital.

You will be expected to function according to your state law and the accepted standards for home health aides. Your employer will have specific policies that define your job. This is called a *job description*. The job description also lists the procedures you can perform. You should receive a written copy of your job description before you start to work.

The job description must follow state law. In other words, the agency can allow you to do only those things that are in the law. You can perform only those procedures listed in your job description. Also, you must do only what you have been trained to do. For example, applying a warm compress is part of your job. But you have not learned how to apply warm compresses. You cannot perform the procedure until you have had the necessary training.

You must follow the laws, standards, and agency policies. Otherwise the client, a family member, or property could be harmed. You could be considered negligent in your duties if harm occurs. *Negligence* is the unintentional harming of another person or his or her property. You can be sued for negligence. If found guilty, you may have to pay money to the injured person. The amount of money is determined by the judge. If you are thorough and careful, you can prevent negligence.

Examples of Negligent Acts

- Failure to report changes in the client's condition to your supervisor
- Leaving a client's home without a relief person, if one is assigned
- Damage or loss of the client's property
- Burning a client's skin because a procedure was done wrong
- Injuring the client because of failure to take proper safety measures

You are responsible for your own actions. If you break a law or are negligent, you may be arrested or sued. You can avoid legal action if you follow these guidelines.

GENERAL GUIDELINES

1. Perform only tasks you are trained to do.
2. Ask your supervisor if you are not sure about a procedure.
3. Follow your agency's rules.
4. Follow the client's care plan unless instructed otherwise by your supervisor.
5. Do not perform any task that is not in your job description.
6. Do not force clients to follow a routine or procedure.
7. Protect your client's rights.
8. Report all changes in the client's condition promptly.
9. Report and record accurately all care provided.
10. Consider safety at all times.

INCIDENTS

Despite good training and work habits, incidents can happen. *Incidents* are accidents or unusual occurrences. They involve the client, family, or employee. Examples of incidents are

- A client falls.
- You burn your hand while preparing the client's meal.
- A client accuses you of stealing money or personal belongings.

When an incident occurs, report it immediately. Ignoring accidents or mistakes can harm the client, the agency, or you. Incidents must be reported as soon as possible for several reasons:

1. Prompt reporting helps you give a clear picture of the incident while it is fresh in your mind. This protects you and the client.
2. Your supervisor can handle client or family complaints better if he or she is aware of the problem.
3. Unsafe situations must be corrected to prevent future accidents.
4. There may be a lawsuit because of the incident. The agency's insurance company needs to know what happened.

When an incident happens, you need to complete an incident report (Fig. 2-8). Tell what happened, the time, and the mental and physical condition of the client. You also need to tell how the client tolerated the incident. State the facts related to the incident. *Do not give opinions.* For example, you enter the home and find the client on the floor. You should report that the client was found lying on the floor. Do not report that the client probably fell. The agency keeps the incident report in case there is a lawsuit. *Do not* write in the client's chart that an incident report has been filed.

Wills

More clients are choosing to die at home rather than in hospitals. Your clients may be thinking about how their property and family will be cared for after they die. Many clients have wills. A *will* is a legal document that states what happens to money and property after a person's death.

You may be asked to witness a client signing his or her will. Individuals named in the will cannot witness its signing. If you are asked to witness a will, keep in mind the following guidelines:

1. Notify your supervisor before you act as a witness.
2. Do not give the client legal advice.
3. Do not help the client with the wording of the will.
4. Do not make comments about the contents of the will.
5. Write down your actions and what happened.

Summary

You play a very special role in home care. With your help, many people can live at home during illness, disability, or old age. The client, the family, and your employer all depend on you to provide good care.

You must understand what you can and cannot do as a home health aide. Whenever you are in doubt or have a question, *ask your supervisor.* You may be responsible for home maintenance, shopping and cooking, and personal care. Being flexible, dependable, and skillful are just a few of the qualities and characteristics you need to have.

You will learn many personal things about your clients. You must keep this information confidential. Your clients are discussed only with your supervisor or other team members.

Your behavior is guided by both ethics and laws. You can avoid legal action if you follow rules, act in an ethical manner, and perform only those tasks you have been trained to do.

INCIDENT REPORT

<u>3/20/88</u>
Date of Report

<u>3/20/88</u>
Date of Incident

<u>11 AM</u>
Time of Incident

<u>George Smith</u>
Name of Party Involved in Incident

<u>333 Knight Way, Kingsvale</u>
Address

<u>(326) 555-0011</u>
Telephone

<u>76</u>
Age

<u>M</u>
Sex

Exact Location of the Incident: <u>Living room in client's home</u>

Describe the Incident: <u>While helping client transfer from hospital bed to wheelchair, client cut (R) lower leg on wheel chair leg extender</u>

Equipment Involved: <u>Wheel chair - family had w/c adapted - sharp metal edge on adapted leg extender</u>

Did Injury Occur? ☑ yes ☐ no Describe: <u>5 cm. laceration (R) lower leg</u>

Action Taken: <u>Controlled bleeding, notified supervisor, client taken to emergency room for treatment</u>

Client Condition Before Incident:
☑ Normal
☐ Senile

☐ Disoriented
☐ Sedated

☐ Unconscious
☐ Other (specify) _____

Nature of the Incident:
☐ Slip or Fall
☐ Burn
☐ Illness from Food

☐ Medication
☑ Cut
☐ Client Induced

☐ Personal Articles
☐ Other (specify) _____

Witnesses (include address): <u>None</u>

<u>Jane Brown</u> HHA
Name of Person Completing Form

<u>Sarah Wilbert</u> RN, Supervisor
Reviewed by: Name & Title

Fig. 2-8 An incident report.

Study Questions

1. A client, family member, or supervisor asks you to perform an unfamiliar task. What would you do? You are asked to do something health aides are not allowed to do. How should you respond?

2. Mrs. Smith, age 67, returned home from the hospital with casts covering her left leg and her right arm. She lives alone. Her daughter visits every evening after work. The physician has ordered nursing care, physical therapy, occupational therapy, and home health aide services. How can you help this client? What tasks can you perform?

3. What personal qualities and characteristics are most important for home health aides? Why?

4. Sue and Ellen work for the same home health agency. They have taken care of the same client at different times. They are good friends and care very much about a client named Mrs. Adams. They meet for lunch at a restaurant. Sue seems to have something on her mind and seems sad. Ellen asks her what is wrong. Sue says that Mrs. Adams only has a short time to live. Ellen is concerned about her friend and encourages her to discuss her feelings. How do you feel about this situation? What if the person sitting behind them is a friend or relative of the client? How would you handle this situation and why?

Circle T if the statement is true and F if it is false.

T F 5. You must do everything your supervisor tells you to.

T F 6. All agencies allow home health aides to perform the same procedures and tasks.

T F 7. You should have a written job description before you start to work.

T F 8. You should never pour medication from the bottle unless your supervisor tells you to.

T F 9. You can take verbal or telephone orders from doctors.

T F 10. You can tell the client and family about the diagnosis and treatment decided on by the doctor.

T F 11. Home health aides show empathy by feeling sorry for clients.

T F 12. You must show respect for the values, beliefs, and feelings of clients.

T F 13. You should take drugs only under the advice and supervision of a doctor.

T F 14. Alcohol should never be consumed while on duty.

T F 15. Jewelry is considered part of your uniform.

T F 16. Laws are ethical standards of what is right and wrong conduct.

T F 17. A person who breaks a law may be punished by being sent to prison or by paying a fine.

T F 18. Negligence occurs when a client is careless and is injured.

T F 19. Home health aides are always responsible for their own actions.

T F 20. Assault is attempting or threatening to touch another person without that person's consent.

T F 21. False imprisonment is the illegal restraint of another person's movement.

T F 22. A client has the right to have the information about treatment and care kept private and confidential.

T F 23. Home health aides cannot witness the signing of a will.

Answers

5. False	10. False	15. False	20. True
6. False	11. False	16. False	21. True
7. True	12. True	17. True	22. True
8. False	13. True	18. False	23. False
9. False	14. True	19. True	

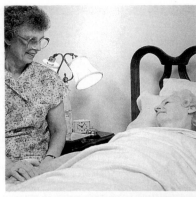 

3 Communicating Effectively

Chapter Highlights	What you will learn to do
How people communicate	■ Compare verbal and nonverbal communication
Communicating with clients	■ Describe examples of barriers to communication
Communicating with the client's family and friends	■ Describe factors that can affect communication with the client
	■ Explain the rules for communicating with clients
	■ Explain the importance of the client's family and friends
	■ Describe common reactions of family and friends to a client's illness
	■ Explain how to deal with conflict from the client and family

Key Terms

Body language Messages sent through facial expressions, gestures, and posture
Cliche A pat answer or common expression
Communication The giving and receiving of information by two or more people

Nonverbal communication The sending of messages without using words
Verbal communication Using words and language to communicate

How People Communicate

Communication is the giving and receiving of information by two or more people. It is an important function of human beings. The ability to communicate allows you to:

- Express your feelings and desires
- Make your needs known
- Learn new information
- Get tasks done

Communication is an important part of your job. You use communication to:

- Establish and maintain relationships with clients, families, team members, and your supervisor
- Gain understanding of the client and family's needs
- Explain what you will be doing in the home
- Report and record your activities and client observations

People communicate with each other all the time. You are aware of communicating when you are talking or writing. Using words and language is called *verbal communication*. You may not be aware that your facial expressions, gestures, and posture also communicate messages. This is called *body language* (Fig. 3-1). Sending messages without using words is called *nonverbal communication*. Besides body language, nonverbal communication involves such things as touch, tone of voice, and smells.

Communication exists when someone sends a message (the sender) and someone else receives it (the receiver). Problems occur when the sender and receiver have different meanings for words or ideas. For example, the word "rain" means different things to people. To some it means water from the sky. To others it means a supply of drinking water. Some view rain as an inconvenience because the roof leaks or because an outdoor event must be canceled. The sender and receiver need to understand a word or idea the same way in order to communicate.

Feedback is a way to check the accuracy of communication. Feedback can be verbal or nonverbal. One verbal method of feedback is to ask others to repeat what you said. This will tell you if the other person *understood* what you said. You can then restate your ideas if you were misunderstood. You may be unsure

of what someone else has said. You can say, "I'm not sure I understand what you mean" or "Are you saying that. . .?" This immediately tells the sender whether or not you understood the message.

The following examples show how you can use feedback to communicate with the client:

You arrive at Mrs. Black's home. Your assigned duties include bathing, skin care, helping Mrs. Black walk with a walker, and helping her dress. She says she is too tired and asks you to return another day. You ask, "Are you saying you're too tired for a bath this morning?" Mrs. Black tells you that she was awake all night with a backache. You asked Mrs. Black a question to check your understanding of her message. As a result you can help her feel more comfortable and get your job done.

Your client is an 80-year-old bedbound woman. She has two grown children. They visit about once a week to do her shopping and errands. One day she be-

Fig. 3-1 The home health aide is giving messages with her body language. Her posture is poor, she has a sad look on her face, and she is using gestures.

gins complaining about her children. She says that they do not care about her because they never come to visit. She says they are too busy to see a "sick old woman." You are alarmed because she seems very upset. You sit down and talk to her. "Mrs. Smith, it sounds like you're very angry at your children." You have shown that you are interested in her. You have checked your understanding of her message. Your actions have also encouraged Mrs. Smith to express her feelings. As a result, you will gain a better understanding of her needs.

Verbal and nonverbal communication can occur at the same time. Though you may be speaking, your body language is also giving messages. For example, you ask Mr. Town if he is having pain. He says, "No." However, he is holding his side and wincing with each movement. His verbal message is different from his nonverbal message. He is giving you mixed messages. You can often tell from body language how someone feels before a word is spoken. Most people are unaware of sending nonverbal messages. For this reason nonverbal messages more accurately indicate how a person feels. When verbal and nonverbal messages match, communication is clear. Confusion results when the messages are different. The mixed message blocks communication. Other blocks, or barriers, include:

Giving opinions or advice. When you give opinions or advice, you are making judgments about the other person. Allow clients and family members to express their feelings and concerns. Do not give your opinion or suggest ways to handle a matter.

Lack of trust. Sometimes you will not have an answer to a client's question. Do not lie or guess. If you do, clients will not trust you. Simply tell the client you do not have the answer, but you will ask your supervisor. Then ask your supervisor for help. Always get back to the client with an answer. Sometimes it will be necessary to have a nurse or doctor speak to the client.

Changing the subject. A client brings up concerns and you change the subject. You are giving the message, "I'm not comfortable hearing or talking about that subject." The client gets the message not to talk about that topic. This blocks communication. Try not to change the subject. Let clients express their concerns.

Lack of feedback. Feedback promotes communication by checking the information given. Give and ask for feedback often. Without feedback, people do not know if their messages are understood.

Cliches. A cliche is a pat answer or common expression. Examples are "Everything will be okay" and "Your doctor knows best." When you use cliches, clients feel unimportant. A client may say "Life is no longer worth living. I just want to die!" Answering, "Don't worry, things will get better" does not encourage the client to express feelings and worries. You need to encourage clients to talk about their feelings. "Tell me about it" invites the client to talk to you.

Being judgmental. You must not make judgments about a person's feelings, concerns, or ideas. You must not show disapproval of what a client says or does. If you do, clients may not share their thoughts with you.

Communicating with Clients

The client is a member of the home health care team. Although you may enjoy visiting with clients, you have a professional relationship with them. You have a reason for entering a client's home. That reason is to give care as directed by your supervisor. Your communication with the client has a purpose. Your conversation with a client must center on the client and his or her care.

Illness can affect how well you and the client communicate. The need for home care means that clients cannot meet all of their own basic needs. This is hard for most people to accept. Clients have many emotions. These may include anger, fear, frustration, helplessness, and despair. These emotions can make communication difficult. Other factors include:

- The type of illness or disability
- The seriousness of the condition
- Previous experiences with illness
- Age
- Position in the family (mother, father, child, breadwinner, etc.)
- Personality
- Money problems

Emotions also affect how the client reacts to you. Unfortunately, you may not be warmly welcomed by the client. Your presence reminds the client that things have changed and may never be "normal" again. Your client may seem sad, angry, or even hostile. You need to think about how you might feel in the client's place. Try to understand the causes of your client's feelings.

You may have a hard time working with some clients. They may be physically and emotionally draining. You may feel frustrated and angry as a result. Good communication will help you deal with these clients.

Communicating with clients and families is very different from talking to friends. You have a professional relationship with the client. The client expects services from you, not friendship. These general guidelines will help you communicate more effectively in your work.

GENERAL GUIDELINES

1. Your client deserves your respect. Do not be rude or argue.

2. Be courteous to your client. Be polite, considerate, and cooperative.
3. Control your emotions, even if your client is rude or difficult. Try to find the cause of the client's behavior. Is the client worried or frustrated? Ask your supervisor to help you deal with the situation.
4. Use tact. Try to say and do the right thing at the right time. This means *thinking* before you act or speak.
5. Give and receive feedback. This promotes good communication.
6. Make sure your verbal and nonverbal messages communicate the same thing. Otherwise you will confuse and frustrate the client. For example, do not make a face while telling a client that her home is lovely.
7. Control the volume (loudness) and tone of your voice. They affect the meaning of your words.
8. Speak clearly and distinctly. Do not whisper, mumble, or shout. Clients with hearing problems may have difficulty hearing you.
9. Control how fast you talk. Speaking too fast or slow can frustrate clients.
10. Be honest with your client. Answer questions clearly and honestly. Know the things you should not discuss with your client. Sometimes you will have to share client information with the family or your supervisor. You may not want the client to hear the conversation. Make sure you have privacy and that the client cannot hear you.
11. Remember that your client has many interests and talents. Encourage the client to pursue these areas. The illness is just one part of the person's life.
12. Use touch to communicate (Fig. 3-2). Many people are afraid of being avoided or rejected because of their illness. A simple touch can say that someone cares. However, some people do not like to be touched. Watch your client's body language. That

will tell you if the client is comfortable with your touch.
13. Be aware of body language. Both you and the client send messages through body language. Be careful that your posture, tone of voice, and gestures do not show irritation or impatience.
14. Communicate in writing or with a spelling board when needed (Fig. 3-3). A spelling board contains the alphabet, numbers, and symbols. The client points to pictures or spells out words to communicate with others.
15. Make sure the call bell is within the client's reach (see Chapter 8). Always answer the client's call promptly. Remember that every minute may seem like forever when waiting for someone else to meet basic needs.

Communicating with the Client's Family and Friends

Family and friends should be included whenever possible during times of illness. However, the first concern is always the client. You must be sensitive to how your client feels. Many clients want the support and company of loved ones (Fig. 3-4). Others may be embarrassed or upset. They may refuse to see people. Find out how the client feels about visitors. Follow the client's wishes whenever possible. If a client continually refuses to see even close relatives, tell your supervisor. There may be a problem that needs attention.

These guidelines will help you plan the client's care with visiting time:
- Make sure the client, family, and visitors are aware of the care schedule. Sometimes procedures must be done at certain times. Or you may be in the home only a short time.
- Provide privacy. This is especially important for cou-

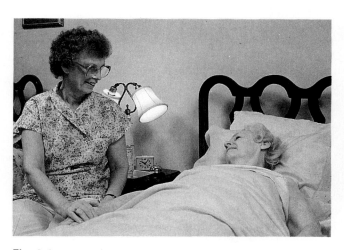
Fig. 3-2 Home health aide uses touch to comfort a client.

Fig. 3-3 Spelling board.

Fig. 3-4 Client visiting with friends.

Fig. 3-5 Aide knocks before entering a client's room.

ples who have sexual relationships. Knock and announce your presence before entering a room (Fig. 3-5).

- Suggest that visitors leave if the client seems tired or upset. Be sure to ask politely. Clients are often uncomfortable asking visitors to leave.

Friends and family often ask questions about the client's condition. This is a difficult situation for you for two reasons. First, the client has the right to privacy. Second, the doctor and nurse are responsible for giving the family information about the client. You can give the family information as directed by your supervisor. Otherwise, politely refer questions to your supervisor.

Family members may have opinions about the client's care. The client may also have ideas about care. Requests from the client and family may be different from the treatment plan. You need to tell your supervisor of these differences. The supervisor is responsible for giving you your directions. Remember to do only what you have been trained to do. The supervisor may have to talk to the client and family about needed care.

Each family has its own style. Over the years family routines are established. Members have their own position and role in the family. You may not like the way family members treat your client. However, you should not interfere. Illness affects the client's behavior. It may also affect how family members treat the client. You may be uncomfortable with their behavior. Or you may not approve of their behavior. However, you must treat each family member with respect and courtesy. Discussing your feelings and observations with your supervisor may be helpful.

In home care you work in client homes. Therefore you are in their territory. You enter their homes and family life. Some homes are loving and supportive. In others you may find tension and conflict between family members. These may have been going on for

years. The tension and conflict will probably not improve with the client's illness. Nor will your presence change the mood in the home.

Family members are also affected by the illness. They may resent their loved one for being sick. They may resent the burden placed on the family and home life. They may also resent their loved one's weakness and dependence on others. There may be loss of income. The illness may inconvenience family members. These can all cause anger, guilt, and frustration. As a result, families or clients may express their anger at you or your work. They may yell at you or criticize you. However, the client and family may not realize what is really happening.

Though this kind of situation is common, it is difficult to handle. You must not take things personally. You may find yourself becoming angry. However, you must not yell back or walk out. Think about the situation. Is the criticism deserved? Correct your actions if necessary. However, your actions and behavior may be correct and respectful. Then you are not the problem. The problem is the anger, guilt, and frustration caused by the illness.

You and your supervisor may need to talk to those involved. Let them talk freely and openly. Do not judge them. Often people will calm down very quickly when they feel someone cares.

Summary

Communication is one of the most important things people do. You will use communication skills to develop relationships with the client and family. You will also use the skills to share information with them and other team members. Conversation can be both verbal and nonverbal. Messages sent through facial expressions, gestures, and posture may be different from what is being said. How the client feels can affect how well you communicate with one another. You can encourage communication by giving feedback. However, you must be a good listener.

Family and friends are important to the client's recovery. When people are ill or suddenly disabled, lifestyles change. Conflict may result. Dealing with conflict can be difficult. You can decrease tension by staying calm. Try to understand that you are not the problem. That will help you provide the best possible care.

This chapter has given you some basic information about communication. Communication will also be discussed in other chapters in relation to specific problems or issues. Chapter 4 discusses how to use communication skills to report and record your observations and activities.

Study Questions

1. Give examples of how people communicate:
   - Verbally
   - With gestures
   - Through facial expressions
   - Through body language

2. Give three examples of communication. Describe barriers and how you would reduce or eliminate each.

3. Your new client, Mr. Rose, is 89 years old. A stroke left him paralyzed on his right side. He has difficulty understanding and remembering things. He is very confused. He cannot speak well. His children want him to stay at home as long as possible. What measures would you take to communicate with Mr. Rose?

4. Your client, Mrs. Gray, is a nice woman in her early 60s. She has been alert and talkative. She was discharged from the hospital three months ago. When in the hospital she had a large portion of her intestine removed due to cancer.

   The doctor made a home visit while you were there. The only change is that she has been napping more often during the day. The doctor examines Mrs. Gray. He tells you and Mrs. Gray that there may be more cancer. He also says that Mrs. Gray is too weak to have another operation now.

   Mrs. Gray's daughter visits after the doctor has left. She notices her mother gets tired rather quickly. She pulls you aside and says, "The doctor and my mother won't tell me anything. My mother doesn't seem well. Is she dying? Please tell me. You're the only one I can talk to." What should you do?

Circle T if the statement is true and F if the statement is false.

T F 5. Verebal communication involves the use of the written or spoken word.

T F 6. Verbal communication is the truest reflection of a person's feelings.

T F 7. Messages can be sent by facial expressions, gestures, posture, body language, and touch.

T F 8. Touch means different things to different people.

T F 9. Communication can occur if the sender and the receiver use and understand different languages.

T F 10. Changing the subject promotes communication.

T F 11. You should give an opinion when the client is expressing fears and concerns.

T F 12. Listening is important for effective communication.

T F 13. Pat answers, such as "Don't worry," encourage the client to express feelings and concerns.

T F 14. Clients and visitors should be allowed privacy when visiting.

Answers

5. True	8. True	11. False	13. False
6. False	9. False	12. True	14. True
7. True	10. False		

4

Communicating in the Home Health Agency

Chapter Highlights	**What you will learn to do**
Basic medical terminology	■ Use medical terms and abbreviations
The client's record	■ Describe the purposes of the client's record
Reporting and recording observations	■ Describe the forms in the client's record
Case conferences	■ Explain the differences between signs and symptoms
	■ Ask clients about their signs and symptoms
	■ Identify changes to watch for in the client's condition
	■ Describe the information you need to give when reporting a problem
	■ Explain recording guidelines
	■ Explain the purpose of case conferences

Key Terms

Abbreviation A shortened word
Care plan A written plan that lists the client's problems and goals and activities to improve the client's condition
Client record The written account of a client's care
Prefix A word element placed at the beginning of a word
Root The main part of a word

Sign An observed change in a client's condition; something that you can see, hear, feel, or smell
Suffix A word element placed at the end of a word
Symptom Something the client feels that you cannot see, hear, feel, or smell

Basic Medical Terminology

Using medical terminology will help you communicate with your supervisor and other team members. You will not have to learn every medical term. However, you need to understand the terms commonly used in health care. Your communication will be more clear and concise if you use medical terms.

Many medical terms are from the Greek and Latin languages. Most terms are a combination of prefixes, root words, and/or suffixes. A *prefix* is a word element placed at the beginning of a word. A *root* is the main part of the word. A *suffix* is a word element placed at the end of another word. Table 4-1 shows how word elements are combined to form medical terms.

Prefixes

A prefix is placed at the beginning of a word. Prefixes change the meaning of words (see Table 4-1). They are never used alone. Table 4-2 lists common prefixes and their meanings.

Roots

The *root* of the medical term contains the basic meaning of the word. It can be combined with another root, with prefixes, and with suffixes to form medical terms.

A vowel may be added when two roots are combined or when a suffix is added to a root. The vowel is called a *combining vowel* and is usually an "o." An "i" is sometimes used so the word is easier to pronounce. An "i" is used when there is no vowel between the two combined roots or between the root and the suffix.

Common roots and their combining vowels are listed in Table 4-3.

Suffixes

A *suffix* is placed at the end of a root to change the meaning of the word. Suffixes cannot be used alone. When translating medical terms, you need to begin with the suffix. The common suffixes are listed in Table 4-4.

Table 4-1 Forming Medical Terms

PREFIX	ROOT	SUFFIX	COMBINATION
hyper- (too much)	-glyc- (sugar)	-emia (blood condition)	hyperglycemia (high blood sugar)
brady- (slow)	-cardia (heart)		bradycardia (slow heart rate)
	hemat- (blood)	-uria (urine condition)	hematuria (blood in the urine)
	gastro- (stomach)	-ostomy (surgical opening)	gastrostomy (surgical opening into the stomach)
dys- (difficult)	-pnea (breathing)		dyspnea (difficulty breathing)
	thermo- (heat)	-meter (measure)	thermometer (instrument that measures heat or temperature)

Table 4-2 Prefixes

PREFIX	MEANING
a-, an-	without or not
ab-	away from
ad-	toward
ante-	before, forward
anti-	against
auto-	self
bi-	double, two
brady-	slow
circum-	around
contra-	against, opposite
de-	down, from, away from, not
dia-	across, through, apart
dis-	separation, away from
dys-	bad, difficult, abnormal
ecto-	outer, outside
en-	in, into, within
endo-	inner, inside
epi-	over, on, upon
eryth-	red
ex-	out, out of, from, away from
hemi-	half
hyper-	excessive, too much, high
hypo-	under, decreased, less than normal
in-	in, into, within, not
inter-	between
intra-	within
intro-	into, within
leuk-	white
macro-	large
mal-	bad, illness, disease
mega-	large
micro-	small
mono-	one, single
neo-	new
non-	not
olig-	small, scanty
para-	abnormal
per-	by, through
peri-	around
poly-	many, much
post-	after, behind
pre-	before, in front of, prior to
pro-	before, in front of
re-	again
semi-	half
sub-	under
super-	above, over, excess
supra-	above, over
tachy-	fast, rapid
trans-	across
uni-	one

Table 4-3   Common Roots

ROOT (COMBINING VOWEL)	MEANING
abdomin(o)	abdomen
aden(o)	gland
adren(o)	adrenal gland
angi(o)	vessel
arterio	artery
arthr(o)	joint
broncho	bronchus, bronchi
card, cardi(o)	heart
cephal(o)	head
chole, chol(o)	bile
chrond(o)	cartilage
colo	colon, large intestine
cost(o)	rib
crani(o)	skull
cyan(o)	blue
cyst(o)	bladder, cyst
cyt(o)	cell
dent(o)	tooth
derma	skin
duoden(o)	duodenum
encephal(o)	brain
enter(o)	intestines
fibr(o)	fiber, fibrous
gastr(o)	stomach
gloss(o)	tongue
gluc(o)	sweetness, glucose
glyc(o)	sugar
gyn, gyne, gyneco-	woman
hem, hema, hemo, hemat(o)	blood
hepat(o)	liver
hydr(o)	water
hyster(o)	uterus
ile(o), ili(o)	ileum
laparo	abdomen, loin, or flank
laryng(o)	larynx
lith(o)	stone
mamm(o)	breast, mammary gland
mast(o)	mammary gland, breast
meno	menstruation
my(o)	muscle
myel(o)	spinal cord, bone marrow
necro	death
nephr(o)	kidney
neur(o)	nerve
ocul(o)	eye
oophor(o)	ovary
ophthalm(o)	eye
orth(o)	straight, normal, correct
oste(o)	bone
ot(o)	ear
ped(o)	child, foot

Continued

Table 4-3—cont'd. Common Roots

ROOT (COMBINING VOWEL)	MEANING
pharyng(o)	pharynx
phleb(o)	vein
pnea	breathing, respiration
pneum(o)	lung, air, gas
proct(o)	rectum
psych(o)	mind
pulmo	lung
py(o)	pus
rect(o)	rectum
rhin(o)	nose
salping(o)	eustachian tube, uterine tube
splen(o)	spleen
sten(o)	narrow, constriction
stern(o)	sternum
stomat(o)	mouth
therm(o)	heat
thoraco	chest
thromb(o)	clot, thrombus
thyr(o)	thyroid
toxo	poison
toxic(o)	poison, poisonous
trache(o)	trachea
uro	urine, urinary tract, urination
urethr(o)	urethra
urin(o)	urine
uter(o)	uterus
vas(o)	blood vessel, vas deferens
ven(o)	vein
vertebr(o)	spine, vertebrae

Table 4-4 Common Suffixes

SUFFIX	MEANING
-algia	pain
-asis	condition, usually abnormal
-cele	hernia, herniation, pouching
-centesis	puncture and aspiration of
-cyte	cell
-ectasis	dilation, stretching
-ectomy	excision, removal of
-emia	blood condition
-genesis	development, production, creation
-genic	producing, causing
-gram	record
-graph	a diagram, a recording instrument
-graphy	making a recording
-iasis	condition of

Continued

Table 4-4—cont'd. Common Suffixes

SUFFIX	MEANING
-ism	a condition
-itis	inflammation
-logy	the study of
-lysis	destruction of, decomposition
-megaly	enlargement
-meter	measuring instrument
-metry	measurement
-oma	tumor
-osis	condition
-pathy	disease
-penia	lack, deficiency
-phasia	speaking
-phobia	an exaggerated fear
-plasty	surgical repair or reshaping
-plegia	paralysis
-rrhage, -rrhagia	excessive flow
-rrhaphy	stitching, suturing
-rrhea	profuse flow, discharge
-scope	examination instrument
-scopy	examination using a scope
-stasis	maintenance, maintaining a constant level
-stomy, -ostomy	creation of an opening
-tomy, -otomy	incision, cutting into
-uria	condition of the urine

Abbreviations

Abbreviations are shortened words. They are used to save time and space. Your agency has a list of acceptable abbreviations. You can use them when recording client observations. If you are not sure of an abbreviation, write out the entire word. Communication will not be accurate if an abbreviation is used incorrectly. The abbreviations common in health care are listed in Table 4-5.

The Client's Record

The client's record is written evidence of the care a client has received. The record is often called the *chart*. The care provided, the client's response, and the effect of care are included. The written account of specific activities, events, or observations is called *documentation*. Writing in the record is called *recording* or *charting*. The record contains documentation from members of the health team involved in the client's care. The record is a legal document.

Purpose

Careful, accurate documentation is important to the client, doctor, health team, agency, and you. There are several important reasons for the client's record.

1. Documentation gives written evidence of the care provided, the client's response, and the effect of care.
2. Plans for further care and changes in care are written. Other members of the health team can read the record and be up to date.
3. Members of the health team can communicate with each other. The doctor and team members base plans for care on information in the chart.
4. Care can be reviewed and evaluated.
5. Services are documented as required by Medicare and insurance companies.
6. The record can be used in a court of law to prove the care given and observations.
7. Facts about the client's care can be recalled when necessary. Team members may not remember every detail from two weeks ago or last month.

TABLE 4-5 Common Abbreviations

ABBREVIATION	MEANING
@	at
A, Ax	axillary
a	before
abd.	abdomen
$\overline{ac}$, Ac	before meals
ADL	activities of daily living
ad lib	as desired
am, AM	morning
amb.	ambulatory, capable of walking
amt.	amount
approx.	approximately
AP	apical pulse
app't	appointment
as tol	as tolerated
bid	twice a day
BM	bowel movement
BRP	bathroom privileges
BR	bed rest
C	centigrade
$\overline{c}$	with
CA	cancer
Ca	calcium
CAD	coronary artery disease
cath.	catheter
CBC	complete blood count
cc	cubic centimeter
CHF	congestive heart failure
c/o	complains of
cm	centimeter
CNS	central nervous system
CO_2	carbon dioxide
COPD	chronic obstructive pulmonary disease
CPR	cardiopulmonary resuscitation
C-section	cesarean section
CVA	cerebrovascular accident
d/c	discontinue
Disch.	discharge
DME	durable medical equipment
DOA	dead on arrival
Dr.	doctor
drsg.	dressing
Dx	diagnosis
ECG, EKG	electrocardiogram
EEG	electroencephalogram
EENT	eyes, ears, nose, and throat
ER	emergency room
ETOH	alcohol
F	Fahrenheit
FBS	fasting blood sugar
FF	force fluids
ft.	feet
f/u	follow up

Continued

TABLE 4-5—cont'd.   Common Abbreviations

ABBREVIATION	MEANING
FUO	fever of unknown origin
FWB	full weight bearing
fract., fx	fracture
gal	gallon
G.I.	gastrointestinal
gtt(s)	drops
G tube	gastrostomy tube
GYN	gynecology
H_2O	water
hr	hour
hs, HS	hour of sleep
HHA	home health aide, home health agency
HNV	has not voided
ht	height
in	inch
I&O	intake and output
irr	irregular
IV	intravenous
kg	kilogram
L	liter, left
Lt	left
lab	laboratory
lbs, #	pound
Lg, lge	large
Liq.	liquid
LLQ	left lower quadrant
LMP	last menstrual period
LOC	level of consciousness, loss of consciousness
LPN	licensed practical nurse
LUQ	left upper quadrant
LVN	licensed vocational nurse
MD, M.D.	medical doctor
meds	medications
MI	myocardial infarction
ml	millileter
MS	multiple sclerosis
Na	sodium
NaCl	sodium chloride (salt)
N/A salt, NAS	no added salt
NG	nasogastric tube
NKA	no known allergies
NKDA	no known drug allergies
noc, NOC	at night
NPO, N.P.O.	nothing by mouth
N/S	normal saline
N/V	nausea and vomiting
NWB	nonweight bearing
O_2	oxygen
OB	obstetrics
obs.	observation
OD	right eye
OOB	out of bed

Continued

TABLE 4-5—cont'd.   Common Abbreviations

ABBREVIATION	MEANING
ortho	orthopedics
OS	left eye
OT., O.T.	occupational therapy, occupational therapist
OU	both eyes
oz	ounce
$\overline{p}$	after
P	pulse
p.c.	after meals
Peds	pediatrics
PERL, PEARL	pupils equal and reactive to light
pm, PM	afternoon
po	by mouth
prn, p.r.n.	as needed, whenever necessary
PT, P.T.	physical therapy, physical therapist
pt	patient, pint
PWB	partial weight bearing
q	every
qam., q am	every morning
qd	every day
qh	every hour
q2h	every two hours
q3h	every three hours
q4h	every four hours
qhs, QHS	every night at bedtime
qid, Q.I.D.	four times a day
qod	every other day
qs	quantity sufficient
qt	quart
R	respiration, rectal temperature, right
Rt.	right
RLQ	right lower quadrant
RN	registered nurse
ROM	range-of-motion
RUQ	right upper quadrant
Rx	prescription or treatment ordered by the doctor
$\overline{s}$	without
sm.	small
SOB	shortness of breath
ss	one half
stat	immediately
S&A	sugar and acetone
STD	sexually transmitted diseases
tbsp	tablespoon
tid, TID	three times a day
TPR	temperature, pulse, and respiration
tsp	teaspoon
V.D.	venereal disease
VS	vital signs
WBC	white blood count
w/c	wheelchair
wt	weight
x	times

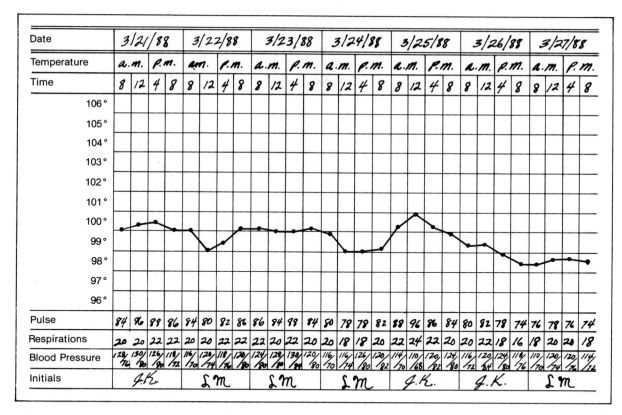

Fig. 4-1 Graphic sheet.

Forms

The record contains several forms. They are used by health team members to plan and evaluate the client's care. You might not use each form. However, you should be familiar with them. Your supervisor will show you how to use your agency's forms. Ask for help if you are not sure how to complete them.

Graphic sheet—Used to record temperature, pulse, respirations and blood pressure (Fig. 4-1). This sheet may also include the client's weight, urine output, and frequency of bowel movements.

Nursing notes or progress notes—Used to record observations, treatments, care provided, and the client's response to care. Any contact with the client is recorded. This includes phone conversations and home visits. These forms may have lines for writing (narrative form) or check lists (Fig. 4-2). Check lists for home health aides include types of bathing: bed bath, shower, or tub bath. They may also include type of activity: ambulated with assistance, with walker, cane, etc. Nurses, therapists, and home health aides may use separate progress notes. Physical therapists may have check lists specific to exercise.

Care plan—A written plan that lists the client's problems and goals and activities to improve the client's condition (Fig. 4-3). The care plan is developed by the nurse. It continually changes as the client's condition changes. Each client has a care plan.

ADL Sheet—The activities of daily living (ADL) sheet lists daily functions such as bathing, grooming, mouth care, meals, exercise, and toileting (Fig. 4-4). The form is used to record the amount of assistance a client needs for each activity. This form also tells the amount and kind of care the client needs.

Work plan—Assigns household and personal care duties over one week (see Chapter 9, page 118). It describes what needs to be done (bathing, meals, linen change, cleaning) and who will perform each task (aides, family members, or the client). The work plan also states when the tasks should be completed. This form is useful for clients receiving 8 or more hours of care daily. It is also helpful when several different aides care for the same client.

Physician order sheet—Used by the doctor to write the orders for client's care (Fig. 4-5). Medication, treatment, therapy, and activity orders are written on the order sheet. Orders are changed by the physician as the client's condition changes.

Initial assessment sheet—Describes the client's condition when the first contact was made with the agency (Fig. 4-6). The form contains the client's name, date, time, description of the problem, physical needs,

HOME HEALTH AIDE VISIT RECORD

Johnson, James   3/14/88   11:00 AM
Client Name   _Date_   _Time of Visit_

SUMMARY

11⁴⁵AM - Client reports that he's "feeling stronger today."
Assisted client with shower, mouth care & skin care. Noted a
red rash on the client's lower back - reported to supervisor at
11²⁵ a.m.
12³⁰ changed bed linens & straightened bedroom. Prepared lunch -
client's appetite good. Ambulated with assistance.

1½ hrs.   3248 - 3258   ⟨10 mi⟩
Total Visit Time   _Mileage_
none   Sue Smith   HHA
A _Supplies Used_   _Signature & Title_

HOMECARE SERVICES

HOME CARE & HOSPICE AGENCY

Smith, Mary

Home Health Aide Visit—Care Given   _Last Name_   _First Name_
☐ HHA Supervision Completed

ACTIVITY	EXERCISES	HYGIENE	SKIN CARE	DIET
☐ Ambulated	☐ Passive ROM	☒ Bed Bath	☒ Massage	Feeder: ☐ Yes ☒ No
☐ Walker	☐ Active ROM	☐ Sponge Bath	☐ Sheepskin	Solids: ☐ Good
☒ Up in Chair	☐ Other___	☐ Shower	☒ Linen Change	☒ Fair
☐ Wheel Chair	☐ Other___	☐ Tub	☐ Turn and Position	☐ Poor
☐ Commode		☐ Shampoo	☐ (X's) ___	Fluids: ☒ Good
		☒ Oral Hygiene	☐ Other ___	☐ Fair
		☐ Shaving	☐ ___	☐ Poor

BOWEL MOVEMENT: Frequency per 24 hrs. _None_   ☐ Incontinence
URINARY OUTPUT: Frequency per 24 hrs. _Catheter_   ☐ Incontinence
VITAL SIGNS: BP 140/80   T 98⁴   P 76   R 16
Observations: 10 am - found client lying in bed soiled c̄ urine - noted
urine leaking around catheter. Client states she is constipated.
Notified supervisor of client's condition.

Travel Time: _15 min_   Time w/pt. (include charting): _2 hours_
              3/16/88   Joan Blake, HHA
B   _Date_   _Signature/Title_

Fig. 4-2 Nursing notes. **A,** Narrative form. **B,** Check list.

HOME HEALTH AIDE CARE PLAN

Jessie Miller _____ 3/13/88
Client   Date

CVA _____ 3 Times per week _____ Donna May
Diagnosis   Frequency of Care   Case Manager

PERSONAL CARE	TOTAL	ASSIST
Bath: ☐ shower ☐ tub ☑ partial bed ☐ complete bed		✓
Oral Hygiene: ☐ total mouth care ☑ dentures		✓
Hair: ☑ shampoo ☐ frequency 1/wk ☑ comb & brush	✓	
Shave: ☐ face ☐ underarms ☐ legs		
Skin Care: ☑ lotion ☐ powder ☑ massage		✓
Nail Care: ☑ clean & file ☑ fingers ☐ toes		✓
Dressing: ☐ pajamas ☑ street clothes		✓
Elimination: ☐ toilet ☐ commode ☐ urinal ☑ bedpan		✓
TREATMENTS & TASKS		
Hot and Cold Applications: ☐ heating pad ☐ ice pack		
Medications: ☑ admin. by family ☐ admin. by client ☐ prepoured		✓
Dressing Changes: ☐ frequency		
Empty Catheter/Ostomy Bag: ☐ record observations		
Monitor Bowel Function: ☐ enema, type		
Catheter Care: ☐ type		
Test Urine & Record		
ROM Exercises: ☑ active ☐ passive ☐ resistive		✓
Fluids: ☐ encourage ☐ limit ☐ record I&O		
Vital Signs: ☐ frequency of visit q visit	✓	
ACTIVITY & LIMITATIONS		
☐ bedrest ☐ BRP ☐ position & turn _____ hrs ☐ transfer bed ☑ transfer chair ☐ hoyer lift ☐ walk ☐ crutches ☐ cane ☐ wheelchair		✓
HOMEMAKING		
☑ linen change ☐ laundry ☑ light housekeeping ☐ meal preparation ☐ diet _____ ☐ shopping		✓

Fig. 4-3 Care plan.

ACTIVITIES OF DAILY LIVING ASSESSMENT

Mary Allen _____ 3/30/88 _____ Fractured left hip
Name   Date   Diagnosis

LEVEL OF ABILITY:

I = Independent   S = Supervision Needed   A = Assistance Needed   U = Unable   NA = Not Applicable

BATHING:	NA Tub	NA Shower	A Sponge	NA Bed				
GROOMING:	A Skin Care	I Oral Hygiene	A Dressing	I Eating				
MOBILITY:	NA Cane	S Walker	NA Crutch	U Stairs				
	A Sitting	S Standing	NA Wheelchair	S Ambulation	A Transfers			

HOME ASSESSMENT

Environmental Hazards ___ Unable to navigate stairs ___

Rugs Wall to wall   Stairs 10   Furniture _____   Toilet Raised seat

Other
Needs ___ 10 steps to upstairs bedroom — converted dining room into
bedroom during recovery period

Mary Jones, RN _____ 3/31/88
Signature of Nurse   Date

Fig. 4-4 ADL sheet.

HOME HEALTH SERVICES
PHYSICIAN'S ORDERS

Brown, Jack
Name

_3/3/88 @ 11 AM_
Date

☒ Telephone Order   ☐ Visit Change   ☐ Physical Therapy

☐ Verbal Order   ☒ Increase   ☐ Occupational Therapy

☐ Initial Referral   ☐ Decrease   ☐ Speech Therapy

☒ Addendum to Treatment Plan   ☐ R.N.   ☐ Social Services

☐ Interruption of Service   ☒ H H A   ☐ Laboratory

☐ Discharge Patient   ☐ Supplies   ☐ Respiratory

    ☐ Medications

☒ Special Orders

HHA to visit 3 times a week × 3 weeks

☒ Comments

Condition is worsening, weakness has increased, having difficulty getting out of bed. Needs assistance with bathing, skin care, oral hygiene and transfers

Signature of Nurse _Mary Jones RN_

MD Name _MARK DOUGLAS_   Date Sent: _3/7/88_

MD Signature _M. Douglas_   Date: _3/8/88_

Fig. 4-5 Physician's order sheet.

INITIAL ASSESSMENT SHEET

Requested Visit Date 3/12/88
Pt. Name _Judy Black_
Address _3 Sunhill_
City, State, Zip _Northtown MI 59786_
Phone # _555-3344_
Birthdate _2/14/42_
☐ Male ☒ Female
Hospital _Lakeview_
Adm. _3/2/88_ Dc. _3/12/88_

Health Insurance Type & Number
MCare A or B _—_
Medi-Cal _—_
Private _BC-40006-223_
Fee Information Given
☒ Yes ☐ No
Hospice Discussed with
☐ Patient ☐ Family
by _NA_

Referred by _Dr. Brown_
Agency _—_
Phone _555-6000_
Physician _Dr. Brown_
Address _17 Northway_
City, State, Zip _Oakville MI 59788_
Phone # _555-6000_
Date of Last MD Visit _3/12/88_

Referral Diagnosis and Date of Onset _fx pelvis, fx femur (L), fx (R) arm_ _12/8_
Prognosis _Good_ Does Pt. Know? _—_ Family _—_
Medical HX and Other Diagnoses _Involved in auto accident & multiple fractures, discharged from hospital with an open draining wound (R) side chest, (L) leg in balanced suspension traction - (R) arm casted above elbow, history of insulin dependent diabetes_

Services Requested and Frequency: ☒ RN ☒ HHA ☒ MSW ☒ OT ☒ PT ☐ ST ☐ HMKR
(RN): assess wound healing, change dressing qod X 2 wks (HHA): provide personal care daily X 3 wks (PT): muscle strengthening exercises (OT): instruct in ADL
Precautions/Restrictions (Activity, Exercise, Weightbearing) _bed bound - in continuous traction, needs ROM exercises_

Home Environment/Psycho-Social Factors _lives with husband who works fulltime during daytime hours - husband has a back problem limiting his ability to provide personal care for his wife_

Nearest Relatives/Who to Notify in Emergencies—Name/Address/Phone _George Black - husband work phone 555-4321_

Equipment/Supplies: ☒ Need to order: _hospital bed, sheepskin, bed pan, trapeze_
☐ Pt. currently has:

Occupation (current or previous) _Accountant_ Diet _Reg Diabetic_
Medications _NKDA_
Other Information/Directions _MSW should see this client to help arrange additional homemaker assistance in the home during the husband's absence_
reg insulin 10 units q AM
Keflex 500 mg QID X 14 days
Tylenol #3 one-two tabs 3-4 hrs PRN pain
Dulcolax supp PRN constipation

Referral Taken By _Nancy Smith_ _RN_ _3/12/88_
Name Title Date

Fig. 4-6 Initial assessment sheet.

activity level, allergies, nutritional needs, habits and preferences, sleep habits, medications, communication problems and abilities, and other important information.

Client information sheet—Gives the client's age, birth date, address, marital status, insurance carrier, and doctor (Fig. 4-7). The form may also list the names, addresses, and phone numbers of persons to contact in an emergency.

Reporting and Recording Observations

You spend more time with the client than any other team member. You will be responsible for recog-

nizing changes in the client's condition. You may be the first to notice such changes. The changes can be an improvement or worsening of a condition.

Home health aides are the eyes and ears of a home health agency. Your observations about the client provide important information to the nurse and doctor. The information is used to plan the client's care. You must report and record your observations accurately.

You will use your senses to observe the client. Your senses of sight, hearing, smell, and touch will tell you a great deal about the client's condition. A *sign* is a change you see, hear, feel, or smell. A *symptom* is how the client feels. You cannot see, hear, feel, or smell what the client feels. The following are examples of signs and symptoms.

CLIENT INFORMATION SHEET

Client _____

Address _____

City, State, Zip_____

Telephone _____

Directions _____

Marital Status_____ Sex_____

Birth Date_____ Age_____

Medicare # _____

Private Ins. Co. _____

Primary DX_____ Onset_____

Operative Procedures _____

Primary Physician _____

Address _____

Telephone _____

Acute Hospital _____

Extended Care Facility _____

Nearest Relative or Friend _____

Address _____

Relationship_____ Telephone_____

Person at Home to Help _____

Language Spoken _____

Contact Person _____

Telephone _____

Medicaid/Medical # _____

Policy #_____

Secondary DX_____

Other MD _____

Address _____

Telephone _____

From_____ To_____

From_____ To_____

Services Requested: ☐ RN ☐ LVN/LPN ☐ PT ☐ OT ☐ ST ☐ MSW ☐ HHA ☐ HM

Physician's Verbal Orders _____

Other Relevant Information _____

Diet_____ LOC_____ Vision/Hearing Problems_____

Allergies: Food_____ Drugs_____

Physical Assistance Needed:

BATHING
☐ Bed
☐ Shower
☐ Partial
☐ Complete
☐ Other _____

AMBULATION
☐ Cane
☐ Walker
☐ Wheelchair
☐ Assistance of 1 or 2 _____
☐ Activity Limitation _____

TOILET
☐ Independent
☐ Incontinent
☐ Catheter
☐ Commode
☐ Bathroom

EATING
☐ Feeds Self
☐ Needs Help
☐ Other _____

Alertness: ☐ Alert ☐ Confused at Times ☐ Senile

Homemaking Needs: ☐ Cooking ☐ Laundry ☐ Shopping ☐ Housekeeping (Heavy/Light) ☐ Other _____

Anticipated Start of Care: _____   Date of Intake:_____

Referred by _____   Case Manager_____

Fig. 4-7 Client information sheet.

Signs	Symptoms
Skin rash	Pain
Wound drainage	Discomfort
Bleeding	Fatigue
Pale skin	Nervousness
Sweating	Emotional upset
Cough	Headache
Hoarse voice	Abdominal cramping
Bad breath	Blurred vision
Hot, dry skin	Dizziness

Observe your clients each time you are with them. Table 4-6 lists the basic observations you will need to make and report to your supervisor. The best time for observation is when you give personal care. Watch your client. Notice how he or she moves around, his or her skin condition, and how the client responds to you. Some clients always walk with a limp, shake, or forget your name. Know what is normal for your client so you can recognize changes.

Changes in the client's condition may be sudden or gradual. Remember that medications can cause many changes in a client's condition. Watch for sudden changes in mood or activity after a client takes a new medication. Report all changes. Remember, your responsibility is to observe and report, not to solve or diagnose a problem. Your supervisor will assess the situation and take appropriate action. Make sure you record your observations immediately so you do not forget important details. Also, record who you talked to and when you reported your observations (recording is discussed on page 42).

Some clients will tell you about their pain or problem right away. Others will be more private. They might not want to bother you. They may feel like com-

TABLE 4-6   Basic Observations

General changes
Elevated temperature
Mood changes
Excessive food or fluid intake
Vital sign changes
Excessive fatigue
Listlessness

Skin, nails, and hair
Changes in color, texture, or odor
- Red, blue, gray, yellow, purple, green, or black skin changes
- Bumps, lumps, cuts, bruises, bleeding, sores, rashes, peeling
- Foul odor
Swelling
Change in moisture
- Moist, clammy skin
- Dry, flaky skin
- Brittle hair and nails
Change in temperature; hot or cold
Loss of hair
Insects on the body or in the hair

Musculoskeletal
Change in walking pattern
- Limping
- Shuffle
- Paralysis
- Weakness
- Unsteadiness
- Balance problems
- Inability to walk
Pain with movement
Swelling of limbs and joints
Red, white, or shiny hot areas over joints
Deformity
Loss of function
Cold or hot extremity
Obvious injury to a limb

Nervous system
Shaking body or limbs, twitching, numbness, paralysis
Eye changes
- Sensitivity to light, blurred or double vision
- Red or yellow vision
- Glassy or dull appearance to the eyes
- Fixed stare
- Unequal pupil size, pupils pinpoint or dilated
Headache
Pain spreading down the back, legs, or arms
Discharge from the eyes or ears
Client is slow to respond or cannot awaken (especially after a head injury)

Circulatory system
Swelling
- In ankles or feet
- In the neck, axillae (underarms), or groin
Change in color
- Blue or white nail beds
- Face is gray, pale, red, or white
Change in vital signs
- Significant increase or decrease in blood pressure: systolic BP less than 90 mm Hg, or greater than 150 mm Hg; diastolic greater than 90 mm Hg
- Rapid or slow pulse rate: greater than 100 or less than 60 beats per minute
- Pulse rate weak or irregular
Chest pain spreading to the neck, jaw, shoulders, or arms

Respiratory system
Changes in respiratory rate
- Slow, deep breathing
- Rapid breathing
- Shortness of breath
Noisy breathing
Productive cough
- Sputum red, green, yellow, brown, or black
- Sputum thick or thin
- Sputum has a foul odor
Painful breathing
Congestion
Sore throat
Runny nose

Digestive system
Mouth and tongue changes
- Dry mouth
- Cracks, sores, or bleeding
- Swelling
- Change in color
- Tongue covered with white coating
Bad breath
Complaints of abdominal pain
Nausea or vomiting
Abdominal bloating (distention)
Poor appetite
Difficulty eating, chewing, swallowing
Blood in the stool or vomitus
Diarrhea or constipation
Abnormal stools
- Black, yellow, red, or clay colored stools
- Foul smell
- Hard, dry stools
Painful or difficult bowel movements
Excessive hiccuping or belching
Excessive gas

Urinary system
Difficulty urinating
Painful urination
Abnormal urine
- Brown, red, orange color
- Cloudy urine   *Continued*

TABLE 4-6—cont'd.   Basic Observations

- Sediment in the urine
- Foul odor
Frequent urination
Incontinence
No urine output in 6 to 8 hour period
Incontinence when coughing, laughing, or vomiting
Pain in the pelvic area or lower back
Inability to empty bladder completely

Reproductive system
Excessive bleeding during menstrual periods
Excessive cramping
Vaginal discharge

- Green, yellow, brown, white, or cheesy discharge
- Foul odor
Irregular menstrual periods
Breast changes
- Lumps
- Discolored or hard patches
- Change in shape of breast or nipple
- Pain
- Discharge from nipples
Discharge from penis
Swollen testicles, female labia, or breasts
Sores or skin breakdown on the genitals

plainers if they mention their discomforts. Make sure you give clients the chance to tell you how they feel. Do not decide how they feel for them. Listen carefully and provide support as needed. Assure clients that the information is important. Also, tell them that you will share the information with your supervisor.

Clients need to give you as much information as possible. You may need to ask a client to describe a problem. Here are some questions you can ask:
- What is the problem (pain, difficulty breathing, vomiting, bleeding, etc.)?
- Where is the problem? Ask the client to point to the area.
- Has the problem occurred before? When?
- How long have you had the problem?
- What makes it worse or better?
- What has been done to correct the problem? Did it help?

You will need to report your observations to your supervisor. Some problems do not require immediate attention. Others need prompt medical care. Make sure you know your agency's policies on calling an ambulance. Be prepared when you are reporting a problem. Know the answers to these questions before you call your supervisor:
1. What is the specific observation? How is it different than the client's normal pattern?
2. When was the problem discovered? By whom?
3. How severe is the problem?
4. How well is the client handling the problem?
5. What are the client's vital signs?
6. What, if anything, have you done to help solve the problem?

Your supervisor will assess the situation based on the information you give, the client's condition, and the plan of care. You may be asked to continue observing the client for additional changes. Or you may be instructed to perform a specific action. Sometimes your

supervisor or another nurse will visit the client to assess the situation. Your client may need to go to the hospital for further evaluation.

Your agency will have policies describing how to report client changes. The policies may involve recording your observations. In most agencies your supervisor will review your charting as soon as you turn it in to the agency. If you think a problem is serious and cannot wait, notify your supervisor immediately. If you are not sure if you should report a change, it is best to report it anyway.

In most cases you will report to a specific person. Make sure you know how to reach your supervisor. Many offices close at 5 PM. There should be an "on-call" staff to assist you 24 hours a day. On-call staff provide service after the office closes. They are available for emergencies. The agency may have an answering service to take messages after the office is closed. When you leave a message, include the following information:
- Your name
- The date and time
- The name and age of the client
- The client's address, phone number, and nearest cross street
- Brief description of the problem
- How long you will remain at the client's residence
- Where you can be reached in 10 minutes, half an hour, and in one hour

Recording

Each agency has specific policies about home health aides charting. Some agencies have checkoff lists. Others have lined paper for you to record your observations and activities. Objective and subjective recording may be used to describe a client's condition.

Objective recording is what you see, hear, smell, and feel (signs). It can be measured. For example, two people observe the same wound. They both should describe it the same way because they observe the same thing. They record a wound that is "3 cm wide and foul-smelling."

Subjective recording is what the client tells you (symptoms). You cannot see, hear, feel, or smell a client's headache. But you can record what the client tells you about the headache. You should record the client's own words whenever possible. Use quotation marks to show that you are quoting the client.

Below are some examples of objective and subjective reporting.

Objective Reporting
- The client's skin is moist and hot.
- The client's breathing is 26 respirations per minute.
- The client's urine is cloudy and has a foul odor.
- The client is speaking in a loud voice and is crying.

Subjective Reporting
- The client states, "My left calf hurts."
- The client says, "I didn't sleep all night."
- The client is complaining of pain in his left arm.
- The client says she is very worried about her children.

The record of your observations should give a clear picture of how the client feels and looks. There should also be a clear picture of what you have done to help the client. Your language should be simple and clear. Stick to the facts. However, give enough information to cover all important details. Remember, if something is not charted, it is assumed that the task was not done. The client's chart is proof that you have completed assigned tasks. Your recording is reviewed by your supervisor, the state, and insurance reviewers (Blue Cross, Medicare, etc.). They read charting to make sure the care given is necessary and appropriate. If someone fails to properly document activities, the agency may not be paid for the care.

The following guidelines apply to all charting.

GENERAL GUIDELINES

1. Charting should be specific and describe the complaint or situation. To write "The client is not feeling well" gives little useful information. More specific information is needed. "The client reports a throbbing headache on the left side" is a better statement.
2. Avoid general words such as "normal," "good," and "adequate." The words have different meanings to different people.
3. Write neatly.
4. Record all entries in black ink. Do not use a pencil. Only black ink photocopies well.
5. Start all entries with the date and time.
6. Finish all entries with your full signature and title.
7. Record observations when:
   a. The client's condition changes
   b. The client shows a lack of improvement

c. There is a response to a medication or treatment
d. You complete a procedure
8. Note the time when you noticed the change. Also note when the client first noted or reported the problem.
9. Chart at least every two hours. Gaps in charting may suggest that care was not given. Also, details are easily forgotten.
10. Do not write between the lines or leave empty spaces.
11. Record the client's own words whenever possible. Use quotation marks to show that you are quoting the client.
12. Write notes in the proper time sequence:
    9 AM - assisted Mrs. Brown to the commode.
    10 AM - assisted Mrs. Brown into the shower.
    10:30 AM - gave back massage.
13. Record all attempts to notify your supervisor of a client problem or change. If you are unable to reach your supervisor or other designated person, leave a message. Document the message, who you spoke with, the date, and the time.
14. Do not block out charting errors with correction tape or fluid, scribbling, or erasing. If you make an error, draw a line through the wrong entry, write "error," and initial the change (Fig. 4-8).
15. Use only abbreviations accepted by your agency. Write the entire word if you are unsure of an abbreviation.
16. Write "cont." or "continued" when continuing charting on another page. Write the time and date at the beginning of the new page.
17. Make sure the client's name is on each page of the chart.
18. Chart only your own activities and observations. Do not chart for another person. Your signature means that you made the entry and gave the documented care.
19. Never chart a procedure or treatment until it has been completed.

EXAMPLE: RECORDING YOUR OBSERVATIONS

You arrive at Mrs. Jones's home at 9:30 AM. Mrs. Jones is still in bed. She complains of a backache that she has had for two days. She tells you, "I feel terrible and haven't slept a wink all night." She refuses breakfast. You perform these tasks during your visit:
- Take vital signs
- Assist with a tub bath
- Make the bed
- Help the client dress
- Clean the client's bedroom, bathroom, and kitchen
- Report the client's complaints to your supervisor

Vital signs are blood pressure 120/80, pulse 86 beats per minute, respirations 20, temperature 98.8° F.

HOME HEALTH AIDE VISIT RECORD

Janet Brown   3/21/88   9 AM
_____   _____   _____
Client Name   Date   Time of Visit

SUMMARY

0930 - *Assisted with client's bedbath*

Noted bruised area over ~~R~~ error 9B Ⓛ *shoulder*

Client states she "fell last night" - reported incident

& observations to supervisor

1000 - *Prepared ~~lunch~~ error 9B breakfast - client's appetite good*

1030 - *VS T98 error 9B 140/90 98⁴ 82-16*

1½ hours   10
_____   _____
Total Visit Time   Mileage

none   *J. Brown HHA*
_____   _____
Supplies Used   Signature & Title

Fig. 4-8 The charting is crossed out and marked "error." The correct entry is then made.

During her bath you notice a fine red rash on her back and chest. You ask her about the rash and she tells you it itches.

Your charting might look something like this:
02/24/88
9:30 AM—Upon arrival found Mrs. Jones lying in bed c/o a backache x 2 days. She states, "I feel terrible and haven't slept a wink all night." VS—BP 120/80, TPR 98.8-86-20. Supervisor notified of client complaints.
10:00 AM—Client walked to the BR c̄ assistance. Assisted client with tub bath. Noted a fine red rash on the client's back and chest. Client states that the rash itches.
10:30 AM—Completed cleaning of bedroom, bathroom, and kitchen.
11:00 AM—Left Mrs. Jones lying in bed. She states she is comfortable and "feeling a little better." Client also states that her backache is better. Notified supervisor of client's condition and rash.

Case Conferences

Case conferences are formal, regular meetings. They are attended by all members of the health care team. The group meets to review how well clients are progressing. Clients are discussed individually. Team members involved with a client discuss the client's problems, needs, and progress. Client care plans are developed and changed as needed. The group may have new ideas for dealing with difficult situations. Home health aides often provide important information about clients. Case conferences are also a good time to evaluate your understanding of the client's needs. It is a time for sharing ideas and concerns.

The following is an example of a case conference:

Mrs. Moss is 66 years old. She recently returned home from the hospital after a serious car accident. She needs help walking because of severe weakness in both legs. She has a wound infection. She needs daily dressing changes and IV medications. She lives with her husband. He has taken time off work to care for her. He is a very neat housekeeper. He insists on giving all his wife's personal care.

The nurse visits Mrs. Moss to change the dressings. The nurse is teaching Mr. Moss how to start and stop the medication. The physical therapist is working with Mrs. Moss to increase muscle strength. The husband refused the help of a home health aide at first. He believed he could care for his wife himself.

Mr. Moss hurt his back lifting Mrs. Moss out of bed. Any heavy lifting causes severe pain in his lower back. He agreed to have a home health aide assist with his wife's personal care. Over the last two weeks Mr. Moss has become depressed. He often states that he is "failing his wife." He also says that he should be caring for her because he always promised he would when needed. He has become hostile towards the aide. He also interferes with the HHA's duties.

At case conference Mrs. Moss's case is presented. The physical therapist reports that Mrs. Moss is gaining strength. She can walk 10 feet with a walker before tiring. The therapist also reports that Mrs. Moss is concerned about her husband's behavior and depression. The RN reports that the wound has signs of healing. The nurse has been trying to teach Mr. Moss how to change the dressing. He is also being taught how to give IV medications. The nurse reports that the husband's willingness to participate has decreased. The husband says that he is afraid of making a mistake and does not want to hurt his wife.

The team agrees that he is more depressed. They also agree that he will be hard to teach at this time. The HHA reports that Mr. Moss has become more difficult to deal with. The aide reports that Mrs. Moss is not receiving the care she needs because Mr. Moss interferes.

The social worker suggests that she visit Mr. Moss. The social worker will help him cope with his wife's physical problems and needs. Mr. Moss will also be encouraged to explore his feelings about his wife's condition and his role in providing her care.

The team suggests that Mr. Moss try to help with those things that will not hurt his back. They include personal grooming, dressing changes, and encouraging his wife to practice her exercises. Each team member will try to get Mr. Moss involved in some part of his wife's care. The social worker will refer Mr. Moss to other counseling resources if necessary. His depression is expected to improve when he is more involved in his wife's care. Team members will report on the client's progress and the husband's response to the plan.

Summary

You have learned basic medical terminology and abbreviations. They will help you communicate in a clear and concise manner. You are responsible for reporting and recording information about the client's condition. You are the eyes and ears of the agency. You spend more time with the client than any other team member. You are often the first person to recognize changes in the client's condition. When you give care, you can observe changes in the client's behavior, habits, and physical condition. You must report these changes to your supervisor. You should communicate often with your supervisor and other team members. This allows you to share observations and gain new information about your client. Case conferences are a good way for team members to discuss the care and problems of clients.

Study Questions

1. Name signs and symptoms for each body system. What is the difference between a sign and a symptom?

2. Describe the things you should report to your supervisor.

3. Explain why it is important to report and record your observations and activities.

4. A client says "my stomach hurts." What questions should you ask to gain more information about the problem?

5. You are unable to reach your supervisor to discuss a client problem. What should you do? Why?

6. Give examples of objective and subjective recording.

Write the definition of the following prefixes.

7. a- _____
8. dys- _____
9. post- _____
10. olig- _____
11. hyper- _____
12. pre- _____
13. hemi- _____
14. hypo- _____

Write the definition of the following suffixes.

15. -algia _____
16. -itis _____
17. -ostomy _____
18. -ectomy _____
19. -emia _____
20. -osis _____

21. -rrhage _____
22. -penia _____
23. -pathy _____
24. -otomy _____

Write the definition of the following roots.

25. crani _____
26. cardio _____
27. mast _____
28. urino _____
29. pnea _____
30. cyano _____
31. arterio _____
32. colo _____
33. arthro _____
34. gastro _____
35. gluco _____
36. hemo _____
37. hystero _____
38. hepato _____
39. myo _____
40. nephro _____
41. phlebo _____
42. osteo _____
43. neuro _____
44. pneumo _____
45. psycho _____
46. thoraco _____

Match the item in column A with the item in column B.

Column A
47. _____ Intravenous
48. _____ Apnea
49. _____ Hemiplegia
50. _____ Thoracotomy
51. _____ Arthritis
52. _____ Bronchitis
53. _____ Anuria
54. _____ Hematuria
55. _____ Hysterectomy
56. _____ Hemorrhage

Column B
A Inflammation of a joint
B Blood in the urine
C Excessive flow of blood
D Paralysis on one side
E Surgical removal of the uterus
F No breathing
G Inflammation of the bronchi
H Incision into the chest
I No urine
J Within a vein

Write the abbreviation for the following terms.

57. As desired   _____
58. Complains of   _____
59. Twice a day   _____
60. Hour of sleep   _____
61. Intake and output   _____
62. Nothing by mouth   _____
63. When necessary   _____
64. Postoperative   _____
65. Every   _____
66. Wheelchair   _____

Circle T if the statement is true and F if the statement is false.

T F 67. The client's record cannot be used in a lawsuit because of the right to privacy.

T F 68. Information is collected about the client by using the senses of sight, hearing, touch, and smell.

T F 69. The care plan contains a summary of the medications and treatments ordered by the doctor.

T F 70. Case conferences are held to develop or revise the client's care plan.

T F 71. The client's record is used to communicate information about the client.

T F 72. The record is a written account of the client's illness and response to treatment.

T F 73. The record is a written account of care given by the health team.

T F 74. Blood pressure is recorded on the graphic sheet.

T F 75. When recording information you should erase if you make an error.

T F 76. Use the client's exact words whenever possible when recording.

T F 77. Record only what you have observed and done yourself.

T F 78. To save time, chart a procedure before it is completed.

Answers

7. Without, not
8. Bad, difficult, abnormal
9. After, behind
10. Scanty, small
11. Excessive, too much
12. Before, prior to
13. Half
14. Decreased, less than normal
15. Pain
16. Inflammation
17. Creation of an opening
18. Removal of, excision
19. Blood condition
20. Condition
21. Excessive flow
22. Lack, deficiency
23. Disease
24. Incision, cutting into

25. Skull
26. Heart
27. Breast
28. Urine
29. Breathing, respiration
30. Blue
31. Artery
32. Colon, large intestine
33. Joint
34. Stomach
35. Glucose, sweetness
36. Blood
37. Uterus
38. Liver
39. Muscle
40. Kidney
41. Vein
42. Bone

43. Nerve
44. Lung
45. Mind
46. Chest
47. J
48. F
49. D
50. H
51. A
52. G
53. I
54. B
55. E
56. C
57. ad lib
58. c/o
59. b.i.d.
60. H.S. (h.s.)

61. I&O
62. NPO
63. p.r.n.
64. postop (post op)
65. q
66. w/c
67. False
68. True
69. False
70. True
71. True
72. True
73. True
74. True
75. False
76. True
77. True
78. False

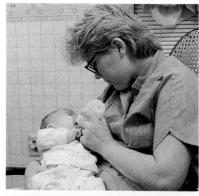

Understanding the Needs of Clients

5

What you will learn to do

■ Describe basic needs and how to help clients meet them

■ Describe how culture and religion affect health and illness

■ Explain what you should do when a client's culture and religion are different from yours

■ Identify and describe eight stages of growth and development

■ Describe the differences between sex and sexuality

■ Explain how injury, illness, and aging can affect sexuality and how to promote a client's sexuality

■ Explain how to deal with a sexually aggressive client

■ Describe how children react to illness and how to meet their emotional needs

- List the physical and emotional effects of aging
- Discuss why some elderly people may need home health care
- Describe the role of the home health aide in caring for ill and disabled clients

Key Terms

Bias An opinion, judgment, or attitude
Aging The process of growing older
Culture Values, beliefs, and customs that are passed down from one generation to the next
Disability Permanent loss of a physical or mental function
Esteem Worth and value
Extended family The nuclear family plus grandparents, aunts, uncles, and cousins
Menarche The start of menstruation
Menopause When menstruation stops
Need That which is required or desirable for life and mental well-being
Nuclear family Mother, father, and children who live together

Puberty When reproductive organs begin to function and secondary sex characteristics appear
Self-esteem When a person thinks that he or she is a worthwhile and valuable person
Sex The physical activities involving the organs of reproduction; the activities are done for pleasure or to have children
Sexuality That which relates to one's sex; physical, psychological, social, cultural, and spiritual factors that affect a person's feelings and attitudes about his or her sex

Needs

A *need* is something that is required or desirable for life and mental well-being. All human beings have the same basic needs. These needs are arranged in order of importance. The lower-level needs must be met before higher level needs. These basic needs, from the lowest level to the highest, are shown in Fig. 5-1. If one or all of the needs are not met, the person will have problems functioning. Illness or death may occur.

Normally people meet their own needs every day. Illness, disease, and injury make it hard for people to meet their own needs. When ill, they usually seek help from doctors, nurses, and other health workers.

Physical needs are necessary for life. These needs are:

Oxygen—all parts of the body need oxygen to function.
Water—the body contains a large amount of water. Water must be taken in to make up for water lost from the body.
Food—provides energy for the body.
Elimination—poisons are produced as the body uses food for energy. The body gets rid of the poisons through urination and bowel movements.
Rest—sleep is needed to restore energy. The body has time to heal. Body functions slow down for a period of time.

Safety and security relate to the need for shelter, clothing, and protection from harm and danger. Individuals need to be protected from cold, heat, wind, rain, and snow. They need to feel safe from harm and

danger that could affect life or the body. Harm and danger could be an accident, illness, fall, or disease. People also need to feel safe and secure in their minds. They need to know what to expect and what will happen.

The other needs relate to the mind and feelings. Sometimes they are called *psychological needs*. They involve emotions, social relationships, and the intellect. If a psychological need is not met, the person may become ill physically or mentally.

Love and belonging—to feel loved, cared about, and wanted by others. A person needs to have affection and to feel close to others.
Esteem and self-esteem—*esteem* means belief in someone's worth and value. *Self-esteem* means that a person thinks that he or she is a worthwhile and valuable person. Human beings want others to think well of them. They also need to think well of themselves.
Self-actualization—people need to learn and create. The person achieves what he or she is capable of doing. This need is not necessary for life itself. However, it is important to mental well-being.

When ill or injured, people may have difficulty meeting their basic needs. They may be unable to do common, everyday tasks. These include eating, dressing, bathing, walking, and even talking. These people may need home health care. You will help them meet their basic needs. You must be concerned with the client's physical and psychological needs. The client's care plan will list activities to help the client meet basic needs.

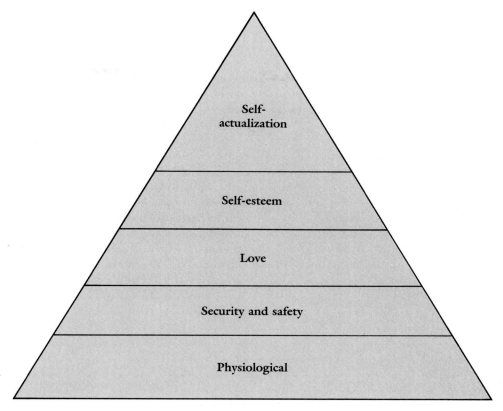

Fig. 5-1 The basic needs for life. These needs, from the lowest to the highest level, are physical needs, the need for safety and security, the need for love and belonging, the need for esteem, and the need for self-actualization. (From Sorrentino, S.A.: Mosby's textbook for nursing assistants, ed. 2. St. Louis, 1987, The C.V. Mosby Co.)

At times certain needs seem more important than others. For example, a husband is caring for his wife. He does everything to keep her clean and well-fed. However, she wants to do some things herself. In trying to be a good husband and caregiver, he does not let her do anything for herself. In doing so, he pays more attention to her physical needs than her psychological needs. However, her need for esteem (to do things herself), is more important to her.

Culture

Culture is the values, beliefs, and customs passed down from one generation to the next. Language, food habits, dress, work, and behavior are influenced by culture. Culture is also affected by neighborhoods and communities.

Families usually pass on their culture to the next generation. The family is made up of individuals who live together. They are usually related by blood or marriage. A family can also be a group of friends or a single parent and children. Parents and children who live together are called a *nuclear family*. An *extended family* includes the nuclear family plus grandparents, aunts, uncles, and cousins. Family members usually support, love, and protect one another. They teach their children about life and how to behave in society.

Families are as different from each other as individuals. They have cultural ideas about food and rules for behavior. Families also have attitudes about health and illness. Their cultural practices influence how basic needs are met. You may meet families with attitudes different from yours. Their ways of doing things may also be different. Remember, you are a guest in the client's home. Do not expect a family to do things your way. Try to understand their customs and practices.

People tend to mix with others who have similar likes and dislikes. This limits contact with other cultures. People are often uncomfortable with others who are different from themselves. The discomfort can lead to unfavorable *bias*. Bias is an opinion, judgment, or attitude. Bias often occurs when something is unfamiliar. If you are not familiar with your client's culture, unfavorable bias may occur. Discuss your concerns with your supervisor. Learn as much as possible about your client's culture, likes, dislikes, and attitudes. You can give better care if you understand your client's cultural practices.

Religion

Religion relates to spiritual beliefs and practices. Religion may influence food choices, living arrangements, health care, and days of worship. Therefore, religion also influences meeting basic needs.

Many religions have special ceremonies when a child is born or when a person dies. Religion may be important in your client's life. During illness the clergy can provide spiritual and psychological support. If the client cannot go to church, the pastor, priest, or rabbi will visit the client at home. Provide privacy during these visits.

Accept your client's religious beliefs and practices without bias. For example, some religious groups do not eat meat. Others eat only specially prepared meat. Still others eat meat on certain days of the week. Usually the family will tell you about their special dietary practices. The client's care plan will also give guidelines for special diets.

Growth and Development

No matter what their age, all human beings have the same basic needs. Age is a factor in how well an individual can meet his or her needs. An infant must receive total care from others. The infant must be fed, bathed, diapered, dressed, held, etc. The baby must be protected from danger. The baby's psychological needs are met when being held and cared for. They are also met when the caregiver responds to the baby's cry.

As children grow older, they learn to take care of themselves. However, they still need help. Two-year-olds may be able to feed themselves. But they cannot shop for food or make meals. Six-year-olds can dress, bathe, and play with others. However, they still need the care and supervision of adults.

As individuals grow older, they are able to meet their own basic needs. Less and less help is needed from others. The peak of independence (functioning alone) is reached during the adult years. However, as a person grows older, changes occur in the body. The changes weaken the body. Therefore, the elderly are more likely to become ill. They often have difficulty meeting their basic needs.

You may be assigned to care for clients of all ages. You need to be aware of the abilities of the different age groups. That will help you better understand their needs.

Table 5-1 presents 8 stages of growth and development. Normal characteristics are given for each age group. (Text continues on p. 57.)

Table 5-1   Growth and Development

STAGE	AGE	CHARACTERISTICS AND BEHAVIORS
Infancy	0-1 years	Rapid physical, psychological, social growth
		Depends on caregiver to meet basic needs (Fig. 5-2)
		Clothing, food, warmth, and toileting
		Holding, rocking, and comforting
		Gentle handling
		Responding to crying
		Talking to infant
		Calling infant by name
		Singing or playing music to infant
		Begins to eat solid food
		Begins to trust others
		Responds to mother, father, and others who are familiar
		Learns by sucking, touching, and looking at things around him or her
		Learns to crawl and then to walk
		Begins to talk
		Likes a stimulating environment
		Bright toys and objects (rattles, colored blocks, big beads, big balls, soft dolls and animals, books with big, bright pictures)
		Looking in a mirror

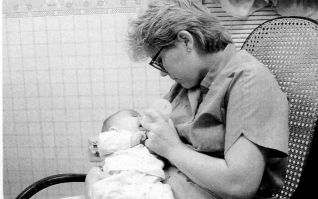

Fig. 5-2 An infant is being held and bottle-fed. Physical needs, the need for safety and security, and the need for love and belonging are being met.

Continued

Table 5-1—cont'd. Growth and Development

STAGE	AGE	CHARACTERISTICS AND BEHAVIORS
Infancy	0-1 years	Being played with Singing and music Being talked to and smiled at Needs a safe environment to roll, play, crawl, etc. Needs to be protected from danger: suffocation, poisoning, choking, burns, injury from toys
Toddler	1-3 years	Walks, crawls, runs, and jumps Learns and uses more words; "no" and "mine" are said often Has specific likes and dislikes for such things as food and toys Uses words or points to make needs known (drink, go, more, cookie, hot) Begins to develop fine motor skills 　Scribbles 　Builds towers with blocks 　Turns book pages 　Can feed self with a spoon (Fig. 5-3) Starts toilet training Has temper tantrums Imitates parents (says and does what they do) Less dependent on caregiver; can do some things alone Needs help with physical needs such as food, water, rest, toilet training Needs to play and explore in a safe environment Needs protection from auto accidents, drowning, burns, poisoning, suffocation, choking, falls, and injuries from sharp objects (toys, tools, and household objects) Learns safety practices about electrical outlets; stoves; machines; containers under the sink, in the garage, and in the medicine cabinet Needs to be treated and disciplined in a consistent manner Needs toys that fit age and abilities: dolls, dishes, pots and pans, trucks, children's furniture, books, push-pull toys, puzzles, finger paints, crayons, paper, balls, play dough Likes to hear stories and look at story books Will watch children's television programs Needs to be held, comforted, and hugged for safety, security, and psychological needs Needs to have caregiver respond when he or she asks for help or cries
Preschool	3-6 years	Becomes aware of own body and differences between the sexes; may play "doctor and nurse" games

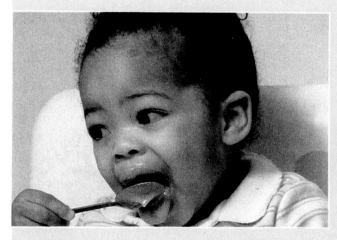

Fig. 5-3 Toddler is able to use a spoon. (From Sorrentino, S.A.: Mosby's textbook for nursing assistants, ed. 2, St. Louis, 1987, The C.V. Mosby Co.)

Continued

Table 5-1—cont'd. Growth and Development

STAGE	AGE	CHARACTERISTICS AND BEHAVIORS
Preschool	3-6 years	Asks questions about everything and the meaning of words; needs simple answers

Fig. 5-4 Three-year-olds enjoy cutting paper and using coloring books and crayons. (From Sorrentino, S.A.: Mosby's textbook for nursing assistants, ed. 2, St. Louis, 1987, The C.V. Mosby Co.)

Fig. 5-5 Three-year-olds are able to do some personal care activities. (From Sorrentino, S.A.: Mosby's textbook for nursing assistants, ed. 2, St. Louis, 1987, The C.V. Mosby Co.)

Fig. 5-6 Four-year-olds play "dress-up" and imitate adults. (From Sorrentino, S.A.: Mosby's textbook for nursing assistants, ed. 2, St. Louis, 1987, The C.V. Mosby Co.)

Becomes more coordinated; can run, skip, hop, catch a ball, skate, jump rope, and ride a tricycle.

Hand coordination increases: can use scissors, begins to print a few letters, can lace shoes (Fig. 5-4)

Wants to please parents or caregiver; wants to do things right

Is impatient and jealous and has mood swings; becomes calmer later in this stage

Relates to family members

Uses imagination in play and story telling; may have an imaginary playmate

Able to dress, bathe, tend to toileting, and other personal care activities (Fig. 5-5)

Begins to learn the difference between right and wrong

Learns to play with others

May go to nursery school

May have fears about monsters, ghosts, and boogeymen; may need a night light

Likes to have stories read to him or her

Learns safety rules for crossing streets, playing near streets, and other dangers

Can do simple tasks and errands around the house

Needs activities that promote muscle development, coordination, and learning of safety rules

Running

Climbing

Skating

Swimming

Sledding

Riding a tricycle

Playing in a sandbox and on playground equipment

Needs to use imagination (make-believe) and imitate adults (Fig. 5-6)

Dress-up

Playing with dolls

Doctor and nurse kits

Trains, planes, cars, and trucks

Telephones

Enjoys educational programs for children on television

Needs activities that develop hand coordination: books, crayons, puzzles, clay, and blocks

Continued

Table 5-1—cont'd. Growth and Development

STAGE	AGE	CHARACTERISTICS AND BEHAVIORS
School age	6-12 years	Is becoming more active, skilled, and graceful; needs activities that promote physical development: swimming, biking, skating, running, jumping rope, ballet (Fig. 5-7)
		Enters school
		Learns reading, writing, arithmetic, science, and history
		Is becoming more independent
		Able to meet personal care needs
		Wants to do household tasks and chores (Fig. 5-8)
		May babysit or have a paper route
		Friends (peers) and acceptance are very important (Fig. 5-9)
		Will act and dress like friends
		Prefers to be with friends rather than family
		Wants praise and rewards for achievements and accomplishments
		Becomes involved in group activities: teams, scouts, groups of friends, and clubs
		Plays games with rules: team sports and board games
		Likes previously learned activities such as swimming and biking
		Likes to read books
		Curious about male and female activities and responsibilities (jobs, family responsibilities, household chores)
		Curious about sex; needs sex education
		Begins to develop morals, values, and a conscience
		Learns acceptable behavior
		Learns manners
		Learns to judge right and wrong

Fig. 5-7 Six-year-olds enjoy being active. (From Sorrentino, S.A.: Mosby's textbook for nursing assistants, ed. 2, St. Louis, 1987, The C.V. Mosby Co.)

Fig. 5-8 School-age children enjoy household chores. (From Sorrentino, S.A.: Mosby's textbook for nursing assistants, ed. 2, St. Louis, 1987, The C.V. Mosby Co.)

Fig. 5-9 Belonging to a peer group is important to school-age children. (From Sorrentino, S.A.: Mosby's textbook for nursing assistants, ed. 2, St. Louis, 1987, The C.V. Mosby Co.)

Continued

Table 5-1—cont'd. Growth and Development

STAGE	AGE	CHARACTERISTICS AND BEHAVIORS
School age	6-12 years	Needs to have rules and restrictions enforced by parents Makes friends with members of own sex Rapid growth in height and weight (especially for girls) late in this stage Needs to do things that involve hand coordination: building model planes and cars, sewing, crafts
Adolescence	12-18 years	Stage between childhood and adulthood; begins with *puberty*, when reproductive organs begin to function and secondary sex characteristics appear *Girls* *Menarche* the start of menstruation (see Chapter 6, page 89) Breasts begin to grow Increase in height and weight Pubic and axillary (underarm) hair Hips widen *Boys* Increase in height and weight Testicles enlarge Pubic and axillary (underarm) hair Hair on face, chest, legs, and elsewhere on the body Nocturnal emissions ("wet dreams") in which the penis becomes erect and semen is released Voice deepens Rapid physical, emotional, and sexual growth Must adjust to changes in the body and the body's appearance Becomes independent of parents in decisions and activities Parties and dances Has a job Learns to drive a car More activities outside the home Does not share thoughts or feelings with parents Wants privacy Argues with parents Begins to date Belonging to a group is very important; gives a sense of belonging Dating and relationships with the opposite sex become very important; may "go steady" Emotional reactions are hard to control; may be happy one moment and sad and crying the next

Continued

Table 5-1—cont'd. Growth and Development

STAGE	AGE	CHARACTERISTICS AND BEHAVIORS

Adolescence	12-18 years	Develops an identity: determines who he or she is in terms of appearance, body, morals, attitudes, values, roles, and relationships
		Begins to think about a career and what to do after high school
		Increases ability to think, reason, and evaluate
		Sexual activities begin: hand holding, kissing, caressing, and touching (petting); some are more active sexually
		Sex education is important to prevent unwanted pregnancy and sexually transmitted diseases (see Chapter 21)
		Questions the morals, ethics, and values of adults, especially those of parents
		Needs to have guidance from parents about dating, when to be home, smoking, drinking alcohol, and the use of drugs
		Needs to be allowed activities common in this age group
		    Parties and dances
		    Talking on the telephone (Fig. 5-10)
		    Music
		    Experimenting with clothing, make-up, and hair styles
		    Fads of the age group
		Needs to have good nutrition and eating patterns; excess eating and fad diets should be discouraged
		Needs to have an adult available when he or she needs to talk or needs comforting
		Needs to pay attention to personal hygiene; deodorants and bathing are important as sweat glands become very active

Young adulthood	18-40 years	Functions independently of parents Full physical growth and development by age 30; gradual declines after 30 Sex is intimate and related to feelings for the partner; not just a physical need or urge Marriage and having children usually occur Children are raised Lives in a home other than parents' home Has a job and earns money to support self and family Becomes involved in community activities and politics Ethics, morals, and values are well established Few illnesses or health problems Divorce is common Needs to avoid practices that could cause health problems later: smoking, drinking too much alcohol, drug abuse, poor eating habits

Fig. 5-10 Teenagers enjoy talking on the telephone. (From Sorrentino, S.A.: Mosby's textbook for nursing assistants, ed. 2, St. Louis, 1987, The C.V. Mosby Co.)

Continued

Table 5-1—cont'd. Growth and Development

STAGE	AGE	CHARACTERISTICS AND BEHAVIORS
Adulthood	40-65 years	Body functions begin to slow down Signs of aging begin to appear: graying hair, baldness, tooth loss, muscle weakness, gradual loss of height *Menopause* occurs in women: menstruation stops and the woman is no longer able to have children Illnesses and diseases develop Children become independent; they marry, have children, and have homes of their own Becomes a grandparent Deals with aging parents and the death of parents More leisure time when children leave home; time for hobbies such as fishing, painting, golf, volunteer work, etc. (Fig. 5-11) Continues to be active in community and politics Women may return to work after raising a family Gets ready for retirement (home, finances, and leisure activities)

Late adulthood	65 years and older	Adjusts to retirement
		Declines in body function and signs of aging continue in all body systems
		Illness and disease are common
		Some need assistance with basic physical and safety needs; may be too weak to care for self
		At risk for falls, burns, and accidents
		Relationships change
		    Spouse (husband or wife), relatives, and friends die
		    Relatives and friends may move to a retirement community or to senior citizen housing
		Adjusts to reduced income because of retirement
		Change in living arrangements may be necessary: live with children, retirement community, senior citizen housing, nursing home
		Has friends in own age groups; still needs to be with people of all ages, especially children (Fig. 5-12)

Fig. 5-11 Adults have more leisure time. (From Sorrentino, S.A.: Mosby's textbook for nursing assistants, ed. 2, St. Louis, 1987, The C.V. Mosby Co.)

Fig. 5-12 The elderly need to be with children. (From Sorrentino, S.A.: Mosby's textbook for nursing assistants, ed. 2, St. Louis, 1987, The C.V. Mosby Co.)

Sexuality

Health care has changed in the last several years. In the past clients were viewed as having only physical problems. Therefore, physical needs were the first and often the only concern. Little attention was paid to the psychological or social effect of the disorder on the client. The needs of love and belonging, esteem, and self-actualization were overlooked. Now attention is given to physical, psychological, social, and spiritual needs.

There is another part of the person which involves the physical, psychological, social, and spiritual. That part is sexuality. Health care now recognizes the effect of illness and injury on a person's sexuality.

There are differences between sex and sexuality. *Sex* can be defined as the physical activities involving the organs of reproduction. The activities are done for pleasure or to have children. *Sexuality* involves the whole personality and the body. A person's attitudes and feelings are involved. Besides physical and psychological factors, sexuality is influenced by social, cultural, and spiritual factors. The way a person behaves, thinks, dresses, and responds to others is related to the individual's sexuality.

Sexuality is present from birth. When the infant's sex is identified, a boy or girl name is given. Blue is used for boys, and pink for girls. Toys often reflect sexuality. Dolls are for girls. Trains and baseball bats are for boys. By two years of age children are aware of their own sex. By three years of age they know the sex of other children. As children grow older, they learn male and female roles. They learn what boys or girls are to do from their parents (Fig. 5-13). Children learn early that there are certain behaviors for boys and certain behaviors for girls.

As children grow older, they are more curious about the human body and how it works. Bodily changes during adolescence bring a greater interest about sex and the body.

Sex takes on more meaning as young adults mature. Attitudes and feelings are an important part of sex. Decisions about sexuality become very important. Decisions relate to choosing a partner, sex before marriage, and birth control.

Sexuality continues to be important into adulthood and old age. Changes in attitudes and the need for sex occur as a person grows older. Life circumstances change. Some of these changes may include divorce, death of a spouse, injury, and illness.

Injury and Illness

Sexuality and sex involve the mind and the body. Injury and illness can affect the way the body works. The mind can also be affected. A person who has had disfiguring surgery may feel unclean, unwhole, unattractive, or mutilated. The person's attitude about sex

Fig. 5-13 This little girl is learning female roles from her mother. (From Sorrentino, S.A.: Mosby's textbook for nursing assistants, ed. 2, St. Louis, 1987, The C.V. Mosby Co.)

may change. The person may not feel worthy of being loved or may not feel attractive. These feelings affect the person's ability to be close and intimate with another. Therefore, the person may develop sexual problems that are psychological in nature. The individual can be helped to overcome these feelings. Time, understanding, and a caring partner are very helpful. Some may need counseling or psychiatric help.

Many illnesses and injuries affect the nervous, circulatory, and reproductive systems. Surgery can also affect these systems. If one or more of these systems are affected, the client may have changes in sexual ability. Most chronic illnesses also affect sexual functioning.

You may care for clients with disorders that affect sexual functioning. Changes in sexual functioning will have a great impact on the client. Fear, anger, worry, and depression often occur. These will be seen in the client's behavior and comments. You need to understand that the client's feelings are normal and expected.

Sexuality and the Elderly

There is a common notion in our society that sex, love, and intimacy are for the young. Young people fall in love, hold hands, embrace, and have sex. Older people are not supposed to need sex, love, and affection. Another, similar notion is the idea that older people are not capable of having sexual activities. Fortunately, these ideas are untrue. Sexual relationships are psychologically and physically important to the elderly (Fig. 5-14).

Love, affection, and intimacy are needed throughout life. As other losses occur, feeling close to another human being may take on more importance. Children leave home. Friends and relatives die. There is loss of job due to retirement. Health problems may be

Fig. 5-14 Love and affection are important to the elderly. (From Sorrentino, S.A.: Mosby's textbook for nursing assistants, ed. 2, St. Louis, 1987, The C.V. Mosby Co.)

developing. Adding to these losses are decreasing physical strength and changes in appearance.

The organs of reproduction change during the aging process. However, the changes do not eliminate sexual needs or abilities.

Elderly people may not have sexual intercourse often. Some never have intercourse. This does not mean that they do not have sexual needs or desires. Their needs may be shown in other ways. Hand-holding, touching, caressing, and embracing are ways of showing closeness and intimacy.

Having a sexual partner is also important. Death and divorce result in loss of a sexual partner. Or the partner may be ill at home, in a hospital, or in a nursing home. These situations are seen in adults of all ages.

Meeting the Client's Sexual Needs

Sexuality is part of the total person. Illness or injury does not mean that sexuality is unimportant. Some clients are so ill that sexual activity is impossible. However, others may want and be able to have sexual activity with their partners. Sexual activity does not always imply intercourse. Sexual activity may occur in other ways. Nursing personnel used to discourage any form of sexual expression, particularly among the elderly. Hand-holding was okay. But the client and partner were not to get any closer. Fortunately the importance of sexuality in health and illness is now recognized. The home health team plays an important role in allowing clients to meet their sexual needs. The following measures are appreciated by clients. They are carried out in cooperation with your supervisor.

1. Allow the person to practice his or her grooming routines. This includes applying make-up, nail polish, and body lotion, and wearing cologne. Hair care and shaving are also important. Women may want

to shave their legs and underarms and pluck their eyebrows. Men may wish to use after-shave lotion. The client may need help with these activities.
2. Allow the client a choice in clothing. Street clothes, rather than gowns or pajamas, may be very appropriate if the person's condition permits.
3. Avoid exposing the client. Care and procedures should be performed so that the client is not exposed unnecessarily. The client must be draped and screened appropriately.
4. Accept the person's sexual relationships. The client may not have the same sexual attitudes, values, or practices as you. However, you cannot expect the client to follow your standards. The client may have a homosexual, premarital, or extramarital relationship. The client may have more than one sexual partner. You must not make judgments or gossip about the client's relationships.
5. Allow for privacy. You can usually tell when two people want to be alone. Be sure to let them know how much time they can expect alone. For example, you can remind them when to expect a meal tray or a treatment. This gives them an idea of when to expect someone. Knocking before you enter any client's room is a common courtesy. It shows respect for privacy.
6. Allow elderly individuals their right to be sexual. The measures described previously apply to the elderly as well as to other age groups.
7. Allow couples to share the same room. The couple should not be separated. They have lived together for years. They should be allowed to share the same bed if the client's condition permits.
8. Allow single elderly people to develop new relationships. Death and divorce result in loss of a sexual partner. The widowed or divorced client may develop a new relationship. Instead of trying to keep the two people apart, measures should be taken to allow them time together.

The Sexually Aggressive Client

Some clients try to have their sexual needs met by you. Clients may flirt, make sexual advances or comments, expose themselves, or touch you. You will probably be angry or embarrassed when these situations occur. These reactions are normal. Often there are reasons for the client's behavior. Understanding the client's behavior may help you deal with the situation.

Illness, injury, surgery, or aging may threaten the male client's sense of manhood. He may try to reassure or prove to himself that he is still attractive and able to perform sexually. He may do so by behaving sexually toward you.

Sometimes sexually aggressive behaviors are due to confusion or disorientation. Nervous system disorders, medications, fever, and poor vision can cause confusion and disorientation. The client may confuse you with his or her sexual partner. Or the client may be unable to control behavior because of changes in mental function. Under normal conditions the person could control any urges toward you. However, changes in the brain may make control difficult. Sexual behavior in these situations is usually very innocent on the client's part.

Sometimes clients may touch you inappropriately. Their purpose in touching is sexual. However, touch may be the only way the client can get your attention. Consider the following situation. Mr. Green is paralyzed on one side of his body. He is unable to speak. You have your back to him and are bending over. Your buttocks are the closest part of your body to him. To get your attention he touches your buttocks. The client's touch is not sexual in this situation.

A client's sexual advances may be on purpose. You will need to deal with the situation in a professional manner. However, there is no best way to deal with advances. The following suggestions may be helpful.

1. Discuss the situation with your supervisor. The supervisor may have some ideas to help you deal with or understand the client's behavior.
2. Ask the client not to touch you in places where you were touched.
3. Explain to the client that you have no intention of doing what has been suggested.
4. Explain to the client that his or her behavior makes you uncomfortable. Then politely ask the client not to act in that way.
5. Allow privacy if the client is becoming sexually aroused. Provide for the client's safety (raise side rails, place the call bell within reach, etc.). Then tell the client when you will return.

Caring for Children

As a home health aide you may care for children in the home. Children may need home care because:

- The primary caregiver (parent, grandparent, aunt, uncle, guardian) cannot care for the child. Reasons may include illness, disability, mental health problems, or death.
- The primary caregiver will be out of the home.
- The child needs more care than the primary caregiver can give or knows how to do.
- The primary caregiver needs to learn about child care.
- The child has been abused or neglected.

You may babysit if the primary caregiver is ill. Or you may care for a sick child. Your supervisor will assign you specific duties. The family may ask you to do other things. Discuss their requests with your supervisor.

Signs and symptoms of disease occur very rap-

Fig. 5-15 The sick infant needs to be held and cuddled.

idly in children. They may respond in several ways. They may feel bad but do not understand why. They may be scared, cry, look sad, and show anger. Children have active imaginations. They may think they are being punished. Older children may fear permanent injury, loss of a body part (arm or leg), or death.

You need to meet the ill child's emotional needs. The following guidelines will help you.

- Give the child clear explanations of what you are doing. Get feedback to check the child's understanding (see Chapter 3, page 21).
- Touch and comfort according to the child's needs. Young children need lots of hugging. Older children may want to be left alone for a while.
- Hold and cuddle infants (Fig 5-15). That helps to soothe and comfort them.
- Respond when the baby cries or when the child calls for you.
- Allow the child to play. Play should fit the child's age and condition (Fig. 5-16). Ask your supervisor what the child can do.
- Encourage the child to talk about what he or she is thinking. Listen to what the child is saying.
- Give the child lots of attention. It helps the child feel safe, secure, and wanted.

The bodies of infants and children contain a lot of water. Many illnesses cause fever, diarrhea, and vomiting. All cause a loss of fluid from the body. The fluid loss can be very quick and very serious. A sick child will need to drink extra fluid. The extra fluid meets normal needs and replaces lost fluid.

Getting a sick child to drink is not always easy. The following ideas may be helpful.

- Find out what the child likes to drink. Give those fluids if allowed in the child's diet.
- Offer fluids in small, colorful cups and glasses. Children like glasses with cartoon, movie, and storybook characters.

Fig. 5-16 The three-year-old is playing in bed. Playing with a coloring book and crayons is a quiet activity for the sick child.

Fig. 5-18 Home health aide is making popsicles with fruit juice.

A

B

Fig. 5-17 **A,** A cartoon is taped to the bottom of a glass. **B,** The child drinks the milk to find the picture.

- Use the child's favorite cup.
- Use colorful straws.
- Have the older child keep track of how much he or she drinks.
- Tape a bright picture to the underside of a clear glass. Fill the glass with milk or juice. Encourage the child to find the "surprise" at the bottom (Fig. 5-17).
- Make popsicles out of fruit juices (Fig. 5-18). The child may like sucking on a popsicle rather than drinking juice.
- Offer Jello, popsicles, ice cream, milk shakes, snow cones, and soda drinks.

The sick child may have a loss of appetite (*anorexia*). This is very common in children. Often anorexia is the first symptom of illness. Though eating is important, it is best not to force the child to eat. Let the child guide you in determining food needs. The following guidelines will help you meet the child's need for food.

- Give food and fluids high in calories. These include sodas, clear soups, Jello, crackers, hard candy, ice cream, milk shakes, and toast.
- Ask the child what he or she likes to eat.
- Let the child help in planning meals.
- Let the child help make the meal if possible.
- Make meal time fun. Serve food in fancy cups, colored plates, or on "special" family dishes. Decorate food (Fig. 5-19). Use cookie cutters to make sandwiches into different shapes. Let the child have a "picnic." Or serve the meal on a tray in front of the television.
- Take advantage of "hungry" periods. Serve nutritious foods such as meat, potatoes, fruit, vegetables, frozen yogurt, and peanut butter cookies.
- Have friends and relatives bring "treats" from the child's favorite store or restaurant.

Special Age Considerations

Remember that preschool children are in a period of discovery and growth. They are learning new

Fig. 5-19 The home health aide is using pickles, ketchup, and mustard to make a face on a hamburger.

Fig. 5-20 An elderly client receiving home care.

skills. They also want to do things without help. The sick child may actually need your help with dressing, feeding, or toileting. This is especially true if the child is very weak or unable to move around. An uncooperative child can be frustrating. Do not be impatient with the child. Let the child do as much as possible. Also let the child decide what and when something will be done whenever possible.

Peers are important to the school-age child. The child wants to be like everyone else and to have friends. Illness can interfere with the child's need to be like others. You cannot change the child's medical condition. However, you can encourage the child to talk about his or her feelings. You need to give support and listen to the child's concerns, fears, and disappointments. Allow the child to be involved with his or her care as much as possible. Give praise and encouragement. Be sure to explain to the child what you are doing and why.

The adolescent experiences many physical and emotional changes. It is a time of constant conflict. While struggling for independence and identity, the adolescent also wants to depend on parents. Adolescents normally have a hard time controlling their emotions. Illness may make the adolescent even more emotional. The adolescent may be embarrassed about body changes. Be sure to allow as much privacy as possible. When caring for adolescents, show patience, tolerance, and acceptance. Encourage the teenager to talk about concerns, fears, and interests.

Caring for the Elderly

Aging is the process of growing older. It is a normal process and affects everyone. Aged refers to being old. In general, the aged are 65 years and older.

They are referred to as the *elderly*. There are more and more elderly people. People are living longer than in the past. They are also working longer, retiring later, and leading more active lives in their later years. Most elderly people enjoy good health. Some are ill but continue to live at home. However, independent functioning may be difficult.

Everyone is different. Some people live very active, healthy, happy lives until they die. Others develop many health problems as the body ages. Certain changes normally take place as a person ages. Hearing and sight decrease. Bones become brittle and break easily. Joints become stiff and painful. Muscles weaken. The ability to move about is reduced. Food requirements are less as activity decreases. Appetite decreases. Less sleep is needed than during the younger years.

Some elderly have emotional problems. They may feel insecure, lonely, useless, unloved, or unwanted. Some feel they are a burden to their children. The elderly no longer have their jobs to make them feel worthwhile. Their spouses, relatives, and friends may be dying. They may find it hard to keep up the home. Some lose their homes because they cannot maintain them or because they cannot pay taxes. Many elderly have fears about losing their homes. Some are forgetful. They feel frustrated when they cannot remember things. This can be a very hard time for the elderly. Although they are older, they can still feel, think, care, and love. The elderly have the same basic needs as everyone else. They need to feel loved, secure, and accepted.

The elderly are the main users of home care services. Sometimes you may provide relief for family members or caregivers. This allows them to leave the home for a while. Sometimes the client needs help with home maintenance and personal care (Fig. 5-20). Sometimes someone is needed 8 to 24 hours a day to make sure the client is safe. Many elderly only need help a couple hours a week.

You need to practice the following when caring for the elderly:

- Treat the client with respect.
- Do not criticize the client because you think he or she is confused.
- Take the time to listen. You can learn a great deal about a lifetime of events.
- Do not change the client's routines or do things your way.
- Do not rush.

Caring for the Ill and Disabled

Most of your clients will have some form of disability or illness. *Disability* refers to the permanent loss of a physical or mental function. Examples include blindness, deafness, mental retardation, inability to walk, and speech disorders. Disabilities may be present at birth. They may also be caused by injuries to the brain or other body part.

Illness refers to the loss of good health. A serious illness can affect the family's ability to care for the client. Illness and disability may require changes in the home. A person who cannot move because of a car accident may need special equipment. A hospital bed and other equipment may need to be bought or rented. Hospital beds often do not fit through bedroom doors. Therefore they remain in living rooms. As a result, the client's personal care (bathing, toileting, and meals) takes place in the living room (Fig. 5-21).

A sick person has many fears and anxieties. There is fear of death, disability, chronic illness, and loss of function. Some clients are able to explain why they are afraid. Others keep their feelings to themselves. They fear being laughed at for being afraid. A client with a broken leg may be afraid of having a limp or not being able to walk again. Clients who have had surgery for cancer may fear that more cancer will be found. These fears and anxieties are normal and expected. You need to appreciate how clients are affected by illness. Think about how you would feel and react if you had the client's illness and problems. That will help you have empathy for the client.

The following guidelines will help you care for ill and disabled clients.

1. Follow the instructions given by your supervisor. Also follow the client's care plan.
2. Be professional. Be honest and show concern.
3. Allow clients to do as much for themselves as possible.
4. Protect the client's privacy.
5. Pay attention to details. The client may focus on the illness and the care you give. He or she may be concerned if caregivers do procedures differently.

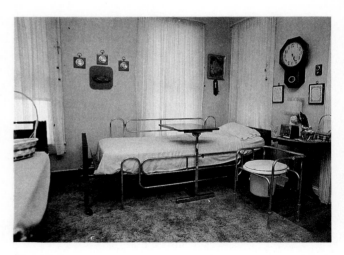

Fig. 5-21 The family's living room has become the client's room. Note the hospital bed, commode, and overbed table.

6. Give the client opportunities to talk about concerns and fears. If the client does not want to talk, do not press the issue.
7. Remember that clients may be upset about their condition. Be patient and understanding. They need time to think through their feelings.
8. Do not give advice.
9. Report and record your observations (see Chapter 4).
10. Tell your supervisor when there is a change in the client's condition. Also report if there are problems in the home.

Summary

All human beings have the same basic needs. These needs are necessary for life. They are physical needs, the need for safety and security, love and belonging, esteem, and self-actualization. These needs continue throughout life. However, the ability to meet basic needs depends on the client's age and state of health.

Culture and religion influence health and illness practices. Therefore, they also influence how basic needs will be met. Culture and religion influence behavior, thinking, and feeling. These beliefs affect eating habits, living arrangements, family, clothing, work, and health habits. Your client's culture and religion may be different from yours. However, you are a guest in the client's home. Accept the client's beliefs and practices without bias.

Sexuality is important to people of all ages. Illness and injury can affect a person's sexuality. However, everyone has the need to be loved, have affection, and be close to another human being.

You may be assigned to care for children, the elderly, and ill or disabled clients. These clients have many feelings, fears, and concerns about their conditions. You need to know the normal behaviors for each age group. A review of growth and development is very important when you are assigned to children.

Study Questions

1. Identify the needs not being met in each of the following situations. Describe how you can help the client meet those needs.
   - A 48-year-old man must stay in bed. He has a broken leg and both arms are broken. His wife works during the day.
   - A 67-year-old woman has a hard time walking. This limits her ability to leave the home. Her husband recently died after 48 years of marriage.
   - A 22-year-old man injured his spinal cord in a diving accident. He cannot move his arms or legs.
   - A 32-year-old woman is pregnant. She is on bed rest until she delivers in 4 weeks. Her husband is an alcoholic. He sometimes abuses his wife and children, ages 3, 6, and 9. There is very little money for food and clothing for the winter.

2. Describe some of the differences in caring for children and caring for the elderly.

3. You are assigned to a 3-year-old. What toys should you let the child play with?

4. A client is of the Baptist faith. You are a Catholic. Identify the things you should and should not do.

5. You are assigned to a 70-year-old widow. Every day a gentleman friend visits her. He is 75 years old. What should you do?

6. A 52-year-old male client is paralyzed from the waist down. Mary Monroe is assigned to care for him every day from 8 a.m. to 5 p.m. while his wife works. He keeps trying to touch Mary's breasts. He also asks her to kiss him and to lie in bed with him. What should Mary do?

Circle T if the statement is true and F if it is false.

T F 7. Physical needs are essential for life.
T F 8. Food, clothing, and shelter are physical needs.
T F 9. Love and belonging are not important to sick people.
T F 10. Self-actualization is the need to learn and create.
T F 11. The client's culture and religion will probably influence how basic needs are met.
T F 12. The nuclear family consists of parents, children, grandparents, aunts, uncles, and cousins.
T F 13. The start of menstruation is called puberty.
T F 14. Changes in the reproductive organs occur with aging. These changes make sexual activity impossible.

T F 15. Adolescence is a time of rapid physical, emotional, and sexual growth.
T F 16. Children can develop signs and symptoms of disease very fast.
T F 17. Sick children need a lot of attention.
T F 18. Sick children do not need explanations about care.

Select the *best* answer.

19. Preschool children can do all of the following *except*
   a. Dress, bathe, and tend to toileting
   b. Run, skip, hop, and ride a tricycle ·
   c. Play board games and other games with rules
   d. Use their imaginations when playing

20. The peer group becomes important to
   a. Preschoolers
   b. School age children
   c. Teenagers
   d. Young adults

21. Sexuality is important to
   a. Small children
   b. Teenagers and young adults
   c. Middle aged adults
   d. Persons of all ages

22. Which of the following will *not* promote a client's sexuality?
   a. Allowing the person to practice normal grooming routines.
   b. Having the client wear a hospital gown.
   c. Allowing the client and his/her partner privacy.
   d. Showing acceptance of the client's relationships.

23. You are to give a sick child extra fluid. You should do all of the following *except*
   a. Give the child his or her favorite drinks if allowed
   b. Provide large glasses and cups
   c. Use the child's favorite cup
   d. Make popsicles out of fruit juices

24. You are to care for an elderly client. You should
   a. Treat the client with respect
   b. Avoid visiting with the client
   c. Change the client's routines to fit your schedule
   d. All of the above

25. When caring for ill and disabled clients you should
   a. Follow your supervisor's instructions
   b. Allow clients to do as much for themselves as possible
   c. Let the client talk about his or her concerns
   d. All of the above

Answers

7. True	10. True	13. False	16. True	18. False	20. b	22. b	24. a
8. False	11. True	14. False	17. True	19. c	21. d	23. b	25. d
9. False	12. False	15. True					

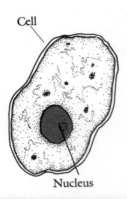
Cell

Nucleus

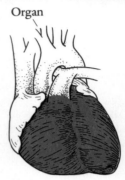
Organ

6

Understanding How the Body Functions

What you will learn to do

- Describe the functions of cells, tissues, and organs
- Explain how body systems work together
- Explain how understanding body functions will help you give safe care
- Describe the integumentary system and the changes that occur with aging
- Identify what you need to observe about the skin, nails, and hair
- Describe the musculoskeletal system and how it is affected by aging
- Identify what to observe about the musculoskeletal system
- Describe the nervous system and how it is affected by aging
- Identify observations to make about the nervous system
- Describe the circulatory system and the circulatory changes that occur with aging

- Identify the observations that mean a problem with the circulatory system
- Describe the respiratory system and how it is affected by aging
- Describe the observations you need to make about a client's breathing
- Describe the digestive system and the changes which occur with aging
- Identify the observations that may mean a problem with the digestive system
- Describe the urinary system and the changes that occur with aging
- Describe what to observe about the urinary system
- Describe the male and female reproductive systems and the observations that need to be made
- Describe the effects of aging on the reproductive system
- Know the basic function of each endocrine gland and how aging affects the endocrine system
- Describe the observations that may indicate an endocrine problem

Key Terms*

Artery A blood vessel that carries blood away from the heart

Capillary A tiny blood vessel; food, oxygen, and other substances pass from the capillaries to the cells

Cell The basic unit of the body

Digestion The process of physically and chemically breaking down food so it can be absorbed for use by the cells of the body

Hemoglobin The substance in red blood cells that gives blood its color; hemoglobin carries oxygen in the blood

Hormone A chemical substance secreted by the glands into the bloodstream

Menstruation The process in which the endometrium (lin-ing) of the uterus breaks up and is discharged from the body through the vagina

Metabolism The burning of food for heat and energy by the cells

Organ Groups of tissues with the same function

Peristalsis Involuntary muscle contractions in the digestive system

Respiration The process of supplying the cells with oxygen and removing carbon dioxide from them

System Organs that work together to perform special functions

Tissue Groups of cells with the same function

Vein A blood vessel that carries blood back to the heart

You will care for clients who need help meeting their basic needs. Their bodies may not function properly because of illness, disease, or injury. Aging can also affect how the body functions. You will give care and perform procedures to promote comfort, healing, and recovery. You need to have a basic knowledge of the body's normal structure and function. This will help you understand certain signs and symptoms, reasons for care, and the purpose of procedures.

Cells, Tissues, and Organs

The Cell

The *cell* is the basic unit of the body. Cells are so small that a microscope is needed to see them.

Cells need oxygen, food, and water to survive. They have many functions that help the cell and body survive. Cells vary in size, shape, and function (Fig. 6-1). For example, certain blood cells carry oxygen throughout the body. They have a different function from nerve cells. Nerve cells send messages back and forth between body parts and the brain.

Cells contain many structures (Fig. 6-2). One substance is called *protoplasm*, which means "living matter." Protoplasm contains all the water, structures, and substances within the cell. The *nucleus* is in the center of the cell. The nucleus is the cell's control center. It directs cell activity and is responsible for cell reproduction.

Mitosis is the process in which a cell divides or reproduces itself (Fig. 6-3). Cell reproduction is necessary for body growth and repair. A healing wound is an example of how cells reproduce to replace injured cells.

The fluid around the nucleus is called *cytoplasm*. The *cell membrane* is the cell's outer covering. It gives the cell shape and holds structures in the cell.

---

*Students are responsible for only those terms mentioned in the text. Additional terms used in labeling figures throughout this chapter are for illustrative purposes only.

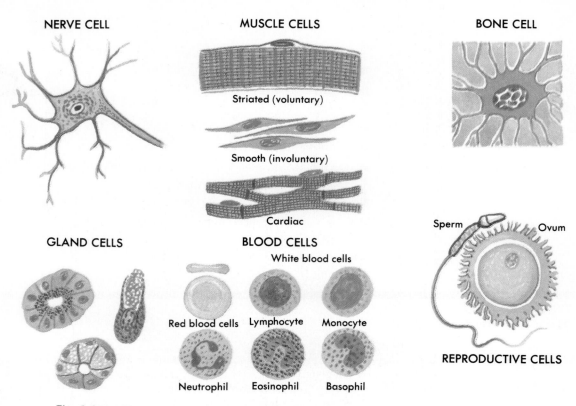

Fig. 6-1 The different types of cells. (From Anthony, C.P., and Thibodeau, G.A.: Textbook of anatomy and physiology, ed. 11, St. Louis, 1983, The C.V. Mosby Co.)

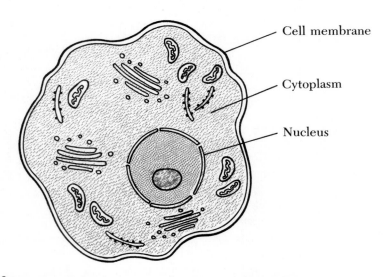

Fig. 6-2 Parts of a cell. (From Sorrentino, S.A.: Mosby's textbook for nursing assistants, ed. 2, St. Louis, 1987, The C.V. Mosby Co.)

Tissues

Some cells have similar functions. These cells are grouped together to form *tissues*. There are four basic types of body tissues.

1. *Epithelial tissue* covers the internal and external sur-

faces of the body. Epithelial tissue lines the nose, mouth, respiratory tract, stomach, and intestines. Skin, hair, nails, and glands are also epithelial tissue.

2. *Connective tissue* anchors, connects, and supports

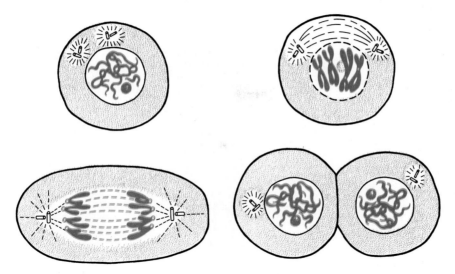

Fig. 6-3 Cell division. (From Sorrentino, S.A.: Mosby's textbook for nursing assistants, ed. 2, St. Louis, 1987, The C.V. Mosby Co.)

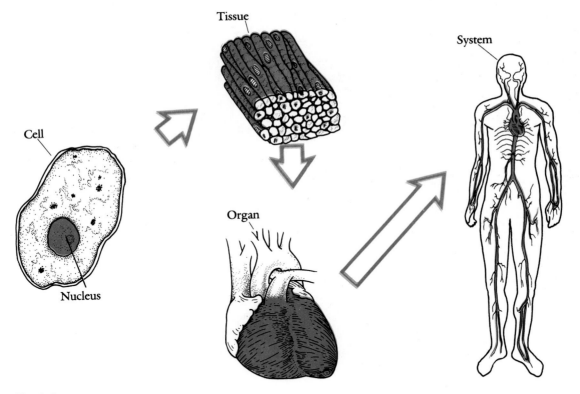

Fig. 6-4 Organization of the body. (From Lafleur, M., and Starr, W.K.: Understanding medical language: a student-directed approach, St. Louis, 1984, The C.V. Mosby Co.)

other body tissues. Connective tissue is found in every part of the body. Bones, tendons, ligaments, and cartilage are connective tissues. Blood is a form of connective tissue.

3. *Muscle tissue* allows the body to move by stretching and contracting. There are three types of muscle tissue (see page 73).

4. *Nerve tissue* receives and carries messages to the brain and back to the body.

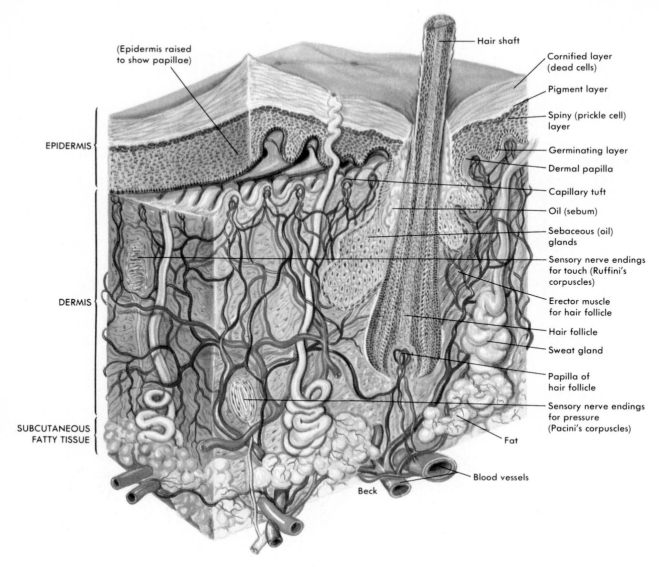

(Epidermis raised
to show papillae)

Hair shaft

Cornified layer
(dead cells)

Pigment layer

Spiny (prickle cell)
layer

EPIDERMIS

Germinating layer

Dermal papilla

Capillary tuft

Oil (sebum)

Sebaceous (oil)
glands

Sensory nerve endings
for touch (Ruffini's
corpuscles)

DERMIS

Erector muscle
for hair follicle

Hair follicle

Sweat gland

Papilla of
hair follicle

Sensory nerve endings
for pressure
(Pacini's corpuscles)

SUBCUTANEOUS
FATTY TISSUE

Fat

Blood vessels

Beck

Fig. 6-5 The layers of the skin. (From Mosby's medical and nursing dictionary, ed. 2, St. Louis, 1986, The C.V. Mosby Co.)

Organs

Organs are formed by groups of tissues. Examples of organs include the heart, brain, liver, and kidneys. Systems are formed by organs that work together for special functions (Fig. 6-4). The mouth, esophagus, stomach, and intestines make up the digestive system. The parts work together to digest food. All body systems work together. Changes in one system usually affect one or more of the other systems.

Intergumentary System

The skin, nails, and hair make up the integumentary system. The skin is the largest organ in the body. There are two skin layers (Fig. 6-5). The epidermis is the outer layer. Cells of the epidermis constantly flake off.

They are replaced by new cells. Pigment gives the epidermis color. Dark skin has more pigment than lighter skin.

The inner layer is the dermis. It contains blood vessels and nerves. The dermis also contains hair roots, oil glands, and sweat glands. Hair is all over the body except for the palms of the hands and soles of the feet. At the root of each hair is an oil gland. Oil glands secrete an oily substance that keeps the hair and skin soft and shiny.

Sweat glands are deep in the epidermis. They open onto the skin through small openings called pores. These glands secrete sweat. Sweat is made up of water, salt, and a small amount of wastes. Sweat glands are all over the body. However, some areas have more sweat glands than others. The palms of the hands, underarms, forehead, and soles of the feet have many sweat glands. These areas become very moist when a person is active, nervous, or hot.

The skin has the following functions:

1. Covers and protects the body. Germs, chemicals, and other substances cannot enter the body. Water and other body structures are held in the body.
2. Protects the organs from injury.
3. Senses heat, cold, pain, and pressure through nerve endings in the dermis.
4. Helps control body temperature. Blood vessels dilate (widen) when temperature outside the body is high. More blood is brought to the skin for cooling during evaporation. Also, the body is cooled as sweat evaporates. When blood vessels constrict (narrow), heat is kept in the body because less blood reaches the skin.

Skin care is important to your clients (see Chapter 14). Changes in the skin occur with aging. Special skin care may be needed. For example, people normally use soap when bathing. However, soap tends to dry the skin. Dry skin is normal with aging. If soap is used, the skin will dry more. Therefore, daily bathing with soap is avoided. Table 6-1 lists the changes that occur in the skin, hair, and nails with aging. Nursing care measures are also listed.

Table 6-1 Physical Effects of Aging

SYSTEM	CHANGES	NURSING CARE
Integumentary	Lines, folds, and wrinkles (skin loses its elastic nature and fatty tissue layer)	
	Dry skin (oil and sweat glands are less active)	Avoid daily bathing
		Complete bath twice a week; partial baths on other days
		Mild soaps
		No soap on arms, legs, chest, back, and abdomen
		Lanolin-based lotion or bath oil to prevent itching
	Sensitive to cold (loss of fatty tissue layer)	Provide sweaters, lap blankets, socks, extra blankets; protect from drafts and cold; higher thermostat settings; *Do not use hot water bottles or heating pads*
	Nails become thick and tough	Nail and foot care
		Toenails cut by someone trained to do so
	Graying hair	
	Hair thins on both men and women	
	Hair is dryer	Brush hair regularly
		Shampoo less often than in younger years
Musculoskeletal	Gradual muscle atrophy	
	Decreasing strength	
	Bones are brittle and can break easily	Diet high in protein, calcium, and vitamins
		Protect from injury
		Prevent falls
		Turn and move gently
		Support when walking and getting out of bed
	Joints become stiff and painful	Exercises as ordered by the physician and nurse

Continued

Table 6-1—cont'd.   Physical Effects of Aging

SYSTEM	CHANGES	NURSING CARE
Musculoskeletal (cont'd.)	Changes cause gradual loss of height, loss of strength, and decreased ability to move about	Encourage to be as active as possible
Nervous	Senses of taste and smell dull; appetite decreases	
	Less sensitive to touch and pain (injuries and disease may go unnoticed)	Protect from injury Apply heat and cold applications carefully (see Chapter 18) Inspect skin for signs of breakdown and give good skin care (see Chapter 14)
	Blood flow to the brain is reduced—short memory, forgetfulness, response is slower, confusion, dizziness, tires easily	Keep mentally active Reality orientation (see chapter 21) Nap during the day
	Hearing loss	See Chapter 21
	Vision loss	See Chapter 21
Cardiovascular	Heart pumps with less force (may be unable to meet body's demand for oxygen when active)	Rest periods during the day Plan activities to avoid overexertion Should not walk long distances, carry heavy objects, or climb stairs
	Arteries narrow and are less elastic (less blood flows to body tissues)	Exercises as ordered to prevent blood clots (see Chapter 19) Activities and diet as ordered by the doctor Place items used often within the client's reach
Respiratory	Respiratory muscles weaken—signs and symptoms with activity; may not have the strength to cough; respiratory infections or diseases may develop	Avoid heavy bed linens (they prevent deep breaths) Turn and reposition (see Chapter 10) Deep breathing exercises as ordered (see Chapter 19) Semisitting position if difficulty breathing Keep as active as possible
	Lung tissues are not as elastic	
Digestive	Difficulty swallowing (decreased saliva)	
	Decreased appetite	Good oral hygiene and denture care

Continued

Table 6-1—cont'd. Physical Effects of Aging

SYSTEM	CHANGES	NURSING CARE
	Fried and fatty foods hard to digest (decreased amount of digestive juices)	Needs to avoid dry, fried, and fatty foods
	Indigestion (decreased secretion of digestive juices)	
	Chewing difficulties (tooth loss and dentures that fit poorly)	Pureed or ground food
		Avoid foods high in fiber (fruits and vegetables with skins and seeds, apricots, and celery)
	Gas and constipation (peristalsis decreases, causing slower emptying of stomach and colon)	Foods that prevent constipation (see Chapter 17)
Urinary	Kidney function decreases	Increase fluid intake as ordered by the doctor
	Kidneys atrophy from a reduced blood supply	Client should drink most fluids by 5:00 PM to avoid need to urinate at night
		Bladder training (see Chapter 15)
		Indwelling catheter (see Chapter 15)
	Urinary incontinence (the inability to control the passage of urine from the bladder)	
Reproductive	*Male*—decrease in hormone testosterone	Allow the client to be sexual (see Chapter 5)
	Atrophy of tissues	Understand the psychological effect on the client (see Chapter 5)
	Takes longer for an erection	
	Longer time between erections	
	Decreased frequency of sex	
	Female—decreased secretion of estrogen and progesterone	
	Menopause—stops menstruating (ends the possibility of pregnancy)	
	Reproductive tissues atrophy	
	Takes longer to become sexually excited	
	Decreased frequency of sex	
Endocrine	Pancreas does not secrete enough insulin; elderly may develop diabetes	Observe for signs and symptoms of diabetes (see Chapter 21)

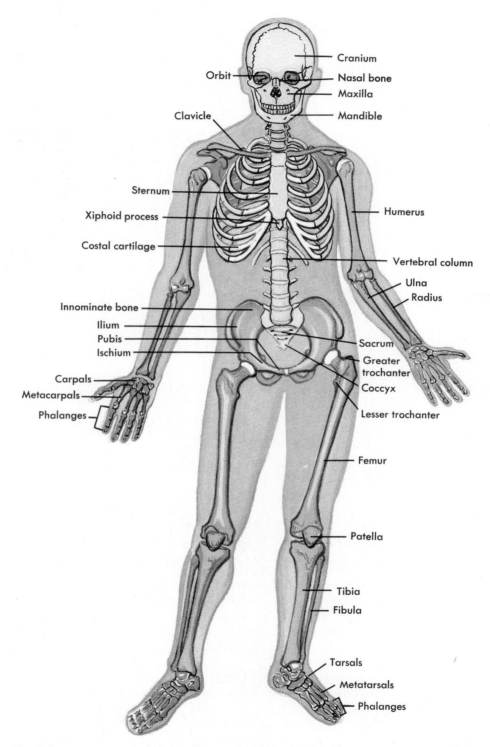

Fig. 6-6 Bones of the body. (From Mosby's medical and nursing dictionary, ed. 2, St. Louis, 1986, The C.V. Mosby Co.)

You need to observe the following about the client's skin:

1. Is the skin pale or flushed?
2. Is the skin cool, warm, or hot?
3. Is the skin dry or moist?
4. What color are the lips and nails?
5. Are there any sores, bruises, or reddened areas? Where are they located?

Musculoskeletal System

The musculoskeletal system gives the body form and support. It also protects the body and allows the body to move. This system is made up of bones, joints, and muscles.

There are 206 bones in the human body (Fig. 6-6). Healthy bones are hard and strong. The centers of bones are hollow. A substance called *bone marrow* is inside the hollow centers. Bone marrow produces blood cells. Bones are grouped according to their shape.

- *Long bones* bear the weight of the body. The bones of the legs are long bones.
- *Short bones* allow skill and ease of movement. Short bones are found in the wrists, fingers, ankles, and toes.
- *Flat bones* protect the organs of the body. Ribs, bones of the skull, pelvic bones, and shoulder blades are flat bones.
- *Irregular bones* allow various degrees of movement. The vertebrae in the spinal column are irregular bones.

The point at which two or more bones meet is called a *joint* (Fig. 6-7). Joints allow movement. Examples of joints include the knee, ankle, hip, wrist, elbow, shoulder, and neck. There are also joints in the fingers and toes. Connective tissue at the end of long bones is called *cartilage*. The cartilage cushions the joint so the bone ends do not rub together. Bones are held together at the joint by *ligaments*. Ligaments are strong bands of connective tissue.

There are over 500 muscles in the human body (Figs. 6-8 and 6-9). Some muscles are voluntary and others are involuntary. *Voluntary* muscles can be consciously controlled. Muscles that are attached to bones are voluntary. They are called *skeletal muscles*. The muscles of your arm do not work unless you move your arm; likewise for the muscles of your legs. Skeletal muscles are *striated*; that is, the muscles appear striped or streaked. *Involuntary muscles* work automatically. They cannot be consciously controlled. Involuntary muscles control the action of the stomach, intestines, blood vessels, and other body organs. Involuntary muscles are also called *smooth muscles*. They are smooth in appearance. *Cardiac muscle* is found in the heart. Although it is an involuntary muscle, it appears striated like skeletal muscle.

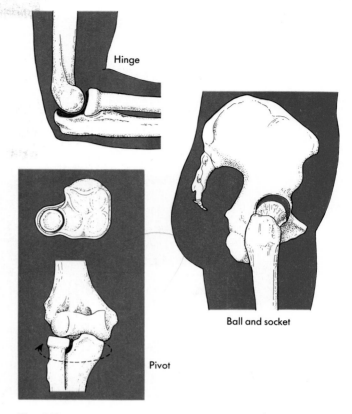

Fig. 6-7 Types of joints. (From Austrin, M.: Young's learning medical terminology step by step, ed. 6, St. Louis, 1987, The C.V. Mosby Co.)

Muscles perform 3 important body functions:
- The movement of body parts
- The maintenance of posture
- The production of body heat

Tendons connect muscles to bones. Tendons are strong, tough connective tissue. When muscles contract (shorten), tendons at each end of the muscle cause the bone to move. There are many tendons in the body; the Achilles tendon is shown in Fig. 6-9. Some muscles are constantly contracted to maintain the body's posture. When muscles contract they burn food for energy. This causes heat to be produced. The more muscle activity, the more heat produced in the body. Shivering is a way the body produces heat when exposed to cold. The shivering sensation is the result of rapid, general muscle contractions.

Sometimes muscles are not used because of injury and disease. When they are not used, they tend to waste away. In other words, they tend to shrink or decrease in size. This is called *atrophy* (See Fig. 11-18). *Contractures* can also develop. A contracture is the abnormal shortening of a muscle. The contracted muscle is fixed in position. It is permanently deformed and cannot be stretched back to its normal position (See Fig. 11-17).

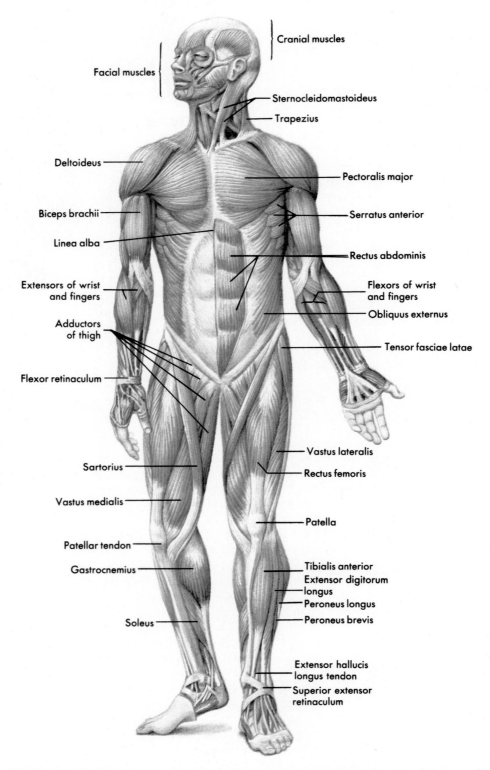

Cranial muscles

Facial muscles

Sternocleidomastoideus

Trapezius

Deltoideus

Pectoralis major

Biceps brachii

Serratus anterior

Linea alba

Rectus abdominis

Extensors of wrist and fingers

Flexors of wrist and fingers

Adductors of thigh

Obliquus externus

Tensor fasciae latae

Flexor retinaculum

Sartorius

Vastus lateralis

Rectus femoris

Vastus medialis

Patella

Patellar tendon

Gastrocnemius

Tibialis anterior

Extensor digitorum longus

Peroneus longus

Peroneus brevis

Soleus

Extensor hallucis longus tendon

Superior extensor retinaculum

Fig. 6-8 Anterior view of the muscles of the body. (From Mosby's medical and nursing dictionary, ed. 2, St. Louis, 1986, The C.V. Mosby Co.)

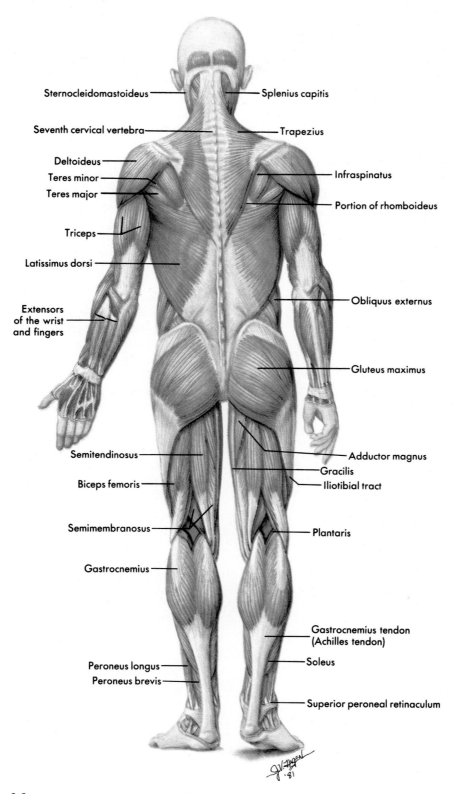

Sternocleidomastoideus —— —— Splenius capitis

Seventh cervical vertebra —— —— Trapezius

Deltoideus ——
Teres minor —— —— Infraspinatus
Teres major —— —— Portion of rhomboideus

Triceps ——

Latissimus dorsi ——

—— Obliquus externus

Extensors
of the wrist ——
and fingers

—— Gluteus maximus

Semitendinosus —— —— Adductor magnus
—— Gracilis
Biceps femoris —— —— Iliotibial tract

Semimembranosus —— —— Plantaris

Gastrocnemius ——

—— Gastrocnemius tendon
(Achilles tendon)
Peroneus longus —— —— Soleus
Peroneus brevis ——

—— Superior peroneal retinaculum

Fig. 6-9 Posterior view of the muscles of the body. (From Mosby's medical and nursing dictionary, ed. 2, St. Louis, 1986, The C.V. Mosby Co.)

Aging also causes changes in the musculoskeletal system. These changes and the necessary nursing care are listed in Table 6-1. You need to make the following observations about your client's musculoskeletal system:

1. Can the client move his or her arms and legs?
2. Does the client complain of pain in muscles, joints, or bones?
3. Does the client walk normally or with a limp?
4. Are the client's movements shaky or jerky?

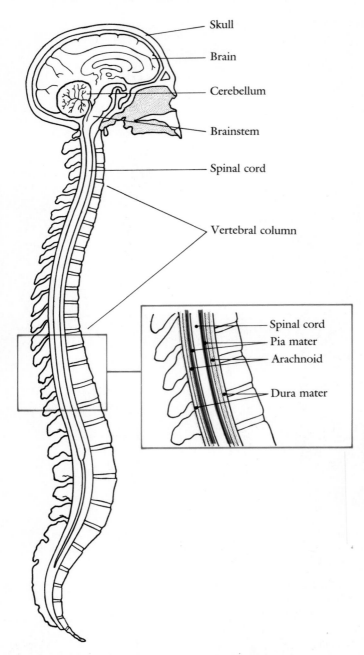

Fig. 6-10 Nervous system. (From Sorrentino, S.A.: Mosby's textbook for nursing assistants, ed. 2, St. Louis, 1987, The C.V. Mosby Co.)

Nervous System

The nervous system controls body functions. The main parts of the nervous system are the *brain*, the *spinal cord*, and the *nerves* (Figs. 6-10 and 6-11). Nerves carry messages, or impulses, to and from the brain. The nerves are connected to the spinal cord. The nerve cell, called a *neuron*, is the basic unit of the nervous system (Fig. 6-12). Neurons carry messages back and forth between the brain and the body. For example, a neuron gets the message of heat, cold, touch, smell, hearing, vision, balance, hunger, or thirst. The message travels from the neuron to a nerve. The nerve connects to the spinal cord and travels to the brain. If the body must respond, the brain sends a message back to the body part.

The Central Nervous System

The nervous system has two divisions: the central nervous system and the peripheral nervous system. The central nervous system consists of the brain and spinal cord. The brain is covered by the skull. The main parts of the brain are the *cerebrum*, the *cerebellum*, and the *brainstem* (Fig. 6-13).

The cerebrum is the largest part of the brain. It is the center of thought and intelligence. The cerebrum is divided into two halves called the *right* and *left hemispheres*. The *right hemisphere* controls the movement and activities of the *left* side of the body. The *left hemisphere* controls the body's *right* side.

The outside of the cerebrum is called the *cerebral cortex*. The cerebral cortex controls the highest functions of the brain. These include reasoning, memory, the conscious, speech, voluntary muscle movement, vision, hearing, sensation, and other activities.

The cerebellum regulates and coordinates body movements. Smooth movements and balance are controlled by the cerebellum. Injury to the cerebellum causes jerky movements, loss of coordination, and muscle weakness.

The brainstem connects the cerebrum to the spinal cord. The brainstem controls heart rate, breathing, the size of blood vessels, swallowing, coughing, and vomiting.

The spinal cord lies within the spinal column. The cord is approximately 18 inches long. The pathways in the cord conduct messages to and from the brain.

The brain and spinal cord are covered and protected by connective tissue called *meninges*. The meninges consist of three layers. There is a space between the middle and inner layers. The space is filled with fluid. This fluid is called *cerebrospinal fluid*. The cerebrospinal fluid protects the structures of the brain and spinal cord.

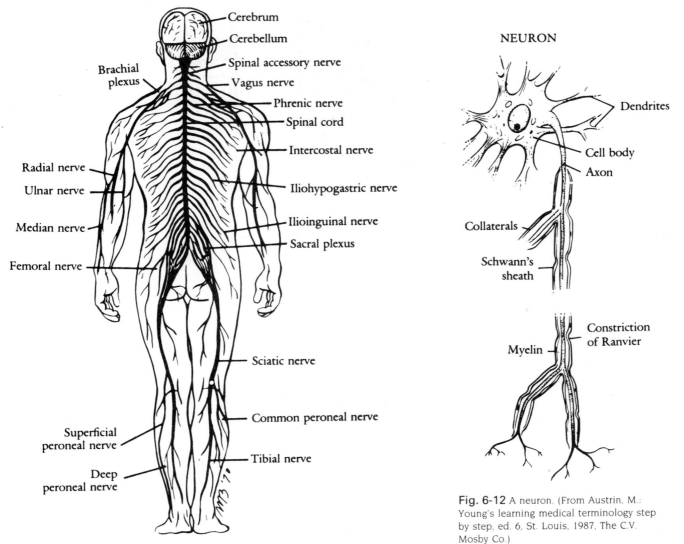

NEURON

Fig. 6-11 Nerves. (From Austrin, M.: Young's learning medical terminology step by step, ed. 6, St. Louis, 1987, The C.V. Mosby Co.)

Fig. 6-12 A neuron. (From Austrin, M.: Young's learning medical terminology step by step, ed. 6, St. Louis, 1987, The C.V. Mosby Co.)

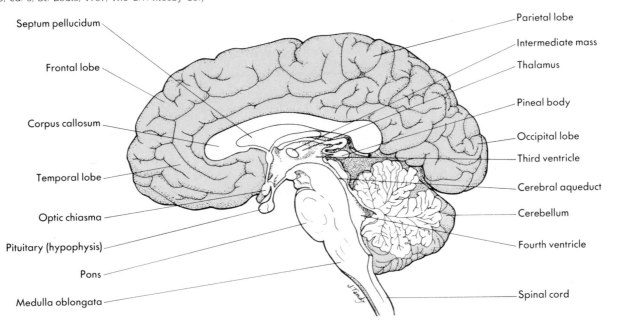

Fig. 6-13 The brain. (Modified from Austrin, M.: Young's learning medical terminology step by step, ed. 6, St. Louis, 1987, The C.V. Mosby Co.)

The Peripheral Nervous System

The peripheral nervous system consists of the nerves throughout the body. The nerves send messages to and from the brain. Messages involve smell, vision, hearing, pain, touch, temperature, pressure, and voluntary muscle control.

Some peripheral nerves control involuntary muscles and their body functions. Examples include the heartbeat, blood pressure, intestinal contractions, and glandular secretions. They occur automatically without conscious effort. They can speed up or slow down depending on the situation. For example, when you are angry, frightened, excited, or exercising, the functions speed up. When you relax the functions slow down.

The Sense Organs

The five major senses are sight, hearing, taste, smell, and touch. Neurons for taste are in the tongue and are called *taste buds*. Neurons for smell are located in the nose. The dermis contains neurons for touch, especially in the toes and fingertips.

The *eye* contains the structures for vision. The bones of the skull, the eyelids and eyelashes, and tears protect the eyes from injury. The structures of the eye are shown in Fig. 6-14. The *sclera*, the white of the eye, is the outer layer. The iris gives the eye its color. The opening in the middle of the iris is the *pupil*. Pupil size varies with the amount of light entering the eye. The pupil constricts (narrows) in bright light. It dilates (widens) in dim or dark places. The inner layer of the eye is called the *retina*. The nerves for vision are in the retina.

The *ear* functions in hearing and balance. The ear has three main parts: the *external ear*, *middle ear*, and *inner ear*. The structures of the ear are shown in Fig. 6-15. Sound waves pass through the external ear into the *auditory canal*. The many glands in the auditory canal secrete a waxy substance. The waxy substance is called *cerumen* (ear wax). The auditory canal extends about I inch to the *eardrum*. The eardrum, called the *tympanic membrane*, separates the external and middle ear.

The middle ear contains the *eustachian tube* and three small bones. The eustachian tube connects the middle ear and the throat. Air enters the eustachian tube so that there is equal pressure on both sides of the eardrum. The three small bones amplify sound received from the eardrum. They also send the sound to the inner ear.

The inner ear consists of the *semicircular canals* and the *cochlea*. The cochlea, which looks like a snail shell, contains fluid. The fluid carries the sound waves from the middle ear to the *auditory nerve*. The auditory nerve then carries the message to the brain.

The three semicircular canals are involved with balance. They sense the position of the head and changes in position. They send messages to the brain about the position of the body.

Like other body systems, the nervous system is

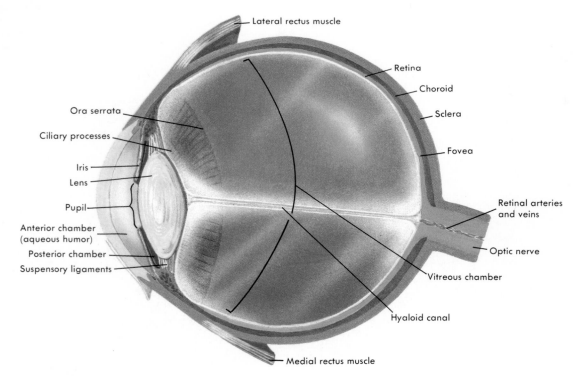

Lateral rectus muscle
Retina
Choroid
Sclera
Ora serrata
Fovea
Ciliary processes
Iris
Lens
Retinal arteries and veins
Pupil
Anterior chamber (aqueous humor)
Posterior chamber
Suspensory ligaments
Optic nerve
Vitreous chamber
Hyaloid canal
Medial rectus muscle

Fig. 6-14 The eye. (From Mosby's *medical and nursing dictionary*, ed. 2, St. Louis, 1986, The C.V. Mosby Co.)

affected by injury and the aging process. Unlike other cells, nerve cells cannot be replaced when they die. Therefore, aging and injury can seriously affect nervous system function. Table 6-1 identifies the changes which occur with aging.

The following observations relate to the function of the client's nervous system.

1. Is the client easy or difficult to wake up?
2. Can the client state his or her name?
3. Can the client accurately identify others?
4. Does the client answer questions properly?
5. Does the client speak clearly?
6. Does the client follow instructions the right way?
7. Can the client squeeze your fingers with each hand?
8. Can the client move his or her arms and legs?
9. Are the client's movements shaky or jerky?
10. Does the client complain of spots, flashes, or blurred vision?
11. Is the client sensitive to bright lights?
12. Is there drainage from the client's ears?
13. Is the client able to hear?
14. Does the client have bowel and bladder control?

Circulatory System

The blood, heart, and blood vessels make up the circulatory system. The heart pumps blood through the blood vessels. The circulatory system performs many important functions.

- Blood carries food, oxygen, and other substances to the cells.
- Blood removes waste products from the cells.
- Regulation of body temperature is aided by the blood and blood vessels. Heat from muscle activity is carried by the blood to other parts of the body. Blood vessels in the skin dilate (widen) if the body needs to be cooled. They constrict (narrow) if heat needs to be kept in the body.
- The circulatory system produces and carries cells that defend the body from harmful disease-causing germs.

The blood contains cells and a liquid called *plasma*. Plasma is mostly water. It carries blood cells to the other body cells. Plasma also carries food, hormones (see page 91), and chemicals to the cells. Waste products are also carried in the plasma.

Red blood cells give the blood its red color. Red blood cells pick up oxygen in the lungs. When blood is bright red, the red blood cells are full of oxygen. As the blood circulates through the body, oxygen is given to the cells. The cells release carbon dioxide (a waste product). The carbon dioxide is picked by the red blood cells. When red blood cells are filled with carbon dioxide, the blood appears dark red.

There are about 25 trillion red blood cells in the body. These cells live for 3 or 4 months. The bone marrow produces new red blood cells. About one million new red blood cells are produced every second.

White blood cells are colorless. They protect the body against infection. At the first sign of infection, white blood cells rush to the infected area. The body produces more white blood cells when there is an infection. White blood cells are also made in the bone marrow. They live about 9 days.

Platelets are needed for blood clotting. They are

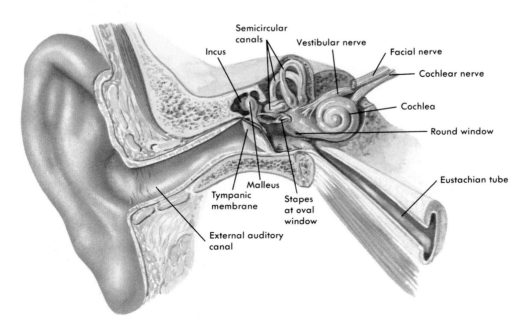

Fig. 6-15 The ear. (From Mosby's medical and nursing dictionary. ed. 2. St. Louis. 1986. The C.V. Mosby Co.)

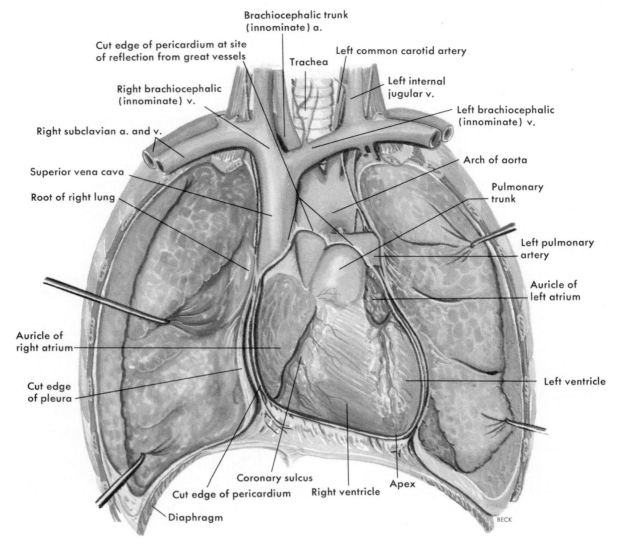

Brachiocephalic trunk
(innominate) a.

Cut edge of pericardium at site
of reflection from great vessels

Trachea

Left common carotid artery

Right brachiocephalic
(innominate) v.

Left internal
jugular v.

Left brachiocephalic
(innominate) v.

Right subclavian a. and v.

Arch of aorta

Superior vena cava

Pulmonary
trunk

Root of right lung

Left pulmonary
artery

Auricle of
left atrium

Auricle of
right atrium

Cut edge
of pleura

Left ventricle

Coronary sulcus

Apex

Cut edge of pericardium

Right ventricle

Diaphragm

BECK

Fig. 6-16 Location of the heart in the chest cavity. (From Anthony, C.P., and Thibodeau, G.A.: Textbook of anatomy and physiology, ed. 11, St. Louis, 1983, The C.V. Mosby Co.)

also produced by the bone marrow. A platelet lives about 4 days.

The heart is a muscle. It pumps blood through the blood vessels to the tissues and cells of the body. The heart lies in the middle to lower part of the chest toward the left side (Fig. 6-16). The heart is hollow with 4 chambers (Fig. 6-17). The upper chambers receive blood. They are called the *atria*. The *right atrium* receives blood from body tissues. The *left atrium* receives blood from the lungs. The lower chambers are called *ventricles*. The ventricles pump blood. The *right ventricle* pumps blood to the lungs for oxygen. The *left ventricle* pumps blood to all parts of the body.

There are two phases of heart action, systole and diastole. During *diastole*, the resting phase, the chambers fill with blood. During *systole*, the working

phase, the heart contracts. Blood is pumped through the blood vessels when the heart contracts.

Blood flows to tissues and cells through the blood vessels. There are three groups of blood vessels: arteries, capillaries, and veins. *Arteries* carry blood away from the heart. Arterial blood is rich in oxygen. The *aorta* is the largest artery of the body. The aorta receives blood directly from the left ventricle. The aorta branches off into other arteries. These arteries carry blood to all parts of the body (Fig. 6-18). The arteries branch off into smaller parts within the tissues. The smallest branch of an artery is called an *arteriole*.

Arterioles connect with blood vessels called *capillaries*. Capillaries are very tiny vessels. Food, oxygen, and other substances pass from the capillaries into the cells of the body. Waste products, including carbon

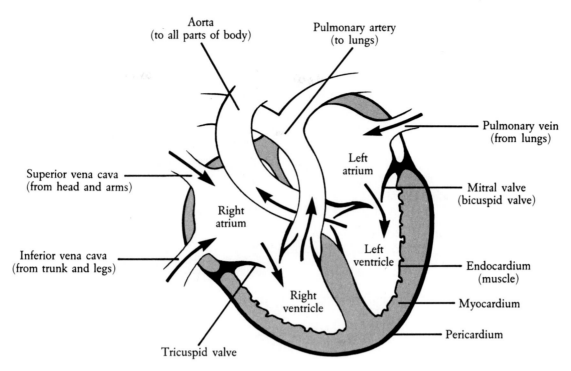

Fig. 6-17 Structures of the heart. (From Sorrentino, S.A.: Mosby's textbook for nursing assistants, ed. 2, St. Louis, 1987, The C.V. Mosby Co.)

dioxide, are picked up from the cells by the capillaries. The waste products are carried back to the heart by the veins.

Veins return blood to the heart. They are connected to the capillaries by *venules*. Venules are small veins. The venules join together to form veins. The many branches of veins also join together near the heart to form two main veins (Fig. 6-19). The two main veins are the *inferior vena cava* and the *superior vena cava*. Both empty into the right atrium. The inferior vena cava carries blood from the legs and trunk. The superior vena cava carries blood from the head and arms. Venous blood is dark red in color. It has little oxygen and a lot of carbon dioxide.

Blood flow through the circulatory system is diagrammed in Fig. 6-17. It can be summarized as follows. Venous blood, poor in oxygen, empties into the right atrium. Blood then flows into the right ventricle. The right ventricle pumps blood into the lungs to pick up oxygen. Oxygen-rich blood from the lungs enters the left atrium. Blood from the left atrium passes into the left ventricle. The left ventricle pumps the blood to the aorta. The aorta branches off to form other arteries. Arterial blood is carried to the tissues by arterioles and to the cells by capillaries. The cells and capillaries exchange oxygen and food for carbon dioxide and waste products. The capillaries connect with venules. Venules carry blood containing carbon dioxide and waste prod-

ucts. The venules form veins. The veins return blood to the heart.

There are many cardiovascular diseases. Some are discussed in Chapter 21. Aging also affects the cardiovascular system (see Table 6-1). These changes can lead to health problems and disease. When caring for clients, you need to make the following observations:
1. Measure the client's blood pressure, pulse, and respirations (see Chapter 13).
2. Is the client complaining of chest pain?
3. Is the client pale (white) or cyanotic (bluish color to the skin)? What is the color of the nail beds?
4. Is the client short of breath when active or resting?
5. Is the client dizzy when he or she sits or stands up after lying down?
6. Are the client's ankles, feet, hands, or fingers swollen?

Respiratory System

Oxygen is needed for survival. Every cell of the body needs oxygen. The respiratory system brings oxygen into the lungs. This system also rids the body of carbon dioxide. *Respiration* is the process of supplying the cells with oxygen and removing carbon dioxide from them. Respiration involves *inhalation* (breathing in) and *exhalation* (breathing out). The terms *inspiration*

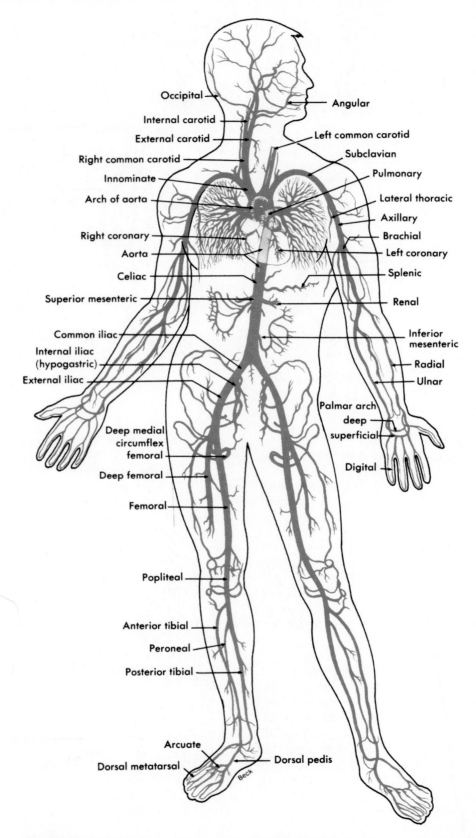

Fig. 6-18 Arterial system. (From Anthony, C.P., and Thibodeau, G.A.: Textbook of anatomy and physiology, ed. 11, St. Louis, 1983, The C.V. Mosby Co.)

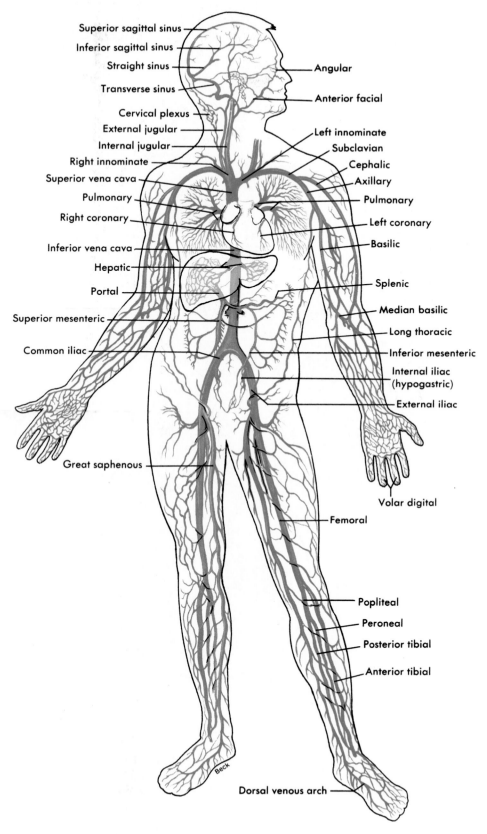

Superior sagittal sinus
Inferior sagittal sinus
Straight sinus
Transverse sinus
Cervical plexus
External jugular
Internal jugular
Right innominate
Superior vena cava
Pulmonary
Right coronary
Inferior vena cava
Hepatic
Portal
Superior mesenteric
Common iliac
Great saphenous

Angular
Anterior facial
Left innominate
Subclavian
Cephalic
Axillary
Pulmonary
Left coronary
Basilic
Splenic
Median basilic
Long thoracic
Inferior mesenteric
Internal iliac
(hypogastric)
External iliac
Volar digital
Femoral
Popliteal
Peroneal
Posterior tibial
Anterior tibial
Dorsal venous arch

Beck

Fig. 6-19 Venous system. (From Anthony, C.P., and Thibodeau, G.A.: Textbook of anatomy and physiology, ed. 11, St. Louis, 1983, The C.V. Mosby Co.)

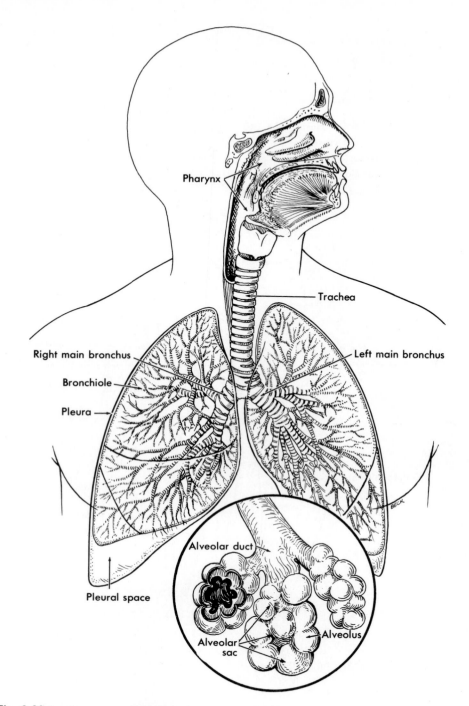

Fig. 6-20 Respiratory system. (From Anthony, C.P., and Thibodeau, G.A.: Textbook of anatomy and physiology, ed. 11, St. Louis, 1983, The C.V. Mosby Co.)

(breathing in) and *expiration* (breathing out) are also used. The respiratory system is shown in Fig. 6-20.

Air enters the body through the *nose*. The air then passes into the *pharynx* (throat). This structure is a tube-shaped passageway for air and food. Air passes from the pharynx into the *larynx* (voice box). The *epiglottis* acts like a lid over the larynx. The epiglottis prevents food from entering the airway during swallowing. Dur-

ing inhalation the epiglottis lifts up to let air pass over the larynx. Air passes from the larynx into the *trachea* (windpipe). The trachea branches off into the *right bronchus* and the *left bronchus*. Each bronchus enters a lung. Upon entering the lungs the bronchi divide many times into smaller and smaller branches. Eventually they end in tiny one-celled air sacs called *alveoli*.

The alveoli look like small clusters of grapes.

They are supplied with capillaries. Oxygen and carbon dioxide are exchanged between the alveoli and capillaries. The blood in the capillaries picks up oxygen from the alveoli. Then the blood returns to the heart's left side and is pumped to the rest of the body. The alveoli pick up carbon dioxide from the capillaries. The carbon dioxide is exhaled.

Breathing is necessary for life. Therefore, breathing problems can threaten life. Diseases, chest injuries, and some changes due to aging can affect breathing. The changes due to aging are listed in Table 6-1. Cigarette smoking and air pollution can cause serious lung diseases and breathing problems. Respiratory diseases are discussed in Chapter 21.

You need to watch your clients for signs and symptoms of breathing problems. You need to make the following observations.
1. Do both sides of the client's chest rise and fall with respirations?
2. Is the client breathing fast, slow, or irregular? What is the client's respiratory rate (see Chapter 13)?
3. Is breathing noisy?
4. Is the client having difficulty breathing?
5. Does the client cough up mucus (sputum)? How much and what is the color of the mucus?
6. Does the client have a cough? How frequent? Is the cough dry or does the client cough up mucus (a productive cough)?

Digestive System

The digestive system breaks down food so that it can be used by the cells. This process is called *digestion*. The system also rids the body of solid wastes. The digestive system is also called the *gastrointestinal system* (Fig. 6-21).

Digestion starts in the *mouth*. The *teeth* cut, chop, and grind food into small pieces for digestion and swallowing. The *tongue* aids in chewing and swallowing. *Taste buds* are on the tongue. They sense sweet, sour, bitter, and salty tastes. *Salivary glands* in the mouth secrete *saliva*. The saliva moistens foods so it is easier to swallow. The saliva also begins digesting food.

The tongue pushes food into the *pharynx* (throat) during swallowing. Contraction of the pharynx pushes food into the *esophagus*. The esophagus is about 10 inches long. Involuntary muscle contractions move food down the esophagus into the stomach. The involuntary muscle contractions are called *peristalsis*.

The *stomach* is in the upper left part of the abdomen. Stomach muscles stir and churn food into even smaller particles. The stomach lining secretes *gastric juices*. Food is mixed and churned with the gastric juices. This forms a semiliquid substance called *chyme*.

Peristalsis pushes the chyme from the stomach into the small intestine.

The *small intestine* is about 20 feet long. It has three parts. The first part is the *duodenum*. The duodenum adds more digestive juices to the chyme. One juice is called *bile*. Bile is a greenish liquid. It is made in the *liver* and stored in the *gallbladder*. Juices from the *pancreas* and small intestine are also added to the chyme. The digestive juices break down food so that it can be absorbed.

Peristalsis moves the chyme through the other two parts of the small intestine: the *jejunum* and the *ileum*. Tiny projections called *villi* line the small intestine. The villi absorb the digested food into the capillaries. Most food absorption occurs in the jejunum and ileum.

Some chyme is not digested. Undigested chyme passes from the small intestine into the *large intestine*. The large intestine is also called the *large bowel* or the *colon*. The colon absorbs most of the water from the chyme. The remaining semisolid material is called *feces*. Feces consist of a small amount of water and solid wastes. These are the waste products of digestion. Peristalsis moves the feces from the colon to the *rectum*. Feces leave the body through the *anus*.

The digestive system is less effective as the body ages. The changes of aging are listed in Table 6-1. These changes often cause eating and elimination problems. Food and elimination are basic physical needs. Therefore, you need to observe for problems. You need to make the following observations.
1. Does the client eat the entire meal?
2. How much food on the tray is eaten?
3. Does the client complain of nausea?
4. Is the client vomiting? What does the vomited material look like?
5. Is the client belching?
6. Does the client complain of abdominal pain?
7. Does the client have difficulty swallowing?
8. How often does the client have a bowel movement?
9. What is the amount, color, and consistency of bowel movements?
10. Is the client's abdomen soft or hard?

Urinary System

The respiratory system, the digestive system, and the skin remove wastes from the body. The digestive system rids the body of solid wastes. The lungs rid the body of carbon dioxide. Water and other substances make up sweat. There are other wastes in the blood from body cells burning food for energy. The urinary system has two functions:
- To remove waste products from the blood
- To maintain water balance within the body

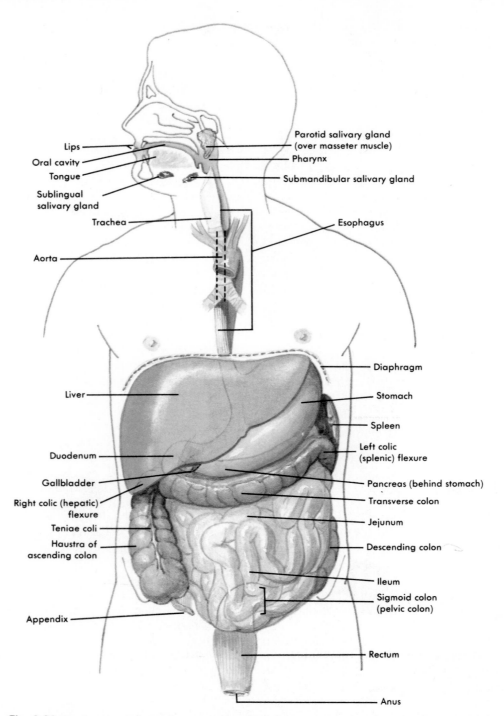

Fig. 6-21 The digestive system. (From Mosby's medical and nursing dictionary, ed. 2, St. Louis, 1986, The C.V. Mosby Co.)

The structures of the urinary system are shown in Fig. 6-22.

The *kidneys* are 2 bean-shaped organs in the upper abdomen. They lie against the muscles of the back on each side of the spine.

Each kidney has over a million tiny *nephrons* (Fig. 6-23). The nephron is the basic working unit of the

kidney. Each nephron has tiny *tubules*. Blood passes through the tubules and is filtered. Most of the water and other needed substances are reabsorbed by the blood. The remaining fluid and wastes form *urine* in the tubule.

Each kidney has a tube called the *ureter*. Each ureter is about 10 to 12 inches long. The ureters carry

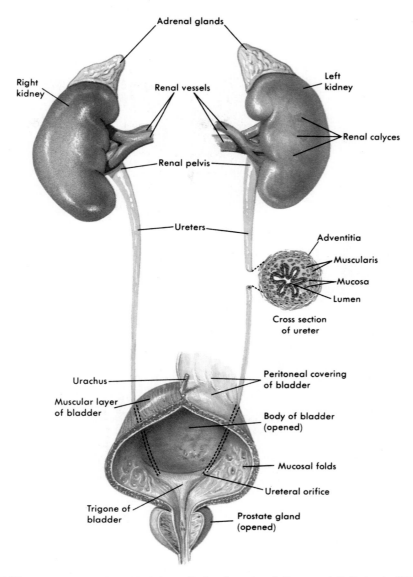

Fig. 6-22 Urinary system. (From Mosby's medical and nursing dictionary, ed. 2, St. Louis, 1986, the C.V. Mosby Co.)

urine from the kidneys to the *bladder*. The bladder is a hollow muscular sac. It lies in the lower part of the abdomen toward the front. The bladder stores urine until the desire to urinate is felt. Urine passes from the bladder through the *urethra*. The opening at the end of the urethra is the *meatus*. Urine passes from the body through the meatus. Urine is a clear yellowish fluid.

The aging process also affects the urinary system (see Table 6-1). Urinary elimination is a basic physical need. You need to be alert for problems with the urinary system. The following observations need to be made.

1. Does the client have pain, burning, or urinary urgency?

2. Does the client have a hard time urinating?
3. How often does the client urinate?
4. What is the amount of urine?
5. What is the color of the urine?
6. Is the urine clear?
7. Does the urine have an odor?
8. Are there any particles in the urine?

Reproductive System

Human reproduction involves the union of a female sex cell and a male sex cell. Males and females have different reproductive structures. The differences allow for reproduction.

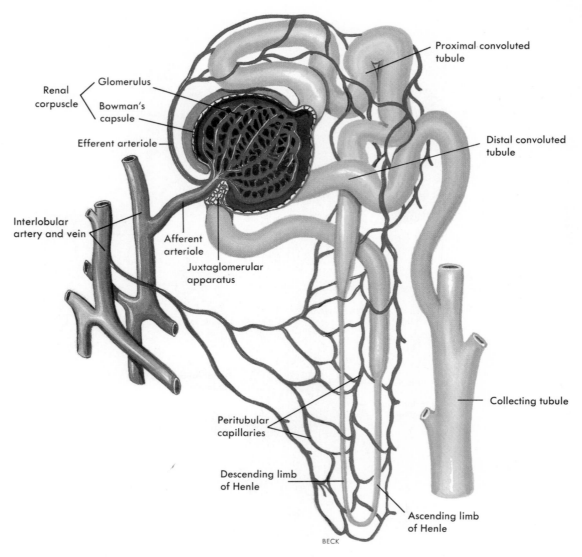

Fig. 6-23 A nephron. (Anthony, C.P., and Thibodeau, G.A.: Textbook of anatomy and physiology, ed. 11, St. Louis, 1983, The C.V. Mosby Co.)

The Male Reproductive System

The male reproductive structures are shown in Fig. 6-24. The *testes* (*testicles*) are the male sex glands. Sex glands are also called *gonads*. The testes produce male sex cells. Male sex cells are called *sperm* cells. The testes also produce *testosterone*, the male hormone. This hormone is needed for the reproductive organs to function. Testosterone is also needed for the development of secondary sex characteristics in the male (see Chapter 5). The testes are outside the body. They are located between the thighs in a sac called the *scrotum*.

Sperm travel through a tube called the *vas deferens*. Eventually each vas deferens joins a *seminal vesicle*. The two seminal vesicles store sperm and produce *semen*. Semen is a fluid that carries sperm from the male

reproductive tract. The seminal vesicles unite to form the *ejaculatory duct*. The ejaculatory duct passes through the prostate gland.

The *prostate gland* lies just below the bladder. The gland secretes a fluid into the semen. The ejaculatory ducts join the *urethra* as they leave the prostate. The urethra also runs through the prostate. The urethra is the outlet for both urine and semen. The urethra is in the penis.

The *penis* is outside the body. When the man becomes sexually excited, tissues of the penis fill with blood. This causes the penis to become larger, hard, and erect. The erect penis can then enter the female's vagina. The semen containing sperm is then released into the vagina.

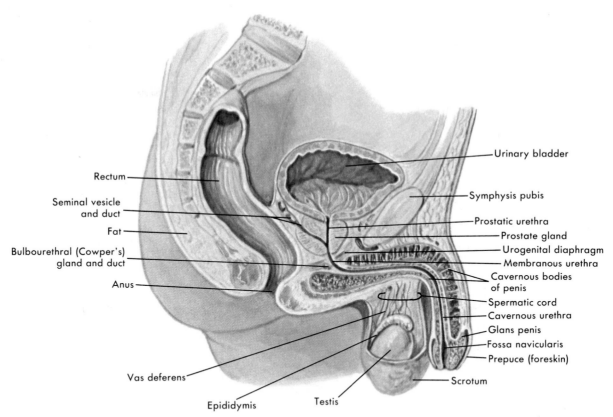

Rectum

Seminal vesicle and duct

Fat

Bulbourethral (Cowper's) gland and duct

Anus

Vas deferens

Epididymis

Testis

Urinary bladder

Symphysis pubis

Prostatic urethra

Prostate gland

Urogenital diaphragm

Membranous urethra

Cavernous bodies of penis

Spermatic cord

Cavernous urethra

Glans penis

Fossa navicularis

Prepuce (foreskin)

Scrotum

Fig. 6-24 Male reproductive system. (From Mosby's medical and nursing dictionary, ed. 2, St. Louis, 1986, The C.V. Mosby Co.)

The Female Reproductive System

The female reproductive system is shown in Fig. 6-25. The 2 female gonads are called the *ovaries*. There is an ovary on each side of the uterus. The ovaries produce and contain the *ova* (eggs). The ova are the female sex cells. One ovum (egg) is released monthly during the woman's reproductive years. The release of an ovum from an ovary is called *ovulation*. The ovaries also secrete the female hormones *estrogen* and *progesterone*. The female reproductive system needs these hormones to function. They are also needed for the development of female secondary sex characteristics (see Chapter 5).

When an ovum leaves an ovary it is picked up by one of the *fallopian tubes*. There is a fallopian tube on each side. The ovum travels through the fallopian tube to the *uterus*. The uterus is a hollow muscular organ. It is located behind the bladder and in front of the rectum. The narrow section of the uterus is called the *cervix*. The lining of the uterus is called the *endometrium*. Many blood vessels are in the endometrium. If sex cells from the male and female unite into one cell, the cell will implant into the endometrium. There it will grow

into a baby. The unborn baby grows and gets nourishment in the uterus.

The cervix projects into the *vagina*. The vagina opens to the outside of the body. The vagina receives the penis during sexual intercourse. It is also part of the birth canal.

The *mammary glands*, or *breasts*, are reproductive organs because they secrete milk after childbirth. They are located on the outside of the chest. They are made up of glands and fat (Fig. 6-26). The milk drains out of the nipples.

MENSTRUATION

The endometrium is rich in blood to feed the cell that grows into an unborn baby (*fetus*). If a woman does not become pregnant, the endometrium breaks up. It leaves the body through the vagina. This process is called *menstruation*. Menstruation occurs about every 28 days. Therefore, it is also called the *menstrual cycle*.

The first day of the cycle begins with menstruation. Blood flows from the uterus through the vaginal opening. Menstrual flow usually last for 3 to 7 days. Ovulation occurs during the next phase. An ovum is

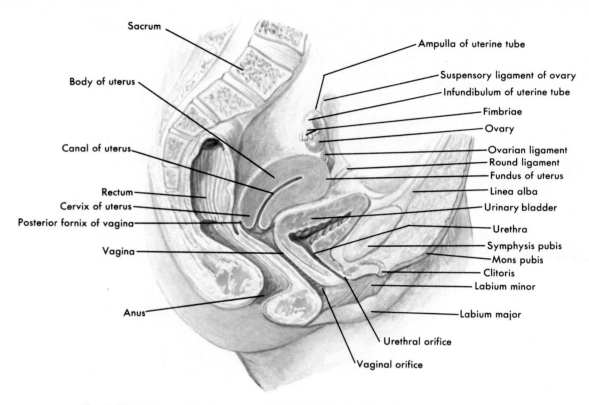

Fig. 6-25 Female reproductive system. (From Mosby's medical and nursing dictionary, ed. 2, St. Louis, 1986, The C.V. Mosby Co.)

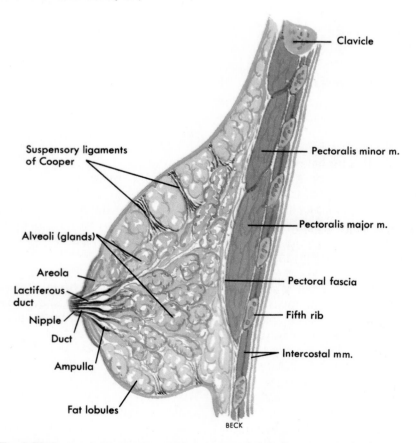

Fig. 6-26 The female breast. (From Anthony, C.P., and Thibodeau, G.A.: Textbook of anatomy and physiology, ed. 11, St. Louis, 1983, The C.V. Mosby Co.)

released by an ovary. Ovulation usually occurs on or about the fourteenth day of the cycle. Meanwhile, the ovaries secrete estrogen and progesterone (the female hormones). These hormones cause the endometrium to thicken for pregnancy. If pregnancy does not occur, the hormones decrease in amount. Blood supply to the endometrium decreases because of lower hormone levels. The endometrium breaks up and is discharged through the vagina. Another menstrual cycle begins.

The reproductive system is important for sex and sexuality (see Chapter 5). Disease, injury, and aging (see Table 6-1) can affect this system. Some women have problems getting pregnant. The cause of the problem may be in the male or the female. The inability to get pregnant can affect the couple psychologically.

The following observations relate to the reproductive system.

1. Is there drainage from the nipples?
2. Is there discharge from the penis or vagina? What is its color? Does it have an odor?
3. How long does the woman's menstrual flow last?
4. Does the woman complain of pain during menstruation?
5. Is there vaginal bleeding between menstrual periods?
6. Are there sores on the penis or outside of the vagina?
7. Is the penis or vagina red, swollen, or irritated?
8. Does the client complain of pain, burning, or other discomfort?

Endocrine System

The endocrine system is made up of the *endocrine glands* (Fig. 6-27). These glands secrete chemicals called *hormones* into the bloodstream. The hormones regulate the activities of other organs and glands in the body. Table 6-2 lists the endocrine glands and their functions.

Hormones of one gland affect other body systems. Aging causes the glands to secrete less hormones. Body functions then decrease and slow down. Table 6-1 lists the changes in the endocrine system related to aging.

Endocrine disorders cause many signs and symptoms. These signs and symptoms may be very obvious. Sometimes they are very hard to detect. Endocrine disorders can cause physical and psychological signs and symptoms. You need to observe for the following.

1. Is the client weak or tired?
2. Does the client eat often and a lot? Does the client have a poor appetite?
3. Is the client's blood pressure high or low (see Chapter 13)?
4. Does the client urinate a lot?

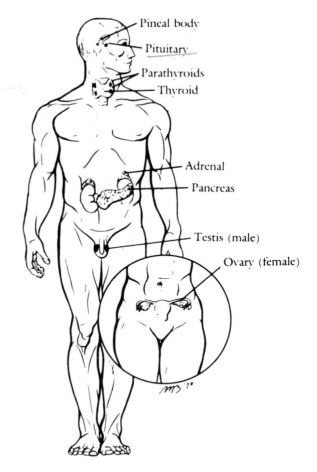

Fig. 6-27 Endocrine system. (From Austrin, M.: Young's learning medical terminology step by step, ed. 6, St. Louis, 1987, The C.V. Mosby Co.)

5. Does the client drink a lot of fluid? Does the client complain of being thirsty?
6. Does the client complain of numbness, tingling, or cramps in the fingers, toes, arms, or legs?
7. Is there a change in the client's skin color?
8. Is the client nervous, restless, or sad? Does the client act differently from before?

Summary

The human body has many systems. Each system has its own structures and functions. The systems work together to perform body functions and to survive. When one system is diseased or injured, other systems are affected. Aging also affects each body system. The body signals when something is wrong. These signals can be observed.

Reviewing this chapter may be helpful as you learn to be a home health aide. Each procedure involves the client's body and your body. You need to understand the body's structure and function in order to give good and safe care.

Table 6-2 Endocrine Glands

GLAND	FUNCTION
Pituitary (the master gland)	Regulates growth of muscles, bones, and other organs Regulates functioning of the thyroid gland Regulates growth, development, and function of the reproductive system Prevents kidneys from getting rid of too much water
Thyroid gland	Regulates *metabolism*, the burning of food for heat and energy by the cells; too little thyroid hormone causes slowing of body functions, slowed movements, and weight gain. Too much of the hormone causes increased metabolism, excess energy, and weight loss
Parathyroid glands	Regulate body's use of calcium, which is needed for nerve and muscle function
Adrenal glands	Cause body to produce energy quickly during emergencies—heart rate, blood pressure, muscle power, and energy all increase Regulate use of carbohydrates (see Chapter 17) Control body's response to stress and inflammation Regulate the amount of salt and water that is absorbed and lost by the kidneys
Pancreas	Regulates the amount of sugar in the blood available for use by the cells
Gonads	Functioning of the reproductive system

Study Questions

Circle the *best* answer.

1. The basic unit of body structure is the
   a. Cell
   b. Neuron
   c. Nephron
   d. Ovum

2. The outer layer of the skin is called the
   a. Dermis
   b. Epidermis
   c. Integument
   d. Myelin

3. Which is *not* a function of the skin?
   a. Providing the protective covering for the body
   b. Regulating body temperature
   c. Sensing cold, pain, touch, and pressure
   d. Providing the shape and framework for the body

4. Which part of the musculoskeletal system allows movement?
   a. Bone marrow
   b. Bones
   c. Joints
   d. Ligaments

5. The highest functions of the brain take place in the
   a. Cerebral cortex
   b. Medulla
   c. Brainstem
   d. Spinal nerves

6. Besides hearing, the ear is involved with
   a. Regulating body movements
   b. Balance
   c. Smoothness of body movements
   d. Controlling involuntary muscles

7. Which part of the heart pumps blood to the body?
   a. Right atrium
   b. Right ventricle
   c. Left atrium
   d. Left ventricle

8. Which blood vessels carry blood away from the heart?
   a. Capillaries
   b. Veins
   c. Venules
   d. Arteries

9. Oxygen and carbon dioxide are exchanged
   a. In the bronchi
   b. Between the alveoli and capillaries
   c. Between the two lungs
   d. In the trachea

10. Food is made easier to swallow by
    a. Bile
    b. Gastric juices
    c. Chyme
    d. Saliva

11. Most of the absorption of food takes place in the
    a. Stomach
    b. Small intestine
    c. Colon
    d. Large intestine

12. Urine is formed by the
    a. Jejunum
    b. Kidneys
    c. Bladder
    d. Liver

13. Urine passes from the body through
    a. The ureters
    b. The urethra
    c. The anus
    d. Nephrons

14. The male sex gland is called the
    a. Penis
    b. Semen
    c. Testis
    d. Scrotum

15. The male sex cell is the
    a. Semen
    b. Ovum
    c. Gonad
    d. Sperm

16. The female sex gland is the
    a. Ovary
    b. Fallopian tube
    c. Uterus
    d. Vagina

17. The discharge of the lining of the uterus is called
    a. The endometrium
    b. Ovulation
    c. Fertilization
    d. Menstruation

18. The endocrine glands secrete substances called
    a. Hormones
    b. Mucus
    c. Semen
    d. Insulin

Answers

1. a	6. b	11. b	15. d
2. b	7. d	12. b	16. a
3. d	8. d	13. b	17. d
4. c	9. b	14. c	18. a
5. a	10. d		

Controlling Infection in the Home

7

Chapter Highlights	What you will learn to do

How infections spread

Preventing the spread of infections

Isolation precautions

- Explain how an infection develops
- List the signs and symptoms of an infection
- Identify 6 conditions that microorganisms need to live and grow
- Describe how microorganisms are spread and measures that prevent the spread of infection
- Perform the handwashing procedure
- Perform the procedure for wet-heat sterilization
- Explain the purpose of isolation and describe isolation techniques
- Put on a gown, mask, and gloves and double bag garbage

Key Terms

Asepsis The absence of pathogens
Clean technique Medical asepsis
Contamination The process by which an object or area becomes unclean
Disinfection The process by which pathogens are destroyed
Infection A disease that results when microorganisms invade and grow in the body
Medical asepsis The techniques and practices used to prevent the spread of pathogens from one person or place to another person or place; clean technique

Microorganism A small living plant or animal that cannot be seen without a microscope; a microbe
Nonpathogen A microorganism that does not usually cause an infection
Pathogen A microorganism that is harmful and able to cause an infection
Sterile Having no pathogenic or nonpathogenic microorganisms
Sterilization The process by which all microorganisms are destroyed

How Infections Spread

Infection is a major health hazard. Some infections cause a short illness. Other infections are very serious and can cause death. Infections are very dangerous to infants and the elderly. You need to protect the client and yourself from infection.

Organisms are living things. A *microorganism* is a small (micro) living plant or animal (organism). It can be seen only with a microscope. Microorganisms, also called *microbes*, are everywhere. They can be found in the air, food, soil, and water and inside and outside the body. Microorganisms are also on animals, clothing, and furniture. Some microorganisms are harmful. They cause infections and are called *pathogens*. A *nonpathogen* is a microorganism that does not usually cause an infection.

Microorganisms must have the following to live and grow:

- A *host*—The host is where the microorganism lives and grows. A host can be a person, animal, food, water, plant, soil, or other material.
- *Water*—Microorganisms need a moist area.
- *Warmth*—microorganisms grow best at body temperature. They are destroyed by heat. Cold does not kill microorganisms. However, cold slows their growth.
- *Oxygen*—Like other living things, microorganisms need oxygen to live. However, some microorganisms cannot live where there is oxygen.
- *Darkness*—Microorganisms like dark areas. They are destroyed by light.
- *Food*—Microorganisms need food to live and grow.

Some microorganisms live and grow in certain places. There are microorganisms that normally live in the respiratory tract, in the intestines, on the skin, and in other areas outside the body. They do not cause infections when in their natural area. If the nonpathogen leaves its natural location, it becomes a pathogen. *Escherichia coli* is a microorganism normally found in the large intestine. If the E. *coli* enters the urinary system or other body part, it can cause an infection.

Infection

An *infection* is a disease that results when microorganisms invade and grow in the body. The infection may involve a body part or the whole body. The client may have some or all of the following signs and symptoms: fever, pain or tenderness, fatigue, loss of appetite, nausea, vomiting, diarrhea, rash, sores on mucous membranes, redness and swelling of a body part, and discharge or drainage from the infected area. You must report signs and symptoms of an infection to your supervisor.

The development of an infection depends on several factors. First, there must be a *source*. The source is a pathogen that can cause disease. The pathogen must have a *reservoir* where it can grow and multiply. Humans and animals are reservoirs for microorganisms. The pathogen must be able to leave the reservoir. In other words, it must have an *exit*. The exits in the human body are the respiratory, gastrointestinal, urinary, and reproductive tracts, breaks in the skin, and the blood.

After leaving the reservoir, the pathogen must be *transmitted* (spread or carried) to another host. Methods of transmission are shown in Fig. 7-1. They include:

- *Air*—Dust particles or drops of moisture from coughing, sneezing, or talking
- *Contact*—giving personal care; handling equipment (bedpans, emesis basins, stethoscopes, etc.); linens, dishes, glasses, silverware, and food; handling body fluids (urine, feces, vomitus, drainage from wounds, respiratory secretions, blood, etc.)
- *Insects*—insect bites (mosquitoes, fleas, ticks, lice) or food that has been touched by insects
- *Animals*—animal bites, eating meat from an infected animal, or touching an infected animal
- *Food and water*—drinking contaminated water, eating spoiled food, eating unwashed food

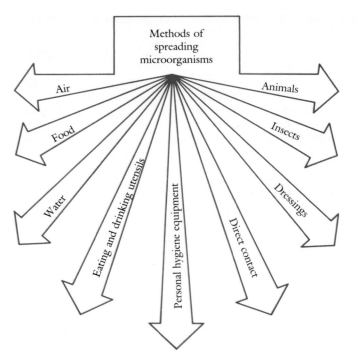

Fig. 7-1 Methods by which microorganisms can be spread. (From Sorrentino, S.A.: Mosby's textbook for nursing assistants, ed. 2, St. Louis, 1987, The C.V. Mosby Co.)

The pathogen then needs to enter the body. Microorganisms enter the body the same way that they exit. Whether or not the pathogen will grow and multiply depends on the *body's ability to resist infection*. The human body has the natural ability to protect itself from infection. A person's ability to resist infection relates to age, sex, nutrition, fatigue, general health, medications, and if there are other illnesses.

Preventing the Spread of Infections

Asepsis means the absence of all disease-producing microorganisms (the absence of pathogens). Certain practices result in asepsis. These practices are known as *medical asepsis* or *clean technique*. Medical asepsis means the techniques and practices used to prevent pathogens from spreading from one area to another. Medical asepsis is different from disinfection and sterilization. *Disinfection* involves destroying pathogenic microorganisms. *Sterilization* destroys *all* microorganisms. *Sterile* means having no microorganisms, either pathogenic or nonpathogenic.

Contamination is when an object or area becomes unclean. In medical asepsis, an object or area is considered "clean" when it is free of pathogens. An object or area is contaminated ("dirty") if pathogens are present. A sterile object or area is contaminated when pathogens or nonpathogens are present.

Common Aseptic Practices

You have an important role in maintaining cleanliness. You must be concerned with your own personal cleanliness. You must also keep your clients and their homes clean. Table 7-1 lists common aseptic practices. They will help you prevent the spread of infection to the client, the family, and yourself.

Table 7-1   Common Aseptic Practices

1. Wash your hands before and after you touch the client.
2. Wash your hands after urinating, having a bowel movement or changing tampons or sanitary napkins.
3. Wash your hands before handling or preparing food.
4. Wash fruits and vegetables before serving them.
5. Encourage each family member to use his or her own towels, washcloths, toothbrush, drinking glass, and other personal care items.
6. Use disposable cups and dishes for clients with infection.
7. Encourage the client to cover the nose and mouth with tissues when coughing, sneezing, or blowing the nose. Make sure there is a plastic or paper bag for used tissues (Fig. 7-2).
8. Practice good personal hygiene yourself. Bathe, wash your hair, and brush your teeth regularly (see Chapter 2)
9. Encourage clients to wash their hands often. They should wash their hands after toileting and before eating.
10. Wash cooking and eating utensils with soap and water after they have been used.
11. Clean cooking and eating surfaces with soap and water or a disinfectant.

Fig. 7-2 A paper bag is nearby for used tissues.

Fig. 7-3 The home health aide is checking the date of a food label.

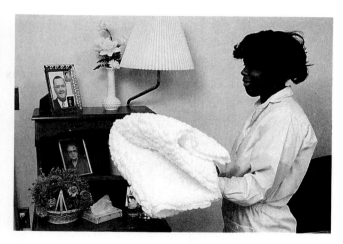

Fig. 7-4 The aide holds equipment away from her uniform.

Fig. 7-5 The aide is wearing gloves and a disposable apron.

12. Do not leave food sitting out and uncovered. Close all food containers. Refrigerate foods that will spoil.
13. Do not use food that smells bad or looks discolored.
14. Check the expiration date on food. Do not use it if the date has passed (Fig. 7-3).
15. Clean the kitchen and bathroom as described in Chapter 9.

16. Change water in flower vases daily.
17. Remove dead plants and flowers from the home.
18. Dust furniture with a damp cloth and use a damp mop for floors. This helps prevent the movement of dust in the air.
19. Empty garbage every day. Use large, sturdy plastic bags or wrap the garbage in several thicknesses of newspaper. Place the garbage outside the home. If possible, put the bags in plastic or metal garbage containers.
20. Wear disposable gloves if you have open cuts or sores on your hands.
21. Hold equipment and linens away from your uniform (Fig. 7-4).
22. Do not shake linens. This helps prevent the movement of dust.
23. Clean from the cleanest area to the dirtiest. This prevents soiling a clean area.
24. Clean away from your body and uniform. Dusting, brushing, or wiping toward yourself transmits microorganisms to your skin, hair, and uniform.
25. Pour contaminated liquids directly into sinks or toilets. Avoid splashing the liquid onto other areas.
26. Do not sit on the client's bed if the client has an infection. You will pick up microorganisms and carry them to the next surface that you sit on.
27. Wear disposable gloves when you will have contact with the client's body fluids. This includes when giving enemas, cleaning the client's genital area, handling vomitus, and giving mouth care.
28. Wear a disposable apron (Fig. 7-5) when you will be in contact with the client's body fluids.

HANDWASHING

Handwashing is the most important and the easiest way to prevent the spread of infection. You use your hands in almost every activity. They are easily contaminated and can spread microorganisms if they are not washed before and after giving care. Good handwashing involves three things:

Soap—bar or liquid soap from a dispenser
Water—clean, warm running water
Friction—rubbing the hands together

Fig. 7-6 A paper towel is used to turn the faucet off. (From Sorrentino, S.A.: Mosby's textbook for nursing assistants, ed. 2, St. Louis, 1987, The C.V. Mosby Co.)

Fig. 7-7 A nail file is used to clean under the fingernails. (From Sorrentino, S.A.: Mosby's textbook for nursing assistants, ed. 2, St. Louis, 1987, The C.V. Mosby Co.)

To wash your hands properly you need to follow these rules:

1. Wash your hands under warm running water.
2. Hold bar soap during the entire procedure. After washing your hands, rinse the soap under running water. After rinsing, drop the soap into the soap dish. Be careful not to touch the soap dish during or after the procedure.
3. Do not use the client's personal soap for yourself.
4. Keep your hands and forearms lower than your elbows during the procedure. If they are held up, dirty water can run from your hands to your elbows.
5. Clean your thumbs, knuckles, sides of the hands, little fingers, and underneath the nails. Use a nail brush or nail file to clean under fingernails (Fig. 7-7).
6. Dry your hands with paper towels. Use a clean hand towel if there are no paper towels.
7. Faucets are considered "dirty." Use a paper towel to turn off the water (Fig. 7-6). The paper towel keeps your hand clean.

8. Apply lotion after handwashing. This prevents chapping and dry skin.
9. Consult your supervisor if you have a skin condition that gets worse with soap and frequent handwashing. You may have to wear disposable gloves.

Procedure: Handwashing

1. Gather equipment: soap, paper towels, nail brush or nail file, and a wastebasket.
2. Place bar soap and nail brush (or nail file) on a paper towel on the sink. Put other paper towels in a clean, dry area nearby.
3. Push your wristwatch 4 to 5 inches above your hand.
4. Turn on the faucet. Adjust water to a warm, comfortable temperature.

Fig. 7-8 Hands are lower than the elbows for handwashing. (From Sorrentino, S.A.: Mosby's textbook for nursing assistants, ed. 2, St. Louis, 1987, The C.V. Mosby Co.)

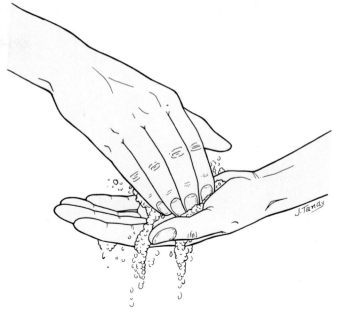

Fig. 7-9 The tips of the fingers are rubbed against the palms to clean underneath the fingernails. (From Sorrentino, S.A.: Mosby's textbook for nursing assistants, ed. 2, St. Louis, 1987, The C.V. Mosby Co.)

5. Wet your wrists and hands. Keep your hands lower than your elbows throughout the procedure (Fig. 7-8).
6. Apply soap to your hands.
7. Rub your palms together to work up a good lather.
8. Wash each hand and wrist thoroughly. Clean between the fingers. Clean under fingernails by rubbing the tips of your fingers against your palms (Fig. 7-9).
9. Wash for 1 to 2 minutes using friction and rotating motions.
10. Clean under the fingernails with the nail brush (or nail file) as in Fig. 7-7.
11. Rinse your wrists and hands under running water. Water should flow from the arms to the hands.
12. Return the soap to the soap dish.
13. Dry your wrists and hands with paper towels. Pat dry.
14. Turn off the faucet with the paper towels.
15. Discard the paper towels in the waste basket.

CARE OF SUPPLIES AND EQUIPMENT

Disposable equipment is very common in health care. Disposable equipment is usually used once and then discarded. However, some disposable equipment can be used several times by a client. Examples include disposable bedpans, urinals, wash basins, water pitchers, and drinking cups. Disposable equipment helps reduce the spread of infection.

Larger and more costly equipment is usually not disposable. It has to be disinfected or sterilized for reuse. However, it has to be cleaned first. Cleaning reduces the number of microorganisms to be destroyed and removes organic material. Organic material includes blood, pus, drainage from wounds, and body secretions or excretions. Follow these guidelines when cleaning equipment.

1. Rinse the item in cold water to remove organic material. Heat causes organic material to become thick, sticky, and hard to remove.
2. Use soap and hot water to wash the item.
3. Use a brush if necessary.
4. Rinse and dry the item.
5. Disinfect or sterilize the item.
6. Disinfect equipment used in the cleaning procedure.

DISINFECTION

Disinfection is the process in which pathogens are destroyed. However, disinfection does not destroy spores. *Spores* are microorganisms that are protected by

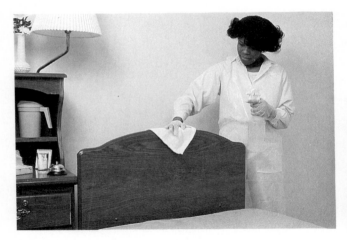

Fig. 7-10 The client's bed is cleaned with a disinfectant.

Fig. 7-11 Wet-heat sterilization. Items in the pot are covered with cold water.

a hard shell. Spores are killed by very high temperatures.

Boiling in water. This method is simple and cheap. Small items can be disinfected by placing them in boiling water for at least 15 to 20 minutes.

Chemical disinfectants. These are generally used for cleaning equipment and for housekeeping. They are used to clean commodes, wheelchairs, and the client's hospital furniture (Fig. 7-10). There are many types of chemical disinfectants. You should wear waterproof gloves when using a disinfectant. The gloves will prevent skin irritation. Some chemical disinfectants have special precautions for storage and use. You need to read labels and consult your supervisor about disinfectants.

STERILIZATION

Sterilization kills all nonpathogens, pathogens, and spores. Very high temperatures are used. Microorganisms grow best at body temperature and are destroyed by heat.

You may have to sterilize items, such as baby bottles, in the home. Pressure cookers can be used to sterilize objects. Wet-heat sterilization is sometimes used.

Procedure: Wet-heat sterilization

1. Gather equipment
   a. Large pot with lid
   b. Tongs
   c. Items to be sterilized
   d. Cold water
2. Make sure you have cleaned all items to be sterilized.
3. Wash your hands.
4. Place the pot on the stove.
5. Place items in the pot. Cover the items with cold water. Make sure the water level is at least 1 inch below the rim (Fig. 7-11).
6. Place the lid on the pot. Make sure handles are turned in toward the stove.
7. Bring the water to a boil. Continue boiling for 20 minutes. Do not lift the lid during this time.
8. Turn the heat off. Let the pot cool. Do not lift the lid. You could be burned by escaping steam. Leave the equipment in the pot until needed.
9. Remove the items with tongs. Put the items in their proper place.

Isolation Precautions

Sometimes other measures are needed to prevent the spread of microorganisms. *Isolation techniques* prevent the spread of pathogenic microorganisms from one area to another. Pathogens are kept within a certain area, usually the client's room. Isolation techniques are ordered by the doctor. Your supervisor will tell you when they are needed.

Isolation precautions are used to prevent the spread of a *communicable* or *contagious disease.* Such diseases are caused by pathogens that spread easily. Common communicable diseases are measles, mumps, chicken pox, syphilis, gonorrhea, and AIDS (acquired immune deficiency syndrome). Clients may have respiratory, wound, skin, gastrointestinal, or blood infections that are highly contagious. Isolation techniques are used for these clients. Some communicable diseases are discussed in Chapter 21.

Isolation techniques are sometimes used to protect a client. Age, weakness, illness, and certain medications can make some clients very susceptible to infection. Their ability to fight an infection is reduced. If an infection develops, it can be very dangerous to the client.

There are several isolation techniques. Each requires different procedures. All require handwashing before and after client contact. Your supervisor will instruct you on the type of isolation for your client. These are the main isolation techniques:

1. *Drainage and secretion precautions* prevent the spread of pathogens found in wounds or wound drainage. Gloves and a gown are worn by those who will have contact with the wound or drainage. Supplies and dressings are double bagged.
2. *Respiratory isolation* is used to prevent the spread of pathogens through the air. Masks are worn. Tissues and supplies in contact with respiratory secretions are double bagged.
3. *Enteric precautions* prevent the spread of pathogens through feces. A gown and gloves are worn by those having contact with the client or the client's urine, feces, bedpan, toilet, urinal, and linens. Urine and feces are flushed down the toilet immediately. Dishes, garbage, and supplies are double bagged.
4. *Blood/body fluid precautions* are used when body fluids are infected. Gowns and gloves are worn to prevent contact with the client's blood or body fluids. Dishes, garbage, and supplies are double bagged.
5. *Strict isolation* is used when communicable diseases are spread by direct contact or through the air. Gowns, masks, and gloves are worn. Urine and feces are flushed down the toilet immediately. Dishes, garbage, and supplies are double bagged.

Gowns, Gloves, and Masks

You may have to wear a gown, gloves, or a mask when isolation is ordered. These protect the client from your microorganisms. They also protect you from getting the client's microorganisms. You need to remember the following about gowns, gloves, and masks:

1. The gown should be long enough and large enough to cover your uniform.
2. The inside of the gown is "clean." The outside is contaminated. Touch only the inside of the gown.
3. A wet gown is contaminated. You need to take it off and put a new one on.
4. Do not touch the outside of the gown when taking it off.
5. Turn the gown inside out as you take it off. Remember, the outside is "dirty" and the inside is "clean." Turning the used gown inside out will keep the "dirty" side away from others (Fig. 7-12).

Fig. 7-12 Gowning technique. **A,** Arms and hands are put through the sleeves. **B,** Strings tied at the back of the neck. **C,** Gown overlapped in the back so entire uniform is covered.

Continued

Fig. 7-12, cont'd. D. Gown is turned inside out as it is removed. (From Sorrentino, S.A.: Mosby's textbook for nursing assistants, ed. 2, St. Louis, 1987, The C.V. Mosby Co.)

6. The front of the mask is considered contaminated. Do not touch the front of the mask.
7. The mask must cover your nose and mouth.
8. Avoid coughing, sneezing, and unnecessary talking when wearing a mask.
9. Change the mask if it gets wet or contaminated.
10. Do not touch the inside of the mask when taking it off. Touch only the ties during removal.
11. Bring the strings together when removing the mask. This folds the inside of the mask together (Fig. 7-13).
12. Dry your hands before putting on gloves. Gloves are very hard to put on when hands are wet.
13. Touch only the top rim or the inside of gloves when putting them on (Fig. 7-14, A).
14. Remove gloves by pulling the top parts over your hands. The gloves will be inside out. The parts that touched the client will now be on the inside (Fig. 7-14, B).
15. Gloves are removed first, then the gown. Take the face mask off last.
16. Discard gloves, gown, and face mask in a waste basket.
17. Wash your hands before leaving the area.

Double Bagging

Double bagging involves placing contaminated items in two bags. This allows for the safe removal of contaminated items from the client's room and home. Ideally, two people do the double bagging. One person is inside the room; the other at the doorway outside the room. The person inside the room places contaminated items in a plastic bag. The bag is then sealed. The person outside the room holds open another bag. This bag is considered clean. The person inside the room stands at the doorway and places the contaminated bag into the clean bag (Fig. 7-15). Perhaps a family member can help you. If you are alone, you have to double bag alone. Open the second bag ("clean" bag) as much as possible. Then place the contaminated bag in the bag. Try not to let the "dirty" bag touch the outside of the "clean" bag (Fig. 7-16).

Other Precautions

The isolation techniques used will depend on the microorganism and the way it is spread. Your supervisor may tell you to do one or several of the following.
1. Ask family and visitors to wash their hands before entering the client's room.
2. Use disposable dishes, cups, and eating utensils for the client.
3. Flush urine and feces down the toilet immediately.
4. Double bag items as directed by your supervisor.
5. Wear gloves when you will touch the client's blood and body fluids.
6. Wash your hands immediately if they are contaminated with the client's blood or body fluids.
7. Wash your hands before entering and after leaving the room.
8. Clean blood spills promptly. Use a solution of 5.25% sodium hypochlorite diluted 1:10 with water. (You should get instructions from your supervisor for this step.)
9. Consider floors to be contaminated. Anything that is or has been on the floor is contaminated.
10. Use a mop with a disinfectant solution for cleaning floors. Floor dust is contaminated. A wet mop keeps dust down.
11. Prevent drafts. Pathogens are carried in the air by drafts.
12. Use paper towels to handle contaminated equipment and objects. Your hands or gloves will stay clean.
13. Avoid touching your hair, nose, mouth, eyes, and other body parts when caring for a client in isolation.
14. Wash the client's linens and clothing separately. Do not wash them with the family's laundry. Linens should be washed in hot water with detergent. Be sure to follow laundry instructions on clothing labels.
15. Do not touch any clean area or item if your hands are contaminated.
16. Place clean items or objects on paper towels.
17. Do not shake linen.
18. Use paper towels to turn faucets on and off.

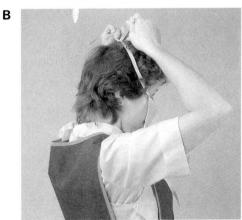

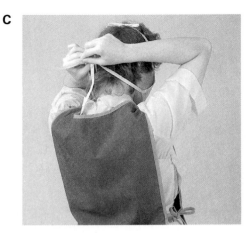

Fig. 7-13 **A,** Mask is positioned so mouth and nose are covered. **B,** Upper strings tied on the back of the head. **C,** Lower strings tied at the neck. **D,** Strings of face mask brought together so the inside of the mask will be folded together after being removed. (From Sorrentino, S.A.: Mosby's textbook for nursing assistants, ed. 2, St. Louis, 1987, The C.V. Mosby Co.)

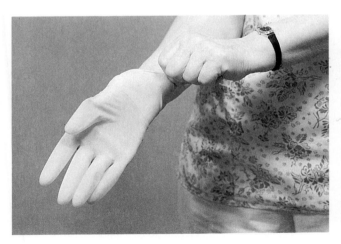

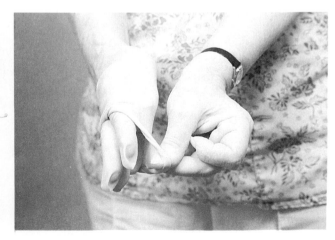

Fig. 7-14 **A,** Glove is pulled on by touching the top part. **B,** Glove is pulled over the hand during removal. The glove is being turned inside out.

Fig. 7-15 Double bagging. One person is in the client's room at the doorway. The other is outside the room. The "dirty" bag is placed inside the "clean" bag.

19. Tell your supervisor if you have any cuts, open skin areas, a sore throat, vomiting, or diarrhea.
20. Spend extra time with the client when possible. The client may feel very alone, unclean, and unwanted. Show the client that he or she is cared about and worthwhile.

Fig. 7-16 Aide is double bagging alone. The aide is careful not to touch the outside of the "clean" bag with the "dirty" bag.

Summary

Preventing the spread of infection is very important to the client, the community, and you. You must be conscientious about your work. Your employer and clients depend on you to practice measures to prevent the spread of infection. One act of carelessness can spread microorganisms and put your client in danger. The reverse is also true. You can develop the same infection that the client has. The most important infection control measure is handwashing. Handwashing before and after contact with the client greatly reduces the spread of microorganisms.

Study Questions

1. List the areas in homes where microorganisms can grow.
2. Describe how you can prevent the spread of infection.

Circle T if the statement is true and F if it is false.

T F 3. A pathogen can cause an infection.
T F 4. An infection occurs when microorganisms invade and grow in the body.
T F 5. Sterilization is the same as clean technique.
T F 6. An object is sterile if nonpathogens are present.
T F 7. Hands should be washed under warm running water.
T F 8. Hands and forearms are held up during handwashing.
T F 9. You should clean under your fingernails when washing your hands.
T F 10. Disposable equipment helps reduce the spread of infection.

Circle the *best* answer.

11. A pathogen needs all of the following to grow *except*
   a. Water
   b. Nourishment
   c. Oxygen
   d. Light
12. Microorganisms grow best where it is
   a. Warm and dark
   b. Warm and light
   c. Cool and dark
   d. Cool and light
13. The client with an infection may have
   a. Fever, nausea, vomiting, rash, and/or sores
   b. Pain or tenderness, redness, and/or swelling
   c. Fatigue, loss of appetite, and/or a discharge
   d. All of the above

14. Microorganisms can enter and leave the body through the
    a. Respiratory tract and/or breaks in the skin
    b. Gastrointestinal system and/or the blood
    c. Reproductive system and/or urinary system
    d. All of the above

15. When cleaning equipment you should
    a. Rinse the item in cold water before cleaning
    b. Wash the item with soap and hot water
    c. Use a brush if necessary
    d. All of the above

16. You are doing wet-heat sterilization. You should do all of the following *except*
    a. Cover the items in the pot with cold water
    b. Boil the water with a lid on the pot
    c. Allow the water to boil for 20 minutes
    d. Remove the lid so the water cools faster

17. Isolation techniques
    a. Prevent infection
    b. Destroy pathogens
    c. Keep pathogens within a certain area
    d. Destroy pathogens and nonpathogens

18. You are to wear an isolation gown. You can touch
    a. The front of the gown
    b. The inside of the gown
    c. The sleeves
    d. The back of the gown

19. The following statements are about isolation. Which is *false*?
    a. Floors are contaminated.
    b. Paper towels are used to handle contaminated items.
    c. Garbage is double bagged.
    d. Gowns, masks, and gloves are always necessary.

20. A client has a communicable disease. You are to wash the client's laundry and the family's laundry. You should
    a. Wash everything together
    b. Wash everything in hot water
    c. Wash the client's laundry separately
    d. Send the family's laundry to the dry cleaners

Answers

3. True	8. False	13. d	17. c
4. True	9. True	14. d	18. b
5. False	10. True	15. d	19. d
6. False	11. d	16. d	20. c
7. True	12. a		

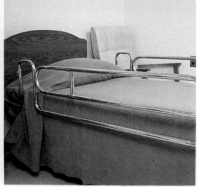

8 Safety

What you will learn to do

- Explain why some people cannot protect themselves
- Protect infants and children from harm
- Identify safety measures that prevent accidents in the home
- Prevent equipment-related accidents
- Describe the safety measures related to fire and oxygen
- Function in the event of a fire
- Use a fire extinguisher
- Explain the importance of the client's call bell
- Travel safely

Key Terms

Coma A state of being completely unaware of one's surroundings; the person in a coma cannot react or respond to people, places, or things

Ground That which carries leaking electricity to the earth and away from the electrical appliance

Suffocation The stopping of breathing that results from lack of oxygen

106

Safety is a basic need. This need is present when driving a car, walking down a street, or when sick at home. Everyone wants to be safe from accidents and dangers. Many people think that homes are free of dangers and hazards. This is not true. Many accidents happen in the home. Some cause death.

The Safe Environment

A safe environment is one in which a person has a very low risk of illness or injury. The person feels safe and secure physically and psychologically. There is little risk of infection, falling, being burned or poisoned, or other injuries. The person is comfortable in relation to noise, temperature, and smells. There is enough lighting and enough room to move about. The person is not afraid.

Why Some People Cannot Protect Themselves

Some people cannot protect themselves. You need know what factors increase a client's risk of an accident. That way you can provide for the client's safety.

Age

Children and the elderly need to be protected from injury. Infants are helpless. They depend on others for protection. Young children have not yet learned what is safe and dangerous. They like to explore their surroundings, to put things in their mouths, and to touch and feel new things. Therefore, falls, drinking poisonous fluids, choking, burns, and other accidents are common in children. The following safety measures are important when caring for infants and children.

1. Do not leave infants or young children alone. Do not leave them alone in strollers, walkers, high chairs, infant seats, bathtubs, or wading pools. Children in cribs should be checked often.
2. Make sure crib side rails are up and locked in place.
3. Place safety plugs in electrical outlets (Fig. 8-1). Children cannot stick their fingers or small objects into openings with safety plugs.
4. Keep cords and electrical equipment away from children. This includes cords from window blinds.
5. Store household cleaners and medicines in locked storage areas. Children should not be able to reach the storage areas (Fig. 8-2).
6. Childproof caps should be on medicine containers and household cleaners.
7. Do not let children play with toys that have loose parts, buttons, and sharp edges. A child can choke on or be cut by such toys.

Fig. 8-1 Safety plug in an electrical outlet. (From Sorrentino, S.A.: Mosby's textbook for nursing assistants, ed. 2, St. Louis, 1987, The C.V. Mosby Co.)

8. Keep one hand on a child in a crib, on a scale, or on a table if you need to look away for a moment (Fig. 8-3).
9. Fasten the safety strap when a child is in a high chair.
10. Do not prop baby bottles on a rolled towel or blanket. Hold the baby and bottle during feedings.
11. Keep plastic bags and wraps away from children. They can cause suffocation.
12. Use guardrails at the top and bottom of stairs. This prevents small children from climbing up and down stairs.

Many elderly people are in danger of having accidents. This is because of the changes in their bodies from aging. Movements are slower and unsteady. Balance may be affected, causing the person to fall easily. The person may be unable to move quickly and suddenly to avoid danger. Other factors cause accidents and injuries in the elderly.

AWARENESS OF SURROUNDINGS

People need to be aware of their surroundings to protect themselves from injury. Some clients are completely unaware of their surroundings. These clients are unconscious or in a *coma*. A person in a coma cannot react or respond to people, places, or things. The client relies on others for protection.

Some elderly people are confused and disoriented. Certain diseases and injuries cause confusion and disorientation. These people may not understand what is happening to and around them. They can be dangerous to themselves and others.

Vision

People with poor vision have difficulty seeing objects. They can fall or trip on toys, furniture, or electrical cords. They may have problems reading labels on medicine and other containers. Taking the wrong medicine, the wrong dose, or poisoning could occur.

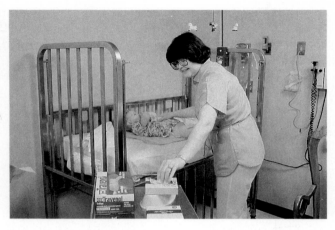

Fig. 8-3 One hand is kept on the child while the aide looks away. (From Sorrentino, S.A.: Mosby's textbook for nursing assistants, ed. 2, St. Louis, 1987, The C.V. Mosby Co.)

Fig. 8-2 A, These household cleaners are within the reach of children when placed in cabinets under the sink. They should be located in high, locked cabinets that are not used for the storage of food. **B,** The medicine chest in this bathroom contains many medicine containers. Like household products, they should be in a high place that is locked and out of the reach of children. (From Sorrentino, S.A.: Mosby's textbook for nursing assistants, ed. 2, St. Louis, 1987, The C.V. Mosby Co.)

Hearing

People with impaired hearing (deafness) may not hear warning signals. Fire alarms, smoke detectors, emergency vehicle sirens, and tornado sirens may not be heard. They may have difficulty hearing oncoming cars and car horns. They may not know that they should move to a safe place.

Smell and touch

Age and illness can affect smell and touch. People with a reduced sense of smell may not be able to smell smoke or gas. Those with a reduced sense of touch may be burned easily. They have difficulty telling heat from cold.

Paralysis

Paralyzed clients may not be able to sense pain, heat, or cold. They may be aware of their surroundings and danger. However, they may be unable to move away from the danger.

Medications

Medications can have different side effects on different people. Side effects include loss of balance, reduced awareness, confusion, disorientation, drowsiness, and incoordination. These sensations may be new and frightening to clients. They may be afraid, uncooperative, or act strange.

Safety in the Home

Most accidents in the home can be prevented. Common sense and simple safety measures can prevent accidental injuries. You should check to see that safety measures have been taken in the client's home. Consult your supervisor if there are safety hazards.

Falls

Falls are the most common accidents in the home. They are common among the elderly. Most falls occur in bedrooms and bathrooms. Common causes are slippery floors, throw rugs, poor lighting, cluttered floors, furniture that is out of place, and slippery bathtubs and showers. The following help prevent falls in the home.

1. There is good lighting in rooms and hallways.

2. There are hand rails on both sides of stairs, in halls, and in bathrooms.
3. There is wall-to-wall carpeting or carpeting that is tacked down. "Throw rugs" should be avoided.
4. Nonskid shoes and slippers are worn.
5. Nonskid waxes are used on hardwood, tiled, or linoleum floors.
6. Floors are not cluttered with toys and other objects.
7. Electrical cords and extension cords are out of the way.
8. Furniture is left in place and not rearranged.
9. A telephone and lamp are at the bedside.
10. Nonskid bathmats are in tubs and showers.
11. Weak clients are helped to walk, get out of bed, get out of the tub or shower, and with other activities.
12. The client's call bell (see page 113) is within reach.
13. Cracked steps, loose hand rails, and frayed carpets are reported.
14. Frequently used items are within the client's reach.
15. Night-lights are in the client's room and in hall-ways.
16. The client's bed is in the low position, except when bedside care is being given. The distance from the bed to floor is less if the client falls or gets out of bed.
17. Floors are kept free of spills and excess furniture.
18. Crutches, canes, and walkers have nonskid tips (see Chapters 10, 11).
19. Wheels on beds and wheelchairs are locked when transferring clients to or from them.
20. Gates are used at the tops and bottoms of stairs when there are infants and toddlers. The child should not be able to put his or her head through the gate bars.

SIDE RAILS

Hospital beds have side rails. Rails can be bought for regular beds from medical equipment companies. Side rails can be raised or lowered. They are locked in place in the raised position by levers, latches, or buttons. They protect the client from falling out of bed. The client can use them to move and turn in bed. Side rails can be half the length or the full length of the bed (Fig. 8-4). If the half length is used (see Fig. 12-3, page 173), there are usually two rails on each side. One is for the upper part of the bed and the other for the lower part.

Side rails are necessary for clients who are unconscious, sedated with medication, confused, or disoriented. Side rails should be kept up at all times for these clients, except when giving bedside care.

HAND RAILS

Hand rails are helpful in hallways (Fig. 8-5) and bathrooms. They provide support for clients who are weak or unsteady when walking. They also give support when sitting down on or getting up from a toilet. Hand rails along bathtubs can be used when getting in and out of the tub. All stairways should have hand rails.

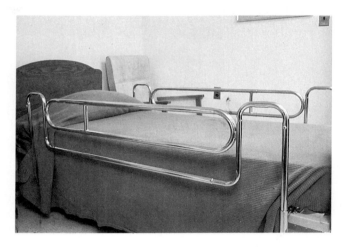

Fig. 8-4 Full-length side rails.

Fig. 8-5 An elderly woman uses the handrail for support when walking.

Fig. 8-6 Fireplaces cause many home fires.

Fig. 8-7 Pot handles are turned inward. (From Sorrentino, S.A.: Mosby's textbook for nursing assistants, ed. 2, St. Louis, 1987, The C.V. Mosby Co.)

Your client may not have hand rails where they are needed. Be sure to tell your supervisor about this problem. The supervisor can help the client and family decide if they are needed and where to get them.

Burns

Burns are a major cause of death among children and the elderly. Common causes of home fires are smoking in bed, spilling hot liquids, children playing with matches, charcoal grills, fireplaces, and stoves (Fig. 8-6).

The following safety measures can prevent burns:
1. Keep matches out of the reach of children.
2. Supervise the play of children.
3. Never leave children at home alone.
4. Teach children fire prevention measures and the dangers of fire.
5. Turn the handles of pots on stoves so they do not point outward where people stand and walk (Fig. 8-7).
6. Supervise the smoking of clients who cannot protect themselves.
7. Do not allow smoking in bed.
8. Keep space heaters and materials that can catch on fire away from children.
9. Set the hot water heater no higher than 120° F for elderly clients.
10. Label or color code hot and cold faucets (red for hot, blue for cold).

Poisoning

Accidental poisoning is another major cause of death. Children are the most frequent victims. Aspirin and household products are the most common poisons. Poisoning in adults may be due to carelessness or poor vision when reading labels. Sometimes poisoning is a suicide attempt. Poisoning can be prevented by:

1. Having childproof caps on all medicine containers and household products
2. Labeling all medicine containers and household products clearly
3. Storing poisonous materials in a place that is high, locked, and out of the reach of children
4. Storing poisonous materials in their original containers, not in food containers
5. Keeping medicines out of purses where children may find them
6. Making sure that there is enough light to accurately read labels

Suffocation

Suffocation is when breathing stops because of the lack of oxygen. Death will occur if the person does not start breathing. Common causes of suffocation include choking, drowning, inhaling gas or smoke, strangulation, and electrical shock. Safety measures to help prevent suffocation are:
1. Taking small bites and chewing food slowly and thoroughly
2. Checking exhaust systems on cars regularly
3. Having gas odors promptly investigated by competent repairmen
4. Opening doors and windows if you smell gas
5. Resting for at least 1 hour after eating and before exercising, activity, or swimming
6. Having all electrical cords and appliances in good repair
7. Keeping electrical appliances away from sinks and bathtubs
8. Keeping plastic bags away from children

Accidents Due to Equipment

Equipment made of glass or plastic must be intact. Check equipment for cracks, chips, and sharp or

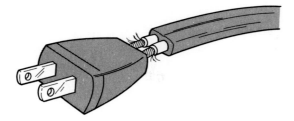

Fig. 8-8 A frayed electric wire. (From Sorrentino, S.A.: Mosby's textbook for nursing assistants, ed. 2, St. Louis, 1987, The C.V. Mosby Co.)

rough edges before use. These can easily cut, stab, or scratch clients. Damaged equipment should not be used or given to clients. Consult your supervisor, describe the defect, and discard the item as instructed.

Electrical equipment must work properly and be in good repair. Frayed cords (Fig. 8-8) and overloaded electrical outlets (Fig. 8-9) can cause electrical shocks. The shocks can cause death. Fires may also result. Frayed cords and equipment that do not work right must be repaired by someone trained to do so.

Three-pronged plugs (Fig. 8-10) may be used on some appliances and equipment. Two of the prongs carry electricity. The third prong is the ground. A *ground* carries leaking electricity to the earth and away from the piece of equipment. With a ground, leaking electricity cannot be conducted to a person, causing electrical shocks and possible death. Tell your supervisor if you get a shock when using a piece of equipment or an appliance. The item needs to be repaired.

The Spread of Microorganisms

Infection is a major health hazard. Infections are caused by microorganisms. Illness increases the risk of infection. The infection adds to that individual's health problems. Chapters 7 and 9 describe how microorganisms are spread and the measures to prevent their spread.

Fire Safety

Faulty electrical equipment and wiring, overloaded electrical circuits, and smoking are the major causes of fire in the United States. Fire is a constant danger in the home.

Fire and the Use of Oxygen

Three things are needed to start and maintain a fire: heat (a spark or flame), a material that will burn, and oxygen. A certain amount of oxygen is in the air. However, some clients need more oxygen than what is in the air. Doctors will order supplemental oxygen for these clients. Supplemental oxygen comes in portable oxygen tanks. (Oxygen therapy is discussed in Chapter

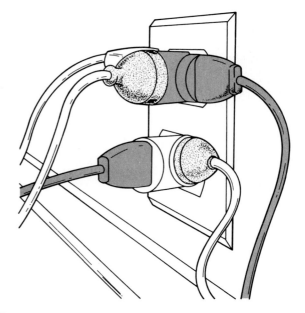

Fig. 8-9 An overloaded electrical outlet. (From Sorrentino, S.A.: Mosby's textbook for nursing assistants, ed. 2, St. Louis, 1987, The C.V. Mosby Co.)

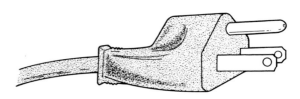

Fig. 8-10 A three-pronged plug. (From Sorrentino, S.A.: Mosby's textbook for nursing assistants, ed. 2, St. Louis, 1987, The C.V. Mosby Co.)

18). Because oxygen is needed for fire, special safety measures are practiced when oxygen is used in the home.

1. "No Smoking" signs are placed where oxygen is used.
2. Family and visitors are politely reminded not to smoke.
3. The client is not allowed to have smoking materials, (cigarettes, cigars, and pipes), matches, or lighters.
4. Electrical equipment must be turned off before being unplugged. Sparks occur when electrical appliances are unplugged while still turned on.
5. Wool blankets and synthetic fabrics that cause static electicity are removed from the room. The client should wear a cotton gown, pajamas, or clothes. You should wear cotton uniforms.
6. Electric equipment is removed from the room. This includes electric razors, hair dryers, and heating pads.
7. Materials that ignite easily are removed from the room. These include oil, grease, alcohol, and nail polish remover.

8. The oxygen tank is kept away from heat sources.
9. A fire extinguisher is kept nearby.

Fire Prevention

Fire prevention measures have been described in relation to children, burns, equipment-related accidents, and the use of oxygen. These and other fire safety measures are summarized as follows:

1. Follow the fire safety precautions for the use of oxygen.
2. Be sure all ashes and cigar and cigarette butts are out before emptying ashtrays.
3. Provide ashtrays to clients who are allowed to smoke.
4. Empty ashtrays into a metal container partly filled with sand or water. Do not empty ashtrays into wastebaskets or plastic containers lined with paper or plastic bags.
5. Supervise the smoking of clients who cannot protect themselves. This includes confused, disoriented, and sedated clients.
6. Follow the safety practices for using electrical equipment.
7. Supervise the play of children and keep matches out of their reach.

What to Do If There Is a Fire

Each agency has policies and procedures explaining what to do if there is a fire. You must become familiar with these policies and procedures. The following guidelines will help you protect the client and yourself if there is a fire.

1. Have fire emergency numbers near the client's phones.
2. Plan escape routes from each room.
3. Know where fire extinguishers are and how to use them.
4. Know where fire alarm boxes are located.
5. Turn off any oxygen or electrical equipment in the general area of the fire.
6. Get the client and others out of the house.
7. Call the fire department.
8. Try to fight a small fire if you can. Leave right away if the fire gets out of control.
9. Close doors as you leave the home.
10. Crawl, keeping your head close to the floor, if you are in an area filled with smoke (Fig. 8-11).
11. Cover your face with a damp cloth or towel if in smoke-filled areas (Fig. 8-12).
12. Feel doors before you open them. Do not open the door if it is hot or if smoke is coming around the door.
13. Open cool doors slightly. Keep your head to the side (Fig. 8-13). Close the door if smoke or heat rushes at you.

Fig. 8-11 Crawl to leave a smoke-filled room.

Fig. 8-12 Aide covers her face with a towel so she does not breathe in smoke.

14. Stuff blankets, clothes, towels, linens, coats, or other cloth at the bottom of the door if you are trapped inside (Fig. 8-14). Open a window slightly for air. Hang a piece of clothing or sheet out the window to attract attention.

You should be able to use a fire extinguisher. Local fire departments often give demonstrations on how to operate fire extinguishers. Some agencies require all employees to demonstrate how to use a fire extinguisher.

There are different kinds of extinguishers for different kinds of fires: oil and grease fires; electrical fires; and paper and wood fires. A general procedure for using a fire extinguisher follows.

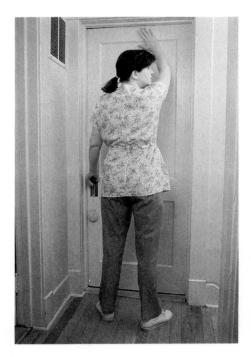

Fig. 8-13 A door is opened slightly to see if there is fire and smoke in the other room. The aide keeps her head turned to the side.

Fig. 8-14 Towels are stuffed at the bottom of a door to prevent smoke from entering the room.

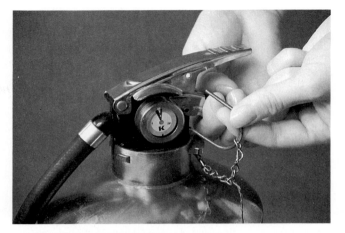

Fig. 8-15 **A,** The safety pin of a fire extinguisher is removed. **B,** The top handle of the fire extinguisher is pushed down. **C,** The hose of the fire extinguisher is directed at the base of the fire. (From Sorrentino, S.A.: Mosby's textbook for nursing assistants, ed. 2, St. Louis, 1987, The C.V. Mosby Co.)

Procedure: Using a fire extinguisher

1. Pull the fire alarm.
2. Get the nearest fire extinguisher.
3. Carry the fire extinguisher upright.
4. Take the extinguisher to the fire.
5. Remove the safety pin (Fig. 8-15, A).
6. Push the top handle down (Fig. 8-15, B).
7. Direct the hose at the base of the fire (Fig. 8-15, C).

The Call Bell

The client must have a way to signal to others when help is needed. The call bell allows the client to call for help. The bell should be loud enough to be heard in different parts of the house. Some clients have buzzers (Fig. 8-16). These do not cost too much and are easy to install. Other clients have tap bells (Fig. 8-17). Table bells can be bought in attractive styles and colors (Fig. 8-18). Whatever is used, it should always be within the client's reach. There should also be a bell or buzzer in the client's bathroom. The call bell should always be on the client's good side.

Your Own Safety

Home health aides usually travel alone. You will often go to a client's home by yourself. You may be assigned to a home in a remote area, in a bad neighborhood, or in an area that is considered "safe." You may work before the sun comes up or after the sun sets. Therefore, you may have to travel in the dark. No matter when you walk, drive, or use public transportation by yourself, you need to protect yourself from harm. Table 8-1 lists personal safety measures that should be a part of your normal, everyday routine.

Fig. 8-16 Buzzer system.

Fig. 8-17 Tap bell. (From Sorrentino, S.A.: Mosby's textbook for nursing assistants, ed. 2, St. Louis, 1987, The C.V. Mosby Co.)

Fig. 8-19 Aide uses the peephole to see who is at the door.

Fig. 8-20 "Send Police" sign in a car window.

Fig. 8-18 Table bell.

TABLE 8-1 Personal Safety Measures

Strangers at the client's door or at your door

- Use a peephole if there is one (Fig. 8-19).
- Yell "I'll get it" even if you are alone.
- Ask for identification before you open the door. Do not be afraid to ask utility workers, salespeople, repairmen, delivery people, or others for identification. Anyone coming to the door should be able to show you identification.
- Do not allow strangers in to use the telephone. Offer to make the call for the person. Use this measure even if the stranger says it is an emergency.
- Do not let strangers into a security entrance of an apartment building. The person may say that he or she is there for a neighbor. If you let the person in, he or she has access to the entire building.

Telephone calls

- Do not give information to "wrong numbers." They may ask who is speaking or the phone number that was reached. Do not give this information. Ask the number the person is trying to call.
- Do not let strangers know that you or the client will be alone.
- Do not let strangers know that the client is ill or disabled.
- Hang up if you receive threatening calls.
- Notify the police if threatening calls continue. Keep a record of the date and time of each call. Also record what was said. Share this information with the police.

Driving

- Keep your car in good driving condition.
- Make sure your spare tire is properly inflated.
- Have enough gas in your car in case of detours or traffic jams. You should always have at least a half a tank of gas.
- Have money in case you need to buy gas, take a cab or other transportation, or make an emergency phone call.
- Plan your route. Use highly traveled streets and highways whenever possible. Share this information with your supervisor and a member of your family.
- Know where police and fire stations are in your clients' neighborhoods.
- Drive to the nearest police, fire, or gas station if you are being followed. Do not drive home, turn onto a side street, or turn into a strange driveway.
- Call your supervisor when you arrive at and leave a home.
- Keep your car doors locked while driving.
- Do not keep your purse or other valuables on the front seat.
- Keep windows up while driving. Use the air conditioner or vent for ventilation.
- Do not pick up hitchhikers.
- Do not stop to help another driver. Drive to the nearest phone and call the police.
- Park in well-lighted areas.
- Lock your car doors when you leave your car.
- Have the key ready to unlock the car door before you get to the car.
- Look inside the car and in the back seat before you unlock or get in the car.

Car trouble

- Put on your emergency flashers.
- Raise the hood of the car.
- Stay in the car and keep the doors locked. Open a window a short way for ventilation.
- Place a "Send Police" sign in a window (Fig. 8-20).
- Ask the person who stops to call the police. Do not go with the person.

Public transportation

- Use well-lighted bus or train stops that are used often.
- Wait at a stop where there are other people. Do not wait alone. Walk an extra block to another stop where others are waiting if necessary.
- Sit near the driver.
- Watch who gets off the bus with you. If you are suspicious, do not get off. Go to another stop where you feel safe.

Walking

- Do not walk in alleys, remote areas, or near buildings or bushes.
- Do not walk with strangers.
- Avoid walking alone at night whenever possible.
- Know where to find pay phones. Always have a quarter ready.
- Plan your route so that you will use well-lighted streets. Your route should be the shortest and safest to where you want to go.
- Do not hitchhike or accept rides from strangers.
  Walk in the street at night and toward oncoming traffic.
- Wear light-colored clothing when walking at night.
- Carry some money in your pocket. Do not carry all of your money in your wallet or purse.
- Carry a shriek alarm or whistle.
- Keep your house key or car key in your hand.
- Walk like you are confident and know where you are going.
- Make sure you watch what is going on around you.

Arriving home

- Keep headlights on and your car doors locked until you have checked the parking area or your garage.
- Have your house or apartment key in your hand.
- Ask the driver to wait until you are inside before he or she leaves.
- Do not go inside if something seems out of place or unusual. Go to a safe place to call the police.

Summary

Most accidents can be prevented. Knowing the common safety hazards and accidents, being aware of people who need protection, and exercising common sense all help promote safety. Remember that infants, young children, and the elderly have a greater risk of accidents than other people.

Fire is a safety hazard. Exercising safety precautions in relation to smoking and electrical equipment helps prevent fires. Extra precautions are needed when oxygen is being used. Clients who smoke present additional fire safety concerns. Be sure you know what to do if there is a fire.

You must be aware of your own safety when walking, driving a car, or using public transportation. The simple safety measures described in this chapter will help you feel safer and more secure.

Study Questions

1. Identify the safety hazards in your home. How would you correct them?

2. Plan escape routes from your home in case there is a fire.

3. A stranger comes to the client's door. He says that he is from the water company. Explain what you should do.

Circle T if the statement is true and F if it is false.

T F 4. A safe environment is one in which a person has low risk of becoming ill or injured.

T F 5. Young children are in danger of having accidents. They have not learned what is safe and what is dangerous.

T F 6. Childproof caps are needed only on medicine containers.

T F 7. Household cleaners should be kept in locked storage areas that are out of the reach of children.

T F 8. Safety plugs in electrical outlets protect children from shocks.

T F 9. Aging causes body changes that make an elderly person more likely to have accidents.

T F 10. A client in a coma is not in danger of accidents.

T F 11. Smell, touch, sight, and hearing can help prevent accidents.

T F 12. Medications are a cause of some accidents.

T F 13. Falls can be prevented in the home by making sure there is enough lighting.

T F 14. Clients should wear bedroom slippers to prevent skidding and slipping on floors.

T F 15. Burns can be prevented by supervising the play of children.

T F 16. People should not smoke in bed.

T F 17. Poisonous products should be clearly labeled and stored in their original containers.

T F 18. Poisonings occur in adults because of poor lighting when reading labels.

T F 19. Having electrical cords and appliances in good repair can prevent suffocation.

T F 20. The spread of infection is not a hazard in the home.

T F 21. Side rails should be kept up even when giving care.

T F 22. The client's bed should be kept in the low position except when giving bedside care.

T F 23. You should check glass and plastic equipment for damage.

T F 24. Two-pronged plugs are necessary to properly ground electrical equipment.

T F 25. A spark or flame, a material that will burn, and oxygen are needed to start and maintain a fire.

T F 26. Smoking is not allowed where oxygen is being used.

T F 27. Wool blankets are used for clients receiving oxygen.

T F 28. You should supervise the smoking of a client who is confused or sedated.

T F 29. Oxygen should be turned off if it is being used in the area of a fire.

T F 30. You should try to put out a fire before calling the fire department.

T F 31. You should give your number if you get a "wrong number."

T F 32. You should leave your car door unlocked. This lets you get in the car faster.

T F 33. You have car trouble. You should leave the car after raising the hood.

T F 34. You are waiting for a bus. You should find a bus stop where you will not be with strangers.

T F 35. You are walking at night. You should walk in the same direction as the traffic.

Answers

4. True	12. True	20. False	28. True
5. True	13. True	21. False	29. True
6. False	14. False	22. True	30. False
7. True	15. True	23. True	31. False
8. True	16. True	24. False	32. False
9. True	17. True	25. True	33. False
10. False	18. True	26. True	34. False
11. True	19. True	27. False	35. False

9 Home Maintenance

Chapter Highlights	What you will learn to do
The home environment	■ Identify the housekeeping responsibilities of home health aides
Laundry	■ Explain the importance of a clean home
	■ Describe how to work efficiently in the home
	■ Describe four types of cleaning products and how to use them safely
	■ Clean a kitchen, bathroom, and the client's room
	■ Describe four types of laundry products
	■ Describe the guidelines for doing laundry and how to remove stains
	■ Do laundry

All-purpose cleaner A product used for all types of cleaning; used on walls, floors, counters, stoves, refrigerators, sinks, tubs, outside of the toilet, and appliances

Cleanser A product used for hard-to-clean surfaces such as sinks, tubs, and toilets

Detergent A product used for laundry and dishwashing

Soap A product used for laundry and dishwashing

Specialty cleaner A product used for certain surfaces and cleaning problems; there are special cleaners for windows, laundry stains, toilet bowls and ovens

Your housekeeping responsibilities depend on the services of your agency. The needs of the client and family also affect what you do. Your responsibilities may include:

1. Light housekeeping so rooms are clean and neat.
2. Laundry. Clothes and linens belonging to the client and family need to be washed, ironed, and mended.
3. Shopping for food and household items.
4. Fixing and serving meals. This includes feeding the helpless client.
5. Using home appliances to give personal care and do housekeeping.

The Home Environment

Your housekeeping tasks relate to the health and safety of the client and family. A clean home is important to them. People feel better in a clean, fresh atmosphere. A clean home:

1. Controls the spread of microorganisms and infection.
2. Prevents accidents due to clutter.
3. Saves time and energy when things are in their place and can be found easily.
4. Prevents the problem of insects and rodents.
5. Promotes comfort and relaxation.
6. Saves the family time and worry about keeping the home clean.

You will not do heavy housekeeping. This includes moving furniture, waxing floors, shampooing carpets, washing windows, cleaning rugs or drapes, painting walls, and carrying firewood, coal, or ash containers. A cleaning service may be needed for these tasks. Your supervisor can help the client and family make necessary arrangements.

Organizing Your Work

Your supervisor will meet with the client and family to determine what housekeeping tasks need to be done. You may be included in the meeting. They will decide what tasks family members will do and what you will do. Then you and your supervisor will develop a work plan. The plan will list each task, how often it is done, and who will do the task (Fig. 9-1). The plan also shows who will do your tasks when you are not there. The work plan will change as the client's needs change.

The client or family may ask you to do something that is not part of the work plan. Be sure to discuss the request with your supervisor. The request may cost the client more money. Or it may be beyond your role as a home health aide.

Housekeeping tasks include cleaning the client's room, the kitchen, bathroom, and other rooms. Some tasks are done weekly. These include vacuuming, washing floors, polishing furniture, and changing bed linens (Fig. 9-2). Certain tasks are done daily or several times a day to keep the home neat and orderly. Newspapers, toys, and magazines are picked up as needed. Ashtrays and wastebaskets are emptied as indicated. Beds are made and furniture is dusted daily. Daily cleaning should take about an hour. The amount of time needed for cleaning depends on the size of the home.

Organizing client care and housekeeping tasks are important. Client care is your first concern. However, assigned housekeeping duties must be completed. Careful planning must be done. You should have a list of all client care activities and tasks to be done that day. Cleaning can be done after client care. Housekeeping tasks can also be done while the client is sleeping, visiting, or watching television.

You may have to clean, shop, and fix meals. The following hints will help you save time and work more efficiently:

1. Follow the work plan.
2. Collect all supplies and equipment needed for a client care activity or housekeeping task.
3. Use a pail, tray, shopping bag, or laundry basket to carry supplies and equipment from one room to another (Fig. 9-3).
4. Keep paper and pencil in your pocket. Jot down household items that need to be bought or replaced.
5. Secure a shopping list to a bulletin board, refrigerator door, or other convenient spot. Note food, cleaning supplies, paper products, and other household items that need to be bought. Ask family members to use the list.
6. Wipe up spills and crumbs as soon as possible. Spilled liquid and hardened food are more difficult to remove.

WORKPLAN

Mrs. Johnson
CLIENT

_3/6 - 3/20_
PERIOD COVERED

TASK	SUN	MON	TUE	WED	THUR	FRI	SAT
Assist with Toileting	Daughter	Mary	Barbara	Mary	Barbara	Mary	Daughter
Assist with Dressing	Daughter	Mary	Barbara	Mary	Barbara	Mary	Daughter
Assist with Bathing	Daughter	Mary	Barbara	Mary	Barbara	Mary	Daughter
Shampoo Hair					Barbara T		
Change Linens						Mary	
Laundry						Mary	
Clean Bedroom		Susan			Susan		
Clean Bathroom		Susan			Susan		
Clean Kitchen		Susan			Susan		
Vacuum Carpets					Susan		
Sweep Floors					Susan		
Dust					Susan		
Prepare Breakfast	Daughter	Mary	Barbara	Mary	Barbara	Mary	Daughter
Prepare Lunch	Daughter	Mary	Barbara	Mary	Barbara	Mary	Daughter
Prepare Dinner X 2 days	Daughter		Barbara		Barbara		Daughter
Grocery Shopping				Susan B.			

Fig. 9-1 Work plan.

Fig. 9-2 Some housekeeping tasks, such as vacuuming, are done weekly. (From Sorrentino, S.A.: Mosby's textbook for nursing assistants, ed. 2, St. Louis, 1987, The C.V. Mosby Co.)

Fig. 9-3 Aide uses a pail to carry cleaning supplies from one room to another. (From Sorrentino, S.A.: Mosby's textbook for nursing assistants, ed. 2, St. Louis, 1987, The C.V. Mosby Co.)

7. Plan major tasks for certain days. Do not try to shop, do laundry, vacuum, and wash floors on the same day.

8. Use time well. Client care can be given, a meal prepared, or the kitchen cleaned while clothes are in the washer or dryer.

9. Observe safety rules at all times (see Chapter 8).

10. Practice good body mechanics at all times (see Chapter 10).

11. Practice measures to prevent the spread of infection (see Chapter 7).

12. Vacuum or sweep carpets at least once a week and when needed. Use short, overlapping strokes on heavily soiled areas.

13. Sweep up crumbs and other bits of debris before mopping the floor.

14. Do not leave spills or puddles of water on the floor.

15. Shake out small rugs outside.

16. Pick up and put away clothes, toys, dishes, and other items as often as necessary.

Another way to save time and energy is to make good use of storage space. Items should be stored where they will be used. For example, towels should be near the bathroom. Linens should be near bedrooms. Pots and pans should be near the stove. The client's home may not be organized well. You should not rearrange things just to suit your needs. You need to ask the client for permission or suggest ways to rearrange things.

Cleaning Products, Supplies, and Equipment

Cleaning products are used to clean and protect surfaces and materials. They also protect people. Cleaning surfaces and materials control the spread of microorganisms. Therefore, people are protected from microorganisms that can cause infections.

There are four basic types of cleaning products.

1. *All-purpose cleaners* are used for all types of cleaning. They can be used on walls, floors, counters, stoves, and refrigerators. They can be used to clean sinks, tubs, the outside of the toilet, and appliances.

2. *Soaps and detergents* are used for laundry and dishwashing.

3. *Cleansers* are used for hard-to-clean surfaces such as sinks, tubs, and toilets. They come in powders, foams, and liquids. Powdered cleansers can scratch and dull sinks and tubs. Therefore, they should not be used on those surfaces. Spray-on foam should be used instead.

4. *Specialty cleaners* are for certain surfaces and cleaning problems. For example, there are special cleaners for windows, laundry stains, toilet bowls, and ovens. Whenever you use a cleaning product, you must read the instructions on the label. Incorrect use of a product can harm the surface, material, or you. The label will tell you:

- How to use the product
- What surfaces or materials to use it on
- What to do if the product gets in your eyes
- What to do if someone accidentally drinks or eats the product

You need to follow these guidelines when using cleaning products:

1. Do not mix cleaning agents with each other. You could cause a harmful chemical reaction. The mixing could produce a dangerous gas. The gas could cause death or seriously injure your eyes, nose, or lungs.

2. Do not leave cleaners on surfaces any longer than directed on the label. The surface could be damaged.

3. Do not scrub surfaces forcefully. Some surfaces are easily damaged.

4. Change water when it is dirty. This prevents streaks and film on surfaces.

5. Store cleaners as directed on the label. Make sure they are in a locked cabinet out of the reach of children (Fig. 8-2 on page 108).

6. Leave the product in its original container and do not remove labels. Do not store cleaners in food or drinking containers.

7. Wear rubber gloves when using cleaners if you have sensitive skin.

8. Check the label to see if a cleaner is flammable (able to catch fire). If it is, store it away from heat (oven, clothes dryer, toaster, water heater, pilot lights, furnace, etc.). Do not allow people to smoke near the cleaner. Do not use the cleaner near the stove, clothes dryer, furnace, oven, pilot lights, curling iron, or electric rollers.

9. Call for help in case of accidental poisoning. Have the number of the local ambulance, hospital emergency room, and poison control center near the telephone. Have the container in your hand when you call for help. You will need to identify the product, list the ingredients, and tell how much was ingested.

10. Rinse your eye for 15 minutes with water if a cleaning product gets in your eye. Put your head over the sink. Turn your head to the side so that the injured eye is down toward the sink. Leave the water running and open the drain. Hold your eye open with one hand. Allow a constant, gentle stream of water to flow over the eye (Fig. 9-4).

Besides cleaning products, you will need the following supplies and equipment:

- Broom and/or vacuum cleaner
- Rags
- Water

Fig. 9-4 Aide's head is turned so that the injured eye is toward the sink. A gentle stream of water flows over the open eye.

- Sponges
- Toilet brush
- Mop
- Dustpan
- Garbage bags
- Garbage can

The supplies and equipment available will vary in each home. Some homes have brooms rather than vacuums, or rags rather than mops. You may like to use certain products. However, the client and family have their own preferences. You need to use the products and equipment already in the home. Do not make the client and family buy products to suit your needs. You need to make do with what is on hand. Most cleaning supplies and equipment will do the job. Remember how infections spread and keep the home as clean as possible. You can clean the home when you use good planning and common sense.

Cleaning the Kitchen

The kitchen is cleaned often. You should clean up after each meal. Cleaning the kitchen should not wait until the end of the day. Housekeeping tasks in the kitchen involve:

- Disposing of garbage
- Storing leftovers
- Washing dishes
- Wiping surfaces
- Cleaning floors, cabinets, and drawers

Cans, boxes, and paper trash go into a paper or plastic bag. Garbage, consisting of food or wet items, should be put in a container lined with a plastic bag. Some homes have trash compactors. They save storage space by crushing trash and garbage. Trash compactors help keep kitchens fresh and clean (Fig. 9-5). All garbage should be emptied at least once a day. Remember

that garbage attracts microorganisms, insects, rodents, and animals.

Garbage disposals are ideal for food and liquid garbage (Fig. 9-6). They grind up food and empty it into the sewage system. This helps control infection. Follow these guidelines when using a garbage disposal.

Fig. 9-5 A trash compactor.

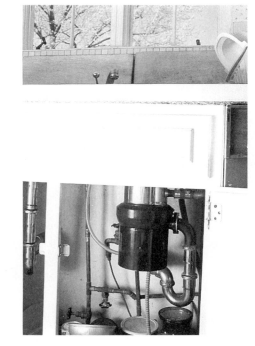

Fig. 9-6 Garbage disposals are located under sinks.

1. Put only soft food scraps in the disposal. Discard gristle, fruit pits, and bones in the garbage.
2. Check the disposal before starting it for foreign objects. Silverware, bones, and cooking utensils may have fallen in by mistake.
3. Turn the water on before you start the disposal. The water must be on to wash food particles down the drain.
4. Use the disposal guard if there is one. This protects your face and eyes from particles that may fly out during the grinding process.
5. Never put your hand in the disposal while it is running. The blades rotate very fast and could seriously cut your fingers and hand.
6. Turn the disposal off before you turn the water off.

Leftover food should be placed in small containers. The containers are covered with lids, foil, or plastic wrap. Leftovers are refrigerated as soon as possible and used within the next 2 to 3 days.

Dishwashing is another method of infection control. If a dishwasher is not available, dishes are washed by hand. Dishes are easier to clean if they are rinsed first. Eggs and milk should be rinsed off with cold water. Hot water is used for other foods. Burned-on foods in pots and pans should be softened first. Fill the utensil with water and add detergent or vinegar. Then put the item on the stove to simmer.

Dishes are washed in hot, soapy water. If possible use a plastic dishpan so you do not chip dishes and glasses. When washing dishes, the cleanest items are washed first. The order is usually glasses, silverware, dishes, and then pots and pans. Dishes are rinsed in a pan of hot water. Or you can put them in a dish rack and pour hot water over them (Fig. 9-7). Allow washed items to air-dry.

Many homes have a dishwasher. The appliance cleans the dishes with hot water and a special detergent. Remember these guidelines when using a dishwasher:

1. Dishes are scraped or rinsed before being loaded into the dishwasher. Make sure large food particles are removed.
2. Place cups and glasses face down on the rack (Fig. 9-8). Otherwise they will catch water.
3. Avoid overcrowding the dishwasher. If items are too close, the detergent and water cannot get in between them.
4. Use only special dishwasher detergent.
5. Wait until there is a full load before turning on the wash cycle. This saves water and electricity.
6. Do not put pots and pans or cast iron, wood, or plastic items in the dishwasher. China and crystal should not be put in the dishwasher.
7. Let dishes air-dry to save energy. Stop the dishwasher after the dishes have been rinsed and then open the door.

Dishes used by clients with infections are washed separately. They are not washed with those used by the rest of the family. Dishes are put away after they have dried.

Counter tops, tables, the stove, refrigerator, and other appliances need to be wiped clean. Make sure counter-top appliances (toaster, blender, food processor, can opener) are unplugged before you clean them. A sponge or dishcloth moistened with warm water and a detergent is used. Grease, spills, and splashes from cooking must be thoroughly removed. Some people also use liquid surface cleaners after wiping the surfaces. The sink is cleaned with a cleanser.

Uncarpeted floors are damp-mopped at least once a week. Spills are wiped up immediately. A dust mop or broom can be used for routine sweeping. A dustpan is used to collect dust and crumbs. Sweeping is done daily or more often if needed.

Fig. 9-7 Hot water is sprayed over dishes to rinse them.

Fig. 9-8 Cups and glasses are loaded face down in the dishwasher.

Kitchen drawers and cabinets and the items in them are cleaned 3 or 4 times a year. Drawers and cabinets can be kept orderly by storing and putting items away neatly. The outside of cabinets and drawers are wiped clean weekly and as needed.

Cleaning the Bathroom

The bathroom is a good place for the growth and spread of microorganisms. Therefore you must clean the bathroom thoroughly.

Every family member has a role in keeping the bathroom clean. Aseptic measures must be practiced whenever the bathroom is used. The toilet is flushed after each use. The sink is rinsed after washing, shaving, or oral hygiene. The tub or shower is wiped out after each use. Hair is removed from the sink, tub, or shower. Towels are hung out to dry or placed in a hamper. Water spills are wiped up.

The bathroom is cleaned every day. Routine bathroom cleaning involves cleaning all surfaces (Fig. 9-9). A disinfectant, specialty cleaner, or a solution of water and detergent is used. The surfaces to be cleaned include:

1. The toilet bowl, seat, and outside areas
2. The floor
3. The sides, walls, and curtain or door of the tub or shower
4. Towel racks
5. Holders for toilet tissue, toothbrushes, and soap
6. The mirror
7. The sink
8. Windowsills

When cleaning the toilet, use a brush if one is available (Fig. 9-10). Be sure to clean under the rim, under the seat, and behind the seat. Use a sponge to

Fig. 9-10 A brush is used to clean the toilet.

clean the sides and the tank. The sponge should be used *only* for the toilet, and for no other purpose.

The floor is mopped or vacuumed if carpeted. The wastebasket is emptied. Clean towels and washclothes are placed on the towel racks. You may open bathroom windows for a short time and use air freshener. These help to eliminate odors and give a fresh smell to the bathroom. Bath mats, the wastebasket, and the laundry hamper or basket are washed weekly. Finally, toilet and facial tissue are replaced whenever needed.

The Client's Room

The client may stay in one room or a section of the home. Cleaning this area is very important. A fresh, neat, uncluttered atmosphere will help your client relax and feel better. You need to do the following:

1. Change soiled linens immediately.
2. Make the bed every day and straighten linens as often as necessary.
3. Change linens at least once a week and more often if the client is bed-bound.
4. Change the water in flower vases every day.
5. Remove old newspapers.
6. Dust every day.
7. Empty wastebaskets every day.
8. Make sure the client has a supply of tissues.
9. Wash the client's water pitcher and glass every day.

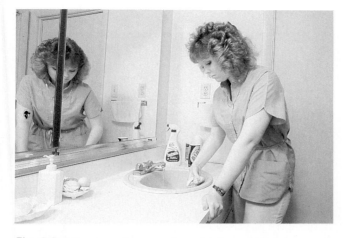

Fig. 9-9 Bathroom surfaces are cleaned daily to control the spread of microorganisms. (From Sorrentino, S.A.: Mosby's textbook for nursing assistants, ed. 2, St. Louis, 1987, The C.V. Mosby Co.)

10. Open windows to air out the room if weather or the client's condition permits.
11. Clean the bed frame with a disinfectant at least once a week.
12. Sweep or vacuum floors every day.

Laundry

Doing laundry is an important role of the home health aide. People feel better wearing clean clothes. They sleep better on clean sheets. Washing clothes and linens also helps prevent the spread of infection. If the client has an infection, his or her laundry is washed separately.

Laundry Products

Several laundry products are available. The basic types are detergents, fabric softeners, bleach, and prewashes.

Detergents come in powders and liquids. They can be used for general laundry. Read the instructions on the package before using detergent. They will tell you how much to use and when to add the detergent to the wash cycle. They will also tell you if the product is safe for the fabrics being washed. There are light-duty and heavy-duty detergents. Light-duty detergents are used for delicate items such as lingerie and wool sweaters. Heavy-duty detergents are used for sturdy items such as sheets, towels, and general laundry.

Fabric softeners come in liquids and powders. They take the stiffness out of fabrics and create a feeling of freshness. Follow the package instructions when using a fabric softener. Some fabric softeners come in strips of cloth. These go in the dryer. The softener is released from the cloth strip during the drying process. They are simple to use. Just pull a strip from the box and toss it into the dryer with the laundry.

Bleach removes stains and brightens fabrics. Bleach is also a disinfectant. Bleach is used with detergent. It is not used alone and is not poured directly onto a fabric. There are three kinds of bleach: liquid chlorine, powdered chlorine, and oxygen or all-purpose bleach. Bleach is very powerful for stain removal. However, it can damage fabrics if used incorrectly or on the wrong fabrics. Always read the clothing labels for washing instructions before using bleach. Do not use bleach on delicate fabrics or wools. Do not mix bleach with a fabric softener. Combining the two products could damage the fabric.

Prewash aids are used to remove stains. These products come in liquids, powders, and sprays. Read the package instructions before using the product. Also check the garment label for washing instructions. Some prewashes are sprayed or poured on the stained area.

Others require soaking. Make sure you remove caked-on material before using a prewash.

Laundry Methods

Most garments have a care label inside at the neck or a seam (Fig. 9-11). The label gives washing and drying instructions. The washing method is based on the fabric and its color. Instructions tell how to wash, dry, and iron the garment. Labels may say "wash in cold water," "tumble dry," "hand wash," "do not use bleach," "dry at low temperatures," "dry clean only," "use a cool iron," or "wash separately." You should read all labels before washing garments.

Laundry can be washed in a washing machine or by hand or dry-cleaned. A washing machine cleans and disinfects laundry better than hand washing. It also saves time. If the client does not have a washing machine, you can wash the laundry by hand or take it to a public laundry. Consult your supervisor to see what you should do. Make sure you know how to use the washing machine. If you do not know how to use it, ask for help or read the manufacturer's instructions. Most manufacturers put instructions on the inside of the lid (Fig. 9-12).

Dry cleaning is a special process. Steam and chemicals are used to clean clothes. It is done at special dry cleaning stores. The client or family may have clothes that need to be dry-cleaned. Ask your supervisor what you should do with these garments.

Dry laundry immediately after washing. Mildew will form on wet clothing that is allowed to sit. Put clothes in a clothes dryer or hang them outside. Some clients prefer that clothes be dried outside. This gives clothes a fresh smell and saves energy. Be sure to check the label for drying instructions.

Follow these guidelines when doing laundry:
1. Consult the client and family about the use of detergents, bleaches, fabric softeners, and prewashes.

Fig. 9-11 Washing instructions on a clothing label.

Fig. 9-12 Washing machine instructions are on the inside of the lid.

2. Check clothing labels for washing instructions.
3. Sort clothes before washing. Separate white clothes, blends, and dark clothes. Towels and sheets are usually washed separately.
4. Check items for spots and stains.
5. Shake or rinse out excess debris before washing items (grass, sand, dirt, food, vomitus, feces, etc.).
6. Check pockets to make sure they are empty.
7. Button, hook, snap, or zip clothes.
8. Remove belts and adornments if possible to prevent loss or damage.
9. Wash items at the correct temperature and washing action (check label instructions).
10. Dry clothes immediately after washing.
11. Remove permanent-press items promptly from the dryer. Fold or hang them on hangers.
12. Dampen items to be ironed. Ironing is easier when items are damp.
13. Iron or fold clothing to prevent unnecessary wrinkling and creasing.
14. Make sure you use the correct iron setting (check the clothing label).
15. Iron items that require the lowest iron setting first.
16. Do not leave the iron on the fabric or unattended. The fabric could be scorched, a fire could start, and children could be injured.
17. Mend clothing when necessary.
18. Put freshly laundered and ironed clothing and linens neatly in drawers and closets.

Stain Removal

Stains should be treated as soon as possible. Flushing nongreasy stains with water helps keep the stain from setting. Then use an appropriate stain remover as soon as possible. Stain removers include pre-wash products, white vinegar, ammonia, chlorine bleach, and hydrogen peroxide. These should be used only if safe for the fabric. Never mix two stain removers. Consult your supervisor about how to remove a particular stain. Then wash the item or have it dry-cleaned. Follow these guidelines when removing stains:

1. Check the care label for special washing instructions.
2. Send garments to the dry cleaners if they cannot be washed. Do not try to remove stains from garments that need to be dry-cleaned. Make sure the dry cleaner is informed of the type of stain and its location.
3. Test the cleaning agent on a hidden part of the garment (seam, facing, collar, belt, pocket). The test is done to see if the agent is safe for the fabric.
4. Use as little cleaning agent as possible.
5. Do not use hot water. Hot water sets stains and makes them very hard to remove.
6. Place the garment face down (inside out) on a clean surface. An ironing board is a good place to work. Put a towel on the ironing board under the garment. Move the towel as you work so that the garment is always on a clean surface (Fig. 9-13).
7. Try a prewash product on stains first. Most prewashes work on common stains.

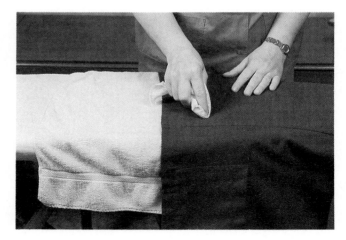

Fig. 9-13 A stain is removed. A towel is placed on an ironing board. The garment is turned inside out and is placed on the towel.

Summary

Housekeeping tasks may be part of your assignment. However, the client is your first concern. Activities must be organized to allow enough time for client care and housekeeping tasks. Try to follow the work plan developed by your supervisor. Remember that the client must have a safe, clean living area. The client's home and property must be treated with care and respect. The home is not reorganized and rearranged to meet your needs and personal preferences. Use the equipment and supplies on hand for client care and housekeeping tasks.

Be sure to follow label instructions carefully. These instructions include those found on cleaning products, laundry products, and clothing labels.

Study Questions

1. You are assigned to do the following housekeeping tasks: laundry; dusting; and cleaning the bathroom, kitchen, the client's room, and other rooms in the home. Write out a work plan for each day of the week.

2. You are to do the laundry for the entire family. Explain how you will do this task.

3. The client keeps all cleaning products, laundry products, and dishwashing products in the garage. Bath towels, kitchen towels, and linens are kept in a cedar chest in one of the bedrooms. Brooms, mops, buckets, and the vacuum cleaner are kept in a hall closet. Describe how you would organize your work.

Circle the *best* answer.

4. You may be responsible for all of the following *except*
   a. Doing laundry for the client and family
   b. Grocery shopping
   c. Vacuuming, washing floors, and dusting
   d. Moving furniture, waxing floors, and washing windows

5. A clean home
   a. Controls the spread of infection
   b. Prevents accidents
   c. Promotes comfort and relaxation
   d. All of the above

6. Daily cleaning should take about
   a. 1 hour
   b. 2 hours
   c. 3 hours
   d. 4 hours

7. You are assigned the following. Which is the *most* important?
   a. Laundry
   b. Cleaning the bathroom
   c. Caring for the client
   d. Cleaning the kitchen

8. All of the following will save time and energy *except*
   a. Cleaning spills at the end of the day
   b. Collecting all supplies needed for an activity
   c. Keeping a shopping list
   d. Sweeping before mopping the floor

9. Which should you use to clean the toilet?
   a. All-purpose cleanser
   b. Specialty cleaner for the toilet
   c. Soap
   d. Detergent

10. You are going to use a cleaning product. Which of the following should you do first?
    a. Store the cleaner out of the reach of children
    b. Read the label instructions
    c. Put on rubber gloves
    d. Mix the product with another cleaning product

11. Which statement is *false*?
    a. Cleaning products should be left in their original containers.
    b. Flammable products should be kept away from heat.
    c. Flush your eye with water if a cleaning product gets in your eye.
    d. Cleaning agents can be mixed together for a stronger cleaner.

12. Which is the *best* way to dispose of food?
    a. Put it in a plastic garbage bag.
    b. Put it in a trash compactor.
    c. Use a garbage disposal.
    d. Wrap it in several thicknesses of newspaper and then place it in a paper bag.

13. Leftover food should be used within
    a. 2 to 3 days
    b. 4 to 5 days
    c. One week
    d. Two weeks

14. You are going to wash dishes. Which should you wash *first*?
    a. Plates and bowls
    b. Glasses
    c. Silverware
    d. Pots and pans

15. You are going to use a dishwasher. You should do all of the following *except*
    a. Rinse or scrape dishes before loading them in the dishwasher
    b. Wait until there is a full load before you turn it on
    c. Use a regular dishwashing liquid
    d. Place cups and glasses face down on the rack

16. The bathroom is cleaned
    a. Every day
    b. Twice a week
    c. Once a week
    d. Every two weeks

17. The client's room is cleaned
    a. Every day
    b. Twice a week
    c. Once a week
    d. Every two weeks

18. Prewash products are used to
    a. Soften fabrics
    b. Remove caked-on stains
    c. Remove stains
    d. Wash clothes

19. Before washing garments you should
    a. Check labels for washing instructions
    b. Sort white clothes, blends, and dark clothes
    c. Button, hook, snap or zip clothes
    d. All of the above

20. When ironing you should
    a. Begin with items that require the lowest setting
    b. Check the label for the correct iron setting
    c. Dampen clothes
    d. All of the above

21. A shirt has a stain. You should do all of the following *except*
    a. Check the label for washing instructions
    b. Flush the stain with hot water
    c. Consult your supervisor if necessary
    d. Use as little cleaning agent as possible

Answers

4. d	9. b	14. b	18. c
5. d	10. b	15. c	19. d
6. a	11. d	16. a	20. d
7. c	12. c	17. a	21. b
8. a	13. a		

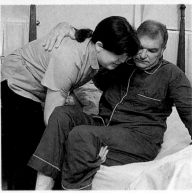

10 Body Mechanics

Chapter Highlights	What you will learn to do

- ■ Describe the importance and rules of good body mechanics
- ■ Demonstrate good body mechanics
- ■ Explain why position changes are important
- ■ Position clients in the basic bed and sitting positions
- ■ Explain how to reduce friction when moving clients
- ■ Describe the guidelines for transferring clients
- ■ Use a transfer belt
- ■ Help the client who is falling

Key Terms

Base of support The area upon which an object rests

Body alignment The way in which body parts are aligned with one another; posture

Body mechanics Using the body in an efficient and careful way

Dorsal recumbent position The back-lying or supine position

Fowler's position A semisitting position; the head of the bed is raised 45 to 60 degrees

Friction The rubbing of one surface against another

Hemiparesis Weakness on one side of the body

Hemiplegia Paralysis on one side of the body

Involved side The side that does not function well due to weakness, paralysis, or injury; the impaired, affected, or weak side

Lateral position The side-lying position

Paralysis The loss of muscle function or sensation in a body part

Paraplegic A person who is paralyzed from the waist down

Posture The way in which body parts are aligned with one another; body alignment

Quadriplegic A person who is paralyzed from the neck down; function of the arms, trunk, and legs is lost

Sims' position A side-lying position; the upper leg is sharply flexed so it is not on the lower leg and the lower arm is behind the person

Supine position The back-lying or dorsal recumbent position

Transfer belt A belt used to hold onto a client during a transfer or when walking with the client; a gait belt

Uninvolved side The side of the body that is functioning properly; the strong side

When a person is strong and healthy, movement takes little effort. When people are ill, disabled, or injured, even moving in bed can be hard. Many clients will need help to:

- Move up in bed
- Change positions in bed
- Turn over
- Sit on the side of the bed
- Move from the bed to a chair

You may be the only person to help the client. You may move clients who are your size or larger. You need to know how to move them properly. This will prevent injury to the client and yourself.

Principles of Body Mechanics

Body mechanics means using the body efficiently and carefully. Good posture and balance are involved. The strongest and largest muscles of the body are used for work. Good body mechanics prevents fatigue, muscle strain, and injury. Everyday activities require good body mechanics. These include cleaning, doing laundry, getting in and out of a car, and picking up a baby.

The body's major movable parts are the head, trunk, arms, and legs. *Posture*, or *body alignment*, is the way the body parts are aligned with one another (Fig. 10-1). Good body alignment (posture) lets the body move and function with strength and ease. Good alignment is important even when standing, sitting, or lying down.

Base of support is the area upon which an object rests. The feet are the base of support for humans. A good base of support is needed for balance. For exam-

ple, it is hard to balance yourself on one foot. Staying in that position for a long time is also hard. Your base of support will be wider if you stand with your feet apart. A wide base of support makes you balanced and stable (see Fig. 10-1).

The strongest and largest muscles are in the shoulders, upper arms, hips, and thighs. Use these muscles to lift and move heavy objects. If smaller and weaker muscles are used, strain and exertion are placed on them. This causes fatigue and injury (Fig. 10-2, A). Strong hip and thigh muscles are used when you bend your knees or squat to lift a heavy object (Fig. 10-2, B). Do not bend over from the waist when lifting. This uses the small muscles of the back. Instead, hold items close to your body and base of support. This uses upper arm and shoulder muscles (Fig. 10-3). Holding items away from the body strains the smaller muscles of the lower arms.

General guidelines for good body mechanics

1. Maintain a wide base of support. Stand with your feet about 12 inches apart.
2. Make sure you have good posture.
3. Use the stronger and larger muscles of your body. These are in the shoulders, upper arms, thighs, and hips.
4. Hold objects close to your body when lifting, moving, or carrying them.
5. Lift and carry objects with your palms up (see Fig. 10-3). This uses the larger muscles in your upper arms. Weaker lower arm muscles are used when the palms are down.
6. Avoid unnecessary bending and reaching. Stand close to your work area. If possible, have the work

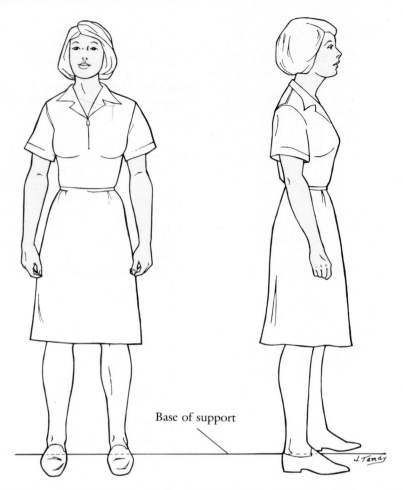

Fig. 10-1 Front and side view of an adult in good body alignment. Feet are apart for a wide base of support. (From Sorrentino, S.A.: Mosby's textbook for nursing assistants, ed. 2, St. Louis, 1987, The C.V. Mosby Co.)

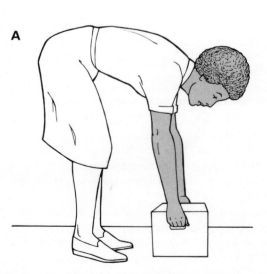

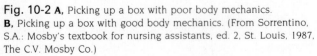

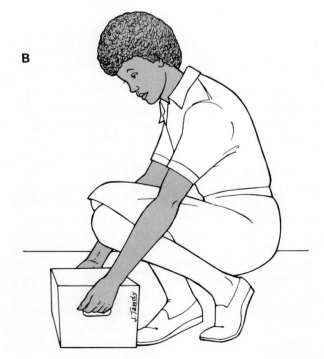

Fig. 10-2 A, Picking up a box with poor body mechanics.
B, Picking up a box with good body mechanics. (From Sorrentino, S.A.: Mosby's textbook for nursing assistants, ed. 2, St. Louis, 1987, The C.V. Mosby Co.)

area level with your waist. The height of hospital beds and tables can be adjusted (see Chapter 12).

7. Face your work area. This prevents unnecessary twisting.
8. Avoid lifting whenever possible. Push, slide, or pull heavy objects when you can.
9. Use both hands and arms when lifting, moving, or carrying heavy objects.
10. Turn your whole body when you change directions. Do not twist your back or neck.

11. Work with smooth, even movements. Avoid sudden or jerky motions.
12. Get help, if possible, to lift or move heavy clients. A family member may be able to help.
13. Squat to lift heavy objects from the floor (Fig. 10-2, B). Push against the strong hip and thigh muscles to stand.
14. Wear low-heeled shoes. They give a wider base of support than high heels.

Fig. 10-3 Box being carried close to the body and base of support. (From Sorrentino, S.A.: Mosby's textbook for nursing assistants, ed. 2, St. Louis, 1987, The C.V. Mosby Co.)

Positioning

Clients must be properly positioned when in bed and sitting in chairs. They look, feel, and function better when in good alignment. Proper positioning helps prevent many complications. These include pressure areas on bony parts (see Chapter 14) and body deformities (see Chapter 11). Good body alignment also helps circulation and breathing.

The doctor may order certain positions for a client, or the doctor may not allow the client to lie in a certain position. Some clients can change their own positions. Others need help. Clients are repositioned every hour or every two hours. Your supervisor and the client's care plan will tell you about position changes and how often to turn the client. Be sure to use good body mechanics and get help if it is needed. Also be sure to explain to the client what you are going to do. Be gentle when moving the client and protect the client's privacy. The client must be able to reach the call bell after repositioning.

Basic Positions

Fowler's position is a semisitting position (Fig. 10-4).

- Raise the head of the bed 45 to 60 degrees
- Keep the spine straight
- Support the head with a small pillow
- Support the arms with pillows

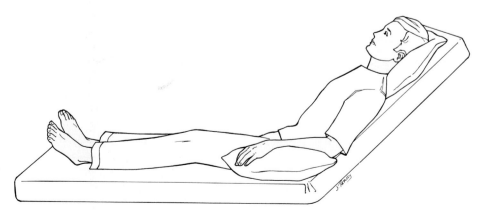

Fig. 10-4 Fowler's position. (From Sorrentino, S.A.: Mosby's textbook for nursing assistants, ed. 2, St. Louis, 1987, The C.V. Mosby Co.)

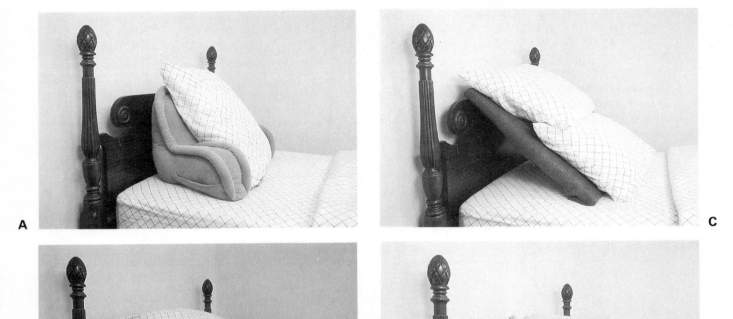

Fig. 10-5 Devices to position a client in Fowler's position. **A,** Pillow-armrest. **B,** Plywood covered with a blanket, flannel, or other fabric. **C,** A foam wedge pillow. **D,** Sofa cushions.

Fig. 10-6 Supine position. (From Sorrentino, S.A.: Mosby's textbook for nursing assistants, ed. 2, St. Louis, 1987, The C.V. Mosby Co.)

Some clients do not have hospital beds. The devices shown in Fig. 10-5 can be used for Fowler's position.

The *supine (dorsal recumbent) position* is the back-lying position (Fig. 10-6).
- The bed is flat
- Support the head and shoulders on a pillow
- Place the arms and hands at the sides
- Support the arms with regular-size pillows
- Support the hands on small pillows with the palms down
- Place a folded or rolled towel under the small of the back (if instructed to do so)

- Place a small pillow under the thighs (if instructed to do so)

Clients lie on their abdomens in the *prone position* (Fig. 10-7).
- The head is turned to one side
- Place a small pillow under the head
- Place a small pillow under the abdomen
- Place a small pillow under the lower legs (or position the client so the feet hang over the end of the mattress as in Fig. 10-8)
- Flex the arms at the elbows so the hands are near the head

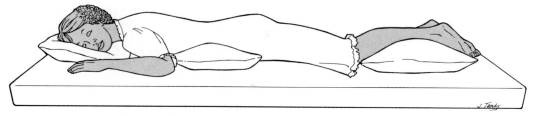

Fig. 10-7 Prone position. (From Sorrentino, S.A.: Mosby's textbook for nursing assistants, ed. 2, St. Louis, 1987, The C.V. Mosby Co.)

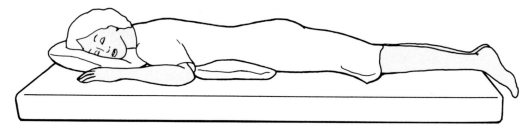

Fig. 10-8 Client in prone position with feet hanging over the edge of the mattress. (From Sorrentino, S.A.: Mosby's textbook for nursing assistants, ed. 2, St. Louis, 1987, The C.V. Mosby Co.)

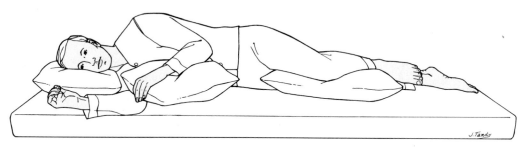

Fig. 10-9 Lateral position. (From Sorrentino, S.A.: Mosby's textbook for nursing assistants, ed. 2, St. Louis, 1987, The C.V. Mosby Co.)

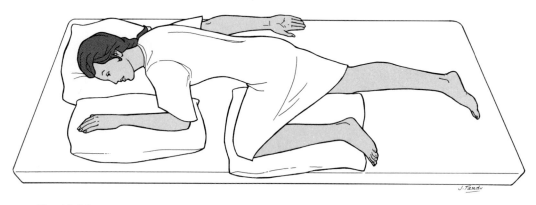

Fig. 10-10 Sims' position. (From Sorrentino, S.A.: Mosby's textbook for nursing assistants, ed. 2, St. Louis, 1987, The C.V. Mosby Co.)

The *lateral position* is the side-lying position (Fig. 10-9)
- Place a pillow under the head and shoulders
- Support the upper leg and thigh with pillows
- Place a small pillow under the upper hand and arm
- Position a pillow against the back

Sims' position is a side-lying position (Fig. 10-10).
- Flex the upper leg so it is not on the lower leg
- Position the lower arm behind the client
- Place a pillow under the head and shoulder
- Support the upper leg with a pillow
- Place a pillow under the upper arm and hand

Fig. 10-11 Client positioned in a chair. Feet are flat on the floor, calves do not touch the chair, back is straight and against the chair.

Fig. 10-12 Pillow is used to support the paralyzed arm. Note that the wrist is at a slight upward angle.

Positioning in a Chair

Many clients are able to sit in chairs. They must hold their upper bodies and heads erect (Fig. 10-11). They will be in poor alignment if they cannot stay erect.

- The back and buttocks are against the back of the chair
- Position the feet flat on the floor or on wheelchair footrests
- Position the back of the knees and calves slightly away from the edge of the seat
- Put a small pillow between the client's lower back and the chair (if instructed to do so)
- Position paralyzed arms on pillows
- Position wrists so that they are at a slight upward angle (Fig. 10-12)

Lifting and Moving Clients in Bed

Some clients cannot move alone. These clients need your help moving in bed. Sometimes two or three people are needed to move a client.

The rules of body mechanics must be followed when moving and lifting clients in bed. They need to be protected from injury. Be sure to keep clients in good body alignment when moving them. They should be positioned in good body alignment after being moved.

Friction must be reduced to protect the client's skin. *Friction* is the rubbing of one surface against another. When being moved in bed, the client's skin rubs against the sheet. This can cause scratching and skin injury. The client can develop an infection or decubitus ulcers (see Chapter 14).

There are several ways to reduce friction when moving clients in bed. You can roll or lift clients instead of sliding them. A *turning sheet* (lift or pull sheet) can be used. A drawsheet can be used as a turning sheet (see Chapter 12). Or a sheet or blanket can be folded to extend from the client's shoulders to above the knees. You may be instructed to sprinkle talcum powder or cornstarch on the client's skin or sheets.

GENERAL GUIDELINES FOR LIFTING AND MOVING CLIENTS

1. Ask your supervisor if there are special ways to move or lift the client. These may be ordered by the doctor or on the client's care plan.
2. Decide how you will move the client and if you need help.
3. Keep the client covered to protect the right to privacy.
4. Protect any tubes or drainage containers connected to the client. Tubes should move easily with the client.
5. Use good body mechanics at all times.
6. Explain to the client what you are going to do.
7. Encourage the client to help as much as possible.
8. Be careful where you place your hands. Do not touch painful or tender areas.
9. Lift or roll clients instead of sliding them.
10. Be gentle. Do not jerk or jar clients.
11. Lower clients gently if you have lifted them. Do not let go until the client is on the bed or chair.
12. Stop if the procedure causes the client pain. You may be doing something wrong or the client may be in poor alignment. Get more help if necessary.

Raising the Client's Head and Shoulders

You may have to tie the back of a gown, turn or remove a pillow, or give care. You may have to raise your client's head and shoulders to do these tasks. The client's head and shoulders are raised by locking arms with the client. You may need help if the client is heavy or hard to move.

Procedure: Raising the client's head and shoulders

1. Wash your hands.
2. Explain to the client what you are going to do.
3. Lock the bed wheels.
4. Raise the bed to a good working level for you. Use good body mechanics.
5. Make sure the opposite side rail is raised. Lower the side rail near you.
6. Have the client put his or her near arm under your near arm and behind your shoulder. His or her hand should rest on top of your shoulder (Fig. 10-13).
7. Put your near arm under the client's near

arm. Your hand should be on the client's shoulder.
8. Put your free arm under the client's neck and shoulders (Fig. 10-14).
9. On the count of three pull the client up to a sitting or semisitting position (Fig. 10-15).

Continued

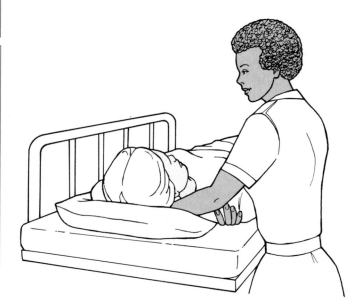

Fig. 10-14 Far arm of aide under client's neck and shoulders. Near arm under client's near arm. (From Sorrentino, S.A.: Mosby's textbook for nursing assistants, ed. 2, St. Louis, 1987, The C.V. Mosby Co.)

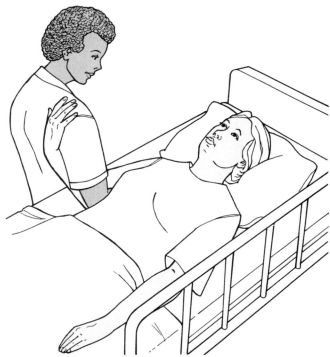

Fig. 10-13 Raising the client's head and shoulders by locking arms with the client. Client's near arm under aides near arm and behind the shoulder. (From Sorrentino, S.A.: Mosby's textbook for nursing assistants, ed. 2, St. Louis, 1987, The C.V. Mosby Co.)

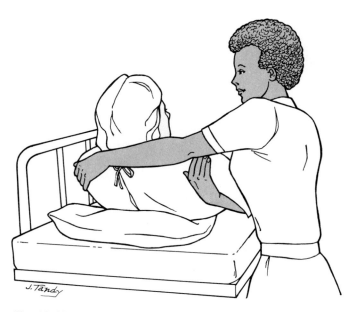

Fig. 10-15 Client raised to semisitting position by locking arms. (From Sorrentino, S.A.: Mosby's textbook for nursing assistants, ed. 2, St. Louis, 1987, The C.V. Mosby Co.)

10. Support the client with your near arm as you straighten or remove the pillow, tie the gown, etc. (Fig. 10-16).
11. Help the client lie down. Give support with your locked arm. Support the neck and shoulders with your other arm.
12. Make sure the client is comfortable and in good alignment.
13. Place the call bell within the client's reach.
14. Raise the side rail near you.
15. Lower the bed.
16. Wash your hands.

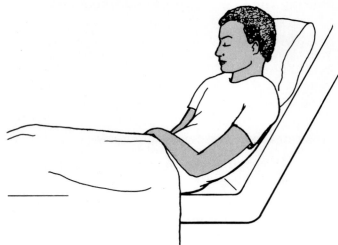

Fig. 10-17 Client in poor body alignment after sliding down in bed. (From Sorrentino, S.A.: Mosby's textbook for nursing assistants, ed. 2, St. Louis, 1987, The C.V. Mosby Co.)

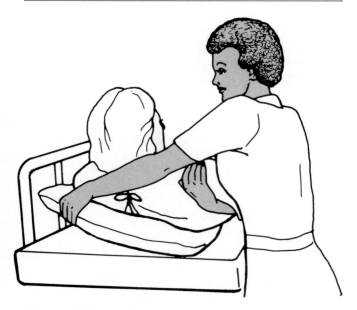

Figure 10-16 Aide lifts the pillow while client is raised to a semisitting position. (From Sorrentino, S.A.: Mosby's textbook for nursing assistants, ed. 2, St. Louis, 1987, The C.V. Mosby Co.)

Moving a Client Up in Bed

Many clients have the head of their beds raised. This often causes them to slide down toward the middle and foot of the bed. They need to be moved up in bed for good body alignment and comfort (Fig. 10-17). You can usually move children and lightweight adults up in bed without help. Sometimes the client is able to help.

Procedure: Moving the client up in bed

1. Wash your hands.
2. Explain to the client what you are going to do and what he or she can do to help.

3. Lock the bed wheels.
4. Raise the bed to a good working level for you. Use good body mechanics.
5. Lower the head of the bed so it is as flat as possible.
6. Place the pillow against the headboard if the client can be without it. This prevents his or her head from hitting the headboard when being moved up.
7. One person (Fig. 10-18):
   a. Make sure the side rails are up.
   b. Stand at the head of the bed with your feet about 12 inches apart. Point the foot near the foot of the bed in that direction.
   c. Roll the top of the drawsheet close to the client's head. Grasp the drawsheet with both hands.
   d. Bend your hips and knees while keeping your back straight.
   e. Rock backward, pulling the drawsheet and client up toward the head of the bed.
8. Two people (Fig. 10-19):
   a. Stand on one side of the bed. Have your helper stand on the other.
   b. Lower the side rails.
   c. Roll the drawsheet close to the client's side.
   d. Stand with your feet about 12 inches apart. Point the foot near the head of

Continued

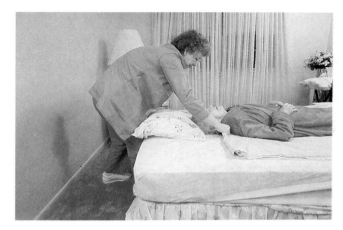

Fig. 10-18 Aide uses a drawsheet to pull the client up in bed.

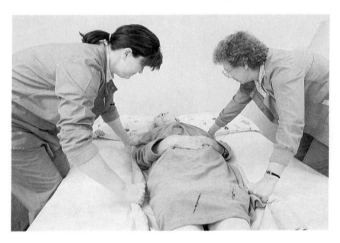

Fig. 10-19 Two people use a drawsheet to pull the client up in bed.

    the bed in that direction. Face that direction.
   e. Bend your hips and knees while keeping your back straight.
   f. Explain that you and your helper will move on the count of three.
   g. Move the client to the head of the bed on the count of three. Gently lift and pull the drawsheet and the client toward the head of the bed.
   h. Repeat steps d through g if necessary.
  9. Put the pillow under the client's head and shoulders. Straighten linens.
10. Make sure the client is comfortable and in good alignment.
11. Place the call bell within the client's reach.
12. Make sure the side rails are up.
13. Lower the bed.
14. Wash your hands.

Procedure: Moving the client up in bed with the client's help

1. Wash your hands.
2. Explain to the client what you are going to do and what he or she can do to help.
3. Lock the bed wheels.
4. Raise the bed to a good working level for you. Use good body mechanics.
5. Lower the head of the bed so it is flat as possible.
6. Place the pillow against the headboard if the client can be without it. This prevents his or her head from hitting the headboard when being moved up.
7. Make sure that the opposite side rail is raised. Lower the side rail near you.
8. Stand with your feet about 12 inches apart. Point the foot near the head of the bed in that direction. Face that direction.
9. Bend your hips and knees. Keep your back straight.
10. Place one arm under the shoulders and the other under the client's thighs.
11. Ask the client to bend the knees. The client's feet should be firm against the mattress.
12. Ask the client to position both hands against the mattress.
13. Ask the client to push with the hands and feet on the count of three.
14. Move the client to the head of the bed on the count of three. Shift your body weight from your back leg to your front leg (Fig. 10-20).

Continued

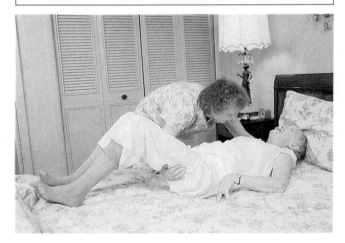

Fig. 10-20 Client helps in moving up in bed. Feet and hands are firm on the mattress.

15. Put the pillow under the client's head and shoulders.
16. Straighten linens. Make sure the client is comfortable and in good alignment.
17. Place the call bell within the client's reach.
18. Raise the side rail.
19. Lower the bed.
20. Wash your hands.

Moving the Client to the Side of the Bed

You will have to reach over the client during certain procedures. A bed bath is one example. You should have to reach as little as possible when using good body mechanics. You will not have to reach as much if the client is close to you.

A client lying in the middle of the bed needs to be moved to the side before being turned. Otherwise, the client will be on the side of the bed after turning rather than in the middle. A client should lie in the middle of the bed for good alignment.

The client should be supine when being moved to the side of the bed. The client is moved in segments. This is easily done by one person. Do not use this procedure for clients with spinal cord injuries or those recovering from spinal surgery.

Procedure: Moving the client to the side of the bed

1. Wash your hands.
2. Explain to client what you are going to do.
3. Lock the bed wheels.
4. Raise the bed to a good working level for you. Use good body mechanics.
5. Lower the head of the bed so it is as flat as possible.
6. Stand on the side to which you will be moving the client.
7. Make sure the opposite side rail is raised. Lower the one near you.
8. Stand with your feet about 12 inches apart. One foot should be in front of the other. Flex your knees.
9. Cross the client's arms over the chest.
10. Place your arm under the client's neck and shoulders. Grasp the far shoulder.
11. Place your other arm under the middle of the client's back.

12. Move the upper part of the client's body toward you. Rock backward and shift your weight to your rear leg (Fig. 10-21, A).
13. Place one arm under the client's waist. Place the other under the thighs.
14. Move the lower part of the client's body toward you by rocking backward (Fig. 10-21, B).
15. Repeat the procedure for the legs and feet as in Fig. 10-21, C. Your arms should be under the thighs and calves.
16. Make sure the client is comfortable and in good alignment. Place the pillow under the head and shoulders.
17. Place the call bell within the client's reach.
18. Raise the side rail near you.
19. Lower the bed.
20. Wash your hands.

Turning Clients

Clients have to be turned onto their sides to prevent the complications from bedrest and to receive care. Certain medical and nursing procedures require a side-lying position. The side the client will lie on depends on the client's condition and the situation.

Procedure: Turning a client

1. Wash your hands.
2. Explain to client what you are going to do.
3. Lock the bed wheels.
4. Raise the bed to a good working level for you. Use good body mechanics.
5. Stand on the side of the bed opposite to which you will turn the client. Make sure the opposite side rail is up.
6. Lower the side rail near you.
7. Move the client to the side of the bed near you.
8. Cross the client's arms over the chest. Cross his or her ankles so the top foot faces the direction of the turn (Fig. 10-22).
9. Raise the side rail.
10. Go to the other side of the bed. Lower the side rail.
11. Stand with your feet about 12 inches apart. Flex your knees and keep your back straight.
12. Place one hand on the far shoulder and the other on the client's far hip (see Fig.

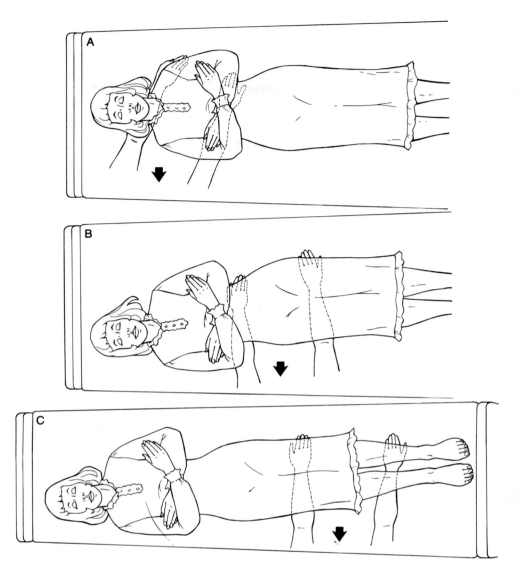

Fig. 10-21 A, Client moved to side of bed in segments. Upper part moved first as aide has one arm under client's neck and shoulders and other under middle of client's back. **B,** Aide has one arm under client's waist and other under thighs to move client's lower body to side of the bed. **C,** Client's legs and feet moved to side of bed. Aide has one arm under client's thighs and other under the calves. (From Sorrentino, S.A.: Mosby's textbook for nursing assistants, ed. 2, St. Louis, 1987, The C.V. Mosby Co.)

10-22). Or grasp the drawsheet on the far side of the client (Fig. 10-23).
13. Roll the client toward you gently.
14. Make sure the client is comfortable and in good body alignment (Fig. 10-24, page 141).
   a. Position a pillow against the back for support.
   b. Put pillow under head and shoulder.

   c. Place a pillow in front of the bottom leg. Place the top leg on the pillow in a flexed position.
   d. Support his or her arm and hand with a small pillow.
15. Place the call bell within the client's reach.
16. Raise the side rail.
17. Lower the bed.
18. Wash your hands.

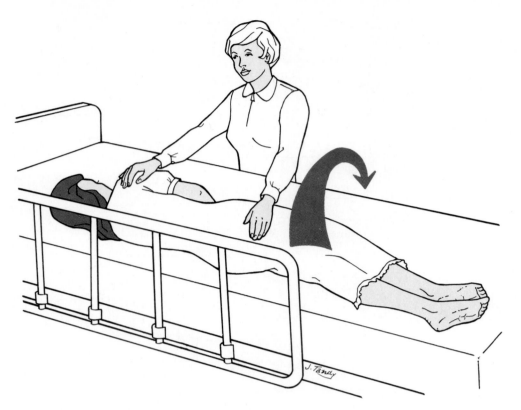

Fig. 10-22 Client being turned toward aide. Client's ankles are crossed so that the top foot points in the direction of the turn. (From Sorrentino, S.A.: Mosby's textbook for nursing assistants, ed. 2, St. Louis, 1987, The C.V. Mosby Co.)

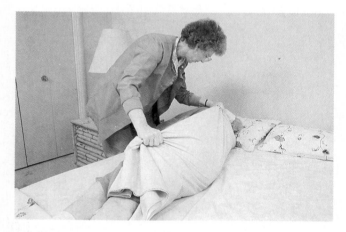

Fig. 10-23 Aide using drawsheet to turn a client.

Sitting on the Side of the Bed

Clients sit on the side of the bed, or *dangle*, for many reasons. Some clients increase activity in stages. They go from bedrest, to sitting on the edge of the bed, and then to sitting in a chair. Walking is the next step. Sitting on the side of the bed is one of the first steps in getting out of bed. It is also a step in transferring to a chair or wheelchair.

Two people may be needed to help a client sit on the side of the bed. Some clients have problems with balance or coordination. These clients need to be supported. The client should lie down if fainting occurs. You must make certain observations while the client is dangling. The client's pulse and respirations are taken. You need to observe for difficulty in breathing, pallor, or cyanosis (bluish coloring). Also note complaints of dizziness or light-headedness.

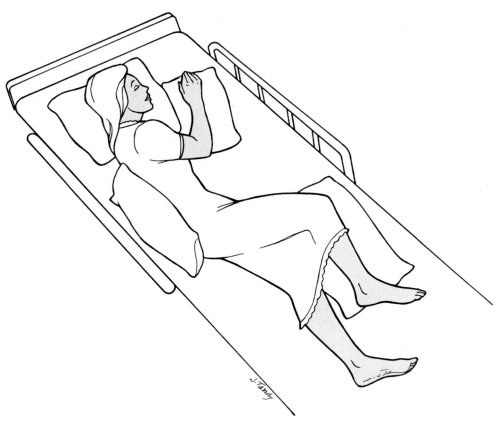

Fig. 10-24 Client positioned on side in middle of the bed. Pillow in front of bottom leg with top leg on pillow in flexed position; pillow against the back; small pillow supports arm and hand; pillow under head and shoulder. (From Sorrentino, S.A.: Mosby's textbook for nursing assistants, ed. 2, St. Louis, 1987, The C.V. Mosby Co.)

Procedure: Helping the client sit on the side of the bed

1. Explain to the client what you are going to do. Also explain what he or she can do to help.
2. Collect the following equipment:
   a. Robe and slippers or shoes
   b. Footstool if the client is very short
3. Wash your hands.
4. Decide which side of the bed will be used.
5. Move furniture if necessary to provide enough moving space for you and the client.
6. Make sure the client is supine. Lock the bed wheels.
7. Raise the bed to a good working level for you. Use good body mechanics.
8. Help the client move up in bed.
9. Prepare the client to get out of bed.

   a. Fan-fold top linens to the foot of the bed.
   b. Put the slippers or shoes on the client.
10. Ask the client to move to the side of the bed. Help if necessary.
11. Raise the head of the bed so that the client is in a sitting position.
12. Slide one arm under the client's neck and shoulders. Grasp the far shoulder. Place your other hand under the far knee (Fig. 10-25).
13. Turn the client a quarter of a turn. As the legs go over the side, the trunk will be upright (Fig. 10-26).
14. Ask the client to push both fists into the mattress (Fig. 10-27). This supports him or her in the sitting position.
15. Do not leave the client alone. Provide support if necessary.
16. Ask how the client feels. Be sure to check
Continued

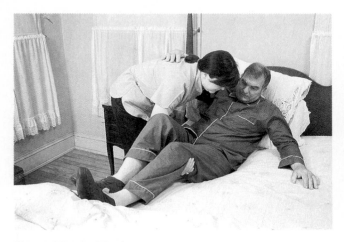

Fig. 10-25 Client prepared to sit on side of bed. Client in Fowler's position, aide grasping far shoulder and far knee with arms.

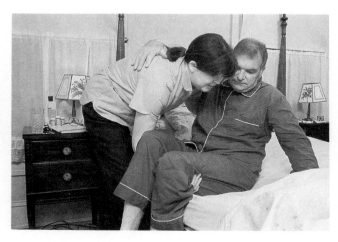

Fig. 10-26 Client upright with legs over edge of mattress.

the pulse and respirations. Help the client lie down if necessary.

17. Help the client put on a robe.
18. Lower the bed to its lowest possible position if the client will get out of bed.
19. Reverse the procedure to return the client to bed.
20. Lower the head of the bed after the client has returned to bed. Help him or her move to the center of the bed.
21. Remove the slippers.
22. Make sure the client is comfortable and in good alignment. Return top linens to their proper position.
23. Place the call bell within the client's reach.
24. Lower the bed.
25. Put away the robe and slippers.
26. Return furniture to its proper location.
27. Wash your hands.
28. Report the following:
    a. How well the client tolerated the activity
    b. The length of time he or she dangled
    c. Pulse and respiratory rates while dangling
    d. The amount of help he or she needed
    e. Other observations or client complaints

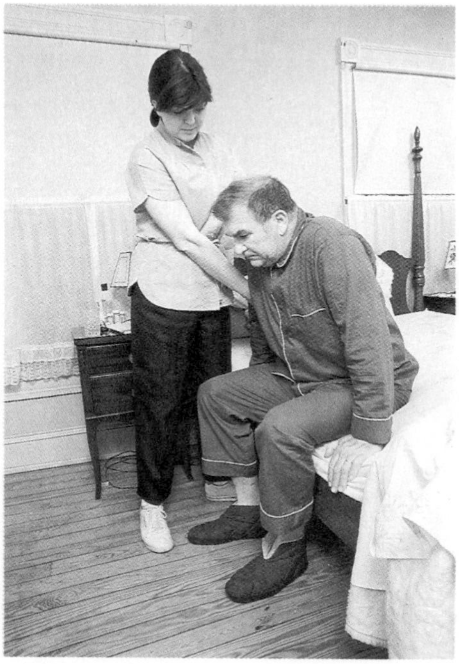

Transferring Clients

Clients often need to be moved from their beds to chairs, wheelchairs, or to the toilet. The amount of help needed depends on the client's condition. Some clients need only support. Others must be

Fig. 10-27 Client supporting self with fists pushed into mattress.

moved from one place to another. The following terms relate to a client's *mobility* (the ability to move about):

- *Hemiparesis*—weakness on one side of the body; an arm or a leg may be very weak
- *Paralysis*—the loss of muscle function or sensation in a body part
- *Paraplegic*—a person who is paralyzed from the waist down
- *Quadriplegic*—a person who is paralyzed from the neck down; function of the arms, trunk, and legs is lost
- *Hemiplegia*—paralysis on one side of the body

- *Involved side*—the side that does not function well due to weakness, paralysis, or injury; the impaired, or weak affected side
- *Uninvolved side*—the side of the body that is functioning properly; the strong side

If mobility is affected, a client will need help transferring. One, two, or three people may be needed to transfer the client.

GENERAL GUIDELINES FOR TRANSFERRING CLIENTS

1. Follow the rules for good body mechanics (see page 129).
2. Follow the rules for lifting and moving clients (see page 134).
3. Arrange the room so there is enough space for a safe transfer.
4. Place the chair or wheelchair correctly for a safe and easy transfer.
5. Know your limitations. Do not try to transfer a large or helpless client by yourself.
6. Allow the client to do as much as possible. This helps the client physically and psychologically.
7. Explain exactly what you want the client to do. This helps the client know what to expect and what to do.
8. Help the client back to bed if he or she is weak, dizzy, or faint.
9. Practice safety at all times.
10. Make sure the client is wearing shoes or nonskid slippers.

Transfer Belts

A *transfer belt* is useful when transferring a semihelpless or helpless client. The belt helps you control and support the client during the transfer. The belt is applied around the client's waist. Your supervisor or the physical therapist can arrange to have a transfer belt in the home.

The belt can also be used to support a client who is walking. Then it is called a *gait belt*.

Procedure: Applying a transfer (gait) belt

1. Wash your hands.
2. Explain to the client what you are going to do.
3. Help the client to a sitting position.
4. Apply the belt around the client's waist over clothing. Do not apply the transfer belt over bare skin.

---

5. Tighten the belt so it is snug. The belt should not cause discomfort or difficulty breathing.
6. Make sure breasts are not caught under the belt.
7. Place the belt buckle off-center or in the back (Fig. 10-28).
8. Prepare to transfer the client.

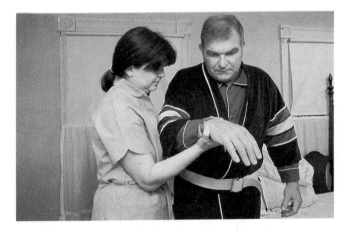

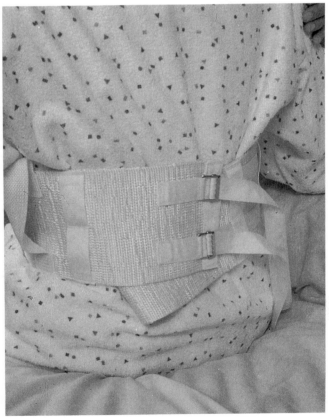

Fig. 10-28 Transfer belt. **A,** Belt is positioned off center in the front. **B,** Belt buckle is positioned at the back. (B from Sorrentino, S.A.: Mosby's textbook for nursing assistants, ed. 2, St. Louis, 1987, The C.V. Mosby Co.)

Transferring a Client to a Chair or Wheelchair

Safety is very important when transferring a client to a chair or wheelchair. You must protect the client from falling. The client should wear street shoes or nonskid slippers. This prevents the client from sliding or slipping on the floor. The chair or wheelchair must be able to support the client's weight. The chair should have a high back and arms (Fig. 10-29). You may need help, depending on the client's mobility, condition, and size. Encourage the client to help in the transfer whenever possible. This helps increase muscle strength.

Chairs and wheelchairs may have vinyl seats and backs. The vinyl holds body heat. This causes the client to be warmer and perspire more. You can cover the back and seat with a folded bath blanket. Or you can put a pillow on the seat. This increases the client's comfort when sitting in the chair.

You should help the client out of bed on his or her strong side. For example, Mr. Smith's left side is weak and the right side strong. Help him out of bed on his right side. During the transfer, the strong side moves first and pulls the weaker side along. Transferring from the weak side causes an awkward and unsafe transfer.

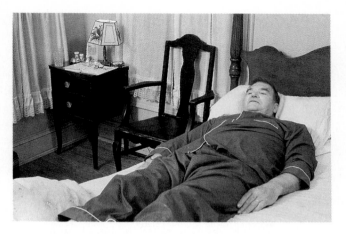

Fig. 10-29 The client's chair should have a high back and arms for support. Note that the chair is even with the headboard.

Procedure: Transferring a client to a chair or wheelchair

1. Explain to the client what you are going to do and what he or she can do to help.
2. Collect the following equipment:
   a. One or two bath blankets
   b. Robe and shoes
   c. Transfer (gait) belt if needed
   d. Pillow
3. Wash your hands.
4. Decide which side of the bed will be used. Remember to transfer the client from his or her strong side. Move furniture if necessary so there is enough room.
5. Place the chair or wheelchair at the head of the bed. The back of the chair should be even with the headboard (see Fig. 10-29).
6. Put the pillow or folded bath blanket on the seat. Lock the wheels and raise the footrests of the wheelchair.
7. Lower the bed. Lock the bed wheels.

8. Fan-fold top linens to the foot of the bed.
9. Help the client sit on the side of the bed. Make sure his or her feet touch the floor.
10. Help the client put on a robe.
11. Apply the transfer belt if it is to be used.
12. Help the client stand.
    a. Do the following if you are using a transfer belt:
       1. Stand in front of the client.
       2. Ask the client to place his or her hands on your shoulders.
       3. Grasp the transfer belt at each side.
       4. Brace your knees against the client's knees; block his or her feet with your feet (Fig. 10-30).
       5. Pull the client up into a standing position as you straighten your knees (Fig. 10-31).
    b. Do the following if you do not have a transfer belt:
       1. Stand in front of the client.
       2. Place your hands under his or her arms. Your hands should be around the shoulder blades (Fig. 10-32).
       3. Ask the client to push the fists into the mattress and lean forward on the count of three.
       4. Brace your knees against the client's knees and block his or her feet with your feet.
       5. Pull the client up into a standing position on the count of three.
       Continued

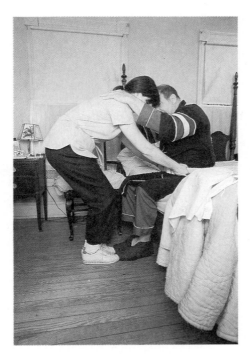

Fig. 10-30 Prevent the client from sliding or falling by blocking the client's knees and feet with your own knees and feet.

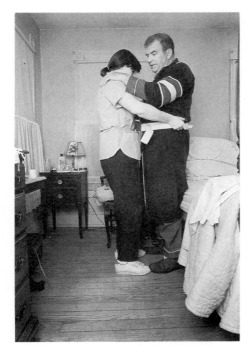

Fig. 10-31 Client pulled up into a standing position and supported by holding transfer belt and blocking client's knees and feet.

Fig. 10-32 Client being prepared to stand. Hands placed under client's arms and around to shoulder blades.

Straighten your knees as you pull the client up.

13. Support the client in the standing position. Hold the transfer belt or keep your hands around the client's shoulder blades. Continue to block the client's feet and knees with your feet and knees. This helps prevent a fall.

14. Turn the client so he or she can grasp the far arm of the chair. His or her legs will touch the edge of the chair as in Fig. 10-33.

15. Continue to turn the client until he or she can reach the other armrest.

16. Lower the client into the chair as you bend your hips and knees (Fig. 10-34). The client helps by leaning forward and bending the elbows and knees.

17. Make sure the buttocks are to the back of the seat. Position the client in good alignment.

18. Position the feet on the footrests of the wheelchair.

19. Cover the client's lap and legs with a bath blanket. Make sure the blanket does not hang on the floor or over the wheels of a wheelchair.

20. Remove the transfer belt.

21. Place the chair as preferred by the client.

22. Make sure the call bell and other necessary items are within the client's reach.

23. Wash your hands.

Continued

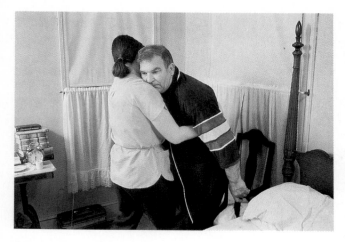

Fig. 10-33 Client supported as he grasps far arm of chair. Legs are against the chair.

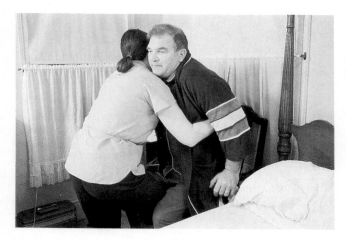

Fig. 10-34 Client holds armrests, leans forward, and bends elbows and knees while lowered into chair.

24. Report the following to the nurse:
    a. The pulse rate if taken before or after the transfer
    b. How well the client tolerated the activity
    c. Complaints of light-headedness, pain, discomfort, difficulty breathing, weakness, or fatigue
    d. The amount of help needed to transfer the client
25. Reverse the procedure to return the client to bed.

Mechanical Lifts

Mechanical lifts are used to transfer helpless clients. They are also used for clients that are too heavy to lift alone. The client may be transferred from bed to a chair, bathtub, toilet, or car. There are different kinds of lifts. However, they all work the same basic way. Follow your supervisor's instructions when using a mechanical lift.

Procedure: Using a mechanical lift

1. Explain to the client what you are going to do.
2. Collect the following equipment:
   a. Mechanical lift
   b. Arm chair or wheelchair
   c. Slippers
3. Wash your hands.
4. Center the sling under the client. Turn him or her from side to side as if making an occupied bed to position the sling (see Chapter 12). The lower edge of the sling should be behind the knees (Fig. 10-35).
5. Place the chair at the head of the bed. The chair should be even with the headboard and about one foot away from the bed. Place a folded bath towel or blanket on the chair.
6. Lock the bed wheels. Lower the bed.
7. Raise the head of the bed so the client is in a sitting position. Or support the client in a sitting position if the bed cannot be raised.
8. Tighten the release valve so that it is closed (Fig. 10-36).
9. Raise the lift so it can be positioned over the client.
10. Spread the legs of the lift to widen the base. Lock the legs in position.
11. Position the lift over the client (Fig. 10-37).
12. Attach the sling to the straps or chains. Fasten the hooks away from the client's skin (Fig. 10-38).
13. Attach the sling to the swivel bar (Fig. 10-39).
14. Cross the client's arms over the chest. Allow him or her to hold onto the straps or chains. Do not let the client hold the swivel bar.
15. Pump the lift up until the client and sling

Continued

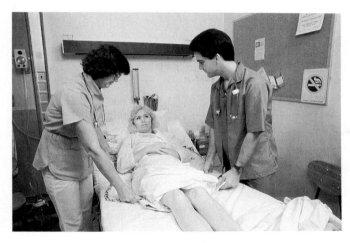

Fig. 10-35 Sling of mechanical lift is positioned under the client. The lower edge of the sling is behind the client's knees.

Fig. 10-36 Release valve of mechanical lift in closed position. (From Sorrentino, S.A.: Mosby's textbook for nursing assistants, ed. 2, St. Louis, 1987, The C.V. Mosby Co.)

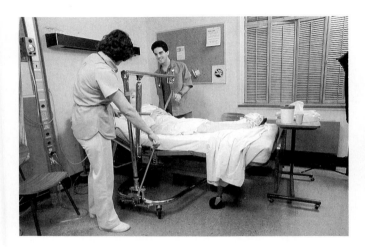

Fig. 10-37 Lift positioned over client and legs of lift are spread to widen base of support.

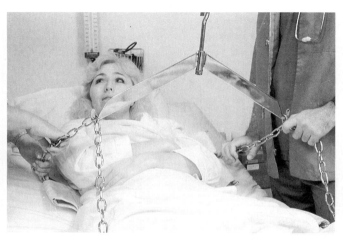

Fig. 10-38 Sling attached so the hooks are turned away from the client's body.

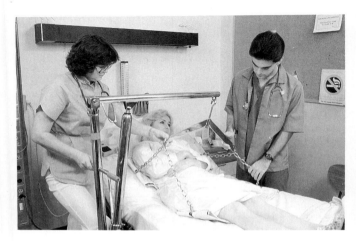

Fig. 10-39 Sling attached to a swivel bar.

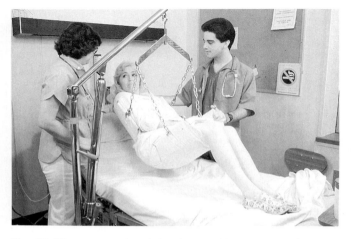

Fig. 10-40 Lift is raised until the sling and client are off of the bed.

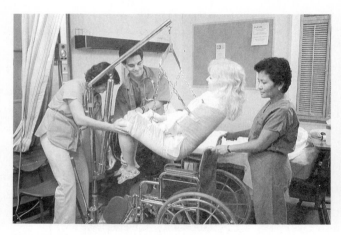

Fig. 10-41 Client's legs are supported as client and lift are moved away from the bed.

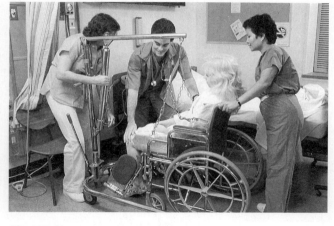

Fig. 10-42 Client guided into a chair.

are free of the bed (Fig. 10-40). Make sure the lift can support the client's weight.

16. Move the lift and client away from the bed (Fig. 10-41).

17. Position the lift so the client's back is toward the chair.

18. Open the release valve slowly. Gently lower the client into the chair (Fig. 10-42).

19. Lower the bar to unhook the sling from the lift. Leave the sling under the client if possible.

20. Put the slippers on the client. Position the feet on the footrests if a wheelchair is used.

21. Cover the client's lap and legs with a bath blanket. Make sure the blanket does not hang on the floor or over the wheels.

22. Place the chair as the client prefers.

23. Make sure the call bell and other necessary items are within the client's reach.

24. Wash your hands.

25. Report the following:
    a. The pulse rate if taken before and after the procedure
    b. Complaints of light-headedness, pain, discomfort, difficulty breathing, weakness, or fatigue
    c. How well the client tolerated the activity

26. Reverse the procedure to return the client to bed.

The Falling Client

Sometimes clients begin to fall during transfers or when walking. They may be weak, light-headed, or dizzy. They may faint. Falling can be caused by slip-ping or sliding on spills, waxed floors, and throw rugs or by wearing the wrong shoes (see Chapter 8). There is a natural tendency to want to stop the client's fall. However, trying to prevent a fall could cause greater harm. Twisting and straining to stop the fall can injure you or the client. Head injuries from falls are common. Remember that balance is lost as a person is falling. If you try to prevent the fall, you can lose your balance. Thus both of you could fall or cause the other to fall.

When a client begins to fall, help him or her to the floor. Easing the client to the floor lets you control the direction of the fall. You will also be able to protect the client's head.

Procedure: Protecting the client during a fall

1. Stand with your feet apart. Keep your back straight.

2. Bring the client close to your body as quickly as possible. Use the gait belt if one is worn. If one is not worn, wrap your arms around the client's waist. You can also hold the client under the arms (Fig. 10-43).

3. Move your leg so that the client's buttocks rest on the leg (Fig. 10-44). Move the leg near the client.

4. Lower the client to the floor. Allow him or her to slide down your leg to the floor (Fig. 10-45). Bend at your hips and knees as you lower the client.

5. Call for help if someone else is in the home.

6. Check the client for injuries.

Continued

Fig. 10-43 Support the falling client by holding him under his arms.

Fig. 10-44 The client's buttocks are on the aide's leg.

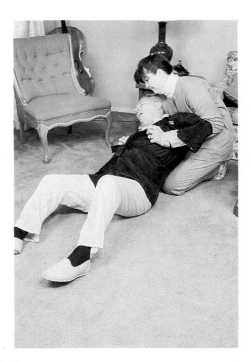

Fig. 10-45 The client is eased to the floor on the aide's leg.

7. Help the client back to bed if he or she is alert and able (Fig. 10-46).
   a. Help the client to a sitting position.
   b. Help the client to a kneeling position.
   c. Ask the client to place the stronger foot on the floor.
   d. Wrap your arms around the client's back.
   e. Ask the client to push off the floor with the foot. Help the client into a standing position. Make sure you use good body mechanics.
8. Call an ambulance if the client is unconscious, is unable to move, or complains of pain in a body part.
9. Call your supervisor. Report the following:
   a. What happened
   b. The client's condition
   c. If you called an ambulance or helped the client back to bed
   d. The client's pulse before and after the fall
   e. How the client tolerated activity before the fall
   f. Any complaints prior to the fall
   g. The amount of help needed by the client to transfer
10. Complete an incident report as required by your agency.

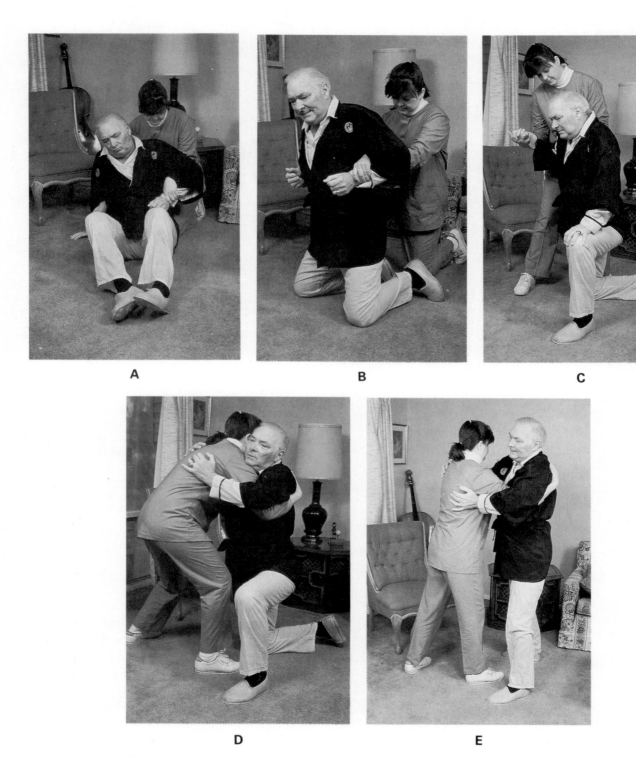

A   **B**   **C**

D   **E**

Fig. 10-46 The client is helped up after falling. **A,** The client sits. **B,** The client kneels. **C,** The client places one foot on the floor. **D,** Aide wraps her arms around the client's back. **E,** The client is helped to stand as he pushes off the floor with his foot.

Summary

You will lift, move, and transfer clients. You must use good body mechanics in everything you do. Body mechanics helps protect you and the client from injury.

Positioning clients in good alignment is important. Some clients cannot change their own positions. They rely on you for moving and turning. Good body alignment promotes their comfort and physical well-being.

You have learned several ways to move, lift, transfer, and position clients in bed. Client comfort and safety must always be considered during these activities. Be sure you know of any position restrictions that may be ordered for a client. Also be sure to protect the client from falling. Encourage the client to help as much as possible in repositioning or transfers.

Study Questions

1. Explain why good body mechanics is important for the client and yourself.

2. Describe the principles of body mechanics as they apply to:
   a. Turning a client in bed
   b. Transferring a client to a chair
   c. Carrying groceries
   d. Doing laundry
   e. Helping the falling client

3. Explain why position changes are important.

Circle T if the statement is true and F if it is false.

T F   4. Body mechanics is the way body segments are aligned with one another.

T F   5. Good body mechanics helps protect you and your clients from injury.

T F   6. Base of support is the area upon which an object rests.

T F   7. Objects should be kept away from the body when lifting, moving, or carrying them.

T F   8. You should face the direction in which you are working to prevent unnecessary twisting.

T F   9. When possible, you should push, slide, or pull heavy objects rather than lift them.

T F   10. You should consult your supervisor for any special ways to position or move a client.

T F   11. A turning sheet should extend from the client's shoulders to above the knees.

T F   12. A client should be moved to the side of the bed before being turned.

T F   13. A transfer belt is part of a mechanical lift.

T F   14. A client should be moved from the weak side of the body.

T F   15. The head of the bed is elevated 45 to 60 degrees for the supine position.

T F   16. The Sims' position is a side-lying position.

Circle the *best* answer.

17. Body mechanics involves all of the following *except*
    a. Good posture
    b. Balance
    c. The small muscles of the back
    d. The large muscles of the body

18. The small muscles of the body are located in the
    a. Back
    b. Shoulders
    c. Upper arms
    d. Hips and thighs

19. Which will *not* reduce friction?
    a. Sliding the client.
    b. Lifting the client.
    c. Rolling the client.
    d. Using a turning sheet.

20. A client is to be transferred from the bed to a chair. The client should
    a. Be barefoot
    b. Wear socks
    c. Wear slippers
    d. Wear street shoes

21. A client is to be positioned in a chair. Which statement is *false*?
    a. The client's back and buttocks should be against the back of the chair.
    b. The client's feet should be flat on the floor or wheelchair footrests.
    c. A paralyzed arm should rest on the client's lap.
    d. The backs of the knees and calves should be away from the chair.

Answers

4. False	9. True	14. False	18. a
5. True	10. True	15. False	19. a
6. True	11. True	16. True	20. d
7. False	12. True	17. c	21. c
8. True	13. False		

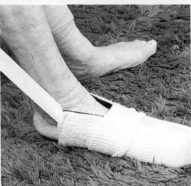

11 Activity

Chapter Highlights	What you will learn to do
Activity	■ Help a client walk
Inactivity	■ Describe how four walking aids are used
Rehabilitation	■ Describe the complications of inactivity
	■ Describe the devices used to maintain the body in alignment
	■ Explain how to prevent muscle atrophy and contractures
	■ Perform range-of-motion exercises
	■ Describe the process of rehabilitation

Key Terms

Activities of daily living The activities a person does every day

Atrophy A decrease in size or a wasting away of tissue

Contracture The abnormal shortening of a muscle

Embolus A blood clot that travels through the bloodstream until it lodges in a distant blood vessel

Footdrop Plantar flexion

Plantar flexion The foot is bent; footdrop

Prosthesis An artificial replacement for a missing body part

Range-of-motion The movement of a joint to the extent possible without causing pain

Rehabilitation The process of restoring the disabled individual to the highest level of physical, psychological, social, and economic functioning possible

Thrombus A blood clot

Activity is important for physical and psychological well-being. Activity involves the things we do every day. It also includes exercise. Most people perform daily activities and exercise without help. Illness, surgery, and injury can limit exercise and activity. There may be loss of function or weakness of a body part. Some clients are bed-bound. These clients need help with everyday activities. Some have to use crutches, walkers, or canes. Some have to relearn activities such as dressing and eating.

Activity

The things we do every day are called *activities of daily living* (ADL). These activities include bathing, oral hygiene, eating, elimination, and moving about. Almost every activity of daily living involves walking.

Ambulation

Ambulation is the act of walking. You may care for clients who are weak and unsteady due to illness, injury, surgery, or aging. Such clients may need support while walking.

Clients who have been confined to bed will slowly begin activity. Activity is increased in steps. First the client will dangle (sit on the side of the bed). The next step is sitting in a bedside chair. Then the client will walk short distances. For example, the client may walk from the bedroom to the bathroom. Eventually the client will walk about in the home. These clients will probably need support as they increase activity.

Using a transfer (gait) belt is advised if the client is weak or unsteady. Or you can use the client's belt if it is wide and sturdy (Fig. 11-1). Clients may wish

to have hand rails installed on stairs and in hallways (see Fig. 8–5 on page 109). These give additional support when walking.

Procedure: Helping the client walk

1. Explain to the client what you are going to do. Also explain how the client can help.
2. Wash your hands.
3. Collect the following:
   a. Robe and shoes
   b. Transfer (gait) belt
   c. Walking aid if needed (see page 154)
4. Decide which side of the bed to use.
5. Move furniture so there is enough moving space.
6. Make sure the bed is in the low position. Lock the bed wheels.
7. Fold top linens to the foot of the bed.
8. Help the client put the shoes on.
9. Help the client sit on the side of the bed. (See *Helping the client sit on the side of the bed*, page 141.)
10. Help the client put on the robe.
11. Apply the transfer belt. (See *Applying a transfer [gait] belt*, page 143).
12. Help the client stand. (See *Transferring the client to a chair or wheelchair*, page 144).
13. Give the client his or her walking aide if one is used.
14. Stand at the client's side while he or she gains balance. Hold the belt at the side and back.
15. Encourage the client to use good posture.
16. Help the client walk. Walk at his or her weak side. Support the client with the transfer belt (Fig. 11-2). Support the client as in Fig. 11-3 if a transfer belt is not used.
17. Encourage the client to walk normally. Ask him or her to allow the heel of the foot to strike the floor first. Discourage shuffling, sliding, or walking on tiptoe. Do not rush him or her.
18. Report the following:
   a. The distance walked
   b. The amount of help needed
   c. How well the client tolerated the activity
   d. Complaints of fatigue, pain, dizziness, or light-headedness

Fig. 11-1 A wide belt is used as a transfer belt.

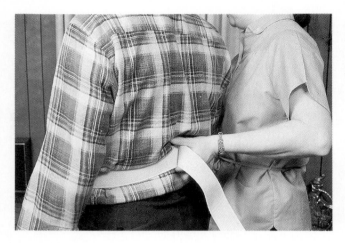

Fig. 11-2 Transfer belt is used to support a client while walking.

Fig. 11-3 Aide has one arm around client's waist. The other arm is holding the client's forearm.

Walking Aids

Walking aids are used to support the body. They include crutches, canes, and walkers. Walking aids are ordered by the doctor. The type of aid ordered depends on the client's condition, ability to walk, and amount of support needed. The physical therapist or the nurse will teach the client to use the walking aid. However, the client may need support even when using a walking aid.

CRUTCHES

Crutches (Fig. 11-4) are used when the client cannot use one leg. They may also be ordered when one or both legs need to gain strength. Some clients with permanent leg weakness can use crutches. Crutches may be needed on a temporary or permanent basis.

Safety is important when crutches are used. The client may fall. Certain safety measures must be followed.

1. The crutches must fit. A nurse or physical therapist will fit the client with crutches. If they do not fit right, the client can fall. Back pain, nerve damage, and injuries to the underarms and palms are other risks.
2. Crutch tips must be on the crutches. They must not be wet or worn down.
3. Crutches are checked for flaws. Check wooden crutches for cracks. Check aluminum crutches for bends. Bolts on both types must be tight.
4. Street shoes are worn. They should be flat and have nonskid soles.
5. The client's clothes must fit well. Loose clothing can get caught between the crutches and underarms. Loose clothing can also hang forward. This blocks the client's view of the floor, feet, and crutch tips.
6. The safety rules to prevent falls must be followed (see Chapter 8).

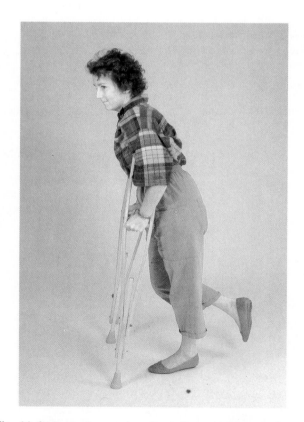

Fig. 11-4 Client using crutches. (From Sorrentino, S.A.: Mosby's textbook for nursing assistants, ed. 2, St. Louis, 1987, The C.V. Mosby Co.)

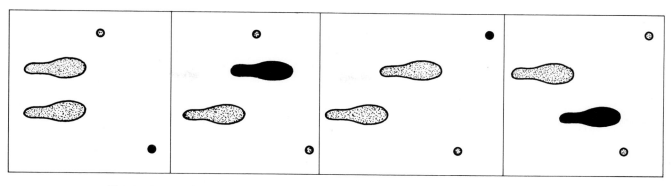

Fig. 11-5 Four-point alternating gait. (From Potter, P.A., and Perry, A.G.: Fundamentals of nursing: concepts, process, and practice, St. Louis, 1985, The C.V. Mosby Co.)

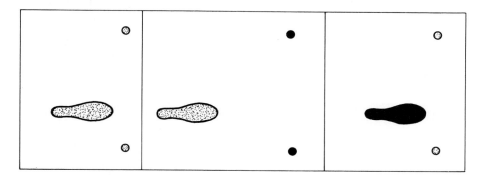

Fig. 11-6 Three-point gait. (From Potter, P.A., and Perry, A.G.: Fundamentals of nursing: concepts, process, and practice, St. Louis, 1985, The C.V. Mosby Co.)

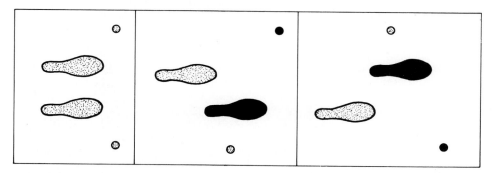

Fig. 11-7 Two-point gait. (From Potter, P.A., and Perry, A.G.: Fundamentals of nursing: concepts, process, and practice, St. Louis, 1985, The C.V. Mosby Co.)

There are five basic methods (gaits) for crutch walking. The method used depends on the client's problem and condition.

Four-point alternating gait (Fig. 11-5) is used when the client can stand (bear weight) on both feet. The gait involves the following sequence:

Step 1. Right crutch forward

Step 2. Left foot forward

Step 3. Left crutch forward

Step 4. Right foot forward

Three-point gait (Fig. 11-6) is used when the client can bear weight on one foot. The affected leg

does not touch the ground. The sequence is:

Step 1. Both crutches and weak leg forward

Step 2. The good leg forward

Two-point gait (Fig. 11-7) is used when the client can bear weight on both feet. The sequence is:

Step 1. Right crutch and left foot forward

Step 2. Left crutch and right foot forward

Swing-to-crutch gait (Fig. 11-8) requires the client to bear some weight on both feet. Strong upper arm muscles are needed. The client uses the arms to lift the body to the crutches. The sequence is:

Step 1. Move the crutches forward

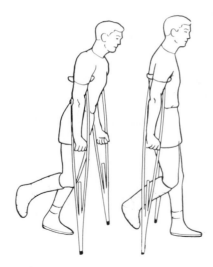

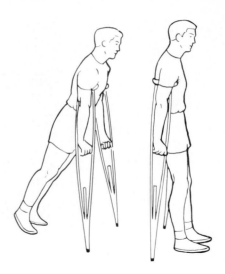

Fig. 11-8 Swing-to-crutch gait. (From Long, B.C., and Phipps, W.J.: Essentials of medical-surgical nursing: a nursing process approach, St. Louis, 1985, The C.V. Mosby Co.)

Fig. 11-9 Swing-through-crutch gait. (From Long, B.C., and Phipps, W.J.: Essentials of medical-surgical nursing: a nursing process approach, St. Louis, 1985, The C.V. Mosby Co.)

Fig. 11-10 A, Single-tipped cane. **B,** Tripod cane. **C,** Four-point (quad) cane. (From Sorrentino, S.A.: Mosby's textbook for nursing assistants, ed. 2, St. Louis, 1987, The C.V. Mosby Co.)

Step 2. Lift and swing the body forward to the crutches

Swing-through-crutch gait (Fig. 11-9) requires the client to bear some weight. Strong upper arms are needed to lift and swing the body through the crutches. The body is swung forward past the crutches. The sequence is:

Step 1. Move the crutches forward

Step 2. Lift and swing the body through past the crutches

CANES

A cane is used when there is weakness on one side of the body. It helps with balance and support. There are single-tipped canes and canes with three and four points (Fig. 11-10).

The single-tipped cane is held on the strong side. (If the left leg is weak, the cane is held in the right hand). The tip of the cane should be about 6 to 10 inches (15-25 cm) to the side of the foot. The grip is usually at hip level (Fig. 11-11). The sequence for walking is:

Fig. 11-11 Grip of cane is held at hip level. (From Sorrentino, S.A.: Mosby's textbook for nursing assistants, ed. 2, St. Louis, 1987, The C.V. Mosby Co.)

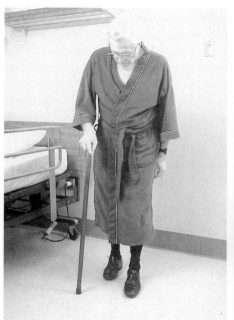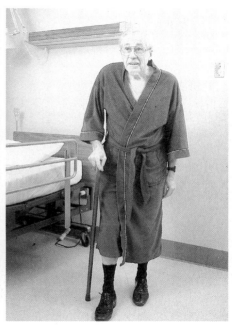

Fig. 11-12 Walking with a cane. **A,** The cane is moved forward about one foot. **B,** Leg opposite the cane (weak leg) is brought forward even with the cane. **C,** Leg on the cane side (strong leg) is moved ahead of the cane and weak leg. (From Sorrentino, S.A.: Mosby's textbook for nursing assistants, ed. 2, St. Louis, 1987, The C.V. Mosby Co.)

Step 1. Move the cane forward about 12 inches (Fig. 11-12, A)

Step 2. Move the weak leg (opposite the side of the cane) forward even with the cane (Fig. 11-12, B)

Step 3. Move the strong leg forward and ahead of the cane and weak leg (Fig. 11-12, C)

Three-point and four-point canes are usually held on the strong side. They provide more support than single-tipped canes. However, they are harder to move.

WALKERS

A walker is a four-point walking aid (Fig. 11-13). It gives more support than a cane. Many people like walkers better than canes. Walkers make them feel safer and more secure. The walker is picked up and moved about 6 inches in front of the client. The client then moves the right and then the left foot up to the walker (Fig. 11-14).

Baskets, pouches, and trays can be attached to the walker (Fig. 11-15) so that clients can carry needed items themselves. This allows greater independence. The client's hands are free to grip the walker.

BRACES

Braces may be used to support a weak body part (Fig. 11-16). They can also be used to prevent movement or to prevent or correct deformities. Braces are made of metal, plastic, or leather. They are applied over the ankle, knee, or back. Bony points under the

Fig. 11-13 A walker.

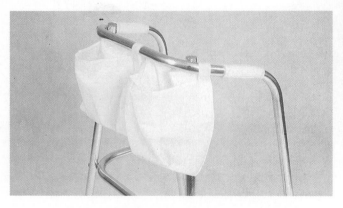

Fig. 11-15 Walker attachments. (From Sorrentino, S.A.: Mosby's textbook for nursing assistants, ed. 2, St. Louis, 1987, The C.V. Mosby Co.)

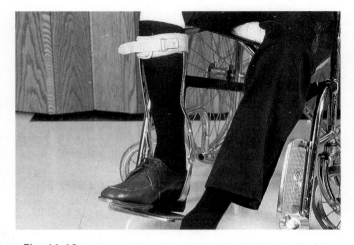

Fig. 11-16 Leg brace. (From Sorrentino, S.A.: Mosby's textbook for nursing assistants, ed. 2, St. Louis, 1987, The C.V. Mosby Co.)

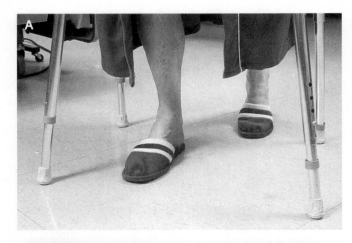

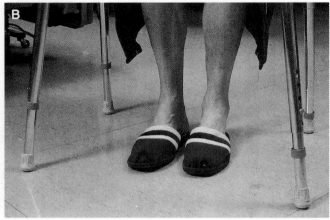

Fig. 11-14 Walking with a walker. **A,** The walker is moved about 6 inches in front of the client. **B,** Both feet are moved up to the walker. (From Sorrentino, S.A.: Mosby's textbook for nursing assistants, ed. 2, St. Louis, 1987, The C.V. Mosby Co.)

brace must be protected. Otherwise skin breakdown can occur. The nurse or physical therapist will tell you how to protect the bony points.

Inactivity

Some clients are confined to bed. They need rest to recover from illness or injury. Some are too weak to get up. Others are unable to move because of paralysis. Inactivity affects the normal function of every body system. Serious complications can include the following:

- *Decubitus ulcers* are areas where the skin and tissues are broken down (see Fig. 14-40 on page 236). They are caused by a lack of blood flow to the part because of pressure. Decubitus ulcers (decubiti) are also called bedsores or pressure sores. They are discussed in Chapter 14.

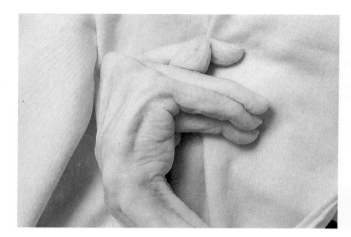

Fig. 11-17 A contracture. (From Sorrentino, S.A.: Mosby's textbook for nursing assistants, ed. 2, St. Louis, 1987, The C.V. Mosby Co.)

- *Constipation and fecal impaction* are problems with bowel elimination. Peristalsis slows down with inactivity. This slows the movement of feces through the large intestine. These are discussed in Chapter 15.
- *Contracture* is the abnormal shortening of a muscle. The contracted muscle is fixed into position (Fig. 11-17). The part is permanently deformed and cannot be stretched. The individual is permanently deformed and disabled. Contractures can develop in wrists, fingers, arms, legs, ankles, and the neck.
- *Atrophy* is the decrease in size or the wasting away of tissue. Muscle atrophy is a decrease in size or a wasting away of the muscle (Fig. 11-18).
- *Blood clots* occur when blood flow is sluggish. Activity and exercise increase circulation. Inactivity slows circulation. Blood clots (*thrombi*) can form in veins (Fig. 11-19, A). The blood clot (*thrombus*) can break loose and travel through the bloodstream. It then becomes an embolus. An *embolus* is a blood clot that travels through the blood vessels until it lodges in a distant vessel (Fig. 11-19, B). An embolus from a vein eventually lodges in the lungs (pulmonary embolus). A pulmonary embolus can cause severe respiratory problems and death.
- *Pneumonia* is an inflammation of the lungs. Secretions pool in the lungs when a client is inactive. The alveoli become filled with fluid. The client with pneumonia is very ill. Pneumonia is discussed in Chapter 21.
- *Osteoporosis* is a bone disorder in which the bones become porous and brittle. Inactivity does not allow for the proper use of bone. For bone to be formed properly, it must be used. If not, the bone is absorbed. It becomes porous and brittle. The bones can break very easily. Osteoporosis is discussed in Chapter 21.
- *Depression* involves the client's mood. The person feels sad, discouraged, and unhappy.

These complications must be prevented. Otherwise the client will develop more health problems.

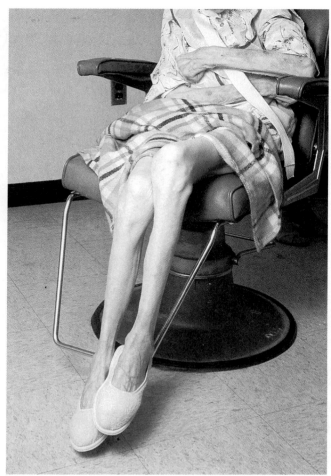

Fig. 11-18 Muscle atrophy. (From Sorrentino, S.A.: Mosby's textbook for nursing assistants, ed. 2, St. Louis, 1987, The C.V. Mosby Co.)

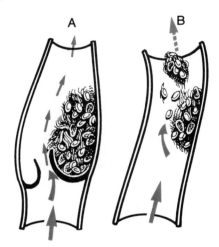

Fig. 11-19 A, A blood clot is attached to the wall of a vein. The arrows show the direction of blood flow. **B,** Part of the thrombus has broken off. It has become an embolus. The embolus will travel in the bloodstream until it lodges in a distant vessel. (Modified from Long, B.C., and Phipps, W.J.: Essentials of medical-surgical nursing: a nursing process approach, St. Louis, 1985, The C.V. Mosby Co.)

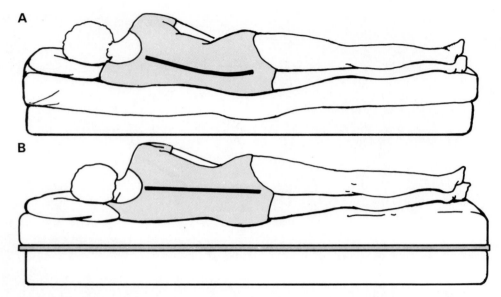

Fig. 11-20 A, Mattress sagging without bed boards. The client's back is not straight. **B,** Bed boards are placed under the mattress. No sagging occurs. The client's back is straight. (From Sorrentino, S.A.: Mosby's textbook for nursing assistants, ed. 2, St. Louis, 1987, The C.V. Mosby Co.)

Positioning clients in good body alignment is essential. Range-of-motion exercises are also very important.

Positioning

Body alignment and positioning were discussed in Chapter 10. Supportive devices may be needed to keep the client in good body alignment. They support and keep the client in a particular position.

Bed boards are placed under the mattress. They prevent the mattress from sagging (Fig. 11-20). Bed boards are usually made of plywood and are covered with canvas or some other material. There are two sections for hospital beds. One section is for the head of the bed and the other for the foot. The two sections allow the head of the bed to be raised. A sheet of plywood is needed for a regular bed.

A *footboard* is placed at the foot of the mattress (Fig. 11-21). It prevents *plantar flexion*. In plantar flexion the foot (plantar) is bent (flexion). *Footdrop* is another term for plantar flexion. To prevent footdrop the bottom of the feet are positioned flush against the footboard. The feet are in good body alignment as in the standing position. The footboard can be used as a bed cradle to keep top linens off the feet. Your supervisor will help the client get a footboard if one is needed.

Trochanter rolls prevent the hips and legs from turning outward (external rotation). They are shown in Fig. 11-22. Bath blankets (thin flannel blankets) are used to make trochanter rolls. The blanket is folded to the desired length and rolled up. The loose end is placed under the client from the hip to the knee. Then the roll is tucked along the side of the body. Pillows can be used instead of trochanter rolls.

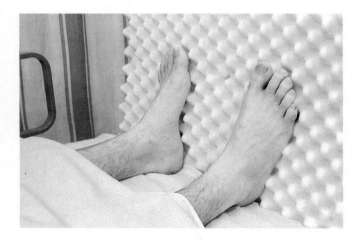

Fig. 11-21 Footboard. The client's feet are flush with the board to keep them in normal alignment. (From Sorrentino, S.A.: Mosby's textbook for nursing assistants, ed. 2, St. Louis, 1987, The C.V. Mosby Co.)

Handrolls help prevent contractures of the thumb, fingers, and wrist. A handroll can be made by rolling up a washcloth (Fig. 11-23). Commercial handrolls are available (Fig. 11-24). Firm sponges and rubber balls can be used.

A *bed cradle* is often used to keep top linens off the feet (Fig. 11-25). The weight of linens on the feet can cause footdrop and decubiti. A sturdy cardboard box can be used as a bed cradle (Fig. 11-26). The footboard of the bed can be used as a bed cradle. Top linens are draped over the footboard as in Fig. 11-27.

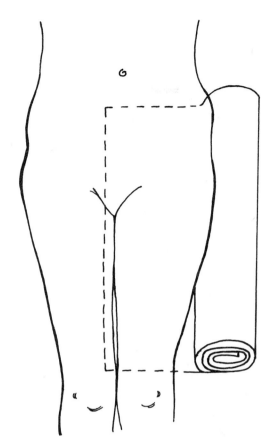

Fig. 11-22 Trochanter roll made from a bath blanket. The roll extends from the hip to the knee. (From Sorrentino, S.A.: Mosby's textbook for nursing assistants, ed. 2, St. Louis, 1987, The C.V. Mosby Co.)

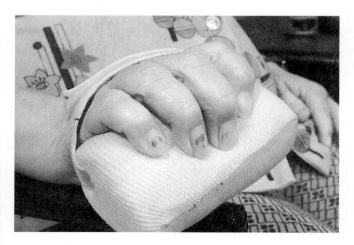

Fig. 11-24 Handroll. (From Sorrentino, S.A.: Mosby's textbook for nursing assistants, ed. 2, St. Louis, 1987, The C.V. Mosby Co.)

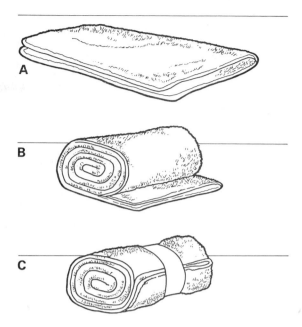

Fig. 11-23 Handroll is made by rolling up a washcloth. **A,** Fold the washcloth in half. **B,** Roll up the washcloth. **C,** Tape the rolled washcloth. (From Sorrentino, S.A.: Mosby's textbook for nursing assistants, ed. 2, St. Louis, 1987, The C.V. Mosby Co.)

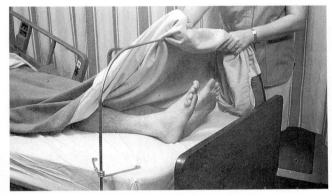

Fig. 11-25 A bed cradle is placed on top of the bed. Linens are brought over the top of the cradle. (From Sorrentino, S.A.: Mosby's textbook for nursing assistants, ed. 2, St. Louis, 1987, The C.V. Mosby Co.)

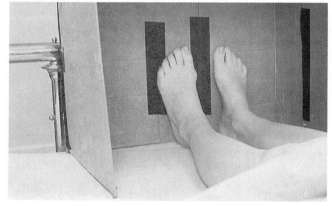

Fig. 11-26 Cardboard box used as a bed cradle.

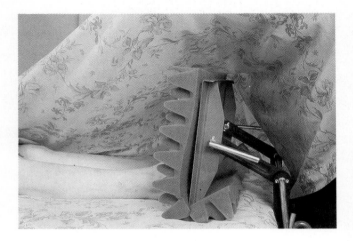

Fig. 11-27 The footboard of the bed is used as a bed cradle.

Exercise

Exercise helps prevent contractures, atrophy, and the complications from bed rest and inactivity. Some exercise occurs when clients perform activities of daily living. Turning and moving in bed without help is also a form of exercise. However, other exercises are needed for muscles and joints.

Range-of-motion (ROM) is the movement of a joint to the extent possible without causing pain. Range-of-motion exercises involve exercising the joints through their complete range-of-motion.

Range-of-motion exercises may be active, passive, or active-assistive:

- *Active* range-of-motion exercises are done by the client.
- *Passive* exercises require another person to move the joints through their range-of-motion.
- *Active-assistive* exercises are done by the client with some help from another person.

Range-of-motion exercises involve these movements:

- *Abduction*—moving a body part away from the body
- *Adduction*—moving a body part toward the body
- *Extension*—straightening a body part
- *Flexion*—bending a body part
- *Hyperextension*—excessive straightening of a body part
- *Dorsiflexion*—bending backward
- *Rotation*—turning the joint
- *Internal rotation*—turning the joint inward
- *External rotation*—turning the joint outward
- *Pronation*—turning downward
- *Supination*—turning upward

Range-of-motion exercises are normally done during activities of daily living. However, some clients cannot perform their own ADLs. Therefore, the doctor or nurse may order range-of-motion exercises. The nurse or physical therapist will teach the client and family how to do them. A family member can do the exercises when you are not there. Your supervisor and the client's care plan will tell you:

- Which joints to exercise
- If the exercises are active, passive, or active-assistive
- How often they are to be done (2 or 3 times a day)
- How many times to do each exercise (usually 5 or 6 times)

GENERAL GUIDELINES FOR RANGE-OF-MOTION EXERCISES

Range-of-motion exercises can injure a client if they are not done correctly. You need to practice the following rules:

1. Follow the client's care plan and your supervisor's instructions.
2. Expose only the body part being exercised.
3. Use good body mechanics.
4. Support the part being exercised. Hold the body part with the palms of your hands.
5. Move the joint slowly, smoothly, and gently.
6. Do not force a joint beyond its present range-of-motion or to the point of pain.

Procedure: Performing range-of-motion exercises

1. Explain to the client what you are going to do. Also explain how the client can help.
2. Wash your hands.
3. Raise the bed to a good working height for you. Use good body mechanics.
4. Lower the side rail.
5. Position the client in the supine position if allowed. Make sure the client is in good alignment.
6. Cover the client with a bath blanket. Fold top linens to the foot of the bed.
7. Exercise the neck (Fig. 11-28):
   a. Place your hands over the client's ears to support the head.
   b. Flex the neck: bring the head forward so the chin touches the chest.
   c. Extend the neck by straightening the head.
   d. Hyperextend the neck: bring the head backward until the chin is up.
   e. Rotate the neck: turn the head from side to side.
   f. Move the head to the right and to the left for lateral flexion.

Continued

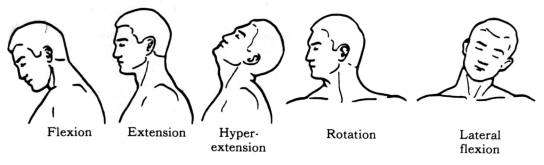

Fig. 11-28 Range-of-motion exercises for the neck.

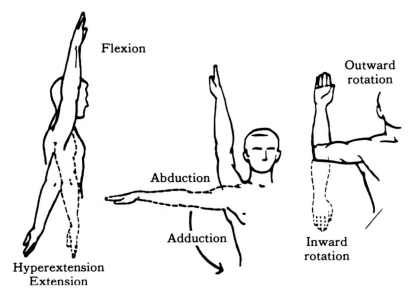

Fig. 11-29 Range-of-motion exercises for the shoulder.

g. Repeat flexion, extension, hyperextension, rotation, and lateral flexion 5 to 6 times.
8. Exercise the shoulder (Fig. 11-29):
   a. Hold the client's wrist with one hand and the elbow with the other.
   b. Flex the shoulder: raise the arm straight in front and over the client's head.
   c. Extend the shoulder: bring the arm down to the client's side.
   d. Hyperextend the shoulder: move the arm behind the body. This step can be done if the client is standing or sitting in a straight-back chair.
   e. Abduct the shoulder: move the straight arm away from the side of the body.
   f. Adduct the shoulder: move the straight arm to the side of the body.
   g. Rotate the shoulder internally: bend the elbow and place it at the same level as the shoulder. Move the forearm down toward the body.
   h. Rotate the shoulder externally: move the forearm toward the head.
   i. Repeat flexion, extension, hyperextension, abduction, adduction, and internal and external rotation 5 to 6 times.
9. Exercise the elbow (Fig. 11-30):
   a. Hold the client's wrist with one hand and the elbow with the other.
   b. Flex the elbow: bend the arm so that shoulder is touched.
   c. Extend the elbow by straightening the arm.
   d. Repeat flexion and extension 5 to 6 times.
10. Exercise the forearm (Fig. 11-31):
    a. Turn the client's hand so the palm is down for pronation.

Continued

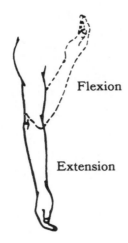

Fig. 11-30 Range-of-motion exercises for the elbow.

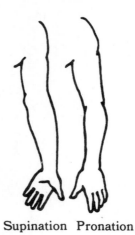

Supination Pronation

Fig. 11-31 Range-of-motion exercises for the forearm.

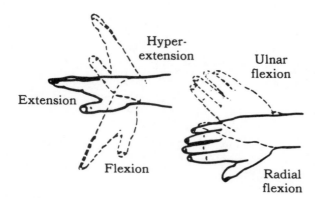

Fig. 11-32 Range-of-motion exercises for the wrist.

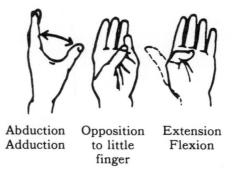

Abduction   Opposition   Extension
Adduction   to little   Flexion
               finger

Fig. 11-33 Range-of-motion exercises for the thumb.

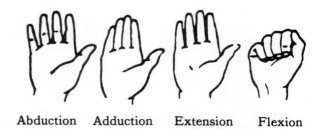

Abduction   Adduction   Extension   Flexion

Fig. 11-34 Range-of-motion exercises for the fingers.

    b. Supinate the joint: turn the hand so the palm is up.

    c. Repeat pronation and supination 5 to 6 times.

11. Exercise the wrist (Fig. 11-32):

    a. Hold the wrist with both hands.

    b. Flex the wrist by bending the hand down.

    c. Extend the wrist by straightening the hand.

    d. Hyperextend the wrist by bending the hand back.

    e. Turn the hand toward the thumb for radial flexion.

    f. Turn the hand toward the little finger for ulnar flexion.

    g. Repeat flexion, extension, hyperextension, and radial and ulnar flexion 5 to 6 times.

12. Exercise the thumb (Fig. 11-33):

    a. Hold the client's hand with one hand and the thumb with your other hand.

    b. Abduct the thumb: move it out from the inner part of the index finger.

    c. Adduct the thumb: move it back next to the index finger.

    d. Touch each finger tip with the client's thumb for opposition.

    e. Flex the thumb: bend it into the client's hand.

    f. Extend the thumb: move it out to the side of the fingers.

Continued

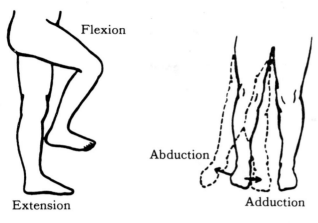

Fig. 11-35 Range-of-motion exercises for the hip.

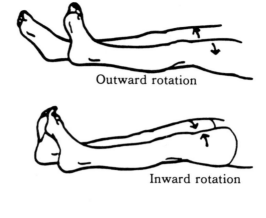

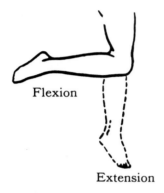

Fig. 11-36 Range-of-motion exercises for the knee.

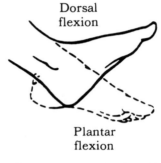

Fig. 11-37 Range-of-motion exercises for the ankle.

g. Repeat flexion, extension, abduction, adduction, and opposition 5 to 6 times.
13. Exercise the fingers (Fig. 11-34):
   a. Abduct the fingers: spread them and the thumb apart.
   b. Adduct the fingers: bring the fingers and thumb together.
   c. Extend the fingers: straighten them so that the fingers, hand, and arm are straight.
   d. Flex the fingers to make a fist.
   e. Repeat abduction, adduction, extension, and flexion 5 to 6 times.
14. Exercise the hip (Fig. 11-35):
   a. Place one hand under the client's knee and the other under the ankle to support the leg.
   b. Flex the hip by raising the leg.
   c. Extend the hip by straightening the leg.
   d. Abduct the hip: move the leg away from the body.

   e. Adduct the hip: move the leg toward the other leg.
   f. Rotate the hip internally: turn the leg inward.
   g. Rotate the hip externally: turn the leg outward.
   h. Repeat flexion, extension, abduction, adduction, and inward and outward rotation 5 to 6 times.
15. Exercise the knee (Fig. 11-36):
   a. Place one hand under the knee and the other under the ankle to support the leg.
   b. Flex the knee by bending the leg.
   c. Extend the knee by straightening the leg.
   d. Repeat flexion and extension of the knee 5 to 6 times.
16. Exercise the ankle (Fig. 11-37):
   a. Place one hand under the foot and the other under the ankle to support the part.

Continued

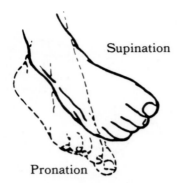

Fig. 11-38 Range-of-motion exercises for the foot.

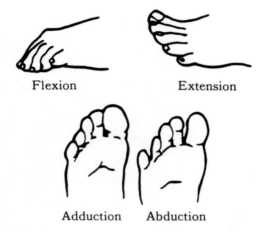

Fig. 11-39 Range-of-motion exercises for the toes.

19. Cover the leg and raise the side rail.
20. Go to the other side of the bed. Lower the side rail.
21. Repeat steps 8 through 18.
22. Make sure the client is in a comfortable position.
23. Cover the client with top linens. Remove the bath blanket.
24. Raise the side rail.
25. Lower the bed to its lowest horizontal level.
26. Make sure the call bell is within reach.
27. Wash your hands.
28. Report the following to the nurse:
   a. The time the exercises were performed
   b. The joints that were exercised
   c. The number of times each exercise was done
   d. Complaints of pain, or signs of stiffness or spasm
   e. How much the client participated in the exercises

Note: Figs. 11-28 to 11-39 are taken from Phipps, W.J., Long, B.C., and Woods, N.F.: Medical-surgical nursing: concepts and clinical practice, ed. 2, St. Louis, 1983, The C.V. Mosby Co.

   b. Dorsiflex the foot: pull it forward and push down on the heel at the same time.
   c. Plantar flex the ankle: turn the foot down or point the toes.
   d. Repeat dorsal flexion and plantar flexion 5 to 6 times.
17. Exercise the foot (Fig. 11-38):
   a. Turn the outside of the foot up and the inside down to pronate the foot.
   b. Turn the inside of the foot up and the outside down to supinate the foot.
   c. Repeat pronation and supination 5 to 6 times.
18. Exercise the toes (Fig. 11-39):
   a. Flex the toes by curling them.
   b. Extend the toes by straightening them.
   c. Abduct the toes by pulling them together.
   d. Repeat flexion, extension, abduction, and adduction 5 to 6 times.

Rehabilitation

Disease, injury, and surgery can cause loss of a body function. Or a body part can be lost. Loss of a body part can cause loss of function. So can the complications from bed rest and inactivity. Activities of daily living may be difficult or seem impossible. The individual may be unable to return to a job. The client may be unable to care for children, family members, or the home. The person may be totally or partially dependent on others.

The client's care will focus on preventing and reducing the degree of disability. The person will also be helped to adjust to the disability. *Rehabilitation* is the process of restoring the disabled individual to the highest level of physical, psychological, social, and economic functioning possible.

Rehabilitation and the Whole Person

Rehabilitation involves the whole person. A physical illness or injury always has some social and psychological effect. A physical handicap has similar effects. How would you feel if an automobile accident left you paralyzed from the waist down? Would you be angry, afraid, or depressed? Would you deny that this has happened to you? Could you do your usual activities?

Fig. 11-40 Eating utensils with cuffs for individuals with special needs. Note that some have cuffs that fit over the hand. (From Sorrentino, S.A.: Mosby's textbook for nursing assistants, ed. 2, St. Louis, 1987, The C.V. Mosby Co.)

Fig. 11-41 Self-help devices can be attached to splints. (From Sorrentino, S.A.: Mosby's textbook for nursing assistants, ed. 2, St. Louis, 1987, The C.V. Mosby Co.)

Could you dance, exercise, shop, or go to school? Could you go to church or visit your relatives and friends? Could you return to your present job? Could you find other employment with your remaining skills and abilities?

Rehabilitation helps a person adjust to the disability physically, psychologically, socially, and economically. The person's abilities are emphasized, not the disability. Complications that can cause further disability must be prevented. Therefore, rehabilitation begins when the client first enters the hospital. The process continues in a nursing home or with home care.

PHYSICAL CONSIDERATIONS

A major goal is for the person to perform activities of daily living. The need for self-help devices is evaluated by an occupational therapist.

The hands, wrists, and arms may be affected by disease or injury. Self-help devices may be needed. Equipment can often be changed or developed to meet the individual's needs. There are special eating utensils. Glass holders, plate guards, and silverware with curved handles or cuffs (Fig. 11-40) are available. Devices can be attached to a special splint (Fig. 11-41). Electric toothbrushes are helpful. They make the back-and-forth motions for tooth brushing. Longer handles can be attached to combs, brushes, and sponges. There are also self-help devices for fixing meals, using kitchen appliances, dressing, writing, dialing telephones, and for many other activities (Fig. 11-42). See the Appendix for other self-help devices.

The legs may be involved. Some clients need to use walking aids. They can walk with crutches, walkers, canes, or braces. Both legs may be paralyzed or amputated. A wheelchair will be necessary. If possible, the person is taught how to transfer from the bed to

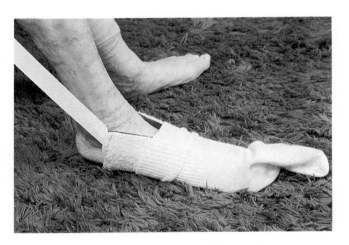

Fig. 11-42 This device holds socks or stockings in place.

the wheelchair without help. Other transfers will be taught. These include transfers to and from the toilet, bathtub, sofas and chairs, and in and out of cars.

The person with a missing body part may need a prosthesis. A *prosthesis* is an artificial replacement for the missing body part (Fig. 11-43). The individual is taught how to use the prosthesis. Artificial eyes are available. There are breast prostheses for women who have had a breast removed. New technology will result in better prostheses. The goal is to have a prosthesis that functions and looks like the missing body part.

PSYCHOLOGICAL AND SOCIAL CONSIDERATIONS

Self-esteem and relationships are often affected by a disability. Changes in appearance and function may cause the person to feel unwhole, unattractive, unclean, or undesirable to others. The client may be depressed, angry, and hostile.

Successful rehabilitation depends on the per-

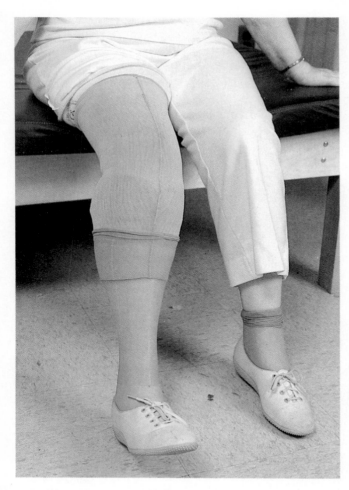

Fig. 11-43 Lower leg prosthesis. (From Sorrentino, S.A.: Mosby's textbook for nursing assistants, ed. 2, St. Louis, 1987, The C.V. Mosby Co.)

son's attitude, acceptance of limitations, and motivation. The individual needs to focus on the remaining abilities. Discouragement and frustration are common. Progress may be slow or efforts unsuccessful. Each new task that must be learned is a reminder of the disability. Old fears and emotions may again be experienced. The client needs help in accepting the disability and its limitations. Support, reassurance, encouragement, and sensitivity from others are important.

ECONOMIC CONSIDERATIONS

The client may be unable to return to his or her job. Rehabilitation can help many clients work again. The person is evaluated for work abilities, past work experiences, interests, and talents. The process of rehabilitation may restore a job skill or a new skill may be learned. The goal is for the person to become employed. The client is given help in finding a job when ready for employment.

The Rehabilitation Team

Rehabilitation requires a team effort. The client, the doctor, nursing team, other health professionals, and the family are part of the team. All help the disabled person become independent. A physical therapist, occupational therapist, speech therapist, social worker, and dietician may be involved. A vocational counselor evaluates the person's ability to perform a job and return to work.

RESPONSIBILITIES OF THE HOME HEALTH AIDE

Home health aides are important in the rehabilitation process. You need to practice the following points:

1. Follow the instructions and directions given by your supervisor.
2. Report signs and symptoms of complications from bed rest and inactivity.
3. Keep the client in good body alignment at all times.
4. Prevent decubitus ulcers (see pp. 236-238).
5. Turn and reposition the individual as directed.
6. Perform range-of-motion exercises as instructed.
7. Encourage the person to perform as many ADLs as possible and to the extent possible.
8. Give praise when even a little progress is made.
9. Provide emotional support and reassurance.
10. Practice the techniques developed by other members of the rehabilitation team when assisting the person.
11. Make sure you know how to apply the client's self-care devices.
12. Try to understand and appreciate the individual's situation, feelings, and concerns.
13. Do not pity or give the person sympathy.
14. Concentrate on the person's abilities, not the disabilities.
15. Remember that muscles will atrophy if they are not used.
16. Practice the task that the client must perform. By performing the task yourself you can guide and direct the client better.
17. Make sure you know how to use and operate special equipment.
18. Have a hopeful and positive attitude.

Summary

Exercise and activity are necessary for physical and psychological well-being. A weak client may need some help in walking. Some clients need walking aids on a permanent or temporary basis. Doctors may prescribe crutches, canes, walkers, or braces.

Complications can be caused by a lack of activity or exercise. They can also occur when a person is confined to bed. You will be responsible for positioning and exercising clients. The exercises are done to prevent complications, especially muscle atrophy and contractures. Muscle atrophy can make ambulation difficult. A leg contracture may make normal ambulation impossible.

Emphasizing abilities is an important part of rehabilitation. Contractures, atrophy, decubiti, and other complications must be prevented. Therefore, good care is necessary. You also need to know the techniques taught to the disabled person. This lets you guide the individual during care. Finally, you must remember that the more the individual can do alone, the better off that person will be.

Study Questions

1. Explain how you can prevent complications from inactivity.
2. A 24-year-old male client is paralyzed from the waist down. He was in a motorcycle accident 4 months ago. He was a swim coach at the local high school. He is married with a 2-year-old son. Rehabilitation is part of his home care. Discuss what you can do to help him.

Circle the *best* answer.

3. Which statement about ambulation is *false*?
   a. A transfer belt is used if the client is weak
   b. The client should shuffle at first
   c. Walking aids may be needed
   d. You should walk at the client's weak side

4. A single-tipped cane is used
   a. At waist level
   b. On the strong side
   c. On the weak side
   d. On either side

5. You are getting a client ready to walk with crutches. You should do all of the following *except*
   a. Check the crutch tips
   b. Have the client wear slippers or socks
   c. Tighten the bolts on the crutches
   d. Help the client as needed

6. Passive range-of-motion exercises are performed by
   a. The client
   b. A member of the health team
   c. The client with the assistance of another
   d. All of the above

7. You are to do range-of-motion exercises. You should do all of the following *except*
   a. Support the extremity being exercised
   b. Move the joint slowly, smoothly, and gently
   c. Force the joint through full range-of-motion
   d. Exercise only the joints indicated by the nurse

8. Flexion involves
   a. Bending the body part
   b. Straightening the body part
   c. Moving the body part toward the body
   d. Moving the body part away from the body

9. Rehabilitation is concerned with
   a. Physical disabilities
   b. Physical capabilities
   c. The whole person
   d. Psychological, social, and economic functioning

10. Physical rehabilitation begins with the prevention of
   a. Anger, frustration, and depression
   b. Contractures, decubiti, and other complications
   c. Illness and injury
   d. Loss of self-esteem

11. Mr. Williams is in a rehabilitation program. Activities of daily living should be
   a. Done by Mr. Williams to the extent possible
   b. Done by the home health aide
   c. Postponed until he regains use of his legs
   d. Supervised by the physical therapist

12. The process of rehabilitation emphasizes
   a. The disability
   b. The individual's limitations
   c. The person's abilities
   d. All of the above

13. The disabled person may
   a. Feel undesirable or unattractive
   b. Be angry and hostile
   c. Be depressed
   d. All of the above

14. Which statement is *false*?
   a. Disabled people are never able to work again
   b. Disabled people may need to learn a new job skill
   c. Disabled clients are evaluated for their ability to work
   d. Disabled clients can be given help to find a job

15. The home health aide
   a. Plans the rehabilitation program
   b. Supplies prostheses
   c. Praises the person when even slight progress is made
   d. Does as much as possible for the disabled person

Circle T if the statement is true and F if it is false.

T   F   16. Single-tipped canes and four-point canes give equal support.

T F 17. When a client uses a cane, the feet are moved first.

T F 18. A walker is moved in front of the client. Then the right and left feet are moved.

T F 19. A client has a brace. Bony areas need to be protected from skin breakdown.

T F 20. A bed cradle keeps linens off the feet.

T F 21. Trochanter rolls prevent contractures of the hands.

T F 22. Footboards help prevent footdrop.

Answers

3. b	8. a	13. d	18. True
4. b	9. c	14. a	19. True
5. b	10. b	15. c	20. True
6. b	11. a	16. False	21. False
7. c	12. c	17. False	22. True

12 Bedmaking

Chapter Highlights	What you will learn to do

Chapter Highlights

Beds

Linens

Making beds

What you will learn to do

■ Care for clients in hospital beds, water beds, and regular beds

■ Identify when bed linens should be changed

■ Explain the purpose of cotton and plastic drawsheets

■ Describe the rules for handling linens and making beds

■ Make a closed, open, and occupied bed

Key Terms

Drawsheet A sheet placed over the middle of the bottom sheet; it helps keep the mattress and bottom linens dry, and can be used to turn and move clients in bed

Mitered corner A way of tucking linens under the mattress to help keep the linens straight and smooth

Plastic drawsheet A drawsheet made of plastic; it is placed between the bottom sheet and the cotton drawsheet to keep the mattress and bottom linens clean and dry

Many clients spend a lot of time in bed. Remember the fairy tale about the princess and the pea? The princess was so sensitive that she could not sleep because of a small pea under many mattresses. Clients are also sensitive about how their beds feel. Every crumb, wrinkle, or soiled area is annoying. This disturbs the client's rest. Bedmaking is important for your client's rest and comfort.

Beds

Some clients rent hospital beds when illness or recovery will be long. Other clients use their regular beds.

Good body mechanics is very important when making beds or giving care. If the client has a regular bed, body mechanics is even more important. You will have to bend and reach more with a regular bed. Beds may be in awkward places. A bed may be pushed against a wall, in a small cramped room, or in the living room. Safety measures are always important.

Hospital Beds

Hospital beds are operated electrically or manually. They can be raised and lowered. This allows care to be given without unnecessary bending or reaching. The low level lets the client get out of bed with ease. The head of the bed can also be raised or lowered.

Electric beds are easy to use. They are also expensive. The client and care givers can change bed positions with the hand controls (Fig. 12-1). The client and family must use the controls safety. They need to know what positions are safe and unsafe for the client. They should be warned about raising the bed to a high level. The high level should be used only to give care. Otherwise, the bed should be kept in the low position. The distance to the floor is less if the client falls or has to get out of bed.

Manually operated beds have hand cranks. They are located at the foot of the bed (Fig. 12-2). The left crank raises or lowers the head of the bed. The right crank adjusts the knee portion. The center crank raises or lowers the entire bed. The cranks are pulled up for use. They are kept down at all other times. Cranks in the up position are a safety hazard. People can bump into them when walking by.

BED POSITIONS

There are three basic bed positions.
- *Fowler's position*—a semisitting position. The head of the bed is elevated 45 to 60 degrees (Fig. 12-3).
- *Semi-Fowler's position*—the head of the bed is raised 45 degrees. The knee portion is raised 15 degrees (Fig. 12-4). This position is comfortable and it prevents clients from sliding down in bed. However, raising the knee portion can cause circulatory problems. You

Raises knee portion

Raises head of bed

Raises and lowers bed horizontally

Fig. 12-1 Controls for an electric bed. (From Sorrentino, S.A.: Mosby's textbook for nursing assistants, ed. 2, St. Louis, 1987, The C.V. Mosby Co.)

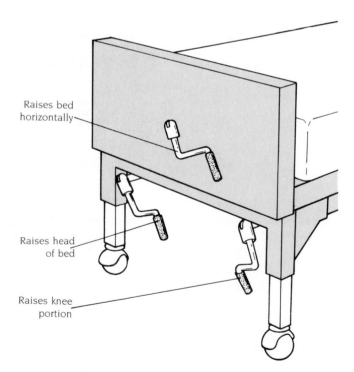

Raises bed horizontally

Raises head of bed

Raises knee portion

Fig. 12-2 Manually operated hospital bed. (From Sorrentino, S.A.: Mosby's textbook for nursing assistants, ed. 2, St. Louis, 1987, The C.V. Mosby Co.)

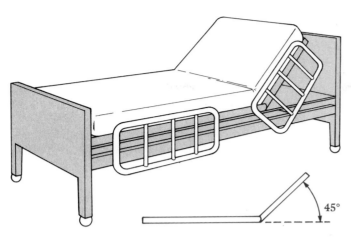

Fig. 12-3 Fowler's position. (From Sorrentino, S.A.: Mosby's textbook for nursing assistants, ed. 2, St. Louis, 1987, The C.V. Mosby Co.)

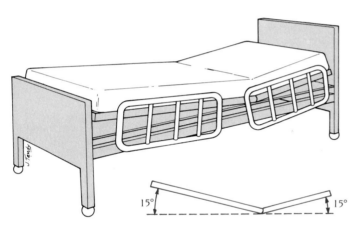

Fig. 12-4 Semi-Fowler's position. (From Sorrentino, S.A.: Mosby's textbook for nursing assistants, ed. 2, St. Louis, 1987, The C.V. Mosby Co.)

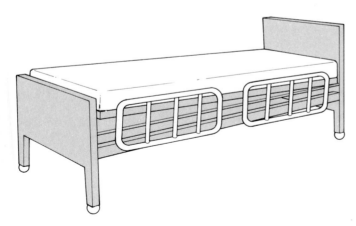

Fig. 12-5 Trendelenburg's position. (From Sorrentino, S.A.: Mosby's textbook for nursing assistants, ed. 2, St. Louis, 1987, The C.V. Mosby Co.)

need your supervisor's permission to use this position for a client. Some agencies define semi-Fowler's position as follows: the head of the bed is elevated 30 degrees; the knee portion is *not* raised. Make sure you know which definition is used by your agency.

- *Trendelenburg's position*—the head of the bed is lowered and the foot is raised (Fig. 12-5). This position is not used unless ordered by the doctor or nurse. Blocks can be put under the lower legs of regular beds and hospital beds. Some hospital beds are made so that the entire bed frame can be tilted to this position.

SAFETY CONSIDERATIONS

Hospital beds usually have wheels on the legs. Each wheel has a lock. This locks the wheel in place to prevent the bed from moving (Fig. 12-6). Make sure the wheels are locked when giving care. They should also be locked when transferring a client to and from the bed. The client can be injured if the bed moves accidentally.

The importance of side rails on beds was discussed in Chapter 8.

Water Beds

Some clients have water beds. A *water bed* is a mattress filled with water and enclosed in a sturdy frame (Fig. 12-7). Water beds reduce pressure on the skin. Some people find water beds to be very relaxing and comfortable. Follow these guidelines when a client has a water bed.

1. Keep all sharp objects away from the mattress. Pens, hair and bobby pins, jewelry, safety pins, and other sharp objects can easily puncture the mattress.
2. Use good body mechanics when helping a client out of a water bed. Getting out of a water bed can be difficult.

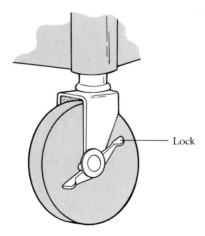

Fig. 12-6 Lock on a bed wheel. (From Sorrentino, S.A.: Mosby's textbook for nursing assistants, ed. 2, St. Louis, 1987, The C.V. Mosby Co.)

Fig. 12-7 Water bed.

3. Find out what temperature the water should be. Ask your supervisor for this information. Then watch the thermostat on the bed so the water does not get too hot or too cold. Be sure to check the thermostat every day.
4. Ask the client or family what you should do in case there is a leak. They may have a repair kit. Or a water bed store may have to be called for service.

Mattresses

A good mattress is important. The mattress should be firm and give good support. Bed boards may be needed if the mattress sags (see Fig. 11-20 on page 160). Hospital mattresses are usually coated with a plastic material. This protects the mattress from water, food, and body fluids.

Mattresses for regular beds do not have protective coatings. Some clients will want to protect the mattress. Mattress protectors can be bought from home health care suppliers and in some department stores. Large sheets of plastic can be bought at department, discount, or hardware stores. Plastic tablecloths and shower curtains can be used. Large pieces of plastic are often used to cover furniture during shipping. Furniture stores may give this plastic away.

Like other household furnishings, the mattress needs attention. Protecting with plastic is one way to help it last longer. The following guidelines are also helpful.
1. The mattress should be covered with a mattress pad. A mattress pad is needed if the mattress is covered with plastic.
2. The mattress should be turned at least once a month. This allows both sides to be used evenly. Turning the mattress from end to end also allows for even use. Be sure to have someone help you turn the mattress.
3. The bed should be stripped and allowed to air out

at least once a week. The bed is also stripped whenever linens are wet or soiled all the way to the mattress pad. If possible, expose the mattress to the sun and open windows in the room.
4. Brush or vacuum the mattress weekly if the client spends a lot of time in bed.

Linens

Linens need special care and attention. Medical asepsis is important when handling linens and making beds. Your uniform is considered dirty. Therefore, always hold linens away from your body and uniform (Fig. 12-8). Never shake linens in the air. Shaking them causes the spread of microorganisms. Clean linens are placed on a clean surface. Never put dirty linen on the floor.

You should collect linens in the order they are used. Be sure to collect enough linen. If your client has two pillows, you will need two pillowcases. Extra blankets may be needed to keep the client warm. You should collect linens in the following order:
1. Mattress pad
2. Bottom sheet (flat sheet or fitted sheet)
3. Plastic drawsheet
4. Cotton drawsheet
5. Top sheet (flat sheet)
6. Blanket
7. Bedspread
8. Pillowcase(s)

Not all linens will be changed every time the bed is made. The mattress pad, plastic drawsheet, blanket, and bedspread may be reused. They are reused if they are not soiled, wet, or very wrinkled. Your client may use fitted bottom sheets. If only flat sheets are used, the top sheet can be reused as the bottom sheet. *Remember, linens that are wet, damp, or soiled must be changed right away.*

Drawsheets may be used. A *cotton drawsheet* is placed over the middle of the bottom sheet. It helps keep the mattress and bottom linens clean. A *plastic drawsheet* is placed between the bottom sheet and the cotton drawsheet. It helps keep the mattress and bottom linens clean and dry. Plastic drawsheets, like the ones used in hospitals and nursing homes, can be bought. Sheets of plastic, shower curtains, or plastic tablecloths can be used instead. The plastic must not have any holes.

Certain clients need plastic drawsheets. These include clients with bowel or bladder control problems or those who have a lot of drainage from wounds. If a plastic drawsheet is used, a cotton one is needed. Plastic drawsheets hold heat and make the client perspire more. The cotton drawsheet keeps the client's skin from contact with the plastic drawsheet. The cotton draw-

Fig. 12-8 Linens are held away from the body and uniform.

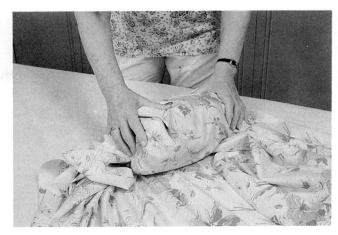

Fig. 12-9 Roll linens away from you when removing them from the bed.

sheet absorbs perspiration. Plastic drawsheets are also hard to keep tight and free of wrinkles. This adds to the client's discomfort.

Some clients use disposable bed protectors instead of plastic drawsheets. These help keep the bottom linen and the mattress clean and dry. However, they are expensive and are used only once. A disposable bed protector must be discarded when it gets wet or soiled.

A cotton drawsheet may be used without a plastic one. Mattresses covered with plastic cause some clients to perspire heavily. A cotton drawsheet helps absorb moisture. Cotton drawsheets are often used to move and position clients in bed (see Chapter 10). When used for this purpose, the drawsheet is not tucked in at the sides.

The use of blankets will depend on the client and outside temperature. The elderly are more sensitive to cold. They may need more blankets. Ill clients may also need to be warmer. In warm weather, lightweight blankets may be enough for some clients. Some may just want a top sheet. In cold weather, wool or wool blend blankets are usually needed. Some clients prefer a down comforter. Be sure to check with the client and your supervisor about the use of blankets. Each client's needs are different. A lot will depend on the client's condition, the outside temperature, and the temperature in the home. However, if a blanket is used, a top sheet must be between the blanket and the client.

Your housekeeping responsibilities may include making the beds of family members. Be sure to ask them their preferences about the use of blankets.

Laundering Linens

Clean linen is important for the client's comfort and infection control. Each client should have clean sheets at least once a week. If the client is bed-

bound, linens should be changed more often. Change the bed whenever the sheets get wet or soiled.

Chapter 9 discusses laundry and stain removal. Be sure to check label instructions when washing blankets and bedspreads. Linens do not have to be ironed. However, it is important to fold them as soon as they are dry. This helps avoid unnecessary wrinkling.

GENERAL GUIDELINES FOR HANDLING LINEN AND MAKING BEDS

1. Use good body mechanics at all times.
2. Follow the rules of medical asepsis.
3. Always wash your hands before handling clean linen. Wash them after handling dirty linen.
4. Never shake linens. Shaking linens causes the spread of microorganisms.
5. Hold linens so that they do not touch your uniform. Dirty and clean linen should never touch uniform.
6. Roll linens up away from you when removing them. The side that touched the client will be inside the roll. The side that was away from the client will be on the outside (Fig. 12-9).
7. Never put dirty linen on the floor or on clean linen. Ask the client or family where to put dirty linen.
8. Do not use worn or torn linen. A tear can easily become larger. Tears are uncomfortable and dangerous for the client.
9. Mend torn linen. Do not use safety pins for tears.
10. Rewash linen that has visible soap residue. The soap can irritate the client's skin.
11. Use the right size linen. For example, use queen size sheets and blankets for a queen size bed.
12. Use fitted bottom sheets when possible. They stay in place better and wrinkle less than flat sheets.
13. Use the top sheet for the bottom sheet if there is a shortage of linen. The top sheet on the bed can be reused if it is clean. Folded top sheets can also be used as drawsheets.

Fig. 12-10 All the linens match.

Fig. 12-11 A closed bed.

14. Match linens if possible (Fig. 12-10). The bottom and top sheets and pillowcases should match. Do not use a floral sheet on the bottom, a striped sheet on top, and a colored pillowcase.
15. Keep bottom linens tight and free of wrinkles.
16. Make sure the cotton drawsheet completely covers the plastic drawsheet. A plastic drawsheet should never touch the client's body.
17. Straighten and tighten loose sheets, blankets, and bedspreads whenever necessary.
18. Make as much of one side of the bed as possible before going to the other side. This saves time and energy.
19. Check linens for crumbs after meals and remove them.
20. Change linens when they become wet, soiled, or damp.

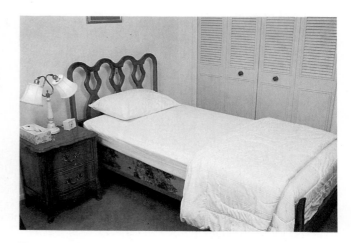

Fig. 12-12 Open bed.

Making Beds

Beds are made in the following ways:
- *Closed bed*—A bed that is not being used. Top linens are not folded back. This bed is made for those who will be out of bed most of the day (Fig. 12-11).
- *Open bed*—Top linens are folded back so that the client can get into bed. A closed bed becomes an open bed by folding back top linens (Fig. 12-12).
- *Occupied bed*—A bed that is made with the client in it (Fig. 12-13).

The bed is usually made in the morning after the client's bath. The bed can be made while the client is in the shower or tub. The client may have a hospital bed, or twin, regular, queen, or king size bed. The procedures which follow apply to any size bed. However, they are written for hospital beds. The procedures also include plastic and cotton drawsheets. You should consult your supervisor about their use.

Fig. 12-13 Occupied bed.

Fig. 12-14 Aide reversing stack of linens so that the item used first is on the top. (Remember, you collected the linens in the order they are used. Therefore, the item you used first is on the bottom.) **A,** Arm placed over the top of the stack of linens. **B,** Stack of linens turned over onto the arm. (From Sorrentino, S.A.: Mosby's textbook for nursing assistants, ed. 2, St. Louis, 1987, The C.V. Mosby Co.)

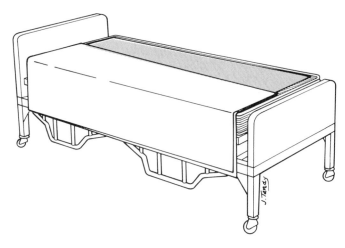

Fig. 12-15 Bottom sheet placed on the bed with the center fold in the middle of the bed. The lower edge of the sheet is even with the bottom of the mattress. Hem stitching is toward the mattress pad. (From Sorrentino, S.A.: Mosby's textbook for nursing assistants, ed. 2, St. Louis, 1987, The C.V. Mosby Co.)

Procedure: Making a closed bed

1. Wash your hands.
2. Collect clean linen:
   a. Mattress pad (if needed)
   b. Bottom sheet (flat sheet or fitted sheet)
   c. Plastic drawsheet
   d. Cotton drawsheet
   e. Top sheet (flat sheet)
   f. Clean blanket and bedspread if needed
   g. Pillowcases
3. Place clean linen on a chair. The mattress pad should be on the top of your stack and the pillowcases on the bottom (Fig. 12-14). The chair should be on the side you will be working on.
4. Raise the bed to a comfortable working level for you. Use good body mechanics.
5. Move the mattress against the headboard.
6. Put the mattress pad on the mattress. Or straighten the old one if a clean one is not needed.
7. Place the bottom sheet on the mattress pad (Fig. 12-15):
   a. Unfold the sheet lengthwise.
   b. Place the center fold in the middle of the bed.
   c. Fitted sheet:

1. Pull a corner over the top of the mattress.
2. Straighten the sheet as you move to the foot of the bed.
3. Pull a corner over the bottom of the mattress.
   d. Flat sheet:
   1. Place the lower edge even with the bottom of the mattress.
   2. Place the larger hem at the top of the mattress and the small hem at the bottom.

Continued

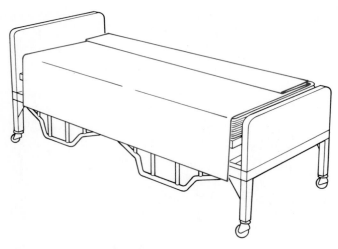

Fig. 12-16 Bottom sheet fan-folded to the other side of the bed. (From Sorrentino, S.A.: Mosby's textbook for nursing assistants, ed. 2, St. Louis, 1987, The C.V. Mosby Co.)

3. Face the hem stitching toward the mattress pad.

8. Pick the sheet up from the side to open it. Fan-fold it toward the other side of the bed as in Fig. 12-16.

9. Go to the head of the bed. Tuck the top sheet under the mattress. You will have to lift the mattress slightly. Make sure the sheet is tight and smooth.

10. Make a mitered corner at the head of the bed:
    a. Raise the side of the sheet onto the mattress (Fig. 12-17, A). The top edge should be tucked in and smooth and tight as in step 9.
    b. Tuck the remaining part under the mattress (Fig. 12-17, B).
    c. Bring the raised part down off the bed (Fig. 12-17, C).
    d. Tuck the entire side of the sheet under the mattress (Fig. 12-17, D).

11. Place the plastic drawsheet on the bed. It should be about 14 inches from the top of the mattress.

12. Open the plastic drawsheet. Fan-fold it toward the other side of the bed.

13. Place a cotton drawsheet over the plastic drawsheet. The cotton drawsheet must cover the entire plastic drawsheet (Fig. 12-18).

14. Open the cotton drawsheet. Fan-fold it toward the other side of the bed.

15. Tuck the plastic and cotton drawsheets un-der the mattress. Tuck each in separately if it is easier for you.

16. Go to the other side of the bed.

17. Miter the top corner of the bottom flat sheet. Or pull corners of the fitted sheet over the mattress.

18. Pull the bottom sheet tight so there are no wrinkles. Tuck in the sheet.

19. Pull the plastic and cotton drawsheets tight so there are no wrinkles. Tuck them in together or pull each tight and tuck in separately (Fig. 12-19).

20. Go to the side of the bed that you started on.

21. Put the top sheet on the bed:
    a. Unfold it lengthwise.
    b. Place the center fold in the middle of the bed.
    c. Place the large hem at the top and even with the top of the mattress.
    d. Open the sheet. Fan-fold the extra part toward the other side of the bed.
    e. Face the hem stitching toward the outside.
    f. Do not tuck the bottom of the top sheet in yet.
    g. Never tuck top linens in on the sides.

22. Place the blanket on the bed:
    a. Unfold it so that the center fold is in the middle.
    b. Put the upper hem about 6 to 8 inches from the top of the mattress.
    c. Open the blanket. Fan-fold the extra part toward the other side of the bed.
    d. Tuck in the bottom sheet and blanket at the foot of the bed. (Do this step if the bedspread is not to be tucked in.) They should be smooth and tight. Make a mitered corner.

23. Place the bedspread on the bed:
    a. Unfold it so that the center fold is in the middle.
    b. Place the upper hem even with the top of the mattress.
    c. Open the bedspread and fan-fold the extra part toward the other side of the bed.
    d. Make sure the bedspread is even and covers all top linens.
    e. Tuck in the top sheet, blanket, and bedspread together at the foot of the bed (if the bedspread is the type to be tucked in). They should be smooth and tight. Make a mitered corner.

Continued

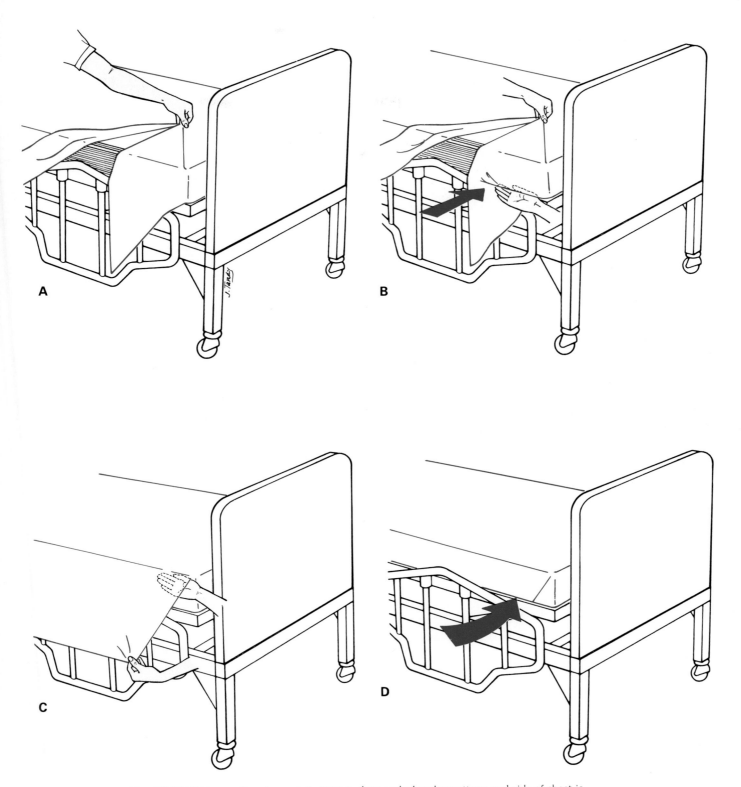

Fig. 12-17 Making a mitered corner. **A,** Bottom sheet tucked under mattress and side of sheet is raised onto mattress. **B,** Remaining portion of sheet is tucked under mattress. **C,** Raised portion of sheet is brought off the mattress. **D,** Entire side of sheet is tucked under mattress. (From Sorrentino, S.A.: Mosby's textbook for nursing assistants, ed. 2, St. Louis, 1987, The C.V. Mosby Co.)

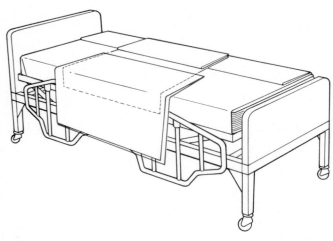

Fig. 12-18 Cotton drawsheet placed over plastic drawsheet. Plastic drawsheet is completely covered by cotton drawsheet. (From Sorrentino, S.A.: Mosby's textbook for nursing assistants, ed. 2, St. Louis, 1987, The C.V. Mosby Co.)

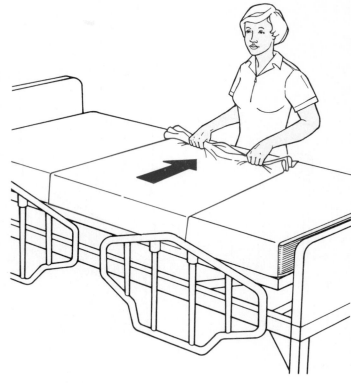

Fig. 12-19 Drawsheet pulled tight to remove wrinkles. (From Sorrentino, S.A.: Mosby's textbook for nursing assistants, ed. 2, St. Louis, 1987, The C.V. Mosby Co.)

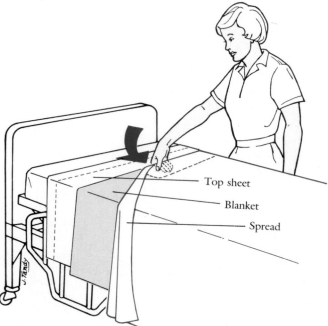

Top sheet

Blanket

Spread

Fig. 12-20 Top hem of the bedspread is turned under the top hem of the blanket to make a cuff. (From Sorrentino, S.A.: Mosby's textbook for nursing assistants, ed. 2, St. Louis, 1987, The C.V. Mosby Co.)

24. Go to the other side of the bed.
25. Straighten all top linen. Work from the head of the bed to the foot.
26. Tuck in the top sheet and blanket (and bedspread) together. Make a mitered corner.
27. Turn the top hem of the bedspread under the top hem of the blanket. This makes a cuff (Fig. 12-20).
28. Turn the top sheet down over the bedspread. Hem stitching should be down.
29. Place the pillow on the bed.
30. Open the pillowcase so that it lies flat on the bed.
31. Put the pillowcase on the pillow as follows:
    a. Grasp the corners of the pillow with one hand at the seam and tag end of the pillow.
    b. Make a V-shaped end with the corners (Fig. 12-21, A).
    c. Open the pillowcase with the other hand (Fig. 12-21, B).
    d. Using the "V" end of the pillow, guide

Continued

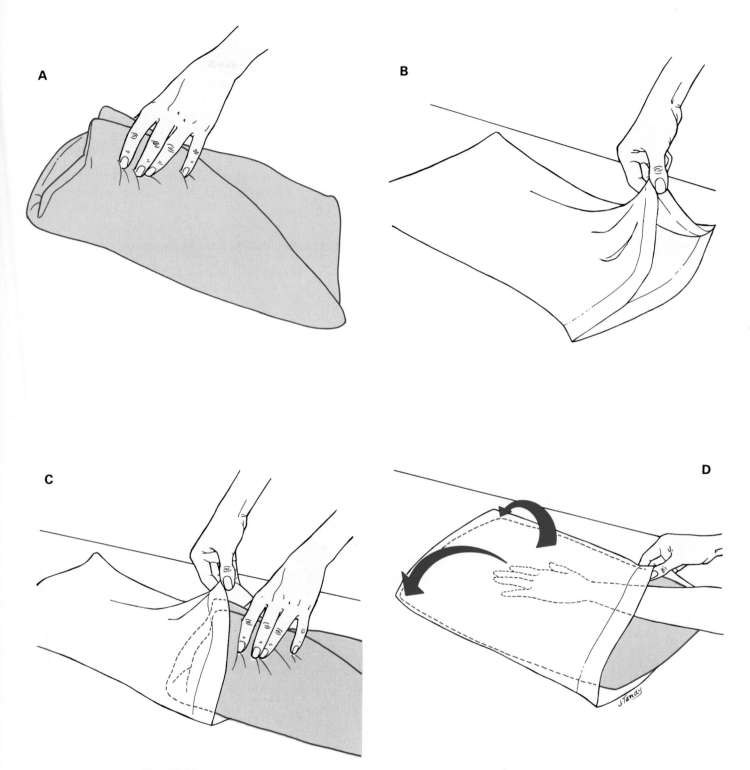

Fig. 12-21 Putting a pillowcase on the pillow. **A,** Grasp the corners of the pillow at the seam end and form a "V" with the pillow. **B,** Pillowcase flat on the bed with aide opening the pillowcase with the free hand. **C,** "V" end of the pillow is guided into the pillowcase. **D,** "V" end of the pillow falls into the corners of the pillowcase. (From Sorrentino, S.A.: Mosby's textbook for nursing assistants, ed. 2, St. Louis, 1987, The C.V. Mosby Co.)

the pillow into the pillowcase until the corners are reached (Fig. 12-21, C).
   e. Let the corners of the pillow fall into the corners of the pillowcase (Fig. 12-21, D).
   f. Fold any extra pillowcase material under the pillow at the seam end of the pillowcase.
32. Place the pillow on the bed. The open end is away from the door and the seam is toward the head of the bed.
33. Lower the bed.
34. Wash your hands.

Procedure: Making an open bed

1. Wash your hands.
2. Collect the equipment as for a closed bed.
3. Make a closed bed.
4. Fan-fold top linens to the foot of the bed (Fig. 12-22).
5. Lower the bed.
6. Wash your hands.

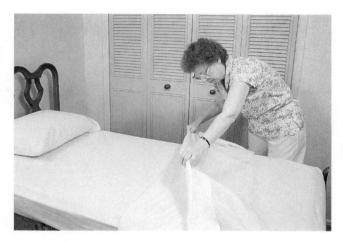

Fig. 12-22 Top linens of closed bed fan-folded to the foot of the bed to make an open bed.

The Occupied Bed

An occupied bed is made when a client cannot get out of bed. The client must be kept in good body alignment during the procedure. You should know about any restrictions in the way you move or position the client. Be sure to explain each step of the procedure to the client before it is done.

The client will have to be on one side of the bed while you make the other side. There are several ways to get the client to the other side of the bed. The way you choose will depend on the client's condition and ability to move.
1. Ask the client to roll to the other side of the bed. Help as necessary.
2. Move the client to the side of the bed (see *Moving the client to the side of the bed* on page 138).
3. Pull the client to the side of the bed with the draw-sheet.
4. Ask the client to pull himself or herself to the side of the bed using the side rail. Help the client as needed.

Procedure: Making an occupied bed

1. Explain to the client what you are going to do.
2. Wash your hands.
3. Collect clean linen:
   a. Mattress pad (if needed)
   b. Bottom sheet (flat sheet or fitted sheet)
   c. Plastic drawsheet
   d. Cotton drawsheet
   e. Top sheet (flat sheet)
   f. Blanket and bedspread (if needed)
   g. Pillowcase(s)
   h. Bath blanket
4. Place the linen on the bedside chair.
5. Offer the client the bedpan or urinal before beginning.
6. Raise the bed to a good working height for you. Use good body mechanics.
7. Lower the head of the bed to a level appropriate for the client. The bed should be as flat as possible.
8. Lower the side rail on your side. The opposite side rail should be up.
9. Loosen top linens at the foot of the bed.
10. Remove the bedspread and blanket separately. Fold each if they are to be reused:
   a. Fold the top edge of the linen to the bottom edge (Fig. 12-23, A).
   b. Fold the far side to the near side (Fig. 12-23, B).
   c. Fold the top edge to the bottom edge again (Fig. 12-23, C).
   d. Place the item over the back of a chair (Fig. 12-23, D).
11. Cover the client with a bath blanket. This

Continued

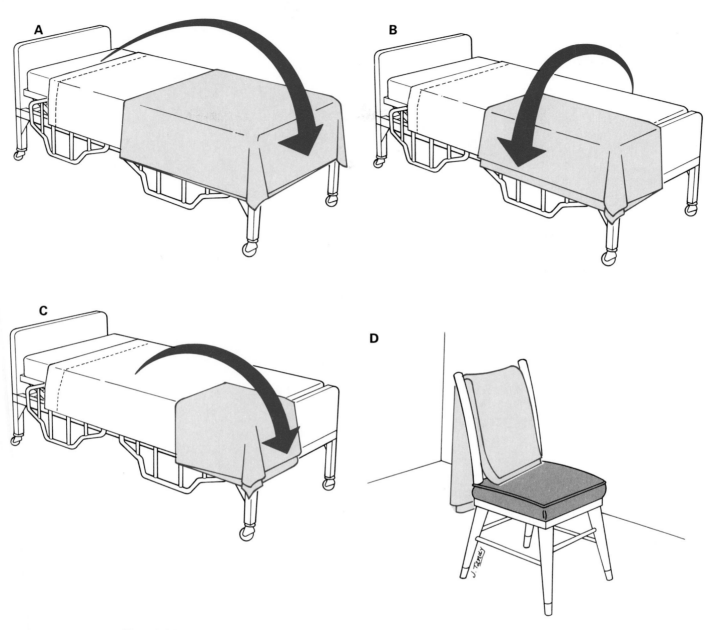

Fig. 12-23 Folding linen for reuse. **A,** Top edge of blanket folded down to the bottom edge. **B,** Blanket folded on the far side of the bed to near side. **C,** Top edge of blanket folded down to bottom edge again. **D,** Folded blanket placed over back of straight chair. (From Sorrentino, S.A.: Mosby's textbook for nursing assistants, ed. 2, St. Louis, 1987, The C.V. Mosby Co.)

provides warmth and privacy. You can use the top sheet or a regular blanket if you do not have a bath blanket.

a. Unfold a bath blanket over the top sheet.

b. Ask the client to hold onto the bath blanket. If he or she cannot help, tuck the top of the bath blanket under the shoulders.

c. Grasp the top sheet under the bath blanket at the client's shoulders. Bring the sheet down to the foot of the bed. Remove the sheet from under the blanket (Fig. 12-24).

12. Move the mattress to the head of the bed.

13. Position the client on the side of the bed away from you. Adjust the pillow so it is

Continued

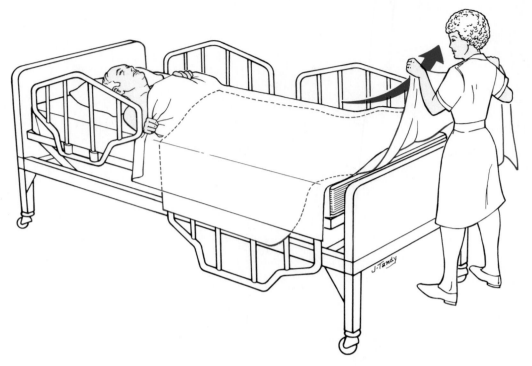

Fig. 12-24 Client holding onto bath blanket. Aide at foot of the bed removing the top sheet from under the bath blanket. (From Sorrentino, S.A.: Mosby's textbook for nursing assistants, ed. 2, St. Louis, 1987, The C.V. Mosby Co.)

comfortable for the client. It should be on the far side of the bed.

14. Loosen bottom linens from the head to the foot of the bed.

15. Fan-fold bottom linens one at a time toward the client. The cotton drawsheet is first and then the plastic drawsheet, bottom sheet, and mattress pad (Fig. 12-25). Do not fan-fold the mattress pad if it will be reused.

16. Place a clean mattress pad on the bed. Unfold it lengthwise so the center is in the middle of the bed. Fan-fold the top part toward the client. If the mattress pad is to be reused, straighten and smooth any wrinkles.

17. Place the bottom sheet on the mattress pad. Hem stitching is away from the client. Unfold the sheet so the center is in the middle of the bed. The smaller hem of a flat sheet should be even with the bottom of the mattress. Fan-fold the top part toward the client.

18. Make a mitered corner at the head of the bed (if a flat sheet is used). Tuck the sheet under the mattress from the head to the foot of the bed.

19. Pull the fan-folded plastic drawsheet toward you over the bottom sheet. Tuck the excess drawsheet under the mattress. Do the following if a clean plastic drawsheet is to be used (Fig. 12-26):
    a. Place the plastic drawsheet on the bed about 14 inches from the top of the mattress.
    b. Fan-fold the top part toward the client.
    c. Tuck in the excess drawsheet under the mattress.

20. Place the cotton drawsheet over the plastic drawsheet. Make sure it covers the entire plastic drawsheet. Fan-fold the top part toward the client. Tuck the excess drawsheet under the mattress.

21. Raise the side rail on the side you are working on.

22. Go to the other side of the bed and lower the side rail.

23. Position the client on the side of the bed away from you. Adjust the pillow for the client's comfort.

24. Loosen bottom linens. Remove each piece of used linen.

25. Straighten and smooth the mattress pad.

continued

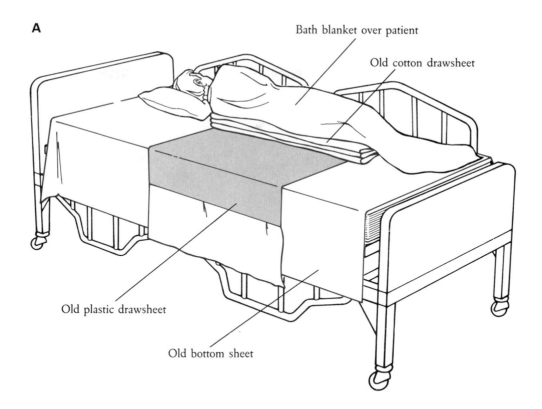

A

Bath blanket over patient

Old cotton drawsheet

Old plastic drawsheet

Old bottom sheet

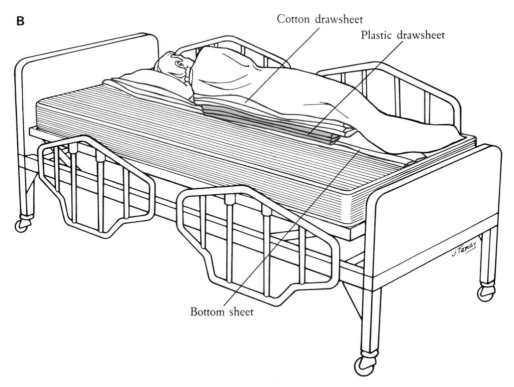

B

Cotton drawsheet

Plastic drawsheet

Bottom sheet

Fig. 12-25 Occupied bed. **A,** Cotton drawsheet fan-folded and tucked under client. **B,** All bottom linens tucked under client. (From Sorrentino, S.A.: Mosby's textbook for nursing assistants, ed. 2, St. Louis, 1987, The C.V. Mosby Co.)

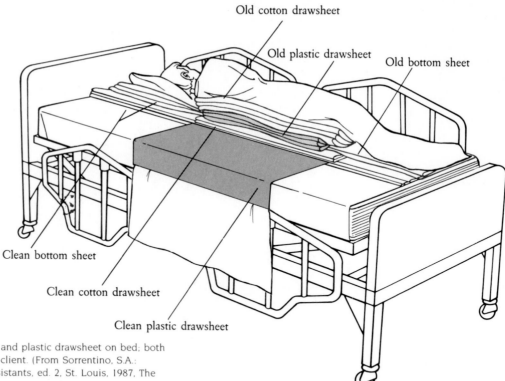

Old cotton drawsheet

Old plastic drawsheet

Old bottom sheet

Clean bottom sheet

Clean cotton drawsheet

Clean plastic drawsheet

Fig. 12-26 Clean bottom sheet and plastic drawsheet on bed; both are fan-folded and tucked under client. (From Sorrentino, S.A.: Mosby's textbook for nursing assistants, ed. 2, St. Louis, 1987, The C.V. Mosby Co.)

26. Pull the clean bottom sheet toward you. Make a mitered corner at the head of the bed. Tuck the sheet under the mattress from the head to the foot of the bed.
27. Pull the plastic and cotton drawsheets tightly toward you. Tuck both under the mattress together or tuck each in separately.
28. Position the client in the supine position in the center of the bed. Adjust the pillow for the client's comfort.
29. Put the top sheet on the bed. Unfold it lengthwise. Make sure the center is in the middle of the bed. The large hem should be even with the top of the mattress. The hem stitching should be on the outside.
30. Ask the client to hold the top sheet so you can remove the bath blanket. Tuck the sheet under the shoulders if the client cannot help you. Remove the bath blanket.
31. Place the blanket on the bed. Unfold it so that the fold is in the middle of the bed. Unfold the blanket so it covers the client. The upper hem should be 6 to 8 inches from the top of the mattress.
32. Place the bedspread on the bed. The center should be in the middle of the bed. Unfold

it so it covers the client. Be sure the top hem is even with edge of the mattress.
33. Turn the top hem of the bedspread under the top hem of the blanket to make a cuff.
34. Bring the top sheet down over the bedspread to form a cuff.
35. Go to the foot of the bed.
36. Lift the mattress corner with one arm. Tuck the top sheet, blanket, and bedspread under the mattress together. Be sure the linens are loose enough to allow movement of the client's feet. Make a mitered corner.
37. Raise the side rail. Go to the other side of the bed.
38. Lower the side rail.
39. Straighten and smooth top linens.
40. Tuck the top linens under the mattress as in step 36. Make a mitered corner.
41. Change the pillowcase(s).
42. Raise the side rail.
43. Raise the head of the bed to a level appropriate for the client. Make sure the client is comfortable.
44. Lower the bed.
45. Remove dirty linens from the room.
46. Wash your hands.

Summary

You have learned how to make different kinds of hospital beds. You have also learned the principles involved in bedmaking and in the handling of linens. The client's condition or equipment may require changes in these procedures. However, the principles must be followed. The client's comfort and safety must be the focus of bedmaking. Remember that the client spends a lot of time in bed. Therefore, it is important for the bed to be neat, clean, and free of wrinkles. A well-made bed will make your client more comfortable.

Be sure to handle linens properly so that you do not spread microorganisms. You also need to follow the rules of medical asepsis, bedmaking, and good body mechanics. They help you to make a bed safely and easily.

Study Questions

Circle T if the statement is true and F if it is false.

T F 1. Linens must be changed whenever they become soiled, wet, or damp.

T F 2. A hospital bed should be kept in the low position except when giving care.

T F 3. A client has a manual hospital bed. The cranks should be kept in the up position.

T F 4. A client has a water bed. You need to keep sharp items away from the mattress.

T F 5. All mattresses are coated with plastic.

T F 6. A mattress should be turned so it wears evenly.

T F 7. Linens are held away from your body and uniform.

T F 8. Dirty linens can be put on the floor to avoid contact with clean linen.

T F 9. A cotton drawsheet is always used when a plastic drawsheet is used.

T F 10. To remove crumbs from the bed, the linens are loosened and shaken in the air.

T F 11. The hem stitching of the bottom sheet should be downward, away from the client.

T F 12. The plastic drawsheet is placed on the bed so that it is 6 to 8 inches from the top of the mattress.

T F 13. Cotton drawsheets must completely cover plastic drawsheets.

T F 14. The upper hem of the bedspread should be even with the top of the mattress.

T F 15. A closed bed can be made into an open bed by fan-folding the top linens to the foot of the bed.

T F 16. When making an occupied bed, the side rail opposite you should be up at all times.

T F 17. A cotton drawsheet is never used unless a plastic drawsheet is used.

T F 18. A client's sheet is torn. You should use a safety pin to close the tear.

Answers

1. True	6. True	11. True	15. True
2. True	7. True	12. False	16. True
3. False	8. False	13. True	17. False
4. True	9. True	14. True	18. False
5. False	10. False		

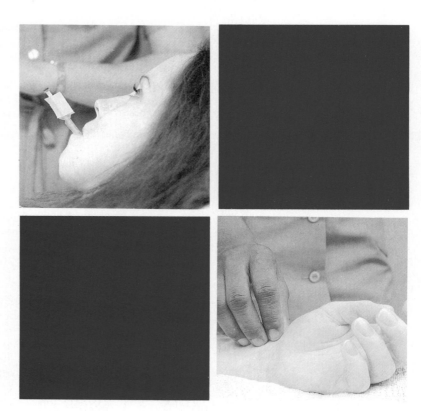

13

Vital Signs

Chapter Highlights	What you will learn to do
Measuring and reporting vital signs	■ Explain why vital signs are measured
Temperature	■ Identify the factors that affect vital signs
Pulse	■ Identify when vital signs should be measured
Respiration	■ Describe the equipment used to measure vital signs
Blood pressure	■ Know the normal ranges for vital signs in adults and children
Vital signs in children	■ Identify the sites for taking a pulse
	■ Describe normal and abnormal respiratory patterns
	■ Explain the guidelines for measuring blood pressure
	■ Report and record vital signs in adults and children
	■ Perform the procedures described in this chapter

Key Terms

Blood pressure The amount of force exerted against the walls of an artery by the blood

Diastolic pressure Pressure in the arteries when the heart is relaxing and filling with blood

Pulse The beat of the heart felt at an artery; the beat is produced as a wave of blood passes through the artery

Pulse deficit The difference between the apical pulse rate and the radial pulse rate

Respiration The breathing of air in and out of the lungs

Sphygmomanometer Instrument used to measure blood pressure

Stethoscope Instrument used to listen to the heart and other body sounds

Systolic pressure Pressure in the arteries when the heart is contracting

Temperature The amount of heat in the body

Vital signs Temperature, pulse, respirations, and blood pressure

*V*ital *signs* are temperature, pulse, respirations (TPR), and blood pressure (BP). They are measurements of how well the body is functioning. The *temperature* (T) measures the amount of heat in the body. The *pulse* (P) is defined as the beat of the heart felt at an artery. The beat is produced as a wave of blood passes through the artery. A pulse can be felt every time the heart beats. *Respiration* (R) is breathing of air in and out of the lungs. B*lood pressure* is the amount of force exerted against the walls of an artery by the blood. Changes in vital signs can show if the client is getting better or worse.

Measuring and Reporting Vital Signs

Vital signs indicate changes in normal body function. They are also used to determine a client's response to treatment. Life-threatening conditions can be recognized from vital signs. Each vital sign has a normal range. Measurements outside the normal range must be reported. You also need to know what is normal for your client. What is normal for one client may be abnormal for another. For example, the normal adult pulse rate is 70 to 80 beats per minute. Mr. Jones usually has a pulse rate of 60 to 66 beats per minute. A pulse rate of 76 is considered normal. However, it is abnormal for Mr. Jones. Vital signs tell more when compared to the client's previous measurements. You must report vital signs that are different from a client's previous measurements.

When to Measure Vital Signs

Vital signs are measured when you visit the client to give personal care. Your supervisor will tell you how often to take a client's vital signs. This information is also on the client's care plan. Some clients have vital signs measured once or twice a day. Others have them taken four times a day. The frequency is related to the client's health. Clients who need minimal personal care will have vital signs measured less frequently. Sicker clients have vital signs measured more often. This is because their conditions can change rapidly.

A person's vital signs vary during a 24-hour period. Many factors affect vital signs. These include sleep, activity, eating, weather, noise, exercise, medications, fear, anxiety, and illness. Vital signs are usually lower in the morning when the client is less active. They are higher in the afternoon when the client is more active. Try to measure the client's vital signs at the same time each day. That way the vital signs are taken under similar conditions. The measurements will mean more when compared to previous vital signs.

When one vital sign changes, the others usually change. For example, a child has a fever (elevated temperature). The child's pulse will probably be faster. The child is likely to breathe more rapidly. One vital sign does not give enough information. All vital signs should be taken to give more information about body function.

Vital signs may be taken at times other than when instructed. These vital signs should be reported to your supervisor right away. Vital signs are taken when the client:

- Has fallen or been injured
- Complains of feeling ill
- Shows signs of illness such as pain, congestion, sore throat, vomiting, diarrhea, or skin rash
- Shows a change in behavior, the ability to move, or the ability to respond
- Has a sudden change in condition

Reporting and Recording

When vital signs are measured, they are recorded right away. Your agency has forms for recording vital signs. However, you may not have a form with you. You need to keep a note pad and pencil in your pocket to make notes. These notes are used to report to your supervisor and to chart in the client's record. You need to note the following:

- The client's name
- Date and time the vital signs were taken
- The vital signs
- A brief description about how the client looks and feels

Temperature, pulse, respirations, and blood pressure are often referred to as TPR/BP. This abbreviation is used to record vital signs. For example, a client's vital signs are:

- Temperature—98.6° F
- Pulse—84 beats per minute
- Respirations—16 per minute
- Blood pressure—120/70 mm Hg

The measurements are recorded as: TPR 98.6-84-16 BP 120/70.

You do not need to report vital signs every time they are taken. If they are within normal range, recording them in the client's record will do. However, changes in a client's vital signs must be reported. Vital signs are also reported when there is a change in the client's condition (see page 189). If you are not sure if vital signs should be reported, call your supervisor. Report anything that concerns you. It is better to report vital signs than not to report them.

Temperature

Temperature measures the amount of heat in the body. Body heat is constantly produced by the muscles. Heat is lost from the body through the skin and lungs. As you breathe and sweat, your body releases heat. With exercise, muscle movement increases body heat. You sweat more and breathe faster to rid the body of the extra heat. This is how the body maintains a balance between the heat produced and the heat lost. Therefore, body temperature remains fairly stable. Sometimes the body cannot maintain this balance.

Normal Temperature Ranges

The Fahrenheit (F) and Centigrade or Celsius (C) scales are used to measure temperature. The common sites for measuring body temperature are the mouth, rectum, and axilla (underarm). Normal body temperature is 98.6° F (37° C) when measured orally. Rectal temperatures are one Fahrenheit degree higher (99.6° F). Axillary temperatures are one Fahrenheit degree lower (97.6° F) than oral temperatures. Normal ranges of body temperature for adults are:

- Oral–97.6° to 99.6° F (36.5° to 37.5° C)
- Rectal–98.6° to 100.6° F (37.0° to 38.1° C)
- Axillary–96.6° to 98.6° F (36.0° to 37.0° C)

Body temperature tends to be lower in the morning and higher in the afternoon. Several factors affect body temperature. These include age, weather,

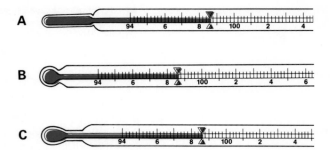

Fig. 13-1 Types of glass thermometers. **A,** The long or slender tip. **B,** The stubby tip (the rectal thermometer). **C,** The pear-shaped tip. (From Sorrentino, S.A.: Mosby's textbook for nursing assistants, ed. 2, St. Louis, 1987, The C.V. Mosby Co.)

exercise, pregnancy, the menstrual cycle, emotions, and illness.

Types of Thermometers

Body temperature is measured with a thermometer. There are glass, disposable, and electronic thermometers.

GLASS THERMOMETERS

The glass thermometer (clinical thermometer) is commonly used in the home. It is a hollow glass tube with a bulb at one end. The bulb is filled with mercury. When the bulb touches a warm surface, the mercury rises in the tube. The temperature reading is the point where the mercury stops.

There are three types of glass thermometers. Each has a different bulb or tip (Fig. 13-1). *Long or slender* tip thermometers are used for oral and axillary temperatures. They are not used for rectal temperatures. The long tip could injure rectal tissue. *Stubby* and *pear-shaped* tip thermometers have round, stubby bulbs. They can be used for oral, axillary, and rectal temperatures. The round bulb is safer for insertion into the rectum. Once a thermometer has been used rectally, it should never be used for oral or axillary temperatures. To avoid confusion, manufacturers often color-code the top of rectal thermometers in red.

Glass thermometers are available in Fahrenheit and Centigrade scales. Some have both scales. Fahrenheit thermometers are marked with long and short lines. Every other long line is an even degree from 94° to 108° F. The short lines indicate 0.2 (two-tenths) of a degree (Fig. 13-2, A). Centigrade thermometers are marked with long and short lines. Each long line represents one degree from 34° to 42° C. Each short line represents 0.1 (one-tenth) of a degree (Fig. 13-2, B).

You may have to convert a temperature in Fahrenheit degrees into Centigrade degrees or vice versa. The following formulas are used for conversions:
To convert from Fahrenheit to Centigrade

- Subtract 32 from the Fahrenheit reading

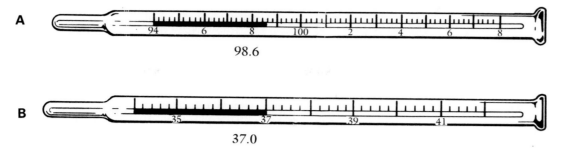

A

98.6

B

37.0

Fig. 13-2 A. Fahrenheit thermometer. The mercury level is at 98.6° F. B. Centigrade thermometer. The mercury level is at 37.0° C. (From Sorrentino, S.A.: Mosby's textbook for nursing assistants, ed. 2, St. Louis, 1987, The C.V. Mosby Co.)

- Multiply the answer by 5
- Divide the answer by 9

To convert from Centigrade to Fahrenheit

- Multiply the Centigrade reading by 9
- Divide the answer by 5
- Add 32

Procedure: Reading a glass thermometer

---

1. Make sure you have good lighting.
2. Make sure your hands are dry so you can hold the thermometer firmly.
3. Hold the thermometer at the stem with your thumb and fingertips (Fig. 13-3).
4. Bring the thermometer to eye level (Fig. 13-4).
5. Rotate the thermometer until you can see the mercury column and the markings clearly.
6. Read the number at the end of the mercury column. Read the thermometer to the nearest degree (long line) and the nearest tenth of a degree (short line). Tenths of a degree are always even numbers on a Fahrenheit thermometer.
7. Record the client's name and the date, time, and temperature.

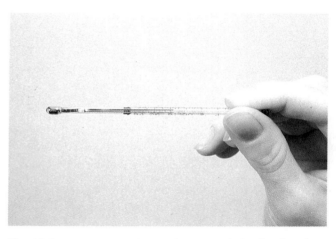

Fig. 13-3 Thermometer is held at the stem with the thumb and fingertips. (From Sorrentino, S.A.: Mosby's textbook for nursing assistants, ed. 2, St. Louis, 1987, The C.V. Mosby Co.)

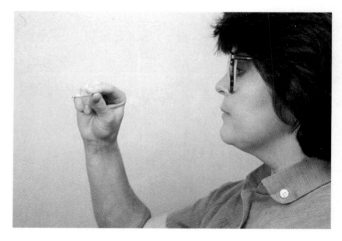

Fig. 13-4 Thermometer is read at eye level. (From Sorrentino, S.A.: Mosby's textbook for nursing assistants, ed. 2, St. Louis, 1987, The C.V. Mosby Co.)

Glass thermometers need special care. Most come with a plastic case for storage (Fig. 13-5). Remember that microorganisms grow best in a warm, moist, dark environment. The plastic case provides such an environment. A glass thermometer is inserted into the mouth, rectum, or axilla. Each area has many microorganisms. Therefore, the thermometer should be

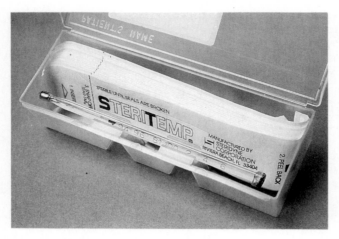

Fig. 13-5 Glass thermometer with storage case.

cleaned before and after use. This prevents the spread of microorganisms. Cleaning the thermometer before use is important. Someone else may have used the thermometer and forgot to clean it.

Methods for cleaning thermometers vary among agencies. The thermometer is usually first wiped with a tissue or cotton ball to remove mucus or fecal material. You need to wipe down from the stem to the bulb. Then it is washed in cold soapy water. Hot water is not used. Hot water causes the mercury to expand so much that the thermometer could break. After cleaning, the thermometer is rinsed under cold running water. Then it is stored in its case. Before being used, the thermometer is washed again in cold soapy water and then rinsed.

Before taking a temperature, shake the thermometer down. This moves the mercury into the bulb. Also check the thermometer for cracks, breaks, or chips which could injure the client.

Procedure: How to use a glass thermometer

1. Collect the following equipment:
   a. Thermometer
   b. Tissues or cotton balls
2. Wash your hands.
3. Apply soap to a tissue or cotton ball.
4. Hold the thermometer at the stem with your thumb and fingertips.
5. Wipe down the thermometer from the bulb to the stem. Use a tissue or cotton ball.
6. Rinse the thermometer under cold, running water.

7. Dry the thermometer with a cotton ball or tissue.
8. Shake down the thermometer. The mercury must be below the lines and numbers.
   a. Hold the thermometer securely at the stem.
   b. Stand away from walls, tables, or other hard surfaces to avoid breaking the thermometer.
   c. Flex and snap your wrist until the mercury is shaken down (Fig. 13-6).
9. Take the client's temperature.
10. Shake down the thermometer again after it has been used.
11. Clean and dry the thermometer as in steps 3 through 7.
12. Store the thermometer in its case.

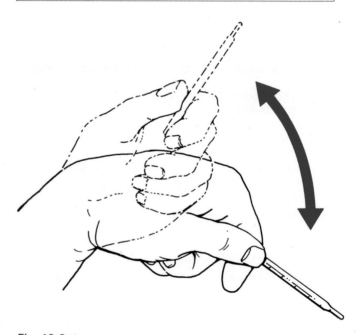

Fig. 13-6 The wrist is snapped to shake down the thermometer. (From Sorrentino, S.A.: Mosby's textbook for nursing assistants, ed. 2, St. Louis, 1987, The C.V. Mosby Co.)

DISPOSABLE THERMOMETERS

Disposable oral thermometers have small chemical dots (Fig. 13-7). The dots change color when heated by the body. The change takes about 45 seconds. The thermometer is used once and discarded.

Temperature-sensitive tape changes color in response to body heat. The color change takes about 15 seconds. It indicates the body's temperature range. A specific temperature reading is not obtained. Like disposable thermometers, temperature-sensitive tape is used only once.

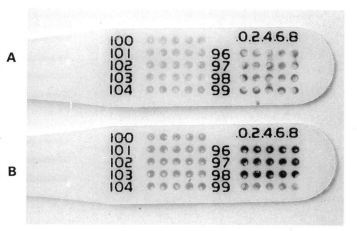

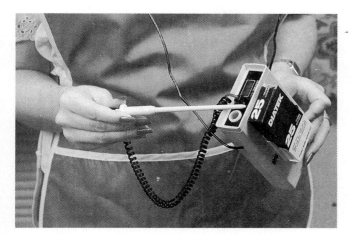

Fig. 13-7 A, Disposable oral thermometer with chemical dots. **B,** The dots change color after the temperature has been taken. (From Sorrentino, S.A.: Mosby's textbook for nursing assistants, ed. 2, St. Louis, 1987, The C.V. Mosby Co.)

Fig. 13-8 An electronic thermometer. (From Sorrentino, S.A.: Mosby's textbook for nursing assistants, ed. 2, St. Louis, 1987, The C.V. Mosby Co.)

ELECTRONIC THERMOMETERS

Electronic thermometers operate on batteries. The temperature is displayed on the front of the thermometer (Fig. 13-8). Electronic thermometers measure body temperature in 2 to 60 seconds.

These thermometers have oral and rectal probes. Disposable probe covers are used to cover the probe. A probe cover is used when the thermometer is placed in the mouth, rectum, or axilla. Probe covers are used only once and then discarded.

Electronic thermometers are expensive. They are accurate, fast, and reduce the spread of infection. They are common in hospitals but not in homes. How-

ever, clients who need their temperatures taken often may wish to buy them.

Measuring Oral Temperatures

Most temperatures are taken orally. This method is the easiest and is preferred by clients. Inaccurate measures are caused by smoking, drinking and eating hot or cold foods or fluids, and by chewing gum. If the client has engaged in any of these activities, wait 15 minutes before taking an oral temperature. Oral temperatures are not taken if the client:

- Is an infant or a child under 4 or 5 years of age
- Is unconscious
- Has had surgery or an injury to the face, neck, nose, or mouth
- Is receiving oxygen
- Breathes through the mouth instead of the nose
- Has a nasogastric tube
- Is delirious, restless, confused, or disoriented
- Is paralyzed on one side of the body because of a stroke
- Has a sore mouth

Procedure: Measuring an oral temperature

1. Explain to the client what you are going to do. Ask him or her not to eat, drink, smoke, or chew gum for 15 minutes.
2. Collect equipment:
   a. Thermometer
   b. Tissue or cotton balls
3. Wash your hands.
4. Wash the thermometer (see *How to use a glass thermometer*, page 192). Check it for cracks, chips, and breaks.
5. Ask the client to sit or lie down.
6. Shake down the thermometer.
7. Place the bulb end of the thermometer under the client's tongue (Fig. 13-9).
8. Ask the client to keep his or her lips around the thermometer. Ask the client not to bite down on the thermometer or to talk. Remind the client to breathe through his or her nose.
9. Leave the thermometer in place for 8 to 9 minutes.
10. Remove the thermometer. Wipe it with tissue or a cotton ball from the stem to the bulb.
11. Read the thermometer.

Continued

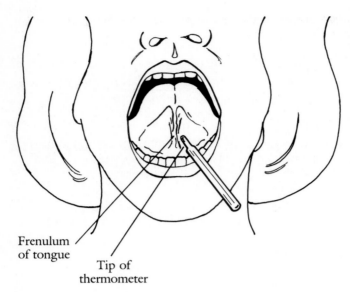

Frenulum
of tongue

Tip of
thermometer

Fig. 13-9 The thermometer is positioned at the base of the tongue next to the frenulum. (From Sorrentino, S.A.: Mosby's textbook for nursing assistants, ed. 2, St. Louis, 1987, The C.V. Mosby Co.)

12. Record the temperature and client observations.
13. Shake down the thermometer.
14. Clean the thermometer and place it in its case.
15. Wash your hands.
16. Report any abnormal temperature to your supervisor.

Measuring Rectal Temperatures

Rectal temperatures are the most accurate. This route is not often used because clients find it embarrassing. Rectal temperatures are taken when oral temperatures cannot be taken (see page 193). There are times when rectal temperatures should not be taken. These include when the client has:

- Diarrhea
- A rectal disorder such as hemorrhoids
- A rectal injury
- Had rectal surgery
- Heart disease

Always use a rectal thermometer for this procedure. The thermometer is lubricated for easier insertion and to prevent tissue injury. A glass thermometer is held in place for 3 to 4 minutes. Holding the thermometer prevents it from being lost in the rectum or broken.

Procedure: Measuring a rectal temperature

1. Explain to the client what you are going to do.
2. Collect equipment:
   a. Rectal thermometer
   b. Tissues or cotton balls
   c. Lubricant
   d. Disposable gloves
   e. Toilet tissue
3. Wash your hands.
4. Clean the thermometer (see *How to use a glass thermometer*, page 192). Check it for cracks, chips, and breaks.
5. Provide for privacy. Ask visitors to leave the room. Close the door.
6. Shake down the thermometer.
7. Position the client in Sims' position.
8. Put on the disposable gloves.
9. Put a small amount of lubricant on a tissue. Lubricate the bulb end of the thermometer.
10. Fold back top linens to expose the anal area. Raise the upper buttock to expose the anus (Fig. 13-10).
11. Insert the bulb end of the thermometer 1 inch into the rectum.
12. Hold the thermometer in place for 3 to 4 minutes (Fig. 13-11).
13. Remove the thermometer.
14. Wipe the thermometer with toilet tissue from the stem to the bulb. Place the thermometer on clean tissue.
15. Place used tissue on several thicknesses of toilet tissue.
16. Wipe the anal area to remove any lubricant or feces. Cover the client.
17. Discard toilet tissue in the toilet.
18. Remove the gloves. Make sure you do not touch the part of the thermometer that was in the client's rectum.
19. Read the thermometer.
20. Record the temperature with an "R" to show a rectal temperature.
21. Clean thermometer and store it in its case.
22. Take the gloves and other used items to the garbage.
23. Wash your hands.
24. Report an abnormal temperature to your supervisor.

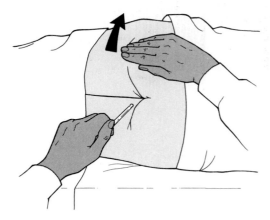

Fig. 13-10 The rectal temperature is taken with the client in Sims' position. The buttock is raised to expose the anus. (From Sorrentino, S.A.: Mosby's textbook for nursing assistants, ed. 2, St. Louis, 1987, The C.V. Mosby Co.)

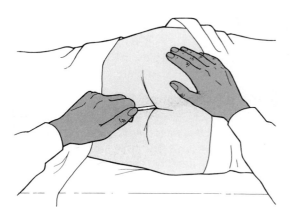

Fig. 13-11 The rectal thermometer is held in place during the measurement. (From Sorrentino, S.A.: Mosby's textbook for nursing assistants, ed. 2, St. Louis, 1987, The C.V. Mosby Co.)

Measuring Axillary Temperatures

Axillary temperatures are taken when oral and rectal methods cannot be used. The axillary method is useful for infants with diarrhea and young, active children. This method is not as accurate as rectal or oral temperatures. The axilla should be dry when the temperature is taken. This site should not be used right after it has been bathed or if the client is sweating. The thermometer must be held in place to keep it in proper position. The client should sit or lie for the procedure. Do not let the client walk around with the thermometer under the arm. A measurement takes 10 to 11 minutes.

Procedure: Measuring an axillary temperature

1. Explain to the client what you are going to do.
2. Collect equipment:
   a. Thermometer
   b. Tissues or cotton balls
   c. Dry washcloth or towel
3. Wash your hands.
4. Clean the thermometer (see *How to use a glass thermometer*, page 192). Check it for cracks, chips, or breaks.
5. Provide for the client's privacy.
6. Expose the client's axilla. You may need to remove the arm from a sleeve.
7. Dry the axilla with the towel or washcloth.
8. Shake down the thermometer.
9. Place the bulb end of the thermometer in the center of the axilla.
10. Ask the client to place or assist the client in placing the arm over the chest. This holds the thermometer in place (Fig. 13-12). Hold the thermometer and arm in place if the client is an infant or child or cannot help (Fig. 13-13).
11. Leave the thermometer in place for 10 to 11 minutes.
12. Remove the thermometer. Wipe it from the stem to the bulb with tissues.
13. Read the thermometer.
14. Record the temperature with an "A" to show an axillary temperature.
15. Help the client put the arm back in the sleeve.
16. Make sure the client is comfortable. Place the call bell within reach.
17. Clean the thermometer and store it in the case.
18. Place the towel or washcloth in the laundry. Discard the tissue.
19. Wash your hands.
20. Report an abnormal temperature to your supervisor.

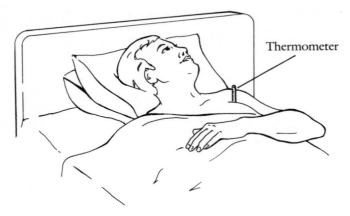

Fig. 13-12 The thermometer is held in place in the axilla by bringing the client's arm over the chest. (From Sorrentino, S.A.: Mosby's textbook for nursing assistants, ed. 2, St. Louis, 1987, The C.V. Mosby Co.)

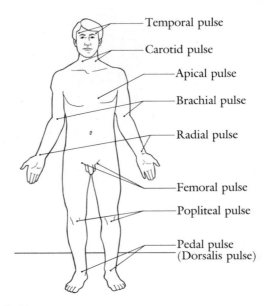

Fig. 13-14 The pulse sites. (From Sorrentino, S.A.: Mosby's textbook for nursing assistants, ed. 2, St. Louis, 1987, The C.V. Mosby Co.)

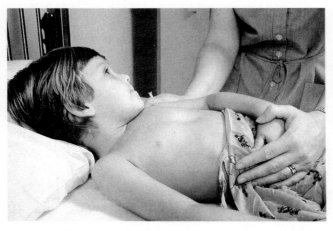

Fig. 13-13 Axillary temperature taken on a child. The nursing assistant holds the thermometer and the child's arm in place. (From Sorrentino, S.A.: Mosby's textbook for nursing assistants, ed. 2, St. Louis, 1987, The C.V. Mosby Co.)

Pulse

When the heart contracts, it pumps blood through the arteries. Each time a wave of blood passes through an artery, a beat can be felt. This beat represents the heartbeat. The pulse is a sign of heart function.

Pulse Sites

There are a number of sites where the pulse can be taken (Fig. 13-14). These are called pulse sites or pulse points. They are located where arteries lie close to the skin and over a bone. The temporal, carotid, brachial, radial, femoral, popliteal, and dorsalis pedis (pedal) arteries are found on both sides of the body. The apical pulse is felt over the apex of the heart. A stethoscope is needed to take an apical pulse. The

radial site is used the most often. It can be taken without disturbing or exposing the client.

Pulse Rate, Rhythm, and Force

The *pulse rate* is the number of heartbeats or pulses felt in one minute. Health, exercise, food, drink, weather, emotions, position, pain, and body temperature are some of the factors that affect heart rate. Some medications cause a faster heart rate. Other drugs slow down the pulse.

The normal pulse rate for adults is 60 to 100 beats per minute. A rate less than 60 or greater than 100 is abnormal. An abnormal rate must be reported to your supervisor immediately. You must also compare the client's previous pulse rates. If the rate is different from previous ones, you need to call your supervisor. For example, Mr. Baker's pulse rate has been between 68 and 72. Now his pulse is 94. A pulse rate of 94 is within the normal range but is not normal for Mr. Baker.

The *rhythm* of the pulse should be regular. That is, a pulse should be felt in a pattern. The same time interval should occur between beats (Fig. 13-15, A). An irregular pulse is when the beats are unevenly spaced or beats are skipped (Fig. 13-15, B).

The *force* of the pulse relates to its strength. A forceful pulse is easy to feel and is described as strong, full, or bounding. Pulses that are hard to feel are often described as weak, thready, or feeble.

Taking a Radial Pulse

The radial pulse is usually used. The first three fingers of one hand are placed against the radial artery.

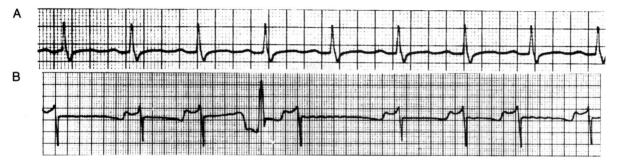

Fig. 13-15 A, The electrocardiogram shows a regular pulse. Each tall wave occurs at a regular interval. **B,** The tall waves in this electrocardiogram occur at irregular intervals. (From Andreoli, K.G., et al.: Comprehensive cardiac care, ed. 5, St. Louis, 1983, The C.V. Mosby Co.)

The radial artery is located on the thumb side of the wrist (Fig. 13-16). Do not use your thumb when taking a pulse; the thumb has a pulse of its own. The pulse in your thumb could be mistaken for the client's pulse. The pulse is counted for 30 seconds. The number is multiplied by 2 for the number of beats per minute. If the pulse is irregular, it must be counted for 1 full minute.

c. The pulse rate
d. The strength of the pulse (strong, full, or bounding; or weak, thready, or feeble)

Procedure: Taking a radial pulse

1. Explain to the client what you are going to do. Ask the client to rest for 5 to 10 minutes if he or she has been active.
2. Collect equipment:
   a. Watch with second hand
   b. Paper and pen
3. Wash your hands.
4. Have the client sit or lie down.
5. Locate the radial pulse with your middle three fingers (see Fig. 13-16). Do not use your thumb.
6. Note if the pulse is strong or weak, and regular or irregular.
7. Count the pulse for 30 seconds. Multiply the number of beats by 2.
8. Count the pulse for 1 full minute if it is irregular.
9. Record the pulse on paper. Note the strength of the pulse and if it was regular or irregular.
10. Wash your hands.
11. Report the following to your supervisor:
    a. A pulse rate less than 60 or greater than 100 beats per minute should be reported immediately
    b. Whether the pulse is regular or irregular

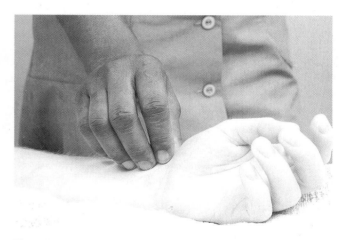

Fig. 13-16 The middle three fingers are used to locate the radial pulse on the thumb side of the wrist. (From Sorrentino, S.A.: Mosby's textbook for nursing assistants, ed. 2, St. Louis, 1987, The C.V. Mosby Co.)

Taking an Apical Pulse

The apical pulse is located on the left side of the chest slightly below the nipple (Fig. 13-17). It is counted for one full minute. This site is used on:
- Infants and children up to about 3 years of age
- Clients who have heart diseases
- Clients who are taking medications that affect the heart
- Clients who have irregular heart rates

A stethoscope is used to take an apical pulse. A *stethoscope* is an instrument used to listen to sounds produced by the heart, lungs, and other body organs. It amplifies sounds so they are easier to hear. The heartbeat normally sounds like a "lub-dub." Each "lub-dub"

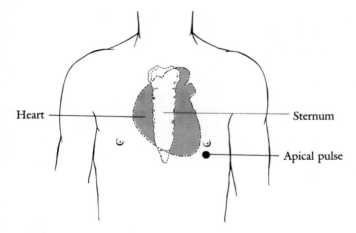

Fig. 13-17 The apical pulse is located 2 to 3 inches to the left of the sternum (breastbone) and below the left nipple. (From Sorrentino, S.A.: Mosby's textbook for nursing assistants, ed. 2, St. Louis, 1987, The C.V. Mosby Co.)

is counted as one beat. Do not count the "lub" as one beat and the "dub" as another.

The parts of a stethoscope are shown in Fig. 13-18. The earpieces should fit snugly to block out other sounds. However, they should not cause pain or discomfort. You will use the same stethoscope for different clients. You may share the stethoscope with other health workers. Therefore, the earpieces and the bell or diaphragm must be cleaned before and after use. This prevents the spread of microorganisms. Alcohol wipes are used for cleaning.

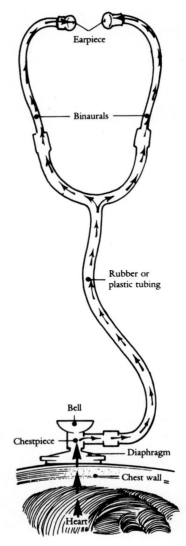

Fig. 13-18 Parts of a stethoscope. (From Malasanos, L., et al.: Health assessment, ed. 2, St. Louis, 1986, The C.V. Mosby Co.)

Procedure: Taking an apical pulse

1. Collect the following equipment:
   a. Stethoscope with diaphragm
   b. Alcohol wipes
   c. Watch with a second hand
   d. Paper and pen
2. Wash your hands.
3. Explain to the client what you are going to do.
4. Turn down the radio or TV.
5. Provide for the client's privacy.
6. Clean the earpieces and diaphragm with alcohol wipes.
7. Position the client in a lying or sitting position.
8. Warm the diaphragm of the stethoscope in your palm.
9. Expose the nipple area of the left chest.
10. Place the earpiece in your ears.

11. Locate the apical pulse. Place the diaphragm 2 to 3 inches to the left of the breastbone and below the left nipple (see Fig. 13-17).
12. Count the pulse for 1 full minute. Note if it is regular or irregular.
13. Cover the client. Remove the earpieces from your ears.
14. Record the client's name and pulse on paper. Note whether the pulse was regular or irregular.
15. Make sure the client is comfortable and the call bell is within reach.
16. Clean the earpieces and diaphragm with alcohol wipes. *Continued*

17. Wash your hands.
18. Report the following to your supervisor:
    a. A pulse rate less than 60 or greater than 100 beats per minute should be reported immediately
    b. Whether the pulse was regular or irregular
    c. The pulse rate
    d. Any unusual heart sounds
19. Record the pulse rate with an "Ap" to show an apical pulse.

Taking an Apical-Radial Pulse

The apical and radial pulse rates should be equal. Sometimes heart contractions are not strong enough to create pulses in the radial artery. The radial pulse may be less than the apical pulse. This is common in clients with heart disease. To see if there is a difference between the apical and radial rates, an *apical-radial pulse* is taken. One person takes a radial pulse while another person takes an apical pulse. The pulses are counted at the same time for one minute.

You may have to take an apical-radial pulse by yourself. First you will take the apical pulse for one minute. Then you will immediately count the radial pulse for one minute. This method is not as accurate as when the pulses are taken at the same time.

The *pulse deficit* is the difference between the apical and radial pulse rates. To get the pulse deficit, subtract the radial rate from the apical rate. The apical pulse is never less than the radial pulse rate. The apical rate, radial rate, and pulse deficit are all recorded.

Respiration

Respiration is the breathing of air in (inhalation) and out of the lungs (exhalation). When air is breathed (inhalation) the chest rises. Oxygen is taken into the lungs. When air is breathed out (exhalation), the chest falls. Carbon dioxide is moved out of the lungs. Each respiration involves one inhalation and one exhalation.

The normal healthy adult has 14 to 20 respirations per minute. Infants and children normally breathe faster than adults (see page 205). The respiratory rate is affected by many of the same factors that affect body temperature and the pulse.

Abnormal Respirations

Normal respirations are quiet, effortless, and regular. Both sides of the chest rise and fall equally. Respiratory and heart diseases, infection, injury, and other diseases can cause abnormal respiratory patterns. These include:

- *Tachypnea*–rapid (tachy) breathing (pnea); respirations are usually greater than 24 per minute
- *Bradypnea*–slow (brady) breathing (pnea); usually less than 10 respirations per minute
- *Apnea*–the lack of or absence (a) of breathing (pnea)
- *Hypoventilation*–respirations are slow, shallow, and sometimes irregular
- *Hyperventilation*–respirations are rapid and deep
- *Dyspnea*–difficult, labored, or painful (dys) breathing (pnea)
- *Cheyne-Stokes*–a breathing pattern in which respirations gradually increase in rate and depth and then become shallow and slow; breathing may stop (apnea) for 10 to 20 seconds
- *Abdominal respirations*–abdominal muscles are used to breathe; the abdomen rises and falls rather than the chest
- *Orthopnea*–the client must sit to breathe comfortably

Counting Respirations

Respirations are counted when the client is at rest. The client should be positioned so you can see the chest rise and fall. Sometimes it is hard to see the chest move. If so, you can put your hand on the client's chest to feel it rise and fall. Breathing can be controlled to a certain extent. Clients may not breathe normally if they know their respirations are being counted. Therefore, they should not know you are counting respirations.

Respirations are usually counted right after taking a pulse. The fingers or stethoscope are kept over the pulse site. The client will think you are still counting the pulse. Respirations are counted for 30 seconds. The number is multiplied by 2 for the number of respirations in 1 minute. If an abnormal pattern is noted, respirations are counted for 1 full minute. Do not try to count respirations while the client is coughing. Wait until the coughing stops.

Procedure: Counting respirations

1. Hold the wrist after taking a radial pulse. Keep the stethoscope in place if you took an apical pulse.
2. Do not tell the client you are counting respirations. If you just need to count respirations, tell the client you are going to take a pulse.
3. Start counting when you see the chest rise.

continued

Each rise and fall counts as one respiration.
4. Observe if respirations are regular and if both sides of the chest rise equally. Also note their depth and if the client has any pain or difficulty in breathing.
5. Count respirations for 30 seconds. Multiply the number by two. Count an infant's respirations for 1 minute.
6. Count an adult's respirations for 1 full minute if they are abnormal or irregular.
7. Record the respiratory rate and other observations.
8. Make sure the client is comfortable and the call bell is within reach.
9. Wash you hands.
10. Report the following to your supervisor:
   a. The respiratory rate
   b. Equality and depth of respirations
   c. If respirations were regular or irregular
   d. If the client has pain or difficulty in breathing
   e. Any respiratory noises
   f. Any abnormal respiratory patterns

Blood Pressure

Blood pressure is the amount of force exerted against the walls of an artery by the blood. Blood pressure is related to the force of heart contractions, the amount of blood pumped with each heartbeat, how fast the heart is beating, and how easily the blood flows through the vessels. The period of heart muscle contraction is called *systole*. The period of heart muscle relaxation is called *diastole*.

Blood pressure measurements involve the systolic and diastolic pressures. The *systolic pressure* is the highest pressure. It represents the amount of force it takes to pump blood out of the heart into the arteries. The *diastolic pressure* is the lowest pressure. It reflects the pressure in the arteries when the heart relaxes. Blood pressure is greater when the heart is pumping. Therefore, the systolic pressure is always greater than the diastolic pressure.

Blood pressure is measured in millimeters (mm) of mercury (Hg). It is recorded as a fraction. The systolic pressure is recorded over the diastolic pressure. For example, the average adult has a systolic pressure of 120 mm Hg and a diastolic pressure of 80 mm Hg. This is written as 120/80 mm Hg.

Factors That Affect Blood Pressure

Blood pressure can change from minute to minute. Age, sex, the amount of blood in the system, and emotions affect blood pressure. So do pain, exercise, body size, and medications. Blood pressure is usually lower in the morning after sleep. It increases with eating and activity. Because it can vary so easily, there are normal ranges for blood pressure. Systolic pressures between 100 and 150 mm Hg are considered normal. Normal diastolic pressures are between 60 and 90 mm Hg.

Persistent measurements above the normal systolic and diastolic pressures are considered abnormal. This condition is known as *hypertension*. You should report any systolic pressure above 150 mm Hg. A diastolic pressure above 90 mm Hg also needs to be reported immediately. Likewise, systolic pressures below 100 mm Hg and diastolic pressures below 60 mm Hg need to be reported. This is called *hypotension*. Some people normally have low blood pressure. However, hypotension usually indicates a serious condition. It can lead to death if not corrected.

Equipment

You will need a stethoscope and sphygmomanometer to measure blood pressure. The *sphygmomanometer* is commonly called the blood pressure cuff. It has three parts (Fig. 13-19):
1. *Inflatable cuff*—it wraps around the client's upper arm.
2. *Rubber bulb with thumbscrew*—the bulb is used to inflate the cuff. The thumbscrew opens and closes. When it is closed, squeezing the bulb inflates the cuff. When the thumbscrew is open, the cuff deflates.
3. *Gauge*—the measuring device for the blood pressure reading.

There are three types of sphygmomanometers: aneroid, mercury, and electronic. The aneroid type has a round dial and a needle that points to the gauge (Fig. 13-19, A). The aneroid manometer is small and easy to carry. The mercury manometer is more accurate than the aneroid type. The mercury type has a column of mercury within a gauged tube (Fig. 13-19, B). It stands upright. Hospitals and doctors' offices often have mercury manometers mounted on walls.

The blood pressure cuff is wrapped around the upper arm. The cuff is inflated to cause pressure over the brachial artery. Blood pressure is measured as the cuff deflates.

Sounds are produced as blood flows through the arteries. A stethoscope is used to hear the sounds in the brachial artery as the cuff deflates. Stethoscopes are not needed with electronic sphygmomanometers.

There are several types of electronic sphygmomanometers (Fig. 13-19, C). Most display the systolic

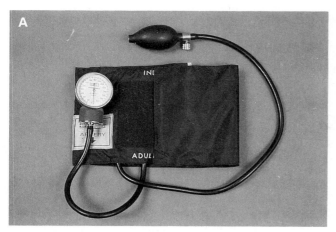

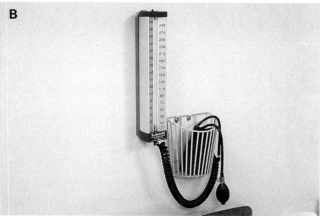

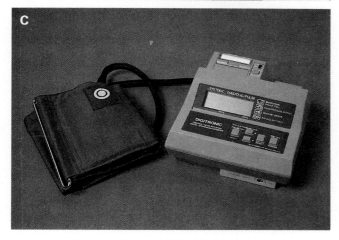

Fig. 13-19 **A,** Aneroid manometer and cuff. **B,** Mercury manometer and cuff. **C,** Electronic sphygmomanometer. (From Sorrentino, S.A.: Mosby's textbook for nursing assistants, ed. 2, St. Louis, 1987, The C.V. Mosby Co.)

and diastolic pressures on the front of the instrument. The pulse is usually displayed also. These instruments are expensive. Some clients have electronic blood pressure equipment. Your supervisor will help you learn how to use the instrument. The manufacturer's instructions will also be helpful.

Measuring Blood Pressure

Blood pressure is normally measured in the brachial artery. The following guidelines are important when measuring blood pressure.

GENERAL GUIDELINES

1. The blood pressure is not taken on an arm with an IV infusion, a dialysis shunt, a cast, or on an injured arm. If a client has had breast surgery, blood pressure is not taken on that side.
2. The client should rest about 15 minutes before you take the blood pressure.
3. The client usually sits or lies when the blood pressure is taken. The doctor may order blood pressure measured in the standing position. Your supervisor will tell you about such an order.
4. Make sure the cuff is the right size and fits properly. The cuff should be wide enough to cover two thirds of the upper arm. It should go around the entire upper arm. Readings will be inaccurate if the cuff does not fit.
5. The cuff is applied to the bare upper arm; it is not applied over clothing. Clothing affects the measurement.
6. The stethoscope diaphragm is placed firmly over the artery. The entire diaphragm must be in contact with the skin.
7. The room should be quiet so that the blood pressure can be heard. Talking, television, radio, and sounds from other rooms can interfere with an accurate measurement.
8. The sphygmomanometer must be clearly visible.
9. The radial artery is located and the cuff is inflated. When you can no longer feel the radial pulse, inflate the cuff an additional 30 mm Hg. This prevents inflating the cuff to a high pressure which is painful to the client.
10. The point at which you do not feel the radial pulse is where you should hear the first sound. The first sound is the systolic pressure. The diastolic pressure is the point where the sound disappears.

Procedure: Taking a blood pressure

1. Collect equipment:
   a. Sphygmomanometer (blood pressure cuff)
   b. Stethoscope
   c. Alcohol wipes
   d. Paper and pen
2. Review the client's prior vital signs. This helps you determine a blood pressure range.
3. Wash your hands.
4. Explain to the client what you are going to do.
5. Provide for the client's privacy.
6. Clean the earpieces and diaphragm of the stethoscope with alcohol wipes.
7. Ask the client to sit or lie down.
8. Position the client's arm so it is at the level of the heart. The palm should be up.
9. Expose the upper arm.
10. Squeeze the cuff to expel any remaining air. Close the thumbscrew.
11. Locate the brachial artery (inner aspect of the elbow).
12. Place the arrow marking on the cuff over the brachial artery (Fig. 13-20, A). Wrap the cuff around the upper arm at least 1 inch above the elbow. The cuff should be even and snug.
13. Place the sphygmomanometer on a flat surface. It should be vertical and at eye level. The aneroid type should be directly in front of you.
14. Place the earpieces of the stethoscope in your ears.
15. Find the radial artery. Inflate the cuff until you can no longer feel the radial pulse. Note this point; this is where you should hear the first blood pressure sound.
16. Inflate the cuff 30 mm Hg beyond the point where you last felt the pulse.
17. Place the diaphragm of the stethoscope over the brachial artery (Fig. 13-20, B).
18. Deflate the cuff at an even rate of 2 to 4 millimeters per second. Turn the thumbscrew counterclockwise to deflate the cuff.
19. Note the point where you hear the first sound. This is the systolic reading. You should hear the sound near the point where the radial pulse disappeared.
20. Continue to deflate the cuff. Note the point

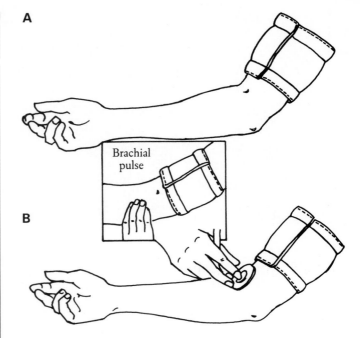

A

Brachial pulse

B

Fig. 13-20 A, The cuff is placed over the brachial artery. **B,** The diaphragm of the stethoscope is placed over the brachial artery. (From Sorrentino, S.A.: Mosby's textbook for nursing assistants, ed. 2, St. Louis, 1987, The C.V. Mosby Co.)

where the sound disappears for the diastolic reading.
21. Deflate the cuff completely. Remove it from the client's arm. Remove the stethoscope from your ears.
22. Record the client's name and blood pressure on paper.
23. Return the cuff to its case.
24. Make sure the client is comfortable and the call bell is within reach.
25. Clean the earpieces and diaphragm of the stethoscope.
26. Wash your hands.
27. Report an abnormal blood pressure to your supervisor. Record it in the proper place. Also report and record the following information:
   a. If the blood pressure was taken standing
   b. Which arm was used
   c. Changes in the client's skin where the cuff was applied (redness, swelling, pain, rash, bruising)
   d. Client complaints of chest pain, headache, nausea, vomiting, difficulty breathing, abdominal pain, or weakness

Table 13-1 Normal Pulse Rates for Children

AGE	AVERAGE PULSE RATE PER MINUTE
Newborn	70-170
1 month to 1 year	80-160
2 years	80-130
4 years	80-120
6 years	75-115
8 to 10 years	70-110
10 to 14 years	60-110
14 to 18 years	60-100

Vital Signs in Children

Vital signs can change very quickly in children. When a child is sick. vital signs are measured often. You need to know what is normal for children of different ages. If vital signs are above or below the normal range, you must call your supervisor immediately.

Temperature

Axillary and rectal temperatures are usually taken on children under 4 or 5 years of age. An oral temperature can be taken if the child this age can keep his or her mouth closed during the procedure. Some preschool children are able to understand and cooperate for an oral temperature. They can sit, lie, or be held for an oral temperature. A child may be more cooperative and quieter if held on your lap.

Axillary temperatures are taken on newborns. They are also indicated for children who cry, fuss, or are uncooperative with the rectal method. As with adults, the thermometer must remain in the axilla for 10 to 11 minutes. As with oral temperatures, children can sit, lie, or be held in your lap.

Rectal temperatures are taken when the child:
- Has a history of seizures
- Cannot understand or cooperate with the oral or axillary method
- Has had a mouth injury or oral surgery
- Has nasal congestion or difficulty breathing
- Is receiving oxygen

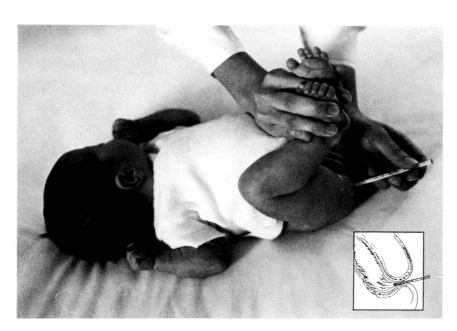

Fig. 13-21 Infant positioned for a rectal temperature. (From Whaley, L.F., and Wong, D.L.: Essentials of pediatric nursing, St. Louis, 1982, The C.V. Mosby Co.)

Table 13-2   Normal Respiratory Rates for Children

AGE	AVERAGE NORMAL RESPIRATORY RATE PER MINUTE
Newborn	35
1 month to 1 year	30
2 years	25
4 years	23
6 years	21
8 years	20
10 years	19
12 years	19
14 years	18
16 years	17
18 years	16-18

(Modified from Whaley, L.F., and Wong, D.L.: Essentials of pediatric nursing, St. Louis, 1982, C.V. Mosby Co.)

Rectal temperatures are not taken when a child has diarrhea or has had rectal surgery. The side-lying or prone position can be used to take a rectal temperature. Infants can be positioned on their backs with knees flexed toward their abdomens (Fig. 13-21). You can hold the infant's feet with one hand. The thermometer is inserted and held in place with your other hand.

As with adults, 98.6° F is the average body temperature for children. Rectal temperatures are one degree higher. Axillary temperatures are one degree lower. You must report an abnormal temperature to your supervisor immediately.

Pulse

Apical pulses are taken on infants and children up to 3 years of age. A radial pulse can be taken on older children. The child should be quiet when the pulse is taken. However, children often cry and become agitated during these procedures. These can affect the pulse rate. Be sure to report and record what the child was doing while you were taking the pulse. Table 13-1 lists the normal pulse rates for children in different age groups.

Respirations

Respirations of infants and children are counted in the same way as for adults. Like adults, children should be quiet when respirations are counted. Respirations can be counted when infants and children are sleeping. If awake, they should be counted before the temperature is taken. Temperature measurements often cause children to cry or fuss.

Infants usually have irregular respiratory patterns. Therefore, their respirations are counted for one minute.

Table 13-2 lists normal respiratory rates for children in different age groups. You must report abnormal rates and signs of breathing difficulties.

Blood Pressure

Blood pressures are lower in children than adults. The lower pressures are related to the child's age, weight, and height. The systolic pressure increases as the child grows older. The diastolic pressure changes very little between ages 6 and 18. As with adults, the child should be at rest when the blood pressure is taken. The child may cooperate more if he or she sits on the mother's lap for the procedure.

The right size cuff is important. The reading will be lower if the cuff is too large. The reading will be too high with a small cuff.

The procedure for measuring blood pressure in children is like that for adults. If you have to take a blood pressure on a young child, your supervisor will give you any special instructions. Your supervisor will take blood pressures on newborns or very small infants.

Table 13-3 gives blood pressure ranges for children of different ages.

Table 13-3 Blood Pressure Ranges for Children

AGE	SYSTOLIC PRESSURE	DIASTOLIC PRESSURE
Newborn	65-90	30-60
6 months to 1 year	65-115	42-80
1 year	65-125	40-90
2 years	70-120	40-90
4 years	75-120	45-85
6 years	85-115	50-60
8 years	90-120	50-65
10 years	90-125	50-65
12 years	95-130	50-70
14 years	100-140	50-70
16 years and up	Same as adult	

Reporting and Recording Vital Signs in Children

Vital signs can change very rapidly in children. Even a slight change can mean a serious problem. Any change in vital signs must be reported to your supervisor. When reporting and recording a child's vital signs, it is important to note what the child was doing at the time. Was the child calm, playing, being held, fussing, crying, or upset? This information helps the nurse assess the child's condition and plan further care.

Summary

Temperature, pulse, respirations, and blood pressure vary from person to person. They can vary within certain normal ranges. Vital signs can change in response to the slightest change in body functions. They are affected by such things as illness, exercise, medications, weather, and emotions. Changes in vital signs can give important information about a person's health. Changes above or below the normal range indicate a disorder or serious illness.

Vital signs are measured each time you visit a client. Sometimes they are taken several times a day. Accuracy is important when measuring, reporting, and recording vital signs.

Study Questions

1. Explain when you should report vital signs.
2. Describe the differences between measuring vital signs in children and adults.

Circle the *best* answer.

3. Which statement is *false*?
   a. The vital signs are temperature, pulse, respirations, and blood pressure.
   b. Vital signs detect changes in normal body function.
   c. Vital signs change only when a person is ill.
   d. Sleep, exercise, medications, emotions, and noise are some of the factors that affect vital signs.

4. Which temperature should you report immediately?
   a. An oral temperature of 98.4° F
   b. A rectal temperature of 101.6° F
   c. An axillary temperature of 97.6° F
   d. An oral temperature of 99.0° F

5. How long should you leave an oral thermometer in place?
   a. 2 to 60 seconds
   b. 3 to 4 minutes
   c. 8 to 9 minutes
   d. 10 to 11 minutes

6. A rectal temperature should not be taken when the client
   a. Is unconscious
   b. Is an infant
   c. Has a nasogastric tube
   d. Has had rectal surgery

7. Which gives the most accurate measurement of body temperature?
   a. Oral temperature
   b. Rectal temperature
   c. Axillary temperature
   d. An electronic thermometer

8. Which is usually used to take a pulse?
   a. The radial pulse
   b. The apical-radial pulse
   c. The apical pulse
   d. The brachial pulse

9. Which should be reported to the nurse immediately?
   a. An adult has a pulse of 120 beats per minute
   b. An infant has a pulse of 130 beats per minute
   c. An adult has a pulse of 80 beats per minute
   d. All of the above

10. Which statement about an apical-radial pulse is *true*?
    a. A stethoscope and sphygmomanometer are used.
    b. Radial pulses can be greater than apical pulses.
    c. Apical pulses can be greater than radial pulses.
    d. Apical and radial pulses are always equal.

11. Normal respirations in the adult are
    a. Between 14 and 20 per minute
    b. Quiet and effortless
    c. Regular and both sides of the chest rise and fall equally
    d. All of the above

12. Difficult, painful, or labored breathing is known as
    a. Tachypnea
    b. Bradypnea
    c. Apnea
    d. Dyspnea

13. Respirations are usually counted
    a. After taking the temperature
    b. After taking the pulse
    c. Before taking the pulse
    d. After taking the blood pressure

14. Which blood pressure is normal for an adult?
    a. 88/54 mm Hg
    b. 210/100 mm Hg
    c. 130/82 mm Hg
    d. 152/90 mm Hg

15. When taking a blood pressure, you should do all of the following *except*
    a. Take it on the arm with an IV infusion
    b. Apply the cuff to a bare upper arm
    c. Turn off the television and radio
    d. Locate the brachial artery

16. Which is recorded as the systolic blood pressure?
    a. The point at which the pulse is no longer felt
    b. The point where the first sound is heard
    c. The point where the last sound is heard
    d. The point 30 mm Hg above where the pulse was felt

17. You are going to take the temperature of a 2-year-old. Which of the following should you do?
    a. Take an oral temperature
    b. Take a rectal temperature
    c. Take an axillary temperature
    d. Take a rectal or axillary temperature

18. A 4-year-old has the following pulse rates. Which should you report immediately?
    a. 86 beats per minute
    b. 98 beats per minute
    c. 118 beats per minute
    d. 130 beats per minute

19. How long should you count an infant's respirations?
    a. 15 seconds
    b. 30 seconds
    c. 60 seconds
    d. 2 minutes

20. A 5-year-old's blood pressure is
    a. Lower than an adult's
    b. The same as an adult's
    c. Higher than an adult's
    d. Not measured

Answers

3. c	8. a	13. b	17. d
4. b	9. a	14. c	18. d
5. c	10. c	15. a	19. c
6. d	11. d	16. b	20. a
7. b	12. d		

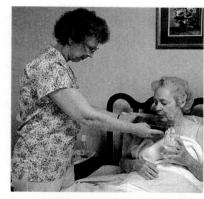

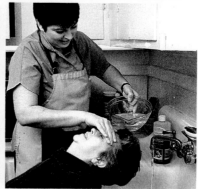

14 Personal Care

Chapter Highlights	What you will learn to do

- Explain the importance of hygiene
- Explain the rules for giving oral hygiene and what you need to observe
- Describe the rules for bathing clients and the observations you should make giving baths
- Describe the safety precautions for clients taking tub baths or showers
- Identify the purposes of a back massage, perineal care, hair care, shaving, and nail and foot care
- Identify the signs, symptoms, and causes of decubiti
- Identify the pressure points of the body in the prone, supine, lateral, Fowler's, and sitting positions
- Describe how to prevent decubitus ulcers
- Perform the procedures described in this chapter

Antiperspirant A skin care product that reduces the amount of perspiration

Aspiration The breathing of fluid or an object into the lungs

Decubitus ulcer An area where the skin and underlying tissues are eroded due to a lack of blood flow; a bedsore or pressure sore

Deodorant A preparation that masks and controls body odors

Perineal care Cleansing the genital and anal areas of the body

Cleanliness is important for comfort, safety, and health. Intact skin prevents microorganisms from entering the body and causing infection. Likewise, the mouth, genital area, and anus must be kept clean and intact. Besides cleansing, personal hygiene prevents body and breath odors, is relaxing, and increases circulation.

Culture and personal preference influence hygiene. Some people like showers. Others like tub baths. Some bathe before going to bed. Others prefer to bathe in the morning. The frequency of bathing also varies among individuals. Some people may not have hot water for bathing. Others may not have the money for soap, deodorant, shampoo, a toothbrush, or toothpaste.

Clients will need help with personal hygiene. You will help with such things as oral hygiene, bathing, hair care, and dressing.

Daily Care of the Client

Hygiene practices are performed as often as necessary to stay clean and comfortable. People normally practice hygiene routinely and out of habit. For example, teeth are brushed and face and hands washed after getting out of bed in the morning. These and other measures may be done routinely before and after meals and at bedtime.

The amount of help needed depends on the client's condition. Some clients are *independent*. They are capable of *self-care*. In other words, they can perform hygiene practices without help. Other clients need minimal, moderate, or maximum assistance. The nurse decides how much help a client needs.

- *Minimal assistance*—clients can perform self-care activities with a little help. Help may be needed in gathering supplies or washing hard-to-reach areas.
- *Moderate assistance*—clients need help with most activities. For example, a client may need help with oral hygiene, bathing, or dressing.
- *Maximum assistance*—personal care is provided. Clients cannot perform any self-care activities. These clients are bedbound, very weak, or physically unable to provide their own care.

You need to report and record the client's ability to assist with personal hygiene. The client's ability to help may change. Such a change is a sign of improvement or a decline in the client's condition.

GENERAL GUIDELINES

These guidelines are important when providing hygiene:

1. Allow the client to be as independent as possible. The client should do as much himself or herself as possible.
2. Follow the client's normal routine. Allow the client to choose the time and order of each activity. For example, one client may shave after bathing. Another may shave before bathing.
3. Use the client's favorite skin care products.
4. Talk to the client as you help with hygiene. This helps put the client at ease. You can also find out important information about the client at this time.
5. Practice good body mechanics at all times.
6. Practice safety at all times.
7. Assist clients taking tub baths or showers. Stay in or near the bathroom as indicated. Make sure the call bell is within the client's reach.
8. Wear gloves for oral hygiene and perineal care. You will have contact with the client's body fluids (saliva, urine, vaginal discharge, feces) during these procedures.
9. Provide personal hygiene whenever necessary. A client may need perineal care after having a bowel movement. Female clients may need perineal care several times a day if menstrual flow is heavy.

Oral Hygiene

Oral hygiene, or mouth care, keeps the mouth and teeth clean. It includes care of the teeth, gums, tongue, and mouth. Mouth care:

- Removes food and debris from around the teeth and gums

- Prevents infection
- Prevents cavities and gum disease
- Prevents mouth odors
- Refreshes the client and increases comfort
- Stimulates circulation in the mouth
- Makes food taste better

The nurse decides the type of mouth care and amount of help a client needs. Oral hygiene is provided upon awakening, after each meal, and at bedtime. Many people also practice oral hygiene before meals. Clients who have dry mouths need oral hygiene often. This includes clients who:

- Are unconscious
- Have fevers
- Breathe through their mouths
- Are receiving oxygen
- Are unable to eat or drink

GENERAL GUIDELINES

The following guidelines are important for good oral hygiene.

1. Use a toothbrush, toothpaste, dental floss, and mouthwash. The toothbrush should have soft or medium bristles.
2. Clients with dentures need a denture cleaner, a denture cup, and a special denture brush or regular toothbrush.
3. Use glycerine swabs for clients with sore and tender mouths and for unconscious clients.
4. Provide the client with a plastic bowl or emesis basin, water glass, straw, tissues, and towels.
5. Wear gloves when providing oral hygiene. Dentists and dental hygienists now wear gloves during dental care. The gloves prevent the spread of infection. Many microorganisms are found in the mouth. Pathogens that spread through sexual contact may be in the mouths of some individuals. You should always wear gloves if there are breaks in the skin on your hands.
6. Adapt the toothbrush if the client has difficulty holding the handle (Fig. 14-1).
7. Allow the client to perform oral hygiene. This includes removing, cleaning, and inserting dentures. Assist as necessary.
8. Prevent choking on water, toothpaste, or mouthwash. Have the client sit up during oral hygiene. Clients who cannot sit up should be positioned on their sides. Their heads should be turned to the side.
9. Be gentle when brushing teeth and gums. Rough brushing is uncomfortable and may make the gums bleed.
10. Brush all surfaces of the teeth, gums, and tongue.
11. Inspect the mouth, gums, and tongue each time you provide mouth care. Report the following:

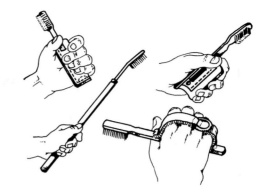

Fig. 14-1 Toothbrushes with different grips.

    a. Dry, cracked, swollen, or blistered lips
    b. Redness, swelling, irritation, sores, or white patches in the mouth or on the tongue
    c. Bleeding, swelling, or excessive redness of the gums
    d. Loose or broken teeth
12. Apply petrolatum jelly or other lubricant to chapped, dry, or cracked lips as directed by your supervisor.

Brushing Teeth

Many clients perform oral hygiene themselves. Others need help only in gathering or setting up equipment. You may have to provide oral hygiene for clients who are very weak or unable to use or move their arms.

Procedure: Brushing a client's teeth

1. Explain to the client what you are going to do.
2. Wash your hands.
3. Collect the following equipment:
    a. Toothbrush
    b. Toothpaste
    c. Water glass with cool water
    d. Dental floss
    e. Mouthwash
    f. Straw
    g. Plastic bowl or emesis basin
    h. Face towel
    i. Paper towels
    j. Disposable gloves
4. Place the paper towels on the work area. Arrange other equipment on the paper towels.
5. Provide for privacy.
6. Assist the client to a sitting position. Po-
Continued

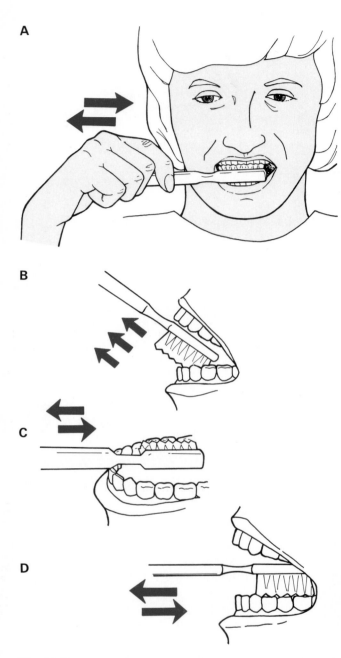

A

B

C

D

Fig. 14-2 A, Position brush horizontally as shown and brush back and forth with short strokes. **B,** Position brush at a 45-degree angle against the inside of the front teeth. Brush from gum to crown of the tooth with short strokes. Reposition the brush until all of the front teeth have been brushed. **C,** Hold the brush horizontally against the inner surfaces of the teeth and brush back and forth. **D,** Position the brush on the biting surfaces of the teeth as shown and brush back and forth. (From Sorrentino, S.A.: Mosby's textbook for nursing assistants, ed. 2, St. Louis, 1987, The C.V. Mosby Co.)

sition the client on the side near you if he or she cannot sit up.

7. Place the towel over the client's chest.
8. Put on the gloves.
9. Apply toothpaste to the toothbrush.
10. Hold the toothbrush over the bowl or emesis basin. Pour a small amount of water over the end of the brush.
11. Brush the teeth gently as described in Fig. 14-2.
12. Allow the client to take a drink of water to rinse his or her mouth. Hold the bowl or emesis basin under the client's chin (Fig. 14-3). Repeat rinsing as necessary.
13. Floss the teeth (see *Flossing the client's teeth,* page 211).
14. Have the client use mouthwash. Hold the bowl or emesis basin under the chin.
15. Remove and discard the gloves.
16. Make sure the client is comfortable, the call bell is within reach, and the side rails are up.
17. Clean and return equipment to its proper place.
18. Wipe off the work area with the paper towels. Then discard the paper towels.
19. Take soiled linen to the laundry.
20. Wash your hands.
21. Note and report your observations (see page 209).

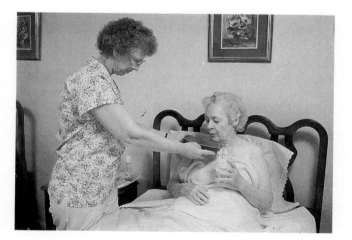

Fig. 14-3 Emesis basin held under the client's chin by the aide.

Flossing

Flossing teeth is part of good oral hygiene. Flossing removes plaque and tartar from the teeth.

These substances cause serious gum disease which leads to loss of teeth. Flossing also removes food between the teeth. Flossing is usually done after brushing but can be done at other times. Some people floss after meals. If flossing is only done once a day, bedtime is the best time to floss.

There are waxed and unwaxed types of dental floss. Waxed floss does not fray as easily as the unwaxed type. Some people find waxed floss easier to use because it slides between the teeth. However, particles of the teeth are more likely to attach to unwaxed floss. Many dentists recommend unwaxed floss, which is thinner than waxed floss.

You will need to floss for clients who cannot tend to oral hygiene.

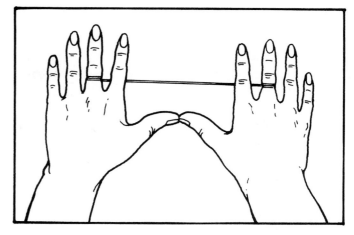

Fig. 14-4 Dental floss is held between the middle fingers to floss the upper teeth. (From Sorrentino, S.A.: Mosby's textbook for nursing assistants, ed. 2, St. Louis, 1987, The C.V. Mosby Co.)

Procedure: Flossing the client's teeth

1. Explain to the client what you are going to do.
2. Wash your hands.
3. Collect the following equipment:
   a. Plastic bowl or emesis basin
   b. Water glass with cool water
   c. Dental floss
   d. Face towel
   e. Paper towels
   f. Disposable gloves
4. Perform steps 4 through 8 in *Brushing a client's teeth*, page 209.
5. Pull the floss from the dispenser until you have a piece 18 inches long. Break off the piece.
6. Hold the floss between the middle fingers of each hand (Fig. 14-4).
7. Stretch the floss with your thumbs.
8. Start at the upper back tooth on the right side. Move the floss gently up and down between the teeth (Fig. 14-5). Work around to the left side.
9. Move to a new section of floss after every second tooth.
10. Hold the floss with your index fingers (Fig. 14-6).
11. Floss the lower teeth. Use back and forth motions and go under the gums as for the upper teeth. Start on the right side and work around to the left side.

Continued

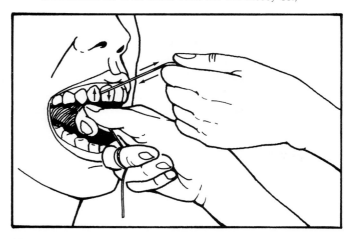

Fig. 14-5 Floss is moved in up and down motions between the teeth. (From Sorrentino, S.A.: Mosby's textbook for nursing assistants, ed. 2, St. Louis, 1987, The C.V. Mosby Co.)

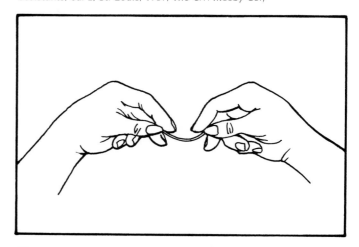

Fig. 14-6 Floss is held with the index fingers to floss the lower teeth. (From Sorrentino, S.A.: Mosby's textbook for nursing assistants, ed. 2, St. Louis, 1987, The C.V. Mosby Co.)

12. Let the client rinse his or her mouth. Hold the bowl or emesis basin under the chin. Repeat rinsing as needed.
13. Remove and discard the gloves.
14. Make sure the client is comfortable, the side rails are up, and the call bell is within reach.
15. Clean and return equipment to its proper place.
16. Wipe off the work area with the paper towels. Then discard the paper towels.
17. Take soiled linen to the laundry.
18. Wash your hands.
19. Note and report your observations (see page 209).

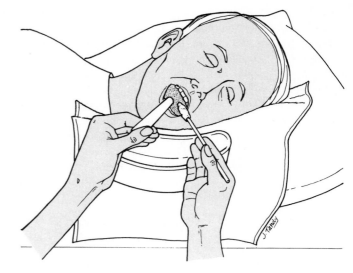

Fig. 14-7 The head of the unconscious client is turned well to the side to prevent the possibility of aspiration. The aide uses a padded tongue blade to keep the mouth open while cleaning the mouth with applicators. (From Sorrentino, S.A.: Mosby's textbook for nursing assistants, ed. 2, St. Louis, 1987, The C.V. Mosby Co.)

Mouth Care for the Unconscious Client

Unconscious clients need special mouth care. They cannot eat or drink and they breathe with their mouths open. They usually receive supplemental oxygen. These factors cause drying of the mouth. They also cause crusts on the tongue and mucous membranes. Mouth care helps keep the mouth clean and moist. It also helps prevent infection.

Lemon glycerine swabs are often used to give mouth care to unconscious clients. However, they have a drying effect. They should not be the only method of mouth care for these clients. Swabs dipped in a small amount of mouthwash, hydrogen peroxide, or a salt solution can be used to clean the mouth. Petrolatum jelly or other lubricant is applied to the lips after cleaning to prevent them from cracking.

Unconscious clients are usually unable to swallow. They need to be protected from choking and aspiration. Aspiration is the breathing of fluid or an object into the lungs. To prevent aspiration, position the client on one side with the head turned well to the side (Fig. 14-7). This position allows fluid to run out of the mouth, reducing the danger of aspiration. Using only a small amount of fluid also helps prevent aspiration.

The client's mouth must be kept open for mouth care. A padded tongue blade can be used for this purpose. To make a padded tongue blade, put two tongue blades together. Then wrap gauze around the top half of the blades and tape the gauze in place (Fig. 14-8). A spoon wrapped with gauze can also be used. Do not hold the mouth open with your fingers. The client can bite down on them. The broken skin lets microorganisms enter your body and cause an infection.

The unconscious client cannot speak or respond to what is happening. However, he or she may

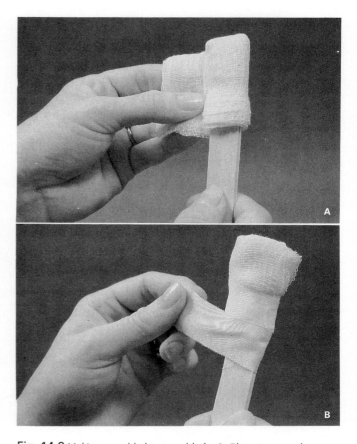

Fig. 14-8 Making a padded tongue blade. **A,** Place two wooden tongue blades together. Wrap gauze around the top half of the two blades. **B,** Tape the gauze in place. (From Sorrentino, S.A.: Mosby's textbook for nursing assistants, ed. 2, St. Louis, 1987, The C.V. Mosby Co.)

be able to hear. Always assume that an unconscious client can hear. Explain what you are doing step by step. Also tell the client when you have completed the procedure and when you are leaving the room.

Mouth care may be necessary every 2 hours. Check with your supervisor and the care plan to see how often it should be done and the solution to be used. Besides receiving mouth care, unconscious clients should be repositioned every 2 hours. Combining mouth care, skin care, and other comfort measures increases their comfort and safety.

Procedure: Providing mouth care for an unconscious client

1. Wash your hands.
2. Collect the following equipment:
   a. Lemon glycerine swabs
   b. Mouthwash or other solution
   c. Swabs or other applicators
   d. Padded tongue blade
   e. Water glass with cool water
   f. Face towel
   g. Plastic bowl or emesis basin
   h. Petrolatum jelly
   i. Paper towels
   j. Disposable gloves
3. Place the paper towels on the work area. Arrange other equipment on top of the paper towels.
4. Explain to the client what you are going to do.
5. Provide for privacy.
6. Lower the side rail near you.
7. Put on the gloves.
8. Position the client on the side toward you. Make sure his or her head is turned well to the side.
9. Place the towel under the client's face.
10. Place the emesis basin or bowl under his or her chin.
11. Separate the upper and lower teeth with the padded tongue blade.
12. Clean the mouth using swabs moistened with mouthwash or other solution (see Fig. 14-7).
    a. Clean the chewing and inner surfaces of the teeth.
    b. Swab the roof of the mouth, the cheeks, and lips.
    c. Swab the tongue.

d. Moisten a swab with water and swab the mouth to rinse.
e. Place used swabs in the emesis basin or bowl.
13. Repeat step 12 using the lemon glycerine swabs.
14. Apply petrolatum jelly to the client's lips.
15. Remove the gloves.
16. Explain that the procedure is over and that you will be repositioning the client. Reposition the client.
17. Raise the side rail. Make sure the hospital bed is the low position.
18. Clean and return equipment to its proper place. Discard disposable equipment.
19. Tell the client that you are leaving the room.
20. Take soiled linen to the laundry.
21. Wash your hands.
22. Note and report your observations (see page 209).

Denture Care

Dentures are cleaned for clients unable to do so themselves. Mouth care should be provided and dentures cleaned as often as natural teeth. Remember that dentures are the client's property. Losing or damaging them is negligent conduct. Replacing or repairing dentures is expensive and time-consuming.

Dentures are slippery when wet. They are held firmly over a basin of water lined with a towel when being cleaned. They can easily break or chip if dropped on a hard surface. Hot water causes dentures to warp. Therefore, hot water is not used to clean or store dentures. Some clients do not wear their dentures. If they are not worn, they should be stored in a container filled with cool water. Dentures can dry out and warp if not stored in water.

Procedure: Denture care

1. Explain to the client what you are going to do.
2. Wash your hands.
3. Collect the following equipment:
   a. Denture brush or toothbrush
   b. Denture cup

Continued

Fig. 14-9 Remove the upper denture by grasping it with the thumb and index finger of one hand. Use a piece of gauze to grasp the slippery denture and to prevent the spread of microorganisms. (From Sorrentino, S.A.: Mosby's textbook for nursing assistants, ed. 2, St. Louis, 1987, The C.V. Mosby Co.)

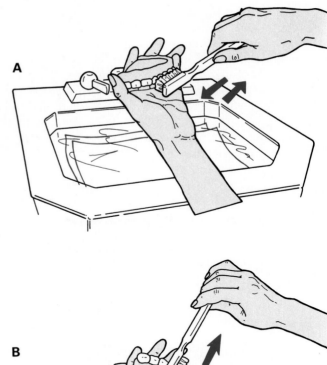

Fig. 14-10 A, The outer surfaces of the upper denture are brushed with back-and-forth motions. Note that the denture is held over the sink, which is filled halfway with water and lined with a towel. **B,** Position the brush vertically to clean the inner surfaces of the denture. Use upward strokes. (From Sorrentino, S.A.: Mosby's textbook for nursing assistants, ed. 2, St. Louis, 1987, The C.V. Mosby Co.)

c. Denture cleaner or toothpaste
d. Water glass with cool water
e. Straw
f. Mouthwash
g. Two face towels
h. Gauze squares
i. Emesis basin or plastic bowl
j. Disposable gloves
k. Denture adhesive (if used)
4. Provide for privacy.
5. Place a towel over the client's chest.
6. Put on the gloves.
7. Ask the client to remove the dentures. Carefully place them in the denture cup.
8. Remove the dentures using gauze squares if the client cannot remove them:
   a. Grasp the upper denture with your thumb and index finger (Fig. 14-9). You may need to break the seal holding it in place. Move the denture up and down slightly to break the seal. Gently remove the denture from the client's mouth once the seal is broken. Place the denture in the cup.
   b. Remove the lower denture. Grasp it with your thumb and index finger. Turn it slightly and lift it out of the mouth. Place the denture in the cup.
9. Take the denture cup to the sink.
10. Rinse each denture under warm running water. Return them to the denture cup.

11. Line the sink with a towel. Fill the sink half full with water.
12. Apply some denture cleaner or toothpaste to the brush.
13. Brush the dentures:
   a. Brush back-and-forth on the outer surfaces (Fig. 14-10, A).
   b. Use upward strokes to brush the inner surfaces (Fig. 14-10, B).
   c. Brush back-and-forth on the biting surfaces.
14. Rinse dentures under warm running water.

Continued

Do not use hot water. Be careful not to drop them.

15. Place dentures in the denture cup. Fill the cup with cool water until the dentures are covered.
16. Bring the denture cup to the client.
17. Position the client for oral hygiene.
18. Help the client brush any remaining permanent teeth. Assist the client to rinse out his or her mouth with a mouthwash. Hold the emesis basin or bowl under the chin.
19. Ask the client to insert the dentures. Apply denture adhesive if used by the client. Insert the dentures if the client cannot do so:
    a. Grasp the upper denture with your thumb and index finger. Raise the upper lip with your other hand and insert the denture. Using your index fingers, gently press on the upper denture to make sure it is in place.
    b. Grasp the lower denture with your thumb and index finger. Pull down slightly on the lower lip and insert the denture. Gently press down on the denture to make sure it is in place.
20. Remove the gloves.
21. Make sure the client is comfortable and the call bell is within reach.
22. Clean and return equipment to its proper place. Discard any disposable equipment.
23. Take soiled linen to the laundry.
24. Wash your hands.
25. Note and report your observations (see page 209).

Bathing

Bathing is an important part of hygiene. It:
- Cleans the skin
- Stimulates circulation
- Helps prevent decubitus ulcers (see page 236)
- Exercises muscles and joints
- Prevents body odors
- Helps prevent infection
- Is refreshing, comforting, and relaxing
- Provides opportunities to observe the client's skin

A client may have a complete or partial bath in bed, a tub bath, or a shower. The method chosen depends on the client's condition, ability to provide self-care, and personal preference. The client's preference also relates to time of day and frequency. A client who bathes in the evening should be allowed to continue the practice if possible.

The frequency of bathing is an individual matter. Some people bathe more than once a day. Others take a complete bath only once or twice a week. Personal preference, condition of the skin, and activity level influence how often a person bathes. Illness also affects the frequency of bathing. Usually illness increases the need for bathing because of fever and increased perspiration. Other illnesses and dry skin may require bathing only every two or three days.

The nurse will indicate on the care plan the type of bath for a client. The doctor may order bath instructions. For example, to keep a cast or dressing dry, the doctor will not allow the client to take a shower or tub bath. A client may request a change in bathing methods. If so, report the request to your supervisor.

Skin Care Products

There are many skin care products. Some are used for cleansing. Others protect the skin from drying or friction. The products used by an individual depend on personal preference and cost.

Soaps cleanse the skin. They remove dirt, dead skin, skin oil, some microorganisms, and perspiration. However, they tend to dry and irritate the skin. Dry skin is easily injured and causes itching and discomfort. The skin must be rinsed well to remove all soap.

Soap is not needed for every bath. Plain water is satisfactory for cleaning, particularly for the elderly, who tend to have dry skin from aging. People with dry skin may prefer soaps that contain bath oils. Soap should not be used if an individual has very dry skin.

Bath oils keep the skin soft and prevent drying. Some soaps contain bath oils, or liquid bath oil can be added to bath water. Bath oils cause showers and tubs to be slippery. Safety precautions must be taken to prevent the client from falling.

Creams and lotions protect the skin from the drying effect of air and evaporation. They do not feel greasy but leave an oily film on the skin. Most creams and lotions are scented.

Powders absorb moisture and prevent friction when two skin surfaces rub together. They are usually applied under the breasts, under the arms, and in the groin area. Powder can be applied between the toes. Powder is applied to dry skin in a thin, even layer. Excessive amounts cause caking and crusts that can irritate the skin. Powders and lotions are not used together. If used together, they can also cause caking and crusts.

Deodorants and antiperspirants are applied to the axillae after bathing. A *deodorant* masks and controls body odors. An *antiperspirant* reduces the amount of perspiration. Deodorants and antiperspirants should not be applied to irritated skin. They do not take the place of bathing.

Observations

When bathing clients or when assisting them to bathe, you should observe the skin. The following observations are reported to the nurse:

1. Color of the skin, lips, nail beds, and sclera (whites) of the eyes (See Chapter 4, *Observations of the skin, nails and hair*)
2. Location and description of any rashes
3. Dry flaky skin
4. Bruises or open areas of the skin
5. Pale or reddened areas, particularly over bony parts
6. Drainage or bleeding from wounds or body openings
7. Change in skin temperature; hot or cold
8. Client complaints of pain or discomfort

GENERAL GUIDELINES

The following rules apply to bed baths, showers, and tub baths.

1. Consult with the nurse for type of bath a client is to have. Also ask what skin care products to use.
2. Collect equipment before starting the procedure.
3. Protect the client's privacy. Close doors and windows.
4. Make sure the client is covered for warmth and privacy.
5. Reduce drafts by closing doors and windows.
6. Protect the client from falling.
7. Use good body mechanics at all times.
8. Make sure water temperature is not too hot, particularly if the client is elderly.
9. Keep soap in the soap dish between latherings. This prevents the water from becoming too soapy. If a tub bath or shower is taken, the client will not slip on the soap.
10. Wash from the cleanest area to the dirtiest. Start with the face and neck and end with the perineal area.
11. Let the client help as much as is safely possible.
12. Rinse the skin thoroughly to remove all soap.
13. Pat the skin dry to avoid irritating or breaking the skin.
14. Change water as often as necessary.
15. Bathe the skin whenever fecal material or urine is on the skin.

The Complete Bed Bath

The *complete bed bath* involves washing the entire body of a client in bed. Clients who are unconscious, paralyzed, in a cast or traction, or weak from illness or surgery usually require bed baths. Complete bed baths are given to clients who cannot bathe themselves.

You should consult with your supervisor about a client's ability to help with the bath. Also ask about any limitations in activity or position. Consider the client's personal preferences whenever possible.

Many clients are embarrassed to have others see their bodies. They may be afraid of being exposed. Every client should be told how a bed bath is given and how the body is covered to protect privacy.

Procedure: Giving a complete bed bath

1. Explain to the client what you are going to do.
2. Offer the bedpan or urinal (see page 250 or page 253).
3. Wash your hands.
4. Place paper towels on the work area. Arrange the following on the paper towels:
   a. Washbasin
   b. Soap dish with soap
   c. Bath thermometer
   d. Orange stick or nail file
   e. Washcloth, two bath towels, two face towels
   f. Bath blanket
   g. Gown, pajamas, or clean clothes
   h. Equipment for oral hygiene
   i. Lotion and powder
   j. Deodorant or antiperspirant
   k. Brush and comb
   l. Other toilet articles as requested by the client
5. Close doors and windows to provide privacy and prevent drafts.
6. Assist the client with oral hygiene. Provide oral hygiene if the client cannot do so.
7. Remove top linen and cover the client with a bath blanket (see *Making an occupied bed*, page 182).
8. Move the client to the side of the bed near you. Let the client have at least one pillow for comfort.
9. Fill the wash basin two-thirds full with water. Water temperature should be 110° to 115° F (43° to 46° C). Place the basin on work area.
10. Lower the side rail.
11. Place a face towel over the client's chest.
12. Make a mitt with the washcloth (Fig. 14-11). Use a mitt throughout the procedure.
13. Wash the client's eyes with water only. Do not use soap. Gently wipe from the inner
Continued

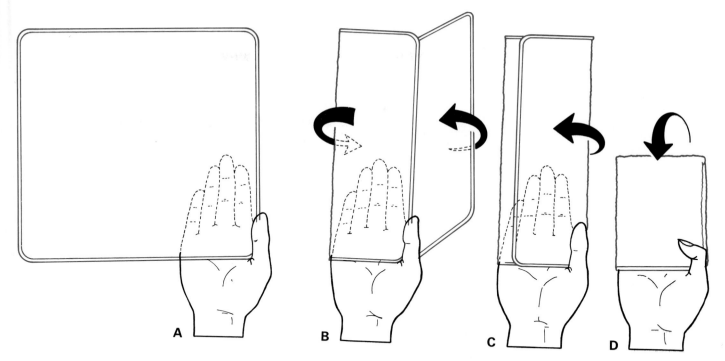

Fig. 14-11 A, Make a mitt with a washcloth by grasping the near side of the washcloth with your thumb. **B,** Bring the washcloth around and behind your hand. **C,** Fold the side of the washcloth over the palm of your hand as you grasp it with your thumb. **D,** Fold the top of the washcloth down and tuck it under next to your palm. (From Sorrentino, S.A.: Mosby's textbook for nursing assistants, ed. 2, St. Louis, 1987, The C.V. Mosby Co.)

corner with a corner of the mitted washcloth (Fig. 14-12). Clean the far eye first. Repeat this step for the eye near you.

14. Ask the client if you should use soap to wash the face. Wash his or her face, ears, and neck. Rinse and dry well using the towel on the client's chest.

15. Remove the gown or pajamas. Do not expose the client.

16. Place a bath towel lengthwise under the far arm.

17. Support the arm with your palm under the client's elbow. His or her forearm should rest on your forearm.

18. Wash the arm, shoulder, and axilla with long, firm strokes (Fig. 14-13). Rinse and pat dry.

19. Place the washbasin on the towel. Put the client's hand into the water (Fig. 14-14). Wash the hand well. Clean under the fingernails with an orange stick or nail file. Encourage the client to exercise the hand and fingers if able and allow this activity.

20. Remove the washbasin and dry the hand well. Cover the arm with the bath blanket.

21. Repeat steps 16 through 20 for the arm near you.

22. Place a bath towel over the client's chest crosswise. Hold the towel in place and pull the bath blanket from under the towel to the waist.

23. Lift the towel slightly and wash the chest (Fig. 14-15). Do not expose the client. Rinse and pat dry.

24. Place the towel lengthwise over the chest and abdomen. Do not expose the client. Pull the bath blanket down to the pubic area.

25. Lift the towel slightly and wash the abdomen (Fig. 14-16). Rinse and pat dry.

26. Pull the bath blanket up to the shoulders, covering both arms. Remove the towel.

27. Change the water. Raise the side rail before you leave the bedside. Lower it when you return.

28. Uncover the far leg. Do not expose the genital area. Place a towel lengthwise under the foot and leg.

29. Bend the knee and support the leg with

Continued

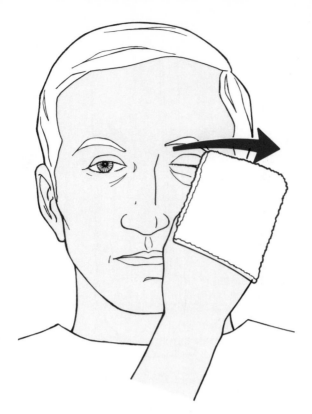

Fig. 14-12 Wash the eyes with a mitted washcloth by wiping from the inner to the outer aspect of the eye. (From Sorrentino, S.A.: Mosby's textbook for nursing assistants, ed. 2, St. Louis, 1987, The C.V. Mosby Co.)

your arm. Wash the leg with long, firm strokes. Rinse and pat dry.

30. Place the basin on the towel near the foot. Lift the leg slightly off the mattress. Slide the washbasin under the foot. Place the foot in the basin (Fig. 14-17). Clean under toenails with an orange stick or nail file.

31. Remove the basin and dry the leg. Cover the leg with the bath blanket and remove the towel.

32. Repeat steps 28 through 31 for the near leg.

33. Change the water. Raise the side rail before you leave the bedside. Lower it when you return.

34. Turn the client onto the side away from you. Keep the client covered with the bath blanket.

35. Uncover the back and buttocks. Do not expose the client. Place a towel lengthwise on the bed along the back.

36. Wash the back. Work from the neck to the buttocks. Use long, firm, continuous strokes (Fig. 14-18). Rinse and dry well.

37. Give a back massage (see page 226). (The client may prefer the back massage after the bath has been completed).

Continued

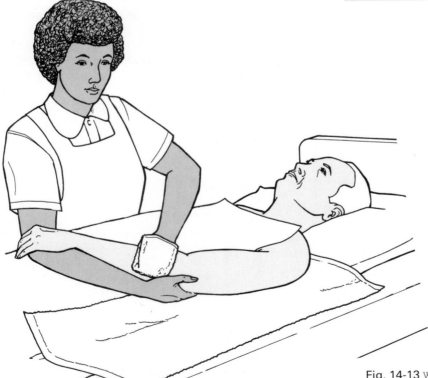

Fig. 14-13 Wash the client's arm with firm long strokes using a mitted washcloth. (From Sorrentino, S.A.: Mosby's textbook for nursing assistants, ed. 2, St. Louis, 1987, The C.V. Mosby Co.)

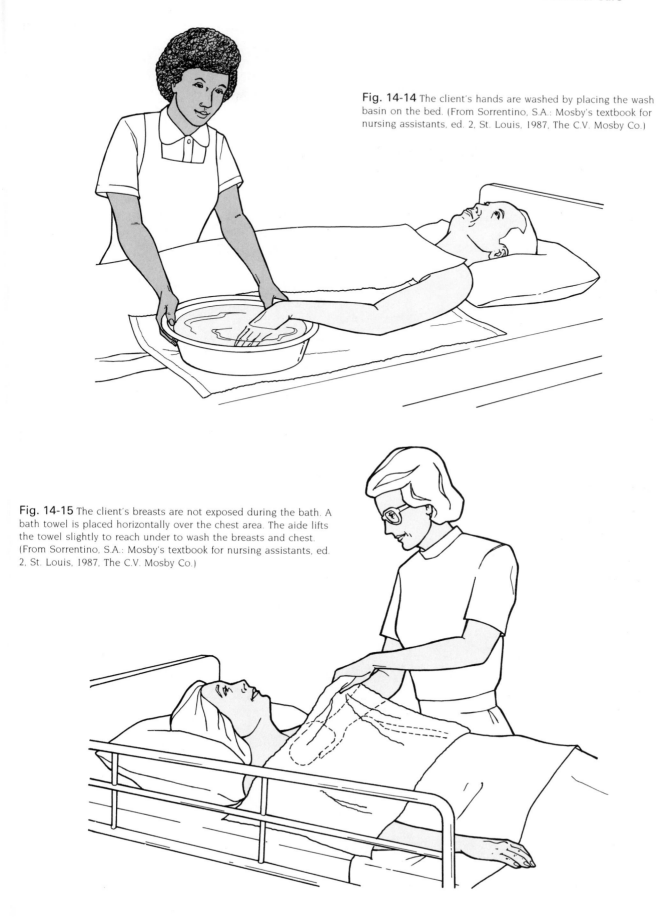

Fig. 14-14 The client's hands are washed by placing the wash basin on the bed. (From Sorrentino, S.A.: Mosby's textbook for nursing assistants, ed. 2, St. Louis, 1987, The C.V. Mosby Co.)

Fig. 14-15 The client's breasts are not exposed during the bath. A bath towel is placed horizontally over the chest area. The aide lifts the towel slightly to reach under to wash the breasts and chest. (From Sorrentino, S.A.: Mosby's textbook for nursing assistants, ed. 2, St. Louis, 1987, The C.V. Mosby Co.)

Fig. 14-16 The bath towel is turned so that it is vertical to cover the breasts and abdomen. The towel is lifted slightly as the aide reaches under to bathe the abdomen. The bath blanket covers the pubic area. (From Sorrentino, S.A.: Mosby's textbook for nursing assistants, ed. 2, St. Louis, 1987, The C.V. Mosby Co.)

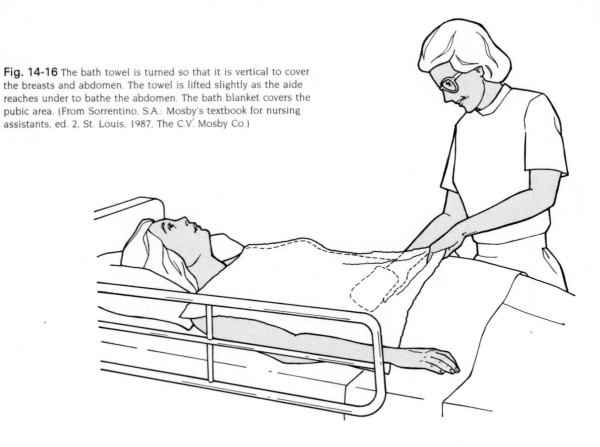

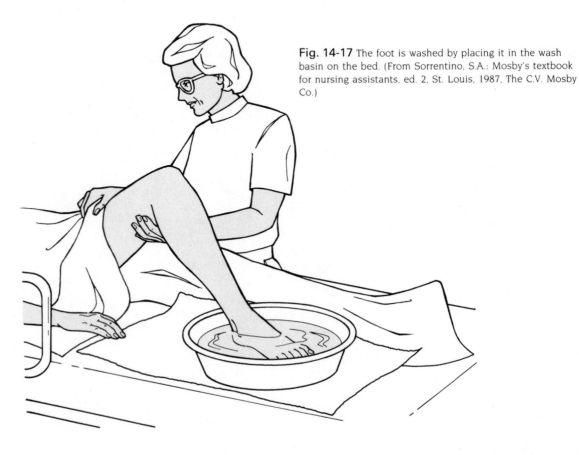

Fig. 14-17 The foot is washed by placing it in the wash basin on the bed. (From Sorrentino, S.A.: Mosby's textbook for nursing assistants, ed. 2, St. Louis, 1987, The C.V. Mosby Co.)

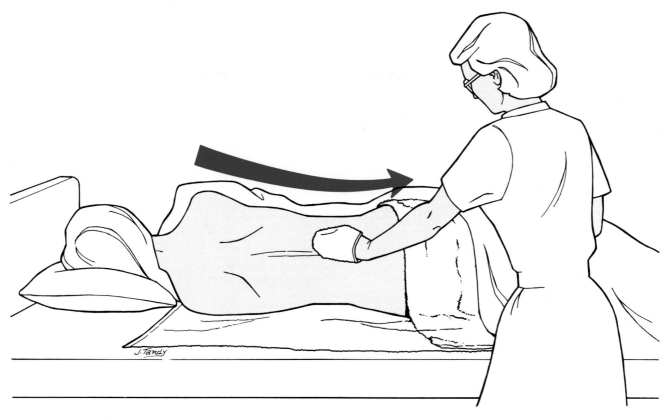

Fig. 14-18 The back is washed with long, firm, continuous strokes. Note that the client is in a side-lying position. A towel is placed lengthwise on the bed to protect the linens from water. (From Sorrentino, S.A.: Mosby's textbook for nursing assistants, ed. 2, St. Louis, 1987, The C.V. Mosby Co.)

38. Turn the client onto his or her back.
39. Change the water for perineal care. Raise the side rail before you leave the bedside. Lower it when you return.
40. Allow the client to wash the genital area. Make sure the client can easily reach the washbasin, soap, and towels. Place the call bell within reach. Ask him or her to signal when through. Make sure the client understands what is to be done. Answer the call bell promptly. Provide perineal care if the client is unable to do so (see pages 227).
41. Give a back massage if you have not already done so.
42. Apply deodorant or antiperspirant if requested.
43. Put a clean gown, pajamas, or clothes on the client.
44. Comb and brush the client's hair.
45. Make the bed. Place the call bell within reach. Make sure the client is comfortable and the side rails are up.
46. Empty and clean the washbasin. Return

equipment and supplies to their proper place.
47. Wipe off the work area with the paper towels. Then discard them.
48. Take soiled linen to the laundry.
49. Wash your hands.
50. Note and report your observations (see page 216).

The Partial Bath

The partial bath involves bathing the face, hands, axillae, genital area, back, and buttocks. These body areas may develop odors or cause discomfort if they are not cleaned. Partial bed baths are given when complete baths are not necessary and when the skin is dry. They are also given when frequent bathing is needed because of urine, feces, perspiration, and other body fluids on the skin.

Some client's can bathe themselves in bed or at the bathroom sink. You will help as needed, particularly in washing the back. The general rules for bathing apply when the client receives a partial bed bath.

Fig. 14-19 The client is bathing himself in bed. The aide has arranged the necessary equipment within the client's reach. (From Sorrentino, S.A.: Mosby's textbook for nursing assistants, ed. 2, St. Louis, 1987, The C.V. Mosby Co.)

Procedure: Giving a partial bath

1. Explain to the client what you are going to do.
2. Offer the bedpan or urinal (see page 250 or page 253).
3. Wash your hands.
4. Collect and arrange equipment as for *Giving a complete bed bath*, page 216.
5. Close doors and windows to provide privacy and prevent drafts.
6. Assist the client with oral hygiene.
7. Remove top linen. Cover the client with a bath blanket or help the client to the bathroom.
8. Fill the washbasin with water. Water temperature should be 110° to 115° F (43° to 46° C).
9. Place the basin on the work area.
10. Position the client so he or she can bathe comfortably. Help him or her sit at the bedside if allowed.
11. Place the work area within the client's reach.
12. Help the client undress.
13. Have the client wash body parts that can be easily reached (Fig. 14-19). Explain that you will wash the back and areas that cannot be reached.
14. Place the call bell within reach. Ask him or her to call when help is needed or when done bathing.
15. Leave the room after washing your hands.
16. Return when you hear the call bell. Knock before entering the room.
17. Change the bath water.
18. Ask the client what was washed. Wash the areas he or she was unable to reach. The face, hands, axillae, genital area, back, and buttocks should be washed.
19. Give a back massage.
20. Apply deodorant or antiperspirant if requested.
21. Help the client dress.
22. Assist the client to comb and brush his or her hair.
23. Make sure the client is comfortable and the call bell is within reach.
24. Make the bed. Empty and clean the wash

basin. Return the basin and other supplies to their proper place.
25. Wipe off the work area with the paper towels. Then discard them.
26. Take soiled linen to the laundry.
27. Wash your hands.
28. Note and report your observations (see page 216).

The Shower

Many clients prefer to shower. Clients with dressings, IVs, or casts are not allowed to shower. The client may need help getting to the shower, gathering equipment, adjusting water temperature, and washing some body areas.

A shower may be part of the bathtub or it may be a walk-in design (Fig. 14-20). Walk-in showers have advantages. Clients can step into them rather than stepping over sides of the bathtubs. Weak and paralyzed clients can be bathed in a shower by using a shower chair. Shower chairs are made of plastic with wheels on the legs. There is a round open area in the seat so water can drain (Fig. 14-21). The wheels must be locked during the procedure to prevent the chair from moving. A straight-backed chair, stool, or lawn chair can be used if a shower chair is not available. Tub benches and hand-held shower nozzles can be used to shower in the bathtub (Fig. 14-22).

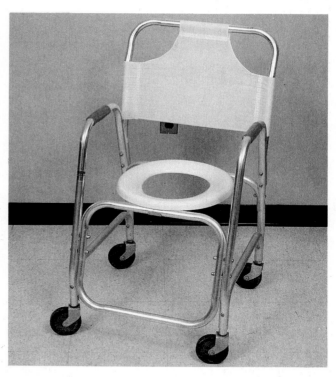

Fig. 14-21 A shower chair has a round opening in the center of the seat. There are wheels with locks on the legs. (From Sorrentino, S.A.: Mosby's textbook for nursing assistants, ed. 2, St. Louis, 1987, The C.V. Mosby Co.)

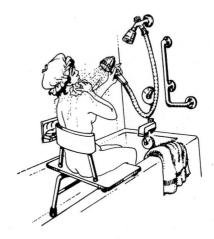

Fig. 14-22 Client taking a shower using a hand-held nozzle. Note the tub bench.

Fig. 14-20 Walk-in shower.

Clients must be protected from falling and chilling when taking showers. Their privacy also needs to be protected. Weak or unsteady clients should not be allowed to stand in the shower or be left unattended. If hand rails (grab bars) have been installed, encourage the client to use them when getting in and out of the shower. The hand rails are especially important if the shower is in the bathtub. Long-handled

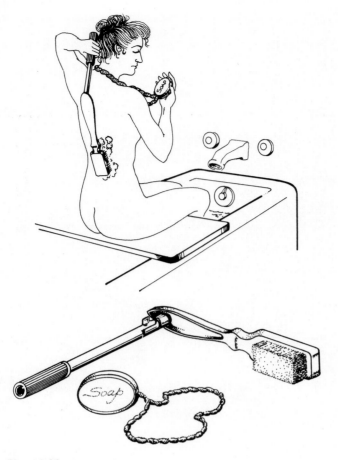

Fig. 14-23 Shower aids.

sponges are helpful for hard to reach areas. Soap-on-a-rope is handy and reduces the possibility of falling on the soap (Fig. 14-23). Clients are not allowed to shower unless the nurse gives approval.

Procedure: Assisting the client to shower

1. Explain to the client what you are going to do.
2. Wash your hands.
3. Place the following in the bathroom:
   a. Washcloth and two bath towels
   b. Soap
   c. Shower cap
   d. Gown, pajamas, or clean clothes
   e. Deodorant or antiperspirant
   f. Other toilet articles as requested by the client
4. Place a rubber bath mat on the floor of the shower. Do not block the drain.

5. Place a bath mat on the floor in front of the shower.
6. Help the client to the bathroom as needed.
7. Turn the shower on. Adjust water temperature and pressure.
8. Help the client undress.
9. Help him or her into the shower. If a shower chair is used, place it in position and lock the wheels.
10. Help the client wash if necessary.
11. Place a towel across a chair or the toilet seat.
12. Wash your hands and leave the room only if the client is able to stand without help. Stay close to the bathroom in case the client calls for help.
13. Return to the bathroom when the client calls you. Knock before entering. Some clients like to take long showers. Check the client every 5 minutes if appropriate.
14. Turn the shower off.
15. Help the client out of the shower and onto the chair.
16. Help the client dry off; pat gently.
17. Help him or her to dress.
18. Help the client return to the room and to bed.
19. Give a back massage.
20. Make sure the client is comfortable.
21. Clean the shower. Discard disposable equipment and return supplies to their proper place.
22. Take soiled linen to the laundry.
23. Wash your hands.
24. Note and report your observations (see page 216).

The Tub Bath

Many people like tub baths because they are relaxing. Clients must be protected from falling when getting in and out of the tub and from burns from hot water. A tub bath can cause a person to feel faint, weak, or tired. These symptoms are more likely to occur if the client has been on bed rest. A bath should not last longer than 20 minutes.

The tub should be cleaned before being used. There must be a bath mat on the bottom of the tub to help prevent falls. For safety, you may want to drain the tub before the client gets out. If the tub is drained first, keep the client covered and protected from exposure and chilling. Changes in the procedure may be necessary for a particular client. Consult your supervisor before assisting a client with a tub bath.

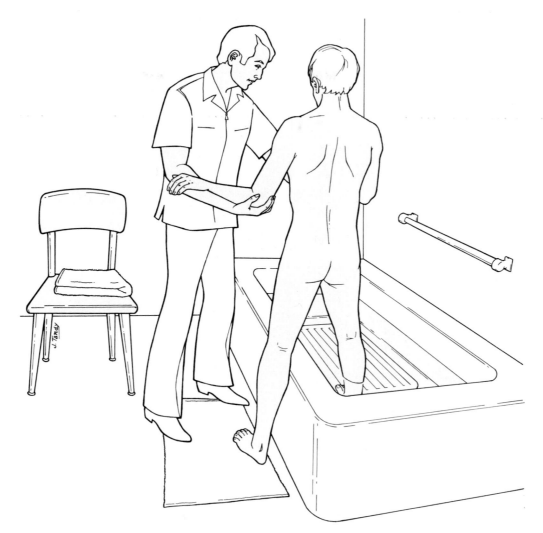

Fig. 14-24 The aide helps the client into the tub to protect the client from falling. Note that there is a bath mat in the tub and that the tub is filled halfway with water. There is a floor mat in front of the tub. (From Sorrentino, S.A.: Mosby's textbook for nursing assistants, ed. 2, St. Louis, 1987, The C.V. Mosby Co.)

Procedure: Assisting the client with a tub bath

1. Explain to the client what you are going to do.
2. Wash your hands.
3. Place the following in the bathroom:
   a. Washcloth and two bath towels
   b. Soap
   c. Bath thermometer
   d. Gown, pajamas, or clean clothes
   e. Deodorant or antiperspirant
   f. Other toilet articles as requested by the client

4. Clean the tub if it needs cleaning.
5. Place a rubber bath mat on the bottom of the bathtub.
6. Place a bath mat on the floor in front of the tub.
7. Assist the client to the bathroom.
8. Have the client sit on the toilet seat or on a chair.
9. Fill the tub halfway. Water temperature should be 105° F (41° C).
10. Help the client undress.
11. Assist the client into the tub (Fig. 14-24).
12. Ask the client to call you when through bathing or when help is needed. Remind

Continued

him or her not to remain in the tub longer than 20 minutes.

13. Place a towel across the chair or toilet seat.
14. Leave the room and wash your hands. Stay nearby in case the client calls for help. Check the client every 5 minutes.
15. Return to the bathroom when he or she calls for you. Knock before entering.
16. Help the client out of the tub and onto the chair.
17. Help the client dry off; pat gently.
18. Help the client dress.
19. Help the client return to the room and to bed.
20. Provide a back massage.
21. Make sure the client is comfortable.
22. Clean the bathtub. Discard disposable equipment. Return supplies to their proper place.
23. Take soiled linen to the laundry.
24. Wash your hands.
25. Note and report your observations (see page 216).

The Back Massage

The back massage, or back rub, involves rubbing the client's back from the neck to the top of the buttocks. A back rub does the following:

- Increases circulation
- Helps prevent decubitus ulcers
- Is soothing and relaxing

The massage is normally given after the bath and at bedtime. A back massage is also given when the client is turned and repositioned. It should last about 4 to 6 minutes. Lotion is used to reduce friction during the massage. Do not use alcohol because it dries the skin. The lotion is warmed before it is applied to the back. You can warm the lotion by:

- Placing the bottle of lotion in the bath water
- Holding the lotion bottle under warm running water
- Rubbing some lotion between your hands

Some clients should not have back massages as described in the following procedure. Back rubs may be dangerous for clients with certain heart diseases, back injuries, back surgeries, skin diseases, and some lung disorders. Your supervisor will tell you if a client cannot have a back massage. Consult your supervisor if you are not sure if a client should have a massage.

Procedure: Giving a back massage

1. Explain to the client what you are going to do.
2. Wash your hands.
3. Collect the following:
   a. Bath blanket
   b. Bath towel
   c. Lotion
4. Close doors and windows to provide privacy.
5. Position the client in the prone or side-lying position.
6. Expose the back, shoulders, upper arms, and buttocks. Cover the rest of the body with the bath blanket.
7. Warm your hands by running warm water over them.
8. Warm the lotion.
9. Apply lotion to the lower back area.
10. Stroke upward from the buttocks to the shoulders. Then stroke down over the upper arms. Stroke up the upper arms, across the shoulders, and down the back to the buttocks (Fig. 14-25). Use firm strokes. Use fast movements to stimulate and slow movements to relax the client. Do not let your hands lose contact with the client's skin.
11. Repeat step 10 for at least 3 minutes.
12. Knead by grasping tissue between the thumb and fingers (Fig. 14-26). Knead half of the back, starting at the buttocks and moving upward to the shoulder. Then knead downward from the shoulder to the buttocks. Repeat on the other half of the back.
13. Massage bony areas. Use circular motions with the tips of your index and middle fingers.
14. Stroke with long, firm movements to end the massage. Tell the client you are finishing the massage.
15. Cover the exposed areas. Remove the bath blanket.
16. Make sure the client is comfortable.
17. Return the lotion to its proper place.
18. Take any soiled linen to the laundry.
19. Wash your hands.
20. Note and report your observations.

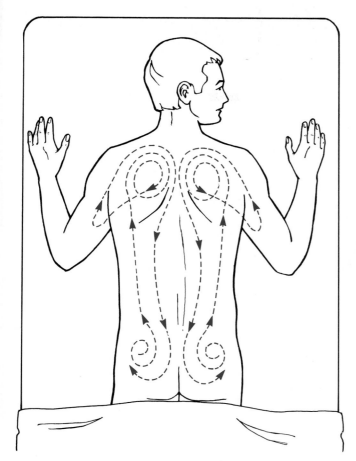

Fig. 14-25 The client lies in the prone position for a back massage. The aide strokes upward from the buttocks to the shoulders, down over the upper arms, back up the upper arms, across the shoulders, and down the back to the buttocks. (From Sorrentino, S.A.: Mosby's textbook for nursing assistants, ed. 2, St. Louis, 1987, The C.V. Mosby Co.)

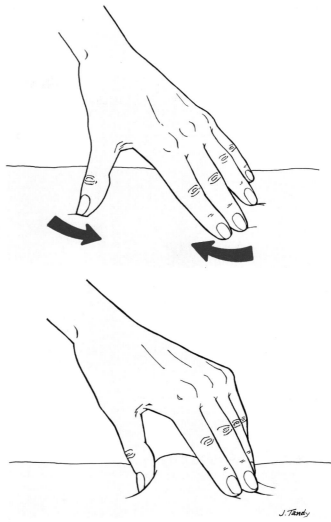

J. Tandy

Fig. 14-26 Kneading is accomplished during the back massage by picking up tissue between the thumb and fingers. (From Sorrentino, S.A.: Mosby's textbook for nursing assistants, ed. 2, St. Louis, 1987, The C.V. Mosby Co.)

Perineal Care

Perineal care involves cleaning the perineum (the genital and anal areas). Perineal care is sometimes called *pericare*. The perineum is warm, moist, and dark. It provides an environment for the growth of microorganisms. Perineal care helps prevent infection, odors, and skin breakdown. It also gives a sense of cleanliness and promotes comfort.

Perineal care is done at least once a day, during the bath. It is also done whenever the area is contaminated with urine or fecal material. Some clients need perineal care more often. Perineal care is done after some surgeries, after childbirth, and during menstruation.

If able, clients should do their own perineal care. Otherwise it is done for them. Perineal care is very private and personal. Many clients and nursing personnel find the procedure embarrassing. This is especially true when it involves a member of the opposite sex. Make sure the client understands the purpose and steps of the procedure before you begin. You need to be sensitive to the client's feelings and need for privacy.

Many clients do not know the terms "perineum" and "perineal." Most people understand one or more of the following terms: "privates," "private parts," "crotch," "genitals," or "the area between your legs."

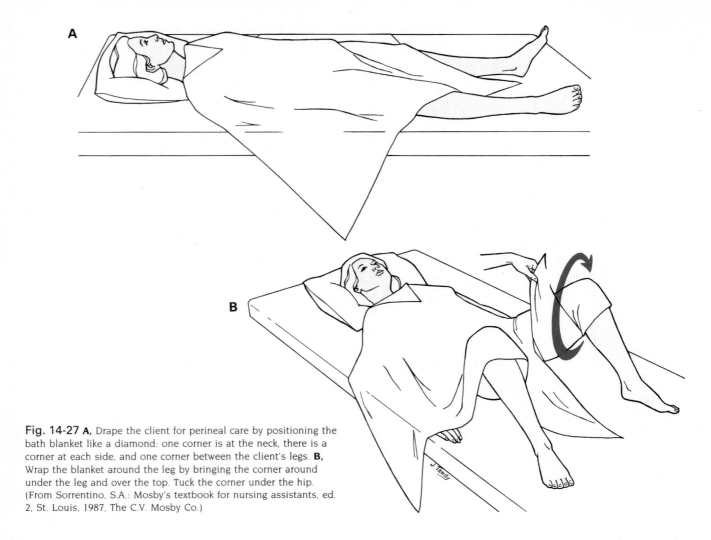

Fig. 14-27 **A,** Drape the client for perineal care by positioning the bath blanket like a diamond: one corner is at the neck, there is a corner at each side, and one corner between the client's legs. **B,** Wrap the blanket around the leg by bringing the corner around under the leg and over the top. Tuck the corner under the hip. (From Sorrentino, S.A.: Mosby's textbook for nursing assistants, ed. 2, St. Louis, 1987, The C.V. Mosby Co.)

Be sure to use a term the client understands. The term should also be in good taste professionally.

The rules of medical asepsis apply to perineal care. You will work from the cleanest area to the dirtiest. The urethral area is the cleanest and the anal area the dirtiest. Therefore, you will clean from the urethra to the anal area. The perineum is very delicate and easily injured. Warm water, not hot, is used. The area must be rinsed thoroughly if soap is used. Then the perineum is patted dry to reduce moisture and promote comfort. Be sure to wear disposable gloves for perineal care.

Procedure: Perineal care

1. Explain to the client what you are going to do.
2. Wash your hands.

3. Place paper towels on the work area. Arrange the following equipment on the work area:
   a. Wash basin
   b. Soap dish and soap
   c. 3 to 10 washcloths or a package of cotton balls
   d. Bath towel
   e. Bath blanket
   f. Bath thermometer
   g. Waterproof pad
   h. Clean gloves
   i. Paper or plastic bag
4. Close doors and windows to provide for privacy.
5. Cover the client with a bath blanket.
6. Position the client in the supine position.
7. Position the waterproof pad under the buttocks.
8. Drape the client (Fig. 14-27).

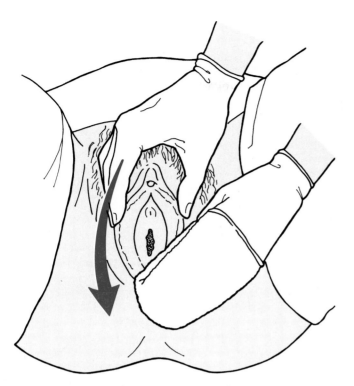

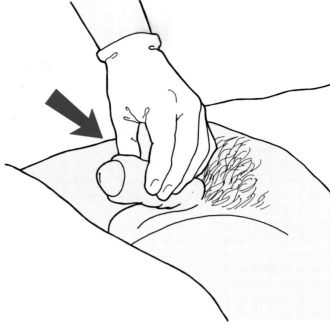

Fig. 14-28 Perineal care is given to the female by separating the labia with one hand. The aide uses a mitted washcloth to cleanse between the labia with downward strokes. (From Sorrentino, S.A.: Mosby's textbook for nursing assistants, ed. 2, St. Louis, 1987, The C.V. Mosby Co.)

Fig. 14-29 The foreskin of the uncircumcised male is pulled back for perineal care. It is returned to the normal position immediately after cleaning. (From Sorrentino, S.A.: Mosby's textbook for nursing assistants, ed. 2, St. Louis, 1987, The C.V. Mosby Co.)

9. Fill the washbasin. Water temperature should be 105° to 109.4° F (41° to 43° C).
10. Place the basin on the work area.
11. Put the washcloths in the water. Squeeze out excess water before using them.
12. Put on the gloves.
13. Fold the corner of the bath blanket between the clients legs onto the abdomen.
14. Female perineal care:
    a. Help the client flex her knees and spread her legs.
    b. Apply soap to a washcloth or cotton ball.
    c. Separate the labia. Clean downward from front to back with one stroke (Fig. 14-28). Set the washcloth or cotton ball aside and prepare a new one. Repeat this step until the area is clean.
    d. Rinse the perineum with a washcloth or cotton ball. Separate the labia. Stroke downward from front to back. Set the washcloth or cotton ball aside. Repeat the step as necessary.
    e. Pat the area dry. Put used cotton balls in the bag.

15. Male perineal care:
    a. Retract the foreskin if the client is uncircumcised (Fig. 14-29).
    b. Apply soap to a washcloth or cotton ball.
    c. Grasp the penis.
    d. Clean the tip of the penis using a circular motion. Start at the urethral opening and work outward (Fig. 14-30). Set the washcloth or cotton ball aside and prepare a new one. Repeat this step as necessary.
    e. Rinse the area with another washcloth or cotton ball.
    f. Return the foreskin to its natural position (if the client is uncircumcised).
    g. Clean the shaft of the penis with firm downward strokes. Rinse the area.
    h. Help the client flex his knees and spread his legs.
    i. Clean the scrotum and rinse well.
    j. Pat dry the penis and the scrotum. Put used cotton balls in the bag.
16. Fold the blanket back between the client's legs.
17. Help the client lower the legs and turn onto the side away from you.

Continued

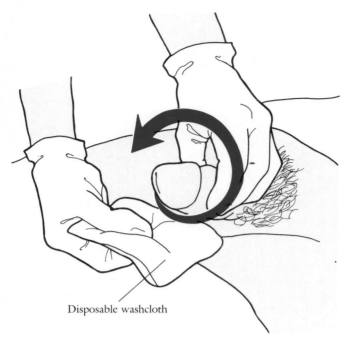

Disposable washcloth

Fig. 14-30 The penis is cleaned with circular motions starting at the urethra. (From Sorrentino, S.A.: Mosby's textbook for nursing assistants, ed. 2, St. Louis, 1987, The C.V. Mosby Co.)

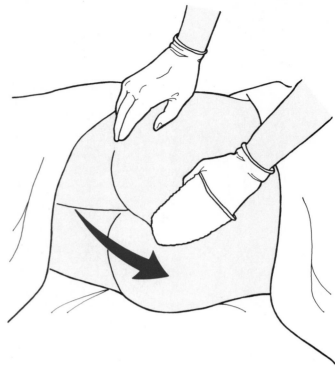

Fig. 14-31 The rectal area is cleaned by wiping from the vagina to the anus. The side-lying position allows the anal area to be cleaned more thoroughly. (From Sorrentino, S.A.: Mosby's textbook for nursing assistants, ed. 2, St. Louis, 1987, The C.V. Mosby Co.)

18. Apply soap to a washcloth.
19. Clean the rectal area. Clean from the vagina (or scrotum) to the anus with one stroke (Fig. 14-31). Set the washcloth aside.
20. Repeat steps 18 and 19 until the area is clean.
21. Rinse the rectal area. Stroke from the vagina (or scrotum) to the anus. Repeat the step as necessary.
22. Pat the area dry with the towel.
23. Remove gloves and discard into the bag.
24. Make sure the client is comfortable. Straighten linens and remove the bath blanket. Make sure the call bell is within reach.
25. Clean equipment. Return equipment and supplies to their proper place.
26. Wipe off the work area with paper towels.
27. Take soiled linen to the laundry. Take disposable supplies to the garbage.
28. Wash your hands.
29. Note and report your observations:
    a. Any odors
    b. Redness, swelling, discharge, or irritation
    c. Complaints of pain, burning, or other discomfort

Shaving

Most men shave every day. A clean-shaven face adds to the client's comfort and well-being. Likewise, most women shave their legs and underarms. If able, clients should shave themselves. Shaving is good exercise. It also gives the client a sense of dignity and control.

Electric shavers or razor blades are used. Electric shavers are easier and safer to use. Do not use them while clients are receiving oxygen. Remember to practice safety rules for using electrical equipment.

The beard and skin are softened before shaving with a razor blade. A warm washcloth or face towel applied to the face for a few minutes softens the skin. Then a lather of soap and water or shaving cream is applied. Be careful not to cut or irritate the skin while shaving.

Beards and mustaches also need daily grooming. Ask the client how he wants his beard or mustache cared for.

A woman's legs and underarms can be shaved after bathing, when the skin is soft. Soap and water or shaving cream provides lather when a razor is used. Some women like to use electric shavers.

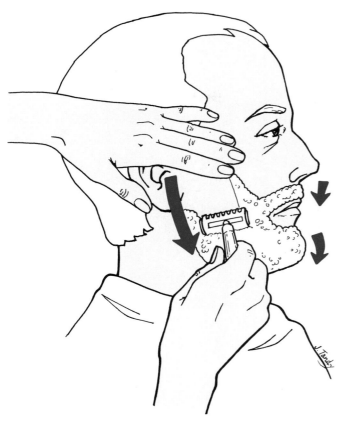

Fig. 14-32 Shaving is done in the direction of hair growth. Longer strokes are used on the larger areas of the face. Short strokes are used around the chin and lips. (From Sorrentino, S.A.: Mosby's textbook for nursing assistants, ed. 2, St. Louis, 1987, The C.V. Mosby Co.)

Procedure: Shaving a client

1. Explain to the client what you are going to do.
2. Wash your hands.
3. Place paper towels on the work area. Arrange the following on the work area:
   a. Washbasin
   b. Bath towel, face towel, and washcloth
   c. Bath thermometer
   d. Safety razor
   e. Mirror
   f. Shaving cream or soap
   g. Shaving brush
   h. After-shave lotion
   i. Tissues

4. Close doors and windows for privacy.
5. Fill the washbasin. Water temperature should be about 115° F (46° C). Place the basin on the work area.
6. Help the client to a semisitting position if allowed.
7. Place the bath towel over the chest.
8. Wash the client's face. Do not dry.
9. Place a washcloth or face towel in the washbasin. Wet it thoroughly and then wring it out.
10. Apply the washcloth or towel to the client's face for 3 to 5 minutes.
11. Apply shaving cream to the face with your hands. Or apply a generous amount of lather with a shaving brush.
12. Tighten the razor blade to the razor.
13. Hold the skin taut with your other hand.
14. Shave in the direction of hair growth. Use longer strokes around the chin and lips (Fig. 14-32).
15. Rinse the razor often and wipe with tissues.
16. Apply direct pressure to any bleeding areas.
17. Wash off remaining shaving cream or soap. Dry with a towel.
18. Apply after-shave lotion if requested by the client.
19. Make sure the client is comfortable and the call bell is within reach.
20. Clean and return equipment and supplies to their proper place. Wipe off the work area with the paper towels. Discard disposable supplies.
21. Take soiled linen to the laundry.
22. Wash your hands.
23. Report any nicks or bleeding to your supervisor.

Hair Care

Illness and disability may prevent people from practicing routine hair care measures. Clients should have help with hair care whenever it is necessary. Hair care:
- Cleans the hair and scalp
- Loosens surface dirt and dandruff
- Stimulates circulation to the scalp
- Improves the client's appearance
- Adds to the client's comfort

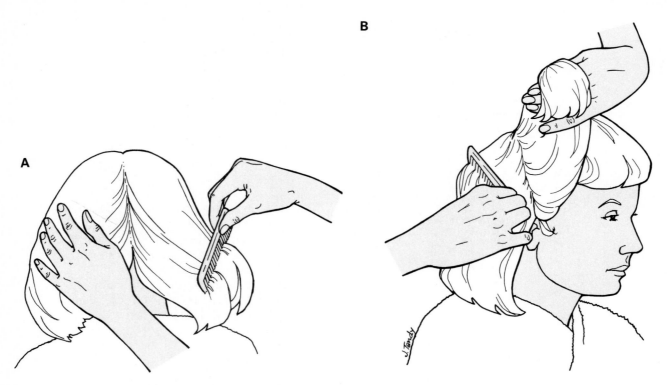

Fig. 14-33 **A,** The hair is parted down the middle and divided into two main sections. **B,** A main section is then parted into two smaller sections. (From Sorrentino, S.A.: Mosby's textbook for nursing assistants, ed. 2, St. Louis, 1987, The C.V. Mosby Co.)

Brushing and Combing Hair

Brushing and combing are usually done after the bath and whenever needed. Clients should do their own hair care if able. However, they should have as much help as necessary. Hair care is done for clients unable to do so. Be sure to consider the client's preferences when styling hair.

Long hair is easily matted and tangled during bedrest. Daily brushing and combing help prevent this problem. Braiding hair also prevents matting and tangling. Do not braid hair unless the client gives permission. You must never cut hair to remove mats or tangles.

When giving hair care, protect the client's garments by laying a towel across the shoulders. The towel collects falling hair.

Procedure: Brushing and combing hair

1. Explain to the client what you are going to do.
2. Arrange the following near the client:
   a. Comb and brush
   b. Bath towel
   c. Other toilet articles as requested
3. Wash your hands.
4. Provide for privacy.
5. Help the client to a sitting position if possible.
6. Place a towel across the client's shoulders. Place a towel across the pillow if he or she is in bed.
7. Ask the client to remove eyeglasses. Put them in the glass case.
8. Part the hair. Divide it into two sections (Fig. 14-33, A). Then divide a side into two sections (Fig. 14-33, B).
9. Brush from the scalp to the hair ends (Fig. 14-34).

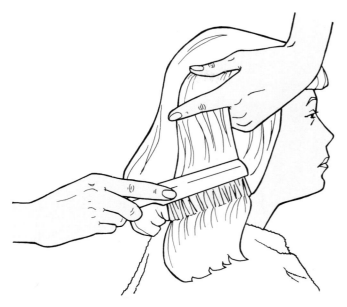

Fig. 14-34 The hair is brushed by starting at the scalp and brushing down to the hair ends. (From Sorrentino, S.A.: Mosby's textbook for nursing assistants, ed. 2, St. Louis, 1987, The C.V. Mosby Co.)

Fig. 14-35 The client is seated in front of the sink for a shampoo. The client is facing away from the sink. A towel is placed under the client's neck to protect it from the edge of the sink.

10. Style the hair as the client prefers.
11. Remove the towel.
12. Allow the client to put on eyeglasses. Help him or her assume a comfortable position.
13. Clean and return equipment to its proper place. Take soiled linen to the laundry.
14. Wash your hands.

Shampooing

Many people wash their hair at least once a week. Some shampoo two or three times a week, and others shampoo every day. Condition of the hair and scalp, hair style, and personal preference influence the frequency of shampooing. The shampoo and hair conditioner used are also a matter of personal preference.

The care plan will tell you when to wash a client's hair. If a client asks for a shampoo, tell your supervisor. Do not give a shampoo unless your supervisor tells you to.

Hair can be washed at the sink, in the tub or shower, or in bed. The nurse decides which method to use. The method depends on the client's condition, safety, and personal preference. Hair should be dried and styled as quickly as possible after shampooing. Fe-

male clients may want their hair curled or rolled up before drying.

Shampooing during the shower or tub bath. If allowed, clients can shampoo during their showers. A hand-held nozzle allows shampooing in a shower chair or during a tub bath. An extra towel, shampoo, and hair conditioner (if requested) should be within the client's reach. Be sure to help as necessary.

A shampoo at the sink. Clients who can sit in chairs can usually be shampooed at a sink. The chair is placed so the person faces away from the sink. The client's head is tilted back over the edge of the sink (Fig. 14-35). A folded towel is placed over the sink edge to protect the person's neck. A water pitcher or hand-held nozzle is used to wet and rinse the hair.

A shampoo in bed. This method is used for those who cannot sit in chairs. The client's head and shoulders are moved to the edge of the bed if the position is allowed. A rubber or plastic trough is placed under the client's head. The trough protects the linens and mattress from water. The trough also allows water to drain into a basin placed next to the bed (Fig. 14-36). A water pitcher is used to wet and rinse the hair. Ask your supervisor if your agency has plastic shampoo tray for client use.

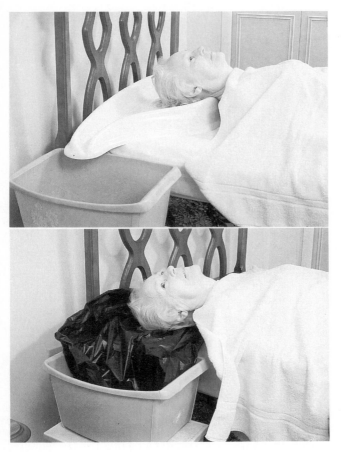

Fig. 14-36 **A,** A trough is placed under the head when shampooing the client in bed. The trough is directed to the side of the bed to allow water to drain into a collecting basin. **B,** A plastic trash bag can be used as a trough.

Procedure: Shampooing the client's hair

1. Explain to the client what you are going to do.
2. Wash your hands.
3. Arrange the following in a convenient place:
   a. Two bath towels
   b. Face towel or washcloth folded lengthwise
   c. Shampoo
   d. Hair conditioner if requested
   e. Pitcher or hand-held nozzle
   f. Equipment for the shampoo in bed (if needed)
      1. Trough
      2. Basin or pail
      3. Bath blanket
      4. Waterproof bed protector
      5. Bath thermometer
   g. Comb and brush
   h. Hair dryer
4. Provide for privacy.
5. Position the client for the method you are going to use.
6. Brush and comb hair thoroughly to remove snarls and tangles (see *Brushing and combing hair, page* 232).
7. Get water. Water temperature should be about 110° F (43° to 44° C).
8. Have the client hold a face towel or washcloth over the eyes.
9. Wet the hair completely. Use the pitcher or nozzle.
10. Apply a small amount of shampoo.
11. Work up a lather. Start at the hairline and work toward the back of the head.
12. Massage the scalp with your fingertips.
13. Rinse the hair.
14. Repeat steps 10 through 13.
15. Apply conditioner. Rinse as directed on the container.
16. Wrap the client's head with a bath towel. Dry his or her face with the towel or washcloth used for the eyes.
17. Help the client raise the head if appropriate.
18. Rub hair and scalp with the towel. Use another towel if the first one gets too wet.
19. Comb the hair to remove snarls and tangles. A female client may want hair curled or rolled up.
20. Dry the hair as quickly as possible.
21. Help the client assume a comfortable position.
22. Clean and return equipment to its proper place. Discard disposable equipment. Take soiled linen to the laundry.
23. Wash your hands.

Care of Nails and Feet

Ill, disabled, and elderly clients may have difficulty caring for their nails and feet. Foot problems can result from poor circulation, disease, poor-fitting shoes, and toenails that are not trimmed properly. Breaks in the skin are caused by hangnails, ingrown nails (nails that grow in at the side), and nails torn away from the skin. These breaks let microorganisms enter the body.

Long or broken nails can scratch the skin or snag clothing. Dirty feet, socks, or stockings can harbor microorganisms and can cause offensive odors. Nail and foot care helps to:

- Prevent infection
- Prevent injury
- Prevent odors
- Promote cleanliness

Cleaning and trimming nails are easier after they have been soaked. Be very careful when clipping and trimming fingernails to prevent damaging nearby tissues. Do not use scissors to cut fingernails. Home health aides to not cut toenails.

Procedure: Nail and foot care

1. Explain to the client what you are going to do.
2. Wash your hands.
3. Place paper towels on your work area. Arrange the following on the paper towels.
   a. Washbasin
   b. Bath thermometer
   c. Bath towel, face towel, and washcloth
   d. Emesis basin or small bowl
   e. Nail clippers
   f. Orange stick
   g. Emery board or nail file
   h. Lotion or petrolatum jelly
   i. Bath mat or newspapers
4. Provide for privacy.
5. Help the client sit in a chair or at the bedside.
6. Place a bath mat, newspapers, or towel under the feet.
7. Fill the wash basin. Water temperature should be 109° to 111° F (43° to 44° C). Add cool water if the client complains that the water is too hot.
8. Place the basin on the bath mat. Help the client put the feet into the basin.
9. Position a table in front of the client. The table should be low and close to the client. Place paper towels on the table.
10. Fill the emesis basin or bowl. Water temperature should be 109° to 111° F (43° to 44° C).
11. Place the basin (or bowl) on the table.
12. Place the client's fingers in the basin (Fig. 14-37).
13. Let the feet and fingernails soak for 20 to

Fig. 14-37 A client receiving nail and foot care. The feet are soaking in a foot basin and the fingers are soaking in the emesis basin.

30 minutes. Rewarm the water in 10 to 15 minutes.
14. Clean under fingernails with the orange stick. Then remove the basin and dry the fingers.
15. Clip fingernails straight across with the nail clippers (Fig. 14-38).
16. Shape nails with an emery board or nail file. Push cuticles back with the orange stick or a washcloth (Fig. 14-39).
17. Remove the table from in front of the client.
18. Scrub callused areas of the feet with the washcloth.
19. Remove the feet from the washbasin. Dry thoroughly.
20. Apply lotion or petrolatum jelly to the feet.
21. Help the client assume a comfortable position. Make sure the call bell is within reach.
22. Clean and return equipment and supplies to their proper place. Discard disposable supplies.
23. Take soiled linen to the laundry.
24. Wash your hands.
25. Report your observations to your supervisor:
   a. Reddened, irritated, blistered, or callused areas
   b. Breaks in the skin

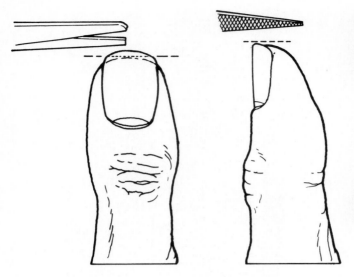

Fig. 14-38 Fingernails are clipped straight across. A nail clipper is used for the procedure. (From Sorrentino, S.A.: Mosby's textbook for nursing assistants, ed. 2, St. Louis, 1987, The C.V. Mosby Co.)

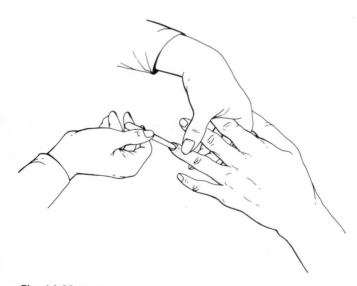

Fig. 14-39 The cuticle is pushed back with an orange stick. (From Sorrentino, S.A.: Mosby's textbook for nursing assistants, ed. 2, St. Louis, 1987, The C.V. Mosby Co.)

Decubitus Ulcers

Decubitus ulcers (decubiti) are areas where the skin and underlying tissues are eroded (Fig. 14-40). They are caused by a lack of blood flow. They are also called *bedsores* and *pressure sores*. Decubiti are seen most often in elderly, paralyzed, bedbound, obese, or very thin and

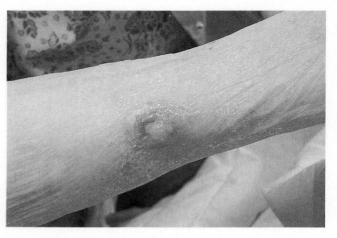

Fig. 14-40 A decubitus ulcer. (From Sorrentino, S.A.: Mosby's textbook for nursing assistants, ed. 2, St. Louis, 1987, The C.V. Mosby Co.)

malnourished clients. Others at risk include:

- Clients who cannot control their bowels or bladders
- Clients who have a decreased ability to feel heat, cold, or pressure
- Heavily sedated clients
- Clients with poor circulation
- Diabetic clients (see Chapter 21)
- Clients with casts or in traction

The first sign of a decubitus ulcer is pale or white skin or a reddened area. The client may complain of pain, burning, or tingling in the area. Some clients do not feel any abnormal sensations.

Sites

Decubitus ulcers usually develop over bony areas (Fig. 14-41). These are areas where bone lies close to the skin surface. The bony areas are also called pressure points. They bear the weight of the body in a particular position. Pressure from the weight of the body can reduce the blood supply to the area. In obese clients, decubiti can develop in areas where skin is in contact with skin. Friction results when skin is in contact with skin. Decubiti can develop between abdominal folds, the legs, and the buttocks, and underneath the breasts.

Causes

Pressure and friction are common causes of skin breakdown and decubiti. Other factors include breaks in the skin, poor circulation to an area, moisture, perspiration, poor hygiene, dry skin, and irritation by urine and feces. Inactivity and staying in one position for a long time are also risk factors.

Decubitus ulcers develop in four stages (Fig. 14-42). The area becomes larger with each stage.

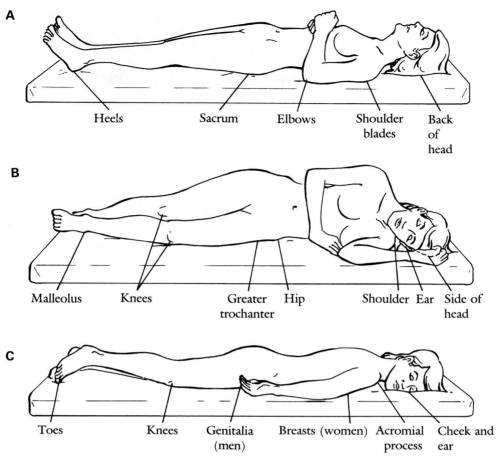

Fig. 14-41 Pressure points in: **A,** The supine position. **B,** The lateral position. **C,** The prone position. (From Sorrentino, S.A.: Mosby's textbook for nursing assistants, ed. 2, St. Louis, 1987, The C.V. Mosby Co.)

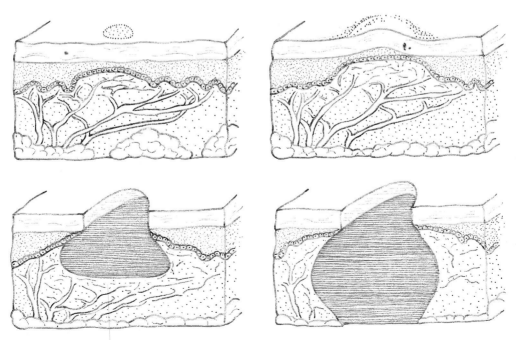

Fig. 14-42 Stages of a decubitus ulcer. (From Potter, P.A., and Perry, A.G.: Fundamentals of nursing: concepts, process, and practice, St. Louis, 1985, The C.V. Mosby Co.)

- *Stage* 1—Reddened skin. The color returns to normal when pressure is relieved or after gentle massage.
- *Stage* 2—The skin stays reddened. There may be some swelling or a blister. Tissue damage occurs.
- *Stage* 3—The sore extends through the skin layers into underlying tissues. Capillaries are also destroyed.
- *Stage* 4—Muscle is destroyed. The sore extends to the bone. The bone may be visible.

Prevention

Preventing decubitus ulcers is much easier than trying to heal them. Good nursing care, cleanliness, and skin care are essential. The following guidelines can help prevent skin breakdown and decubiti.

GENERAL GUIDELINES

1. Encourage exercise and movement.
2. Reposition the client every 2 hours. Use pillows for support.
3. Provide good skin care. Avoid harsh, irritating soaps. Make sure the skin is dry after bathing.
4. Keep the skin free of urine and feces. Give perineal care as necessary after the client urinates or has a bowel movement.
5. Keep the skin dry. Sweat and wound drainage can irritate the skin.
6. Apply lotion to dry areas such as the hands, elbows, legs, ankles, and heels. Do not apply lotion between the toes.
7. Give a back massage when the client is repositioned.
8. Keep linens clean, dry, and free of wrinkles.
9. Apply powder to areas where skin touches skin.
10. Do not irritate the skin. Avoid scrubbing or vigorous rubbing when bathing or drying the client.
11. Massage reddened or pale pressure points. Massage gently in a circular motion using lotion.
12. Use pillows and blankets to prevent skin from being in contact with skin. This reduces moisture and friction.
13. Encourage the client to eat his or her meals. Good nutrition is important for tissue growth and repair.
14. Report any signs of skin breakdown or decubiti immediately.

Treatment

Treatment of decubitus ulcers is directed by the doctor. Drugs, treatments, and special equipment may be ordered to promote healing. Your supervisor and the care plan will tell you about the client's treatment. You may be involved in using the following equipment.

Fig. 14-43 Sheepskin.

Sheepskin is placed on top of the bottom sheet (Fig. 14-43) to protect the skin from the bed linens. Friction is reduced between the skin and bottom sheet. Air circulates between the fur to help keep the skin dry. Sheepskin comes in various sizes for placement under the shoulders, buttocks, or heels. It is also called lamb's wool.

A *bed cradle* is a metal frame placed on the bed and over the client. Top linens are brought over the cradle. This keeps the weight of the linen off the client's legs and feet (see Fig. 11-25). The top linens are tucked in at the bottom of the mattress and mitered. They should also be tucked under both sides of the mattress to protect the client from air drafts and chilling. A cardboard box can be used as a bed cradle (see Fig. 11-26).

Heel and elbow protectors are made of foam rubber or sheepskin. They fit the shape of the heel or elbow (Fig. 14-44). They provide extra padding and prevent friction between linens and the heel or elbow.

Flotation pads or cushions (Fig. 14-45) are similar to water beds. They are made of a gel-like substance. The outer case is heavy plastic. Flotation pads are used for chairs and wheelchairs. The pad is placed in a pillowcase to prevent contact between the plastic and the skin. Flotation pads are expensive.

The *egg-crate mattress* is a foam pad that looks like an egg carton (Fig. 14-46). The peaks in the mattress distribute the client's weight more evenly. The small pockets let the air circulate under the client. The mattress is placed on top of the regular mattress and covered with a sheet.

A *water bed* lets the client "float" on top of the mattress (Fig. 14-47, page 240). Body weight is distributed along the entire length of the body. Therefore, pressure on bony points is avoided.

An *air mattress* is inflated with air (Fig. 14-48).

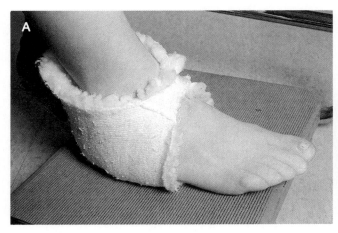

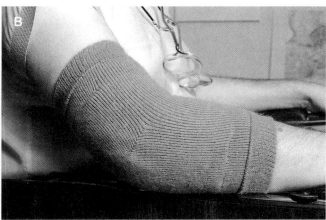

Fig. 14-44 A, Heel protector. B, Elbow protectors. (From Sorrentino, S.A.: Mosby's textbook for nursing assistants, ed. 2, St. Louis, 1987, The C.V. Mosby Co.)

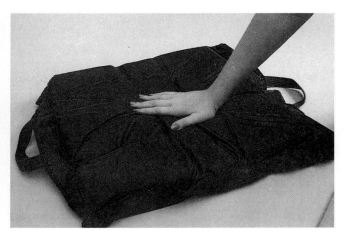

Fig. 14-45 Flotation pad. (From Sorrentino, S.A.: Mosby's textbook for nursing assistants, ed. 2, St. Louis, 1987, The C.V. Mosby Co.)

Fig. 14-46 Egg-crate mattress. (From Sorrentino, S.A.: Mosby's textbook for nursing assistants, ed. 2, St. Louis, 1987, The C.V. Mosby Co.)

Fig. 14-47 Water bed.

Fig. 14-48 Air mattress.

Body weight is distributed like with a water bed. The air mattress goes on top of the regular mattress. Air mattresses are made of plastic. An air mattress is covered with a sheet so the plastic is not in contact with the client's skin.

Trochanter rolls and *footboards* are also used to prevent and treat decubiti (see Chapter 11).

Dressing

Home care clients may wear normal, everyday clothes. Bedbound clients usually wear nightgowns or pajamas. Some women also like bed jackets. Clients should be encouraged to wear clothes during the day. This helps them feel better and improves their sense of well-being.

Allow clients to choose what they will wear. However, encourage the client to choose clothing that is comfortable and easy to put on and take off. Clothing should not restrict movement. It should be appropriate for the weather or temperature in the home. Clothes, gowns, and pajamas should be changed whenever they are damped or soiled.

Some clients are able to dress and undress themselves. Others need help. The following rules are important when dressing or undressing clients.
1. Provide for privacy. Do not expose the client.
2. Encourage the client to help as much as possible. Dressing is a form of exercise.
3. Remove clothing from the strongest or "good" side first.
4. Put clothing on the weakest side first.

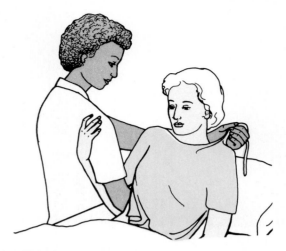

Fig. 14-49 The sides of the garment are brought to the client's back. (From Sorrentino, S.A.: Mosby's textbook for nursing assistants, ed. 2, St. Louis, 1987, The C.V. Mosby Co.)

Procedure: Dressing the client

1. Explain to the client what you are going to do. Also explain how the client can help.
2. Wash your hands.
3. Get a bath blanket and necessary clothing.
4. Provide for privacy.
5. Position the client in the supine position.
6. Cover the client with the bath blanket. Do not expose the client during the procedure.
7. Put on garments that open in the back.
   a. Slide the garment onto the arm and shoulder of the weak side.
   b. Slide the garment onto the arm and shoulder of the strong side.
   c. Raise the client's head and shoulders by locking arms with the client.
   d. Bring the sides to the back of the client (Fig. 14-49).
   e. Do the following if the client is in a side-lying position:
      1. Turn the client toward you.
      2. Bring the side of the garment to the client's back (Fig. 14-50, A).
      3. Turn the client away from you.
      4. Bring the other side to the client's back (Fig. 14-50, B).
   f. Fasten buttons, snaps, ties, or zippers.
   g. Position the client in the supine position.
8. Put on garments that open in the front.
   a. Slide the garment onto the arm and shoulder on the weak side.
   b. Raise the client's head and shoulders by locking arms with him or her. Bring the side of the garment around to the back (Fig. 14-51). Lower the client to the supine position. Slide the garment onto the arm and shoulder of the strong arm.
   c. If the client cannot raise the head and shoulders:
      1. Turn the client toward you.
      2. Tuck the garment under him or her.
      3. Turn the client away from you.
      4. Pull the garment out from under him or her.
      5. Turn the client back to the supine position.

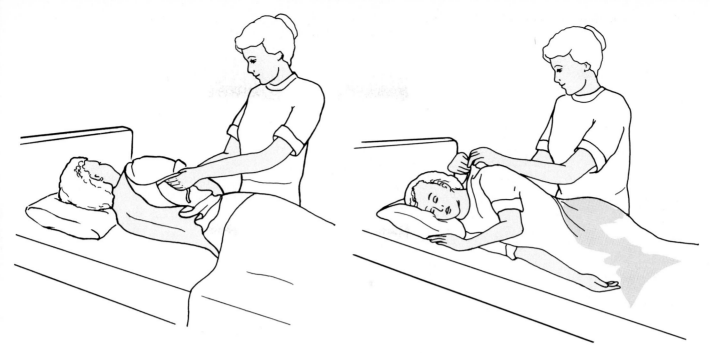

Fig. 14-50 A, The side-lying position can be used to put on garments that open in the back. The client is turned toward the aide and the garment is put on the arms. The side of the garment is brought to the client's back. B, The client is then turned away from the aide. The other side of the garment is brought to the back and fastened. (From Sorrentino, S.A.: Mosby's textbook for nursing assistants, ed. 2, St. Louis, 1987, The C.V. Mosby Co.)

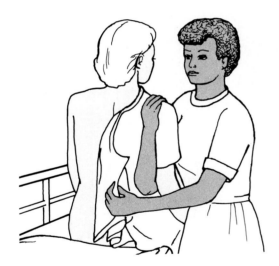

Fig. 14-51 A front-opening garment is put on with the client's head and shoulders raised. (From Sorrentino, S.A.: Mosby's textbook for nursing assistants, ed. 2, St. Louis, 1987, The C.V. Mosby Co.)

        6. Slide the garment over the arm and
           shoulder of the strong arm.
        d. Fasten buttons, snaps, ties, or zippers.
     9. Put on pullover garments.
        a. Position the client in the supine posi-
           tion.

        b. Bring the garment neck over the client's
           head.
        c. Slide the garment arm and shoulder
           onto the weak side.
        d. Raise the client's head and shoulders.
        e. Bring the garment down.
        f. Slide the garment arm and shoulder
           onto the strong side.
        g. If the client cannot assume a semisit-
           ting position:
           1. Turn the client toward you.
           2. Tuck the garment under him or her.
           3. Turn the client away from you.
           4. Pull the garment out from under him
              or her (Fig. 14-52).
           5. Return the client to the supine posi-
              tion.
           6. Slide the garment arm and shoulder
              onto the strong side.
        h. Fasten buttons, snaps, ties, or zippers.
     10. Put on pants or slacks.
        a. Slide pants over the client's feet and up
           the legs.
        b. Ask him or her to raise the hips and
           buttocks off the bed if able.
                                          Continued

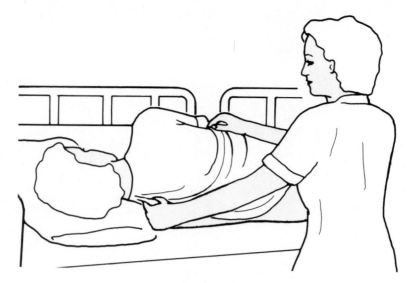

Fig. 14-52 A pullover garment is put on the client. The garment is brought down over the client. (From Sorrentino, S.A.: Mosby's textbook for nursing assistants, ed. 2, St. Louis, 1987, The C.V. Mosby Co.)

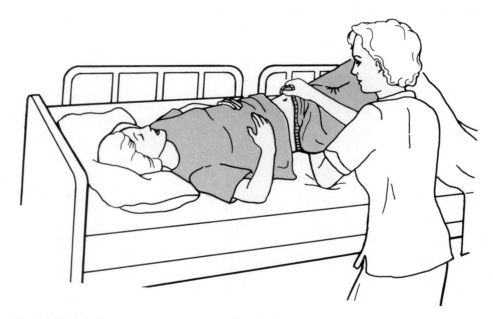

Fig. 14-53 The client lifts the hips and buttocks so the pants can be put on. (From Sorrentino, S.A.: Mosby's textbook for nursing assistants, ed. 2, St. Louis, 1987, The C.V. Mosby Co.)

c. Bring the pants up over the buttocks and hips (Fig. 14-53).
d. Ask the client to lower the hips and buttocks.
e. If the client cannot raise the hips and buttocks:
  1. Turn him or her onto the strong side.
  2. Pull pants over the buttock and hip on the weak side (Fig. 14-54).
  3. Turn the client onto the weak side.
  4. Pull them over the buttock and hip on the strong side (Fig. 14-55).
  5. Return him or her to the supine position.

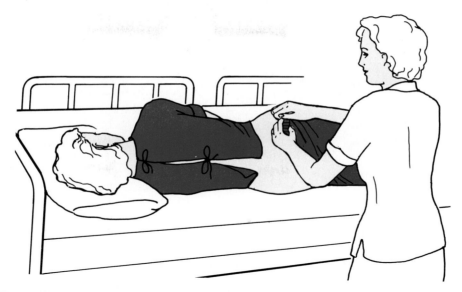

Fig. 14-54 The client is turned so the pants can be put on one side. (From Sorrentino, S.A.: Mosby's textbook for nursing assistants, ed. 2, St. Louis, 1987, The C.V. Mosby Co.)

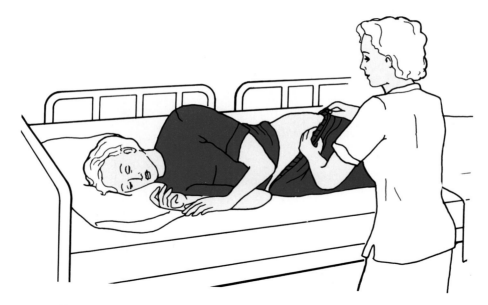

Fig. 14-55 Client turned to other side so pants can be brought up over hip and buttocks. (From Sorrentino, S.A.: Mosby's textbook for nursing assistants, ed. 2, St. Louis, 1987, The C.V. Mosby Co.)

    f. Fasten buttons, ties, snaps, the zipper, or the buckle.
11. Put socks and shoes or slippers on the client.
12. Help the client assume a comfortable position.
13. Remove the bath blanket. Make sure the call bell is within reach.
14. Take soiled clothing to the laundry.

15. Note and report your observations to the nurse.
16. Reverse the procedure to undress the client.

Dressing the Client with an IV

Some clients receive intravenous infusions. Special measures are needed when dressing these clients. The arm with the IV and the IV bottle must be handled carefully. A client may wear a special gown when receiving IV infusions. These gowns open along the entire sleeve and close with ties or snaps. Others wear regular hospital gowns or their own nightgowns, pajamas, or clothing. The sleeve opening must be large enough for the bottle. Remember to dress the side with the IV first and the strong arm last.

Procedure: Dressing the client with an IV

1. Follow steps 1 through 6 in *Dressing the client*, page 240.
2. Unfasten the garment.
3. Remove the garment from the arm without the IV.
4. Gather up the sleeve with the IV. Slide the sleeve over the IV site and tubing. Remove the client's arm and hand from the sleeve (Fig. 14-56, A).

5. Keep the sleeve gathered. Slide your arm along the tubing to the IV bottle (Fig. 14-56, B).
6. Remove the IV bottle from the pole. Slide the bottle and tubing through the sleeve (Fig. 14-56, C). Do not pull on the tubing. Keep the bottle above the client's arm.
7. Hang the IV bottle on the pole.
8. Gather the sleeve of the clean garment. This sleeve will be put on the arm with the IV infusion.
9. Remove the IV bottle from the pole. Quickly slip the gathered sleeve over the bottle at the garment shoulder (Fig. 14-56, D). Hang the bottle on the pole.
10. Slide the gathered sleeve over the tubing, hand, arm, and IV site. Then slide the sleeve onto the client's shoulder.
11. Put the other side of the garment on the client. Fasten the garment.
12. Check to see if the IV is working properly.
13. Help the client finish dressing. See *Dressing the client*, page 240.

Fig. 14-56 **A,** The gown is removed from the uninvolved arm. The sleeve on the arm with the IV is gathered up, slid over the IV site and tubing, and removed from the arm and hand.

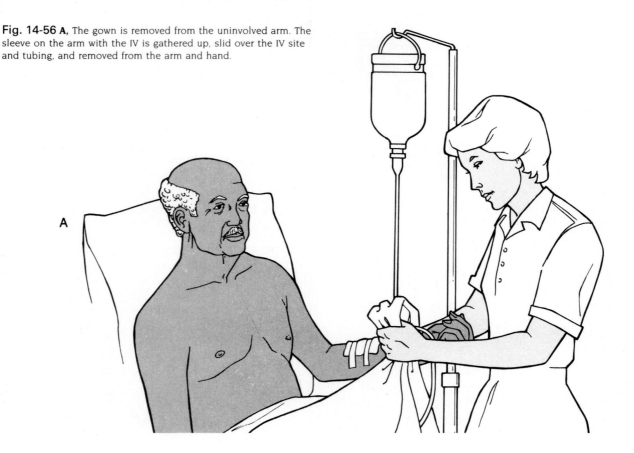

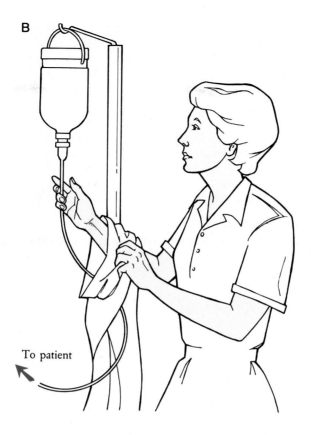

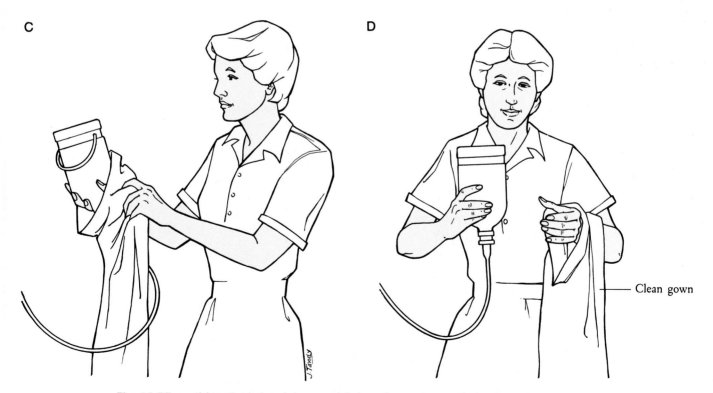

Fig. 14-56 cont'd B, The gathered sleeve is slid along the IV tubing to the bottle. **C,** The IV bottle is removed from the pole and passed through the sleeve. **D,** The gathered sleeve of the clean gown is slipped over the IV bottle at the shoulder part of the gown. (From Sorrentino, S.A.: Mosby's textbook for nursing assistants, ed. 2, St. Louis, 1987, The C.V. Mosby Co.)

Summary

Assisting clients with personal care is an important responsibility of the home health aide. The client's physical and mental well-being are affected by good personal hygiene. Cultural and personal preferences influence hygiene practices. These practices should be allowed when possible.

The skin must be kept clean and intact. This increases comfort and prevents infection. Oral hygiene, bathing, back massages, perineal care, hair care, and nail and foot care are important to the client physically and psychologically. Shaving and wearing clean clothes are also appreciated. Clients should do as much self-care as possible. You must help as necessary. Providing personal care gives you time to get to know the individual. The skin can also be observed at this time.

Decubitus ulcers result from poor care. Once they develop, they are very hard to heal. The ulcers are serious and can cause death. The client is faced with longer nursing and medical care. The bills for such care can be very high. You must help prevent decubiti. If they occur, you must follow the directions outlined by the nurse for treating them. Remember, it is easier to prevent decubiti than to treat and heal them.

Study Questions

1. A client has a mouth odor. When observing the mouth, you see food debris on the teeth. You also notice white patches on the tongue. Explain what you will do and why.

2. A client is to have a complete bed bath. The client has a decubitus ulcer on his right hip. He just had a bowel movement in the bed. It does not look like mouth care has been given for awhile. There are crusts on his lips and food debris on his teeth. Identify the order in which you will give care. Explain your reasons for giving care in that order. How should you position the client for his bath? Describe what to report to your supervisor.

3. Mrs. Johnson is paralyzed from the waist down. She uses a wheelchair. You are to help her take a shower. She also wants a shampoo and her legs and underarms shaved. Then you have to help her dress. She has dentures. Describe how you will help Mrs. Johnson. Include the safety measures that must be practiced.

Circle T if the statement is true and F if it is false.

T F   4. Cleanliness and skin care are necessary for comfort, safety, and health.
T F   5. A back massage is given only after the bath.
T F   6. Hard-bristled toothbrushes should be used.
T F   7. Unconscious clients receive mouth care in the supine position.
T F   8. Use your fingers to keep the mouth of an unconscious client open during mouth care.
T F   9. Dentures are washed in hot water.
T F 10. Bath oils are used to cleanse and soften the skin.
T F 11. Powders absorb moisture and prevent friction.
T F 12. Deodorants reduce the amount of perspiration.
T F 13. Tub baths should not last longer than 20 minutes.
T F 14. You can give permission for tub baths or showers.
T F 15. A weak client can be left alone in the shower if in a shower chair.
T F 16. Back rubs relax muscles and stimulate circulation.
T F 17. Perineal care helps prevent infection.

T F 18. Use scissors to cut a client's fingernails and toenails.
T F 19. White or reddened skin is the first sign of a decubitus ulcer.
T F 20. Decubiti usually occur over bony areas of the body.
T F 21. Pressure is a cause of decubiti.
T F 22. Garments are removed from the strong side first.

Read each question carefully and circle the *best* answer.

23. You have brushed a client's teeth. You should report
    a. Bleeding, swelling, or excessive redness of the gums
    b. Irritations, sores, or white patches in the mouth or on the tongue
    c. Lips that are dry, cracked, swollen, or blistered
    d. All of the above

24. Soaps do all of the following *except*
    a. Remove dirt and dead skin
    b. Destroy pathogens
    c. Remove skin oil and perspiration
    d. Dry the skin

25. Which action is *incorrect* when bathing an individual?
    a. Cover the client to provide warmth and privacy.
    b. Rinse the skin thoroughly to remove all soaps.
    c. Wash from the dirtiest to the cleanest area.
    d. Pat the skin dry.

26. Bath water for a complete bed bath should be
    a. 100° F
    b. 105° F
    c. 110° F
    d. 120° F

27. You are to give a back massage. Which is *false*?
    a. The massage should last about 4 to 6 minutes.
    b. Lotion should be warmed before being applied.
    c. The hands should always be in contact with the skin.
    d. Alcohol should be used to prevent friction.

28. A client's hair can be washed
    a. In the tub or shower
    b. In bed
    c. While sitting in a chair
    d. All of the above

29. Before shaving a male client with a razor blade you should
    a. Dry his face thoroughly
    b. Apply a cold washcloth to his face
    c. Soften his skin
    d. Apply after-shave lotion
30. When shaving clients you should
    a. Shave in the direction of hair growth
    b. Use long strokes around the chin and lips
    c. Use short strokes on the larger areas of the face
    d. All of the above

31. All of the following prevent decubiti *except*
    a. Repositioning the client every 2 hours
    b. Applying lotion to dry areas
    c. Scrubbing and rubbing the skin vigorously
    d. Keeping bed linens clean, dry, and free of wrinkles
32. A client is to get dressed. Which is *false*?
    a. The client should choose the clothes.
    b. Clothes should be comfortable.
    c. Clothing should not restrict movement.
    d. Clothing must open and fasten in the back.

Answers

4. True	12. False	19. True	26. c
5. False	13. True	20. True	27. d
6. False	14. False	21. True	28. d
7. False	15. False	22. True	29. c
8. False	16. True	23. d	30. a
9. False	17. True	24. b	31. c
10. False	18. False	25. c	32. d
11. True			

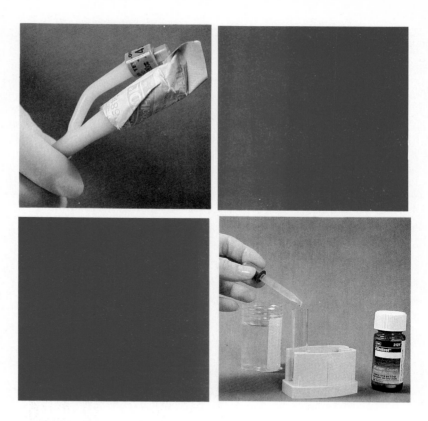

15 Elimination

Key Terms

Catheter A tube used to drain or inject fluid through a body opening

Catheterization The process of inserting a catheter

Colostomy An artificial opening between the colon and abdomen

Constipation The passage of a hard, dry stool

Defecation The process of excreting feces from the rectum through the anus; a bowel movement

Diarrhea The frequent passage of liquid stools

Enema The introduction of fluid into the rectum and lower colon

Fecal impaction The prolonged retention and accumulation of fecal material in the rectum and lower colon

Fecal incontinence The inability to control the passage of feces and gas through the anus; anal incontinence

Feces The semisolid mass of waste products in the colon

Flatulence The excessive formation of gas in the stomach and intestines

Flatus Gas or air in the stomach or intestines

Ileostomy An artificial opening between the ileum (small intestine) and the abdomen

Micturation The process of emptying the bladder; urination or voiding

Stool Feces that have been excreted

Urinary incontinence The inability to control urination

Urination The process of emptying the bladder; micturation or voiding

Voiding Urination or micturation

Elimination is a basic need. The body eliminates wastes through perspiration, breathing, urine, and feces. People cannot control the elimination of wastes through perspiration and breathing. However, the elimination of urine and feces can be controlled. Normal elimination is important for health and mental well-being.

Urinary Elimination

The healthy adult eliminates about 1000 to 1500 ml (2 to 3 pints) of urine a day. The amount of urine produced is affected by:

- The amount of fluid ingested
- The type of fluid ingested
- The amount of salt in food and fluids
- Age
- Illness
- Activity
- Drugs
- Body temperature
- Amount of perspiration
- Weather temperature

Coffee, tea, alcohol, and some drugs cause the body to produce more urine. A diet high in salt causes the body to retain water. Less urine is produced when water is retained. When a person perspires a lot, less urine is produced. Illness, activity, and weather temperature can increase perspiration. The kidneys become less efficient as the body ages. Therefore, the elderly produce less urine.

The act of eliminating urine is called *urination*. It is also called *micturation* and *voiding*. Clients may use slang terms for urination. Listen to your clients to find out what words they use. This is very important when caring for children. Most 4-year-olds will not respond if asked to "urinate." When working with adults, use professional terms. Most adults understand the words "urine," "urinate," and "urination." Foreign-speaking clients may not understand these terms. Your supervisor will help you communicate with these clients.

Reporting and Recording

Certain observations about a client's urine must be made. They are reported to your supervisor and recorded according to your agency's policy.

- *Frequency*—Most people urinate before going to bed, upon awakening, and before meals. Some urinate every 2 to 3 hours. Others void every 8 to 12 hours. Urination should not be necessary during sleep unless a lot of urine is produced.
- *Amount*—Adults normally urinate 1000 to 1500 ml a day. The amount is influenced by the factors listed on this page. You must report if the client:
  1. Is voiding frequently in small amounts
  2. Is voiding frequently in large amounts
  3. Voids less than 600 ml in 24 hours

  You may have to measure the amount of urine voided (see *Intake and output*, Chapter 17).
- *Odor*—Urine normally has a faint, aromatic odor. Some foods give urine a stong odor. Asparagus is an example. Bacteria in the urine cause a strong ammonia smell. This is seen in incontinent clients (see page 254) and those with urinary tract infections.
- *Color*—Normal urine is light yellow to amber in color. Urine is lighter when it is less concentrated and darker when more concentrated. Concentration relates to the amount of water in the urine. Bleeding, some foods, and some drugs can change the color of urine. Report any abnormal color to your supervisor.
- *Clarity*—This relates to the clearness of urine. Normal urine is clear. Abnormal urine is cloudy. It may contain pus, blood, bacteria, or other particles. You must report cloudy urine.

Maintaining Normal Urination

Some clients cannot get up to use the bathroom. These clients use bedpans, urinals, or commodes (Fig. 15-1). The following measures will help clients maintain normal urination. The rules for medical asepsis also must be practiced.

1. Provide the bedpan, urinal, or commode or help the client to the bathroom as soon as requested. The client may need to void immediately.
2. Help the client assume a normal position for void-

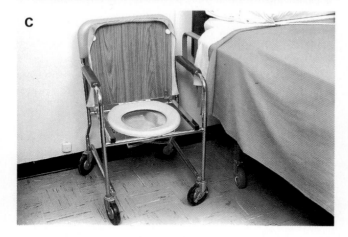

Fig. 15-1 A, Regular bedpan. **B,** Fracture pan. **C,** Urinal. (From Sorrentino, S.A.: Mosby's textbook for nursing assistants, ed. 2, St. Louis, 1987, The C.V. Mosby Co.)

ing if possible. Women void in the sitting or squatting position. Men find it easier to urinate when standing.

3. Make sure the bedpan or urinal is warm.
4. Make sure the client is covered for warmth and privacy.

5. Provide for privacy. Close the doors to the room or bathroom. Close drapes or window shades. Leave the room if the client is strong enough to be alone. Remember that elimination is a very personal and private act.
6. Remain nearby if the client is weak or unsteady.
7. Place the call bell and toilet tissue within the client's reach.
8. Allow the person enough time to void.
9. Run water in a nearby sink if the client cannot start the stream. Or place the client's fingers in some water.
10. Provide perineal care as needed.
11. Cover the bedpan with a towel or bag when carrying it to and from the bathroom.
12. Clean the bedpan, urinal, or commode container with a disinfectant. This prevents odors and the spread of microorganisms.
13. Give the client a washbasin, soap, washcloth, and towel after voiding. Help the client as necessary.
14. Offer the bedpan or urinal at regular intervals. Some clients are embarrassed or too weak to ask.

Bedpans

Bedpans are used by clients who cannot get out of bed. Women use bedpans for urination and bowel movements. Men use bedpans for bowel movements only. Bedpans are usually made of plastic or stainless steel. Stainless steel bedpans tend to be cold. They are warmed before being given to clients.

Besides the standard bedpan, fracture pans are also available (see Fig. 15-1). The *fracture pan* has a thinner rim and is only about half an inch deep at one end. The smaller end is placed under the buttocks (Fig. 15-2). Fracture pans are used for clients with casts or in traction.

Procedure: Giving the client the bedpan

1. Provide for privacy.
2. Collect the following:
   a. Bedpan
   b. Bedpan cover (large paper bag)
   c. Toilet tissue
   d. Disposable gloves
3. Warm the bedpan under warm running water. Dry it with paper towels.
4. Place the equipment on the chair or bed.
5. Explain to the client what you are going to do. Also explain what he or she can do to help.

Continued

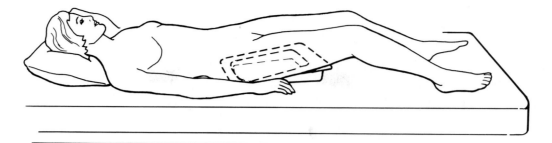

Fig. 15-2 Client positioned on a fracture pan. The smaller end is placed under the buttocks. (From Sorrentino, S.A.: Mosby's textbook for nursing assistants, ed. 2, St. Louis, 1987, The C.V. Mosby Co.)

6. Put on the gloves.
7. Position the client on the back. The head of the bed should be slightly raised. Place extra pillows behind the client if necessary.
8. Fold back top linens. Keep the lower body covered.
9. Have the client flex the knees and raise the buttocks. The client pushes against the mattress with the feet.
10. Slide your hand under the client's lower back. Help him or her raise the buttocks.
11. Slide the bedpan under the client (Fig. 15-3).
12. Do the following if the client cannot help:
    a. Turn the client onto the side away from you.
    b. Place the bedpan firmly against the buttocks (Fig. 15-4, A).
    c. Push the bedpan down and toward the client (Fig. 15-4, B).
    d. Hold the bedpan securely. Turn the client onto his or her back. Make sure the bedpan is centered under the client.
13. Cover the client with the top linens. Help the client to a sitting position. Raise the head of a hospital bed. Place extra pillows behind the client if necessary.
14. Make sure he or she is correctly positioned on the bedpan (Fig. 15-5).
15. Place the toilet tissue and call bell within reach. Ask him or her to call when through or when help is needed.
16. Leave the room and close the door. Remove the gloves and wash your hands.
17. Return when the client calls for you. Knock before entering the room.
18. Lower the head of the bed. Put on gloves.
19. Ask the client to raise the buttocks. Slide the bedpan out from under him or her. Or hold the bedpan securely and turn him or her onto the side away from you.

20. Clean the genital area if the client cannot do so. Clean from front to back with toilet tissue. Give perineal care if necessary.
21. Cover the bedpan. Take it to the bathroom.
22. Measure urine if the client is on intake and output (see Chapter 17). Collect a urine specimen if needed (see Chapter 16). Observe the color, amount, and character of the urine or feces.
23. Empty and rinse the bedpan. Clean it with a disinfectant.
24. Return the bedpan and clean cover to its proper place.
25. Help the client wash the hands.
26. Make sure he or she is comfortable. Place the call bell within reach. Make sure side rails are up if they are needed.
27. Take soiled linen to the laundry. Remove and discard the gloves.
28. Wash your hands.
29. Note and report your observations.

Urinals

Urinals are used by men. They are made of the same materials as bedpans. Plastic urinals have a cap at the top and a hook-type handle. The hook is used to hang the urinal within the client's reach (Fig. 15-6). The urinal can be used when lying, sitting, or standing. If possible, the client should stand. He may need support while standing. Sometimes it is necessary to place and hold the urinal for a client.

Urinals must be emptied promptly. This prevents odors and the spread of microorganisms. A filled urinal can easily spill and cause safety hazards. Urinals are cleaned in the same way as bedpans.

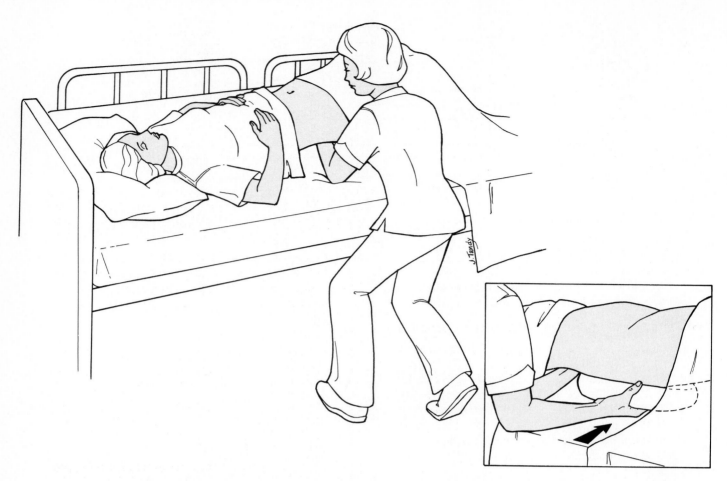

Fig. 15-3 The client raises the buttocks off the bed with the help of the aide. The bedpan is slid under the client. (From Sorrentino, S.A.: Mosby's textbook for nursing assistants, ed. 2, St. Louis, 1987, The C.V. Mosby Co.)

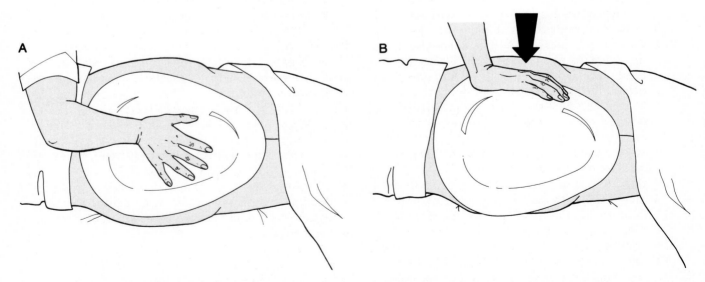

Fig. 15-4 An alternate method of giving the bedpan is used when the client is unable to help. **A,** The client lies on one side and the bedpan is placed firmly against the buttocks. **B,** The aide pushes downward on the bedpan and toward the client. (From Sorrentino, S.A.: Mosby's textbook for nursing assistants, ed. 2, St. Louis, 1987, The C.V. Mosby Co.)

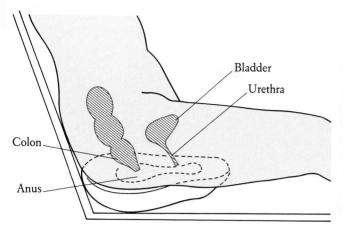

Fig. 15-5 The client is positioned on the bedpan so that the urethra and anus are directly over the opening. (From Sorrentino, S.A.: Mosby's textbook for nursing assistants, ed. 2, St. Louis, 1987, The C.V. Mosby Co.)

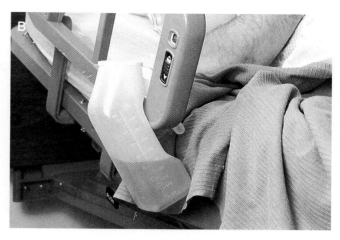

Fig. 15-6 The urinal hangs from the side rail within the client's reach. (From Sorrentino, S.A.: Mosby's textbook for nursing assistants, ed. 2, St. Louis, 1987, The C.V. Mosby Co.)

Procedure: Giving the male client the urinal

1. Put on disposable gloves.
2. Provide for privacy.
3. Help the client stand if he is able. Give him the urinal.
4. Give the client the urinal if he is going to use it in bed. Remind him to tilt the bottom down to prevent spills.
5. Position the urinal between his legs if necessary. Position his penis in the urinal.
6. Place the call bell within reach. Ask him to call when through or when he needs help.
7. Leave the room and close the door.
8. Return to the room when the client calls for you. Knock before entering the room.
9. Cover the urinal. Take it to the bathroom.
10. Measure urine if the client is on intake and output. Collect a urine specimen if needed. Observe the color, amount, and character of the urine.
11. Empty the urinal and rinse it with cold water. Clean the urinal with a disinfectant.
12. Return the urinal to its proper place.
13. Help the client wash his hands.
14. Make sure he is comfortable. Place the call bell within reach. Make sure side rails are up if they are needed.
15. Take soiled linen to the laundry. Remove and discard the gloves.
16. Wash your hands.
17. Note and report your observations.

Commodes

A bedside commode is a chair with a center opening for a bedpan or similar container (see Fig. 15-1). Clients unable to walk to the bathroom may be able to use a bedside commode. The commode lets the client assume the normal position for elimination. The bedpan or container is cleaned like a regular bedpan.

Procedure: Helping the client to the commode

1. Explain to the client what you are going to do.
2. Bring the commode next to the bed. Remove the seat and lid from the container.
3. Help the client sit on the side of the bed. Help him or her put on a robe and slippers.
4. Assist him or her to the commode.
5. Place a blanket over his or her lap for warmth.
6. Place the toilet tissue and call bell within reach.
7. Ask him or her to call when through or when help is needed.
8. Leave the room and close the door. Wash your hands.
9. Return to the room when the client calls for you. Knock before entering the room. Put on the gloves.
10. Wipe the genital area if the client cannot do so.

Continued

11. Help him or her back to bed. Remove the robe and slippers.
12. Cover and remove the container from the commode. Take the container to the bathroom.
13. Check urine and any feces for color, amount, and character. Measure urine if the client is on intake and output. Collect a specimen if one is needed.
14. Clean and disinfect the container. Return the container to the commode.
15. Help the client wash the hands.
16. Make sure he or she is comfortable and the call bell is within reach. Raise the side rails if they are needed.
17. Take soiled linen to the laundry. Remove and discard the gloves.
18. Wash your hands.
19. Note and report your observations.

Urinary Incontinence

Urinary incontinence is the inability to control the elimination of urine. Urine escapes from the bladder. The bladder may empty completely or dribbling may occur. Dribbling is common with laughing, sneezing, coughing, or straining.

Aging, spinal cord damage, nervous system diseases, urinary tract infections, and disorders of the urinary system can cause incontinence. Being unable to wait or to get to the toilet in time are other causes.

Incontinence is embarrassing. Irritation, infection, odors, and decubiti can occur. Incontinent clients must be kept dry, clean, and free of odors. Prompt hygiene and skin care are necessary. Do not let the client remain soiled while you finish another task. Take care of the client immediately. Remember to change wet linens and clothes.

Incontinence can be prevented in some cases. Some clients have problems with mobility and move slowly. Clients who have problems using their hands may be unable to remove clothing in time. Others may have urinary urgency because of an infection. One or more of the following measures may be helpful for these clients.

1. Help the client to the bathroom or offer the bedpan, urinal, or commode at regular times. Most people urinate before bed, upon awakening, and before meals.
2. Help the client to the bathroom or offer the bedpan, urinal, or commode every 1 to 2 hours.
3. Respond quickly when the client tells you that he or she needs to urinate.
4. Keep the bedpan, urinal, or commode within the client's reach. The client may be able to use the device without your help if it is nearby.
5. Encourage the client to wear clothes that can be removed easily.
6. Make sure the client's walking aid (crutches, cane, walker) is nearby.

For some clients, incontinence cannot be prevented. Some need catheters (see page 255). Others use special products for incontinence. These are found in pharmacies, department stores, and medical supply companies. The nurse will help the client and family decide which products to use and where to get them.

- *Incontinent pants* have waterproof pouches (Fig. 15-7). A pad is placed in the pouch. Urine is absorbed by the pad. Pads are changed as needed. The pants are machine washed.
- *Bed protectors* have layers of absorbent material with a plastic backing (Fig. 15-8). These can be placed on beds or furniture.
- *Protective sheets* have more than one layer. Urine drains to the bottom layer. The top layer stays dry. These are helpful at night and for bed-bound clients. Ideally the client has at least two sheets. One is always available while the other is being laundered.

The following measures are important for incontinent clients.

1. Do not bring attention to the client's incontinence. Try to be reassuring and supportive.
2. Remember that the client does not choose to be incontinent.

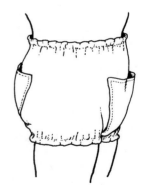

Fig. 15-7 Incontinent pants.

Fig. 15-8 Bed protector.

3. Watch your nonverbal communication. Urine may have a strong odor. Control your facial expressions.
4. Keep the client clean, dry, and odor-free. Provide hygiene and skin care, and change linens and clothes as often as necessary.
5. Use special bed protectors, pads, and sheet as directed.
6. Change padding in special underwear as often as necessary.
7. Following the bladder training program developed for the client (see page 259).
8. Treat the client with respect and dignity. Spend time with the client to show that you care. Do not avoid the client.
9. Open a window if weather permits. A good time to do this is during routine cleaning and when you make the bed. This airs out the room and helps eliminate odors.
10. Use room deodorizers as directed.

Catheters

A *catheter* is a rubber or plastic tube. It is used to drain or inject fluid through a body opening. A urinary catheter is inserted through the urethra into the bladder to drain urine. An *indwelling catheter* (*retention* or *Foley catheter*) is left in the bladder. Urine drains continuously into a collection bag. A balloon near the catheter tip is inflated after insertion. The balloon prevents the catheter from slipping out of the bladder (Fig. 15-9). Connecting tubing joins the catheter to the collection bag. A *catheterization*, the process of inserting a catheter, is done by a nurse or doctor.

The risk of infection is high in clients with catheters. They are used only when necessary. Incontinent clients may need catheters.

Clients with catheters need special care. The main goal is to prevent infection. The following measures are important.

1. Make sure urine can run freely through the catheter or tubing. The tubing should not have kinks.
2. Keep the collection bag *below* the level of the bladder. This prevents urine from flowing backward into the bladder. Attach the collection bag to the bed frame if the client is in bed. Some clients have leg bags.
3. Coil connecting tubing on the bed. Pin it to the bottom linen (Fig. 15-10). This allows urine to flow freely.
4. Tape the catheter to the thigh (see Fig. 15-10). This prevents excessive movement of the catheter. It also reduces friction at the insertion site.
5. Provide catheter care in addition to perineal care. Catheter care is done at least daily or as often as directed (see *Catheter care* on page 256).
6. Empty the collection bag before you leave the home or at time intervals directed by the nurse.

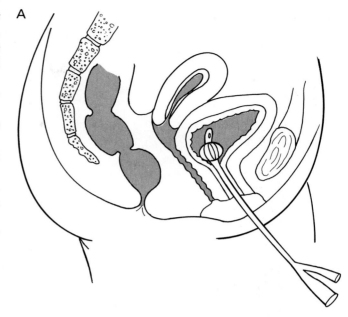

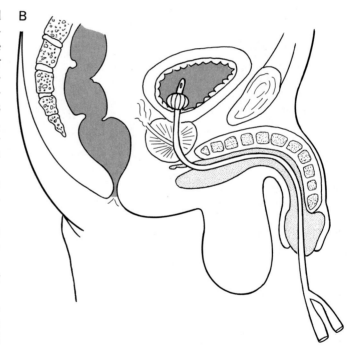

Fig. 15-9 A, The Foley catheter in the female bladder. The inflated balloon at the top prevents the catheter from slipping out through the urethra. **B,** A Foley catheter with balloon inflated in the male bladder. (From Sorrentino, S.A.: Mosby's textbook for nursing assistants, ed. 2, St. Louis, 1987, The C.V. Mosby Co.)

The amount of urine in the bag should be measured and recorded (see *Emptying a urinary collection bag* on page 257).
7. Report client complaints immediately. These in-

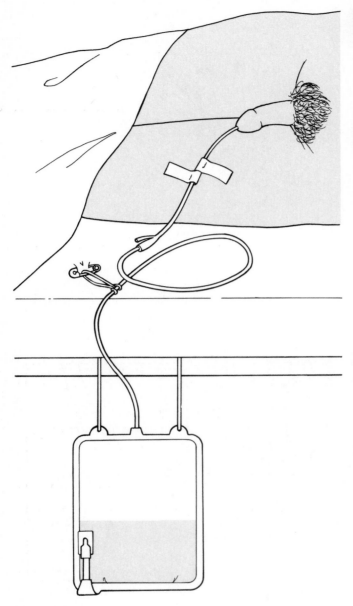

Fig. 15-10 The collecting tubing is coiled on the bed and pinned to the bottom linens. A rubber band is placed around the tubing with a clove hitch. The safety pin is passed through the loops and pinned to the linens. The catheter is taped as shown. Enough slack is left on the catheter to prevent friction at the urethra. (From Sorrentino, S.A.: Mosby's textbook for nursing assistants, ed. 2, St. Louis, 1987, The C.V. Mosby Co.)

clude complaints of pain, burning, the need to urinate, or irritation. Also report the color, clarity, and odor of urine.

8. Report if urine is leaking around the catheter.
9. Keep the catheter and tubing free of mucus, fecal material, and vaginal drainage.
10. Cover the end of the catheter whenever it is separated from the drainage tubing. Use a catheter plug or place it inside an alcohol packet (Fig. 15-11).

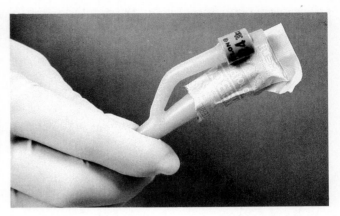

Fig. 15-11 The catheter is plugged when disconnected from the drainage tubing.

11. Move the collection bag when transferring the client. The bag must always be with the client.
12. Observe for breaks in the drainage system. Check for cracked tubing, a leak in the collection bag, leaking urine, and separation of tubing from the catheter.
13. Observe for discharge from the penis, vagina, or urethra.
14. Follow the rules of medical asepsis at all times.

Procedure: Catheter care

1. Explain to the client what you are going to do.
2. Wash your hands.
3. Collect the following:
   a. Equipment for perineal care
   b. Cotton balls or gauze pads
   c. Disposable gloves
   d. Bed protector
   e. Bag
4. Put on the gloves.
5. Provide for privacy. Cover the client with a bath blanket. Fan-fold top linens to the foot of the bed.
6. Drape the client as for perineal care (see Fig. 14-27).
7. Place the bed protector under the buttocks.
8. Perform perineal care (see *Perineal care*, page 228). Check for any crusts, abnormal drainage, or secretions.
9. Separate the labia (female) or retract the foreskin if the male is uncircumcised male (Fig. 15-12).

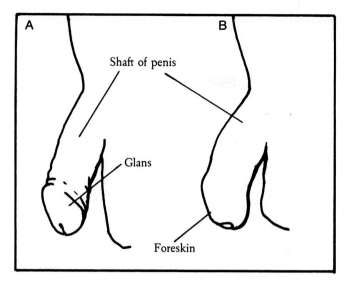

Fig. 15-12 **A,** Circumcised male. **B,** Uncircumcised male. (From Sorrentino, S.A.: Mosby's textbook for nursing assistants, ed. 2, St. Louis, 1987, The C.V. Mosby Co.)

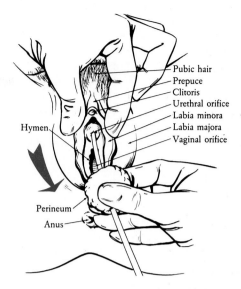

Fig. 15-13 The catheter is cleaned beginning at the meatus. About 4 inches of the catheter is cleaned. (From Sorrentino, S.A.: Mosby's textbook for nursing assistants, ed. 2, St. Louis, 1987, The C.V. Mosby Co.)

10. Apply soap to the cotton balls or gauze pads.
11. Clean from the meatus down the catheter approximately 4 inches (Fig. 15-13). Use a clean cotton ball or gauze pad for each stroke.
12. Make sure the catheter is taped properly. The tubing should be coiled and secured to the bed as in Fig. 15-10.
13. Remove the bed protector.
14. Make sure the client is comfortable. Return top linens to their proper position. Remove the bath blanket.
15. Clean and return equipment to its proper place. Discard disposable equipment.
16. Take soiled linen to the laundry. Remove and discard the gloves.
17. Wash your hands.
18. Note and report your observations.

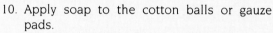

Procedure: Emptying a urinary drainage bag

1. Obtain a graduate (measuring container) and disposable gloves.
2. Wash your hands.
3. Explain to the client what you are going to do.

4. Provide for privacy.
5. Put on the gloves.
6. Place the graduate under the drain of the collection bag. The drain is at the bottom of the bag.
7. Open the clamp on the drain.
8. Allow all urine to drain into the graduate (Fig. 15-14).
9. Close the clamp. Replace the clamped drain in the holder on the bag (see Fig. 15-10).
10. Measure the urine.
11. Rinse the graduate and return it to its proper place. Remove and discard the gloves.
12. Wash your hands.
13. Record the time and amount on the intake and output record.
14. Report the amount and other observations to the nurse.

Leg Bags

Clients who can be up may prefer leg bags. They are hidden under clothing and are smaller than regular drainage bags. A leg bag is connected to the catheter and strapped to the thigh (Fig. 15-15). Leg bags are not used when clients are lying down. The lying position does not let urine drain from the bladder. The leg bag is removed at bedtime and a regular collection bag connected.

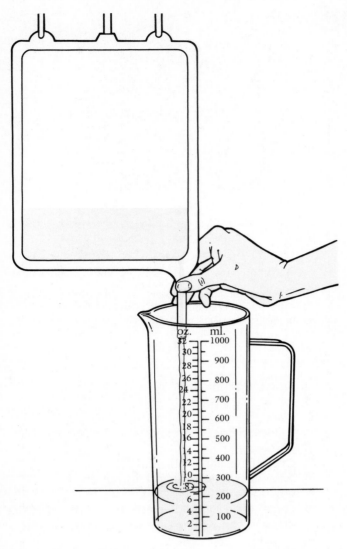

Fig. 15-14 The clamp on the urinary drainage bag is opened and the drain is directed into the graduate. Care is taken not to allow the drain to touch the inside of the graduate. (From Sorrentino, S.A.: Mosby's textbook for nursing assistants, ed. 2, St. Louis, 1987, The C.V. Mosby Co.)

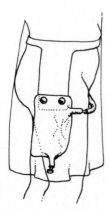

Fig. 15-15 A leg bag for urine collection.

Procedure: Connecting a leg bag	

1. Explain to the client what you are going to do.
2. Wash your hands.
3. Collect the following:
   a. Leg bag
   b. Cap or sterile 4 × 4s
   c. Alcohol packets
   d. Disposable gloves
   e. Waterproof protector
4. Provide for privacy.
5. Ask the client to sit in a comfortable position. Expose the area where the catheter and drainage tubing are joined.
6. Put on the gloves.
7. Open a sterile 4 × 4 and an alcohol packet so they are ready for use.
8. Place a waterproof protector under the area.
9. Disconnect the tubing from the catheter. Let urine drain into the collection bag. Cover the end of the drainage tube with a cap or sterile 4 × 4. Hold the catheter; do not lay it on the bed.
10. Wipe the top end of the leg bag with an alcohol pad.
11. Connect the leg bag to the catheter.
12. Strap the bag to the thigh. Make sure the bag is secure.
13. Empty the drainage bag into a graduate. Measure the amount. Discard the urine.
14. Rinse the drainage bag and allow it to dry.
15. Discard the gloves.
16. Wash your hands.
17. Record the amount of urine and your other observations.

Condom Catheter

A condom catheter goes over the penis. Urine drains from the end of the condom into the drainage tubing (Fig. 15-16). The tubing is connected to a collection bag.

A condom is made of soft rubber. It is secured to the penis with Velcro or elastic. The Velcro or elastic should not be too tight. Otherwise it will interfere with blood supply to the penis. The condom catheter is changed daily or every 2 days. Some states allow home health aides to perform the procedure.

The risk of a urinary tract infection is low. However, be sure to check the penis for irritation. Skin breakdown can lead to an infection.

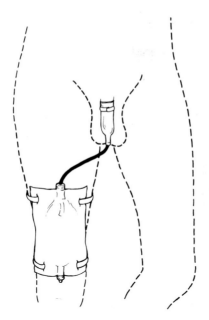

Fig. 15-16 Condom catheters. (From Potter, P.A., and Perry, A.G.: Fundamentals of nursing: concepts, process, and practice, St. Louis, 1985, The C.V. Mosby Co.)

Procedure: Applying a condom catheter

1. Explain to the client what you are going to do.
2. Wash your hands.
3. Collect the following:
   a. Condom catheter
   b. Collection bag
   c. Velcro or elastic band
   d. Equipment for perineal care
   e. Disposable gloves
4. Provide for privacy.
5. Put on the gloves.
6. Help the client lie down. Cover the client with a bath blanket and expose the penis.
7. Provide perineal care (see *Perineal Care*, page 228).
8. Attach the collection bag to the thigh or bed frame.
9. Hold the penis firmly. Roll the condom onto the penis. The condom should be about 2 inches from the head of the penis (see Fig. 15-16).
10. Secure the condom in place with Velcro or the elastic band. The Velcro or elastic should not touch the skin.

11. Connect the drainage tubing to the catheter. If the collection bag is attached to the bed, coil extra tubing to the bed as in Fig. 15-10.
12. Make sure the client is comfortable.
13. Discard disposable supplies. Take soiled linen to the laundry. Remove and discard the gloves.
14. Wash your hands.
15. Note and record your observations.

Bladder Training

Bladder training is used to help incontinent clients regain bladder control. A regular voiding pattern is established.

There are two basic methods for bladder training. One involves having the client use the toilet, commode, bedpan, or urinal at scheduled intervals. The client is allowed 15 or 20 minutes to start voiding. The rules for helping the client maintain normal urination are followed. The normal position for urination should be assumed if possible. Privacy needs to be allowed.

The other method is for clients with indwelling catheters. The catheter is clamped (Fig. 15-17) to prevent urine from draining out of the bladder. The catheter is clamped for 1 hour at first. Eventually it is clamped for 3 to 4 hours at a time. When the catheter is removed, the client uses the toilet, commode, bedpan, or urinal every 3 to 4 hours.

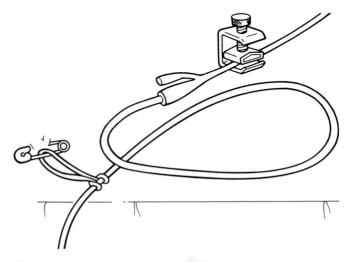

Fig. 15-17 The catheter clamp is screwed into position to prevent urine from draining out of the bladder. The clamp is applied directly to the catheter. Do not apply the clamp to the connecting tubing. (From Sorrentino, S.A.: Mosby's textbook for nursing assistants, ed. 2, St. Louis, 1987, The C.V. Mosby Co.)

Bowel Elimination

Bowel elimination involves the excretion of wastes from the gastrointestinal system. The semisolid mass of waste products in the colon is called *feces*. Defecation or *bowel movement* is the process of excreting feces through the anus. The term *stool* refers to feces that have been excreted.

As for urination, there are many slang terms for having a bowel movement. You will need to determine which words your clients use. Again, it is very important that you know the words that children use. Most adults understand the terms "bowel movement" and "stool" even though they may not use them. Be sure to use professional terms when communicating with adults if possible.

Observations

Describing bowel movements accurately helps the doctor and nurse plan for the client's care. You need to observe the following:

- *Frequency.* A client may have a bowel movement daily, several times a day, or every 2 to 3 days. A client may have a bowel movement in the morning or evening. Frequency varies with each person.
- *Consistency.* Normal stools are soft, formed, and shaped like the rectum. Feces that move through the intestine quickly are watery and unformed. This is called *diarrhea.* Feces that move through the intestine slowly are harder than normal. This is called *constipation.* Stools are described as hard, soft, formed, semiformed, or liquid.
- *Color.* Normal stools are light brown to dark brown. The color is affected by drugs, foods, and certain diseases. Green vegetables may cause green stools. Beets cause red-colored feces. Bleeding in the stomach causes black stools. Iron supplements also cause black stools.
- *Odor.* Feces have a characteristic odor. Foods, drugs, and diseases can affect the odor of stools.

You need to report the following to your supervisor. Be sure to record your observations according to your agency's policies.

- The color, amount, consistency, and odor of a client's stool
- A stool that is abnormal in color. Immediately report a stool that is black or tarry (sticky) in consistency. Ask the client about foods or drugs taken. Also ask the client if he or she is having any pain and where it is located.
- Bright red blood on the toilet tissue
- Liquid or hard stools
- Foul-smelling stools
- A change in the frequency of stools (stools several times a day or no stool for several days)
- Distended (swollen) abdomen
- Complaints of abdominal pain or cramping
- Requests for enemas or laxatives

Factors That Affect Bowel Elimination

Normal defecation is influenced by many factors. The following factors affect regularity, frequency, consistency, color, and odor of stools.

- *Privacy*—Bowel elimination is a private act. Lack of privacy may prevent a person from defecating even though the urge is present.
- *Age*—Infants and toddlers cannot control their bowel movements. Defecation occurs when feces enter the rectum. Bowel training is learned between 2 and 3 years of age. Some elderly lose bowel control because of changes due to aging. Aging can also cause feces to pass slowly through the intestine. This causes constipation.
- *Diet*—A well-balanced diet is important for elimination. A certain amount of bulk is necessary. Bulk comes from foods high in fiber (fruits and vegetables). These foods are not completely digested and leave a residue (bulk). A diet low in residue causes constipation. Gas-forming foods stimulate peristalsis. Increased peristalsis results in defecation. Gas-forming foods include onions, beans, cabbage, cauliflower, radishes, and cucumbers.
- *Fluids*—Feces contain water. Water is absorbed as feces move through the colon. Stool consistency depends on how much water is absorbed. Fluid intake and the amount of urine affect how much water is absorbed in the colon.
- *Activity*—Exercise and activity stimulate peristalsis. Irregular elimination and constipation are often due to inactivity and bed rest. Inactivity may result from disease, surgery, injury, and aging.

Medications—Drugs can be given to control diarrhea or to prevent constipation. Some drugs cause diarrhea or constipation. Drugs given for pain often cause constipation. Antibiotics (drugs that prevent or fight infection) often cause diarrhea.

Common Bowel Problems

Regular bowel movements are important to most clients. Some become more concerned about having bowel movements than about their other health problems. For example, a client may be more concerned about diarrhea than his leg pain. You need to understand the following bowel problems.

Constipation is the passing of a hard, dry, stool. The stool may be large or marble-sized. Stools may be painful to pass. The client may strain to have a bowel movement. The client may also complain of abdominal cramping and a "bloated" feeling. Constipation is common in the elderly. Causes include inadequate fluid intake, a diet low in fiber, some drugs, inactivity, ignoring the urge to defecate, and some diseases. Constipation can lead to fecal impaction.

Fecal impaction is the prolonged retention and accumulation of feces in the rectum. Fecal material becomes hard or putty-like in consistency. Water continues to be absorbed from the hardened feces. Small amounts of fluid leak from the anus. The liquid feces pass around the hardened fecal mass in the rectum. The client may also have abdominal discomfort and rectal pain. Medications and enemas may be ordered. A nurse may have to remove the feces with a gloved finger. Home health aides do not remove feces from the rectum.

Diarrhea is the frequent passage of liquid stools. Feces move through the intestines so fast that water is not absorbed. Clients feel an urgent need to defecate. Some may have difficulty controlling elimination. Abdominal cramping, nausea, and vomiting may also occur. Causes include the "flu," infections, some drugs, irritating foods, and microorganisms in food and water. Some clients have diarrhea with emotional upset.

Fecal incontinence (anal incontinence) is the inability to control the passage of feces and gas from the anus. It can be temporary or permanent, depending on the cause. Common causes include diseases, nervous system injuries, and being unable to get to the bathroom in time. This problem is embarrassing. Clients need good skin care and understanding. A bowel training program may be necessary (see page 263).

Flatulence is the excessive formation of gas in the stomach and intestines. *Flatus* is gas or air in the stomach or intestines. Flatus is expelled through the mouth and anus. If gas is not expelled, the intestines distend. In other words, the intestines swell or enlarge from the gases. The client may have abdominal cramping, shortness of breath, and a swollen abdomen. Causes include gas-forming foods, constipation, medications, and abdominal surgery.

Promoting Bowel Elimination

Certain measures help promote normal bowel elimination. The nurse will plan measures that involve diet, fluids, and exercise. The doctor will order medications or enemas if they are needed. You should routinely practice the following to promote bowel elimination, comfort, and safety.

1. Provide the bedpan or help to the toilet or commode as soon as requested by the client.
2. Provide for privacy. Ask visitors to leave the room. Close doors and pull window shades or curtains. Remember that defecation is a private act. Leave the room if the client can be alone.
3. Make sure the bedpan is warm.

4. Position the client in a normal and comfortable position for defecation. The sitting or squatting position is assumed by both men and women.
5. Make sure the client is covered for warmth and privacy.
6. Allow enough time for defecation.
7. Place the call bell and toilet tissue within reach.
8. Remain nearby if the client is weak or unsteady.
9. Provide perineal care.
10. Wear gloves so your hands do not touch feces.
11. Dispose of fecal material promptly. This reduces odors and prevents the spread of microorganisms.
12. Allow the client to wash the hands after defecating and wiping with toilet tissue.
13. Offer the bedpan after meals if the client has fecal incontinence.

Enemas

An *enema* is the introduction of fluid into the rectum and lower colon. Enemas are ordered by doctors. They are given:

- To remove feces in fecal impaction and constipation
- To clean the bowel of feces before certain surgeries and x-ray procedures
- For flatus and distention
- As part of some bowel training programs

Many people give themselves enemas. However, home health aides usually do not give enemas. If they do, commercial enemas are given.

Commercial enemas are ready to be given (Fig. 15-18). The enema contains about 120 ml (4 ounces) of a solution. The solution stimulates defecation by irritating and distending the rectum. The solution is usually given at room temperature. However, the nurse may ask you to warm the enema in a basin of warm water. The left Sims' position or a left side-lying position is usually used.

The bottle is squeezed and rolled up from the bottom to administer the solution. Squeezing and rolling are continued until all of the solution has been given. Do not release pressure on the bottle. If pressure is released, solution will be withdrawn from the rectum back into the bottle. The client should retain the solution until the urge to defecate is felt. Remaining in the Sims' or side-lying position will help the client retain the enema longer.

You should give a commercial enema only if you have received the proper training. Make sure you have clear instructions. Also review the procedure with your supervisor. Enemas can be dangerous for clients with certain heart and kidney diseases. Be sure to consult your supervisor if an enema is ordered for a client with a heart or kidney disease.

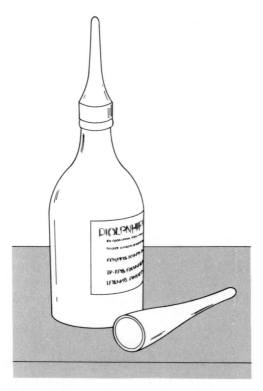

Fig. 15-18 A commercial enema. (From Sorrentino, S.A.: Mosby's textbook for nursing assistants, ed. 2, St. Louis, 1987, The C.V. Mosby Co.)

Procedure: Giving a commercial enema

1. Explain to the client what you are going to do. Also explain how the client can help.
2. Wash your hands.
3. Collect the following equipment:
   a. Commercial enema
   b. Bedpan, commode, or specimen pan
   c. Waterproof bed protector
   d. Toilet tissue
   e. Disposable gloves
   f. Robe and slippers
   g. Specimen container (if needed)
   h. Bath blanket
4. Provide for privacy.
5. Put on the gloves.
6. Cover the client with a bath blanket. Fanfold top linens to the foot of the bed.
7. Position the client in the left Sims' or a comfortable side-lying position.
8. Place the waterproof bed protector under the buttocks.
9. Drape the client to expose the anal area.

10. Place the bedpan near the client.
11. Remove the cap from the enema.
12. Separate the buttocks so you can see the anus.
13. Ask the client to take a deep breath through the mouth.
14. Insert the enema tip 2 inches into the rectum when the client is exhaling (Fig. 15-19). Insert the tip gently.
15. Squeeze and roll the bottle gently. Do not release pressure on the bottle until all of the solution has been given.
16. Remove the tip from the rectum. Put the bottle back into the box tip first.
17. Help the client onto the bedpan. Or help the client to the commode or bathroom.
18. Place the call bell and toilet tissue within the reach. Remind the client not to flush the toilet.
19. Leave the room if it is safe to leave the client alone. Take disposable items with you and discard them.
20. Return to the room when the client calls for you. Knock before entering the room.
21. Observe enema results for amount, color, consistency, and odor.
22. Obtain a stool specimen if ordered.
23. Help the client clean the perineal area if indicated.
24. Empty, clean, and disinfect the bedpan or commode container. Return the bedpan or commode container to its proper place.
25. Remove the waterproof bed protector.

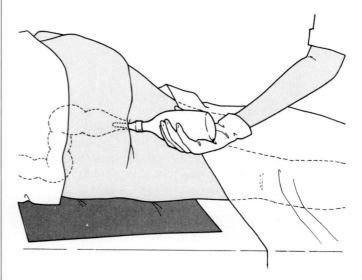

Fig. 15-19 The tip of the commercially prepared enema is inserted 2 inches into the rectum. (From Sorrentino, S.A.: Mosby's textbook for nursing assistants, ed. 2, St. Louis, 1987, The C.V. Mosby Co.)

26. Help the client wash the hands.
27. Return top linens to their proper position. Remove the bath blanket.
28. Make sure the client is comfortable and the call bell is within reach. Raise the side rails if they are needed.
29. Take soiled linen to the laundry. Remove and discard the gloves.
30. Wash your hands.
31. Note and report your observations.

Bowel Training

Bowel training involves two aspects. One is gaining control of bowel movements. The other is developing a regular pattern of elimination. Fecal impaction, constipation, and anal incontinence are prevented. The urge to defecate is usually felt after a meal, particularly breakfast. Therefore, the use of the toilet, commode, or bedpan is encouraged at this time. Other factors that influence elimination are included in the care plan and bowel training program. These include diet, fluids, activity, and privacy. The doctor may order a suppository to stimulate defecation. A *suppository* is a cone-shaped solid medication that is inserted into a body opening. Suppositories melt at body temperature. A nurse inserts a suppository into the rectum. It is inserted about 30 minutes before the time selected for the bowel movement. As with bladder training, the nurse will instruct you about a client's bowel training program.

The Client with an Ostomy

Part of the intestine may be surgically removed. Cancer, diseases of the bowel, and trauma (e.g., stab wounds or bullet wounds) are common reasons for intestinal surgery. Many times it is necessary to perform an *ostomy*. An ostomy is the surgical creation of an artificial opening. The opening is called the *stoma*.

Colostomy

A *colostomy* is an artificial opening between the colon and abdomen. Part of the colon is brought out onto the abdominal wall and a stoma is made. Fecal material and flatus are expelled through the stoma. A colostomy may be permanent or temporary. If the colostomy is permanent, the diseased portion of the colon is removed. A temporary colostomy lets the diseased or injured part of the bowel heal. When healing occurs, the bowel is surgically reconnected.

The location of the colostomy depends on which part of the colon is diseased or injured. Figure 15-20 shows common colostomy sites. The consistency of the stool depends on the location of the colostomy. The stool can be liquid to formed. The more colon remaining to absorb water, the more solid and formed the stool. If the colostomy is near the beginning of the colon, stools will be liquid. A colostomy near the end of the colon will result in a formed stool.

The person needs to wear a colostomy appliance. A colostomy appliance is a disposable plastic bag applied over the stoma. The bag collects feces expelled through the stoma. When the appliance becomes soiled, it is removed and a new one applied. Skin care is given to prevent skin breakdown around the stoma. The appliance has an adhesive backing that is applied to the skin. Many people also secure the appliance to an ostomy belt (Fig. 15-21). Many people manage their own colostomies. However, some need assistance.

Odors must be prevented. Good hygiene is essential. A new bag should be applied whenever soiling occurs. Avoiding gas-forming foods also helps control odors. Deodorants can be put into the appliance. The nurse will tell you which one to use.

Procedure: Caring for the client with a colostomy

1. Explain to the client what you are going to do. Also explain how the client can help.
2. Wash your hands.
3. Collect the following:
   a. Bedpan with cover
   b. Waterproof bed protectors
   c. Bath blanket
   d. Toilet tissue
   e. Clean colostomy appliance
   f. Clean ostomy belt
   g. Washbasin
   h. Bath thermometer
   i. Prescribed soap or cleansing agent
   j. Karaya powder, karaya ring, or other skin barrier if ordered
   k. Deodorant for the appliance
   l. Bag
   m. Paper towels
   n. Disposable gloves
4. Provide for privacy.
5. Put on the gloves.
6. Cover the client with a bath blanket. Fanfold linens to the foot of the bed.
7. Place the waterproof pad under the buttocks. Ask the client to raise the hips if able. *continued*

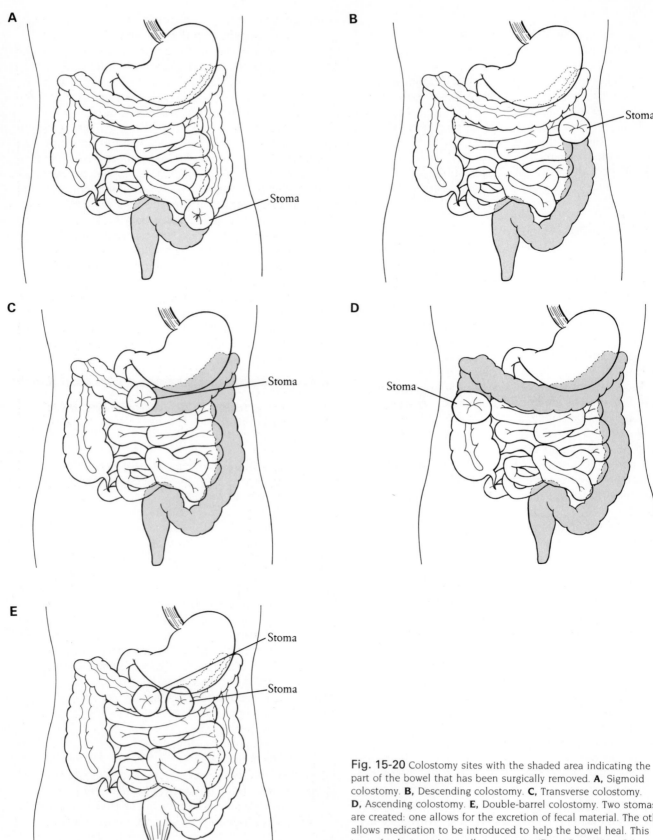

Fig. 15-20 Colostomy sites with the shaded area indicating the part of the bowel that has been surgically removed. **A,** Sigmoid colostomy. **B,** Descending colostomy. **C,** Transverse colostomy. **D,** Ascending colostomy. **E,** Double-barrel colostomy. Two stomas are created: one allows for the excretion of fecal material. The other allows medication to be introduced to help the bowel heal. This type of colostomy is usually temporary. (From Sorrentino, S.A.: Mosby's textbook for nursing assistants, ed. 2, St. Louis, 1987, The C.V. Mosby Co.)

ter. Rinse and pat dry. Use soap or other cleansing agent if ordered.
15. Apply the karaya powder, karaya ring, or other skin barrier.
16. Put a clean colostomy belt on the client.
17. Add the deodorant to the new appliance.
18. Peel back the protector from the adhesive surface of the new appliance.
19. Apply the appliance so that it is centered over the stoma. Make sure it is sealed to the skin. Apply gentle pressure to the adhesive surface from the stoma outward.
20. Connect the belt to the appliance.
21. Remove the waterproof bed protector.
22. Change damp or soiled linen. Return top linens to their proper position. Remove the bath blanket.
23. Make sure the client is comfortable. Make sure the call bell is within reach.
24. Clean the bedpan, washbasin, and other equipment. Return them to their proper places.
25. Collect used disposable equipment and place in the bag.
26. Take the bag to the garbage. Take soiled linen to the laundry. Remove and discard the gloves.
27. Wash your hands.
28. Note and report your observations.

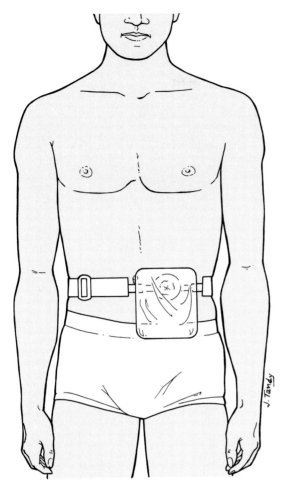

Fig. 15-21 A colostomy appliance in place over the stoma and secured with a colostomy belt. (From Sorrentino, S.A.: Mosby's textbook for nursing assistants, ed. 2, St. Louis, 1987, The C.V. Mosby Co.)

8. Disconnect the appliance from the colostomy belt. Remove the belt.
9. Remove the appliance gently. Place it in the bedpan.
10. Wipe around the stoma with toilet tissue to remove any mucus or fecal material. Place soiled tissue in the bedpan.
11. Cover the bedpan and take it to the bathroom.
12. Empty the contents of the appliance and bedpan into the toilet. Note the color, amount, consistency, and odor of fecal material. Place the appliance in the bag.
13. Fill the washbasin with water. Water temperature should be 115° F (46.1° C). Place the basin on the work area.
14. Clean the skin around the stoma with wa-

Ileostomy

An *ileostomy* is an artificial opening between the ileum (small intestine) and the abdomen. Part of the ileum is brought out onto the abdominal wall and a stoma is made. The entire large intestine is removed (Fig. 15-22). Liquid fecal material drains constantly from an ileostomy. Water cannot be absorbed because the colon has been removed. Feces from the small intestine contain digestive juices. Therefore, it is very irritating to the skin. The ileostomy appliance must fit well so feces do not touch the skin. The appliance is sealed to the skin and is removed every 2 to 4 days. Good skin care is essential.

Disposable and reusable ileostomy appliances are available. The appliance is clamped at the end. Fecal material collects in the bag. To empty the bag, it is directed into the toilet and the clamp removed (Fig. 15-23). The appliance is usually emptied every 4 to 6 hours or when the person urinates. Reusable bags are washed with soap and water and allowed to dry and air out. The care of an ileostomy client is similar to that of a colostomy client.

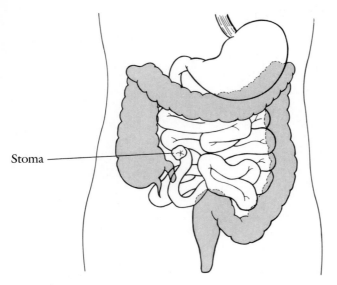

Fig. 15-22 An ileostomy. The entire large intestine is surgically removed during the operation. (From Sorrentino, S.A.: Mosby's textbook for nursing assistants, ed. 2, St. Louis, 1987, The C.V. Mosby Co.)

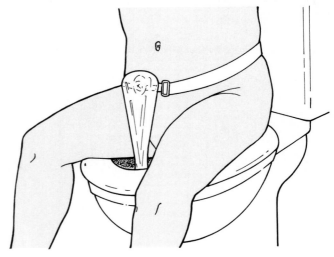

Fig. 15-23 The client with an ileostomy empties the appliance by directing it into the toilet and unclamping the end. (From Sorrentino, S.A.: Mosby's textbook for nursing assistants, ed. 2, St. Louis, 1987, The C.V. Mosby Co.)

Procedure: Caring for the client with an ileostomy

1. Explain to the client what you are going to do. Also explain what the client can do to help.
2. Wash your hands.
3. Collect the following:
   a. Prescribed solvent
   b. Medicine dropper
   c. Clean appliance
   d. Clean belt
   e. Clamp for the appliance
   f. Gauze dressing
   g. Washcloth and towels
   h. Cotton balls
   i. Prescribed soap or other cleansing agent
   j. Karaya ring
   k. Soft brush
   l. Deodorant
   m. Disposable gloves
4. Arrange the equipment in the bathroom.
5. Help the client to the bathroom. Have him or her sit on the toilet.
6. Put on the gloves.
7. Direct the appliance into the toilet (see Fig. 15-23). Remove the clamp from the bottom of the appliance.
8. Let the appliance empty into the toilet.

Wipe the end with toilet tissue. Discard tissue into the toilet. Observe amount, color, consistency, and odor of drainage.
9. Disconnect the appliance from the belt. Remove the belt.
10. Apply a few drops of solvent to the skin around the appliance. Use the medicine dropper. The appliance will loosen and can be gently removed.
11. Cover the stoma with a gauze dressing to absorb drainage.
12. Wet the skin around the stoma. Use a cotton ball soaked with solvent.
13. Clean the skin around the stoma with warm water. Rinse and pat dry. Use soap or other cleansing agent only if ordered.
14. Moisten a karaya ring.
15. Remove the gauze dressing from the stoma.
16. Apply the karaya ring, when it is sticky, to the skin around the stoma.
17. Add deodorant to the appliance.
18. Apply the appliance to the karaya ring. Be sure the bottom of the appliance is clamped.
19. Put a clean belt on the client. Connect the belt to the appliance.
20. Help the client wash the hands.
21. Make sure he or she is comfortable and the call bell is within reach.
22. Clean the used appliance with soap and

water using the soft brush. Wash the belt. Allow both items to dry.
23. Clean and return reusable equipment to its proper place.
24. Collect used disposable equipment and discard in the garbage. Take soiled linen to the laundry. Remove and discard the gloves.
25. Wash your hands.
26. Note and report your observations.

Summary

Elimination is a basic need. Normal urinary and bowel elimination are necesary for health and psychological well-being. So are the hygiene practices that follow elimination. Many factors affect elimination. A major factor is privacy. People normally urinate or have bowel movements in private. Urinating or having a bowel movement with others present is embarrassing. Bowel and bladder control is also very important. Diseases and injuries can result in loss of control. This is also embarrassing and frustrating to clients. These clients need good skin care to prevent odors, decubiti, and infection.

Study Questions

1. You are a 68-year-old female and need home care. You are living with your daughter. She has four teenagers, two boys and two girls. They are watching television in the living room. The dining area has been rearranged for your bedroom. A screen separates the dining and living room. However, the screen does not prevent sounds or conversations from being heard. You need to have a bowel movement and to urinate. You ask the aide for the bedpan. Describe what you might be thinking and feeling in this situation.

2. A 25-year-old male client has an ileostomy. He was engaged to be married. However, his girlfriend broke the engagement 3 months after he came home from the hospital. You are a 21-year-old female. Sometimes you think that the client is making advances toward you. Describe how you would care for this client. Be sure to include his physical, psychological, and social needs.

Circle the *best* answer.

3. Which terms mean urination?
   a. Dysuria and ostomy
   b. Catheterization and incontinence
   c. Micturation and voiding
   d. Catheter and urinal

4. Which statement about urination is *false*?
   a. Urine is normally clear and yellow or amber in color.
   b. Urine normally has an ammonia odor.
   c. People normally urinate before going to bed and upon rising.
   d. A person normally urinates about 1000 ml to 1500 ml a day.

5. Which is *not* a rule for maintaining normal elimination?
   a. Help the individual assume a normal position for urination.
   b. Provide for the person's privacy.
   c. Help the person to the bathroom or commode, or provide the bedpan or urinal as soon as requested.
   d. Always stay with the person who is on a bedpan.

6. The best position for using a bedpan is
   a. Fowler's position
   b. The supine position
   c. The prone position
   d. The side-lying position

7. After a man uses the urinal, you should ask him to
   a. Measure the urine
   b. Use the call bell
   c. Put the urinal on the bedside table
   d. Empty the urinal

8. A client has a catheter. You should do all of the following *except*
   a. Keep the collection bag above the level of the bladder
   b. Make sure the connecting tubing is free of kinks
   c. Coil the connecting tubing on the bed
   d. Tape the catheter to the client's thigh

9. A client has a catheter. Which statement is *false*?
   a. Daily perineal care is enough hygiene.
   b. The rules of medical asepsis must be followed.
   c. The collection bag is emptied when you leave the home.
   d. Complaints of pain, burning, the need to urinate, or irritation must be reported immediately.

10. The goal of bladder training is to
    a. Remove the catheter
    b. Allow the person to walk to the bathroom
    c. Gain voluntary control of urination
    d. All of the above

11. Which statement is *false*?
    a. Regular bowel elimination means that a person must have a bowel movement every day.
    b. Stools are normally brown, soft, and formed.
    c. Diarrhea occurs when feces move through the intestines rapidly.
    d. Constipation results when feces move through the large intestine slowly.

12. Bowel elimination is affected by
    a. Privacy and age
    b. Medications and diet
    c. Fluid intake and activity
    d. All of the above
13. The prolonged retention and accumulation of feces in the rectum is called
    a. Constipation
    b. Fecal impaction
    c. Flatulence
    d. Anal incontinence
14. Which will *not* promote comfortable and safe bowel elimination?
    a. Asking visitors to leave the room
    b. Assisting the client to assume a sitting position
    c. Offering the bedpan after meals
    d. Telling the client that you will return very soon
15. You are going to give a commercial enema. How should you position the client?
    a. Sims' position
    b. Supine position
    c. Squatting position
    d. Fowler's position

16. Bowel training is aimed at
    a. Gaining control of bowel movements
    b. Developing a regular pattern of elimination
    c. Preventing fecal impaction, constipation, and anal incontinence
    d. All of the above
17. Which statement about colostomies is *false*?
    a. Good skin care around the stoma is essential.
    b. Odors can be controlled with deodorant.
    c. The individual will have to wear an appliance.
    d. Fecal material is always liquid in consistency.
18. The ileostomy appliance is usually emptied
    a. Every 4 to 6 hours
    b. Every morning
    c. Every 2 to 3 days
    d. When the doctor gives the order to do so

Answers

3. c	7. b	11. a	15. a
4. b	8. a	12. d	16. d
5. d	9. a	13. b	17. d
6. a	10. c	14. d	18. a

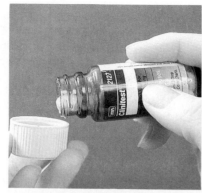

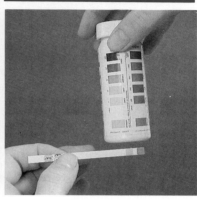

16 Collecting Specimens

Chapter Highlights

Urine specimens

Testing urine

Stool specimens

Sputum specimens

What you will learn to do

- Explain why urine, stool, and sputum specimens are collected
- Describe the rules for collecting specimens
- Collect urine, stool, and sputum specimens
- Test urine for sugar and acetone

Key Terms

Acetone Ketone bodies that appear in the urine due to the rapid breakdown of fat for energy

Calculi Stones

Diabetes mellitus A chronic disease in which the pancreas fails to secrete enough insulin; the body cannot use sugar for energy

Glucosuria Sugar (glucos) in the urine (uria)

Ketone body Acetone

Sputum Mucus secreted by the lungs, bronchi, and trachea during respiratory illnesses or disorders

Specimens are small samples of the body's waste, secretions, or tissue. Urine, feces, and sputum are the most common specimens collected by home health aides. After collection, the specimens are tested or studied in a laboratory. This gives information about body function. The doctor uses the information to diagnose or prescribe treatment. Accuracy is very important. Mistakes can cause a wrong diagnosis or the wrong treatment.

Remember that elimination is very private and personal (see Chapter 15). Almost everyone has had to give a urine sample at one time or another. Starting the stream and urinating into the specimen container can be difficult. Giving the specimen to the health worker can be embarrassing. Put yourself in the client's place when collecting and testing specimens. The client may be embarrassed and concerned about the test results. The client needs privacy, respect, and understanding.

Urine Specimens

Some urine specimens are studied in the laboratory. Others are tested in the home by the client, family, or home health aide. Urine specimens are collected to:

- Check for sugar, acetone, microorganisms, blood, drugs, or other substances
- Help the doctor diagnose the client's problem
- Evaluate the client's condition
- Determine the effectiveness of treatment

GENERAL GUIDELINES

Different types of urine specimens are presented in this chapter. However, the following guidelines apply when collecting any urine specimen.

1. Check the orders with your supervisor to make sure you are collecting the right specimen.
2. Explain the procedure to the client. Make sure he or she understands what needs to be done.
3. Wash your hands before and after collecting the specimen.
4. Wear gloves to avoid contact with the specimen.
5. Collect the specimen at the proper time.
6. Use the proper container for the specimen.
7. Use a clean container for each specimen.
8. Do not touch the inside of the container or lid.
9. Ask the client not to have a bowel movement while a urine specimen is being collected. The specimen must be free of feces.
10. Ask the client to put toilet tissue in the toilet or wastebasket. The specimen should not contain tissue.
11. Provide for privacy. Allow the client to collect the specimen if able. Do not expose the client if you collect the specimen.

12. Practice the measures described in Chapter 15 to promote normal urinary and bowel elimination.
13. Label the container with the client's name, address, date and time of collection, and type of specimen. Provide other information as requested.
14. Store the specimen as instructed or described in the procedure.
15. Note and report your observations about the specimen and the client.
16. Take the specimen to the laboratory if requested.

Routine Urine Specimen

The routine urine specimen is also called the random urine sample. Random urine means that the specimen is collected whenever the client can void. No special measures are required. Simple tests are performed on this type of specimen. The urine can be collected by having the client:

- Void into the specimen container
- Void into a urine catcher, which is shaped like an upside-down hat (Fig. 16-1). This is sometimes called a specimen pan.
- Void into the bedpan or urinal

Many clients can collect the specimen themselves. Weak and very ill clients need help in obtaining the specimen.

Procedure: Collecting a routine urine specimen

---

1. Explain the procedure to the client.
2. Wash your hands.
3. Collect the following:
   a. Bedpan and cover, urinal, or disposable specimen pan

Continued

Fig. 16-1 Urine catcher or specimen pan is placed in the toilet.

    b. Specimen container and lid
    c. Label
    d. Disposable gloves
    e. Paper bag
4. Label the container (see page 270).
5. Put the container and lid in the bathroom.
6. Provide for privacy.
7. Put on the gloves.
8. Ask the client to urinate into the appropriate receptacle. Remind him or her to put toilet tissue into the toilet or wastebasket, not in the bedpan or specimen pan.
9. Take the bedpan or urinal to the bathroom.
10. Measure urine if the client is on intake and output (see Chapter 17).
11. Pour urine into the specimen container until it is about three-fourths full. Dispose of excess urine.
12. Place the lid on the specimen container.
13. Clean and return the bedpan or urinal to its proper place.
14. Help the client to wash the hands.
15. Make sure he or she is comfortable and the call bell is within reach.
16. Place the urine specimen in the paper bag.
17. Remove and discard the gloves.
18. Wash your hands.
19. Place the specimen in the refrigerator until it can be taken to the laboratory.
20. Note and report your observations (see Chapter 15, page 249).

The Clean-Catch Urine Specimen

The clean-catch urine specimen is also called a midstream or clean-voided specimen. Urine is collected before it is contaminated outside the body. Midstream means the sample is taken after the client has started to void.

The perineal area is cleaned before collecting the specimen. This reduces the number of microorganisms in the urethral area. The client begins to void into the toilet, bedpan, urinal, or commode. Then the stream is stopped and the specimen container positioned. The client then voids into the specimen container until the specimen is obtained.

Many clients find it hard to stop the stream of urine. Be sure to wear disposable gloves when collecting a clean-catch urine specimen. You may have to position and hold the specimen container in place after the client starts voiding. If this specimen is ordered, your supervisor will give you a clean-catch specimen kit.

Procedure: Collecting a clean-catch urine specimen

1. Explain the procedure to the client.
2. Wash your hands.
3. Collect the following:
    a. Clean-catch collection kit
    b. Disposable gloves
    c. Bedpan, urinal, or commode if the client cannot use the bathroom
    d. Paper bag
4. Label the container (see page 270).
5. Provide for privacy.
6. Allow the client to complete the procedure if able. Make sure the call bell is within reach.
7. Assist the client if necessary. Put on the gloves.
8. Offer the bedpan or urinal or help him or her to the bathroom or commode.
9. Open the kit. Remove the specimen container and towelettes.
10. Provide perineal care. Use the towelettes or specified solution.
11. Keep the labia separated in the female until the specimen has been collected. If the specimen is collected from an uncircumcised male, keep the foreskin retracted.
12. Collect the specimen:
    a. Ask the client to urinate into the receptacle.
    b. Ask him or her to stop the stream of urine.
    c. Hold the specimen container under the client.
    d. Ask him or her to start urinating again.
    e. Ask the client to stop the stream when urine has been collected.
    f. Allow him or her to finish urinating.
13. Put the lid on the specimen container immediately. Do not touch the inside of the lid.
14. Help the client clean the perineal area. Return the foreskin of the uncircumcised male to its natural position.
15. Clean and return the bedpan or commode it to its proper place. Discard disposable equipment.
16. Help the client wash the hands.
17. Make sure the client is comfortable and the call bell is within reach.
18. Place the specimen container in the paper bag. *Continued*

19. Remove and discard the gloves.
20. Place the bag in the refrigerator until the specimen can be taken to the laboratory.
21. Wash your hands.
22. Note and report your observations (see Chapter 15, page 249).

The 24-Hour Urine Specimen

Occasionally clients are asked to collect all urine during a 24-hour period. This is called a 24-hour-urine specimen. The urine is saved in special containers. The urine must be chilled on ice or refrigerated during the collection period. This prevents the growth of microorganisms. A preservative is added to the container for some tests. Your supervisor will give you specific instructions.

The test begins by asking the client to void; this voiding is discarded. All voidings during the next 24 hours are collected. The procedure and time period for the test must be clearly understood by the client, family, and others involved in the client's care. The general rules for collecting urine specimens must also be followed.

Procedure: Collecting a 24-hour urine specimen

1. Review the procedure with your supervisor. Check to see if a preservative is needed and if the urine is to be preserved on ice.
2. Explain the procedure to the client.
3. Wash your hands.
4. Collect the following:
   a. Urine container for a 24-hour collection
   b. Preservative if needed
   c. Bucket with ice if needed
   d. Funnel
   e. Bedpan, urinal, commode, or specimen pan
5. Label the container (see page 270).
6. Arrange equipment in the client's bathroom. Place a "SAVE ALL URINE" sign in the bathroom.
7. Wear gloves when you will have contact with the client's urine.
8. Offer the bedpan or urinal. Or help the client to the bathroom or commode.
9. Ask the client to void. Discard the speci-

men and note the time. This begins the 24-hour collection period.
10. Record the time when the test began.
11. Ask the client to use the bedpan, urinal, commode, or specimen pan when urinating during the next 24 hours. Remind him or her not to have a bowel movement at the same time and not to put toilet tissue in the receptacle.
12. Measure all urine if the client is on intake and output.
13. Pour urine into the specimen container using the funnel. Do not spill any urine. The test will have to be restarted if urine is spilled or discarded.
14. Add ice to the bucket as necessary.
15. Ask the client to void at the end of the 24-hour period. Pour the urine into the container.
16. Clean and return reusable equipment to its proper place. Discard disposable equipment.
17. Thank the client (and family) for cooperating with the specimen collection.
18. Wash your hands.
19. Note and report your observations (see Chapter 15, page 249).
20. Take the specimen to the laboratory.

Collecting a Specimen from an Infant or Child

Obtaining a urine sample from an infant or small child can be difficult. These children need to have a collection bag applied over the urethra. The procedure does not hurt but it may upset the child. Be sure to explain the procedure to the parents and child.

Procedure: Collecting a urine specimen from an infant or child

1. Explain to the child and parents what you are going to do.
2. Wash your hands.
3. Collect the following equipment:
   a. Disposable collection bag
   b. Washbasin
   c. Sterile cotton balls
   d. Bath towel   *Continued*

e. Two diapers

f. Specimen container

4. Label the specimen container (see page 270).

5. Remove the child's diaper and dispose of it properly.

6. Clean the perineal area. Use a sterile cotton ball for each stroke. Rinse and dry the area.

7. Position the child on the back. Flex the child's knees and separate the legs.

8. Remove the adhesive backing from the collection bag.

9. Apply the collection bag to the perineum. Do not cover the anus (Fig. 16-2).

10. Diaper the child.

11. Elevate the head of the crib if allowed. This position helps urine collect in the bottom of the collection bag.

12. Remove the diaper when the child has urinated.

13. Remove the collection bag gently.

14. Press the adhesive surfaces of the bag together. Or transfer urine to a specimen container through the drainage tab.

15. Clean the perineal area, rinse, and dry well.

16. Diaper the child.

17. Make sure the child is comfortable and crib rails are up.

18. Clean and return equipment to its proper place. Discard disposable equipment.

19. Wash your hands.

20. Place the specimen in the refrigerator until it can be taken to the laboratory.

21. Note and report your observations (see Chapter 15, page 270).

Straining Urine

Stones (*calculi*) can develop in the urinary system. They can be found in the kidneys, ureters, or bladder. The stones may be as small as a pin head or as large as an orange. Some stones cause severe pain and damage to the urinary system. These stones may have to be surgically removed. A stone can pass from the body through urine. All of the client's urine must be strained. If a stone is passed, it is taken to the laboratory to be examined.

Procedure: Straining urine

1. Explain to the client what you are going to do. Also explain that the urinal, bedpan, commode, or specimen pan should be used for voiding.

2. Wash your hands.

3. Collect the following:

a. Disposable strainer or 4 × 4 gauze

b. Specimen container

c. Urinal, bedpan, commode, or specimen pan

4. Arrange equipment in the bathroom. Place a "STRAIN ALL URINE" sign in the bathroom.

5. Wear gloves whenever you will have contact with the client's urine.

6. Offer the bedpan or urinal. Or help the client to the commode or bathroom. Provide for privacy.

7. Ask the client to use the call bell after voiding.

8. Place the strainer or 4 × 4 gauze in the specimen container.

9. Pour urine into the specimen container. The urine will pass through the strainer or 4 × 4 gauze (Fig. 16-3).   *Continued*

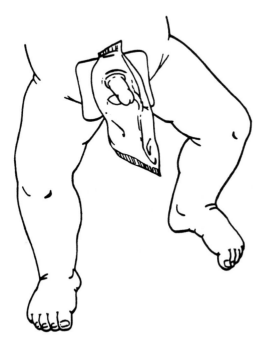

Fig. 16-2 A disposable collection bag is applied to the perineal area of the infant. Urine collects in the bag for a specimen. (From Sorrentino, S.A.: Mosby's textbook for nursing assistants, ed. 2, St. Louis, 1987, The C.V. Mosby Co.)

Fig. 16-3 The disposable strainer is placed in a specimen container. The urine is poured from the receptacle through the strainer into the specimen container. (From Sorrentino, S.A.: Mosby's textbook for nursing assistants, ed. 2, St. Louis, 1987, The C.V. Mosby Co.)

10. Place the strainer or 4×4 gauze in the specimen container if any crystals, stones, or particles appear.
11. Discard the urine.
12. Label the specimen container (see page 270).
13. Help the client clean the perineal area if necessary.
14. Help the client wash his or her hands.
15. Make sure the client is comfortable and the call bell is within reach.
16. Clean and return equipment to its proper place.
17. Wash your hands.
18. Note and report your observations (see Chapter 15, page 270).
19. Take the specimen to the laboratory.

The Fresh-Fractional Urine Specimen

Double-voided specimen is another term for a fresh-fractional urine specimen. This is because the client voids twice. The client voids to empty the bladder which contains "stale" urine. In 30 minutes the client is asked to void again. "Fresh" urine has collected in the bladder since the previous voiding. This second voiding is usually a very small or "fractional" amount of urine.

Fresh-fractional urine specimens are used to test urine for sugar. These tests are described later in this chapter.

Procedure: Collecting a fresh-fractional urine specimen

1. Explain the procedure to the client.
2. Wash your hands.
3. Collect the following:
   a. Bedpan, urinal, commode, or disposable specimen pan
   b. Two specimen containers
   c. Urine testing equipment
   d. Disposable gloves
4. Provide for privacy.
5. Wear gloves whenever you will have contact with the client's urine.
6. Offer the bedpan or urinal. Or help the client to the bathroom or commode.
7. Ask the client to urinate.
8. Take the receptacle to the bathroom.
9. Measure urine if the client is on intake and output. Pour some urine into the specimen container.
10. Test the specimen in case a second one cannot be obtained. Discard the urine.
11. Clean and return the receptacle to its proper place.
12. Help the client wash his or her hands.
13. Make sure the client is comfortable and the call bell is within reach.
14. Wash your hands.
15. Repeat steps 4 through 14 in 20 to 30 minutes.
16. Report the results of the second test and other observations to your supervisor.

Testing Urine

You will probably test the urine of clients with diabetes mellitus. *Diabetes mellitus* is a disease in which the pancreas fails to secrete enough insulin. The lack of insulin prevents the body from using sugar for energy. Sugar builds up in the blood if it cannot be used. Some of the sugar appears in the urine. *Glucosuria* is the medical term for sugar in the urine.

The diabetic client may also have *acetone*, or *ketone bodies*, in the urine. These are caused by the rapid breakdown of fat for energy. Fat is used for energy because the body cannot use sugar due to the lack of insulin.

The doctor orders the type and frequency of urine tests. They are usually done four times a day: 30 minutes before each meal and at bedtime. The doctor uses the test results to adjust the client's medication and diet. You must be accurate when testing urine. The results must be promptly reported to the nurse. Fresh-fractional urine specimens are best for testing urine for sugar and ketones.

GENERAL GUIDELINES

These guidelines are important when testing urine.

1. Perform the tests at the correct times. Most are done 30 minutes before meals and at bedtime.
2. Keep testing materials out of the reach of children. Test tablets and strips are poisonous.
3. Store test materials in a cool, dry place. Moisture can destroy them. Discard test materials that are discolored, darkened, or crumbled.
4. Check the expiration date on the test container. Do not use outdated materials.
5. Follow the instructions on the test container.
6. Time the test as instructed on the test container.
7. Test the sample again if you make a mistake. Accuracy is very important.
8. Use good lighting when comparing the test result to the color chart on the test container.
9. Report the results as instructed. The client may keep a chart of the results. Your supervisor may want to be notified.

The Keto-Diastix

The Keto-Diastix (Fig. 16-4) is used to determine if sugar and ketones (acetone) are in the urine. The plastic strip has two test areas at the bottom. The strip is dipped into a urine specimen. The test areas change color if sugar or ketones are in the urine. The strip is compared to a color chart.

Clinistix, Diastix, and Ketostix are similar to the Keto-Diastix. They are also thin, plastic strips with test areas at the bottom. Instructions on the container tell how long to wait before reading the results.

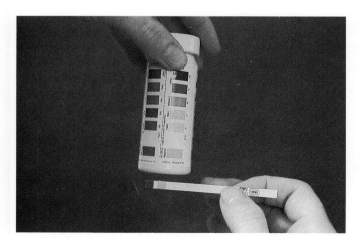

Fig. 16-4 Keto-Diastix. (From Sorrentino, S.A.: Mosby's textbook for nursing assistants, ed. 2, St. Louis, 1987, The C.V. Mosby Co.)

Procedure: Testing urine–Keto-Diastix

1. Explain to the client what you are going to do.
2. Wash your hands.
3. Wear gloves if you will have contact with the client's urine.
4. Collect the following:
   a. Fresh fractional urine specimen (see page 274)
   b. Keto-Diastix
   c. Wristwatch
5. Remove a strip from the bottle. Put the cap back on the bottle immediately. Make sure the cap is tight.
6. Dip the strip into the urine specimen. Completely immerse the test areas for 2 seconds.
7. Remove the strip from the urine after 2 seconds.
8. Tap the edge of the strip gently against the specimen container. This removes excess urine.
9. Wait 15 seconds. Compare the strip with the color chart on the bottle for ketones. The color strip for ketones is buff before testing. Read the results.
10. Compare the strip with the color chart for glucose after 30 seconds. The color strip for glucose is light blue before testing. Read the results.
11. Discard the disposable equipment and the urine specimen.
12. Clean and return equipment to its proper place.
13. Wash your hands.
14. Report and record the results as instructed.

Testape

Testape is one way to test urine for sugar. A strip of tape from the Testape dispenser is dipped into the urine specimen. Then the strip is compared to the color chart on the dispenser.

Procedure: Testing urine—Testape

1. Explain to the client what you are going to do.
2. Wash your hands.
3. Wear gloves if you will have contact with the client's urine.
4. Collect the following:
   a. Fresh-fractional urine specimen (see page 274)
   b. Testape
   c. Wristwatch
5. Tear about 1½ inches of Testape from the dispenser.
6. Dip about ¼ inch of the Testape into the specimen. Remove it immediately.
7. Hold the Testape so that the tested part is downward (Fig. 16-5, A). Do not set the Testape down.
8. Wait 60 seconds.
9. Compare the darkest area of the Testape with the color chart on the dispenser (Fig. 16-5, B).
10. Read the number of the color that matches the Testape.
11. Discard the used Testape and urine.
12. Clean and return equipment to its proper place.
13. Wash your hands.
14. Report and record the results as instructed.

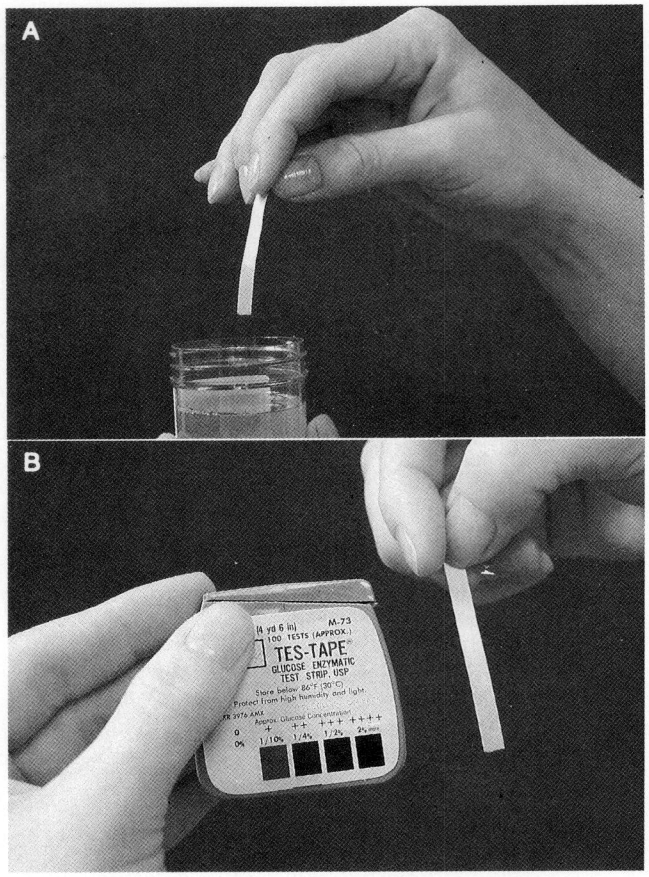

Fig. 16-5 A, The 1½ inch of Testape is held downward after being dipped into urine. **B,** The strip of Testape is compared to the color chart on the Testape dispenser. This determines the amount of sugar in the urine. (From Sorrentino, S.A.: Mosby's textbook for nursing assistants, ed. 2, St. Louis, 1987, The C.V. Mosby Co.)

The Clinitest

The Clinitest is another method of testing urine for sugar. A Clinitest tablet is added to a test tube with urine and water. The solution will change colors depending on the amount of sugar in the urine.

Procedure: Testing urine—the Clinitest

1. Explain to the client what you are going to do.
2. Wash your hands.
3. Wear gloves if you will have contact with the client's urine.
4. Collect the following:
   a. Fresh-fractional urine specimen (see page 274)
   b. Wristwatch
   c. Clinitest kit (test tube, tablets, medicine dropper, test tube holder, and color chart)
   d. Paper towels
   e. Two medicine cups with water
5. Place paper towels over the work area.
6. Arrange the urine specimen, Clinitest equipment, and medicine cups on the paper towels.
7. Place the clean test tube in the test tube holder.
8. Rinse the medicine dropper with water from a cup.
9. Draw urine into the medicine dropper. Keep the medicine dropper in an upright position.

Continued

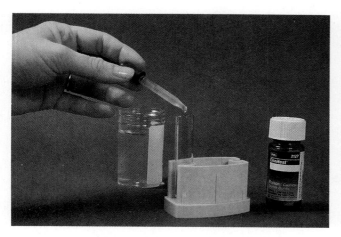

Fig. 16-6 A medicine dropper is used to place urine in the test tube during the Clinitest. (From Sorrentino, S.A.: Mosby's textbook for nursing assistants, ed. 2, St. Louis, 1987, The C.V. Mosby Co.)

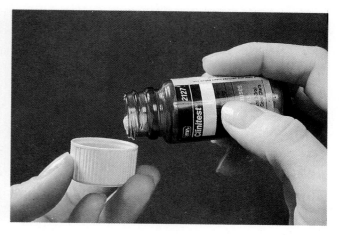

Fig. 16-7 A Clinitest tablet is transferred from the bottle to the bottle cap. The tablet is then dropped from the cap into the test tube. (From Sorrentino, S.A.: Mosby's textbook for nursing assistants, ed. 2, St. Louis, 1987, The C.V. Mosby Co.)

10. Place five drops of urine in the test tube (Fig. 16-6).
11. Rinse the medicine dropper. Use the medicine cup previously used for rinsing. Discard the cup.
12. Draw water into the medicine dropper. Use the other medicine cup for the water.
13. Add 10 drops of water to the test tube.
14. Drop one tablet into the test tube:
    a. Open the bottle.
    b. Hold the bottle in one hand. Hold the bottle cap in the other.
    c. Tap the bottle gently so that a tablet falls into the bottle cap (Fig. 16-7).
    d. Drop the tablet in the cap into the test tube.
    e. Put the bottle cap tightly on the bottle.
    f. Do not let the tablet touch your skin, eyes, mucous membranes, or clothing. The tablet can cause burns and other damage.
15. Watch the boiling reaction. Do not shake or touch the test tube. Keep the test tube away from your eyes.
16. Wait 15 seconds after the boiling has stopped. Then shake the tube gently.
17. Compare the liquid in the test tube with the color chart.
18. Match the color of the liquid with the color chart. Read the number.
19. Discard the contents of the test tube and the urine specimen.
20. Clean the test tube and medicine dropper. Place them in the kit. Place the test tube upside down in the kit.

21. Clean and return other equipment to its proper place.
22. Discard disposable equipment. Wipe off the work area with paper towels.
23. Wash your hands.
24. Report and record the results as instructed.

The Acetest

The Acetest determines if acetone or ketone bodies are in the urine. An Acetest tablet is added to urine. The urine will change color depending on the amount of acetone.

Procedure: Testing urine—Acetest

1. Explain to the client what you are going to do.
2. Wash your hands.
3. Wear gloves if you will have contact with the client's urine.
4. Collect the following:
   a. Fresh fractional urine specimen (see page 274)
   b. Acetest tablets
   c. Medicine dropper
   d. Color chart
   e. Medicine cup with water
   f. Paper towels
   g. Wristwatch

Continued

5. Place the paper towels over the work area.
6. Place the Acetest tablet on the paper towel:
   a. Open the bottle.
   b. Hold the bottle in one hand and the bottle cap in the other.
   c. Tap the bottle gently so that a tablet falls into the cap.
   d. Drop the tablet in the cap onto the paper towel.
   e. Put the bottle cap tightly on the bottle.
   f. Do not let the tablet touch your skin, eyes, mucous membranes, or clothing.
7. Rinse the medicine dropper with water from the medicine cup.
8. Draw some urine into the medicine dropper.
9. Drop one drop of urine onto the tablet.
10. Wait 30 seconds.
11. Compare the tablet with the color chart.
12. Read the result that corresponds with the color match.
13. Discard the paper towel, Acetest tablet, urine, and other disposable equipment.
14. Clean and return the medicine dropper and other equipment to their proper place.
15. Wash your hands.
16. Report and record the results as instructed.

Stool Specimens

A stool specimen is a sample of the client's feces. It is studied for such substances as blood, chemicals, worms, parasites, microorganisms, or fat. The content of stools helps the doctor diagnose and treat a client's health problems. The rules for collecting urine specimens (see page 270) apply when collecting stool specimens. The stool specimen should not be contaminated with urine. Some tests require a warm stool. The specimen should be taken to the laboratory immediately if a warm stool is needed.

Remember that elimination is a private act. Clients may have a hard time having bowel movements when specimens are needed. Be sure to practice the measures to promote normal elimination (see Chapter 15, page 261).

Procedure: Collecting a stool specimen

1. Explain the procedure to the client. Ask the client to let you know when he or she needs to have a bowel movement.
2. Wash your hands.
3. Collect the following:
   a. Bedpan and cover (another bedpan may be necessary if the client needs to urinate) or commode
   b. Urinal
   c. Specimen pan if the client can use the bathroom or commode
   d. Specimen container and lid
   e. Tongue blade
   f. Plastic bag
   g. Toilet tissue
   h. Disposable gloves
4. Label the container (see page 270).
5. Provide for privacy.
6. Put on the gloves.
7. Offer the bedpan or urinal if the client has to urinate first.
8. Assist the client onto the bedpan or to the commode. Place the specimen pan in the toilet under the seat if the client can use the bathroom (see Fig. 16-1).
9. Ask the client not to put toilet tissue in the bedpan, commode, or specimen pan. Provide a plastic bag for toilet tissue.
10. Make sure the call bell and toilet tissue are within reach.
11. Leave the room.
12. Return to the room when the client calls. Knock before entering the room.
13. Use the tongue blade to take about 2 tablespoons of feces from the bedpan to the specimen container (Fig. 16-8).
14. Put the lid on the specimen container. Do not touch the inside of the lid or container.
15. Place the tongue blade inside a plastic bag.
16. Empty, clean, and disinfect the bedpan, commode container, or specimen pan. Return it to its proper place.
17. Help the client wash his or her hands.
18. Make sure the client is comfortable and the call bell is within reach.
19. Remove and discard the gloves.
20. Wash your hands.
21. Note and report your observations.
22. Take the specimen to the laboratory.

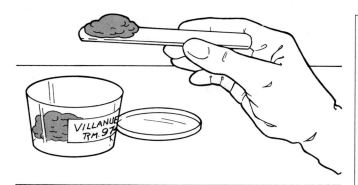

Fig. 16-8 A tongue blade is used to transfer a small amount of stool from the bedpan to the specimen container. (From Sorrentino, S.A.: Mosby's textbook for nursing assistants, ed. 2, St. Louis, 1987, The C.V. Mosby Co.)

Sputum Specimens

Respiratory disorders cause the lungs, bronchi, and trachea to secrete mucus. The mucus is called *sputum* when it is expectorated (expelled) through the mouth. Sputum should not be mistaken for saliva. Saliva is a thin, clear liquid produced by the salivary glands in the mouth. Saliva is often referred to as "spit."

Sputum is studied for the presence of blood, abnormal cells, and microorganisms. The client coughs up sputum from the bronchi and trachea. This can be very painful and hard for the client. A sputum specimen is usually easier to collect in the early morning. Secretions are usually coughed up after awakening.

The client should rinse out his or her mouth with water. This decreases the amount of saliva and removes food particles. *Mouthwash is not used before collecting a sputum specimen.* Mouthwash can destroy some of the microorganisms that may be present.

Collecting a sputum specimen can be embarrassing for the client. Family members may find the sound of the coughing and expectorating to be upsetting or nauseating. Also, the appearance of sputum can be disagreeable to the client and others. For these reasons the client should be allowed privacy during the procedure. The specimen container should be immediately covered and placed in a paper bag.

Procedure: Collecting a sputum specimen

1. Explain to the client that a sputum specimen is needed. Also explain what the client can do to help.

2. Wash your hands.
3. Collect the following:
   a. Sputum specimen container with cover
   b. Tissues
   c. Label
   d. Paper bag
   e. Disposable gloves
4. Label the container (see page 270).
5. Provide for privacy. Close doors to the room. Allow the client to go into the bathroom if able.
6. Put on the gloves.
7. Ask the client to rinse the mouth out with clear water.
8. Have the client hold the container if able. Only the outside of the container should be touched.
9. Ask the client to cover the mouth and nose with tissues when coughing.
10. Ask him or her to take 2 or 3 deep breaths and cough up the sputum.
11. Have the client expectorate the sputum directly into the container as in Fig. 16-9. Sputum should not be in contact with the outside of the container.
12. Collect 1 to 2 tablespoons of sputum unless directed to collect more.
13. Put the lid on the container immediately.

Continued

Fig. 16-9 Client expectorates directly into the center of the specimen container. (From Sorrentino, S.A.: Mosby's textbook for nursing assistants, ed. 2, St. Louis, 1987, The C.V. Mosby Co.)

14. Place the container in the paper bag.
15. Make sure the client is comfortable. Remove the gloves.
16. Wash your hands.
17. Note and report the following:
    a. The amount of sputum collected
    b. How easily the client was able to raise the sputum
    c. The consistency and appearance of the sputum (thick, clear, white, green, yellow, or blood-tinged)
    d. Any other observations
18. Take the specimen to the laboratory.

Summary

Urine, stool, and sputum specimens are tested for various substances. The test results help the doctor diagnose and treat the client's health problems. Some simple urine tests can be done by the client, family member, or home health aide. Remember that accuracy is very important when testing urine.

Specimen collection can be embarrassing to clients. Just as urination and defecation are private acts, so is the collection of specimens. Specimen collection can be even more embarrassing because the urine, stool, or sputum will be seen and studied by others. Clients may also be very concerned about the reason for the tests and the test results. Be sensitive and understanding about the client's feelings when collecting specimens.

Study Questions

1. You are asked to collect a stool specimen and a clean-catch urine specimen from Mrs. Johnson. You also need to strain all urine. Explain how you will perform these procedures.

2. Mr. Adams has diabetes mellitus. His urine is to be tested before meals and at bedtime. The Keto-Diastix test has been ordered. What urine specimen should you collect? Explain how you will test his urine.

3. You are a client receiving home care. The doctor has ordered a stool specimen. Explain how you might feel about a home health aide collecting your stool specimen.

Circle the best answer.

4. When collecting a urine specimen, you should
   a. Label the container with the person's name, address, and other requested information
   b. Use the appropriate container
   c. Collect the specimen at the time specified
   d. All of the above

5. The perineal area is cleaned immediately before collecting a
   a. Routine urine specimen
   b. Clean-catch urine specimen
   c. 24-hour urine specimen
   d. Fresh-fractional urine specimen

6. Urine is tested for sugar and acetone
   a. At bedtime
   b. 30 minutes after meals and at bedtime
   c. 30 minutes before meals and at bedtime
   d. Before breakfast

7. Which is best for sugar and acetone testing?
   a. A routine urine specimen
   b. A clean-catch urine specimen
   c. A 24-hour urine specimen
   d. A fresh-fractional urine specimen

8. Which test measures both sugar and acetone in the urine?
   a. Testape
   b. Clinitest
   c. Acetest
   d. Keto-Diastix

9. You are to collect a stool specimen. You should
   a. Wear disposable gloves
   b. Use a tongue blade to transfer feces from the bedpan to the specimen container
   c. Take about 2 tablespoons of feces for the specimen
   d. All of the above

10. You are to collect a sputum specimen. Which is *false*?
    a. An early morning specimen is best.
    b. You should provide for the client's privacy.
    c. The client should use mouthwash before the procedure.
    d. The sputum is expectorated directly into the specimen container.

Answers

4. d	8. d
5. b	9. d
6. c	10. c
7. d	

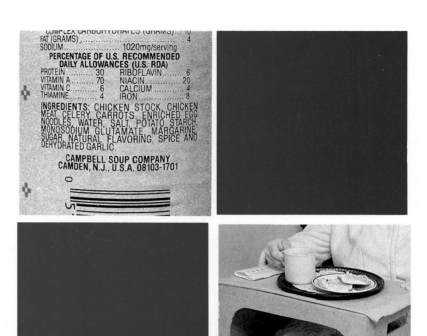

COMPLEX CARBOHYDRATES (GRAMS)....10
FAT (GRAMS) 4
SODIUM...................1020mg/serving
PERCENTAGE OF U.S. RECOMMENDED
DAILY ALLOWANCES (U.S. RDA)
PROTEIN 30   RIBOFLAVIN........6
VITAMIN A.........70   NIACIN............20
VITAMIN C..........6   CALCIUM 4
THIAMINE 4   IRON 8
INGREDIENTS: CHICKEN STOCK, CHICKEN
MEAT, CELERY, CARROTS, ENRICHED EGG
NOODLES, WATER, SALT, POTATO STARCH,
MONOSODIUM GLUTAMATE, MARGARINE,
SUGAR, NATURAL FLAVORING, SPICE AND
DEHYDRATED GARLIC.

CAMPBELL SOUP COMPANY
CAMDEN, N.J., U.S.A. 08103-1701

17

Foods and Fluids

Chapter Highlights	What you will learn to do

Nutrition

Factors affecting nutrition

Special diets

Meal management

Fluid balance

- Identify the foods found in the four basic food groups
- Explain the importance of protein, carbohydrates, and fats in the diet and their major sources
- Describe the functions and dietary sources of vitamins and minerals
- Describe six factors that affect eating and nutrition
- Describe special diets
- Explain meal management in terms of planning, buying, storing, preparing, and serving food
- Describe normal adult fluid requirements and the common causes of dehydration
- Explain what you should do when forced fluids, restricted fluids, or NPO is ordered

- Describe the purpose of intake and output records and the foods that are counted as fluid intake
- Describe between-meal nourishments, tube feedings, intravenous therapy, and total parenteral nutrition
- Perform the procedures in this chapter

Key Terms

Anorexia Loss of appetite
Calorie The amount of energy produced when food is broken down for use
Dehydration A decrease in the amount of water in body tissues
Dysphagia Difficulty or discomfort in swallowing
Edema Swelling of body tissues with water

Intake The amount of fluid taken in by the body
Nutrient A substance that is ingested, digested, absorbed, and used by the body
Nutrition The many processes involved in eating, digesting, absorbing, and using foods and fluids
Output The fluid lost from the body

Food and water are basic physical needs. They are necessary for life and health. The amount and quality of foods and fluids in the diet are important. They affect a person's health and well-being. Poor diet and eating habits put a person at risk for infection, disease, healing problems, and abnormal body functions. Poor physical and mental function increase the risk of accidents and injuries.

Nutrition

Nutrition is the many processes involved in eating, digesting, absorbing, and using foods and fluids. Good nutrition is needed for growth, healing, and maintaining body functions. It begins with the proper selection of foods and fluids. They need to be selected to provide a well-balanced diet and appropriate caloric intake.

Foods and fluids contain nutrients. A *nutrient* is a substance that is ingested, digested, absorbed, and used by the body. Nutrients are grouped into the categories of fats, proteins, carbohydrates, vitamins, and minerals. These essential nutrients are found in the four basic food groups.

Fats, proteins, and carbohydrates give the body fuel for energy. The amount of energy provided by a nutrient is measured in calories. A *calorie* is the amount of energy produced when food is broken down for use. All body functions require energy, even sitting in a chair. The number of calories needed by a person depends on many factors. These include age, sex, activity, climate, amount of sleep, and state of health.

Essential Nutrients

No one food or food group provides all the essential nutrients. A well-balanced diet consists of servings from each of the four basic food groups (see page 284). This ensures an adequate intake of the essential nutrients.

PROTEIN

Protein is the most important nutrient; it is needed for tissue growth and repair. One gram (g) of protein gives the body 4 calories. Protein is found in meat, fish, poultry, eggs, milk and milk products, cereals, beans, peas, and nuts. Foods high in protein are usually the most expensive. Therefore, protein is often lacking in the diets of people with low incomes.

Every body cell is made up of protein. Excess protein intake causes some protein to be excreted in the urine. Some is changed into body fat and some into carbohydrates. Carbohydrates are stored in the liver.

CARBOHYDRATES

Cabohydrates give the body energy. They also provide fiber for bowel elimination. Carbohydrates are found in fruits, vegetables, breads, cereals, and sugar. These foods do not cost much. Rarely are carbohydrates lacking in the diet. One gram of carbohydrate provides 4 calories.

Carbohydrates are broken down into sugars during digestion. The sugars are absorbed into the bloodstream. The fiber is not digested; it makes up the bulky part of chyme for elimination (see Chapter 15, page 260). When carbohydrate intake is excessive, some of the nutrient is stored in the liver. The rest changes into body fat.

FATS

Fats also provide energy. One gram of fat provides 9 calories. Fats serve many functions including:
- Improving the taste of food
- Helping the body use certain vitamins
- Conserving body heat
- Protecting organs from injury

Fat is found in meat, lard, butter, shortenings, salad and vegetable oils, milk, cheese, egg yolks, and nuts. These cost more than carbohydrate sources. Dietary fat not needed by the body is stored as body fat (adipose tissue).

VITAMINS

Vitamins do not provide many calories. However, they are essential nutrients. They are ingested through food and cannot be produced by the body. Vitamins A, D, E, and K can be stored by the body. Vitamin C and the B complex vitamins are not stored. They must be ingested daily. Each vitamin is needed for specific body functions. The lack of a specific vitamin causes signs and symptoms of disease. See Table 17-1 for the sources and major functions of common vitamins.

Table 17-1   Major Functions and Sources of Common Vitamins

VITAMIN	MAJOR FUNCTIONS	SOURCES
Vitamin A	Growth; vision; healthy hair, skin, and mucous membranes; resistance to infection	Liver, spinach, green leafy and yellow vegetables, fruits, fish liver oils, egg yolk, butter, cream, milk
Vitamin B₁ (thiamin)	Muscle tone; nerve function; digestion; appetite; elimination; use of carbohydrates	Pork, liver and other organ meats, breads and cereals, potatoes, peas, beans, and soybeans
Vitamin B₂ (riboflavin)	Growth; healthy eyes; protein and carbohydrate metabolism; healthy skin and mucous membranes	Milk and milk products, organ meats, green leafy vegetables, eggs, breads and cereals
Vitamin B₃ (niacin)	Protein, fat, and carbohydrate metabolism; functioning of the nervous system and digestive system; appetite	Meat, poultry, fish, peanut butter, breads and cereals, peas and beans, eggs, liver
Vitamin B₁₂	Formation of red blood cells; protein metabolism; functioning of the nervous system	Liver and other organ meats, meats, fish, eggs, green leafy vegetables
Folic acid	Formation of red blood cells; functioning of the intestines; protein metabolism	Liver, meats, fish, yeast, green leafy vegetables, eggs, mushrooms
Vitamin C (ascorbic acid)	Formation of substances that hold tissues together; healthy blood vessels, skin, gums, bones, and teeth; wound healing; prevention of bleeding; resistance to infection	Citrus fruits, tomatoes, potatoes, cabbage, strawberries, green vegetables, melons
Vitamin D	Absorption and metabolism of calcium and phosphorus; healthy bones	Fish liver oils, milk, butter, liver, exposure to sunlight
Vitamin E	Normal reproduction; formation of red blood cells; muscle function	Vegetable oils, milk, eggs, meats, fish, cereals, green leafy vegetables
Vitamin K	Blood clotting	Liver, green leafy vegetables, margarine, soybean and vegetable oils, eggs

(From Sorrentino, S.A.: Mosby's textbook for nursing assistants, ed. 2, St. Louis, 1987, The C.V. Mosby Co.)

MINERALS

Minerals are needed for bone and teeth formation, nerve and muscle function, fluid balance, and other body processes. A well-balanced diet supplies the necessary amounts of minerals. See Table 17-2 for the major functions and dietary sources of common minerals.

Food Groups

There are four basic food groups (Fig. 17-1). Essential nutrients are found in varying amounts in each group. No one food provides all the essential nutrients. A well-balanced daily diet includes the recommended number of servings from each food group and all of the essential nutrients. Usually the daily diet includes three regular meals.

MILK AND DAIRY PRODUCTS

This group includes milk and foods and fluids made from whole or skimmed milk (cheese and ice cream). Protein, fat, carbohydrates, calcium, and riboflavin are found in milk and dairy products. Children under 11 years of age should have at least 3 to 4 cups of milk a day. Teenagers need 4 or more cups. Adults need 2 or more cups. Pregnant women and breast-feeding mothers need 6 or more cups of milk a day. This amount meets their own and the babies' nutritional needs.

MEATS AND FISH

Protein, fat, iron, and thiamin are the main nutrients found in meats and fish. A person should have two or more servings daily from this group. The meat and fish group includes beef, veal, lamb, poultry, pork, fish, eggs, and cheese. Alternatives or substitutes for meat and fish are dry beans, peas, nuts, and peanut butter.

Serving size is important when planning a well-balanced diet. This is especially important for meat and fish. They have a lot of calories. Culture, appetite, personal preference, and the recipe affect serving size. A quarter-pound hamburger, a 12-ounce T-bone steak, and a quarter of a chicken are some serving portions advertised by restaurants. Two to three ounces of boned meat, fish, or poultry is one serving from this group. A 12-ounce steak equals 4 to 6 servings of the meat and fish group.

FRUIT AND VEGETABLES

Vitamins A and C, carbohydrates, and small amounts of other nutrients are found in fruits and vegetables. Four or more servings of this food group should be in the daily diet. This group includes fruits, dark green and yellow vegetables, tomatoes, potatoes, and fruit and vegetable juices.

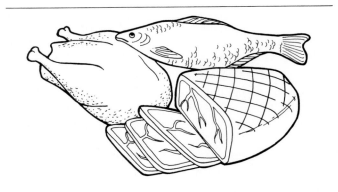

Fig. 17-1 The four basic food groups and the foods included in each group. (From Sorrentino, S.A.: Mosby's textbook for nursing assistants, ed. 2, St. Louis, 1987, The C.V. Mosby Co.)

Table 17-2 Major Functions and Sources of Common Minerals

MINERAL	MAJOR FUNCTION	SOURCE
Calcium	Formation of teeth and bones; blood clotting; muscle contraction; heart function; nerve function	Milk and milk products, green leafy vegetables
Phosphorus	Formation of bones and teeth; use of proteins, fats, and carbohydrates; nerve and muscle function	Meat, fish, poultry, milk and milk products, nuts, eggs
Iron	Allows red blood cells to carry oxygen	Liver and other organ meats, egg yolks, green leafy vegetables, breads and cereals
Iodine	Thyroid gland function; growth; metabolism	Iodized salt, seafood and shellfish, vegetables
Sodium	Fluid balance; nerve and muscle function	Almost all foods
Potassium	Nerve function; muscle contraction; heart function	Fruits, vegetables, cereals, coffee, meats

(From Sorrentino, S.A.: Mosby's textbook for nursing assistants, ed. 2, St. Louis, 1987, The C.V. Mosby Co.)

BREADS AND CEREALS

A well-balanced diet includes four or more servings of bread and cereal. Protein, carbohydrates, iron, thiamin, niacin, and riboflavin are the main nutrients found in this group. Foods in this group include bread, cereal, pasta, and crackers.

Factors Affecting Nutrition

Eating and drinking provide pleasure. They are part of social activities. Food is offered to guests and meals are often shared with family. Familiar foods give people a sense of identity and security. The foods eaten by a person, family, or group are influenced by many factors. Some factors begin in infancy and continue throughout life. Others develop later. Dietary practices are influenced by such things as culture, income, and personal preference. These practices include the selection of food and how it is prepared and served.

You need to know your client's food preferences. These are often related to culture and religion. During illness a client may eat poorly. If you know what the client likes, you can offer those foods and fluids. A special diet may be ordered. The client will accept the diet better if it includes familiar foods.

The factors affecting nutrition are discussed in this section. Only general information is given. A client may not follow every dietary practice of a religion or culture. The United States is a blend of many cultures, religions, and ethnic groups. A client's food habits may reflect this blend.

Culture and Religion

Dietary practices are greatly influenced by culture. The foods available in a region also influence diet. Rice and tea are common in the diets of Chinese, Japanese, Korean, and other peoples of the Far East. Spanish-speaking people eat foods such as tacos, tamales, and burritos. Italians are known for their spaghetti, lasagna, and other pastas. Scandinavians eat a lot of fish. Americans enjoy foods from the meat group, fast foods, and processed foods, such as canned and frozen foods.

Culture also influences how food is prepared. Frying, baking, smoking, or roasting food or eating food raw is influenced by culture. So is the use of sauces and spices. Table 17-3 describes the dietary practices of some cultural and ethnic groups.

Many religions have dietary practices. Selecting, preparing, and eating food are often regulated by religious practices. Some religions require fasting. During a fast all or certain foods are avoided. However, some members of a religious group may not follow each dietary practice of their faith. Others may strictly follow all dietary teachings. You must respect the client's religious practices. Table 17-4 summarizes the dietary practices of the major religions.

Some cultures and religions have certain beliefs about food. Some foods are thought to be cures for certain diseases or ailments.

Table 17-3 Cultural and Ethnic Food Practices

CULTURE	FOOD PRACTICES
Chinese	Common foods include rice, wheat noodles, eggs, fish, meat (especially pork), and a variety of vegetables. Vegetables are never overcooked and meat portions are small. Soy sauce is used frequently. Black tea is a common beverage. Stir-frying and steaming are major cooking methods.
Japanese	Common foods include rice, bean paste, soup, tofu, vegetables, fruit, raw or cooked fish, and pickles. Green tea is the preferred beverage. Cooking methods are similar to the Chinese.
Middle Eastern (Greek, Armenian, Lebanese, Turkish, Syrian)	Common foods include bulgar (cracked wheat), rice, bread, eggplant, tomatoes, lemon, eggs, butter, cheese, and yogurt. Lamb is the favorite meat. Food is not heavily spiced but is rich in fat, especially olive oil. Strong black coffee is heavily sweetened. If a person is of the Moslem religion, pork is not allowed.
Italian	Pasta of various shapes is eaten with many different sauces and cheeses. Northern Italians prefer sauces with a dairy base (cheese, cream, and butter). Southern Italians prefer sauces with a tomato base. Olive oil and garlic are commonly used in cooking. Crusty, white bread and polenta (a cornmeal mush), wine, and ice cream are common. Green vegetables and fruits are used often. Black coffee is popular.
Mexican	A variety of beans (especially pinto), rice, potatoes, peas, and some vegetables are common. Tomatoes are popular and are used ripe or green. Salsa is used frequently. It is a sauce made from vegetables and chile (a type of pepper). Very little milk and meat are eaten.
American Blacks	Hot breads (biscuits, muffins, cornbread) and grits are common. Rice, potatoes, black-eyed peas, and greens (mustard, turnip, collard, and kale) are popular. Vegetables are usually cooked a long time and with some form of pork, fish, poultry, and beef. Foods from the meat group are usually high in bone or connective tissue (neckbones, spareribs, and pig's ears and feet). Buttermilk is common. Little milk or cheese are in the diet. Sweets are eaten frequently. Sweetened and flavored drinks are common in place of fruit juice and milk. Frying, barbecuing, and stewing are common cooking methods.
American Indian	Traditional foods include corn, potatoes, tomatoes, squash, beans, cranberries, wild rice, wild game, fish, and seafood. Soups and stews are popular.

Table 17-4 Religion and Dietary Practices

RELIGION	DIETARY PRACTICE
Adventist (Seventh-Day Adventist)	Coffee, tea, and alcohol are not allowed; beverages with caffeine (colas) are not allowed. Some groups forbid the eating of meat.
Baptist	Some groups forbid coffee, tea, and alcohol.
Christian Scientist	Alcohol and coffee are not allowed.
Church of Jesus Christ of Latter Day Saints (Mormon)	Alcohol and hot drinks such as coffee and tea are not allowed. Meat is not forbidden but members are encouraged to eat meat infrequently.
Greek Orthodox Church	Wednesdays, Fridays, and Lent are days of fasting; meat and dairy products are usually avoided during days of fast.
Islamic (Muslim or Moslem)	All pork and pork products are forbidden. Alcohol is not allowed except for medical reasons.
Judaism (Jewish faith)	Foods must be kosher (prepared according to Jewish law); meat of kosher animals (cows, goats, and sheep) can be eaten; chickens, ducks, and geese are kosher fowl; kosher fish have scales and fins, such as tuna, sardines, carp, and salmon; shellfish cannot be eaten; milk, milk products, and eggs from kosher animals and fowl are acceptable; milk and milk products cannot be eaten with or immediately after eating meat; milk and milk products can be eaten 6 hours after eating meat; milk and milk products can be a part of the same meal with meat—they are served separately and before the meat; kosher foods cannot be prepared in utensils used to prepare nonkosher foods; breads, cakes, cookies, noodles, and alcoholic beverages are not consumed during Passover
Roman Catholic	Fasting for 1 hour before receiving Holy Communion; fasting from meat on Ash Wednesday and Good Friday—some may continue to fast from meat on Fridays

(From Sorrentino, S.A.: Mosby's textbook for nursing assistants, ed. 2, St. Louis, 1987, The C.V. Mosby Co.)

Money

Money is a major factor in selecting foods. People with limited incomes, such as the elderly, usually buy the cheaper carbohydrate foods. Therefore, their diets often lack protein and certain vitamins and minerals.

Appetite

Appetite relates to the desire for food. Hunger is an unpleasant feeling that results from the lack of food. Hunger causes a person to seek food and eat un-til the appetite is satisfied. Aromas and thoughts of food can increase the appetite. Loss of appetite, *anorexia*, can also be experienced. Anorexia can be caused by illness, fear, anxiety, medications, and unpleasant thoughts or sights.

Individual Preference

People usually eat food they like and avoid food they do not like. The taste, smell, texture, and temperature of food influence choice. Food preferences begin in childhood. They are influenced by what is served in the home. As a child grows older, new foods are introduced as a part of school and social activities. Many people decide whether or not they like a food by the way it looks, how it is prepared, its smell, or the recipe ingredients. Food preferences usually expand with age and new social experiences.

Food choices are also influenced by body reactions. Foods that cause allergic reactions, nausea, vomiting, diarrhea, indigestion, or headache are usually avoided.

Illness

Appetite usually decreases during illness and recovery from injuries. However, nutritional needs are usually greater at these times. The body must fight infection, heal tissue, and replace lost blood cells. Nutrients lost through vomiting and diarrhea must be replaced. Some diseases and drugs cause a sore mouth, which makes eating painful. Loss of teeth also affects the ability to chew, especially foods high in protein.

Special Diets

Doctors may order special diets for some clients. This is often called *diet therapy* or a *therapeutic diet*. It is part of the client's treatment plan. A special diet may be ordered because of a nutritional deficiency, a disease, or to eliminate or decrease certain substances in the diet. The doctor, nurses, and dietician all work together to meet the client's nutritional needs. They consider the need for dietary changes, personal preferences, religion, culture, and eating problems.

A special diet may change a client's food intake by:
- Changing the consistency—a liquid or soft diet
- Changing fiber content—a high-fiber or low-residue diet
- Changing calorie intake—a high or low calorie diet
- Changing the kind and amounts of nutrients—a low-sodium or high sodium diet
- Changing the time and number of meals—a diabetic diet
- Omitting certain food because of allergies—an egg-free or wheat-free diet

Special diets are named after the nutrient, substance, or consistency being changed. Table 17-5 describes common therapeutic diets. Some clients do not need special diets. *General diet* is the term used by many agencies when there are no dietary changes.

Special or therapeutic diets may be ordered for clients who have had surgery, and for those with diabetes, diseases of the heart, kidneys, gallbladder, liver, stomach, or intestines. Allergies, obesity, and other disorders also may require therapeutic diets. The sodium-restricted diet and diabetic diet are often ordered. You

will probably have clients on these diets. Therefore, they are described in greater detail.

The Sodium-Restricted Diet

There are 3000 to 5000 mg. of sodium in the average daily diet. The body needs only half this amount daily. Healthy people excrete the excess sodium in urine. However, heart and kidney diseases cause the body to retain the extra sodium.

Sodium restricted diets are usually ordered for clients with heart disease. They may also be ordered for clients with liver disease, kidney disease, certain complications of pregnancy, and when certain drugs are taken. Sodium causes the body to retain water. If there is too much sodium in the body, more water is retained. Body tissues swell with water. There are excess amounts of fluid in the blood vessels. The increased fluid in the tissues and bloodstream forces the heart to work harder. With heart disease, the extra work load can cause serious complications or death. Limiting the amount of sodium in the diet decreases the amount of sodium in the body. Therefore, the body retains less water. Less water in the tissues and blood vessels reduces the amount of work the heart has to perform.

There are five levels of sodium-restricted diets. Levels range from mild to severe. The doctor orders the amount of restriction for the client. Clients need to learn how to figure the amount of sodium in the diet. They also need to know which foods are high and low in sodium. The nurse or dietician will teach clients and families about the diet.

- 2000—3000 *mg. sodium diet (low-salt diet)*. Sodium restriction is mild. Only a small amount of salt is used during cooking. Salt is not added to foods at the table. Highly salted foods and salty seasonings (catsup, celery salt, garlic salt, chili sauce, etc.) are not allowed. Canned and processed foods high in salt, ham, bacon, hot dogs, potato chips, olives, pickles, luncheon meats, and salted or smoked fish are omitted.
- 1000 *mg. sodium diet*. Sodium restriction is described as "moderate." Food is cooked without salt. Foods high in sodium are omitted. Vegetables high in sodium are limited in amount. Salt-free products, such as salt-free bread, are used. Diet planning is necessary.
- 800 *mg. sodium diet*. The same restrictions for the low-salt diet and the 1000 mg. diet are followed. Diet planning is necessary.
- 500 *mg. sodium diet*. Sodium restriction is described as "strict." Restrictions for the lesser restricted diets are followed. In addition, vegetables high in sodium are omitted. Milk is limited to 2 cups a day. Only one egg a day is allowed. The amount of meat is limited to five to six ounces per day. Diet planning is essential.
- 250-*mg. sodium diet*. The diet is described as "severe." It is similar to the 500 mg. sodium diet. However,

Table 17-5 Common Therapeutic Diets

DIET	DESCRIPTION	USE	FOODS ALLOWED
Clear Liquid	Clear liquids that do not leave a residue; nonirritating and nongas-forming	Postoperatively; for acute illness, nausea, and vomiting	Water, tea, and coffee (without milk or cream); carbonated beverages; gelatin; clear fruit juices (apple, grape, and cranberry); fat-free clear broth; hard candy, sugar, and popsicles
Full liquid	Foods that are liquid at room temperature or that melt at body temperature	Advance from clear liquid diet; postoperatively, for stomach irritation, fever, nausea and vomiting	All foods allowed on a clear liquid diet; custard; eggnog; strained soups; strained fruit and vegetable juices; milk; creamed cereals; ice cream and sherbet
Soft	Semisolid foods that are easily digested	Advance from full liquid diet; for chewing difficulties, gastrointestinal disorders, and infections	All liquids; eggs (not fried); broiled, baked or roasted meat, fish or poultry; mild cheeses (American, Swiss, cheddar, cream, and cottage); strained or refined bread and crackers; cooked or pureed vegetables; cooked or canned fruit without skin or seeds; pudding; plain cakes
Low-residue	Food that leave a small amount of residue in the colon	For diseases of the colon and diarrhea	Coffee, tea, milk, carbonated beverages, strained fruit juices; refined bread and crackers; creamed and refined cereal; rice; cottage and cream cheese; eggs (not fried); plain puddings and cakes; gelatin; custard; sherbet and ice cream; strained vegetable juices; canned or cooked fruit without skin or seeds; potatoes (not fried); strained cooked vegetables; and plain pasta
High residue	Foods that increase the amount of residue in the colon to stimulate peristalsis	For constipation and colon disorders	All fruits and vegetables; whole wheat bread; whole grain cereals; fried foods; whole grain rice; milk, cream, butter, cheese; meats

Continued

Table 17-5—cont'd   Common Therapeutic Diets

DIET	DESCRIPTION	USE	FOODS ALLOWED
Bland	Foods that are mechanically and chemically nonirritating and low in roughage; foods served at moderate temperatures; strong spices and condiments are avoided	For ulcers, gallbladder disorders, and some intestinal disorders; postoperatively following abdominal surgery	Lean meats; white bread; creamed and refined cereals; cream or cottage cheese; gelatin, plain puddings, cakes, and cookies; eggs (not fried); butter and cream; canned fruits and vegetables without skin and seeds; strained fruit juices; potatoes (not fried); pastas and rice, strained or soft cooked carrots, peas, beets, spinach, squash, and asparagus tips; creamed soups from allowed vegetables; no fried foods are allowed
High calorie	The number of calories is increased to approximately 4000; includes three full meals and between-meal snacks	For weight gain and some thyroid imbalances	Dietary increases in all foods
Low-calorie	The number of calories is reduced below the minimum daily requirements	For weight reduction	Foods low in fats and carbohydrates and lean meats; avoid butter, cream, rice, gravies, salad oils, noodles, pastries, carbonated and alcoholic beverages, candy, potato chips, and similar foods
High-iron	Foods that are high in iron	For anemia; following blood loss; for women during the reproductive years	Liver and other organ meats; lean meats; egg yolks; shellfish; dried fruits; dried beans; green leafy vegetables; lima beans; peanut butter; enriched breads and cereals
Low-fat (low cholesterol)	Protein and carbohydrates are increased with a limited amount of fat in the diet	For heart disease, gallbladder disease, disorders of fat digestion, and liver disease	Skimmed milk or buttermilk; cottage cheese (no other cheeses are allowed); gelatin; sherbet; fruit; lean meat, poultry, and fish (baked, broiled, or roasted); fat-free

Continued

Table 17-5—cont'd   Common Therapeutic Diets

DIET	DESCRIPTION	USE	FOODS ALLOWED
			broth; soups made with skimmed milk; margarine; rice, pasta, breads and cereals; vegetables; potatoes
High-protein	Protein is increased to aid and promote tissue healing	For burns, high fever, infection, and some liver diseases	Meat, milk, eggs, cheese, fish, poultry; breads, cereals; leafy vegetables
Sodium-restricted	A specific amount of sodium is allowed; there are five basic levels of sodium restriction ranging from mild to severe	For heart disease, fluid retention, and some kidney diseases	Fruits and vegetables and unsalted butter are allowed; adding salt at the table is not allowed; highly salted foods and foods high in sodium are not allowed; the use of salt during cooking may be restricted
Diabetic	The amount of carbohydrates and number of calories are regulated; protein and fat are also regulated	For diabetes mellitus	Determined by nutritional and energy requirements

(From Sorrentino, S.A.: Mosby's textbook for nursing assistants, ed. 2, St. Louis, 1987, The C.V. Mosby Co.)

milk is omitted from the diet. Low-sodium milk can be substituted for regular whole or skim milk.

Food labels give important information about the sodium content of frozen and processed foods (page 293). Be sure to check the label information for sodium content. Do not serve a food that contains more than 250 mg. of sodium to a client on a sodium-restricted diet. Discuss the use of this food with your supervisor.

The Diabetic Diet

The diabetic diet is ordered for clients with diabetes mellitus. As described in Chapter 21, diabetes mellitus is a disease in which there is not enough insulin in the body. Insulin is secreted by the pancreas. It is needed for the body to use sugar. If there is not enough insulin, sugar builds up in the bloodstream rather than being used by body cells for energy. Diabetes is usually treated with insulin therapy, diet, and exercise.

Carbohydrates are broken down into sugar during digestion. The amount of carbohydrates is controlled with the diabetic diet. By controlling the amount of carbohydrates, the person takes in the amount needed by the body. No excess carbohydrate is eaten. The body does not have to use or store the excess. Therefore the diabetic diet involves the right amount and right kind of food for the client. The doctor decides how much carbohydrate, fat, protein, and calories a person needs. Age, sex, activity, and weight are considered when determining the client's diet.

The calories and nutrients allowed are divided among three meals and between-meal nourishments. The client must eat only what is allowed and all that is allowed. This is important so the client does not get too much or too little carbohydrate. The American Diabetes Association (ADA) provides lists of foods that are equal in nutrients and calories. The foods are grouped into six categories: milk, vegetables, fruits, bread, meat foods, and fat. The groups are referred to as "exchange lists" or "exchanges." The exchanges allow for variety in menu planning. For example, a client may not like grapefruit. The client can review the exchange list for fruits and find something more appealing. The client notes that one small orange equals one-half grapefruit. Therefore, the client knows how much to eat. The nurse and dietician help the client and family learn to use the exchange lists.

You need to make sure the client's meal is served on time. The client with diabetes must eat at regular intervals to maintain a certain blood sugar level. Check to see what the client has eaten. If the client has not eaten all the food served, a between-meal nourishment is needed. The nourishment makes up for what was not eaten at the regular meal. The amount of insulin given to the client also depends on how much he or she has eaten during the day. Remind the client to take his or her insulin at the proper time (see *Assisting with medications*, page 306).

Meal Management

Meal management involves planning, buying, storing, preparing, and serving food. The goals are to fix meals that:
- Meet the client's nutritional needs
- Are within the client's food budget
- The client likes
- Include the client's cultural and religious practices

Planning

To help meet the client's nutrtional needs, all meals and snacks should be planned. This also helps you keep track of the food on hand and what needs to be bought.

The four basic food groups are helpful in menu planning. Unless a special diet is ordered, the minimum servings should be in the client's total daily intake. When planning, the client and family should be asked about food preferences. The nurse and dietician will help plan menus if the client is on a special diet.

Meals should be balanced. This helps keep the client's energy level high between meals. A balanced meal includes:
- A *protein* food from the milk or meat groups
- A *carbohydrate* food from the bread and cereal group
- A *fruit or vegetable*

Fats are usually included in the milk and meat groups. They are often used (oils and butter) in preparing meals. Table 17-6 gives examples of balanced meals.

Meals should reflect the client's food habits if possible. Learn about mealtimes from the client and family. A special diet may require changes in favorite foods or mealtime practices. Some clients do not eat three meals a day. Two meals plus nutritious snacks can meet their needs. When planning meals also consider the following:
- *Flavor*. Each food has its own special taste. Serve only one strongly flavored food at a meal. Herbs and spices can add flavor to foods if allowed.
- *Color*. Meals should look appealing. Prepare and serve foods that vary in color. A meal of chicken, white potatoes, and cauliflower looks very bland. A plate of chicken, sweet potatoes, and broccoli is more colorful and attractive.
- *Texture*. Combining textures makes meals more interesting. Food textures include crisp, soft, tender, tough, dry, moist, smooth, and lumpy.
- *Shape*. Foods of different shapes can make meals more interesting. Corn can be served on or off the cob. Hamburger can be made into patties, meat balls, or meatloaf. Potatoes can be baked, mashed, or sliced.
- *Temperature*. Serve foods and beverages with different temperatures such as iced tea, a sandwich, and hot soup.

Shopping for Food

Shopping is easier and quicker if you have a list. Prepare the list from menus, recipes, and the supplies on hand. Also include needed household items (cleaners, soap, toilet tissue, paper towels). Newspaper

---

Table 17-6 Examples of Balanced Meals

MEAL	PROTEIN	CARBOHYDRATE	FRUIT OR VEGETABLE
Breakfast	Milk	Cereal	Banana
Lunch	Tuna	Bread	Vegetable soup
Dinner	Chicken	Potato	Fruit salad
			Broccoli

ads may tell of specials and discounts. If the client has adequate refrigeration and storage space, weekly shopping is usually the most convenient. Consult with the client and family to determine the food budget. Be sure to give all shopping receipts and change to the client.

Grocery stores and food companies give a lot of food information. This information is helpful in making wise purchases.

- *Unit pricing* tells the cost per unit weight or volume of a brand and container size. This information is often on the shelf directly below the food item. Store brands and generic brands are usually cheaper than name brands. Large packages and cans are usually cheaper when comparing cost per unit. However, they may cost more if the entire product is not used. The more food is handled or processed, the higher the cost. For example, individually wrapped cheese slices usually cost more than the same cheese bought in a block.
- *Open dating* is a guide to freshness. The date on the package is the last date the store can sell the product. The date still allows time to use the product at home. Choose foods with the latest date. These products will stay fresher for a longer time.
- *Ingredient labels* are important for people on special diets. They list the ingredients in order of amount (Fig. 17-2). The largest quantity is listed first. The smallest quantity is listed last. The ingredient list is helpful if a client must avoid certain chemicals or foods. For example, a client needs to limit sodium (salt) intake. You should not buy a product that lists sodium near the beginning of the list.
- *Nutrition labels* are required on all foods with nutrients added to them ("enriched" or "fortified" foods). The amount of each nutrient in one serving is listed. You

can compare nutrients and calories in one food with those in another. Nutrition information is separated into two sections (Fig. 17-3). The top section gives nutrition information per serving. The lower section gives the "Percentage of U.S. Recommended Daily Allowance (U.S. RDA)." To be a "significant source" of a nutrient, the food must contain at least 10% of the U.S. RDA for that nutrient. Manufacturers may add other nutrients to the list.

A large part of the food dollar is spent on protein foods. The following can help you spend less for protein and other foods. However, be sure to consider the client's nutritional needs, likes and dislikes, and cultural and religious practices when buying food.

1. Nonfat dry milk is cheaper than regular milk. It can be used for drinking and cooking.
2. Beef cuts from the round and rump are leaner and cheaper than other cuts.
3. Poultry is cheaper than most cuts of meat.
4. Buy foods in bulk (large sizes) if you plan to use it all.
5. Buy fresh fruits and vegetables that are in season.
6. Day-old bread may be cheaper than fresh bread.
7. Check ads for sales and specials.
8. Use coupons for items you would normally buy.

Food Safety

Food must be handled, stored, and prepared carefully. Spoiling and contamination can occur otherwise. The following guidelines should be practiced for all types of food. They will help you prepare attractive, nutritious, and safe meals. Special types of food, such as frozen foods, meats, fruits, and vegetables, have their own safety precautions. They are presented in Table 17-7. Suggested storage times for meat and poultry are presented in Table 17-8.

1. Use a cookbook if you do not know common recipe terms (baste, saute, blend).

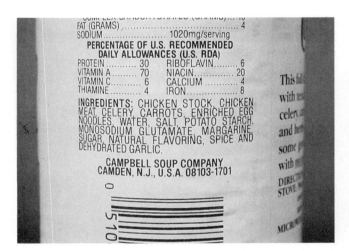

Fig. 17-2 The label indicates that nonfat milk is an excellent source of protein, riboflavin, calcium, and vitamin D. It is a good source of vitamin A, but a poor source of iron and vitamin C. Nonfat milk is low in calories and fat. Therefore, it would be a good choice for a low calorie, low fat diet. Sodium content is low.

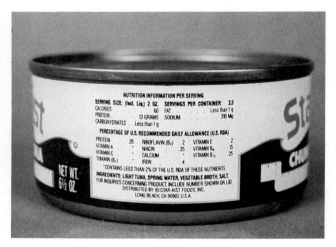

Fig. 17-3 Nutrition label. Note the top and bottom sections.

Table 17-7 Storing and Preparing Food

Frozen Foods and Freezing

Select frozen foods last when grocery shopping. This reduces the possibility of thawing.

Take frozen foods home immediately. Do not do other errands if you have frozen foods with you.

Buy frozen vegetables in large packages. You can use what you need and return the bag to the freezer.

Put frozen foods away first.

Follow package instructions when preparing frozen foods.

Undercook foods that will be frozen for use later. Foods will cook thoroughly during reheating.

Put cooked foods in the refrigerator for a short time before freezing. This chills the food quickly and stops the cooking action.

Label frozen foods. Include the date, the name of the item, and the number of servings.

Do not refreeze foods that have thawed.

Place frozen meat in the refrigerator to thaw. Or thaw in cold water.

Fruits and Vegetables

Buy fruits and vegetables that are in season. They are cheaper when in season. For example, asparagus is in season in May and June. It is cheaper at this time and very expensive in the winter.

Buy only what will be used in a short time. Fruits and vegetables spoil quickly.

Check fruits and vegetables for bruising, spots, decayed areas, and mold. Do not buy damaged products.

Wash fruits and vegetables before serving or cooking them.

Raw fruits and vegetables are the most nutritious. Cooking destroys some of the nutrients.

Store vegetables in a crisper in the refrigerator.

Do not refrigerate potatoes. Store them in a cool place.

Use a minimum of water when cooking vegetables.

Remove damaged leaves from lettuce.

Use water from cooking vegetables for soups.

Cook vegetables whole if possible. This helps prevent nutrient loss.

Prepare vegetables with their skins if possible. Skins and the area just below the skin are rich in nutrients. Skins also help prevent nutrient loss during cooking.

Do not soak cut fruits and vegetables for a long time. This helps prevent loss of nutrients in the water.

Cook vegetables until tender. Do not overcook them.

The Meat Group

Freeze ground meat if it will not be used on the date of purchase.

Do not freeze smoked meats.

Use dry heat cooking methods (roasting, broiling, panbroiling) for tender cuts of meat; use moist methods (braising, stewing, simmering) for less tender cuts:

Roasting—Baking in an oven without adding water; meat may be covered or uncovered

Broiling—Cooking over direct heat

Panbroiling—Cooking meat uncovered in a frying pan; fat is not added

Braising—Browning meat in a small amount of fat; a little water is added and the meat is cooked slowly

Stewing—Browning small pieces (cubes) of meat and then adding water to cover all meat; the meat is cooked slowly

Table 17-7—cont'd Storing and Preparing Food

Simmering—Cooking meat in liquid at a very low temperature (185° F); liquid should barely bubble
Cook meats at low temperatures (300° to 325° F).
Cook fresh pork at 350° F until well done. This destroys harmful microorganisms that can be found in pork.
Use a meat thermometer when cooking roasts (Fig. 17-4). The temperature rises as the roast cooks. Many recipes and cookbooks give the temperature for different degrees of doneness (rare, medium, and well done).
Thaw poultry and fish before cooking.
Wash poultry thoroughly before preparing it for cooking.
Cook poultry and stuffing separately.
Do not overcook fish. It is done when it can be flaked with a fork.

Milk and Milk Products
Keep milk and milk products refrigerated.
Use a double boiler if milk is to be heated.
Do not freeze cheese.
Let cheese warm to room temperature before serving.
Do not keep cottage cheese longer than 3 to 4 days.

2. Measure recipe amounts accurately.
3. Follow recipe instructions carefully.
4. Do not preheat the oven longer than necessary.
5. Use the oven to prepare more than one food.
6. Make food for more than one meal. Store leftovers in the refrigerator if they will be eaten within 1 to 2 days. Otherwise, freeze them.
7. Use the correct size burner for pots and pans.
8. Turn the oven or burner off immediately after use. Turn other appliances off after use also.
9. Use a microwave oven when possible. This decreases energy costs and the amount of heat in the house.
10. Keep storage areas free of insects and rodents.
11. Do not store household chemicals and cleaners with food.

12. Rotate food supplies. Place the oldest items in the front and new items in the back of shelves. The oldest items will be used first.
13. Do not keep food at room temperature for long periods. When you are ready to prepare food, remove it from the refrigerator. Refrigerate leftovers immediately.
14. Wash your hands before you handle food.
15. Practice good personal hygiene (see Chapter 2, page 14). Do not sneeze or cough on food. Keep your hair pulled back and away from your face. Do not touch your face or hair while preparing food.
16. Use mixing utensils to mix food. Do not use your hands.
17. Keep clean food away from dirty food.
18. Wash knives, utensils, and cutting boards between items. For example, wash the knife after you have cut up chicken and before you cut up vegetables.
19. Discard food from containers that leak, bulge, or are very dented. Also discard jars that are cracked or have loose or bulging lids. The food may be contaminated.
20. Wash and rinse can lids before opening to prevent dirt and microorganisms from getting in the food.
21. Do not store acid foods (tomato sauce, citrus juice) in metal containers.
22. Wash your hands after handling one food and before handling another. Be sure to wash your hands after handling raw meat, fish, poultry, and eggs.
23. Wash cutting boards, counter tops, and utensils that have been in contact with raw meat, poultry, fish, and eggs. Use hot, soapy water.

Fig. 17-4 Meat thermometer is inserted into the thickest part of the roast.

Table 17-8 Suggested Storage Times for Meat and Poultry

EATING QUALITY DROPS AFTER THE TIME SHOWN	IN REFRIGERATOR (30°-40° F) DAYS	IN FREEZER (0° F) MONTHS
FRESH MEATS		
Roasts (beef and lamb)	3-5	6-12
Roasts (pork and veal)	3-5	4-8
Steaks (beef)	3-5	6-12
Chops (lamb)	3-5	6-9
Chops (pork)	3-5	3-4
Ground and stew meats	1-2	3-4
Variety meats	1-2	3-4
Sausage (pork)	1-2	1-2
PROCESSED MEATS		
Bacon	7	1
Frankfurters	7	1/2
Ham (whole)	7	1-2
Ham (half)	3-5	1-2
Ham (slices)	3	1-2
Luncheon meats	3-5	1-2
Sausage (smoked)	7	Freezing
Sausage (dry & semidry)	14-21	not recommended
COOKED MEATS		
Cooked meats and meat dishes	3-4	2-3
Gravy & meat broth	1-2	2-3
FRESH POULTRY		
Chicken and turkey (whole)	1-2	12
Chicken (pieces)	1-2	9
Turkey (pieces)	1-2	6
Duck and goose (whole)	1-2	6
Giblets	1-2	3
COOKED POULTRY		
Pieces (covered with broth)	1-2	6
Pieces (not covered)	3-4	1
Cooked poultry dishes	3-4	4-6
Fried chicken	3-4	4

Source: US Department of Agriculture

Serving Meals

Mealtimes are often the highlight of a client's day. They may be a welcome break in an otherwise boring routine. Because eating is a social activity, the client should eat with family and friends if possible.

Weakness and illness can affect a client's appetite and ability to eat. Odors, the sight of unpleasant equipment, an uncomfortable position, the need for oral hygiene, and having to urinate can affect appetite. So can the appearance of the food and serving size.

You can control many of these factors. You should do the following before meals:

1. Plan meals to provide variety in color and texture (see page 292).
2. Serve small portions if the client's appetite is poor. Smaller portions will not overwhelm the client.
3. Set an attractive table or food tray.
4. Assist the client with oral hygiene.
5. Offer the bedpan or urinal or help the client to the bathroom or commode.

6. Help the client wash the hands.
7. Let the client eat at the table, by a window, by the television, or where he or she prefers if possible.
8. Help the client assume a comfortable position for eating.
9. Eliminate any unpleasant noise, odors, or equipment in the area where the client will be eating.
10. Provide a bed tray if the client cannot get out of bed. Bed trays can be bought or made from crates and cardboard boxes (Fig. 17-5).

Feeding Clients

Some clients cannot feed themselves. These clients need to be fed. Weakness, paralysis, casts, and other disabilities may make self-feeding impossible. The situation may be temporary or permanent. Older children and adults are embarrassed, depressed, or angry when they cannot feed themselves. Some may refuse to eat. Preserving their dignity will improve their attitude toward food and eating.

Clients should feed themselves if possible. However, they should follow the limitations ordered by the doctor. Finger foods require less energy and effort to eat. These include fruit slices, raw vegetables, and strips of meat. There are many devices to help people feed themselves (Fig. 17-6). Remember that plastic glasses and cups are lighter and easier to handle than glass items. Be sure to give clients support and encouragement as they try to feed themselves.

When feeding a client you should be comfortably seated. You also need to provide a relaxed mood so the client does not feel rushed. Many people say a prayer before eating. Providing time and privacy for a prayer shows a lot of caring and respect for the client. You also need to ask the client about the order in which foods and fluids should be offered. A spoon is used to feed clients because it is less likely to cause injury than a fork. When a client is being fed, the spoon should only be one-third full. This provides a manageable portion of food for chewing and swallowing.

Many blind people are very aware of food aromas. However, they need to know what is being served. When feeding a blind client, always tell the person what you are offering. If the person does not need to be fed, identify the foods and their location on the tray. Use the numbers on a clock to identify the location of foods (Fig. 17-7).

Meals are times for social contact with others. You should engage the client in pleasant conversation. However, allow the client enough time to chew and swallow.

Fig. 17-6 Feeding devices.

Fig. 17-7 The numbers on the face of a clock are used to help the blind person locate food on the tray. (From Sorrentino, S.A.: Mosby's textbook for nursing assistants, ed. 2, St. Louis, 1987, The C.V. Mosby Co.)

Fig. 17-5 Bed tray.

Procedure: Feeding the client

1. Explain to the client what you are going to do.
2. Wash your hands.
3. Help the client sit comfortably.
4. Bring the tray into the room. Place it on the table.
5. Drape a napkin across the client's chest and underneath the chin.
6. Prepare the food for eating.
7. Tell the client what kind of foods are on the tray.
8. Serve foods in the order preferred by the client. Alternate between solid and liquid foods. Use a spoon for safety as in Fig. 17-8. Allow enough time for chewing. Do not rush the client.
9. Use a straw for liquids if the client cannot drink from a glass or cup. There should be a straw for each liquid. Provide a short straw for a weak client.
10. Converse with the client in a pleasant manner. Encourage him or her to eat as much as possible.
11. Wipe the client's mouth with a napkin.
12. Note how much and what foods the client has eaten.
13. Measure and record intake if applicable.
14. Provide oral hygiene for the client.
15. Make sure the client is comfortable, the call bell is within reach, and the side rails are up. Remove the tray.
16. Wash your hands.
17. Note and report the following:
    a. The amount and kind of food eaten
    b. Complaints of nausea or *dysphagia* (difficulty or discomfort in swallowing)

Between-Meal Nourishments

Many special diets involve between-meal nourishments. Some common nourishments are crackers, milk, juice, a milkshake, a piece of cake, wafers, a sandwich, gelatin, and custard. The nourishment should be served at the time written on the care plan. The necessary eating utensils, a straw, and napkin need to be provided. The same procedure and considerations for feeding clients need to be followed.

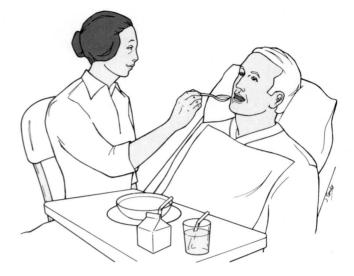

Fig. 17-8 A spoon is used to feed clients. The spoon should be no more than one third full. (From Sorrentino, S.A.: Mosby's textbook for nursing assistants, ed. 2, St. Louis, 1987, The C.V. Mosby Co.)

Fluid Balance

After oxygen, water is the most important physical need for survival. An inadequate intake of water or excessive loss of fluid from the body can cause death. Water enters the body through the ingestion of fluids and foods. The amount of fluid taken in by the body is called *intake*. Water is lost through urine, feces, and perspiration and through the lungs with expiration. *Output* is the fluid lost from the body. Fluid balance must be maintained for health. There must be a balance between intake and output (I&O).

Intake and output must be equal. If fluid intake exceeds fluid output, body tissues swell with water. This is called *edema*. Edema is common in people with heart and kidney diseases. *Dehydration* is a decrease in the amount of water in body tissues. It results when output exceeds intake. Inadequate fluid intake, vomiting, diarrhea, bleeding, excessive sweating, and increased urine production are common causes of dehydration. Some medications and diseases cause excessive urination. Both edema and dehydration must be treated.

Normal Requirements

An adult needs 1500 ml of water daily for survival. 2000 to 2500 ml per day are needed to maintain normal fluid balance. Water needs increase with hot weather, fever, exercise, and illness. Excessive fluid losses from the body also increase the water requirement.

Minimum daily water requirements vary with

age. Infants and young children have a lot of body water. They need more fluids than adults. Therefore, fluid losses cannot be tolerated and will quickly cause death in infants or children.

Special Orders

The doctor may order the amount of fluid that a client can have during a 24-hour period. This is done to maintain fluid balance. It may be necessary to *force fluids*. The client must have an increased amount of fluid. The force fluids order may be general or for a specific amount. Records are kept of the amount ingested. The client is given a variety of fluids that are allowed on the diet. They should be kept within the person's reach and served at the right temperature. You need to regularly offer fluids to clients who have force fluids orders but who cannot feed themselves.

The doctor may *restrict fluids*. Fluids are restricted to a specific amount. Water is offered in small amounts and in small containers. Accurate intake records must be kept. The client with restricted fluid intake needs frequent oral hygiene. This helps keep mucous membranes of the mouth moist.

Some clients can have *nothing by mouth*. The individual cannot eat or drink anything. NPO is the abbreviation for the Latin term *nils per os*, which means nothing by mouth. Clients are usually NPO before and after some surgeries, before some laboratory tests and x-ray procedures, and in the treatment of certain illnesses. Frequent oral hygiene is allowed as long as the client does not swallow any fluid. Usually the client is kept NPO starting at midnight before the scheduled surgery, laboratory test, or x-ray procedure.

Measuring Intake and Output

The doctor or nurse may order that all of a client's fluid intake and output be measured. This involves keeping intake and output (I&O) records (Fig. 17-9). These records give important information about the client's condition. I&O records are also kept when forcing fluids or restricting fluid intake.

Measurement of fluid intake involves measuring all liquid ingested by mouth. Fluids given in IV therapy and tube feedings are also measured. The obvious fluids are measured: water, milk, coffee, tea, juices, soups, and soft drinks. Soft and semisolid foods such as ice cream, sherbet, custard, pudding, creamed cereals, gelatin, and popsicles are also measured. Output includes urine, vomitus, diarrhea, and drainage from wounds.

Intake and output are measured in milliliters (ml) or in cubic centimeters (cc). These are metric system measurements equal in amount. One ounce equals 30 ml. A pint is about 500 ml. There are about 1000 ml in a quart. A measuring cup or a container called a *graduate* is used to measure fluids. A graduate is like a measuring cup or baby bottle and shows calibrations for amounts. Some graduates are marked in ounces and in milliliters or cubic centimeters (Fig. 17-10). Plastic urinals and emesis basins are often calibrated.

You will measure leftover fluids, urine, and vomitus. Containers used to measure urine and vomi-

INTAKE AND OUTPUT RECORD

Client Name Nancy Edder			Date 3/16/88		
ORAL INTAKE			OUTPUT		
Time	Type	Amount	Time	Type	Amount
8A	tea	150 cc	7³⁰A	urine	250 cc
	juice	100 cc			
			9³⁰A	liquid stool	200 cc
10A	H₂O	75 cc	10A	liquid stool	250 cc
12P	tea	100 cc			300 cc
	jello	75 cc	3P	urine	
	soup	150 cc			
2P	water	100 cc	7P	urine	200 cc.
4P	tea	100 cc.	10³⁰P	urine	150 cc.
6P	milkshake	200 cc.			
8P	water	50 cc.			
TOTAL		1100	TOTAL		1350

Fig. 17-9 An intake and output record.

Fig. 17-10 A graduate calibrated in milliliters. The graduate shown is filled to 150 ml. (From Sorrentino, S.A.: Mosby's textbook for nursing assistants, ed. 2, St. Louis, 1987, The C.V. Mosby Co.)

tus should never be used to measure fluid intake. Knowing the capacity of cups, glasses, bowls, pitchers, and other containers used by the client makes measuring intake easier. To determine fluid capacity:

1. Fill the container with water.
2. Pour the water into a measuring cup or graduate.
3. Measure the amount.
4. List each item and the amount contained in each. For example:
   - Soup bowl: ¾ cup = 6 ounces = 180 ml
   - Juice glass: ½ cup = 4 ounces = 120 ml
   - Coffee mug: 1 cup = 8 ounces = 240 ml
   - Water glass: 1¾ cup = 14 ounces = 420 ml

    Clients need to use the urinal, commode, bedpan, or specimen pan for urination. They need to be reminded not to put toilet tissue into the receptacle. Because urine will be measured, the client should not urinate in the toilet.

    You will not be in the home 24 hours a day. Therefore, the client and family must understand that all intake and output must be measured. They must know how to measure intake and output. You can encourage them to measure I&O by placing a fluid capacity list, a measuring device, and an I&O record in the bathroom, the kitchen, and in the client's room. Unless the measurement is recorded right away, it is easily forgotten.

Procedure: Measuring intake and output

1. Wash your hands.
2. Measure intake as follows:
   a. Pour liquid remaining in a container into a measuring cup or graduate.
   b. Measure the amount at eye level.
   c. Check the serving amount from your list of container capacities.
   d. Subtract the remaining amount from the full serving amount.
   e. Repeat steps 2a through 2d for each remaining liquid.
   f. Add the amounts from 2d together. Record this amount and the time on the I&O record.
3. Measure output as follows:
   a. Pour the fluid into the graduate or measure.
   b. Measure the amount at eye level.
   c. Record the amount and the time on the I&O record.
   d. Rinse and return the graduate or measure to its proper place.
   e. Clean and return the bedpan, urinal, emesis basin, or other drainage container to its proper place.
4. Wash your hands.
5. Note and report your observations:
   a. Amount, color, characteristics, and time of vomitus or diarrhea
   b. A sudden increase or decrease in the client's intake or output
   c. A poor appetite or difficulty swallowing, drinking, or voiding
   d. If the client has not voided in 8 hours or cannot void
   e. Unusual observations of urine, vomitus, or stools

Other Methods of Meeting Food and Fluid Needs

    Some clients cannot eat or drink because of illness, surgery, or injury. Other methods must be used to meet their food and fluid needs. These methods require a doctor's order. The nurse is responsible for carrying out the order. The nurse may teach family members the methods described in this section. Home health aides never perform these methods.

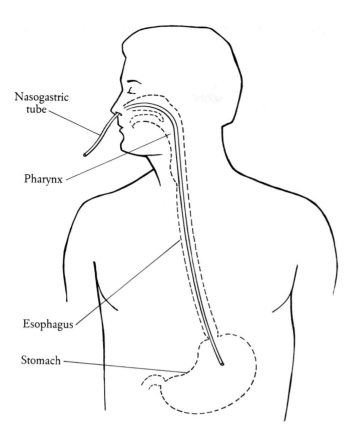

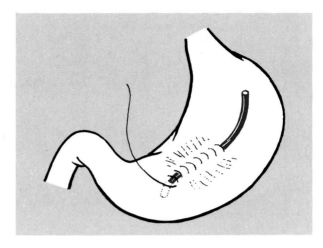

Fig. 17-12 Gastrostomy tube is inserted into the stomach. (From Sorrentino, S.A.: Mosby's textbook for nursing assistants, ed. 2, St. Louis, 1987, The C.V. Mosby Co.)

Fig. 17-11 A nasogastric tube inserted through the nose into the stomach. (From Sorrentino, S.A.: Mosby's textbook for nursing assistants, ed. 2, St. Louis, 1987, The C.V. Mosby Co.)

Tube feedings. A client may be fed through a nasogastric tube (NG tube or Levine tube). The nurse inserts the tube through the client's nose into the stomach (Fig. 17-11). Or a tube may be surgically inserted directly into the stomach (*gastrostomy tube*) as in Fig. 17-12. Commercially prepared or blended fluids are passed through the tube into the stomach. The feeding is given at scheduled times using a syringe or funnel (Fig. 17-13). Or the feeding can be administered continuously using a special pump. *Gavage* is another term for a tube feeding.

Clients with cancer, burns, stroke, or mouth or throat injuries may need tube feedings. Comatose clients may also be candidates for tube feedings.

Tube feedings are given by a nurse or family member. Home health aides do not give tube feedings. However, you may be assigned to care for a client who gets tube feedings. If so, your supervisor will give special instructions.

Intravenous therapy. Many clients receive fluid through a needle inserted in a vein. Minerals and vitamins are often given in the same manner. The abbreviation IV and the term IV *infusion* are common terms

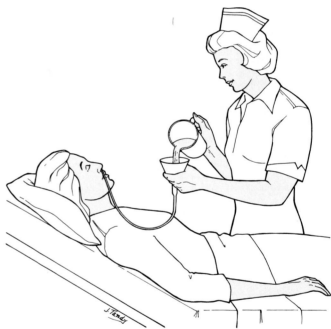

Fig. 17-13 The nurse gives a tube feeding. A funnel is attached to the end of the nasogastric tube. The blended fluid is poured into the funnel. (From Sorrentino, S.A.: Mosby's textbook for nursing assistants, ed. 2, St. Louis, 1987, The C.V. Mosby Co.)

for *intravenous therapy.* The fluid is in a bottle or plastic bag. Clear IV tubing connects the container to the needle in a vein (Fig. 17-14). The amount of fluid given (infused) per hour is ordered by the doctor. The nurse or family makes sure this amount is given. They control the number of drops (the flow rate) per minute. Home health aides are never responsible for IV therapy or for regulating the flow rate.

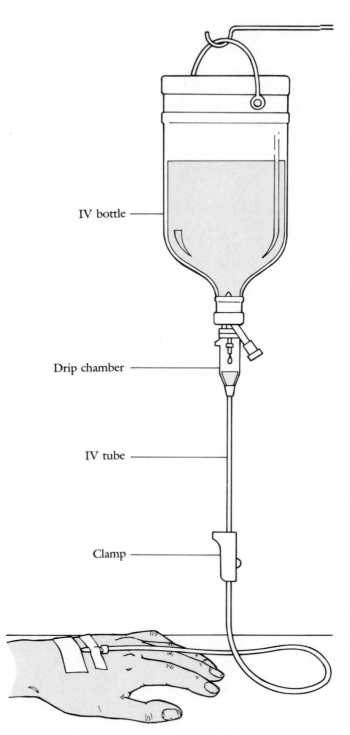

IV bottle

Drip chamber

IV tube

Clamp

Fig. 17-14 Intravenous therapy. The needle is inserted into a vein in the arm or hand. The needle is attached to the bottle by tubing. (From Sorrentino, S.A.: Mosby's textbook for nursing assistants, ed. 2, St. Louis, 1987, The C.V. Mosby Co.)

Parenteral nutrition. Parenteral nutrition is an intravenous feeding. Nourishment is sent directly to the bloodstream. It bypasses the gastrointestinal system. The solution contains all essential nutrients: carbohydrates, proteins, vitamins, and minerals. It is called *total parenteral nutrition* (TPN) or *hyperalimentation.* The solution is far more nutritious than a regular IV solution. TPN is sometimes used for seriously ill and injured clients. Home health aides never administer or regulate TPN solutions.

For TPN, a catheter is surgically inserted into a neck vein. Microorganisms can grow in the solution or at the insertion site. Therefore, microorganisms can easily enter the bloodstream and cause an infection. Infection is a dangerous complication for the client. You must notify your supervisor immediately if the client develops a fever, shortness of breath, or chest pains. Also notify your supervisor if the solution stops dripping or if the dressing is loose.

Summary

Foods and fluids are needed for health and survival. A well-balanced diet contains foods from the four basic food groups. The diet provides the necessary amounts of proteins, carbohydrates, fats, vitamins, and minerals. Eating habits vary among individuals. Habits are affected by many factors including religion and culture. When helping a client meet nutritional needs, you need to consider the factors that affect eating. Also try to make the meal as pleasant as possible for the individual.

Fluid balance is essential for health and life. The amount of fluid taken into the body must equal the amount lost. Fluid is lost through the urine, feces, vomitus, skin, and lungs. Keeping accurate intake and output records will help doctors and nurses evaluate a client's fluid balance.

Clients may depend on you to meet part or all of their food and fluid needs. This includes shopping for food and fixing meals. Some clients need to be fed. You need to remember that meals are usually social activities. The client will enjoy the meal more if refreshed and comfortable.

Study Questions

1. You are assigned to care for Mrs. Weber. She is on a 2000 mg. sodium restricted diet. You are to shop for groceries and prepare meals. She has a small refrigerator. How will you prepare for grocery shopping? Identify the foods she can and cannot eat. Describe how you will prepare her meals safely.

2. You are assigned to care for Mr. Milford. He is semicomatose. He is NPO, receives tube feedings, and is on intake and output. Describe how you will care for this client.

Circle the *best* answer.

3. Nutrition is
   a. Fats, proteins, carbohydrates, vitamins, and minerals
   b. The many processes involved in ingesting, digesting, absorbing, and using food and fluids
   c. The four basic food groups
   d. The balance between fluid intake and output

4. Protein is needed for
   a. Tissue growth and repair
   b. Energy and the fiber for bowel elimination
   c. Body heat and the protection of organs from injury
   d. Improving the taste of food

5. Which foods provide the most protein?
   a. Butter and cream
   b. Tomatoes and potatoes
   c. Meats and fish
   d. Corn and lettuce

6. Eating and nutrition are affected by
   a. A person's culture and religious practices
   b. Personal preferences and the way food is prepared
   c. The amount of money available to buy food
   d. All of the above

7. Sodium-restricted diets are *not* ordered for clients with
   a. Diabetes mellitus
   b. Heart disease
   c. Kidney disease
   d. Liver disease

8. Mrs. Ronan is on a sodium-restricted diet. She wants a little salt on her potato. You should give her the salt.
   a. True
   b. False

9. The diabetic diet controls the amount of
   a. Water
   b. Sodium
   c. Carbohydrates
   d. Nutrients

10. Planning for the diabetic diet involves
    a. Calculating the amount of sodium
    b. Exchange lists
    c. Measuring fluid intake
    d. Giving insulin with meals

11. Which is a guide to freshness?
    a. Unit pricing
    b. Open dating
    c. Ingredient labels
    d. Nutrition labels

12. Which can save money on groceries?
    a. Buying day-old bread
    b. Using coupons
    c. Buying fruits and vegetables that are in season
    d. All of the above

13. Leftovers should be
    a. Refrigerated right away
    b. Left out for later snacking
    c. Discarded
    d. Eaten for your lunch

14. Which statement is *false*?
    a. You can refreeze thawed foods.
    b. Raw fruits and vegetables are the most nutritious.
    c. Poultry must be washed before being cooked.
    d. Milk and milk products must be refrigerated.

15. When preparing food you should
    a. Wash your hands first
    b. Wash knives, utensils, and counter tops after all food has been prepared
    c. Use your hands to mix food thoroughly
    d. Use foods right away if the containers leak, bulge, or are dented

16. Which statement about feeding a client is *false*?
    a. Clients should be allowed to pray before eating.
    b. A fork is used to feed a client.
    c. The client should be asked the order in which foods should be served.
    d. You should engage the client in a pleasant conversation.

17. Fluids are lost from the body through the
    a. Urine and feces
    b. Skin and lungs
    c. Vomitus
    d. All of the above

18. Fluid intake and the fluid output must be equal.
    a. True
    b. False

19. Normal adult fluid requirements are approximately
    a. 1000 to 1500 ml daily
    b. 1500 to 2000 ml daily
    c. 2000 to 2500 ml daily
    d. 2500 to 3000 ml daily

20. A client is NPO. You should
    a. Provide a variety of fluids
    b. Offer fluids in small amounts and small containers
    c. Not give the client fluids
    d. Prevent the client from having oral hygiene

21. Which is *not* counted as liquid food?
    a. Coffee, tea, juices, and soft drinks
    b. Butter, spaghetti sauce, and melted cheese
    c. Ice cream, sherbert, custard, and pudding
    d. Jello, popsicles, soup, and creamed cereals

22. Home health aides are responsible for
    a. Intravenous therapy
    b. Tube feedings
    c. Total parenteral nutrition
    d. None of the above

Answers

3. b	8. b	13. a	18. a
4. a	9. c	14. a	19. c
5. c	10. b	15. a	20. c
6. d	11. b	16. b	21. b
7. a	12. d	17. d	22. d

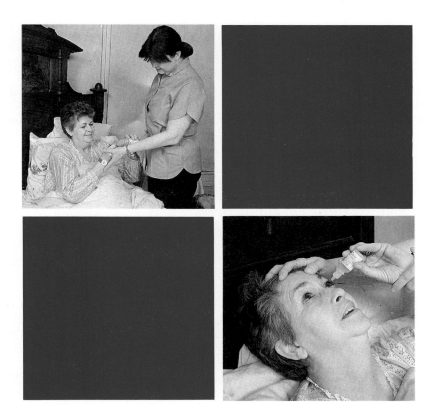

18 Special Procedures

Chapter Highlights

Assisting with medications

Oxygen therapy

Application of heat and cold

What you will learn to do

- Explain how you can assist clients with medications
- Identify medication forms and the routes for taking them
- Describe the rules for assisting clients with medications
- Describe the devices used to administer oxygen
- Explain the rules for caring for a client receiving oxygen
- Identify the purposes, effects, and complications of heat and cold applications
- Describe the role of home health aides in the application of heat and cold
- Explain the rules that apply to heat and cold applications
- Perform the procedures described in this chapter

Key Terms

Constrict To narrow
Dilate To expand or open wider
Medication A chemical substance used to treat disease; a drug

Prescription drugs Drugs that require a doctor's order; the prescription is filled by a pharmacist
Over-the-counter (OTC) drugs Drugs that can be bought without a doctor's order

Assisting with Medications

Medications or *drugs* are chemical substances. They are used to treat diseases. There are many different types of drugs for many different diseases. Drugs can be given for infections and pain. There are also drugs that affect the nervous, cardiovascular, musculoskeletal, reproductive, and other body systems.

Medications can be very helpful. But they can also be very dangerous. For example, a pain medication is helpful because it relieves pain. However, it may also cause drowsiness, dizziness, and fainting. These are called *side effects*. Side effects can be harmful to clients. Different drugs cause different side effects. Skin rashes, ringing in the ears, nausea, vomiting, diarrhea, constipation, gastrointestinal bleeding, itching, dry mouth, high or low blood pressure, blurred vision, and a rapid pulse rate are among the many possible side effects of drugs.

Home health aides do not administer medications. This is the responsibility of the nurse, client, or family. However, you may need to help clients take their medications. If so, you need to make sure the client takes the right medication, the right amount, at the right time, and in the right way.

There are two types of medications: prescription drugs and over-the-counter (OTC) drugs. *Prescription drugs* require a doctor's order. The prescription is filled by a pharmacist. OTC *drugs* can be bought without a doctor's order. They are usually not as strong and cost less than prescription drugs. Aspirin and Tylenol are common over-the-counter drugs. Home health aides do not administer either prescription or over-the-counter drugs.

Prescriptions

Because drug therapy is very complex, *a doctor's order, or prescription, is necessary.* The doctor considers the client's signs and symptoms, diagnosis, age, other health problems, and possible drug side effects when deciding on a medication. The doctor orders the type of drug, the drug *form*, the *dose* (amount), the *time* it is to be taken, how often it is taken (*frequency*), and how it will be taken (*route*).

FORM

Medications come in many different forms. They can be solid or liquid. Table 18-1 describes the different drug forms.

DOSE

The right amount of the medication must be taken. For example, the doctor may order 1 tablet, 2 tablets, or 1 teaspoon of a drug. The dose depends on the drug and the client's age, weight, and condition.

TIME AND FREQUENCY

How the medication works, its side effects, and the reason for the medication influence time and frequency. For example, some drugs irritate the stomach. To reduce the possibility of irritation, they are taken with meals. The doctor may order a medication to be taken:

- @ H.S.   hour of sleep
- q.d.   every day
- q.o.d.   every other day
- q.h.   every hour
- q.2h   every two hours
- q.4h   every four hours
- q.6h   every six hours
- q.8h   every eight hours
- b.i.d.   two times a day
- t.i.d.   three times a day
- q.i.d.   four times a day
- a.c.   before meals
- p.c.   after meals
- With meals
- p.r.n.   when necessary

The exact times medications are taken depends on the client's routine. Your supervisor will tell you what times the client needs to take a medication.

ROUTE

This is the way the medication is taken. The doctor, nurse, client, or family members may give medications through the following routes:

- Oral   by mouth (Fig. 18-1)
- Sublingual   placed under the tongue to be absorbed

Table 18-1 Medication Forms

FORM	FIGURE	DESCRIPTION
Oral Medications		
Capsules	Fig. 18-1, A	Small containers that hold a powder or liquid medicine They are swallowed whole and are taken with water
Lozenges	Fig. 18-1, B	Hard, flavored disks They dissolve in the mouth
Tablets	Fig. 18-1, C	Dried powdered drugs formed into a small, hard disk Some have hard coatings Most are swallowed whole and are taken with water; some are placed under tongue to dissolve
Liquids	Fig. 18-1, D	Water or syrup solutions Some are sweetened with sugar They are swallowed without taking water or other fluid They are measured by teaspoons, tablespoons, medicine cups, or medicine droppers
Topical Medications		
Ointments		Rubbed into the skin They relieve pain
Lotions		Gently patted onto the skin They are used for cleansing, to prevent itching, and to prevent dry skin
Creams		Applied to the skin Some fight infection; others are used for skin rashes
Suppository	Fig. 18-2	Solid cone-shaped medication that melts at body temperature Inserted into a body opening (rectum or vagina)
Drops	Fig. 18-3	Applied into the nose, ear, or eye using a dropper

- *Topical* — applied to a body surface (skin or mucous membrane) (Figs. 18-2, 18-3)
- *Subcutaneous* — injected under the skin (Fig. 18-4, A)
- *Intramuscular* — injected into a muscle (Fig. 18-4, B)
- *Intravenous* — given into a vein (Fig. 18-4, C)

Home health aides *assist* with medications. They do not administer medications. Administering medications means giving the drug to the client without the client's help. It also involves pouring the medication from the bottle into a medicine container. The next step is giving the poured medication to the client. Only RNs and LPNs are allowed to administer medications. They are given this privilege by their state nurse practice acts. Home health aides do not have this privilege. You can assist with, but not administer medications.

Assisting with medications means that you ob-

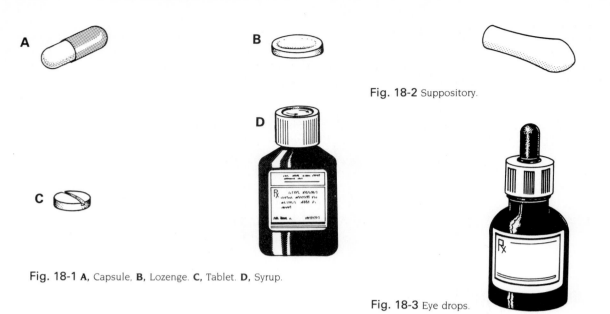

Fig. 18-2 Suppository.

Fig. 18-1 **A,** Capsule, **B,** Lozenge. **C,** Tablet. **D,** Syrup.

Fig. 18-3 Eye drops.

Fig. 18-4 **A,** Subcutaneous injection. **B,** Intramuscular injection. **C,** Intravenous injection.

serve clients taking their own medications. For example, you hand the medicine container to the client. The client takes the correct number of tablets or measures the amount of liquid to be taken. Some clients have *prepoured* medications. These drugs are measured into special containers by the nurse, pharmacist, or family member. The containers have compartments. Each compartment is labeled for a certain day and time (Fig. 18-5). For example, on Tuesday morning the client would take the medication from the compartment labeled "Tuesday 9 a.m."

Prepoured medications help reduce drug errors. They are especially helpful for confused clients or those with poor vision. The client with poor vision may misread a medicine container label. The wrong medication or the wrong dose could be taken. The confused client may not remember taking medications. He or she may take another dose. Forgetting medication or taking too much can seriously harm a client.

Fig. 18-5 Prepoured medications.

GUIDELINES FOR ASSISTING WITH MEDICATIONS

You must be very careful when assisting clients with their medications. The following guidelines will help you perform this responsibility safely.

1. Review the medication plan with your supervisor. The plan will tell you when medications are to be taken. It will also alert you to special considerations. For example, a medication may need to be taken with food.
2. Remember the "five rights" for safely taking medications:
   - The right client
   - The right medication
   - The right time
   - The right route
   - The right dose
3. Read each prescription label carefully. This lets you know who the medication is for. Remember, other family members may also have prescriptions.
4. Know how much of a drug the client must take. For example, Mr. Shaw needs to take 2 tablets of a medication. He pours only 1 from the container. You need to remind him to take another.
5. Keep caps on medicine containers to prevent spilling.
6. Keep medications out of the reach of children and confused adults (see Chapter 8, page 110).
7. Store the client's medications in a specific area. Tell the client and family where the medications are stored. Do not move them around. The client may expect to find a medicine container in a certain place. He or she may take a container without looking at the label.
8. Keep the client's medicines separate from those of other family members.
9. Keep medicines in the original containers.
10. Do not remove labels from prescription or over-the-counter drugs.
11. Do not give a client an unlabeled medicine container.
12. Offer water or other cool liquid to help the client swallow tablets or capsules.
13. Tell your supervisor if the client is taking over-the-counter drugs. Report the name of the drug, the amount taken, and how often it is taken.
14. Know how to store each medicine. Some drugs must be refrigerated. Keep drugs out of sunlight and do not let them freeze. Very hot or cold temperatures can change the chemical structure of the drug.
15. Keep medications dry. Keep them away from moist areas such as bathroom sinks and kitchen counters.

Moisture can soften tablets or change the chemical structure of some drugs.
16. Discard medications that are no longer needed or are out of date. Your supervisor will tell you to discard them. To discard medications, flush them down the toilet or pour them down a drain. Do not discard medications in the trash. Children may find and take them.
17. Notify your supervisor if a client refuses to take a medication.
18. Be honest with clients. Do not say a medication will taste good when it will not.
19. Do not refer to medications as "candy" when dealing with children. They may want more or think all drugs are candy. This can lead to accidental poisoning in children.

Procedure: Assisting with medications

1. Explain to the client what you are going to do.
2. Check the client's medication list. Identify the correct medication, amount, time, and route.
3. Wash your hands.
4. Take the following to the client:
   a. Medication
   b. Teaspoon or tablespoon if needed
   c. Glass of water or other cool liquid
   d. Straw
   e. Tissues or cotton balls if needed
   f. Disposable glove if needed
   g. Equipment for handwashing
5. Provide for privacy. Ask visitors to leave the room.
6. Help the client wash his or her hands.
7. Check the prescription label. Make sure you have the *right* client, the *right* medication, the *right* time, the *right* amount, and the *right* route.
8. Place the medications within the client's reach. Make sure the client has his or her eyeglasses if they are needed.
9. Loosen container lids, tops, or caps. Tell the client the names of each medication.
10. Assist the client with oral medications as necessary (tablets, capsules, liquids):
    a. Support the client's hand if necessary as
    Continued

he or she pours medication into a spoon, cup, or other hand (Fig. 18-6).

b. Give the client the glass of water.

c. Make sure the client swallows the medication.

11. Assist the client with eye medications as necessary:

a. Position the client so that his or her head is tilted back.

b. Know which eye is to receive the medication.

c. Support the client's hand as he or she drops the medication into the lower eyelid (Fig. 18-7).

d. Ask the client to close his or her eyes. This helps distribute the medication.

12. Assist the client with topical medications (ointments, lotions):

a. Help the client remove the dressing if there is one (see Chapter 19, page 323).

b. Wash the area as instructed by your supervisor.

c. Have the client apply the medication.

d. Help him or her with handwashing.

13. Assist the client with a rectal suppository:

a. Help the client unwrap the suppository.

b. Ask the client to put on the disposable glove.

c. Help the client to a side-lying position.

d. Guide the client's hand to the rectal area if necessary.

e. Hold the buttocks together for a few minutes. This helps the client retain the suppository.

f. Help the client assume a comfortable position.

14. Help the client with handwashing.

15. Return medications to their proper place.

16. Remove and discard wrappings and used disposable equipment.

17. Wash your hands.

18. Note and report the following:

a. The medication taken, the time, and the route

b. Any difficulties the client had in taking the medication (difficulty swallowing, hand tremors)

c. Any observed side effects or client complaints

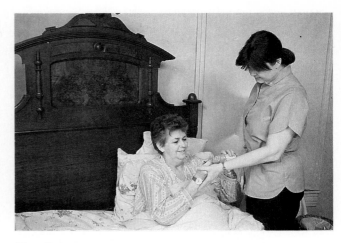

Fig. 18-6 Aide supports the client's hand while she pours a medication.

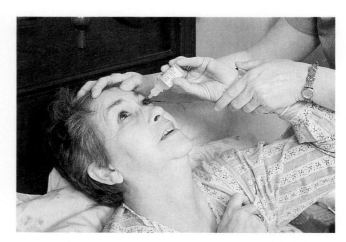

Fig. 18-7 Aide supports the client's hand while she gives herself eye drops.

Oxygen Therapy

Oxygen is a tasteless, odorless, and colorless gas. It is necessary for survival. Death occurs within four minutes if a person stops breathing. During illness the amount of oxygen in the blood may be below normal levels. If so, the doctor will probably order supplemental (extra) oxygen. Acutely ill clients and those with respiratory disorders or heart disease often need supplemental oxygen.

Oxygen is a drug. The doctor orders the following:

- The amount of oxygen to be given
- If oxygen should be given continuously or intermittently (periodically)
- The device used to give the oxygen

Home health aides are never responsible for administering oxygen. However, you may be assigned to clients receiving oxygen therapy. Therefore, you need to know how to safely care for these clients.

Devices Used in the Administration of Oxygen

Oxygen is supplied in tanks (Fig. 18-8). Oxygen is delivered to the client's home by a medical supply company. They make sure the equipment works properly. The nurse or respiratory therapist teaches the client and family how to use the equipment. Small oxygen tanks are also available. Ambulatory or wheelchair clients can use the small tanks when up or out of the home (Fig. 18-9).

There are several devices used to administer oxygen.

- *Nasal catheter* (Fig. 18-10, A)—is inserted by a doctor, nurse, or respiratory therapist. It is inserted through the client's nose to the back of the throat. The nasal catheter can be uncomfortable. Clients need frequent oral hygiene and nasal care.
- *Nasal cannula* (Fig. 18-10, B)—is the most common device and is simple to use. Two small prongs are inserted into the nostrils. The cannula is simple to use. The client can eat and talk with the cannula in place. Extension tubing can be attached to the cannula. This allows the client to move about (Fig. 18-10, C). Nasal irritation can occur if the prongs are too tight.
- *Face mask* (Fig. 18-10, D)—covers the nose and mouth. There are small holes in the sides of the mask. The holes let carbon dioxide escape during exhalation. The mask must be removed for eating and drinking. A nasal cannula is usually used during meals. Face masks can frighten clients and cause feelings of suffocation. Talking can be difficult. The client's face must be kept clean and dry to prevent irritation from the mask.
- *Oxygen tent* (Fig. 18-10, E)—is made of clear plastic and covers a crib or the upper bed. A motor circulates cool air rich in oxygen through the tent. Oxygen tents are not often used.

Fig. 18-9 Client uses a small oxygen tank when up and about.

Fig. 18-8 Oxygen tank. (From Sorrentino, S.A.: Mosby's textbook for nursing assistants, ed. 2, St. Louis, 1987, The C.V. Mosby Co.)

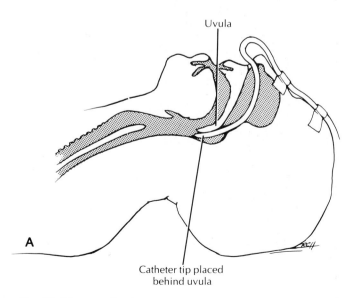

Uvula

A

Catheter tip placed
behind uvula

Fig. 18-10 A, Nasal catheter.

Right nasal prong (1)

B

Left nasal prong (2)

Delivery tube (4)

Restraining band (3)

C

D

E

Fig. 18-10 cont'd. —**B**, Nasal cannula. **C**, Extension tubing allows the client with a nasal cannula to move about. **D**, Face mask. **E**, Oxygen tent.

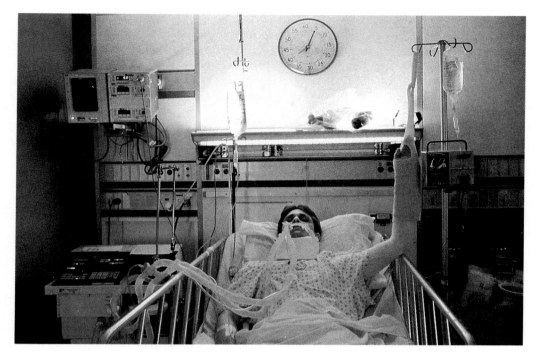

Fig. 18-10 cont'd. —F, Mechanical ventilator. (A and B from Eubanks, D.H. and Bone, R.C., Comprehensive respiratory care: A learning system, St. Louis, 1985, The C.V. Mosby Co. D, E, and F from Sorrentino, S.A.: Mosby's textbook for nursing assistants, ed. 2, St. Louis, 1987, The C.V. Mosby Co.).

- *Mechanical ventilator* (Fig. 18-10, F)—is a machine that helps the client breathe. Ventilators are used for clients with severe breathing problems. Paralyzed clients and those with muscle weakness may be unable to inhale. Ventilators help them breathe.

GENERAL RULES

Nurses and respiratory therapists are responsible for oxygen therapy. You must practice the following rules to safely care for clients receiving oxygen.

1. Follow the safety precautions related to fire and the use of oxygen (see Chapter 8, page 111).
2. Never remove the device used to administer oxygen.
3. Never shut off or increase the flow of oxygen from the tank.
4. Give oral hygiene as directed by the nurse.
5. Make sure the connecting tubing is taped or pinned to the client's gown, pajamas, or clothing. The tubing must be secured in place.
6. Make sure there are no kinks in the tubing.
7. Make sure the client does not lie on any part of the tubing.
8. Observe for signs and symptoms of respiratory distress and abnormal breathing patterns. Immediately report any problems to your supervisor (see Chapter 13).
9. Check the gauge to make sure enough oxygen is in the tank (Fig. 18-11).

Fig. 18-11 Gauge on the oxygen tank shows the amount remaining. (From Sorrentino, S.A.: Mosby's textbook for nursing assistants, ed. 2, St. Louis, 1987, The C.V. Mosby Co.)

Application of Heat and Cold

Heat and cold applications are ordered by the doctor to promote healing and comfort. However, heat and cold applications can cause severe injuries and changes in body function. The risks to the client are great. Therefore, the procedures are considered to be complex nursing functions. Some states and home care agencies do not let home health aides apply heat and cold. Others do. Some states and agencies let home health aides apply cold but not heat applications. You must follow your employer's policies and procedures. The information in this book is intended to give an overview of heat and cold applications.

Heat Applications

Heat applications are usually small. They can be applied to almost any body part. The phrase "local heat application" means that heat is applied to a part of the body. Heat applications can be used to:

- Relax muscles and ease tension
- Relieve pain
- Increase wound drainage
- Promote healing
- Increase blood flow to the area
- Reduce tissue swelling

EFFECTS

When applied to the skin, heat causes blood vessels in that area to *dilate*. Dilate means to expand or open wider (Fig. 18-12). More blood flows through the vessel. More oxygen and nutrients are brought to the tissues for healing. The increased circulation removes toxic (poisonous) substances and waste products faster. Excess fluid is removed from the area more rapidly. The skin feels warm and appears reddened where the heat is applied. These effects are due to increased blood flow.

COMPLICATIONS

Heat applications can help clients. However, complications can occur. High temperatures can cause burns. Pain, excessive redness, and blisters are danger signals. These must be reported immediately. You also must observe for pale skin. When heat is applied too long, blood vessels tend to *constrict* or narrow (see Fig. 18-12, C). Blood flow decreases when vessels constrict. Decreased blood flow reduces the amount of blood available to tissues. A decreased blood supply causes tissue damage and makes the skin appear pale.

Certain clients have a greater risk of complications from local heat applications. They are infants,

very young children, fair-skinned individuals, and the elderly. Their skin is very delicate, fragile, and easily burned. Complications may also occur in those who have a poor ability to sense (feel) heat or pain. Many factors can interfere with sensation. These include circulatory disorders, central nervous system damage, aging, and loss of consciousness. Confused clients and those receiving strong pain medications may also have decreased sensation.

MOIST AND DRY APPLICATIONS

The doctor may order a moist or dry heat application. A *moist heat application* means that water is in contact with the skin. Water is a good conductor of heat. Therefore, the effects of heat are greater and occur faster than with a dry application. Heat penetrates deeper with a moist application. There is less drying of the skin. Temperatures of moist heat applications are lower than dry heat applications. This prevents injury to the client. The following are moist heat applications.

- *Hot compresses and packs*—consist of a washcloth, small towel, or gauze dressing (Fig. 18-13). A compress is applied to a small area. A pack is applied to large body areas. The compress or pack is applied for 20 minutes.
- *Hot soaks*—involve putting a body part into a container of water (Fig. 18-14). They are usually used for small body parts (hand, lower arm, foot, or lower leg). A soak lasts 15 or 20 minutes.
- *Sitz bath*—involves immersing the pelvic area in warm or hot water for 20 minutes (Fig. 18-15). A plastic sitz bath fits onto the toilet seat.

Water does not touch the skin with a *dry heat application*. The risk of burns is less because dry heat does not penetrate as deeply as moist heat. However, higher temperatures are used with dry heat to achieve the desired effect. Therefore, there is still a risk of burns with dry heat. The following are dry heat applications.

- *Hot water bottles*—are filled with water. However, water is not in contact with the client's skin (Fig. 18-16). The hot water bottle is placed in a flannel cover or towel to protect the skin from the bag. The cover may be-

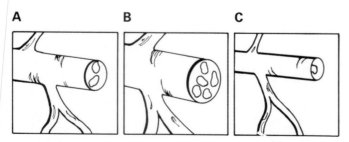

Fig. 18-12 **A,** Blood vessel under normal conditions. **B,** Dilated blood vessel. **C,** Constricted blood vessel. (From Sorrentino, S.A.: Mosby's textbook for nursing assistants, ed. 2, St. Louis, 1987, The C.V. Mosby Co.)

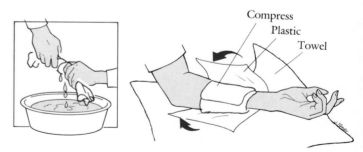

Fig. 18-13 A hot compress is covered with plastic and a bath towel. These keep the compress warm. (From Sorrentino, S.A.: Mosby's textbook for nursing assistants, ed. 2, St. Louis, 1987, The C.V. Mosby Co.)

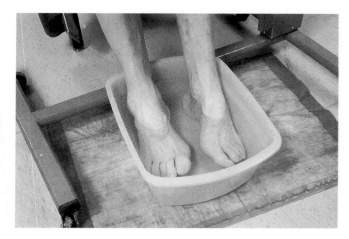

Fig. 18-14 The hot soak. (From Sorrentino, S.A.: Mosby's textbook for nursing assistants, ed. 2, St. Louis, 1987, The C.V. Mosby Co.)

Fig. 18-15 The sitz bath.

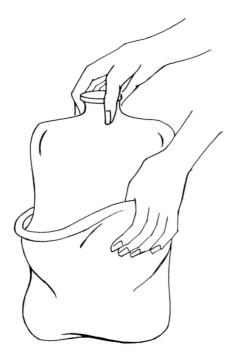

Fig. 18-16 Hot water bottle. (From Sorrentino, S.A.: Mosby's textbook for nursing assistants, ed. 2, St. Louis, 1987, The C.V. Mosby Co.)

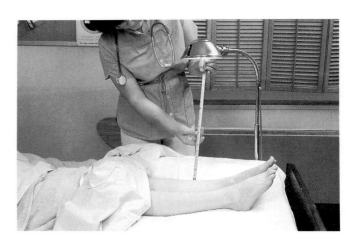

Fig. 18-17 Heat lamp. (From Sorrentino, S.A.: Mosby's textbook for nursing assistants, ed. 2, St. Louis, 1987, The C.V. Mosby Co.)

come moist from perspiration. If so, a dry cover must be applied. Otherwise the dry heat application becomes a moist heat application. This increases the danger of burns and other complications. Hot water bottles are applied for 20 or 30 minutes.

- *Heat lamps*—usually have flexible necks (Fig. 18-17). The lamp is placed at various distances from the body part depending on the bulb wattage. The greater the wattage, the farther away the lamp (Fig. 18-18). The lamp is never covered with bed linens, plastic, or other material.

- *Heating pads*—consist of electric coils covered with a cloth or vinyl material (Fig. 18-19). Low temperature settings should be used. The doctor prescribes the length of application.

General Rules

If you are allowed to apply heat applications, your supervisor will give you the necessary instructions. You must thoroughly understand the purpose, effects, steps, and complications of the procedure. You should have close supervision when applying heat. A nurse should visit the home or be available by phone.

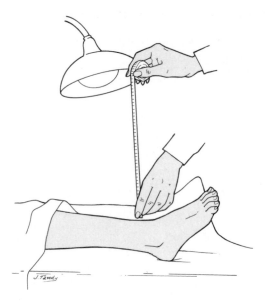

Fig. 18-18 The distance between the heat lamp and the client is measured with a yardstick. (From Sorrentino, S.A.: Mosby's textbook for nursing assistants, ed. 2, St. Louis, 1987, The C.V. Mosby Co.)

Clients must be protected from injury during local heat applications. Those who cannot protect themselves need extra consideration. Serious injury can occur if proper safety precautions are not taken. Practice the following rules to prevent burns and other complications:

1. Do not apply heat unless you have been instructed to do so by your supervisor.
2. Know the procedure and how to operate any necessary equipment.
3. Measure the temperature of moist heat applications with a bath thermometer if possible.
4. Follow agency policies for temperature ranges for heat applications.
5. Know the temperature ranges for warm, hot, and very hot applications. Use the following ranges as guidelines:
   - Warm—93° to 98° F (33.8° to 37° C)
   - Hot—98° to 105° F (37° to 40.5° C)
   - Very hot—105° to 115° F (40.5° to 46.1° C)
6. Ask the nurse what the temperature of the application should be. This is especially important for individuals who are at risk for burns. They include infants, the elderly, and other clients described on page 314. Lower temperatures are usually used for clients at risk.
7. Cover dry heat applications with flannel covers or towels before applying them.
8. Observe the client's skin closely for signs of complications. Immediately report any signs of complications or client complaints of pain or burning.
9. Do not let the client increase the temperature of the application.
10. Know how long the application is to be left in

Fig. 18-19 Heating pad.

place. Carefully watch the time. Set a timer if necessary.
11. Follow the rules of electrical safety when using electrical appliances to apply heat (see Chapter 8, page 111).
12. Do not use pins to secure a heating pad in place. Use tape, ties, or gauze. Pins can puncture the pad and cause an electrical hazard.
13. Expose only the body part where the heat is to be applied. Provide for privacy.
14. Make sure the call bell is within the client's reach.

Cold Applications

Cold applications reduce blood flow to a specific area. They are used to:
- Slow bleeding
- Reduce swelling
- Reduce pain
- Cool the body during a fever

EFFECTS

When cold is applied to the skin, blood vessels *constrict* or narrow (see Fig. 18-12). Decreased blood flow results. When blood flow decreases, less oxygen and nutrients are carried to the tissues. Cold applications are useful immediately after an injury. The decreased circulation reduces the amount of bleeding. Fluid accumulation in the tissues is also reduced. Cold numbs the skin. This helps reduce or relieve pain in the part. The skin looks pale and feels cool in the area of the cold.

COMPLICATIONS

Complications from cold applications include pain, burns and blisters, and cyanosis (a bluish skin color). Burns and blisters can occur from intense cold. They are also caused when dry cold applications are in direct contact with the skin. When cold is applied for a long time, blood vessels tend to dilate. This causes blood flow to increase. Therefore, the prolonged application of cold has the same effect as local heat applications.

Certain people are at risk for complications from local cold applications. They are infants, young children, the elderly, and fair-skinned persons.

MOIST AND DRY APPLICATIONS

Cold applications can be moist or dry. The ice bag is a dry cold application. Moist cold applications penetrate deeper than dry ones. Therefore, temperatures of moist applications do not have to be as cold as dry ones. The cold compress and cold sponge bath are moist applications.

GENERAL RULES

Clients must be protected from injuries due to cold applications. The rules for applying heat apply for cold applications. However, there are the following exceptions:

1. Know the temperature ranges for cool, cold, and very cold applications. Use the following ranges as a guide:
   - Cool—65° to 80° F (18.3° to 26.6° C)
   - Cold—59° to 65° F (15° to 18.3° C)
   - Very cold—59° F and below (15° C and below)
2. Do not let the client lower the temperature of the application.
3. Report client complaints of numbness, pain, or burning. Also immediately report blisters or burns; pale, white, or gray skin; cyanosis; and shivering.

Ice Bags

An ice bag is a dry cold application. The bag is filled with crushed ice or ice chips. Crushed ice allows molding of the bag to the body part. The ice bag is placed in a flannel cover or towel before being applied. If the cover becomes moist, it must be removed and a dry cover applied. Ice bags are left in place for 30 minutes. If the bag is to be reapplied, wait one hour. This gives tissues time to recover from the cold.

Ice collars are used for the neck. Some clients have commercial ice bags. They are filled with a special solution and are kept in the freezer. The commercial ice bag can be refrozen for reuse. Flannel covers or towels are also needed with ice collars or commercial ice bags.

Procedure: Applying an ice bag (collar)

1. Explain to the client what you are going to do.
2. Wash your hands.
3. Collect the following equipment:
   a. Ice bag or collar
   b. Crushed ice or ice chips
   c. Flannel cover or towel
   d. Paper towels
4. Fill the bag with water. Put the stopper in place. Turn the bag upside down to check for leaks. Empty the bag.
5. Fill the bag half to two-thirds full with the crushed ice or ice chips (Fig. 18-20).
6. Remove excess air. Press the bag against a firm surface or bend, twist, or squeeze the bag.
7. Place the cap or stopper on securely.
8. Dry the bag with the paper towels.
9. Place the bag in the flannel cover or towel.
10. Provide for privacy.
11. Apply the bag to the area.
12. Make sure the call bell is within the client's reach.
13. Check the skin every 10 minutes. Check for blisters; pale, white, or gray skin; cyanosis; and shivering. Ask the client about numbness, pain, or burning. Remove the bag if any of these occur. Immediately report signs or symptoms of complications.

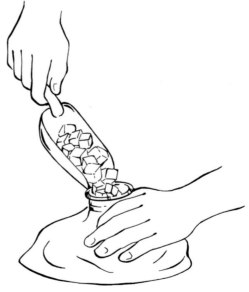

Fig. 18-20 Ice bag is filled with ice. (From Sorrentino, S.A.: Mosby's textbook for nursing assistants, ed. 2, St. Louis, 1987, The C.V. Mosby Co.)

14. Remove the bag after 30 minutes.
15. Make sure the client is comfortable and the call bell is within reach.
16. Clean equipment. Take the flannel cover or towel to the laundry.
17. Wash your hands.
18. Note and report the following:
    a. The time of the application
    b. The site of the application
    c. The length of the application
    d. The client's response
    e. Your observations of the skin

Cold Compresses

Cold compresses are moist cold applications. They consist of a washcloth, small towel, or gauze dressing. A compress is usually applied to a small area. The compress is placed in cold water. After being wrung out it is applied to the specified body part. The application is left in place for 20 minutes and then removed.

Procedure: Applying a cold compress

1. Explain to the client what you are going to do.
2. Wash your hands.
3. Collect the following equipment:
   a. Large basin with ice
   b. Small basin with cold water
   c. Gauze squares, washcloths, or small towels
   d. Waterproof pad or plastic
   e. Bath towel
4. Provide for privacy.
5. Place the small basin with cold water in the large basin with ice.
6. Place the compresses in the cold water.
7. Place a waterproof pad or plastic under the area to receive the compress. Expose the area.
8. Wring out the compress so water is not dripping.
9. Apply the cold compress. Note the time of the application.
10. Check the area every 5 minutes. Check for blisters; pale, white, or gray skin; cyanosis; and shivering. Ask the client about numbness, pain, and burning. Remove the compress if any of these occur. Report signs

and symptoms of complications immediately.
11. Change the compress when it gets warm. Usually compresses need to be changed every five minutes.
12. Remove the compress after 20 minutes.
13. Pat dry the area with the bath towel.
14. Make sure the client is comfortable and the call bell is within reach.
15. Clean equipment. Take dirty linen to the laundry.
16. Wash your hands.
17. Note and report the following:
    a. The time of the application
    b. The site of the application
    c. The length of the application
    d. The client's response
    e. Your observations of the skin

Cold Sponge Baths

The cold sponge bath is used to lower body temperature when there is a high fever. A doctor's order is needed for this procedure. The bath should last 25 to 30 minutes. Body temperature and other vital signs are taken before, during, and after the procedure.

Procedure: Giving a cold sponge bath

1. Explain to the client what you are going to do.
2. Wash your hands.
3. Collect the following equipment:
   a. Bath basin
   b. Bath thermometer
   c. Bath blanket
   d. Two or more bath towels
   e. Two or more washcloths
   f. Thermometer to measure body temperature
   g. Sphygmomanometer and stethoscope
4. Close the door to provide privacy and reduce drafts.
5. Take the client's vital signs. Note them and the time.
6. Place the bath blanket over the top linens. Remove the top linens.
7. Remove the gown or pajamas without exposing the client.

8. Raise the side rails before you leave the bedside.
9. Fill the wash basin two-thirds full with cold water. Measure the water temperature. It should be 68° to 86° F (20° to 30° C). Add ice chips to cool the water if necessary.
10. Place the washcloths in the water. Alternate use of the washcloths during the procedure. Make sure no ice chips stick to them.
11. Lower the side rail.
12. Place a bath towel under the length of the far arm.
13. Sponge the arm for about five minutes using long, slow, and gentle strokes. Pat the arm dry; do not rub dry.
14. Repeat steps 12 and 13 for the arm near you.
15. Place the towel lengthwise over the client's chest and abdomen. Fan-fold the bath blanket to the pubic area.
16. Sponge the chest and abdomen for about 5 minutes. Pat dry. Cover the client with bath blanket. Remove the towel.
17. Measure vital signs. Note them and the time.
18. Stop the sponging and notify the nurse if one of the following occur:
    a. Body temperature is normal or slightly over normal
    b. Shivering
    c. Cyanosis
    d. Other signs and symptoms of cold
19. Place a towel under the length of the far leg.
20. Sponge the leg with long, slow, and gentle strokes for five minutes. Pat the leg dry, cover, and remove the towel.
21. Repeat steps 19 and 20 for the leg near you.
22. Help the client turn onto the side away from you.
23. Place a bath towel on the bed along the length of the client's back and buttocks.
24. Sponge the back and buttocks with long,

slow, and gentle strokes for five minutes. Pat dry and remove the towel.
25. Position the client on his or her back in the center of the bed.
26. Measure vital signs. Note them and the time.
27. Put a clean gown or pajamas on the client. Make the bed. Change any damp or soiled linen.
28. Make sure the client is comfortable and the call bell is within reach.
29. Clean and return equipment to its proper place. Discard disposable equipment. Take dirty linen to the laundry.
30. Measure vital signs 30 minutes after completing the procedure.
31. Wash your hands.
32. Note and report the following:
    a. The time the procedure was started and completed
    b. Vital signs taken before, during, and after the procedure and those taken 30 minutes after the procedure
    c. How the client tolerated the procedure
    d. Other signs and symptoms

Summary

You may have to perform special procedures as a home health aide. They include assisting clients with medications and caring for clients receiving oxygen. These areas are considered complex. If the safety rules are not followed, clients can be seriously harmed. You must be very careful and alert.

Heat and cold applications are also complex procedures. Clients can be injured if proper care is not taken. If you are allowed to apply heat and cold, make sure you protect the client from injury. Close observation of the client is also necessary. Complications of heat and cold can occur easily and quickly. Of all the complications, burns are the most feared and the most serious.

Study Questions

1. You are assigned to Mr. Adams. He is to take his medications at 9 a.m. He takes four different tablets. He also takes a tablet that must dissolve in water and a rectal suppository. His vision is very poor. He also has hand tremors. Describe how you will assist this client.

2. Mrs. Lund has oxygen ordered p.r.n. The oxygen is administered by cannula. Explain how you will help her.

Circle the *best* answer.

3. The following devices are used to administer oxygen. Which device is the simplest and most commonly used?
   a. Nasal catheter
   b. Nasal cannula
   c. Face mask
   d. Oxygen tent

4. A client is receiving supplemental oxygen. You should do all of the following *except*
   a. Follow the safety measures related to fire and the use of oxygen
   b. Turn off the oxygen during meals
   c. Give oral hygiene as directed by the nurse
   d. Make sure there are no kinks in the tubing

5. Local heat applications have all of the following effects *except*
   a. Pain relief
   b. Muscle relaxation
   c. Healing
   d. Decreased blood flow

6. The major complication of local heat applications is (are)
   a. Infection
   b. Burns
   c. Chilling
   d. Decubiti

7. Who has the greatest risk of developing complications from local heat applications?
   a. A 10-year-old boy
   b. A teenager
   c. A 40-year-old woman
   d. An elderly person

8. The statements are about moist heat applications. Which is *false*?
   a. Water is in contact with the skin.
   b. The effects of heat are less than with a dry heat application.
   c. Heat penetrates deeper than with a dry heat application.
   d. The temperature of the application is lower than a dry heat application.

9. The temperature of a hot application is usually between
   a. 65° and 80°F
   b. 93° and 98°F
   c. 98° and 105°F
   d. 105° and 115°F

10. A foot is immersed in a basin of hot water. This is a
    a. Hot compress
    b. Hot pack
    c. Hot soak
    d. Sitz bath

11. Which is a moist heat application?
    a. Hot water bottle
    b. Sitz bath
    c. Heat lamp
    d. Heating pad

12. Local cold applications are used to
    a. Reduce pain, prevent swelling, and decrease circulation
    b. Dilate blood vessels
    c. Prevent infection and the spread of microorganisms
    d. All of the above

13. Which is *not* a complication of local cold applications?
    a. Pain
    b. Burns and blisters
    c. Cyanosis
    d. Infection

14. Which is a dry cold application?
    a. The ice bag
    b. The cold compress
    c. The cold sponge bath
    d. All of the above

15. Before applying an ice bag
    a. The bag is placed in a freezer
    b. The temperature of the bag is measured
    c. The bag is placed in a flannel cover or towel
    d. The client is asked to void

16. Moist cold compresses are left in place no longer than
    a. 20 minutes
    b. 30 minutes
    c. 45 minutes
    d. 60 minutes

17. The cold sponge bath is ordered by the doctor to
    a. Reduce swelling
    b. Relieve pain
    c. Decrease circulation
    d. Lower body temperature

18. The cold sponge bath should last
    a. 15 to 20 minutes
    b. 25 to 30 minutes
    c. 45 to 50 minutes
    d. 60 minutes or longer

Answers

3. b	7. d	11. b	15. c
4. b	8. b	12. a	16. a
5. d	9. c	13. d	17. d
6. b	10. c	14. a	18. b

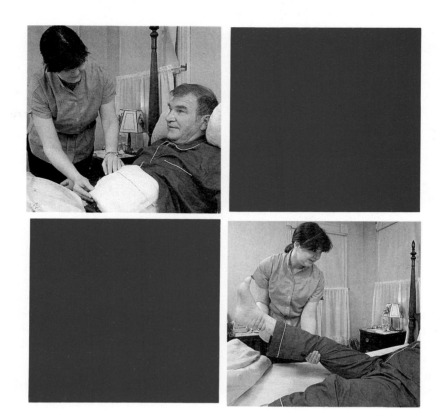

19 The Postoperative Client

Chapter Highlights	What you will learn to do
Psychological care of the client *Physical care of the client*	■ Describe the common fears and concerns of surgical clients ■ Explain how you can promote comfort ■ Explain why dressings are used to cover wounds ■ Explain why postoperative clients should be turned and repositioned ■ Explain the importance of coughing and deep breathing ■ Assist a client with coughing and deep breathing exercises ■ Explain the purpose of leg exercises ■ Assist the client with leg exercises ■ Describe the rules for applying binders and bandages ■ Apply binders, elastic stockings, and elastic bandages

Atelectasis The collapse of a portion of the lung

Embolus A blood clot that travels through the vascular system until it lodges in a distant vessel

Postoperative After the operation or surgery

Preoperative Before the operation or surgery

Thrombus A blood clot

Surgery is done for many reasons: to remove a diseased organ or body part, to remove a tumor, or to repair injured tissue. Surgery is also performed to diagnose disease, to improve appearance, and to relieve symptoms. Whatever the reason, surgery affects the entire body. It also affects the client psychologically.

Home health aides may care for postoperative clients. *Postoperative* means after the surgery. Clients are being sent home soon after surgery. Many of these clients need home care. Your role in caring for surgical clients depends on certain factors. One factor relates to agency policies. Another is whether the surgery was simple or complex. The client's condition is also a factor.

Psychological Care of the Client

Illness or injury cause many fears and concerns. A person's feelings are influenced by past experiences. Some clients have had surgery before. For others it is a new experience. Family and friends who have had surgery often discuss their experiences with the client. Their experiences affect the client. The client may not talk about his or her fears and concerns. The person may be quiet and withdrawn, cry, or talk a lot. Some clients are unusually cheerful or have unusual behavior. These behaviors may be due to one or more fears. The following fears are common among clients before (*preoperative*) and after surgery:

- The fear of cancer
- The fear of body disfigurement
- The fear of disability
- The fear of continued pain
- The fear of bodily exposure
- The fear of tubes, needles, and other equipment
- The fear of complications
- The fear of a prolonged recovery
- The fear that more surgery or other treatments will be needed

What the Client Has Been Told

The doctor tells the client and family about the surgery results. The doctor decides what and when to tell them. Clients usually know the results by the time they go home. However, sometimes a client is not told what was found during surgery. Or the client may not know about a new diagnosis. The family may know but not the client. The opposite is also true. Sometimes the client is told but not the family.

Your supervisor will tell you what the client and family have been told. You must not tell of any diagnosis. Nor should you give incomplete or inaccurate information. Refer any client or family questions to your supervisor.

Responsibilities of the Home Health Aide

You can help the surgical client psychologically. You should do the following:

1. Listen to the client. He or she may need to talk about fears or concerns about recovery.
2. Refer any questions to your supervisor. The client may have questions about the results, care, recovery, or future surgery.
3. Explain procedures and their purpose to the client.
4. Follow the rules of communication described in Chapter 3.
5. Use verbal and nonverbal communication to show you care.
6. Give care and perform procedures efficiently and competently.
7. Report any verbal and nonverbal signs of fear or anxiety in the client to your supervisor.

Physical Care of the Client

Some clients go home the day of or the day after surgery. Some stay in the hospital for a few days or a week. Others need to be in the hospital for several weeks. Home care depends on:

- The type of surgery performed
- The client's age
- The client's general health
- When the surgery was performed

Your supervisor will discuss the client's care with you. You will be told of any special care measures. Postoperative care centers around promoting comfort and preventing complications.

Comfort

Pain is common after surgery. The degree of pain and discomfort depends on the type of surgery. Some clients have a lot of pain postoperatively. Others have only mild discomfort. By the time clients return home, the pain is less. Some clients need mild pain medications. These are ordered by the doctor. Other clients have no pain at all.

The following measure can help promote comfort:

1. Provide a calm, quiet atmosphere. Turn off the television or radio or keep the volume low. Dim lighting or close drapes and window shades. Remind family members that the client is trying to rest.
2. Position the client in good body alignment. Check with your supervisor about any position restrictions.
3. Give the client a backrub before a nap, at bedtime, or when repositioning.
4. Organize the client's care so that he or she has periods of uninterrupted rest.
5. Provide personal care and oral hygiene as necessary.
6. Make sure bed linens are clean, dry, and wrinkle free.
7. Provide distraction if appropriate. The client may need to take his or her mind off the pain. The client may want to talk, watch television, or read a book.
8. Provide care with smooth, even movements. Be gentle.

Dressings

Surgery usually involves cutting into the body. The surgeon will suture (stitch) the area closed. The involved area is called an incision. It is often called the *wound*. Wounds can also occur from accidental injuries. A decubitus ulcer (see Chapter 14, page 236) is also a wound. A wound exists whenever the skin and underlying tissues are damaged.

The wound has to heal. Prevention of infection is very important. Dressings are often used to prevent infection and promote healing. A *dressing* is a gauze bandage that covers a wound (Fig. 19-1). Dressings also absorb wound drainage such as bleeding. Dressings come in different sizes, shapes, and thicknesses. Some wounds do not have dressings. They are left open to the air. This also helps healing. The doctor decides whether or not to use dressings.

Clients may still have dressings when they go home. A nurse is responsible for dressing changes. The client and family may be taught the procedure. Dressing changes involve sterile technique. This means that all objects touching the wound must be free of all pathogens and nonpathogens (see Chapter 7, page 95). The person changing the dressing must know what items must be sterile, what can touch the wound, and what cannot touch the wound.

Dressing supplies must be kept sterile. They

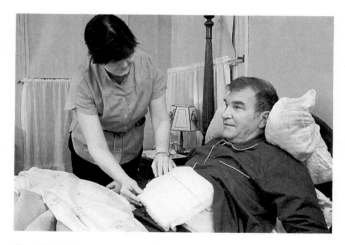

Fig. 19-1 A dressing covers the surgical wound.

should be kept separate from other supplies and equipment. They must also be kept dry.

Prevention of infection is most important. Though you will not change dressings, you will still have contact with the client. Remember to practice good handwashing. Some wounds are left open to the air. Dressings do not protect them from microorganisms.

Positioning

Proper positioning promotes comfort and helps prevent complications. Position restrictions may be ordered. The type of surgery affects positioning. Your supervisor will tell you what positions the client is allowed.

The client is usually positioned for easy and comfortable breathing. The client is also positioned so stress is not placed on the incision. When in the supine position, the client's head and shoulders should be raised slightly. Extra pillows or a backrest may be used (Fig. 19-2). Or the client's head is turned to the side. These positions prevent aspiration if the client vomits.

Your supervisor will tell you how often to reposition the client. Some clients are repositioned every two hours. This helps prevent respiratory and circulatory complications. The client may not want to turn because of pain. You can help ease discomfort by providing necessary support. Also, turn the client with smooth, gentle motions. Use pillows and other devices as instructed to position the client. As healing occurs, the client will have less discomfort. Turning, repositioning, and moving should become easier.

Coughing and Deep Breathing

The postoperative client can develop respiratory complications. There are two major complications. One is pneumonia, an infection in the lung. The other

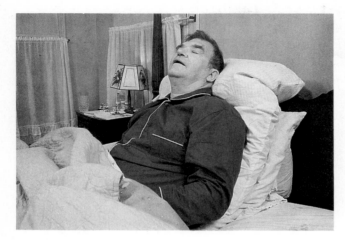

Fig. 19-2 Pillows are used to raise the client's head and shoulders. This position allows easy breathing. It also reduces stress on the incision.

is *atelectasis*, the collapse of a portion of the lung. Atelectasis occurs when mucus collects in the airway. Air cannot get to a part of the lung and the lung collapses. Coughing and deep breathing exercises help prevent these complications. Mucus is removed by coughing. Deep breathing helps air move into most parts of the lungs. The exercises are often ordered for bedbound clients and for those with respiratory disorders.

The client may be afraid to cough and deep breathe. The exercises may be painful. This is especially true after chest and abdominal surgeries. The client may be afraid of breaking open the incision while coughing. However, coughing and deep breathing are necessary to prevent complications.

The frequency of coughing and deep breathing varies. Some doctors order the exercises every one or two hours while the client is awake. Others want coughing and deep breathing done four times a day. Your supervisor will tell you when coughing and deep breathing need to be done. You will also be told how many deep breaths and coughs the client needs to do. This information is also on the client's care plan. Remember that coughing and deep breathing are done only when ordered.

Procedure: Coughing and deep breathing exercises

1. Explain to the client what you are going to do. Also explain what the client can do to help.
2. Provide for privacy.
3. Help the client to a comfortable position. Semi-Fowler's position is usually preferred.

4. Have the client deep breathe:
   a. Have the client place the hands over the rib cage (Fig. 19-3).
   b. Ask the client to exhale until the ribs move as far down as possible.
   c. Ask the client to take a breath as deep as possible. Remind him or her to breathe in through the nose.
   d. Ask the client to hold the breath for 0 to 5 seconds.
   e. Ask the client to exhale slowly through pursed lips (Fig. 19-4). He or she should continue to exhale until the ribs move as far down as possible.
   f. Have the client repeat this step 4 more times. The client should take a total of 5 deep breaths.
5. Ask the client to cough:
   a. Have the client remain in semi-Fowler's position.
   b. Ask the client to interlace the fingers over the incision (Fig. 19-5, A). Or have the client hold a small pillow or folded towel over the incision (Fig. 19-5, B). This is called *splinting* the incision.
   c. Have the client take in a deep breath as in step 5.
   d. Ask the client to cough strongly twice with the mouth open.
6. Help the client assume a comfortable position. Make sure the call bell is within reach.
7. Note and report your observations:
   a. The number of coughs and deep breaths
   b. How well the client tolerated the procedure

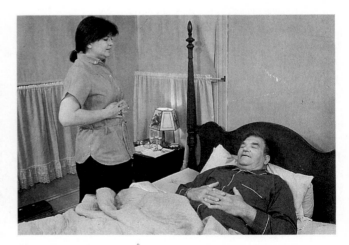

Fig. 19-3 The hands are placed over the rib cage for deep breathing.

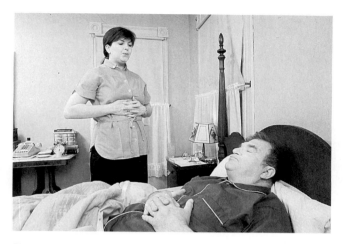

Fig. 19-4 The client exhales through pursed lips during the deep breathing exercise.

A

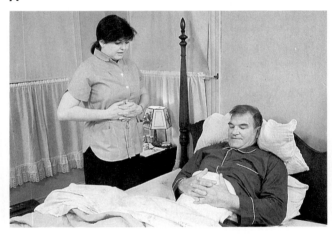

B

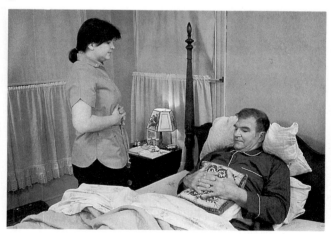

Fig. 19-5 The incision is supported for the coughing exercise. **A,** The client interlaces the fingers over the incisional area. **B,** Or a small pillow can be held over the incision.

Exercise and Activity

Many clients are weak after surgery. They may move slowly because of weakness or discomfort. Some need help walking or getting in out of bed or a chair. Activity restrictions may be ordered. Bending, lifting, driving, house and yard work, and other activities may not be allowed. Therefore, clients may need help with home maintenance, shopping, and meals.

Doctors often order gradual increases in activity (see Chapter 11, page 153). Often special exercises are ordered. These exercises are taught to the client and family in the hospital. A nurse or physical therapist may supervise the exercises in the home. You may be instructed in these special exercises.

Leg exercises are very common after surgery. They help stimulate circulation, especially blood flow in the legs. If blood flow is sluggish, blood clots may form. Blood clots are common in the deep leg veins (Fig. 19-6, A). A blood clot is called a *thrombus* (blood clots are called *thrombi*). A thrombus can break loose and travel in the bloodstream. It then becomes an *embolus*. An *embolus* is a blood clot that travels through the vascular system until it lodges in a distant vessel (Fig. 19-6, B). An embolus from a vein eventually lodges in the lungs (pulmonary embolus). A pulmonary embolus can cause severe respiratory problems and death.

Leg exercises increase venous blood flow. Therefore, thrombi are less likely to develop. Leg exercises are easy to do. You may have to help with them if the client is weak. If the client has had leg surgery, a doctor's order is necessary for the exercises. Leg exercises are done in the supine position. They are done at

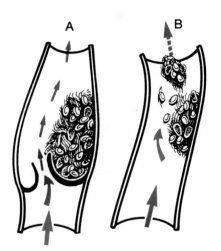

Fig. 19-6 **A,** A blood clot is attached to the wall of a vein. The arrows show the direction of blood flow. **B,** Part of the thrombus has broken off and has become an embolus. The embolus will travel in the bloodstream until it lodges in a distant vessel. (Modified from Long, B.C., and Phipps, W.J.: Essentials of medical-surgical nursing: a nursing process approach, St. Louis, 1985, The C.V. Mosby Co.)

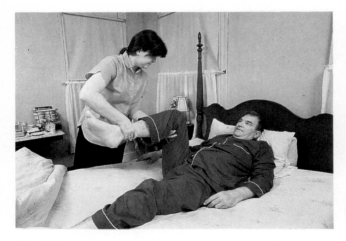

Fig. 19-7 The knee is flexed and then extended during postoperative leg exercises.

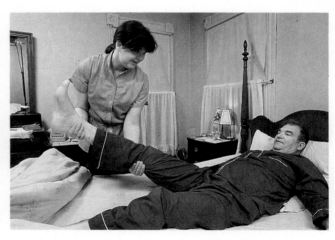

Fig. 19-8 The aide helps the client raise and lower the leg in another postoperative leg exercise.

least every 1 or 2 hours while the client is awake. The following exercises are done 5 times:

1. Ask the client to make circles with the toes. This rotates the ankles.
2. Have the client dorsiflex and plantar flex the feet (see Chapter 11).
3. Have the client flex and extend one knee and then the other (Fig. 19-7).
4. Ask the client to raise and lower one leg off the bed (Fig. 19-8). Repeat this exercise on the other leg.

Binders

Binders promote comfort and prevent injury. They also support body parts, provide pressure, and hold dressings in place. Binders must be applied correctly. If not, they can cause severe discomfort, skin irritation, and circulatory and respiratory complications. Binders are usually applied to the abdomen, breast, and perineal areas.

- *Straight abdominal binder* (Fig. 19-9)—is used for abdominal support. It is also used to hold dressings in place after abdominal surgery. The binder is rectangular in shape. The client is supine when the binder is applied. The top of the binder is positioned level with the client's waist. The lower part is over the hips. Binders are secured in place with pins, hooks, or Velcro.
- *Scultetus binder* (Fig. 19-10)—is rectangular with tails attached to each side. It is used to support the abdomen and incision after abdominal surgery. The binder is applied with the client supine. The tails are overlapped beginning at the bottom and working upward. They are secured in place with one pin at the top.
- *Breast binder* (Fig. 19-11)—supports the breasts after

breast surgery and applies pressure after childbirth. The pressure helps dry up milk in the non-breastfeeding mother. The binder also promotes comfort and gives support when the breasts are swollen after childbirth. The client is supine when the binder is applied. It is pulled snugly across the chest and pinned in place. Then the shoulder straps are pinned in place.

- *T Binder* (Fig. 19-12)—is used to secure dressings in place after rectal or perineal surgery. The single T binder is used for women. Double T binders are used for men. The double T binder can be used for large female perineal dressings. To apply the binder:
  - Bring the waist bands around the waist
  - Pin them in place at the front
  - Bring the tails around between the client's legs and up to the waist
  - Pin the tails in place at the waist

Client safety and the effect of the binder depend on proper application. Do the following when applying binders:

1. Apply the binder so that firm, even pressure is exerted over the area.
2. Make sure the binder fits snugly. However, it should not interfere with breathing or circulation.
3. Keep the body in good alignment.
4. Reapply the binder if it is loose, wrinkled, out of position, or if it causes discomfort.
5. Fasten pins so that they point away from the incision.
6. Change binders that are moist or soiled. They provide an environment for the growth of microorganisms.

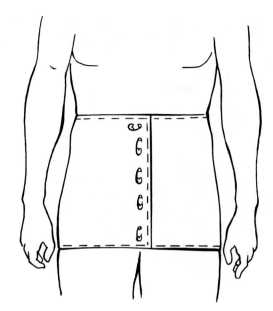

Fig. 19-9 Straight abdominal binder. (From Sorrentino, S.A.: Mosby's textbook for nursing assistants, ed. 2, St. Louis, 1987, The C.V. Mosby Co.)

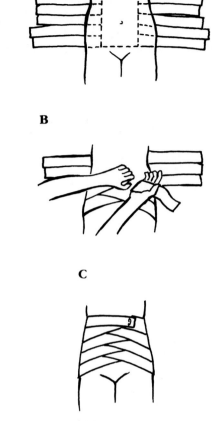

Fig. 19-10 A, Scultetus binder open. **B,** Tails of binder overlapped from bottom to top. **C,** Last tail secured in place at the top with a pin. (From Sorrentino, S.A.: Mosby's textbook for nursing assistants, ed. 2, St. Louis, 1987, The C.V. Mosby Co.)

Fig. 19-11 Breast binder. (From Sorrentino, S.A.: Mosby's textbook for nursing assistants, ed. 2, St. Louis, 1987, The C.V. Mosby Co.)

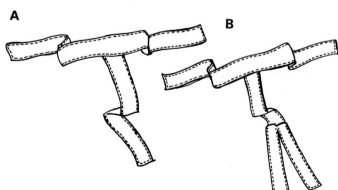

Fig. 19-12 A, Single T binder. **B,** Double T binder. (From Sorrentino, S.A.: Mosby's textbook for nursing assistants, ed. 2, St. Louis, 1987, The C.V. Mosby Co.)

Bandages

Bandages are applied to extremities. They promote comfort and circulation, and provide support and pressure. Like binders, they promote healing and comfort and prevent injury. However, they must be applied properly. Incorrect application can cause severe discomfort, skin irritation, and circulatory and respiratory complications. There are many kinds of bandages. Doctors often order elastic stockings and elastic bandages.

Elastic stockings are often call TED hose or antiembolic stockings. They help prevent thrombi. The elastic exerts pressure on the veins. This promotes venous blood flow to the heart. Elastic stockings are often ordered for clients who are at risk for developing blood clots. They include:
- Postoperative clients
- Clients with heart disease or circulatory disorders
- Bedbound clients
- Pregnant women
- Paralyzed clients
- Stroke victims
- Clients who have had blood clots

The stockings come in many sizes and in thigh-high or knee-high lengths. A nurse measures the client for proper size. Clean stockings are applied before the client gets out of bed. They are removed at least twice a day. Stockings should be washed regularly.

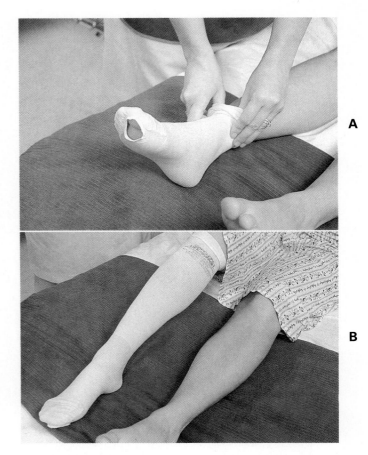

Fig. 19-13 **A,** Stocking gathered and ready for application. **B,** Stocking slipped over toes, foot, and heel. (From Sorrentino, S.A.: Mosby's textbook for nursing assistants, ed. 2, St. Louis, 1987, The C.V. Mosby Co.)

Procedure: Applying elastic stockings

1. Explain to the client what you are going to do.
2. Wash your hands.
3. Provide for privacy.
4. Position the client in the supine position.
5. Expose the legs. Fan-fold top linens back toward the client.
6. Hold the foot and heel of the stocking. Gather up the rest of the stocking in your hands.
7. Support the client's foot at the heel.
8. Slip the foot of the stocking over the client's toes, foot, and heel (Fig. 19-13, A).
9. Pull the stocking up over the leg. The stocking should be even and snug as in Fig. 19-13, B.
10. Make sure the stocking is not twisted and has no creases or wrinkles.
11. Repeat steps 6 through 10 for the other leg.
12. Return top linens to their proper position.
13. Wash your hands.
14. Note and report the time of application.
15. Check the toes every hour for coldness and cyanosis. Also check for client complaints of pain, numbness, or tingling. Remove the stocking if these are noted. Report your observations to your supervisor.

Elastic bandages are used for the same purposes as elastic stockings. They also provide support and reduce swelling following musculoskeletal injuries. The bandage is applied from the lower (distal) part of the limb to the top (proximal) part. Your supervisor will give you directions about the area to be bandaged.

You need to follow the rules listed below when applying elastic bandages:
1. Use a bandage of proper length and width.
2. Make sure the extremity is in good alignment.

3. Face the client during the procedure.
4. Leave fingers or toes exposed if possible. This allows the circulation to be checked.
5. Apply the bandage with firm, even pressure.
6. Check the color and temperature of the part every hour.
7. Reapply the bandage if it is loose or wrinkled.

Procedure: Applying elastic bandages

1. Explain to the client what you are going to do.
2. Wash your hands.
3. Collect the following equipment:
   a. Elastic bandage as determined by the nurse
   b. Tape, metal clips, or safety pins
4. Provide for privacy.
5. Help the client assume a comfortable position. Expose the extremity to be bandaged.
6. Make sure the area is clean and dry.
7. Hold the bandage so that the roll is up and the loose end is on the bottom (Fig. 19-14, A).
8. Apply the bandage to the smallest part of the extremity (wrist, ankle, knee).
9. Make two circular turns around the part (Fig. 19-14, B).
10. Make overlapping spiral turns in an upward direction. Each turn should overlap about two thirds of the previous turn (Fig. 19-14, C).

11. Apply the bandage smoothly with firm, even pressure. The bandage should not be tight.
12. Pin, tape, or clip the end of the bandage to hold it in place.
13. Check the fingers or toes for coldness or cyanosis. Also check for client complaints of pain, numbness, or tingling. Remove the bandage if any of these are noted. Report your observations to your supervisor.
14. Wash your hands.
15. Note and report the following:
    a. The time the bandage was applied
    b. The site of the application
    c. Any other observations

Summary

Postoperative clients often need home care. They may be weak after surgery or have activity restrictions. Help may be needed with home maintenance. Some clients need physical care. Remember that surgery affects the whole person. You must be concerned with a client's physical and psychological care.

Postoperative complications must be prevented. These include respiratory complications, thrombi and emboli, and wound infection. Follow the rules of client safety and medical asepsis to prevent complications. Also help the client with turning, repositioning, coughing and deep breathing, and leg exercises as directed.

A 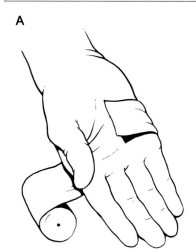 B 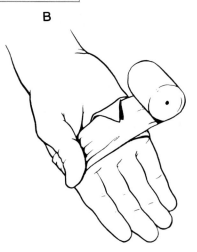 C

Fig. 19-14 **A,** Roll of elastic bandage is up, and loose end is on the bottom. **B,** Bandage applied to smallest part with two circular turns. **C,** Bandage applied with spiral turns in upward direction. (From Parcel, G.S.: Basic emergency care of the sick and injured, ed. 2, St. Louis, 1981, The C.V. Mosby Co.)

Study Questions

1. Mrs. James had abdominal surgery three weeks ago. This is her first day home. She has abdominal dressings and an abdominal binder. The doctor has ordered no bending, lifting, reaching, or driving. Coughing, deep breathing, and leg exercises are to be done every four hours. She also is to wear TED hose. The doctor has ordered pain medications p.r.n. You are assigned to assist with personal care and home maintenance. What other information do you need to safely care for this client? Explain how you will help her.

Circle the *best* answer.

2. You can give psychological care to the postoperative client by explaining
   a. The reason for the surgery
   b. Procedures to the client and why they are being done
   c. The possible postoperative complications
   d. What the doctor is planning for the future

3. The client has some mild discomfort. You can do all of the following *except*
   a. Give a back massage
   b. Provide a quiet atmosphere
   c. Give a pain medication
   d. Position the client in good alignment

4. Which statement is *false*?
   a. Some wounds are left open to the air.
   b. You are responsible for dressing changes.
   c. Handwashing is very important to prevent wound infection.
   d. Microorganisms must not enter the wound.

5. Coughing and deep breathing exercises help prevent
   a. Bleeding
   b. A pulmonary embolus
   c. Respiratory complications
   d. Pain and discomfort

6. The statements are about leg exercises. Which is *true*?
   a. They are done to stimulate circulation.
   b. They are done to prevent thrombi.
   c. They are usually done 5 times every 1 or 2 hours.
   d. All of the above

7. Position changes are usually done
   a. Every 2 hours
   b. Every 3 hours
   c. Every 4 hours
   d. Every shift

8. Binders are applied to
   a. Prevent blood clots in the legs
   b. Prevent wound infection
   c. Provide support and hold dressings in place
   d. Decrease circulation and swelling

9. The scultetus binder is used
   a. On men following rectal surgery
   b. For breast support
   c. To support the abdomen and incision after surgery
   d. Following perineal surgery

10. Elastic stockings are worn to
    a. Prevent blood clots
    b. Hold dressings in place
    c. Reduce swelling after musculoskeletal injury
    d. All of the above

11. When applying an elastic bandage
    a. The extremity needs to be in good alignment
    b. The fingers or toes are covered if possible
    c. It is applied from the largest to smallest part of the extremity
    d. It is applied from the upper to the lower part of the extremity

Answers

2. b	5. c	8. c	10. a
3. c	6. d	9. c	11. a
4. b	7. a		

20

The Mother and Her Newborn

Chapter Highlights	**What you will learn to do**
Infant safety	■ Describe how to meet an infant's safety and security needs
Helping mothers breast-feed	■ Help with breast-feeding
Bottle-feeding babies	■ Sterilize baby bottles
Diapering	■ Bottle-feed an infant
Care of the umbilical cord	■ Burp an infant
Circumcision	■ Diaper a baby
Bathing an infant	■ Give cord care
	■ Care for a circumcision
	■ Bathe an infant

Circumcision The surgical removal of foreskin

Rooting reflex The baby turns his or her head in the direction of a stimulus

Umbilical cord The structure that carries blood, oxygen, and nutrients from the mother to the fetus

Y ou may care for a new mother or an infant. A mother may need help because of complications before or after childbirth. Or there may be other young children. A new baby and other children may be a lot of work. Sometimes mothers just need help with home maintenance.

A review of growth and development will help you care for babies (see Chapter 5, page 50). Remember, babies are helpless. They depend on others to meet their basic needs. Besides physical needs, babies also need to feel safe, secure, love, and belonging. You can help meet the baby's basic needs.

Infant Safety

Babies cannot protect themselves. Like adults, babies need safety and security. They feel secure when warm and when wrapped and held snugly. Responding to their cries and feeding them when they are hungry promotes safety and security. Infant safety is discussed in Chapter 8, page 107. The following measures are also important.

1. Keep the baby warm. Check windows for drafts. Make sure they are securely closed.
2. Keep your nails short and do not wear rings or bracelets. Long nails and jewelry can scratch the baby. (Use a safety pin to secure rings to your uniform.)
3. Use both hands to lift a newborn.
4. Hold the baby securely. Use the cradle hold, football hold, or shoulder hold (Fig. 20-1).
5. Support the baby's head and neck when lifting or holding the baby (see Fig. 20-1). Neck support is necessary for the first 3 months of age.
6. Handle the baby with gentle, smooth movements. Avoid sudden or jerking movements. Do not startle the baby.
7. Hold and cuddle infants. This is comforting and helps them learn love and security.
8. Talk, sing, or play with the baby often. Be sure to talk to the baby during the bath, dressing, and diapering.
9. Respond to the baby's crying. Babies cry when hungry, uncomfortable, wet, frightened, or when they want attention. This is their way of communicating. Responding to their cry helps them feel safe and secure.
10. Do not leave a baby unattended on a table, bed, sofa, or other high surface. Keep one hand on the baby if you must look away (see Fig. 8-3, page 108).
11. Use safety straps for babies in infant seats or high chairs.
12. Make sure the crib is within hearing distance of the caregivers.
13. Keep crib rails up at all times.
14. Do not put a pillow in the crib. Pillows can cause suffocation.
15. Change the baby's position often. Do not always put the baby in the same position. Alternate between the prone and side-lying positions. Support the baby in the side-lying position with a rolled towel or small blanket (Fig. 20-2).
16. Do not lay babies on their backs after a feeding or for sleep. Aspiration can occur in the supine position.
17. Keep pins and small objects out of the baby's reach.

Your observations are important for the infant's safety. Signs and symptoms of illness can develop quickly in babies. Therefore, call your supervisor if the baby cries continually or looks sick. Tell your supervisor if the baby:

- Is flushed, pale, or perspiring
- Has noisy, rapid, difficult, or slow respirations
- Is coughing or sneezing
- Has reddened or irritated eyes
- Turns his or her head to one side or puts a hand to one ear (signs of an earache)
- Is crying or screaming for a long time
- Has skipped feedings
- Has vomited most of the feeding or between feedings
- Has hard, formed stools or watery stools
- Has a rash

Your supervisor may ask you to take the infant's temperature, pulse, and respirations (see Chapter 13). You may be asked for more information. Be sure to tell your supervisor when a sign or symptom began.

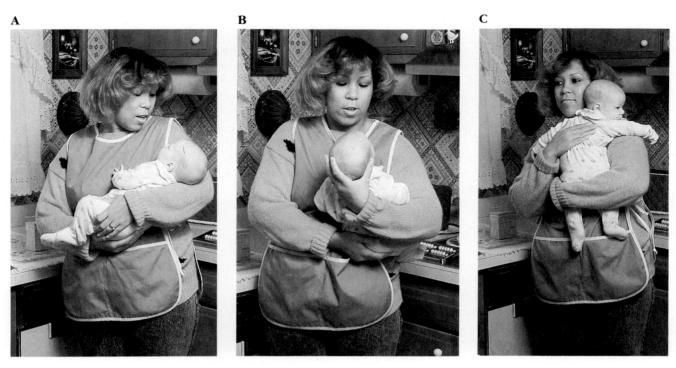

Fig. 20-1 **A,** The cradle hold. **B,** The football hold. **C,** The shoulder hold.

Fig. 20-2 Baby supported in the side-lying position with a rolled towel.

Helping Mothers Breast-Feed

Many mothers breast-feed their babies. Breast-fed babies may need to nurse every 2 or 3 hours. They are fed on demand. In other words, they are fed when hungry rather than on a schedule. Babies nurse for a short time (5 minutes at each breast) at first. Eventually total nursing time may be 20 to 30 minutes.

Hospital nurses help mothers learn to breast-feed. They also teach breast care. Mothers and babies learn how to nurse in a very short time. If the mother or baby is having problems nursing, call your supervisor. A home care nurse may need to help the mother.

The mother may need help getting ready to breast-feed. She may need help with hygiene. Or you may need to bring the baby to her. Give help as nec-essary. Otherwise make sure the call bell is within reach and leave the room. The mother and baby need privacy during breast-feeding. Be sure to stay within hearing distance in case the mother needs you.

You can do the following to help with breast-feeding:

1. Help the mother wash her hands. Handwashing is necessary before she handles her breasts.
2. Help the mother wash her nipples if part of the care plan. Nipples are washed with circular motions from the nipple outward to the breast (Fig. 20-3). Plain water is used. Soap has a drying effect. The nipples can dry and crack.

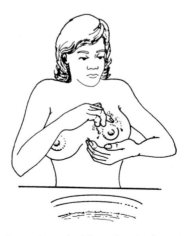

Fig. 20-3 The breast is washed from the nipples outward. Circular motions are used.

3. Help the mother to a comfortable position. She may want to sit up in bed or in a chair. Some mothers like to nurse in the side-lying position (Fig. 20-4).

4. Change the baby's diaper if necessary. Bring the baby to the mother.

5. Make sure the mother holds the baby close to her breast.

6. Have the mother stroke the baby's cheek closest to the breast (Fig. 20-5). This stimulates the *rooting reflex*. The baby turns his or her head toward the stimulus. If the right cheek is stroked, the baby turns his or her head to the right.

7. Have the mother keep breast tissue away from the baby's nose with her thumb or finger (Fig. 20-6).

8. Give her a baby blanket to cover the baby and her breast. This promotes privacy during the feeding.

9. Encourage nursing from both breasts at each feeding. If the baby finished the last feeding at the right breast, the baby begins at the right breast.

10. Remind her how to remove the baby from the breast. She needs to break the seal or suction between the baby and the breast. Ask her to insert a finger in a corner of the baby's mouth (Fig. 20-7). She can also press a finger down on her breast close to the baby's mouth.

11. Help the mother burp the baby if necessary (see page 337). The baby should be burped after nursing at each breast.

12. Have the mother put a diaper pin on the bra strap of the breast last used. This reminds her which breast to use first at the next feeding.

13. Change the baby's diaper after the feeding. Lay the baby in the crib if he or she has fallen asleep.

14. Encourage the mother to wear a nursing bra day and night. The bra supports the breasts and promotes comfort.

15. Encourage the mother to place cotton pads in the bra. The pads absorb leaking milk.

16. Have the mother apply cream (if prescribed) to her nipples after each feeding. The cream prevents nipples from drying and cracking.

17. Help the mother straighten clothing after the feeding if necessary.

The nursing mother needs good nutrition. Remember the following when planning meals or grocery shopping.

1. Calorie intake may be increased. Your supervisor will tell you how much to increase the mother's calorie intake.

2. The mother should drink six or more cups of milk a day. She can drink skimmed or whole milk.

Fig. 20-4 Mother nursing in the side-lying position.

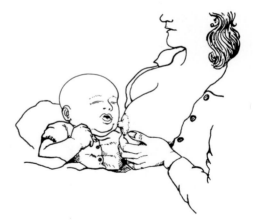

Fig. 20-5 Mother strokes the baby's cheek with her breast. This stimulates the rooting reflex.

Fig. 20-6 The thumb is used to keep breast tissue away from the baby's nose.

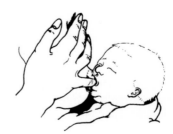

Fig. 20-7 Mother inserts a finger in the baby's mouth to remove the baby from the breast.

3. Include foods high in calcium in the diet.
4. The mother should avoid spicy and gas-forming foods. They can cause cramping and diarrhea in the infant. She should avoid onions, garlic, spices, cabbage, brussels sprouts, asparagus, and beans. Chocolate, cola beverages, and coffee can also cause cramping and diarrhea.

Bottle-Feeding Babies

Formula is given to babies who are not breast-fed. The formula is prescribed by the doctor. Formula is commercially prepared. They provide the essential nutrients needed by the infant.

Formula comes in three forms. The *ready-to-feed* form is ready to use. It can be poured directly from the can into the baby bottle (Fig. 20-8). Water is added to *powdered* and *concentrated* formula. Container directions tell how much formula to use and how much water to add. You can prepare one bottle at a time or enough bottles for the whole day. Extra bottles are capped as in Fig. 20-9 and stored in the refrigerator. These bottles should be used within 24 hours.

Babies must be protected from infection. Therefore, baby bottles, caps, and nipples must be as clean as possible. Bottle-feeding equipment must be carefully washed in hot, soapy water. Complete rinsing is necessary to remove all soap. Some doctors tell mothers to sterilize bottle-feeding equipment. *Sterilization* is the process of killing all microorganisms (pathogens and nonpathogens). Some mothers like to use plastic nursers. These have disposable plastic liners (Fig. 20-10). Plastic nursers do not have to be sterilized.

Fig. 20-8 Ready-to-feed formula is poured from the can into the bottle. A funnel is used to prevent spilling.

Fig. 20-9 Bottles are capped for storage in the refrigerator.

Fig. 20-10 Plastic nursers have disposable liners.

Procedure: Sterilizing bottles

1. Wash your hands.
2. Collect the following equipment:
   a. Bottles, nipples, and caps
   b. Funnel
   c. Can opener
   d. Tongs
   e. Bottle brush
   f. Sterilizer or large pot with cover
   g. Dishwashing soap
   h. Jar with openings in the lid
   i. Other equipment used to prepare formula
   j. Towel
3. Wash bottles, nipples, caps, funnel, can opener, and tongs in hot soapy water. Wash other equipment used to prepare formula.

Continued

4. Clean inside baby bottles with the bottle brush (Fig. 20-11).
5. Squeeze hot soapy water through the nipples (Fig. 20-12). This helps remove formula from them.
6. Rinse all equipment thoroughly in hot water. Be sure to squeeze hot water through nipples to remove soap.
7. Place the nipples and caps in the jar. Put on the lid (Fig. 20-13).
8. Put all equipment into the sterilizer or pot. Stand the bottles and the jar upright.
9. Pour water into the pot. There should be about 2 inches of water in the bottom of the pot or sterilizer (Fig. 20-14).
10. Bring the water to a boil.
11. Cover the pot. Boil for 5 minutes.
12. Remove the pot from the heat. Let the pot cool. Do not remove lid until pot cools.
13. Lay a towel on the counter top.
14. Use the tongs to remove remaining equipment. Stand the bottles upside down to drain. Open the jar. Remove the nipples with the tongs. Place the nipples and caps on the towel (Fig. 20-15).

Fig. 20-13 Nipples and caps are placed in a jar for sterilization.

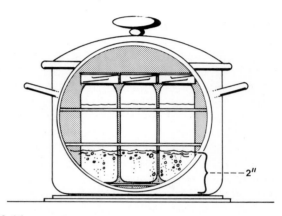

Fig. 20-14 Two inches of water in the bottom of the pot for sterilizing bottles.

Fig. 20-11 A bottle brush is used to clean the inside of the bottle.

Fig. 20-12 Water is squeezed through the nipples during cleaning.

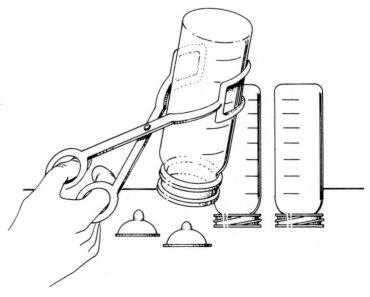

Fig. 20-15 Bottles, caps, and other equipment are allowed to dry after being sterilized.

Feeding the Baby

Babies generally want to be fed every 3 to 4 hours. The amount of formula they take increases as they grow older. Your supervisor or the mother will tell you how much formula a baby should have at each feeding. Babies usually take as much formula as they need. The baby will stop sucking and turn away from the bottle when satisfied.

Babies should not be given cold formula out of the refrigerator. A bottle is warmed before the baby is fed. You can warm the bottle in a pan of water. The formula should feel warm but not hot. You can test the temperature by sprinkling a few drops on your wrist (Fig. 20-16). Do not set the bottle out to warm at room temperature. This takes too long and allows the growth of microorganisms.

These guidelines will help you bottle-feed babies.

1. Warm the bottle so the formula feels warm to your wrist.
2. Assume a comfortable position for the feeding.
3. Hold the baby close to you. Relax and snuggle the baby.
4. Tilt the bottle so the neck and nipple are always filled (Fig. 20-17). Otherwise some air will be in the neck in nipple. The baby will suck air into the stomach. The air causes cramping and discomfort.
5. Do not prop the bottle and lay the baby down for the feeding (Fig. 20-18).
6. Burp the baby when he or she has taken half the formula. Also burp the baby at the end of the feeding.
7. Do not leave the baby alone with a bottle.
8. Discard the formula left in the bottle after feeding.
9. Wash the bottle, cap, and nipple after the feeding (see *Sterilizing bottles*, page 335).

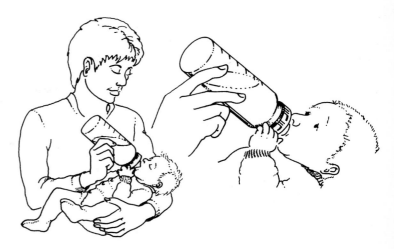

Fig. 20-17 Bottle is tilted so formula fills the bottle neck and nipple.

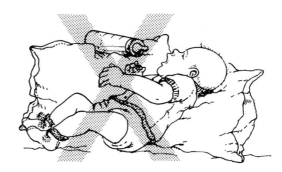

Fig. 20-18 Do not prop the bottle to feed the baby.

Burping the Baby

Babies take in air when they nurse. Bottle-fed babies take in more air than breast-fed babies. Air in the stomach and intestines causes cramping and discomfort. This can lead to vomiting. Burping helps to get rid of the air. Burping a baby is sometimes called *bubbling*.

There are two ways to position the baby for burping (Fig. 20-19). One way is to hold the infant over your shoulder. Be sure to place a clean diaper or towel over your shoulder. This protects your clothing if the baby "spits up." Or you can support the baby in a sitting position on your lap. Hold the towel or diaper in front of the baby. To burp the baby, gently pat or rub the baby's back with circular motions.

Fig. 20-16 Home health aide tests formula temperature. Formula should feel warm on her wrist.

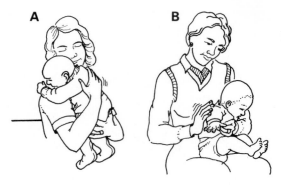

Fig. 20-19 **A,** Baby is held over the aide's shoulder for burping. **B,** Baby is supported in the sitting position for burping.

Diapering

Babies urinate 20 to 30 times a day. Breast-fed babies usually have bowel movements after feedings. Bottle-fed babies may have 3 bowel movements a day. A baby's stools are usually soft and unformed. Hard, formed stools mean the baby is constipated. This must be reported to your supervisor immediately. Watery stools indicate diarrhea. Diarrhea is very serious in infants. Their water balance can be upset quickly (see Chapter 17, page 298). You must call your supervisor immediately if you suspect a baby has diarrhea.

Diaper changes are not necessary every time the baby wets. Changing the diaper after a feeding is usually sufficient. Cloth and disposable diapers are available. Cloth diapers must be washed, dried, and folded for reuse. They are washed daily or every 2 days with a baby detergent. Putting them through the wash cycle a second time without detergent helps remove all soap. If possible, hang diapers outside to dry. This gives them a fresh, clean smell.

Disposable diapers are rolled up and put in the garbage. They are not flushed down the toilet. The use of disposable diapers is more expensive.

Procedure: Diapering a baby

1. Wash your hands.
2. Unfasten the dirty diaper. If a cloth diaper is used, close diaper pins and put them out of the baby's reach.
3. Wipe the genital area with the front of the diaper (Fig. 20-20). Wipe from the front to back.
4. Fold the diaper so urine and feces are well inside. Set the diaper aside.
5. Clean the genital area from front to back. Use a wet wash cloth, disposable wipes, or wet cotton balls. Wash with mild soap and water if there is a lot of feces or if the baby has a rash. Rinse thoroughly and pat the area dry.
6. Give cord care and clean the circumcision (see pages 340-341).
7. Apply cream or lotion to the genital area and buttocks. Do not use too much because caking can occur.
8. Raise the baby's legs. Slide a clean diaper under the buttocks.
9. Fold a cloth diaper so there is an extra thickness in front for a boy (Fig. 20-21, A). For girls, fold the diaper so the extra thickness is at the back (Fig. 20-21, B).
10. Bring the back of the diaper over the front.
11. Make sure the diaper is snug around the hips and abdomen. It should be loose near the penis if the circumcision has not healed. The diaper should be below the umbilicus if the cord stump has not healed.
12. Secure the diaper in place. Use the plastic tabs on disposable diapers (Fig. 20-22, A). Make sure the tabs stick in place. Use baby pins for cloth diapers. Pins should point away from the abdomen (Fig. 20-22, B).
13. Apply plastic pants if cloth diapers are worn. Do not use plastic pants with disposable diapers. They already have waterproof protection.
14. Put the baby in the crib, infant seat, or other safe location.
15. Rinse feces from the cloth diaper in the toilet.
16. Store used cloth diapers in a covered pail or plastic bag. Take the disposable diaper to the garbage.
17. Note and report your observations.

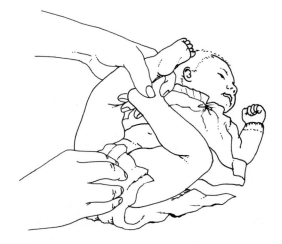

Fig. 20-20 Front of the diaper is used to clean the genital area.

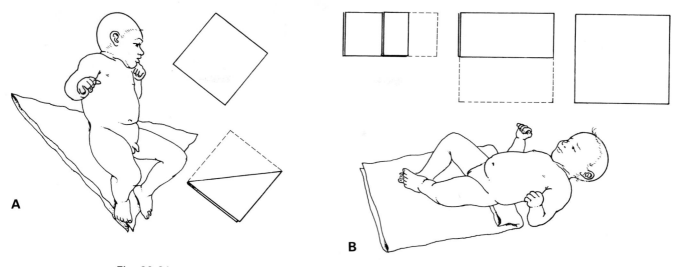

Fig. 20-21 **A,** Cloth diaper is folded in front for boys. **B,** Diaper has a fold in the back for girls.

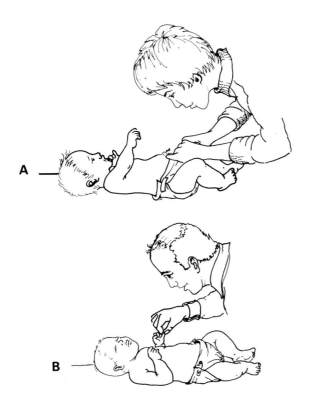

Fig. 20-22 **A,** Disposable diaper secured with plastic tabs. **B,** Pins are used to secure cloth diapers. Pins point away from the abdomen.

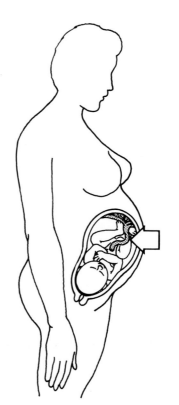

Fig. 20-23 Umbilical cord connects mother and fetus.

Care of the Umbilical Cord

The *umbilical cord* connects the mother and the fetus (unborn baby). It carries blood, oxygen, and nutrients from the mother to the fetus (Fig. 20-23). The umbilical cord is not needed after birth. Shortly after delivery the doctor clamps and cuts the cord. A stump of cord is left on the baby. The stump dries up and falls off in 7 to 10 days. There may be a small amount of blood when the cord comes off.

The cord provides an area for the growth of microorganisms. Therefore, it must be kept clean and dry. Cord care is done at each diaper change. Cord care is continued for 1 to 2 days after the cord comes off. It consists of the following:

1. Keep the stump dry. Do not get the stump wet.

Fig. 20-24 Cord stump is wiped at the base with alcohol.

2. Wipe the base of the stump with alcohol (Fig. 20-24). Use an alcohol wipe or a cotton ball moistened with alcohol. The alcohol promotes drying.
3. Keep the diaper below the cord as in Fig. 20-22. This prevents the diaper from irritating the stump.
4. Report any signs of infection. These include redness, odor, or drainage from the stump.
5. Give sponge baths until the cord falls off. Then the baby can have a tub bath.

Circumcision

Boys are born with foreskin on the penis. The surgical removal of foreskin is called a *circumcision* (see Fig. 15-12 on page 257). The procedure allows good hygiene and is thought to prevent cancer of the penis.

If a circumcision is done, it is usually performed in the hospital before the baby goes home. For those of the Jewish faith, circumcision is a religious ceremony.

The penis will look red, swollen, and sore. However, the circumcision should not interfere with urination. You must carefully check for signs of bleeding and infection. There should be no odor or drainage. Be sure to check the diaper for bleeding. The area should completely heal in 10 to 14 days.

The penis must be thoroughly cleaned at each diaper change. Cleaning is very important if the baby has had a bowel movement. Mild soap and water or commercial wipes can be used. The diaper is loosely applied. This prevents the diaper from irritating the penis. Some doctors advise applying petrolatum to the penis. This protects the penis from urine and feces. It also prevents the penis from sticking to the diaper. Use a cotton swab to apply the petrolatum (Fig. 20-25). Your supervisor will tell you if other measures are needed.

Bathing an Infant

A bath is important for cleanliness. Though babies do not get very dirty, they need good skin care. Baths comfort and relax babies. They also provide a wonderful time to hold, touch, and talk to babies. Remember, stimulation is important for development. Being touched and held helps babies learn safety, security, and love.

Planning is an important part of the bath. You cannot leave the baby unattended if you forget something. Therefore, you must gather equipment, supplies, and the baby's clothes before you begin the bath. Everything you will need should be within your reach.

Safety measures are also very important. You must never leave the baby alone on a table or in the bathtub. Always keep one hand on the baby if you must look away for a moment. The baby must be held securely throughout the bath. Babies are very slippery

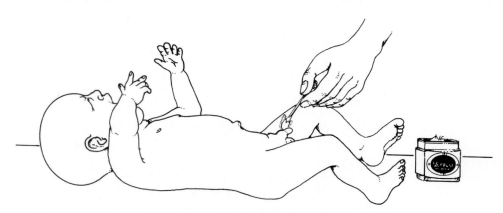

Fig. 20-25 Petrolatum is applied to the circumcised penis.

Fig. 20-26 Aide uses her wrist to test temperature of the bath water.

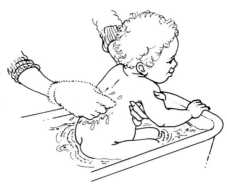

Fig. 20-27 Baby is given a tub bath.

when wet. A wet, squirming baby can be very hard to hold.

Room temperature should be 75° to 80° F for the bath. You may need to turn up the thermostat and close windows and doors about 20 minutes before the bath. The room temperature may be too warm for you. You may want to remove a sweater or roll up your sleeves before starting the bath.

Water temperature needs special attention. Remember that babies have delicate skin and are easily burned. Bath water temperature should be 90° to 100° F. Measure bath water temperature with a bath thermometer. If one is not available, test the water temperature with the inside of your wrist (Fig. 20-26). The water should feel warm and comfortable to your wrist.

Bath time should be part of the baby's daily routine. Some mothers like to bathe their babies in the morning. Others prefer the evening. Evening baths have two important advantages. The bath is comforting and relaxing. This helps some babies sleep longer at night. Working fathers are usually home in the evening. The evening bath lets them be involved. Sometimes fathers will bathe the babies to give mothers time to rest or tend to other children. Be sure to follow the family's routine.

There are two bath procedures for babies. Sponge baths are given until the baby is about 2 weeks old. They are given until the cord stump falls off and the umbilicus and circumcision heal. Remember, the cord must not get wet. The tub bath is given after the cord and circumcision heal (Fig. 20-27).

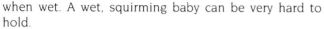

Procedure: The sponge bath

1. Place the following equipment on your work area:
   a. Bath basin
   b. Bath thermometer

c. Bath towel
   d. Two hand towels
   e. Receiving blanket
   f. Washcloth
   g. Clean diaper
   h. Clean clothing for the baby
   i. Cotton balls
   j. Baby soap
   k. Baby shampoo
   l. Baby lotion
   m. Cotton swabs
2. Fill the bath basin with warm water. Water temperature should be 90° to 100° F. Measure water temperature with the bath thermometer or use the inside of your wrist. The water should feel warm and comfortable on your wrist.
3. Undress the baby. Leave the diaper on.
4. Wash the baby's eyes (Fig. 20-28):
   a. Dip a cotton ball into the water.
   b. Squeeze out excess water.
   c. Wash one eye from the inner part to the outer part.
   d. Repeat this step for the other eye with a new cotton ball.
5. Dip a cotton swab into the water. Tap the stick part gently against the basin to remove excess water.
6. Clean inside each nostril (Fig. 20-29). Be gentle and do not push the swab into the nose. Pat dry the baby's face.
7. Moisten the washcloth. Clean the outside and then behind each ear. Be gentle. Do *not* use cotton swabs to clean inside the ears.
8. Rinse and squeeze out the washcloth. Make a mitt with the washcloth (see Fig. 14-11, page 217).
9. Wash the baby's face (Fig. 20-30). Pat dry.
Continued

Fig. 20-28 Baby's eyes are washed with cotton balls. The eye is cleaned from the inner to the outer part.

Fig. 20-29 Nostril cleaned with a cotton swab.

Fig. 20-30 Baby's face washed with a mitted washcloth.

10. Pick up the baby. Hold the baby over the bath basin using the football hold. Support the baby's head and neck with your wrist and hand.
11. Wash the baby's head (Fig. 20-31):
    a. Squeeze a washcloth onto the baby's head.
    b. Apply a small amount of baby shampoo to the head.
    c. Wash the head with circular motions.
    d. Rinse the head by squeezing a washcloth over the baby's head. Be sure to rinse thoroughly.
    e. Use a small hand towel to dry the head.
12. Lay the baby on the table. Remove the diaper.
13. Wash the front of the body. Use a soapy washcloth. Or apply soap to your hands and wash the baby with your hands (Fig. 20-32). Do not get the cord wet. Rinse thoroughly. Pat dry. Be sure to dry all creases.
14. Turn the baby to the prone position. Repeat step 13 for the back and buttocks.
15. Give cord care and clean the circumcision.
16. Apply baby lotion to the baby's body.
17. Put a clean diaper and clean clothes on the baby.
18. Wrap the baby in the receiving blanket.
19. Clean and return equipment and supplies to the proper place. Do this step when the baby is settled.
20. Note and report your observations.

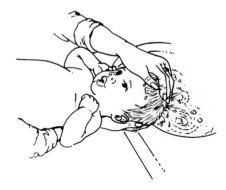

Fig. 20-31 Baby's head is washed over the basin.

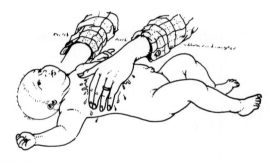

Fig. 20-32 Aide uses her hands to wash the baby.

Procedure: The tub bath

1. Follow steps 1 through 12 in the sponge bath procedure (see page 341).
2. Hold the baby as in Fig. 20-33:
   a. Place your right hand under the baby's shoulders. Your thumb should be over the baby's right shoulder. Your fingers should be under the right arm.
   b. Use your left hand to support the baby's buttocks. Slide your left hand under the thighs. Hold the right thigh with your left hand.
3. Lower the baby into the water feet first.
4. Wash the front of the baby's body. Be sure to wash all folds and creases. Rinse thoroughly.
5. Reverse your hold. Use your left hand to hold the baby.
6. Wash the baby's back as in Fig. 20-27. Rinse thoroughly.
7. Reverse your hold again. Use your right hand to hold the baby.
8. Wash the genital area.
9. Lift the baby out of the water onto a towel.
10. Wrap the baby in the towel. Also cover the baby's head.
11. Pat dry the baby. Be sure you dry all folds and creases.
12. Follow steps 16-20 of the sponge bath (page 342).

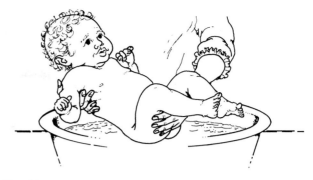

Fig. 20-33 Baby held for the tub bath.

Summary

Caring for new mothers and infants can be a wonderful experience. You may have to help only with home maintenance. Or you may help with other children. However, you must still look out for the infant's safety. Babies cannot protect themselves. They depend on others for their physical needs. They must also feel safe, secure, and loved. Be sure to talk, sing, and play with babies while you meet their basic needs.

Study Questions

1. You are assigned to help a new mother care for her infant. There is another 3-year-old daughter. The father works during the day. The mother has choosen to breast-feed her baby. However, she must remain in bed all day because of a back problem. Her family takes her to the hospital for physical therapy every day. You are to help with the baby, shop for groceries, prepare meals, and clean the home. Describe how you will complete your assignment.

2. You are helping a new mother with home maintenance. She takes care of the baby boy. You feel that she gives unsafe care. For example, she props the bottle on a towel for feeding. The baby cries a lot before the mother picks him up. Describe what you should do.

Circle the *best* answer.

3. A baby's head must be supported for the first
   a. 7 to 10 days
   b. Month
   c. Three months
   d. Six months

4. When holding babies you should
   a. Hold them securely
   b. Cuddle them
   c. Sing and talk to them
   d. All of the above

5. Which statement is *false*?
   a. The crib should be within hearing distance of caregivers.
   b. The baby should have a pillow for sleep.
   c. The baby's position should be changed often.
   d. Crib rails should be up at all times.

6. You should report all of the following to your supervisor *except*
   a. The baby looks flushed and is perspiring
   b. The baby has watery stools
   c. The baby's eyes are red and irritated
   d. The baby spits up when burped

7. The breast-feeding mother should do all of the following *except*
   a. Wash her breasts with soap and water
   b. Hold the baby close to her breast
   c. Stimulate the rooting reflex
   d. Keep breast tissue away from the baby's nose

8. A breast-fed baby should be burped
   a. Every 5 minutes
   b. After nursing from one breast
   c. After nursing from both breasts
   d. After the feeding

9. A baby is bottle-fed. You do the grocery shopping. Which formula should you buy?
   a. The one that is on sale.
   b. The ready-to-feed type.
   c. The one ordered by the doctor.
   d. The powdered form because it lasts longer.

10. You are to sterilize baby bottles. How long should the water boil?
    a. 5 minutes
    b. 10 minutes
    c. 15 minutes
    d. 20 minutes

11. You are to warm a baby bottle. Which statement is *true*?
    a. The bottle is warmed for 5 minutes in the microwave.
    b. The formula should warm at room temperature.
    c. The formula should feel warm on your wrist.
    d. The formula is warmed in a pan for 5 minutes.

12. When bottle feeding a baby you should
    a. Burp the baby every 5 minutes
    b. Save remaining formula for the next feeding
    c. Tilt the bottle so formula fills the neck and nipple
    d. All of the above

13. Diapers are changed whenever the baby urinates.
    a. True
    b. False

14. The cord has not yet healed. The baby's diaper should be
    a. Loose over the cord
    b. Snug over the cord
    c. Below the cord
    d. Disposable

15. The cord stump is cleaned with
    a. Soap and water
    b. Baby shampoo
    c. Plain water
    d. Alcohol

16. The cord and the circumcision are cleaned
    a. Once a day
    b. When the baby has a bowel movement
    c. Three times a day
    d. At every diaper change

17. The cord and circumcision have not healed. The baby should have a sponge bath.
    a. True
    b. False

18. Bath water for the baby should be
    a. 60° to 65° F
    b. 70° to 75° F
    c. 75° to 80° F
    d. 90° to 100° F

19. Which should you use to wash the baby's eyes?
    a. A mitted washcloth
    b. Alcohol wipes
    c. A cotton swab
    d. Cotton balls

20. Cotton swabs are used to clean inside the baby's ears.
    a. True
    b. False

Answers

3. c	8. b	13. b	17. a
4. d	9. c	14. c	18. d
5. b	10. a	15. d	19. d
6. d	11. c	16. d	20. b
7. a	12. c		

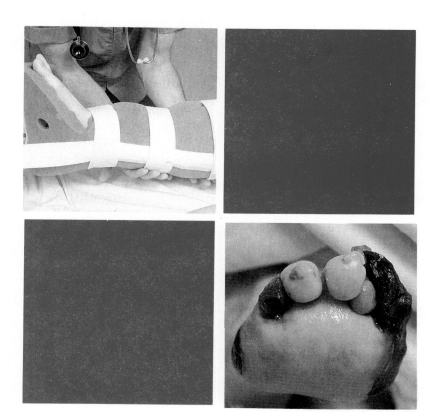

21

Common Health Problems

What you will learn to do

- Identify the warning signs and treatments of cancer
- Explain how to maintain joint function in arthritis
- Explain how to care for clients in casts, traction, and with hip pinnings
- Describe osteoporosis and the care required
- Explain the psychological effect when a limb is removed
- Describe nervous system disorders and the care required
- Describe common respiratory diseases and the care required
- Describe hypertension, its complications, and treatment
- Describe common heart diseases and the care required
- Identify the signs, symptoms, and complications of diabetes mellitus
- Describe common sexually transmitted diseases and their spread

345

Key Terms

Amputation The removal of all or part of an extremity

Benign tumor A tumor that grows slowly and within a localized area; benign tumors usually do not cause death

Closed fracture A fracture in which the bone is broken but the skin is intact; a simple fracture

Compound fracture An open fracture; the bone is broken and the bone has come through the skin

Fracture A broken bone

Gangrene A condition in which there is death of tissue; tissues become black, cold, and shriveled

Malignant tumor A tumor that grows rapidly and invades other tissues; malignant tumors cause death without treatment

Metastasis The spread of cancer to other parts of the body

Stroke A cerebral vascular accident; blood supply to a part of the brain is suddenly interrupted

Tumor A new growth of cells; a tumor can be benign or malignant

This chapter gives basic information about common health problems. Clients with these disorders often need home care. Their care means more if you have some understanding of the disorder. Each disorder is briefly described. The causes, signs and symptoms, and treatment are also described. If more information is needed, a nurse can give you additional explanations.

Reviewing Chapter 6, Understanding How the Body Functions, will be helpful in studying this chapter.

Cancer

Cancer involves a new growth of abnormal cells. The growth is called a *tumor*. Tumors are benign or malignant (Fig. 21-1). *Benign* tumors grow slowly and within localized areas. They do not usually cause death.

Malignant tumors grow fast and into other tissues. They cause death if not treated and controlled. *Metastasis* is the spread of cancer to other parts of the body. It occurs if the cancer is not treated and controlled. Cancer can occur in almost any body part. The most common sites are the lungs, colon, rectum, breast, prostate, and uterus.

There are risk factors for cancer. These include a family history of cancer, exposure to radiation or certain chemicals, smoking, alcohol, certain sexual practices, and viruses.

If found early, cancer can be treated and controlled. The American Cancer Society has identified 7 early warning signs of cancer.

- A change in bowel or bladder habits
- A sore that does not heal
- Unusual bleeding or discharge from a body opening
- A lump or thickening in the breast or other body part

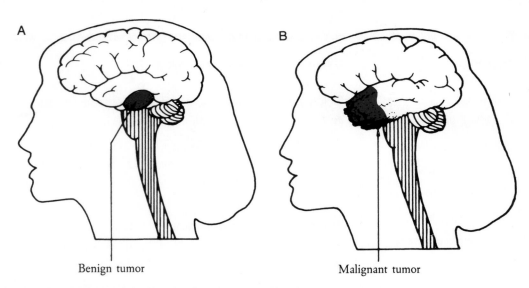

Benign tumor

Malignant tumor

Fig. 21-1 **A,** Benign tumors grow within a localized area.
B, Malignant tumors invade other tissues. (From Sorrentino, S.A.: Mosby's textbook for nursing assistants, ed. 2, St. Louis, 1987, The C.V. Mosby Co.)

- Difficulty swallowing or indigestion
- An obvious change in a wart or mole
- Nagging cough or hoarseness

Cancer is treated by surgery, radiotherapy (radiation therapy), and chemotherapy. The treatment used depends on the type of tumor, its location, and if it has spread. One treatment or a combination may be used.

Malignant tissue is often surgically removed. It is done to cure cancer or to relieve pain in advanced cancer. Surgery can be very disfiguring.

Radiotherapy kills living cells. X-rays are directed at the tumor. Cancer cells and normal cells are exposed to radiation. Both are killed. Radiotherapy is used to cure some cancers. It also controls the growth of cancer cells. Controlling cell growth can relieve or prevent pain. Radiotherapy has side effects. "Radiation sickness" can occur. It involves discomfort, nausea and vomiting, and skin breakdown in the exposed area. The doctor may order special skin care procedures for the client.

Chemotherapy involves drugs which kill cells. Chemotherapy kills normal cells and cancer cells. It is used to cure cancer or to control the rate of cell growth. Side effects can be severe. This is because normal cells are destroyed. The gastrointestinal tract is irritated causing nausea, vomiting, and diarrhea. *Stomatitis*, an inflammation of the mouth, may develop. Hair loss, *alopecia*, may occur. Fewer blood cells are produced. This puts the client at risk for bleeding and infection. The heart, lungs, liver, kidneys, and skin may also be affected.

Cancer clients have many needs. Pain must be controlled. Adequate rest and exercise are needed. Fluid and nutritional status must be maintained. Skin breakdown and elimination problems must be prevented. Constipation is a side effect of pain medications. Diarrhea can occur from chemotherapy. The side effects of radiotherapy and chemotherapy must be dealt with.

The client's psychological and social needs are great. The client may be angry, afraid, and depressed. There may be disfigurement from surgery. The client may feel unwhole, unattractive, or unclean. The client may be dying. Both the client and family need emotional support. Put yourself in the client's place. How would you feel and what would you want if you had cancer? Do not be afraid to talk to the client. Avoiding the client because you are uncomfortable is one of the worst things you can do. Use touch to communicate you care and listen. Often the client needs someone to talk to. Being there when your client needs you is important. You may not have to say anything. You may just need to be there and listen.

Musculoskeletal Disorders

Musculoskeletal disorders affect the ability to move about. Some are due to injury. Others are from the aging process.

Arthritis

Arthritis means joint (arth) inflammation (itis). It is the most common joint disease. Pain and decreased mobility occur in the affected joints. There are two basic types of arthritis.

Osteoarthritis occurs with aging. Joint injury is also a cause. The hips and knees are commonly affected. These joints bear the weight of the body. The joints in the fingers, thumbs, and spine can also be affected. The main symptoms are joint stiffness and pain. Cold weather and dampness seem to increase these symptoms.

Osteoarthritis has no cure. Treatment involves relieving pain and stiffness. Aspirin is often ordered for pain. Local heat applications may also be ordered. Some clients need walking aids (canes, walkers). Help is given as needed with activities of daily living.

Rheumatoid arthritis is a chronic disease. It can occur at any age. Connective tissue throughout the body is affected. The disease affects the heart, lungs, eyes, kidneys, and skin. However, it mainly affects the joints. Usually smaller joints in the fingers, hands, and wrists are involved first. Eventually the larger joints are involved. Severe inflammation causes very painful and swollen joints. Clients usually restrict movement because of the severe pain.

Signs and symptoms are pain, redness, and swelling in the joint area; limitation of joint motion; fever; fatigue; and weight loss. As the disease progresses, more and more joints become involved. Changes in other organs eventually occur.

The treatment goals are to maintain joint motion, control pain, and prevent deformities. Clients need a lot of rest. Bed rest may be ordered if there is a fever. Clients on bed rest are turned and repositioned every two hours. They are positioned to prevent contractures. Eight to 10 hours of sleep are needed each night. Morning and afternoon rest periods are also necessary. Rest is balanced with exercise. Range-of-motion exercises are done. Walking aids may be needed. Splints may be applied to the affected body parts. Safety measures to prevent falls are practiced.

Drugs are ordered by the doctor for pain. Local heat applications may also be ordered. Back massages are relaxing. Positioning to prevent deformities also promotes comfort.

These clients need emotional support. The disease is chronic. Death from other organ involvement is always possible. A good attitude is important. Clients should be as active as possible. The more clients can

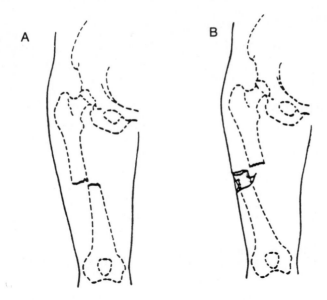

Fig. 21-2 A, Closed fracture. **B,** Open fracture. (From Hood, G.H., and Dincher, J.R.: Total client care: foundations and practice, ed. 6, St. Louis, 1984, The C.V. Mosby Co.)

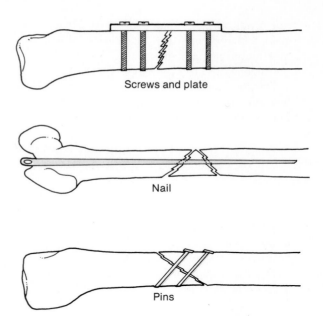

Fig. 21-3 Devices used to reduce a fracture. (From Miliken, M.E., and Campbell, G.: Essential competencies for client care, St. Louis, 1985, The C.V. Mosby Co.)

do for themselves, the better off they will be. A client may need someone to talk to. You need to be a good listener when the client needs to talk.

Fractures

A *fracture* is a broken bone. Fractures may be open or closed (Fig. 21-2). A *closed fracture*, or *simple fracture*, means the bone is broken but the skin is intact. An *open fracture*, or *compound fracture*, means the bone is broken and the bone has come through the skin.

Fractures are caused by falls and accidents. A bone disease called osteoporosis is another cause (see page 352). Signs and symptoms of a fracture are: pain, swelling, limitation of movement, bruising, and color changes at the fracture site. There may be bleeding.

The bone has to heal. The two bone ends are brought into normal position. This is called reduction. *Closed reduction* involves bringing the bone back into place. The skin is not opened. *Open reduction* involves surgery. Nails, pins, screws, metal plates, or wires may be used to keep the bone in place (Fig. 21-3). After reduction, the fracture is immobilized. Movement of the two bone ends is prevented. A cast or traction may be used to immobilize the bone.

CAST CARE

Casts are made of plaster of Paris, plastic, and fiber glass. The cast covers all or part of a limb (Fig. 21-4). Before the cast is applied, the limb is covered with a stockinette material. Material for the plaster of Paris cast comes in rolls. A roll is moistened and then wrapped around the limb. Several rolls may be used. After it is applied, the cast must dry. Plaster of Paris

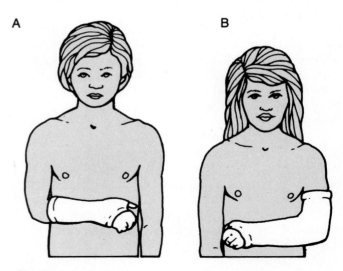

Fig. 21-4 A, Short arm cast. **B,** Long arm cast. (From Sorrentino, S.A.: Mosby's textbook for nursing assistants, ed. 2, St. Louis, 1987, The C.V. Mosby Co.)

casts dry in 24 to 48 hours. A dry cast is odorless, white, and shiny. A wet cast is gray, cool, and has a musty smell. The following rules apply to cast care.

1. Do not cover the cast with blankets, plastic, or other material. The cast gives off heat as it dries. Covers prevent the escape of heat. Burns can occur if the heat cannot escape.
2. Turn the client as directed. Turning promotes even drying of the cast.
3. The cast must maintain its shape. Do not place it

on a hard surface when wet. A hard surface causes the cast to flatten. Pillows are used to support the entire length of the cast (Fig. 21-5). When turning and positioning the client, support the cast with the palms of your hands (Fig. 21-6). If fingers are used, they dent the cast. The dents can cause pressure areas and lead to skin breakdown.

4. Protect the client from rough cast edges. The edges can be covered with tape. This is called petaling. See Fig. 21-7 on page 350. Or the doctor may pull

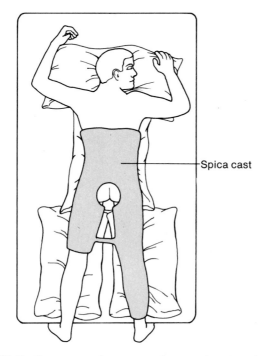

Fig. 21-5 Pillows are used to support the entire length of the wet cast. (From Miliken, M.E., and Campbell, G.: Essential competencies for client care, St. Louis, 1985, The C.V. Mosby Co.)

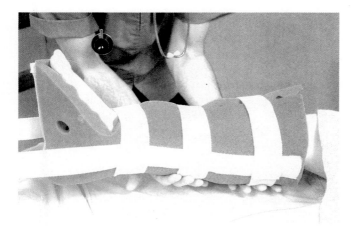

Fig. 21-6 The cast is supported with the palms during lifting. (From Sorrentino, S.A.: Mosby's textbook for nursing assistants, ed. 2, St. Louis, 1987, The C.V. Mosby Co.)

the stockinette up over the cast. Then the stockinette is secured in place with a roll of cast material.

5. Keep the cast dry. Casts lose their shape if they get wet. The cast must be protected from moisture from the perineum. The nurse may apply a waterproof material around the perineal area after the cast dries.

6. Do not let the client put things in the cast. Itching under the cast causes an intense desire to scratch. Skin can be broken by items used in scratching (pencils, coat hangers, knitting needles, back scratchers). The open area under the cast can become infected. Items used in scratching can also cause wrinkles in the stockinette. Or the object can be lost in the cast. Both can cause pressure leading to skin breakdown.

7. Elevate a casted limb on pillows. The limb should be elevated higher than the client's heart. This reduces swelling.

8. Make sure you have enough help when turning and repositioning the client. A cast is heavy and awkward. Balance is easily lost.

9. Lying on the injured side is usually not allowed. The nurse will tell you what positions the client is allowed.

10. Report the following signs and symptoms immediately:
    a. Pain—warns of a decubitus ulcer, poor circulation, or nerve damage.
    b. Swelling and a tight cast—blood flow to the part may be affected.
    c. Pale skin—means reduced blood flow to the part.
    d. Cyanosis—means reduced blood flow to the part.
    e. Odor—there may be an infection.
    f. Inability to move the fingers or toes—the cast may be causing pressure on a nerve.
    g. Numbness—the cast may be causing pressure on a nerve. Or there may be poor blood flow to the part.
    h. Temperature changes—cool skin means poor circulation. Hot skin means inflammation.
    i. Drainage on or under the cast—means an infection under the cast.
    j. Chills, fever, nausea and vomiting—means an infection under the cast.

TRACTION

Traction may be used to immobilize a fracture. Pull from two directions keeps the fractured bone in place. Weights, ropes, and pulleys are used (Fig. 21-8). Traction can be applied to the neck, arms, legs, or pelvis. Traction is also used for muscle spasms, to correct or prevent deformities, and for other musculoskeletal injuries.

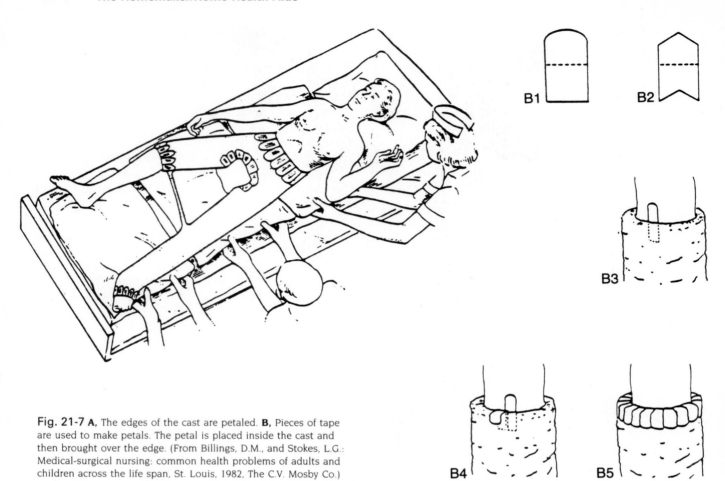

Fig. 21-7 A, The edges of the cast are petaled. **B,** Pieces of tape are used to make petals. The petal is placed inside the cast and then brought over the edge. (From Billings, D.M., and Stokes, L.G.: Medical-surgical nursing: common health problems of adults and children across the life span, St. Louis, 1982, The C.V. Mosby Co.)

Traction is applied by the doctor to the skin or bone. Skin traction involves applying bandages and strips of material to the skin. Weights are then attached to the material or bandage (see Fig. 21-8). Traction applied directly to the bone is called skeletal traction. A pin is inserted through the bone. Special devices are attached to the pin. Weights are attached to the device (Fig 21-9).

Traction may be continuous or intermittent. Continuous traction cannot be removed. Intermittent traction can be removed at times ordered by the doctor.

Follow these rules when caring for clients in traction.
1. Find out if the traction is continuous or intermittent.
2. Keep the client pulled up in bed. This is necessary to maintain the proper pull of the traction.
3. Keep the weights off the floor. The weights should hang from the traction set-up (see Fig. 21-8).

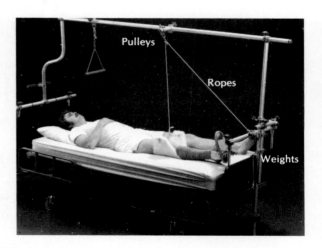

Fig. 21-8 Traction set-up. Note the weights, pulleys, and ropes. (From Perry, A.G., and Potter, P.A.: Clinical nursing skills and techniques, St. Louis, 1986, The C.V. Mosby Co.)

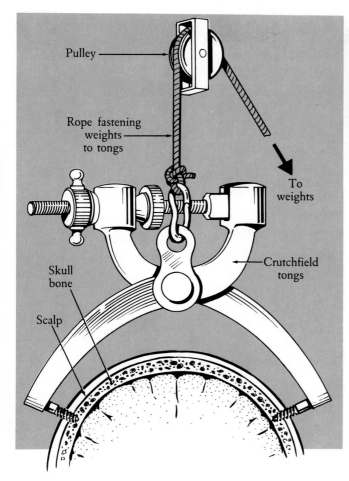

Fig. 21-9 Skeletal traction is attached to the bone. (From Sorrentino, S.A.: Mosby's textbook for nursing assistants, ed. 2, St. Louis, 1987, The C.V. Mosby Co.)

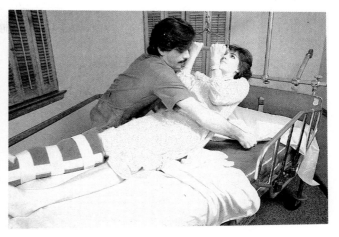

Fig. 21-10 A bed is made from the top down with traction. The client uses the trapeze to lift the buttocks off the bed. Then the linens are pulled down over the bed. (From Sorrentino, S.A.: Mosby's textbook for nursing assistants, ed. 2, St. Louis, 1987, The C.V. Mosby Co.)

disorders and slow healing may complicate the client's condition and care. The client is also at great risk for postoperative complications.

Open reduction is done. A pin is used to fix the fracture in place (Fig. 21-11). This is called a *hip pinning*. A cast or traction is sometimes used. If so, care of the client with a cast or in traction is required. The client with a hip pinning also needs the following care:
1. Give good skin care. Skin breakdown can occur rapidly.

4. Do not remove the weights.
5. Perform range-of-motion exercises to the uninvolved body parts as directed.
6. Usually only the back-lying position is allowed. Check with the nurse about positioning the client.
7. The fracture pan is used for elimination.
8. Give skin care often.
9. Bottom linens are usually put on from the top down. The client can use a trapeze to raise off the bed. Linens are brought under the client at this time (Fig. 21-10).
10. Observe for the signs and symptoms listed under cast care. Report these observations immediately.
11. Observe the area around the pin if skeletal traction is used. Immediately report redness, irritation, drainage, or client complaints of pain at the site.

HIP FRACTURES

Fractured hips are common in the elderly. They are quite serious because healing is slower in older people. The person may have other disorders. These

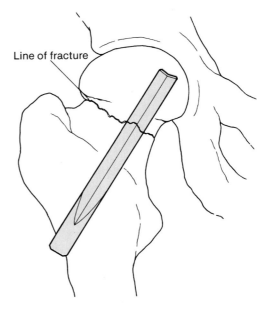

Fig. 21-11 A hip fracture is pinned in place. (From Miliken, M.E., and Campbell, G.: Essential competencies for client care, St. Louis, 1985, The C.V. Mosby Co.)

Line of fracture

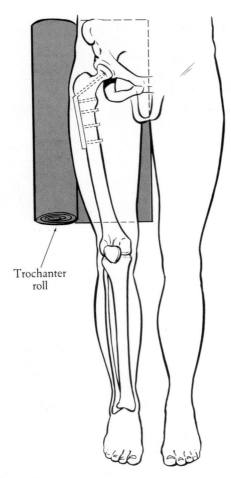

Fig. 21-12 The operated leg is kept abducted following hip pinning. (From Sorrentino, S.A.: Mosby's textbook for nursing assistants, ed. 2, St. Louis, 1987, The C.V. Mosby Co.)

2. Turn and reposition the client as directed. The doctor's orders for turning and positioning depend on the type of fracture and the surgical procedure.
3. Keep the operated leg abducted at all times (Fig. 21-12). The leg is abducted when the client is in the supine position, being turned, or in a side-lying position. Pillows can be used as directed.
4. Prevent external rotation of the hip. Use trochanter rolls or sandbags as directed by the nurse.
5. Provide a straight-back chair with armrests when the client can be up. A low, soft chair is not used.
6. Place the chair on the unoperated side.
7. Assist in transferring the client from the bed to the chair as directed.
8. Do not let the client stand on the operated leg unless permitted by the doctor.
9. Support and elevate the leg as directed when the client is in the chair.

Osteoporosis

Osteoporosis is a disorder in which the bone becomes porous and brittle. It is common in the elderly and in women who have been through menopause. A dietary lack of calcium is a major cause. Bed rest and immobility are other causes. They do not allow for proper bone use. For bone to be formed properly, it must be used to bear weight. If not, calcium is absorbed and the bone becomes porous and brittle.

Signs and symptoms include low back pain, gradual loss of height, and stooped posture. Fractures are a major threat. Bones are so brittle that the slightest stress can cause a fracture. Turning in bed or getting up from a chair can be enough to cause a fracture. Fractures are a great risk if the client falls or has an accident.

Osteoporosis is treated with calcium and vitamins. The hormone estrogen may be given to women. Exercise, good posture, and a back brace or corset are very helpful. Walking aids may be necessary. Bed rest is avoided. Be careful when turning and positioning the client. Also protect the client from falls and accidents. The safety measures described in Chapter 8 must be practiced.

Loss of a Limb

An *amputation* is the removal of all or part of a limb. Amputations are sometimes needed for severe injuries, bone tumors, severe infections, and circulatory disorders.

Gangrene is a condition in which there is death of tissue. Infection, injuries, and circulatory disorders may cause gangrene. They interfere with blood supply. The tissues do not receive enough oxygen and nutrients. Poisonous substances and waste products build up in the affected tissues. Tissues die. They become black, cold, and shriveled (Fig. 21-13), and can fall off. If untreated, gangrene will spread through the body and cause death.

Fingers, the hand, forearm, or entire arm may be removed. Toes, the foot, lower leg, upper leg, or en-

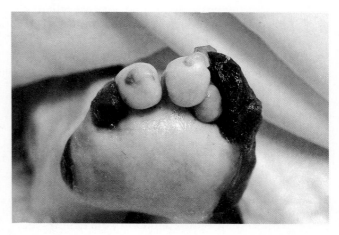

Fig. 21-13 Gangrene. (From Sorrentino, S.A.: Mosby's textbook for nursing assistants, ed. 2, St. Louis, 1987, The C.V. Mosby Co.)

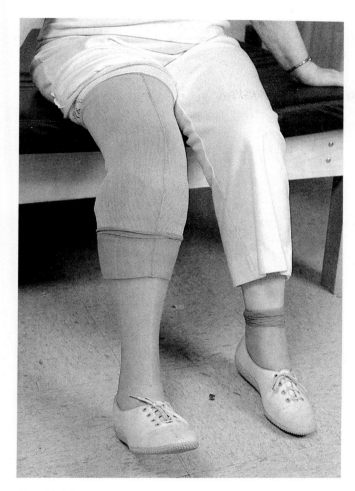

Fig. 21-14 Lower leg prosthesis. (From Sorrentino, S.A.: Mosby's textbook for nursing assistants, ed. 2, St. Louis, 1987, The C.V. Mosby Co.)

Nervous System Disorders

Nervous system disorders can affect mental and physical functions. The ability to speak, understand, feel, see, hear, touch, think, control bowels and bladder, or move may be affected.

Cerebrovascular Accident

A cerebrovascular accident (CVA) is commonly called a *stroke*. Blood supply to a part of the brain is suddenly interrupted. Brain damage occurs. A blood vessel can rupture causing hemorrhage (excessive bleeding) into the brain. Or a blood clot can obstruct blood flow to the brain.

Stroke is more common among the elderly. However, younger people have had strokes. A common cause of stroke is hypertension. Other risk factors include diabetes mellitus, obesity, birth control pills, a family history of stroke, hardening of the arteries, smoking, and stress.

The signs and symptoms of stroke vary. There may be a warning. The client may be dizzy, have ringing in the ears, a headache, nausea and vomiting, and memory loss. Or it can occur suddenly. Unconsciousness, noisy breathing, elevated blood pressure, slow pulse, redness of the face, seizures, and hemiplegia may occur. The victim may lose bowel and bladder control and the ability to speak (*aphasia*).

Emergency care of the stroke victim is described in Chapter 22. If the client survives, some brain damage is likely. The functions lost depend on the area of brain damage (Fig. 21-15). Rehabilitation begins immediately. The client may be dependent on others for care. Care of the client is as follows:

tire leg may be amputated. A lot of psychological support is needed. The client has lost a limb. The client's life is affected by the amputation. Appearance, activities of daily living, moving about, and job are just a few of the affected areas. Put yourself in the client's position. How would you feel if you lost an arm or a leg?

At some point the client will probably be fitted with a prosthesis (Fig. 21-14). Exercises are ordered to strengthen the other limbs. Physical therapy helps the client learn how to use the prosthesis. Occupational therapy may be needed if the client has to use the stump or prosthesis for activities of daily living.

The client may feel that the limb is still there or complain of pain in the amputated part. This is called *phantom limb pain*. The exact cause is unknown. However, it is a normal reaction. The sensation may occur only for a short time after surgery. However, some clients have phantom limb pain for several years.

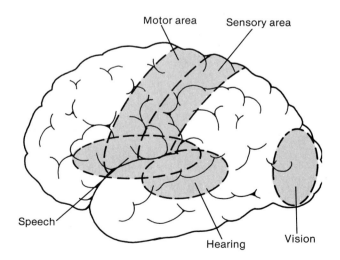

Fig. 21-15 The functions lost from a stroke will depend on the area of brain damage. (From Miliken, M.E., and Campbell, G.: Essential competencies for client care, St. Louis, 1985, The C.V. Mosby Co.)

1. The client is positioned on his or her side to prevent aspiration.
2. Coughing and deep breathing are encouraged.
3. The head of the bed is raised to semi-Fowler's position.
4. Side rails are kept up except when giving care.
5. Turning and repositioning are done every two hours.
6. Elastic stockings are usually ordered to prevent blood clots in the legs.
7. Range-of-motion exercises are done to prevent contractures.
8. A bladder training program is usually started.
9. A bowel training program may be necessary.
10. Safety precautions are practiced (see Chapter 8).
11. Help is given with self-care activities. The client is encouraged to do as much as possible.
12. Methods are developed to communicate with the client. Magic slates, pencil and paper, a picture board, or other methods may be used.
13. Good skin care is given to prevent decubitus ulcers.
14. Speech therapy, physical therapy, and occupational therapy may be ordered by the doctor.
15. Emotional support and encouragement are given. Praise is given for even the slightest client accomplishment.

Parkinson's Disease

Parkinson's disease is a slow and progressive disorder. Part of the brain degenerates. There is no cure. The disease is usually seen in the elderly. Signs and symptoms are: a masklike facial expression, tremors, pill-rolling movements of the fingers, a shuffling gait, stooped posture, stiff muscles, slow movements, slurred speech, monotone speech, and drooling. Mental function is usually not affected early in the disease. As the disease progresses, confusion and forgetfulness may develop.

Drugs specific for Parkinson's disease are ordered. Physical therapy may also be ordered. The client may need help eating and with other self-care activities. Measures to promote bowel elimination are practiced. There is a risk of constipation because of decreased activity and poor nutrition. Safety practices are carried out to protect the client from injury. Remember that mental function may not be affected. The client should be treated and talked to in an adult manner

Multiple Sclerosis

Multiple sclerosis (MS) is a progressive disease. The myelin sheath (nerve covering), spinal cord, and white matter in the brain are destroyed. As a result, messages are not sent to and from the brain in a normal manner.

Symptoms begin in young adulthood. The onset is gradual. There is usually blurred or double vision. Difficulty with balance and walking occur. Tremors, numbness and tingling, weakness, dizziness, urinary incontinence, bowel incontinence or constipation, behavior changes, and incoordination eventually occur. Signs and symptoms become worse over the next several years. Blindness, contractures, paralysis of all limbs (quadraplegia), loss of bowel and bladder control, and respiratory muscle weakness are among the client's many problems. The client becomes totally dependent on others for care.

There is no known cure for multiple sclerosis. Clients are encouraged and allowed to do as much for themselves as possible. The care required depends on the client's needs and condition. Skin care, personal hygiene, and range-of-motion exercises are important. Clients are protected from injury. Measures are taken to promote bowel and bladder elimination. Turning, positioning, coughing, and deep breathing are also important. Other measures are planned as necessary to prevent the complications of bed rest.

Chronic Brain Syndrome

Chronic brain syndrome affects the ability to think and understand. Changes in brain cells occur. The changes may be due to decreased blood flow, atrophy, chemicals, infections, poor nutrition, or aging.

Signs and symptoms develop slowly. They may go unnoticed for a long time. There may be recent memory loss. The person may be unable to remember something that happened yesterday or a few minutes ago. However, events of the long ago past are remembered. Disorientation occurs. The person may not know the date, time, or place. The client may not recognize people or remember names. The ability to concentrate decreases. The person may not be able to follow simple instructions. There is poor judgment. The person may not recognize harmful situations. Attention to personal hygiene decreases.

The client may partially or totally depend on others for basic needs. Supervision and help with activities of daily living are needed. The client must also be protected from injury.

Reality orientation is important for these clients. It promotes awareness of person, time, and place. The following are usually involved:

1. Face the person and speak clearly and slowly.
2. Call the client by name every time you have contact with him or her. Know how the person wants to be addressed (Mr., Mrs., Miss, Ms., first name, or a nickname).
3. State your name and show the individual your name tag.
4. Tell the person the date and time each morning. Repeat the information as often as necessary during the day and evening.
5. Explain what you are going to do and why.

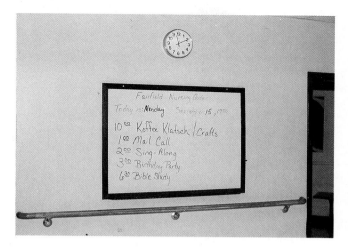

Fig. 21-16 Calendars and clocks are used for reality orientation. Note that they have large numbers.

6. Give clear and simple answers to the person's questions.
7. Ask clear and simple questions. Allow enough time for an answer.
8. Give short, simple instructions.
9. Keep calendars and clocks with large numbers in the home (Fig. 21-16).
10. Encourage the client to wear glasses and a hearing aid if needed.
11. Use touch to communicate with the person (see Chapter 3).
12. Place familiar items and pictures within view.
13. Provide newspapers and magazines. Read to the client if appropriate.
14. Discuss current events with the person.
15. Allow the use of television and radio.
16. Maintain the day-night cycle. Open curtains, shades, and drapes during the day and close them at night. Use a night-light during the night. Regular clothes should be worn during the day rather than gowns or pajamas.
17. Maintain a calm, relaxed, and peaceful atmosphere. Prevent loud noises, rushing, and crowded rooms.
18. Follow the routine set for the client. Meals, bathing, exercise, television programs, and other activities are done on a schedule. This promotes a sense of order. It also helps the client know what to expect.
19. Do not rearrange furniture or the person's belongings.
20. Encourage the client to perform self-care activities.
21. Be consistent. Each team member must follow the program developed for the individual.
22. Remind the person of holidays, birthdays, and other special events.

Alzheimer's Disease

Alzheimer's disease is similar to chronic brain syndrome. Changes in brain tissue are progressive. Unlike chronic brain syndrome, Alzheimer's disease is seen in younger people.

Three stages of Alzheimer's disease have been described.

- *Stage* 1. The client shows memory loss, is moody, has poor judgment, and is disoriented to time.
- *Stage* 2. There is restlessness at night, increased memory loss, and problems with movement and gait. The person cannot judge and recognize things in the environment.
- *Stage* 3. The client has seizures. There is disorientation about person, time, and place. Communication is difficult to understand and does not make sense. Coma and death occur.

A consistent environment is needed. The client is less confused if things stay the same. The same caregivers should take care of the client from day to day. ADLs are done at the same time every day. The client needs calm and quiet. Activities are simple and kept to a minimum. These clients tend to wander and have poor judgment. Therefore, doors and windows must be safely secured. This helps prevent the person from wandering from home. The danger of falling from a window is also prevented.

Care of these clients also includes the following:

1. The client is kept as active as possible.
2. The client is encouraged and assisted with ADLs as needed.
3. Reality orientation is used.
4. Care routines are followed by all caregivers.
5. Bowel and bladder routines are established.
6. The client is spoken to in short, clear sentences.
7. The client is protected from injury.

Head Injuries

The scalp, skull, and brain tissue can be injured. Injuries may be minor. Minor injuries may cause only a temporary loss of consciousness. Other head injuries are more serious. Permanent brain damage or death can occur. Brain tissue can be bruised or torn. Skull fractures can cause brain damage. Hemorrhage can occur in the brain or surrounding structures.

Head injuries are caused by falls, vehicle accidents, industrial accidents, and sport injuries. Other body parts may also be injured. Spinal cord injuries are likely. Head injuries can occur during birth. If the client survives a severe head injury, some permanent damage is likely. There may be paralysis, mental retardation, personality changes, speech problems, breathing difficulties, and loss of bowel and bladder control. These problems require rehabilitation. Care depends on the client's needs and remaining abilities.

Spinal Cord Injuries

Spinal cord injuries can permanently damage the nervous system. Common causes are stab or bullet wounds, vehicle accidents, industrial accidents, falls, or sport injuries.

The type of damage depends on the level of the injury. The higher the level of injury, the greater the loss of function (Fig. 21-17). Muscle function in the legs is lost if injuries occur in the lumbar area. Injuries at the thoracic level cause loss of muscle function below the chest. Clients with injuries at the lumbar or thoracic levels are paraplegics. Cervical injuries may cause loss of function in the arms, chest, and all muscles below the chest. Clients with these injuries are quadriplegics.

If the client lives, rehabilitation is necessary. The emotional needs of the client cannot be overlooked. These clients have severe emotional reactions to paralysis and the loss of function. Paralyzed clients usually need the following care:

1. The client is protected from injury. Falls and burns are major risks. Side rails must be up. Hospital beds are kept in the low position. The call bell must be within reach. Bath water, heat applications, and food must be at the proper temperature.
2. Turning and repositioning are done every two hours.
3. Skin care and measures to prevent decubitus ulcers are practiced.
4. Good body alignment is maintained at all times. Pillows, trochanter rolls, footboards, and other devices are used as needed.

5. Bowel and bladder training programs are carried out.
6. Range-of-motion exercises are done to maintain muscle function and prevent contractures. Other exercises may be ordered.
7. Assistance with food and fluids is given as needed. The client may have to be fed. Self-help devices may be needed.
8. Emotional and psychological support is given. Counselors or psychiatrists may be involved in the client's care.
9. Physical therapy, occupational therapy, and vocational rehabilitation may be ordered. They help the client become independent to the extent possible.

Hearing Problems

Hearing losses range from slight hearing impairments to complete deafness. Hearing is needed for many functions. Learning to talk, speech, responding to others, safety, and awareness of surroundings all require hearing.

EFFECTS ON THE CLIENT

Unless hearing loss is sudden, a person may not be aware of a gradual hearing problem. Others may notice changes in the person's behavior or attitude. However, they may not realize that the changes are due to hearing loss. The symptoms and effects of hearing loss vary.

There are some obvious signs. These include speaking too loudly, leaning forward to hear, and turning and cupping the better ear toward the speaker. The person may answer questions wrong or often ask for words to be repeated. Poor attention and failing grades are early signs of poor hearing in children. Infants with hearing impairments often fail to start learning to talk. This is usually the first sign that baby has a hearing problem.

The psychological and social effects of hearing loss are less obvious. People with hearing problems may respond strangely in conversation and to questions. Therefore, they tend to avoid social situations. This is an attempt to avoid embarrassment. However, loneliness, boredom, and feelings of being left out often result. Only parts of conversations may be heard. They may become suspicious. They think they are being talked about. Or they think that others are talking softly on purpose. Some people with hearing problems try to hog conversations so that they do not have to respond or answer questions.

Hearing loss may cause speech problems. As you talk, you hear yourself. The way you pronounce words and your voice volume depend on how you hear what you are saying. Slurred speech and the improper pronunciation of words may occur. Monotone speech may also occur.

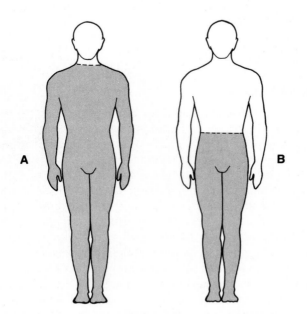

Fig. 21-17 The shaded areas indicate the areas of paralysis. (From Miliken, M.E., and Campbell, G.: Essential competencies for client care, St. Louis, 1985, The C.V. Mosby Co.)

COMMUNICATING WITH THE CLIENT

Hearing impaired people may wear hearing aids or read lips. They may also watch facial expressions, gestures, and body language. Sign language is used by people who are totally deaf. The following can help the person hear or lip read:

1. Gain attention and alert the person to your presence by lightly touching his or her arm. Do not startle or approach the person from behind.
2. Face the person directly when speaking. Do not turn or walk away from the person while you are talking.
3. Stand or sit in good light. Shadows and glares interfere with the person seeing your face clearly.
4. Speak clearly, distinctly, and slowly.
5. Speak in a normal tone of voice. Do not shout.
6. Do not cover your mouth, smoke, eat, or chew gum while talking. These actions affect mouth movements.
7. Stand or sit on the side of the person's better ear.
8. State the topic of conversation or discussion first.
9. Use short sentences and simple words.
10. Write out important names and words.
11. Keep discussions short to avoid tiring the person.
12. Repeat and rephrase statements as necessary.
13. Be alert to the messages you send by your facial expressions, gestures, and body language.
14. Reduce or eliminate background noises.

The person may have speech problems. It may be hard to understand what the person is trying to say. Do not assume that you understand. Nor should you pretend to understand to avoid embarrassing the person. Serious problems can result if you assume or pretend to understand. The following measures will help you communicate with the speech impaired person:

1. Listen and give the person your full attention.
2. Ask questions to which you know the answer. This helps you to become familiar with how the person speaks.
3. Determine the subject being discussed. This helps you understand essential points of the discussion.
4. Ask the person to repeat or rephrase statements if necessary.
5. Repeat what the person has said. Ask if you have understood correctly.
6. Ask the person to write down key words or the message.
7. Watch the person's lip movements during speech.
8. Watch facial expressions, gestures, and body language for clues about what is being said.

HEARING AIDS

A *hearing aid* amplifies sound. It does not correct or cure the hearing problem. The ability to hear is not improved. The person may hear better with a hearing aid. This is because the hearing aid makes sounds louder. Background noises and speech are amplified. These noises must be minimized. Remember that the hearing aid does not make speech clearer, only louder. Measures for communicating with the hearing impaired person apply when a person has a hearing aid.

Hearing aids run on batteries. Sometimes hearing aids do not seem to work properly. Find out if the instrument is turned on or off. Then check the battery position. A new battery may be needed. The earpiece may need cleaning. Or the hearing aid may need repair.

Hearing aids are expensive. They must be handled carefully. The earpiece (Fig. 21-18) is the only part that can be washed. It is washed daily with soap and water. Then it is thoroughly dried before being snapped back into place.

Vision Problems

Vision problems occur in all age groups. Problems range from very mild vision loss to complete blindness. One or both eyes may be affected.

GLAUCOMA

Glaucoma is an eye disease. Pressure within the eye is increased. This damages the retina and optic nerve. The result is visual loss with eventual blindness. The disease may be gradual or sudden. Signs and symptoms include tunnel vision (Fig. 21-19), blurred vision, and blue-green halos around lights. With sudden onset, there is severe eye pain, nausea, and vomiting. Glaucoma is a major cause of blindness. Persons over 40 are at risk for the disease. The cause is unknown.

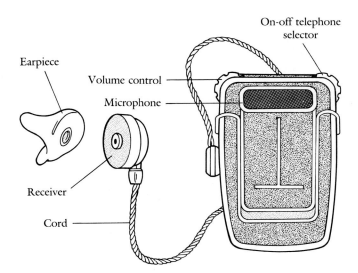

Fig. 21-18 Parts of a hearing aid. (From Sorrentino, S.A.: Mosby's textbook for nursing assistants, ed. 2, St. Louis, 1987, The C.V. Mosby Co.)

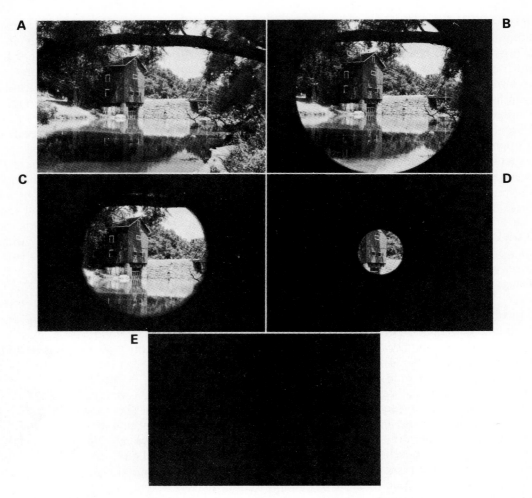

Fig. 21-19 A, Normal vision. **B,** Tunnel vision. **C, D, E,** Visual loss continues with eventual blindness. (From Saunders, W.H., et al.: Nursing care in eye, ear, nose, and throat problems, ed. 4, St. Louis, 1979, The C.V. Mosby Co.)

Treatment involves drug therapy and possibly surgery. The goal is to prevent further damage to the retina and optic nerve. Damage that has already occurred cannot be reversed.

CATARACT

Cataract is an eye disorder in which the lens becomes cloudy (opaque). The cloudiness prevents light from entering the eye. Gradual blurring and dimming of vision occur. Sight is eventually lost. A cataract can occur in one or both eyes. Aging is the most common cause. Surgery is the only treatment.

An eye shield or patch may be worn for several days after surgery. The shield protects the eye from injury. One or both eyes may be covered. Measures for the blind person are necessary when an eye shield is worn. Even if one shield is worn, there may be visual loss in the other eye.

The client is fitted with corrective lenses after surgery. A permanent implant may be done during surgery. Even with corrective lenses or implants there is still some impaired vision.

CORRECTIVE LENSES

Eyeglasses and contact lenses are prescribed for vision problems. Glasses may be needed for certain activities, such as reading or seeing at a distance. Or they may be worn all the time. Contact lenses are usually worn while awake.

Eyeglasses. Lenses are made of hardened glass or plastic. Glass lenses are washed with warm water and dried with soft tissue. Plastic lenses are easily scratched. A special cleaning solution and tissues or cloths are used for plastic lenses.

Glasses are costly. You must protect them from breakage and other damage. When glasses are not worn, they need to be put in their case. The case is put in a safe place.

Contact lenses. Contact lenses fit directly on the eye. Hard and soft contacts are available. Contacts do not break easily, and can be worn for sports. However, they cost more than eyeglasses. They are also easily lost. Contact lenses are removed for activities such as swimming, showering, and sleeping.

People with contacts are taught to insert, remove, and clean them. Clients should do this themselves. Eye damage can easily occur when contacts are inserted or removed. Therefore, you should not perform these measures.

SPECIAL NEEDS OF THE BLIND CLIENT

Blindness can be caused by birth defects, accidents, and eye diseases. It can also be a complication of diseases of other organs and body systems. In most cases blindness is not present at birth. Usually it is acquired later in life. The blind person's life is seriously affected by the loss of sight. Physical and psychological adjustments can be long and hard. Special education and training are needed. Moving about, ADLs, reading Braille, and using a seeing eye dog require training.

Braille is a method of writing that uses raised dots. The dots are arranged to represent each letter of the alphabet. The first 10 letters also represent the numbers 0 through 9 (Fig. 21-20). The person feels the dots with the fingers (Fig. 21-21). Many books, magazines, and newspapers are in Braille. There are also Braille typewriters.

Braille is hard to learn. Books and articles are available on records and tapes. These are often called "talking books." They can be bought or borrowed from libraries.

The blind person can learn to move about with a white cane or a "seeing eye dog" or "guide dog." Both are signs that a person is blind. The dog serves as the eyes of the blind person. The dog is trained to recognize danger and to guide the person through traffic.

You must treat the blind person with respect and dignity—not with pity. Most blind people have adjusted to being blind. They are able to lead independent lives. Some have been blind for a long time. Others have been blind only a short time. Certain practices are necessary when dealing with the blind individual. They are necessary no matter how long the person has been blind.

1. Identify yourself promptly. Give your name, title, and reason for being there. Do not touch the person until he or she is aware that you are in the room.
2. Do not rearrange furniture and equipment.

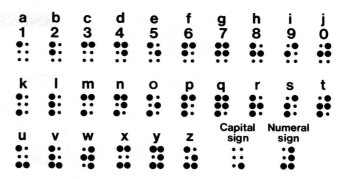

Fig. 21-20 Braille. (From Sorrentino, S.A.: Mosby's textbook for nursing assistants, ed. 2, St. Louis, 1987, The C.V. Mosby Co.)

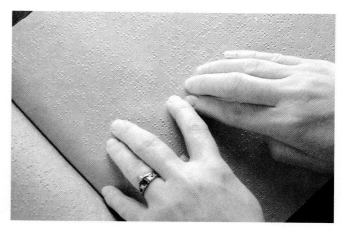

Fig. 21-21 Braille is "read" with the fingers. (From Sorrentino, S.A.: Mosby's textbook for nursing assistants, ed. 2, St. Louis, 1987, The C.V. Mosby Co.)

3. Give step-by-step explanations of procedures. Indicate when the procedure has been completed.
4. Tell the person when you are leaving the room.
5. Leave doors open or shut, never partly open.
6. Assist the person in ambulating by walking slightly ahead of the individual (Fig. 21-22). The person should touch your arm lightly. Never push or guide the blind person in front of you.
7. Warn the person of steps, doors, turns, furniture, curbs, and other hazards when assisting with ambulation.
8. Explain the location of food and beverages on the table or tray. Use the face of a clock (see page 297). Or guide the person's hand to the various items.
9. Help the client cut meat, open containers, butter bread, and with similar activities if needed.
10. Make sure the call bell is always within reach.
11. Provide a radio, "talking books," television, and Braille books for the person's entertainment.

Fig. 21-22 The blind client walks slightly behind the aide and touches the aide's arm lightly.

12. Do not shout or talk in a loud voice. Just because a person is blind does not mean that hearing is impaired.
13. Let the person perform self-care activities if able.

Respiratory Disorders

Some clients with respiratory diseases need home care. The respiratory system brings oxygen into the lungs and removes carbon dioxide from the body. Respiratory disorders interfere with this function. They can threaten life.

Chronic Obstructive Pulmonary Disease (COPD)

Four disorders are grouped under chronic obstructive pulmonary disease (COPD). They are chronic bronchitis, asthma, bronchiectasis, and emphysema. These disorders interfere with the normal exchange of oxygen and carbon dioxide in the lungs.

Chronic bronchitis occurs after repeated episodes of bronchitis (inflammation of the bronchi). Common causes are cigarette smoking and air pollution. "Smoker's cough" in the morning is usually the first symptom. At first the cough is dry. Eventually the client coughs up mucus that may have pus and blood. The cough becomes more frequent. The client may also have difficulty breathing and may tire easily. The mucus and inflamed breathing passages "obstruct" the flow of air into the lungs. The body is unable to obtain normal amounts of oxygen.

Asthma is a disorder in which the air passages narrow. Difficulty in breathing results. Allergies and emotional stress are common causes. Episodes occur suddenly and are called asthma attacks. Besides dyspnea, there is shortness of breath, wheezing, coughing, rapid pulse, perspiration, and cyanosis. The client is usually very frightened during the attack. Fear causes the attack to become worse.

Drugs are used to treat asthma. Emergency room treatment may be necessary for severe attacks. The client and family are taught how to prevent asthma attacks. Repeated attacks can damage the respiratory system.

Bronchiectasis is a disorder in which the bronchi dilate (enlarge). Pus collects in the dilated bronchi. Causes include respiratory infections and aspiration. It may be a complication of measles or whooping cough in children. The client has a chronic, productive cough. Large amounts of sputum, containing pus, are coughed up. The sputum usually has a foul smell. The amount of sputum increases as the disease progresses. Eventually blood may appear in the sputum. Weight loss, fatigue, and loss of appetite can occur. The doctor may order drugs, respiratory therapy, rest, and measures to improve nutrition. The client must be protected from others with respiratory infections. Cigarette smoking is not allowed. It may be necessary to remove the diseased part of the lung.

Emphysema is a disorder in which the alveoli enlarge. The walls of the alveoli become less elastic. Therefore, they do not expand and shrink normally with inspiration and expiration. As a result, some air is trapped in the alveoli during expiration. The trapped air is not exhaled. As the disease progresses, more alveoli become involved. The normal exchange of oxygen and carbon dioxide cannot occur in the affected alveoli.

Cigarette smoking is the most common cause. Signs and symptoms include shortness of breath and "smoker's cough." At first shortness of breath occurs with exertion. Later it occurs at rest. Sputum may con-

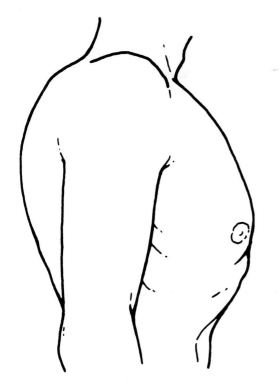

Fig. 21-23 Barrel chest from emphysema. (From Sorrentino, S.A.: Mosby's textbook for nursing assistants, ed. 2, St. Louis, 1987, The C.V. Mosby Co.)

tain pus. As more air is trapped in the lungs, the client develops a "barrel chest" (Fig. 21-23). Clients with emphysema usually prefer to sit upright and slightly forward. Breathing is easier in this position.

The client must stop smoking. Respiratory therapy, breathing exercises, oxygen, and drug therapy may be ordered.

Pneumonia

Pneumonia is an inflammation of lung tissue. The alveoli in the affected area fill with fluid. With fluid in the alveoli, oxygen and carbon dioxide cannot be exchanged normally.

Bacteria, viruses, aspiration, or immobility can cause pneumonia. The client with pneumonia is very ill. Signs and symptoms include fever, chills, painful cough, pain on breathing, and a rapid pulse. There may be cyanosis. The color of sputum depends on the cause. Sputum may be clear, green, yellowish, or rusty-colored.

Drugs are ordered for the infection and for pain relief. The doctor may also order "force fluids" because of the fever. Fluids also help thin mucous secretions. Thin secretions are easier to cough up. Oxygen may be necessary. The client will probably prefer a semi-Fow-

ler's position for breathing. Respiratory isolation may be necessary, depending on the cause of the pneumonia. Mouth care is important. Frequent linen changes may be needed because of fever.

Cardiovascular Disorders

Cardiovascular disorders are the leading cause of death in the United States. Problems may occur in the heart or in the blood vessels.

Hypertension

Hypertension is a condition in which the blood pressure is abnormally high. Narrowed blood vessels are a common cause. When vessels are narrow, the heart must pump with more force to move blood through the vessels. Other disorders can cause high blood pressure. These include kidney disorders, head injuries, some complications of pregnancy, and tumors of the adrenal gland.

Hypertension can damage other body organs. The heart may enlarge to pump with more force. Blood vessels in the brain may burst and cause a stroke. Vessels in the eyes and kidneys may be damaged.

There may be no signs or symptoms at first. Usually hypertension is found when the blood pressure is measured. Signs and symptoms develop as the disorder progresses. There may be headache, blurred vision, and dizziness. Complications of hypertension include stroke, heart attack, kidney failure, and blindness.

The doctor may order drugs to lower the blood pressure. No smoking, regular exercise, and adequate rest will be encouraged. A sodium-restricted diet may be ordered. If the client is overweight, a low-calorie diet is ordered.

Coronary Artery Disease (CAD)

Coronary artery disease is a disorder in which the coronary arteries narrow. One or all of the arteries may be affected. Because the vessels are narrowed, blood supply to the heart muscle is reduced. Atherosclerosis is the most common cause of narrowed coronary arteries. In atherosclerosis, fatty material collects on the arterial walls (Fig. 21-24). This causes the arteries to narrow and obstruct blood flow. Blood flow through an artery may be totally blocked. Permanent damage occurs in the part of the heart receiving its blood supply from that artery.

There are many risk factors for CAD. These include obesity, cigarette smoking, lack of exercise, a diet high in fat and cholesterol, and hypertension. CAD is more likely to occur in older people and in men. People with the type A personality are also at risk. These peo-

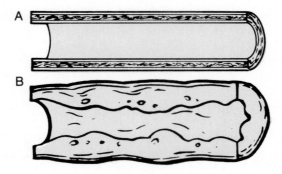

Fig. 21-24 A, Normal artery. **B,** Fatty deposits collect on the walls of arteries in atherosclerosis. (From Sorrentino, S.A.: Mosby's textbook for nursing assistants, ed. 2, St. Louis, 1987, The C.V. Mosby Co.)

ple are aggressive, competitive, and work very hard. They have a hard time relaxing and do things at a fast pace.

The two major complications of CAD are angina pectoris and myocardial infarction (heart attack).

ANGINA PECTORIS

Angina pectoris means "chest pain." Angina means pain, and pectoris means chest. The chest pain is due to reduced blood flow to a part of the heart muscle (myocardium). Angina pectoris is seen when the heart needs more oxygen. Normally blood flow to the heart increases when the heart needs more oxygen. Physical exertion, a heavy meal, emotional stress, and excitement increase the heart's need for oxygen. In CAD, the narrowed vessels prevent increased blood flow.

Chest pain is the major symptom of angina. The pain may be described as a tightness or discomfort in the left side of the chest. The pain may spread to the left jaw and down the inner part of the left arm (Fig. 21-25). The client may be pale, feel faint, perspire, and have dyspnea. These signs and symptoms cause the client to stop activity and rest. Rest usually relieves symptoms in 3 to 15 minutes. Rest reduces the heart's need for oxygen. Therefore, normal blood flow occurs and heart damage is prevented.

Besides rest, angina is treated with a drug called nitroglycerin. A nitroglycerin tablet is taken when an angina attack occurs. The tablet is put under the tongue. It dissolves under the tongue and is rapidly absorbed into the bloodstream. Clients should keep nitroglycerin tablets close at hand.

Clients are taught to avoid situations that can cause angina pectoris. These include overexertion, heavy meals and overeating, and emotional situations. They are advised to stay inside in cold weather and during hot, humid weather. Exercise programs supervised by doctors may be developed. Some clients need

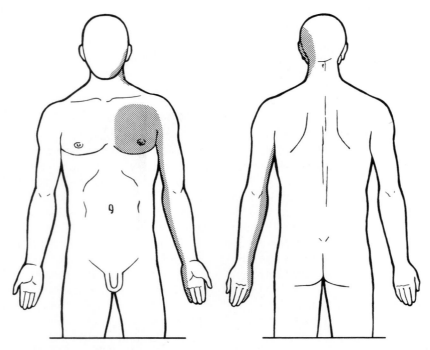

Fig. 21-25 The shaded areas show where the pain of angina pectoris is located. (From Hood, G.H., and Dincher, J.R.: Total client care: foundations and practice, ed. 6, St. Louis, 1984, The C.V. Mosby Co.)

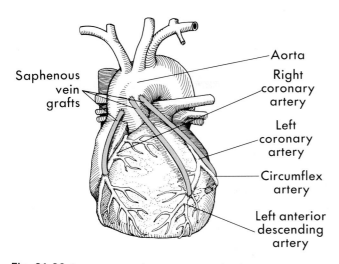

Fig. 21-26 Coronary artery bypass surgery. The diseased part of the artery is bypassed with a vein graft. (From Long, B.C., and Phipps, W.J.: Essentials of medical-surgical nursing: a nursing process approach, St. Louis, 1985, The C.V. Mosby Co.)

coronary artery bypass surgery. The surgery bypasses the diseased part of the artery (Fig. 21-26). This increases blood flow to the heart.

Angina pectoris often leads to a heart attack. Sometimes chest pain is not relieved by rest and nitroglycerin. Then it is probably due to a more serious cause.

MYOCARDIAL INFARCTION (MI)

Myocardial infarction is due to lack of blood supply to the heart muscle (myocardium). Tissue death occurs (infarction). The common term for MI is "heart attack." Coronary, coronary thrombosis, and coronary occlusion are other terms for MI. Blood flow to the myocardium is suddenly interrupted. Usually a thrombus obstructs blood flow through an artery. The damaged area may be small to large. Cardiac arrest can occur (see Chapter 22).

There is sudden, severe chest pain. The pain is usually on the left side. It may be described as crushing, stabbing, or squeezing. Clients often say that it feels like someone is sitting on their chests. The pain may spread to the neck and jaw and down the arm. The pain is more severe and lasts longer than angina. It is not relieved by rest and nitroglycerin. Other signs and symptoms include indigestion, dyspnea, nausea, dizziness, perspiration, pallor, cyanosis, cold and clammy skin, low blood pressure, and a weak and irregular pulse. The client is very fearful and anxious. Some have described a feeling of doom.

Myocardial infarction is an emergency. The goals are to relieve pain, stabilize vital signs, give oxygen, calm the client, and prevent life-threatening com-

plications. Many drugs are given. The client is treated in a coronary care unit (CCU).

Activity is increased gradually. Drug therapy and measures to prevent complications are continued. Cardiac rehabilitation is started. This includes an exercise program, teaching about medications, and diet changes. Changes in life-style and sexual activity may also be necessary. The goal of cardiac rehabilitation is to prevent another heart attack.

Congestive Heart Failure (CHF)

Congestive heart failure occurs when the heart cannot pump blood normally. Blood backs up and causes congestion of tissues. Left-sided or right-sided heart failure, or both can occur. CHF is common in the elderly.

When the left side of the heart fails to pump normally, blood backs up into the lungs. Respiratory congestion occurs. There can be dyspnea, increased amounts of sputum, cough, and gurgling sounds in the lungs. Plus, the heart does not pump enough blood to the rest of the body. Organs get a poor blood supply. Signs and symptoms occur from the organs. Poor blood flow to the brain causes confusion, dizziness, and fainting. Poor blood flow to the kidneys decreases urinary output. The skin becomes pale or cyanotic. Blood pressure falls. A very severe form of left-sided failure is pulmonary edema (fluid in the lungs). Pulmonary edema is an emergency. Death can occur.

The right side of the heart may fail. Blood backs up into the venae cavae and veins. The feet and ankles swell. Neck veins bulge. Congestion occurs in the liver and liver function decreases. Fluid may build up in the abdomen. The heart's right side cannot pump enough blood to the lungs. Therefore, normal blood flow does not occur from the lungs to the heart's left side. Less blood than normal is pumped from the left side of the heart to the rest of the body. As in left-sided failure, the organs get a poor blood supply. Signs and symptoms described in the above paragraph eventually occur.

CHF is usually caused by a weakened heart. MI, hypertension, and damaged heart valves are common causes.

CHF can be treated and controlled. Drugs are given to strengthen the heart and to reduce the amount of fluid in the body. A sodium-restricted diet is ordered. Supplemental oxygen is given. The client will probably prefer a semi-Fowler's or Fowler's position for breathing. The client's care may include the following:
1. Maintaining bed rest or a limited activity program
2. Measuring intake and output
3. Measuring weight daily
4. Restricting fluids as ordered by the doctor
5. Giving good skin care to prevent skin breakdown

6. Performing range-of-motion exercises
7. Assisting with transfers or ambulation
8. Assisting with self-care activities
9. Maintaining good body alignment
10. Applying elastic stockings

The Endocrine System

The most common disorder of the endocrine system is diabetes mellitus. In this disorder the body cannot use sugar properly. For proper use of sugar there must be enough insulin. Insulin is secreted by the pancreas. In diabetes mellitus, the pancreas fails to secrete enough insulin. Sugar builds up in the blood. The cells do not have enough sugar for energy. Therefore, body cells cannot function.

The disorder can occur in children and adults. Persons who have a family history of diabetes are at risk. Aging and obesity increase the risk.

Signs and symptoms include increased urine production, increased thirst, hunger, and weight loss. Urine testing shows sugar in the urine (see Chapter 16). If diabetes is not controlled, complications occur. These include blindness, kidney damage, nerve damage, and circulatory disorders. Circulatory disorders can lead to a stroke, heart attack, and slow healing of wounds. Foot and leg wounds are very serious. Infection and gangrene are common. An amputation may be necessary.

Diabetes mellitus is treated with exercise, diet, and insulin (see Chapter 17). Meals must be served on time. The client needs to eat all foods served. Urine tests (see Chapter 16) are ordered. Good foot care is very important.

Insulin shock can occur if a client gets too much insulin. Diabetic coma develops if a client does not get enough insulin. Table 21-1 summarizes the causes, signs, and symptoms of insulin shock and diabetic coma. Both can lead to death if they are not corrected.

Sexually Transmitted Diseases

Some diseases are spread by sexual contact. They are grouped under the heading of sexually transmitted diseases (STDs). Table 21-2 summarizes the common sexually transmitted diseases. Clients with STDs may seek health care. Some are not aware that they have been infected. Others are aware of having a disease but do not seek treatment. Embarrassment is a common reason for not seeking treatment.

Table 21-1 Insulin Shock and Diabetic Coma

	INSULIN SHOCK	DIABETIC COMA
Causes	Too much insulin Omitting a meal Eating an inadequate amount of food Excessive physical activity Vomiting	Undiagnosed diabetes Not enough insulin Eating too much Insufficient amounts of exercise Stress from surgery, illness, emotional upset, etc.
Signs and symptoms	Hunger Weakness Trembling Perspiration Headache Dizziness Rapid pulse Low blood pressure Confusion Convulsions Cold, clammy skin Unconsciousness	Weakness Drowsiness Thirst Hunger Flushed cheeks Sweet breath odor Slow, deep, and labored respirations Rapid and weak pulse Low blood pressure Dry skin Headache Nausea and vomiting Coma

Table 21-2 Sexually Transmitted Diseases

DISEASE	SIGNS AND SYMPTOMS	TREATMENT
Gonorrhea	Burning on urination Urinary frequency and urgency Vaginal discharge in the female Urethral discharge in the male	Antibiotic medications
Syphilis	*Stage* 1 (10-90 days after exposure): Painless chancre on the penis, in the vagina, or genitalia (Fig. 21-27); the chancre may also be on the lips or inside of the mouth, or anywhere else on the body *Stage* 2 (about two months after the chancre): General fatigue, loss of appetite, nausea, fever, headache, rash, sore throat, bone and joint pain, hair loss, lesions on the lips and genitalia *Stage* 3 (3 to 15 years after infection): Damage to the cardiovascular system and central nervous system, blindness	Antibiotic medications
Genital herpes	Painful, fluid filled sores on or near the genitalia (Fig. 21-28) The sores may have a watery discharge Itching, burning, and tingling in the genital area Fever Swollen glands	No known cure Medications can be given to control discomfort
Venereal warts	Male—warts appear on the penis, anus, or genitalia Female—warts appear near the vagina, cervix, and labia	Application of special ointment which causes the warts to dry up and fall off Surgical removal may be necessary if the ointment is not effective
AIDS (Acquired Immune Deficiency Syndrome)	Seen most commonly in homosexual men, IV drug users, and those who have received contaminated blood prior to blood screening procedures The client is unable to fight off certain infections and cancers Death eventually occurs	No known treatment at this time

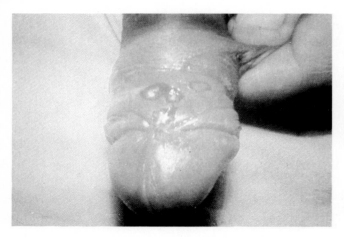

Fig. 21-27 Chancre caused by syphilis. (From Sorrentino, S.A.: Mosby's textbook for nursing assistants, ed. 2, St. Louis, 1987, The C.V. Mosby Co.)

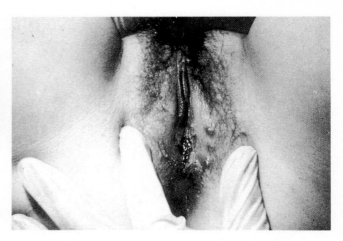

Fig. 21-28 Genital herpes sore. (From Sorrentino, S.A.: Mosby's textbook for nursing assistants, ed. 2, St. Louis, 1987, The C.V. Mosby Co.)

The genital area is usually associated with STDs (Figs. 21-27 and 21-28). However, other body areas may be involved. These include the rectum, ears, mouth, nipples, throat, tongue, eyes, and nose. Most STDs are spread by sexual contact. Some can also be spread through a break in the skin. Contact with the infected person's body fluids (blood, sperm, saliva, feces, wound drainage) is another way of spreading disease. So is the use of contaminated blood or needles.

Isolation procedures may be necessary for some clients. Handwashing before and after client care is essential. Also, be sure to wear disposable gloves when you will have contact with the client's blood or body fluids. This is especially important if you have any breaks in your skin. If gloves are not available, you can use plastic bags, baggies, or even plastic wrap.

Summary

A client may have one or more of the disorders described in this chapter. For example, a client may have arthritis, diabetes, heart disease, osteoporosis, and chronic brain syndrome. Problems increase if a fracture occurs. The client is then at risk for the development of infection, pneumonia, and the complications of bed rest.

Only very basic information was given about each disorder. As a home health aide you are not expected to completely understand your clients' diagnoses. However, the information in this chapter will help you better understand your client's physical, psychological, and social needs.

Study Questions

1. A client has bone cancer. He had his right leg amputated above the knee to remove the tumor. The surgery was 6 months ago. Now the cancer has metastasized to his lungs. Chemotherapy was started 3 weeks ago. Identify the concerns and fears the client may have. What must you consider when caring for this client?

2. A client has a history of angina pectoris. Recently he had a heart attack. Cardiac rehabilitation has been started. You are assigned to do housekeeping tasks and to help with meals. You have also been told to watch for signs and symptoms of angina, heart attack, and congestive heart failure. Why does this client need help with housekeeping and meals? List the signs and symptoms you should watch for. Explain what you should do if the client has chest pain.

Circle the best answer.

3. The spread of cancer to other body parts is called
   a. Malignant tumor
   b. Metastasis
   c. Gangrene
   d. Benign tumor

4. Which is not a warning sign of cancer?
   a. Painful, swollen joints
   b. A sore that does not heal
   c. Unusual bleeding or discharge from a body opening
   d. Nagging cough or hoarseness

5. A client has arthritis. Care will include all of the following *except*
   a. Measures to prevent contractures
   b. Range-of-motion exercises
   c. Local cold applications
   d. Help with activities of daily living

6. Mr. Day has a cast. The cast needs to dry. Which is *false*?
   a. The cast is covered with blankets or plastic.
   b. He is turned as directed so the cast dries evenly.
   c. The entire length of the cast is supported with pillows.
   d. The cast is supported with the palms when it is lifted.

7. A client has a cast. Which should be reported immediately?
   a. Pain, numbness, or inability to move fingers or toes
   b. Chills, fever, or nausea and vomiting
   c. Odor, cyanosis, or temperature changes of the skin
   d. All of the above

8. A client has had a hip pinning. The operated leg should be
   a. Abducted at all times
   b. Adducted at all times
   c. Externally rotated at all times
   d. Flexed at all times

9. The client with osteoporosis is at risk for
   a. Fractures
   b. An amputation
   c. Phantom limb pain
   d. All of the above

10. A client has had an amputation. This affects
    a. Activities of daily living
    b. Appearance
    c. The client's job
    d. All of the above

11. Mr. Smith has had a stroke. Which is *false*?
    a. Blood supply to part of his brain was interrupted.
    b. Hemiplegia may occur.
    c. Aphasia may occur.
    d. Changes in brain tissue are progressive.

12. A client has had a stroke. The nurse tells you to do all of the following. Which one should you question?
    a. Position the client in a semi-Fowler's position.
    b. Do range-of-motion exercises every 2 hours.
    c. Turn, reposition, and give skin care every 2 hours.
    d. Keep the bed in the highest position.

13. A client has Parkinson's disease. Which is *false*?
    a. Parkinson's disease affects part of the brain.
    b. The client's mental function is affected first.
    c. Signs and symptoms include stiff muscles, slow movements, and a shuffling gait.
    d. The client needs to be protected from injury.

14. A client has multiple sclerosis. Which is *false*?
    a. Nerve impulses are sent to and from the brain in a normal manner.
    b. Symptoms begin in young adulthood.
    c. There is no cure.
    d. The client will eventually be paralyzed.

15. Clients with chronic brain syndrome and Alzheimer's disease require similar care. Care should include
    a. Supervision of activities of daily living
    b. Reality orientation
    c. Protection from injury
    d. All of the above

16. Clients with Alzheimer's disease need an environment that is
    a. Calm and quiet
    b. Warm in temperature
    c. Busy and has lots of activity
    d. Changed often

17. Head and spinal cord injuries always cause paralysis.
    a. True
    b. False

18. You are talking to a person with a hearing loss. You should do all of the following *except*
    a. Speak clearly, distinctly, and slowly
    b. Sit or stand where there is good light
    c. Shout
    d. Stand or sit on the side of the better ear

19. You are talking with a hearing-impaired person. You can do all of the following *except*
    a. State the topic of conversation
    b. Cover your mouth, smoke, or chew gum
    c. Use short sentences and simple words
    d. Write out important names and words

20. Mrs. Smith is blind. You should
    a. Touch her to get her attention
    b. Move furniture to relieve boredom
    c. Give step-by-step explanations of procedures
    d. Have her walk in front of you

21. Glaucoma and cataract result in
    a. Decreased mental function
    b. Paralysis
    c. Loss of vision
    d. Breathing difficulties

22. A client has emphysema. Which is *false*?
    a. The client will have dyspnea only with activity.
    b. Cigarette smoking is the most common cause.
    c. The client will probably breathe easier sitting upright and slightly forward.
    d. Sputum may contain pus.

23. A client has pneumonia. Respiratory isolation may be required.
    a. True
    b. False

24. A client has hypertension. Which complication can occur?
    a. Stroke
    b. Heart attack
    c. Kidney failure
    d. All of the above

25. A client has hypertension. Treatment will probably include all of the following *except*
    a. No smoking and regular exercise
    b. A high-sodium diet
    c. A low calorie diet if the client is obese
    d. Medications to lower the blood pressure

26. A client has angina pectoris. Which is *true*?
    a. Damage to the heart muscle occurs.
    b. The pain is described as crushing, stabbing, or squeezing.
    c. The pain is relieved with rest and nitroglycerin.
    d. All of the above

27. A client is having an MI. You know that
    a. The client is having a heart attack
    b. This is an emergency situation
    c. The client may have a cardiac arrest
    d. All of the above

28. A client has congestive heart failure. The following measures have been ordered. Which should you question?
    a. Force fluids
    b. Measure intake and output
    c. Measure weight daily
    d. Perform range-of-motion exercises

29. Which is not a sign of diabetes mellitus?
    a. Increased urine production
    b. Weight gain
    c. Hunger
    d. Increased thirst

30. The statements are about sexually transmitted diseases (STDs). Which is *false*?
    a. STDs are usually spread by sexual contact.
    b. Gloves should be worn if you will be in contact with the client's body fluids.
    c. Signs and symptoms of STDs are always obvious.
    d. Some STDs result in death.

Answers

3. b	10. d	17. b	24. d
4. a	11. d	18. c	25. b
5. c	12. d	19. b	26. c
6. a	13. b	20. c	27. d
7. d	14. a	21. c	28. a
8. a	15. d	22. a	29. b
9. a	16. a	23. a	30. c

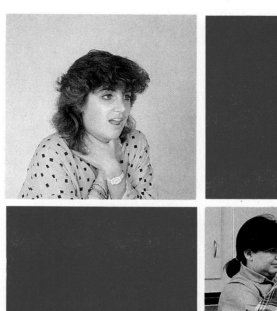

22 Basic Emergency Care

Key Terms

Cardiac arrest The sudden stoppage of breathing and heart action

Convulsion Violent and sudden contractions or tremors of muscles; seizure

First aid Emergency care given to an ill or injured person before medical help arrives

Grand mal seizure Contraction of all muscles at once followed by jerking movements of the body

Hemorrhage Excessive loss of blood from a blood vessel

Petit mal seizure A seizure that usually lasts 10 to 20 seconds and that is characterized by sudden loss of consciousness, twitching of arm and face muscles, and flickering of the eyelids

Poison A substance that can harm body tissues or cause death

Respiratory arrest Breathing stops but the heart continues to pump for several minutes

Seizure A convulsion

Shock A condition that results when there is an inadequate blood supply to the organs and tissues of the body

Home health aides may find emergency situations in homes, in public places, or on the highway. Knowing what to do may mean the difference between a person living or dying. This chapter describes the basic care for common emergencies. You are encouraged to take an American Red Cross Society first aid course. You should also take a basic life support course from the American Heart Association. These courses will better prepare you to give emergency care.

General Rules of Emergency Care

You may need to give first aid. *First aid* is the emergency care given to an ill or injured person before medical help arrives. The goals of first aid are to prevent death and to prevent injuries from becoming worse.

When an emergency occurs, the local Emergency Medical Services (EMS) system must be activated. The system involves emergency personnel (paramedics and emergency medical technicians). They have been trained in emergency care. They know how to treat and transport people with life-threatening conditions. Emergency vehicles are also part of the EMS system. They carry emergency equipment, supplies, and drugs. Emergency personnel communicate by two-way radio with doctors in hospital emergency rooms. The doctors tell the emergency personnel what to do for the victim. In many communities dialing 911 activates the EMS system. Call the fire or police department or telephone operator if your community does not have the 911 system.

Each emergency is different. However, the following rules apply to any kind of emergency:

1. Know your limitations. Do not try to do more than you can. Do not try an unfamiliar procedure. Do what you can at the time.
2. Stay calm. Being calm helps the victim feel more secure.
3. Observe for life-threatening problems. Check for breathing, a pulse, and bleeding.
4. Keep the victim lying down or in the position in which you found him or her. Do not move the victim. You could make an injury worse if you move the victim.
5. Perform necessary emergency measures.
6. Call for help or tell someone to activate the EMS system. An operator will send emergency vehicles and personnel to the scene. Give the following information. Do not hang up until the operator has hung up.
   a. Your location—include the street address and the city or town you are in. Name cross streets or roads and landmarks if possible. Also give the telephone number you are calling from.
   b. What happened (heart attack, accident, etc.)— fire equipment, police, and ambulances may be needed.
   c. How many people need help.
   d. The condition of victims, any obvious injuries, and if there are life-threatening situations.
   e. What aid is being given.
7. Do not remove clothing unless you have to. If clothing must be removed, tear the garment along the seams.
8. Keep the victim warm. Cover the victim with a blanket. Use coats and sweaters if you do not have a blanket.
9. Reassure the conscious victim. Explain what is happening and that help has been called.
10. Do not give the victim any food or fluids.
11. Keep bystanders away. They tend to stare, offer advice, and make comments about the victim's condition. The victim may think the situation is worse than it really is. Onlookers also invade the victim's privacy.

Basic Life Support

A person is clinically dead when the heart and breathing stop. Blood and oxygen are not pumped through the body. Damage to the brain and other organs occurs within 4 to 6 minutes. Sometimes death is expected. It may be expected in clients who have been ill a long time. Breathing and heart action can stop suddenly without warning. This is *cardiac arrest.*

Cardiac arrest is a sudden, unexpected event. It can occur anywhere at any time. People have had cardiac arrests when driving a car, shoveling snow, playing golf and tennis, watching television, and eating. Common causes include heart disease, drowning, electrical shock, severe injury, airway obstruction, and drug overdose.

Respiratory arrest is when breathing stops but the heart continues to pump. If breathing is not restored, cardiac arrest will occur. Causes include drowning, stroke, obstructed airway, drug overdose, electrocution, smoke inhalation, suffocation, injury from lightning, myocardial infarction, and other injuries.

Basic life support involves preventing or promptly recognizing cardiac arrest or respiratory arrest. Basic life support procedures support breathing and circulation. The life-saving measures must be done with speed and skill.

Cardiopulmonary Resuscitation

The three major signs of cardiac arrest are *no pulse, no breathing,* and *unconsciousness.* The victim's skin is cool, pale, and gray. The victim has no blood pressure.

Cardiopulmonary resuscitation (CPR) must be started when cardiac arrest occurs. The goal is to get oxygen to the brain, heart, kidneys, and other organs. CPR has three basic parts (ABCs of CPR): airway, breathing, and circulation.

AIRWAY

Respiratory passages (airway) must be open to restore breathing. The airway is often obstructed (blocked) during cardiac arrest. The victim's tongue falls toward the back of the throat. This blocks the airway. The head-tilt/chin-lift maneuver is used to open the airway (Fig. 22-1):

1. Place one hand on the victim's forehead.
2. Apply pressure on the forehead with your palm to tilt the head back.
3. Place the fingers of your other hand under the bony part of the chin.
4. Lift the chin forward as you tilt the head backward with your other hand.

The head-tilt/chin-lift maneuver is also used for infants and children. However, the head is not hyperextended as in the adult. Rather the head is tilted to a normal (neutral) or "sniffing" position (Fig. 22-2).

Fig. 22-1 The head-tilt/chin-lift maneuver is used to open the airway. One hand is on the victim's forehead and pressure is applied to tilt the head back. The fingers of the other hand are placed under the chin. The chin is lifted forward with the fingers. (From Ellis, P.D., and Billings, D.M.: Cardiopulmonary resuscitation: procedures for basic and advanced life support, St. Louis, 1979, The C.V. Mosby Co.)

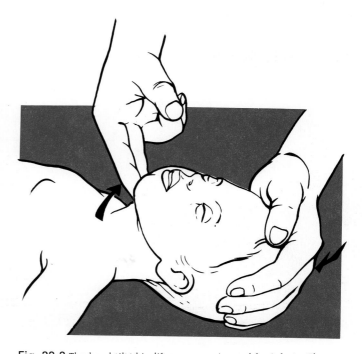

Fig. 22-2 The head-tilt/chin-lift maneuver is used for infants. The infant's head is in a neutral or "sniffing" position. (From Sorrentino, S.A.: Mosby's textbook for nursing assistants, ed. 2, St. Louis, 1987, The C.V. Mosby Co.)

BREATHING

Oxygen is not inhaled when breathing stops. The victim must have oxygen. Otherwise permanent brain and organ damage will occur. Because the victim cannot breathe, breathing must be done for the victim. This is done by *mouth-to-mouth resuscitation* (Fig. 22-3):

1. Open the airway.
2. Pinch the nostrils shut to prevent air from escaping through the nose. Use the thumb and index finger of the hand on the forehead to pinch the nostrils.
3. Take a deep breath.
4. Place your mouth tightly over the victim's mouth.
5. Blow air into the victim's mouth as you exhale. You should see the victim's chest rise as the lungs fill with air.
6. Remove your mouth from the victim's mouth.
7. Take in a quick, deep breath.

Mouth-to-mouth resuscitation is not always possible. The *mouth-to-nose* technique may be necessary. The mouth-to-nose technique is recommended when:

- You cannot ventilate through the victim's mouth
- You cannot open the mouth
- You cannot make a tight seal for mouth-to-mouth resuscitation
- The mouth is severely injured

The airway is opened with the head-tilt/chin-lift method for mouth-to-nose resuscitation. The mouth must be closed. Pressure is placed on the chin to close the mouth. To ventilate, place your mouth over the victim's nose and blow air into the nose (Fig. 22-4).

Some people breathe through openings in their necks. The openings are called *stomas* (Fig. 22-5). *Mouth-to-stoma* ventilation is given during cardiac or respiratory arrest. You will seal your mouth around the stoma and blow air into the stoma (Fig. 22-6). Check for a neck opening to tell if a person is a "neck-breather."

CIRCULATION

Blood flow to the brain and other organs must be maintained. Otherwise permanent damage results. The heart stops beating in cardiac arrest. Blood must be pumped through the body some other way. This is done with chest compression (cardiac massage). Each chest compression forces blood through the circulatory system.

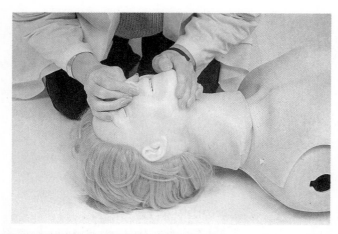
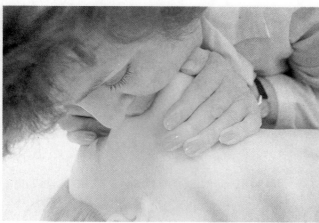

Fig. 22-3 Mouth-to-mouth resuscitation. **A,** The victim's airway is opened and the nostrils pinched shut. **B,** The victim's mouth is sealed by the rescuer's mouth. (From Sorrentino, S.A.: Mosby's textbook for nursing assistants, ed. 2, St. Louis, 1987, The C.V. Mosby Co.)

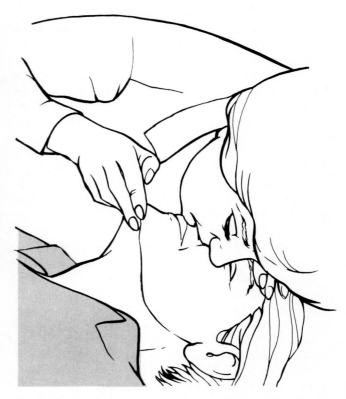

Fig. 22-4 Mouth-to-nose resuscitation. (From Sorrentino, S.A.: Mosby's textbook for nursing assistants, ed. 2, St. Louis, 1987, The C.V. Mosby Co.)

Fig. 22-5 A stoma in the neck. (From Sorrentino, S.A.: Mosby's textbook for nursing assistants, ed. 2, St. Louis, 1987, The C.V. Mosby Co.)

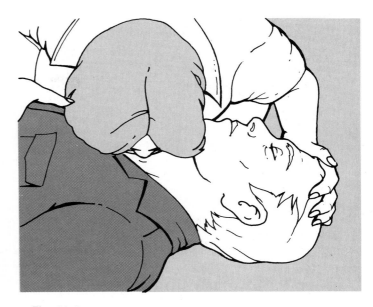

Fig. 22-6 Mouth-to-stoma resuscitation. (From Sorrentino, S.A.: Mosby's textbook for nursing assistants, ed. 2, St. Louis, 1987, The C.V. Mosby Co.)

The heart lies between the sternum (breastbone) and the spinal column. When pressure is applied to the sternum, it moves downward. This compresses the heart between the sternum and spinal column (Fig. 22-7). The victim must be supine and on a hard, flat surface for good compressions. Hand position is also important. Locating proper hand position for adults is shown in Fig. 22-8.

1. Find the lower part of the rib cage on the side near you. Use your index and middle fingers.
2. Run your fingers up along the rib cage to the notch at the center of the chest. The notch is where the ribs and sternum meet.
3. Mark the notch with your middle finger.
4. Place your index finger next to your middle finger on the lower end of the sternum.
5. Place the heel of your hand near the victim's head on the lower half of the sternum. Place it next to your index finger.
6. Remove your index and middle fingers from the notch.
7. Place that hand on top of your hand on the sternum.
8. Extend or interlace the fingers of both hands. This keeps your fingers off the chest.

Your position is important for good chest compressions. Your elbows must be straight. Your shoulders must be directly over the victim's chest (Fig. 22-9). Apply firm downward pressure to depress the sternum 1½ to 2 inches. Then release the pressure

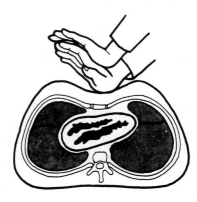

Fig. 22-7 The heart lies between the sternum and spinal cord. The heart is compressed when pressure is applied to the sternum. (From Rosen, P., et al.: Emergency medicine: concepts and clinical practice, St. Louis, 1983, The C.V. Mosby Co.)

without removing your hands from the chest. Compressions are given in a regular rhythm.

PERFORMING CPR

CPR is only done for cardiac arrest. You must determine if cardiac arrest or fainting has occurred. Unresponsiveness, breathlessness, and pulselessness are indications for CPR. Unresponsiveness is determined by tapping or gently shaking the victim and shouting "Are you OK?" If there is no response, the victim is unconscious.

Establishing breathlessness involves three steps:

1. Look at the victim's chest to see if it rises and falls.
2. Listen for the escape of air during expiration. Place your ear by the victim's nose and mouth to listen.

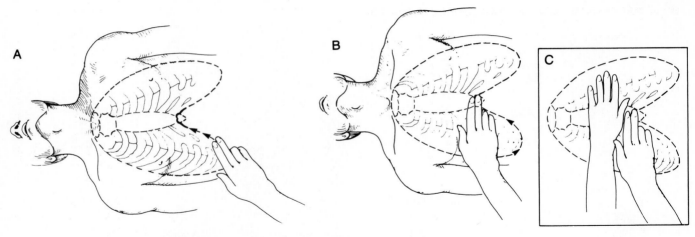

Fig. 22-8 Proper hand position for CPR. **A,** Locate rib cage.
B, Run fingers along rib cage to notch. **C,** Heel of hand placed next to index finger. (From Ellis, P.D., and Billings, D.M.: Cardiopulmonary resuscitation: procedures for basic and advanced life support, St. Louis, 1979, The C.V. Mosby Co.)

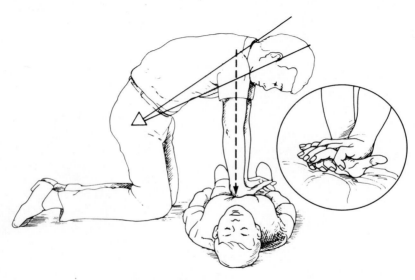

Fig. 22-9 Position of shoulders for CPR. (From Ellis, P.D., and Billings, D.M.: Cardiopulmonary resuscitation: procedures for basic and advanced life support, St. Louis, 1979, The C.V. Mosby Co.)

3. *Feel* for the flow of air. Place your cheek by the victim's nose.

   The carotid artery is used to check for pulselessness. To locate the carotid pulse:
1. Place the tips of your index and middle fingers on the victim's trachea (Fig. 22-10).
2. Slide your fingertips down to the groove of the neck on the side near you.

   CPR can be done alone or with a helper. There are also CPR procedures for infants and young children. *Never* practice CPR on a person. Serious damage can be done. Mannequins are used for learning CPR.

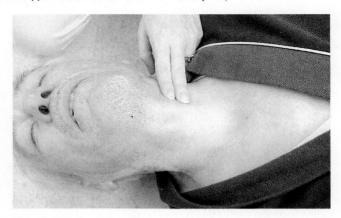

Fig. 22-10 Locating the carotid pulse. Index and middle fingers are placed on the trachea. Then the fingers are moved down into the groove of the neck where the carotid pulse is located. (From Sorrentino, S.A.: Mosby's textbook for nursing assistants, ed. 2, St. Louis, 1987, The C.V. Mosby Co.)

Procedure: Adult CPR—one person

1. Check for unresponsiveness.
2. Call for help.
3. Logroll the victim to the supine position if he or she is face down. Logrolling prevents twisting of the spine (see Chapter 10, page 134). The victim must be on a hard, flat surface. Place the victim's arms alongside the body.
4. Open the airway using the head-tilt/chin-lift maneuver.
5. Check for breathlessness.
6. Give two ventilations. Each should be 1½ seconds long. Allow the victim's chest to deflate between ventilations.
7. Check for pulselessness. This should take 5 to 10 seconds. Use your other hand to keep the airway open with the head-tilt maneuver.
8. Have your helper activate the EMS system.
9. Start cardiac compressions at a rate of 80 to 100 per minute. Give 15 compressions and then two ventilations.
    a. Establish a rhythm and count out loud in a manner you find helpful (try: "one and, two and, three and, four and, five and, six and, seven and, eight and, nine and, ten and, eleven and, thirteen and, fourteen and, fifteen").
    b. Open the airway and given two ventilations.
    c. Repeat this step until you have given four cycles of 15 compressions and two ventilations.
10. Check for a carotid pulse (5 seconds).
11. Give two ventilations if there is no pulse.
12. Repeat step 9. Check for a pulse every 4 to 5 minutes. Do not interrupt CPR for more than 7 seconds.

Procedure: Adult CPR—two rescuers

1. Do the one-person CPR procedure until a helper arrives.
2. Continue chest compressions when the helper arrives. The helper will state, "I know CPR. Can I help?"

3. Indicate you want the person to help but do not stop chest compressions. The helper will kneel on the other side of the victim. Complete a cycle of 15 compressions and 2 ventilations.
4. Stop compressions for 5 seconds. The helper will check for a carotid pulse. The helper will state "No pulse."
5. Perform CPR with your helper as follows (Fig. 22-11):
    a. Helper gives two ventilations.
    b. Give 80 to 100 compressions per minute. Count out loud in a rhythm you find helpful (try: "one- and, two- and, three- and, four- and, five").
    c. Helper gives a ventilation right after the fifth compression. Pause for 1 to 1½ seconds for the ventilation. Then continue chest compressions.
    d. A ventilation is given after every fifth compression. Your helper will check for a pulse during the compressions.
6. Stop compressions at the end of one minute. Your helper will check for breathing and a pulse. After the first minute, stop compressions every few minutes to check for breathing and circulation. Stop compressions for only 5 seconds.
7. Call for a switch in positions when you are tired.
8. Change positions quickly as follows:
    a. Helper gives a ventilation after you give the fifth compression.
    b. Helper moves down to kneel at the victim's shoulder and finds the proper hand position.
    c. Move to the victim's head after giving the fifth compression.
    d. Check for a pulse (5 seconds).
    e. Say, "No pulse."
    f. Given one ventilation before your helper begins chest compressions.
9. Give one ventilation after every fifth compression.
10. Switch positions when the person giving the compressions is tired. Check for a pulse and breathing with every position change.

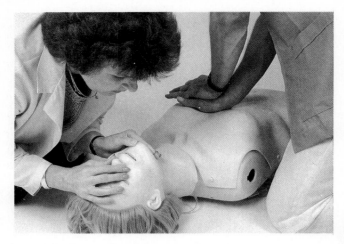

Fig. 22-11 Two people performing CPR. (From Sorrentino, S.A.: Mosby's textbook for nursing assistants, ed. 2, St. Louis, 1987, The C.V. Mosby Co.)

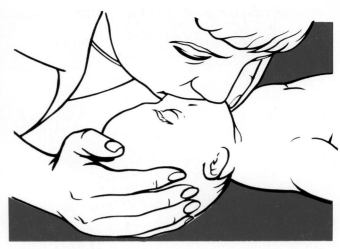

Fig. 22-12 The infant's mouth and nose are covered during mouth-to-mouth resuscitation. (From Sorrentino, S.A.: Mosby's textbook for nursing assistants, ed. 2, St. Louis, 1987, The C.V. Mosby Co.)

Procedure: CPR for infants and children

1. Check for unresponsiveness.
2. Call for help.
3. Turn the victim as a unit. Keep the head and neck straight. Support the head and neck when turning the victim. Position the infant or child supine on a hard, flat surface.
4. Open the airway using the head-tilt/chin-lift maneuver. Do not hyperextend the head. Extension of the head is usually enough to open the airway of an infant or child (see Fig. 22-2).
5. Check for breathlessness.
6. Give two gentle, slow ventilations. Each should take 1 to 1½ seconds. For an infant, cover the nose and mouth with your mouth to give a ventilation (Fig. 22-12). Let the chest deflate between ventilations.
7. Check for pulselessness. Use the brachial artery for infants and the carotid pulse for children. Keep the airway open while you check for a pulse.
8. Have your helper activate the EMS system.
9. Give CPR to an infant as follows:
   a. Locate proper hand position (Fig. 22-13).
      1. Draw an imaginary line between the nipples.
      2. Place the index finger farthest from the infant's head just under the imaginary line.
      3. Place your middle and ring fingers next to your index finger. The area for chest compression is below your middle and ring fingers.
   b. Begin compressions using 2 or 3 fingers. Compress the sternum ½ to 1 inch at least 100 times per minute. Release pressure after each compression. Do not remove your fingers from the infant's chest.
   c. Count out loud in a rhythm that is useful for you (try: "one, two, three, four, five").
   d. Give one ventilation after every fifth compression.
   e. Check for a pulse after 10 cycles of 5 compressions and 1 ventilation.
   f. Continue chest compressions and ventilation if there is no pulse.
   g. Check for a pulse every few minutes.
10. Give CPR to a child as follows (use adult method if the child is large or older than 8 years):
   a. Locate proper hand position as for the adult.
   b. Use the heel of one hand to depress the sternum 1 to 1½ inches (Fig. 22-14).
   c. Give 80 to 100 compressions per minute. Count out loud in a rhythm you find helpful (try: "one and two and three and four and five").
   d. Give a ventilation after every fifth compression.
   e. Check for a pulse after 10 cycles of 5 compressions and 1 ventilation.
   f. Continue chest compressions and ventilations if there is no pulse.
   g. Check for a pulse every few minutes.

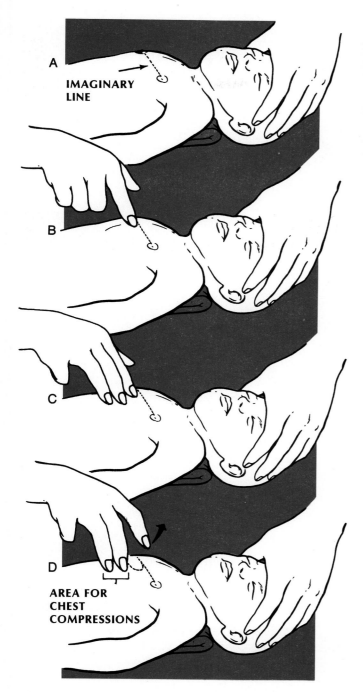

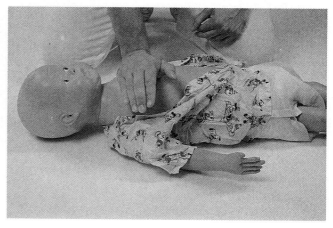

Fig. 22-14 The heel of one hand is used for CPR on a child. The heel is placed over the lower end of the sternum as for an adult. (From Sorrentino, S.A.: Mosby's textbook for nursing assistants, ed. 2, St. Louis, 1987, The C.V. Mosby Co.)

Obstructed Airway

Airway obstruction can lead to cardiac arrest. Air cannot pass through the air passages to the lungs. The entire body does not get oxygen. Airway obstruction, also called choking, often occurs during eating. Meat is the most common food causing airway obstruction. Choking often occurs on large pieces of meat that are poorly chewed. Laughing and talking while eating are also common causes. Adults can choke on dentures. Children have choked on small objects such as pieces of hot dogs, marbles, hard candy, coins, and beads. Airway obstruction can occur in the unconscious client. Common causes are aspiration of vomitus and the tongue falling back into the airway.

When airway obstruction occurs, the victim clutches at the throat (Fig. 22-15). The victim cannot breathe, speak, or cough. The victim appears pale and cyanotic. If conscious, the victim is very frightened. The obstruction must be removed immediately to prevent cardiac arrest. The Heimlich maneuver is done to relieve an obstructed airway. The maneuver involves abdominal thrusts. They can be done with the victim standing or lying. The finger sweep is another maneuver used when an adult is unconscious. You must call for help when a victim has an obstructed airway. Have someone activate the EMS system.

Fig. 22-13 Locating hand position for infant chest compressions. **A,** Imaginary line between the nipples. **B,** Index finger is placed just under the line. **C,** Middle and ring fingers placed next to the index finger. **D,** Area for chest compressions is under the middle and ring fingers. (From Sorrentino, S.A.: Mosby's textbook for nursing assistants, ed. 2, St. Louis, 1987, The C.V. Mosby Co.)

Fig. 22-15 A choking person will usually clutch the throat. (From Sorrentino, S.A.: Mosby's textbook for nursing assistants, ed. 2, St. Louis, 1987, The C.V. Mosby Co.)

Fig. 22-16 Abdominal thrusts with the victim standing. (From Phipps, W.J., Long, B.C., and Woods, N.F.: Medical-surgical nursing: concepts and clinical practice, ed. 2, St. Louis, 1983, The C.V. Mosby Co.)

Procedure: Clearing the obstructed airway—the conscious adult

1. Ask the victim if he or she is choking.
2. Check if the victim can cough or speak.
3. Do the Heimlich maneuver (abdominal thrusts) as follows if the victim is standing or sitting (Fig. 22-16).
   a. Stand behind the victim.
   b. Wrap your arms around the victim's waist.
   c. Make a fist with one hand. Place the thumb side of the fist against the victim's abdomen. The fist is positioned in the middle above the navel and below the end of the sternum.
   d. Grasp your fist with your other hand.
   e. Press your fist and hand into the victim's abdomen with a quick, upward thrust.
   f. Repeat the abdominal thrust until the object is expelled or the victim loses consciousness.

Procedure: Clearing the obstructed airway—the unconscious adult

1. Check for unresponsiveness.
2. Call for help.
3. Logroll the victim to the supine position. The victim's arms should be at his or her sides.
4. Open the airway using the head-tilt/chin-lift maneuver.
5. Check for breathlessness.
6. Give one ventilation. Reposition the victim's head and open the airway if you cannot ventilate. Give one ventilation.
7. Have your helper activate the EMS system.

8. Do the Heimlich maneuver if you could not ventilate the victim.
   a. Kneel next to the victim at the level of his or her thighs.
   b. Place the heel of one hand against the victim's abdomen. Your hand should be in the middle of the abdomen between the lower end of the sternum and the navel.
   c. Place your other hand on top of the hand already on the victim's abdomen (Fig. 22-17).
   d. Press inward and upward to give an abdominal thrust.
   e. Give 6 to 10 abdominal thrusts.
9. Check for a foreign object with the finger sweep maneuver.
   a. Open the victim's mouth using the tongue-jaw lift maneuver (Fig. 22-18):
      1. Grasp the victim's tongue and lower jaw with your thumb and fingers.
      2. Lift the lower jaw upward.
   b. Insert your other index finger into the victim's mouth along the side of the cheek and deep into the throat. Your finger should be at the base of the victim's tongue.
   c. Form a hook with your index finger.
   d. Try to dislodge and remove the foreign object. Do not push the object deeper into the throat.
   e. Grasp the foreign object if it is within reach. Remove the object.
10. Open the airway with the head-tilt/chin-lift method.
11. Give one ventilation.
12. Repeat steps 8 through 11 as long as necessary.

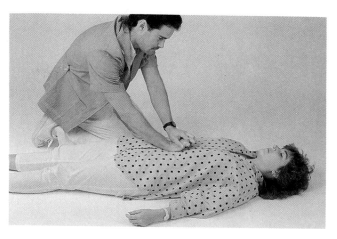

Fig. 22-17 Abdominal thrusts with the victim lying down. (From Sorrentino, S.A.: Mosby's textbook for nursing assistants, ed. 2, St. Louis, 1987, The C.V. Mosby Co.)

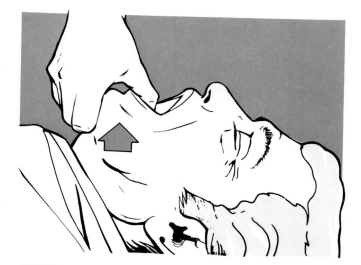

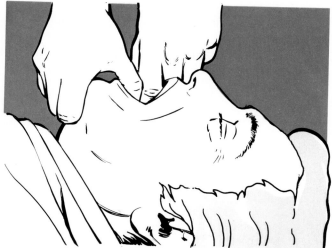

Fig. 22-18 Tongue-jaw lift maneuver. **A,** The victim's tongue is grasped and the jaw lifted forward with one hand. **B,** The index finger of the other hand is used to check for a foreign object. (From Sorrentino, S.A.: Mosby's textbook for nursing assistants, ed. 2, St. Louis, 1987, The C.V. Mosby Co.)

The Heimlich maneuver is not effective for obese persons and pregnant women. Chest thrusts are used if these people have obstructed airways. To do chest thrusts:
1. When the victim is sitting or standing (Fig. 22-19):
   a. Stand behind the victim.
   b. Place your arms under the victim's underarms. Wrap your arms around the victim's chest.
   c. Make a fist. Place the thumb side of the fist on the middle of the sternum.
   d. Grasp the fist with your other hand.
   e. Give backward chest thrusts until the object is expelled or the victim becomes unconscious.

Fig. 22-19 Chest thrusts with the victim standing.

2. When the victim is lying down or unconscious:
   a. Place the victim in the supine position.
   b. Kneel next to the victim.
   c. Position your hands as for chest compression.
   d. Give chest thrusts until the object is expelled or the victim becomes unconscious.

Procedure: Relieving an obstructed airway—the conscious child

1. Ask the child if he or she is choking. Ask "Are you choking?"
2. See if the child can cough or speak.
3. Do the Heimlich maneuver if the child is choking:
   a. Stand behind the child.
   b. Wrap your arms around the child's waist.
   c. Make a fist with one hand. Place the thumb side of the fist against the child's abdomen. Your fist should be in the middle above the child's navel and below the end of the sternum.
   d. Give a quick, inward and upward thrust.
   e. Repeat the abdominal thrusts until the object is expelled or the child loses consciousness.
4. Lie the child down if he or she loses consciousness. (See *Relieving an obstructed airway—the unconscious child*.)

Procedure: Relieving an obstructed airway—the unconscious child

1. Check for unresponsiveness.
2. Call for help.
3. Turn the child as a unit (logroll) if he or she is face down. Be sure to support the head and neck. Position the child on a hard, flat surface.
4. Open the airway with the head-tilt/chin-lift maneuver.
5. Check for breathlessness.
6. Give one ventilation. Reposition the child's head if you could not ventilate the child. Give another ventilation.
7. Have your helper activate the EMS system.
8. Perform the Heimlich maneuver if you cannot ventilate the child (Fig. 22-20).
   a. Kneel at the feet if the child is on the floor. Stand at the feet if the child is on a table.
   b. Place the heel of one hand against the child's abdomen. Your hand should be in the middle and slightly above the navel and below the end of the sternum.
   c. Place your other hand directly on top of the fist on the child's abdomen.
   d. Give a quick, upward thrust.
   e. Give 6 to 10 abdominal thrusts.
9. Check for a foreign object.
   a. Open the mouth using the tongue-jaw lift maneuver.

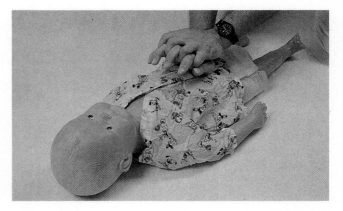

Fig. 22-20 Heimlich maneuver on an unconscious child. (From Sorrentino, S.A.: Mosby's textbook for nursing assistants, ed. 2, St. Louis, 1987, The C.V. Mosby Co.)

b. Look into the child's mouth. Use the finger sweep maneuver *only* if you see a foreign object.

c. Remove the foreign object if it is seen.

10. Open the airway with the head-tilt/chin-lift maneuver.

11. Give one ventilation.

12. Repeat steps 8–11 as long as necessary.

Procedure: Relieving an obstructed airway—the conscious infant

1. See if the infant has an airway obstruction.

2. Hold the infant face down over your forearm or thigh (Fig. 22-21) with one hand.

The infant's head should be lower than the trunk.

3. Give 4 back blows with the heel of one hand. Give the blows between the shoulder blades (Fig. 22-22).

4. Support the infant's back with your free hand. Your other hand should support the infant's neck, jaw, and chest. Turn the infant.

5. Place the infant over your thigh with his or her head lower than the trunk (Fig. 22-23).

6. Give chest thrusts:

a. Locate hand position as for chest compressions.

b. Compress the chest 4 times as for chest compressions but at a slower rate (3 to 5 seconds).

7. Repeat back blows and chest thrusts until the object is expelled or the infant loses consciousness.

Fig. 22-21 Infant is held face down and supported with one hand. The rescuer supports her arm on her thigh. (From Sorrentino, S.A.: Mosby's textbook for nursing assistants, ed. 2, St. Louis, 1987, The C.V. Mosby Co.)

Fig. 22-22 Back blows are given with the heel of one hand. The blows are given between the infant's shoulder blades. (From Sorrentino, S.A.: Mosby's textbook for nursing assistants, ed. 2, St. Louis, 1987, The C.V. Mosby Co.)

Fig. 22-23 The infant is positioned on the rescuer's thigh for chest thrusts. Hand position for chest thrusts in the infant is the same as for chest compressions. (From Sorrentino, S.A.: Mosby's textbook for nursing assistants, ed. 2, St. Louis, 1987, The C.V. Mosby Co.)

Procedure: Relieving an obstructed airway—the unconscious infant

1. Check for unresponsiveness.
2. Call for help.
3. Turn the infant as a unit. Place the infant on a hard, flat surface.
4. Open the airway using the head-tilt/chin-lift maneuver. The infant's head should be in a "sniffing" position. Do not hyperextend the head.
5. Check for breathlessness.
6. Give one ventilation. Reposition the infant's head if you could not ventilate. Give another ventilation.
7. Have your helper activate the EMS system.
8. Give 4 back blows (see *Relieving an obstructed airway—the conscious infant*, page 381).
9. Give 4 chest thrusts (see *Relieving an obstructed airway—the conscious infant*).
10. Check for a foreign body (see *Relieving an obstructed airway—the conscious infant*).
11. Open the airway using the head-tilt/chin-lift maneuver.
12. Given one ventilation.
13. Repeat steps 8–12 as long as necessary.

Hemorrhage

Life and body functions require an adequate blood supply. If a blood vessel is torn or cut, bleeding and blood loss occur. The larger the vessel, the greater the bleeding and blood loss. *Hemorrhage* is the excessive loss of blood from a blood vessel. The person can die if the bleeding does not stop.

Hemorrhage can be internal or external. Internal hemorrhage cannot be seen. Bleeding occurs inside the body. Pain, shock, vomiting blood, coughing up blood, and loss of consciousness are signs of internal hemorrhage. There is little you can do for internal bleeding. Keep the client warm, flat, and quiet until medical help arrives. Do not give fluids.

External bleeding can usually be seen. However, it may be hidden by clothing. Hemorrhage may be from an injured artery or vein. Arterial bleeding is bright red in color and occurs in spurts. There is a steady flow of blood when bleeding is from a vein. Basic emergency care for external hemorrhage involves stopping the bleeding. First apply direct pressure to the bleeding site. If that does not control bleeding, apply pressure to the artery above the bleeding site. To control external hemorrhage:

1. Place a sterile dressing directly over the wound. Use any clean material (handkerchief, towel, cloth, or sanitary napkin) if you do not have a sterile dressing.
2. Apply pressure with your hand directly over the bleeding site (Fig. 22-24). Do not release the pressure until the bleeding is controlled.
3. If direct pressure does not control bleeding, apply pressure over the artery above the bleeding site (Fig. 22-25). Use your first three fingers. For example, if there is bleeding from the lower arm, apply pressure over the brachial artery. The brachial artery supplies blood to the lower arm.

Shock

Shock results when tissues and organs do not get enough blood. Blood loss, heart disease, and severe infection can cause shock. Signs and symptoms of shock include:

- Low or falling blood pressure
- A rapid, weak pulse
- Cold, moist, and pale skin
- Rapid respirations
- Thirst
- Restlessness
- Confusion and loss of consciousness as shock worsens

Shock is possible in any person who is acutely ill or injured. To prevent and treat shock:

1. Keep the victim lying down.

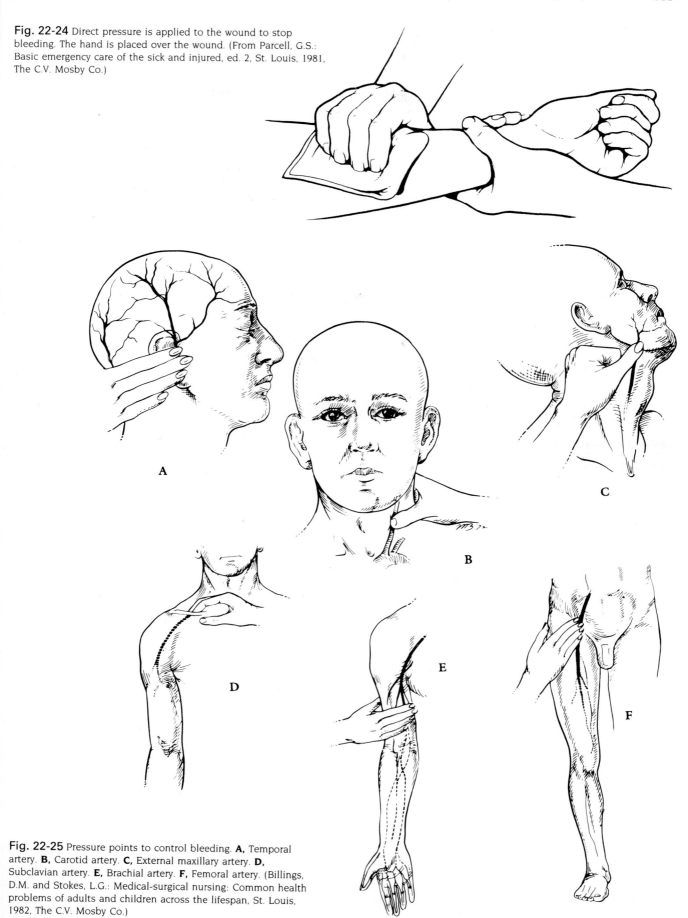

Fig. 22-24 Direct pressure is applied to the wound to stop bleeding. The hand is placed over the wound. (From Parcell, G.S.: Basic emergency care of the sick and injured, ed. 2, St. Louis, 1981, The C.V. Mosby Co.)

Fig. 22-25 Pressure points to control bleeding. **A,** Temporal artery. **B,** Carotid artery. **C,** External maxillary artery. **D,** Subclavian artery. **E,** Brachial artery. **F,** Femoral artery. (Billings, D.M. and Stokes, L.G.: Medical-surgical nursing: Common health problems of adults and children across the lifespan, St. Louis, 1982, The C.V. Mosby Co.)

2. Control hemorrhage.
3. Keep the victim warm. Place a blanket over and under the victim if possible.
4. Reassure the victim.
5. Call for help. Activate the EMS system.

Seizures

Seizures, or convulsions, are violent and sudden contractions or tremors of muscles. They are due to a brain abnormality. The abnormality may be caused by head injury during birth, high fever, brain tumors, poisoning, and central nervous system infections. Head injuries and lack of blood flow to the brain can also cause seizures. Nonhealth care people have used the terms "attack" and "fits" in referring to seizures. Do not use these terms. They tend to create unpleasant and disturbing meanings.

There are grand mal and petit mal seizures. The *grand mal seizure* is the most common. There is contraction of all muscles at once followed by jerking body movements. The seizure begins with a sharp cry. Loss of consciousness follows. Then muscle contractions begin. The legs become stiff and straight, and the arms flex. The jaws and teeth are clenched. The tongue may be caught between the teeth. The eyes roll back and the client may stop breathing. Then jerking movements and breathing begin. Urinary and anal incontinence may occur in this phase. After the seizure, the client usually falls into a deep sleep. Upon awakening, confusion and headache may be experienced.

The *petit mal seizures* usually lasts 10 to 20 seconds. Sudden loss of consciousness, twitching of arm and face muscles, and flickering of the eyelids occur. Petit mal seizures occur most frequently in children and adolescents.

The client must be protected from injury during a seizure. In order to protect the client, perform the following measures:
1. Lower the client to the floor.
2. Place a folded bath blanket or towel under the client's head. Or cradle the client's head in your lap or on a pillow (Fig. 22-26). This prevents the client's head from striking the floor.
3. Turn the head to one side.
4. Loosen tight clothing.
5. Move furniture and equipment away from the client. The client may strike them during the uncontrolled body movements.
6. Do not restrain the client's body movements during the seizure.
7. Insert a padded tongue blade between the teeth if they are not clenched (Fig. 22-27). If the teeth are

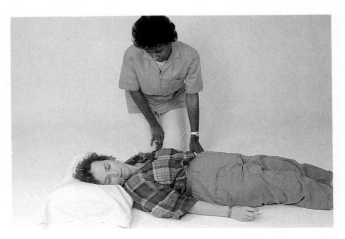

Fig. 22-26 Client's head is protected during a seizure. (From Sorrentino, S.A.: Mosby's textbook for nursing assistants, ed. 2, St. Louis, 1987, The C.V. Mosby Co.)

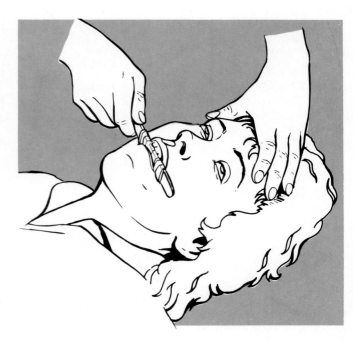

Fig. 22-27 Padded tongue blade is inserted between the client's teeth. (From Sorrentino, S.A.: Mosby's textbook for nursing assistants, ed. 2, St. Louis, 1987, The C.V. Mosby Co.)

clenched, do not try to insert the tongue blade or pry open the teeth. Injury to the teeth and mouth can occur. Use a folded handkerchief or washcloth if you do not have a padded tongue blade.
8. Position the client on one side if possible.
9. Call for help. Do not leave the client during the seizure.

Poisoning

A *poison* is a substance that can harm body tissue or cause death. Certain chemicals, plants, gases, insect bites, snake bites, and animal bites are poisonous. A poison can affect one or more body systems. Signs and symptoms depend on the poison, its amount, and how it enters the body.

Poisoning can be accidental or intentional (on purpose). Accidental poisonings are common in children. They may accidentally ingest detergents, toilet bowl cleaners, bleach, plants, aspirins, and other drugs. Adults and teenagers may take poisons or drug overdoses on purpose. These are suicide attempts.

Indications of poisoning include:

- Smelling strong liquids or chemicals
- Spilled liquids near the victim
- An open or empty medication container near victim
- Plant leaves near a child or in the child's mouth

Quick action is important. Do the following if you suspect poisoning:

1. Activate the EMS system.
2. Maintain an open airway. Give CPR if needed.
3. Call the operator. Ask the operator to call the Poison Control Center. Do not hang up.
4. Tell the Poison Control Center what happened. Answer their questions as thoroughly as possible.
5. Follow instructions given by the Poison Control Center.
6. Save any vomitus and the suspected poison. They are taken to the hospital with the victim.
7. Call your supervisor. Report what has happened, the victim's condition, and your actions.

Burns

Flames, steam, chemicals, electricity, and the sun can all cause burns. Small or large body areas can be burned. Burns can injure the first layer of the skin (epidermis). Or they can be as deep as the bone. Burns can cause serious body damage and threaten life.

You must act quickly. Do the following:

1. Put out the flames. Use a fire extinguisher, water, or smother the flames with a blanket.
2. Pour cool water over the burned area. This cools the burn and stops the burning process. Do not use ice or dry ice.
3. Activate the EMS system.
4. Maintain an open airway. Give CPR if necessary.
5. Remove clothing from the burned area. Do not remove clothing that sticks to the burned area.
6. Keep the burned area wet. Cover the area with a sterile dressing or clean sheet. Keep covering wet.
7. Covered unburned areas with a blanket.
8. Do not apply creams, lotions, butter, salves, or oils to the burned area.
9. Do not give the victim food or fluids.

Fainting

Fainting is the sudden loss of consciousness due to an inadequate blood supply to the brain. Hunger, fatigue, fear, and pain are common causes. Some people faint at the sight of blood or injury. Fainting can also be caused by standing in one place for a long time or being in a warm, crowded room. Dizziness, perspiration, and blackness before the eyes may be experienced before fainting. The person looks pale. The pulse is weak. Respirations are shallow if consciousness is lost. Emergency care for fainting includes the following:

1. Have the person sit or lie down before fainting occurs.
   a. If sitting—have the person bend forward and place his or her head between the knees (Fig. 22-28).
   b. If lying down—elevate the person's legs.
2. Loosen tight clothing.
3. Keep the person lying down if fainting has occurred.
4. Do not let the person get up until symptoms are gone for about 5 minutes.
5. Help the person to a sitting position after recovery from fainting. Observe the person for symptoms of fainting.

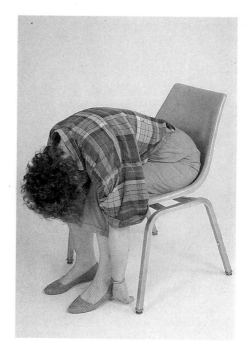

Fig. 22-28 Person bends forward and places head between the knees to prevent fainting. (From Sorrentino, S.A.: Mosby's textbook for nursing assistants, ed. 2, St. Louis, 1987, The C.V. Mosby Co.)

Stroke

Stroke (cerebrovascular accident) is described in Chapter 21. A stroke occurs when the brain is suddenly deprived of blood. Usually a part of the brain is affected. A stroke may be caused by a thrombus, an embolus, or cerebral hemorrhage. Cerebral hemorrhage is due to the rupture of a blood vessel in the brain.

The signs of stroke vary. They depend on the size and location of brain injury. Loss of consciousness or semiconsciousness, rapid pulse, labored breathing, elevated blood pressure, vomiting, and paralysis on one side (hemiplegia) are signs of stroke. The person may have aphasia (the inability to speak). Convulsions may occur.

Emergency care includes the following:
1. Turn the client onto the affected side. The affected side is limp and the cheek appears puffy.
2. Elevate the head without flexing the neck.
3. Loosen tight clothing.
4. Keep the client quiet and warm.
5. Reassure the client.
6. Summon medical help.

Vomiting

Vomiting is the act of expelling stomach contents through the mouth. While not a true emergency, vomiting is a sign of illness or injury. Vomiting can be life-threatening. The vomitus (the material vomited) can be aspirated and obstruct the airway. Shock can also occur if large amounts of blood are vomited.

The following measures will help the vomiting client:
1. Turn the client's head well to one side. This prevents aspiration.
2. Place a basin under the client's chin.
3. Take the vomitus to the bathroom.
4. Have the client use mouthwash and perform oral hygiene. This helps eliminate the taste of vomitus.
5. Eliminate odors.
6. Change linens as necessary.

Observe vomitus for color, odor, and undigested food. Vomitus that looks like coffee grounds has digested blood and indicates bleeding. Measure and report the amount of vomitus to your supervisor. Also record it on the I&O sheet. A specimen is sometimes saved for laboratory study.

Summary

Emergency situations are sudden and unexpected. They are frightening to the victim and to others nearby. Quick action can save the victim's life and prevent injuries from becoming worse. Emergencies can occur anywhere. You may be at the client's side when an emergency occurs. Staying calm, knowing what to do, and calling for help benefit the client physically and psychologically.

You are advised to take a basic life support course and a first aid course. The general rules of emergency care apply to any emergency situation. You may not know how to treat a specific injury. However, you can help the victim by following the general rules of emergency care.

Study Questions

1. You are assigned to care for the Gray family. There are three children: a 3-year-old, a 5-year-old, and a 9-year-old. The mother is paralyzed from the waist down. You find an open bottle of bleach near the 3-year-old. The child is having difficulty breathing. Explain what you should do. Can other family members help? If yes, what can they do to help?

2. Mr. Johnson is 55 years old. He has heart disease. He suddenly falls to the floor. He has no pulse and he is not breathing. Explain what you should do.

3. You have activated the EMS system because a client has been severely burned. Describe what you will tell the operator.

Circle the *best* answer.

4. The goals of first aid are to
   a. Call for help and keep the victim warm
   b. Prevent death and prevent injuries from becoming worse
   c. Stay calm and perform emergency measures
   d. Reassure the victim and keep bystanders away

5. When giving first aid you should
   a. Be aware of your own limitations
   b. Move the victim
   c. Give the victim fluids
   d. Perform any necessary emergency measures

6. Which is *not* a sign of cardiac arrest?
   a. No pulse
   b. No breathing
   c. A sudden drop in blood pressure
   d. Unconsciousness

7. You are to give mouth-to-mouth resuscitation to an adult. You should do all of the following *except*
   a. Pinch the victim's nostrils shut
   b. Place your mouth tightly over the victim's mouth
   c. Blow air into the victim's mouth as you exhale
   d. Cover the victim's nose with your mouth

8. Chest compressions are to be done on an adult. The chest should be compressed
   a. ½ to 1 inch with the index and middle fingers
   b. 1 to 1½ inches with the heel of one hand
   c. 1½ to 2 inches with two hands
   d. With one hand in the middle of the sternum

9. Breathlessness is determined by all of the following *except*
   a. Looking to see if the chest rises and falls
   b. Counting respirations for 30 seconds
   c. Listening for the escape of air
   d. Feeling for the flow of air

10. Which artery is used to check a pulse during adult CPR?
    a. The apical pulse
    b. The brachial pulse
    c. The carotid pulse
    d. The dorsalis pedis pulse

11. How many ventilations are given at the beginning of CPR?
    a. One
    b. Two
    c. Three
    d. Four

12. You are doing CPR alone. Which statement is *false*?
    a. Give 2 ventilations after every 15 compressions
    b. Check for a pulse after one minute
    c. Give 1 ventilation after every fifth compression
    d. Count out loud

13. Cardiac compressions are given to an infant at a rate of
    a. 60 per minute
    b. 75 per minute
    c. 80 per minute
    d. 100 per minute

14. The most common cause of obstructed airway in adults is
    a. A loose denture
    b. Meat
    c. Marbles
    d. Candy

15. If airway obstruction occurs the victim will usually
    a. Clutch at the throat
    b. Be able to speak, cough, and breathe
    c. Be calm
    d. Have a seizure

16. The Heimlich maneuver is used to relieve an obstructed airway. Which statement is *false*?
    a. The victim can be standing, sitting, or lying down.
    b. A fist is made with one hand.
    c. The thrusts are given inward and upward at the lower end of the sternum.
    d. The hands are positioned in the middle between the waist and lower end of the sternum.

17. A victim has an obstructed airway. You should use poking motions to sweep the victim's mouth.
    a. True
    b. False

18. Arterial bleeding
    a. Cannot be seen
    b. Occurs in spurts
    c. Is dark red
    d. Oozes from the wound

19. A victim is hemorrhaging from the left forearm. Your first action should be to
    a. Lower the body part
    b. Apply pressure to the brachial artery
    c. Apply direct pressure to the wound
    d. Cover the victim

20. The signs of shock are
    a. Rising blood pressure, rapid pulse, and slow respirations
    b. Rapid pulse, rapid respirations, and warm skin
    c. Falling blood pressure; rapid pulse and respirations; and skin that is cold, moist, and pale
    d. Falling blood pressure; slow pulse and respirations; thirst; restlessness; and warm, flushed skin

21. A victim is in shock. You should
    a. Give mouth-to-mouth resuscitation
    b. Keep the victim lying down
    c. Remove the victim's clothing
    d. Place the victim in Trendelenburg position

22. The statements relate to grand mal seizures. Which is *false*?
    a. There is contraction of all muscles at once.
    b. The person may stop breathing.
    c. The seizure usually lasts about 10 to 20 seconds.
    d. There is loss of consciousness during the seizure.

23. The client's teeth are clenched during a grand mal seizure. You should
    a. Restrain the person's body movements
    b. Open the airway
    c. Protect the person from injury
    d. Turn the client to the prone position

24. You suspect poisoning. You should
    a. Make the client vomit
    b. Call for help
    c. Wait to see if symptoms develop
    d. Give the client water or milk

25. A client has just been burned. She spilled hot coffee on her hand. You should
    a. Pour cool water on the burn
    b. Apply butter or lotion to the area
    c. Put an ice bag on the area
    d. Open her airway

26. A person is about to faint. Which statement is *false*?
    a. Take the person outside for some fresh air.
    b. Have the person sit or lie down.
    c. Loosen tight clothing.
    d. Elevate the legs if the person is lying down.

27. Emergency care of the stroke victim includes all of the following *except*
    a. Positioning the client on the affected side
    b. Giving the person sips of water
    c. Loosening tight clothing
    d. Keeping the person quiet and warm

28. Vomiting is dangerous because of the danger of
    a. Aspiration
    b. Cardiac arrest
    c. Fluid loss
    d. Stroke

Answers

4. b	11. b	17. b	23. c
5. a	12. c	18. b	24. b
6. c	13. d	19. c	25. a
7. d	14. b	20. c	26. a
8. c	15. a	21. b	27. b
9. b	16. c	22. c	28. a
10. c			

23 The Dying Client

Chapter Highlights	What you will learn to do
Terminal illness	■ Describe terminal illness, hospice care, living wills, and "do not resuscitate" orders
Attitudes about death	■ Identify two psychological forces that influence living and dying
The stages of dying	■ Explain how religion influences attitudes about death
The client's needs	■ Describe the beliefs about death held by the different age groups
The client's family	■ Describe the five stages of dying
Signs of death	■ Explain how you can meet the dying client's psychological, social, spiritual, and physical needs
When a person dies	■ Describe the needs of the family during the dying process
	■ Identify the signs of approaching death and the signs of death
	■ Give postmortem care

Autopsy The examination of the body after death

Coroner A public official responsible for investigating the cause of death

Living will A statement expressing a person's desire not to have life prolonged by artificial means or heroic measures

Postmortem After (post) death (mortem)

Reincarnation The belief that the spirit or soul is reborn in another human body or in another form of life

Rigor mortis The stiffness or rigidity (rigor) of skeletal muscles that occurs after death (mortis)

Terminal illness An illness or injury from which the client is not expected to recover

Dying clients are usually cared for in hospitals and nursing homes. However, more and more people are choosing to die at home. Health care workers see death more often than other people. However, many health workers are unsure of their feelings about death. They are uncomfortable with dying clients and the subject of death. Dying clients represent failure to cure and helplessness. They also remind health care workers that they will die someday.

You must examine your own feelings about death. Your attitudes influence the care you give. You must be able to help meet the client's physical, psychological, social, and spiritual needs.

Terminal Illness

Some illnesses and diseases have no cure. Some injuries are so serious that the body cannot function. Recovery is not expected in these cases. The disease or injury will end in death. A *terminal illness* is one from which the client is not expected to recover.

Doctors cannot accurately predict when a client will die. A person may be given days, weeks, months, or years to live. No prediction is foolproof. Some clients have lived for years after being given a short time to live. Others have died much earlier than expected.

Research and modern technology are expected to produce new cures. However, two very strong psychological forces influence living and dying. They are hope and the will to live. People have died sooner than expected when they have given up hope or lost the will to live.

Hospice Care

Many clients seek hospice care when they are dying (see Chapter 1). Hospices are concerned with the physical, emotional, social, and spiritual needs of dying clients and their families. Hospices do not attempt cures or life-saving procedures. They focus on pain relief and comfort measures. The goal of hospice care is to improve the quality of life for the dying client.

A hospice may be part of a hospital or nursing home or a separate facility. Many hospices offer home care. Hospice services also include follow-up care and support groups for survivors.

Living Wills

Some terminally ill clients have living wills. They state the client's wishes about care if recovery is not expected. A *living will* is a statement expressing a client's desire not to have life prolonged by artificial means or heroic measures. In other words, the client does not want to be kept alive by machines. "Heroic measures" commonly mean CPR. Therefore, the client does not want CPR done.

Some states do not consider living wills to be legal documents. In other words, they have no legal basis. A doctor does not have to follow the client's wishes. However, attitudes about living wills are changing. Some states have laws which recognize living wills. Many doctors, health workers, and agencies do respect the client's wishes. Your supervisor will tell you if a client has a living will.

"Do Not Resuscitate" Orders

When death is expected, the doctor may give a "do not resuscitate" order. This means that CPR (see Chapter 22) will not be done. Nor will the EMS system be activated. The order is usually given when nothing can be done to save, cure, or prolong the person's life. The doctor, client, and family agree not to resuscitate.

Your supervisor will tell you if there is a "do not resuscitate" (DNR) order. Otherwise, you must activate the EMS system and give basic life support when signs of death are present.

Attitudes about Death

Experience, culture, religion, and age influence a person's attitude about death. Many people fear death. Others refuse to believe they will die. Some look forward to and accept death. Attitudes and beliefs about death often change as a person grows older.

People tend to deny that death happens to everyone. Dying people are usually cared for in hospitals and nursing homes. Most of these clients are elderly. Older family members usually do not live with their children. Therefore, many adults and children have not had contact with a dying person. Nor have they watched someone die. The whole process of dying and death seems mysterious and frightening.

Attitudes and practices were different 50 years ago. Family members cared for the dying at home. The family was at the bedside to comfort the dying person and each other. They cared for the body after death and prepared the body for burial. The casket was placed in the parlor (living room). Family and friends gathered to view the body and mourn. Death was viewed as a natural part of life.

Religious beliefs influence attitudes about death. Some believe that there is life after death. This life is free of suffering and hardship. They also believe there will be reunion with family and loved ones. Many people believe there is punishment and suffering for sins and misdeeds in the afterlife. Others do not believe in the afterlife. They believe that death is the end of life. There are also religious beliefs about the form of the human body after death. Some believe the body keeps its physical form. Others believe that only the spirit or soul is present in the afterlife. *Reincarnation* is another belief. This is the belief that the spirit or soul is reborn into another human body or into another form of life. Many people strengthen their religious beliefs when they are dying. Religion is often a source of comfort for the dying client and the family.

Ideas about death change as people grow older. Infants and toddlers have no concept of death. Children aged 3 to 5 become curious about death. They recognize the death of family members, pets, birds, or bugs. However, they think death is temporary. Children often blame themselves when someone or something dies. They think they are being punished for being bad. Children often ask questions about death. Adults often give answers that cause fear and confusion. Children who are told, "He is sleeping," may be afraid to go to sleep.

Between the ages of 5 or 7, death is seen as final. These children think death happens to other people. They also think death can be avoided. Death is associated with punishment and mutilation of the body. They may also associate death with witches, ghosts, goblins, and monsters. These ideas come from fairy tales, cartoons, movies, and television.

Adults have more fears about death than children. They fear pain, suffering, dying alone, invasion of privacy, and loneliness. They also fear being separated from family and loved ones. They worry about who will care for and support loved ones left behind. Adults often resent death.

The elderly usually have fewer fears about death than younger adults. They are more accepting of the fact that death will occur. Friends and family members may have died. Some welcome death as freedom from pain, suffering, and disability. Like younger adults, the elderly are often afraid of dying alone.

The Stages of Dying

Dr. Elisabeth Kubler-Ross has identified five stages of dying. They are denial, anger, bargaining, depression, and acceptance (Fig. 23-1). During *denial* people refuse to believe they are dying. "No, not me" is a common response. The client believes a mistake has been made. The client cannot deal with any problem or decision about the illness or injury. This stage can last for a few hours, days, or much longer. Some people remain in the stage of denial until death.

Anger is the second stage. The person thinks, "Why me?" People behave with anger and rage. They resent those who are alive and healthy. Family, friends, and the health team are usually the target of their anger. They blame others. Fault is found with those who are loved and needed the most. It may be hard to deal with clients during this stage. Remember that anger is normal and healthy. Do not take the client's anger personally. You must control any urge to attack back or avoid the client.

The third stage is *bargaining*. The anger has passed. The client now says, "Yes, me, but . . ." Promises are made to God for more time. The client may want to see a child marry, see a grandchild, or have one more Christmas. Usually more promises are made as the client asks for "just one more" request. This stage

STAGES OF DYING

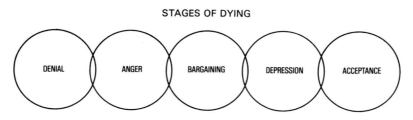

Fig. 23-1 The five stages of dying.

may not be obvious to you. Bargaining is usually done privately and on a spiritual level.

Depression is the fourth stage. The client thinks, "Yes, me." The client is very sad. There is mourning over past losses and the future loss of life. The person may cry or say little. Sometimes a client talks about people and things that will be left behind.

The fifth and final stage of dying is *acceptance* of death. The client has peace and calm. The client has said what needs to be said and has taken care of unfinished business. The person is ready to accept death. A person may be in this stage for many months or years. Acceptance does not mean that death is near.

Dying clients do not always go through all five stages. A person may stay at a certain stage. Or a person may move back and forth between stages. For example, a person who has reached acceptance may move back to bargaining. Then the client may move forward again to acceptance.

The Client's Needs

Dying clients continue to have physical, psychological, social, and spiritual needs. They may want family and friends present. Some want to talk about their fears, worries, and anxieties of dying. Others want to be alone.

Listening and touch are very important when communicating with the dying client. The client is the one who needs to talk and share feelings, worries, and concerns. Just being there and listening are important. Do not worry about saying the wrong thing. Do not feel that you must have the right words to comfort and cheer the person. Nothing really needs to be said. Being with the client is what counts. Touch can show caring and concern when words cannot. Sometimes clients do not want to talk but need to have you nearby. Do not feel that you need to talk. Silence and touch are powerful ways to communicate (Fig. 23-2).

Spiritual needs cannot be overlooked. The person may wish to see a priest, rabbi, or minister. The client may also want to participate in religious practices (Fig. 23-3). Be sure to allow privacy during spiritual moments. Often the clergyman will be with the client and family as death nears. Praying or special ceremonies may be done.

Dying may take a few minutes, hours, days, or weeks. There is a general slowing of body processes and weakness. Changes in the level of consciousness occur. As the client becomes weaker, more care will be needed. The client may totally depend on others for basic needs. You must make every effort to promote physical and psychological comfort. The person should be allowed to die in peace and with dignity.

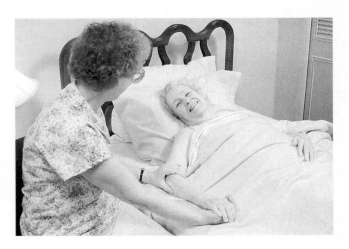

Fig. 23-2 Aide sits silently at the client's side. Touch is used to communicate caring.

Fig. 23-3 Client has religious medals, pictures, and statues within view.

VISION, HEARING, AND SPEECH

Vision becomes blurred and gradually fails. The client naturally turns toward light. A dark room may frighten the client. The eyes may stay half open. Secretions may collect in the corners of the eyes. Because of failing vision you must explain what you are doing to the client. The room should be well lit. However, avoid bright lights and glares. Good eye care is essential (see Chapter 14). If the eyes tend to stay open, an ointment may be ordered. Then the eyes are covered with moistened pads to protect them from injury.

Speech becomes difficult. The client may be very hard to understand or unable to speak. You need to anticipate the client's needs. Do not ask a question that requires a long answer. Ask questions that can be answered with a "yes" or "no." However, keep them to a minimum. Though talking may be hard for the client, you must still talk to the individual.

Hearing is one of the last functions to be lost.

Many people can hear until the moment of death. Even if unconscious, the person may be able to hear. Always assume that dying or unconscious clients can hear. You should speak in a normal voice. Be sure to explain what you are doing and offer words of comfort. Avoid topics that could upset the client.

MOUTH, NOSE, AND SKIN

Oral hygiene is very important for comfort. Routine mouth care is usually adequate if the client can eat and drink. Frequent oral hygiene is necessary:

- As death approaches
- When the client has difficulty taking oral fluids
- If mucus collects in the mouth
- If the client cannot swallow

Crusting and irritation of the nostrils can occur. Common causes are increased nasal secretions, an oxygen cannula, and a nasogastric tube. You must clean the nose carefully.

Circulation fails and body temperature rises as death approaches. The skin feels cool and appears pale. The client perspires more. Good skin care and prevention of decubiti are necessary. Linens, gowns, or pajamas should be changed as often as needed because of perspiration. Only light bed coverings may be needed. Blankets can make the person feel warm and cause restlessness.

ELIMINATION

Dying clients may have urinary and anal incontinence. The bed should be protected (see Chapter 12). Perineal care is important. Some clients are constipated or retain urine. Doctors may order enemas. Urinary catheters may be ordered for urinary retention or incontinence. If so, catheter care is necessary.

COMFORT AND POSITIONING

Promoting the client's comfort is important. Good skin care, personal hygiene, back massages, and oral hygiene help to increase comfort. Some clients have severe pain. These clients need strong pain medications. They are given by nurses or the family.

Frequent position changes and good body alignment promote comfort. Use supportive devices as instructed to maintain alignment. Be careful when turning the client. Turn the client slowly and gently. Clients with breathing problems are usually more comfortable in semi-Fowler's position.

The Client's Family

The family is going through a difficult time. It may be very hard to comfort them. You can show your concern by being available, using touch, and being kind and courteous.

The family will usually spend a lot of time with their loved one. You must respect their right to privacy.

They need as much time together as possible. However, you must not neglect care. You should let family members help give care if they wish to do so. If they do not want to help, you can suggest that they take a break. They can use the time to relax, do errands, or work.

The family may be very tired, sad, and tearful. Watching a loved one die is very painful. So is dealing with the eventual loss of that person. The family needs support and understanding. They must also be treated with courtesy and respect. A clergyman's visit may be comforting to them.

Signs of Death

You need to know the signs of approaching death. They may occur rapidly or gradually.

1. Movement, muscle tone, and sensation are lost. This usually begins in the feet and legs. In time it spreads to the rest of the body. When mouth muscles relax, the jaw drops and the mouth may stay open. There is often a peaceful facial expression.
2. Peristalsis and other gastrointestinal functions slow down. There may be abdominal distention, impaction, anal incontinence, nausea, and vomiting.
3. Circulation fails and body temperature rises. The client feels cool or cold, appears pale, and perspires heavily. The pulse is fast, weak, and irregular. Blood pressure begins to fall.
4. The respiratory system fails. Cheyne-Stokes, slow, or rapid and shallow respirations may be observed. Mucus accumulates in the respiratory tract. This causes the "death rattle" to be heard.
5. Pain decreases as the client loses consciousness. Some people do not lose consciousness until the time of death. The *signs of death* include the absence of a pulse, respirations, and blood pressure. The pupils are fixed and dilated.

When a Person Dies

You may be at the bedside when a client dies. You may be alone or with the family. Or you may find a client dead when you enter the home. You must call your supervisor when a client dies. The supervisor or family will call the doctor and funeral director. If not already present, the clergyman will also be called. Sometimes the coroner is called. A *coroner* is a public official responsible for investigating the cause of death.

The person must be declared dead for legal purposes. This is done by the doctor or coroner. The doctor or coroner may go to the home to declare the person dead. Sometimes the body is taken by ambulance to the hospital emergency room. A doctor declares the client dead at the hospital.

An autopsy may be requested. An *autopsy* is the

examination of the body after death. If requested by the doctor, the family must given written consent. No consent is needed if the autopsy is ordered by the coroner.

Care of the Body After Death

Care of the body after (post) death (mortem) is called *postmortem* care. The purpose is to maintain good appearance and alignment of the body. The body must be positioned in normal alignment before rigor mortis sets in. *Rigor mortis* is the stiffness or rigidity (rigor) of skeletal muscles that occurs after death (mortis). Rigor mortis develops within 2 to 4 hours after death. The family may wish to view the body before it is taken to the morgue or funeral home. The body should appear in a comfortable and normal position for viewing by the family.

Postmortem care is given after the person has been declared dead. If an autopsy is ordered, consult your supervisor. Postmortem care may destroy evidence about the manner or cause of death. Therefore, you may be instructed not to give postmortem care as described here. Some funeral directors prefer to give postmortem care themselves. Your supervisor will tell you what to do in these circumstances.

The right to privacy applies after death as well as during life. So does the right to be treated with dignity and respect.

Procedure: Postmortem care

1. Wash your hands.
2. Collect the following equipment:
   a. Waterproof bed protectors
   b. Washbasin
   c. Bath towels
   d. Washcloth
   e. Tape
   f. Dressings
   g. Disposable gloves
3. Put on the gloves.
4. Make sure the bed is flat.
5. Position the body in the supine position. Make sure the arms and legs are straight. Place a pillow under the head and shoulders (Fig. 23-4).
6. Close the eyes. Gently pull the eyelids over the eyes. Apply a moistened cotton ball gently over the eyelid if the eye will not stay closed.
7. Insert dentures if included in agency policy. If they are not to be replaced, put them in a labeled denture container.
8. Close the mouth. If necessary, place a rolled towel under the chin to keep the mouth closed.
9. Remove all jewelry except for wedding rings. Secure them in place with tape. List the jewelry items that have been removed. Place the jewelry and the list in an envelope for the family.
10. Remove drainage bottles, bags, and containers. Leave tubes and catheters in place if an autopsy is to be performed. Ask your supervisor about removing tubes.
11. Bathe soiled body areas with plain water. Dry the areas thoroughly.
12. Place a disposable bed protector under the buttocks.
13. Remove soiled dressings and replace them with clean ones.
14. Put a clean gown on the body. Make sure the body is positioned as in step 5.
15. Brush and comb the hair if necessary.
16. Cover the body to the shoulders with a sheet if the family is to view the body.
17. Remove all used supplies, equipment, and linens. Straighten the room. Adjust the lighting so it is soft.
18. Allow the family to view the body. Provide for privacy.
19. Remove the gloves and wash your hands.

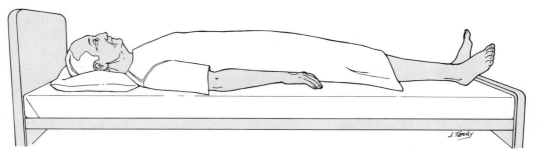

Fig. 23-4 Body in dorsal recumbent position. Arms are straight at the sides. There is a pillow under the head and shoulders. (From Sorrentino, S.A.: Mosby's textbook for nursing assistants, ed. 2, St. Louis, 1987, The C.V. Mosby Co.)

Staying with the Family

The funeral director will take the body to the funeral home. This can be a very hard time for the family. Be sure to stay with them until other family and friends arrive. Remember that being there is important. Use touch and listen.

You may also feel sad. Do not be afraid to show the family your feelings. Sometimes shedding tears or crying with the family is very appropriate. This can be quite comforting to them.

Summary

American society values youth, beauty, and life. The topic of death is usually avoided. When death does occur, medical science is often blamed for failure.

Certain behaviors are common when people do not understand or feel comfortable with death and dying. These behaviors include avoiding the client, nervous conversation, hurried care, and rough handling. You may need to discuss your feelings about death with your supervisor or a member of the clergy. This will help you develop a better attitude about death.

Terminally ill clients should be allowed to die with peace and dignity. Basic needs continue. You must be concerned with the dying person's physical, psychological, social, and spiritual comfort. Visits from the clergy are often appreciated. Dying clients also like when you sit quietly at the bedside and use touch. Remember that silence and touch are ways to communicate with the client and family. The client's right to privacy also needs your attention. This right must be protected both before and after death.

Postmortem care is given after death. Each agency has its own policies and procedures. Postmortem care always includes dignity, respect, and privacy for the body.

Study Questions

1. A client is dying. You are alone with the client. A "DNR" order has been given. Describe how you can meet the client's physical, psychological, social, and spiritual needs. Explain how you will know when the client has died. Describe what you should do after the client has died.

2. A client is dying and the family is present. Explain how you can meet their needs and still allow them privacy.

Circle the *best* answer.

3. Which statement is *true*?
   a. Death from terminal illness is unexpected.
   b. Doctors know the date and time a client will die.
   c. An illness is considered terminal when there is no reasonable hope of recovery.
   d. All severe injuries cause death.

4. Which of the following influence living and dying?
   a. Hope and the will to live
   b. Reincarnation and belief in the afterlife
   c. Denial and anger
   d. Bargaining and depression

5. A "do not resuscitate" order has been given. This means that
   a. The client is in a hospice program
   b. The client has a living will
   c. CPR will not be done
   d. All of the above

6. A client must go to a hospital for hospice care.
   a. True
   b. False

7. Which statement is *false*?
   a. Dying people often prefer home care.
   b. Attitudes about death are influenced by religion.
   c. Infants and toddlers understand death.
   d. Young children often blame themselves when someone dies.

8. Reincarnation is the belief that
   a. There is no afterlife
   b. The spirit or soul is reborn into another human body or another form of life
   c. The body keeps its physical form in the afterlife
   d. Only the spirit or soul is present in the afterlife

9. Adults and the elderly usually fear
   a. Dying alone
   b. Punishment for sins
   c. Reincarnation
   d. The five stages of dying

10. Persons in the stage of denial
    a. Are angry
    b. Make "deals" with God
    c. Are sad and quiet
    d. Refuse to believe they are dying

11. The dying person tries to gain more time in the stage of
    a. Anger
    b. Bargaining
    c. Depression
    d. Acceptance

12. When caring for the dying client, you should
    a. Use touch and listening
    b. Do most of the talking
    c. Keep the room darkened
    d. Speak in a loud voice

13. As death approaches, the last sense to leave the body is
    a. Sight
    b. Taste
    c. Smell
    d. Hearing

14. Care of the dying client includes all of the following *except*
    a. Eye care
    b. Mouth care
    c. Active range-of-motion exercises
    d. Position changes

15. The dying client should be positioned in
    a. The supine position
    b. The Fowler's position
    c. Good body alignment
    d. The dorsal recumbent position

16. Which are *not* signs of approaching death?
    a. Increased body temperature and rapid pulse
    b. Loss of movement and muscle tone
    c. Increased pain and blood pressure
    d. Cheyne-Stokes respirations and the "death rattle"

17. The signs of death are
    a. Convulsions and incontinence
    b. No pulse, respirations, or blood pressure
    c. Loss of consciousness and convulsions
    d. The eyes stay open, there are no muscle movements, and the body is rigid

18. Postmortem care is done
    a. After rigor mortis sets in
    b. After the doctor pronounces the person dead
    c. When the funeral director arrives for the body
    d. After the family has viewed the body

Answers

3. c	7. c	11. b	15. c
4. a	8. b	12. a	16. c
5. c	9. a	13. d	17. b
6. b	10. d	14. c	18. b

A Communicable Diseases

Communicable diseases (also called contagious or infectious diseases) can be transmitted from one person to another. They can be transmitted in the following ways:

- *Direct*—from the infected person
- *Indirect*—from dressings, linens, or surfaces
- *Airborne*—from the client, through sneezing or coughing
- *Vehicle*—ingestion of contaminated food, water, drugs, blood, or fluids
- *Vector*—animals, fleas, ticks

This appendix covers two communicable diseases: AIDS and hepatitis. Tables A-1 and A-2 outline common childhood and adult communicable diseases.

Acquired Immune Deficiency Syndrome (AIDS)

AIDS is caused by a virus. The virus attacks the body's immune system. It affects the person's ability to fight other diseases. There is presently no cure for AIDS and no vaccine to prevent the disease. AIDS eventually causes death.

Those at risk for AIDS are:

- Homosexual or bisexual men with multiple sex partners
- Intravenous drug users
- Recent immigrants from Haiti or Central Africa
- Sex partners who are homosexual, bisexual, intravenous drug users, or immigrants from Haiti or Central Africa
- Children born to infected mothers

AIDS is believed to be transmitted mainly by blood or sexual contact. The AIDS virus has been found in body fluids such as tears and saliva. However, the AIDS virus is usually transmitted by contact with the infected person's semen, blood, and possibly vaginal secretions.

The virus then enters the bloodstream through the rectum, vagina, penis, or mouth. A break in the mucus membrane of the mouth, vagina, or rectum provides a route for the virus to enter the bloodstream. Small breaks in the mucus membrane of the vagina or rectum may occur when the penis, finger, or other objects are inserted. Gum disease can cause breaks in the mucus membrane of the gums.

Intravenous drug users transmit AIDS through the use of contaminated needles and syringes. The virus is carried in the contaminated blood left in the needles or syringes. When needles and syringes are used by others, the contaminated blood enters their bloodsteam.

The Signs and Symptoms of AIDS

Some people carry the AIDS virus without showing signs or symptoms of AIDS. They may not develop the illness for a long time. The signs and symptoms of AIDS include:

- Loss of appetite
- Weight loss greater than 10 pounds without reason
- Fever
- Night sweats
- Diarrhea
- Tiredness, extreme or constant
- Skin rashes
- Swollen glands in the neck, underarms, and groin
- Dry cough
- White spots in the mouth or on the tongue
- Purple blotches or bumps on the skin that look like bruises, but that do not go away

Individuals with AIDS are at risk for other diseases. This is because their bodies do not have the ability to fight disease. The AIDS virus has damaged their immune system, which fights diseases. The person with AIDS is at risk for pneumonia, Kaposi's sarcoma (a type of cancer), and central nervous system damage. The person with central nervous system damage may show memory loss, loss of coordination, paralysis, and mental disorders.

Table A-1 Common Childhood Diseases

DISEASE	SIGNS AND SYMPTOMS	MODE OF TRANSMISSION	INFECTIVE MATERIAL	PROTECTIVE MEASURES
Bacterial Meningitis	Fever, severe headache, stiff neck, sore throat	Direct contact	Oral, nasal secretions	Mask
Chicken Pox (Varicella)	Fever, rash, cutaneous vesicles	Airborne, direct contact with drainage	Respiratory secretions, drainage from vesicles	Mask, good hand-washing
German Measles (Rubella)	Fever, rash	Airborne, direct contact with oral secretions	Oral secretions	Mask
Hepatitis A	Fever, loss of appetite, jaundice, fatigue	Direct contact oral ingestion of virus	Urine, stool	Mask
Measles (Rubeola)	Fever, rash, bronchitis	Airborne, direct contact with secretions	Oral secretions	Gloves, handwashing
Mumps	Fever, swelling of salivary glands (parotid)	Airborne, direct contact	Saliva	Mask
Whooping Cough (Pertussis)	Violent cough at night, whooping sound when cough subsides	Airborne, direct contact	Oral secretions	Mask
Scarlet Fever	Fever, headache, nausea, vomiting	Airborne, direct contact	Oral secretions	Mask

Reprinted and adapted with permission from Heckman, James D.: Emergency Care and the Transportation of the Sick and Injured. ed. 4 Park Ridge, Il., American Academy of Orthopaedic Surgeons, pp 361–362.

Table A-2 Common Adult Diseases

DISEASE	SIGNS AND SYMPTOMS	MODE OF TRANSMISSION	INFECTIVE MATERIAL	PROTECTIVE MEASURES
AIDS	Fever, night sweats, weight loss, cough	Sexual contact, blood, needles	Blood, semen, possibly saliva	Gloves, handwashing
Gonorrhea	Discharge from urethra or vagina, lower abdominal pain, fever	Sexual contact, secretions	Genital-urinary	Gloves if in contact with secretions
Hepatitis B	Fever, fatigue, loss of appetite, nausea, headache	Blood, oral secretions, sexual contact	Blood, saliva, semen	Gloves, handwashing
Non-A, non-B hepatitis	Fever, headache, fatigue, jaundice	Blood	Blood	Gloves, handwashing
Malaria	Cyclic fever, chills, fever	Blood-mosquito vector	Blood	Handwashing
Mononucleosis	Fever, sore throat, fatigue	Mouth-to-mouth kiss	Oral	None
Pneumonia	Fever, cough	Airborne	Sputum	Mask
Syphilis	Genital and cutaneous lesions, nerve degeneration (late)	Sexual contact, blood	Drainage from genital lesions, blood	Gloves, handwashing
Tuberculosis	Fever, night sweats, weight loss, cough	Airborne	Sputum	Mask

Reprinted and adapted with permission from Heckman, James D. Emergency Care and the Transportation of the Sick and Injured. ed. 4 Park Ridge, Il., American Academy of Orthopaedic Surgeons, pp 361–362.

Precautions

Health workers may care for persons with AIDS or for those who are carriers of the AIDS virus. They may have contact with the client's body fluids. Or they may have mouth-to-mouth contact during CPR. Health care workers need to take certain precautions to protect themselves and others from the AIDS virus. The following precautions have been recommended by the Centers for Disease Control in Atlanta, Georgia. *These precautions apply to all client contact.* Remember, you may care for a client who has the AIDS virus but with no symptoms. Or you may care for a client who has not yet been diagnosed as having AIDS.

1. Prevent accidental injury from needles or other sharp objects in contact with the client. These include knives, blades, broken glass, or sharp metal from motor vehicle accidents.
2. Wear latex rubber gloves if you may have contact with a client's body fluids. The body fluids of concern are blood, respiratory secretions, saliva, feces, urine, vomitus, semen, vaginal secretions, menstrual discharge, amniotic fluid, and cerebrospinal fluid.
3. Use a face mask with a one-way valve for any rescue breathing (see Basic Life Support, Chapter 22). Avoid mouth-to-mouth contact.
4. Wash your hands immediately with soap and water if they become contaminated with blood or other body fluids.
5. Wash your hands thoroughly with soap and water before and after client contact.
6. Wear gloves for client care if you have chapped hands, a rash, or skin breaks on your hands.
7. Do not give client care or handle equipment if you have skin lesions or dermatitis. Report the condition to your supervisor immediately.
8. Wear gowns when clothing may be soiled from a client's body fluids, blood, secretions, or excretions.
9. Clean up blood spills promptly with a 5.25% sodium hypochlorite solution diluted 1:10 with water (1 part household bleach and 10 parts water).

Hepatitis

Hepatitis is an inflammatory disease of the liver. There are different types of hepatitis.

- *Type A hepatitis* is usually spread by the fecal-oral route. Food, water, or drinking or eating vessels can be contaminated with feces. The virus is ingested when the person eats or drinks contaminated food or water. It can also be ingested when a person eats or drinks from a vessel contaminated with the virus. Causes include poor sanitation, crowded living conditions, poor nutrition, and poor hygiene practices. The disease is more common in children. You must be careful when handling bedpans, feces, and rectal thermometers.
- *Type B hepatitis* is usually transmitted by blood and sexual contact. The type B virus is present in the blood, saliva, semen, and urine of infected persons. The virus is spread by contaminated blood or blood products and by sharing needles and syringes among IV drug users.

The Signs and Symptoms of Hepatitis

Hepatitis can be mild in severity, or cause death. The signs and symptoms of hepatitis include:

- Loss of appetite
- Weakness, fatigue, exhaustion
- Nausea
- Vomiting
- Fever
- Skin rash
- Dark urine
- Jaundice (yellowish skin color)
- Light-colored stools
- Headache
- Chills
- Abdominal pain

Precautions

As with the AIDS virus, you must protect yourself and others from the hepatitis virus. The precautions outlined for AIDS apply to hepatitis.

B Equipment for Home Care

Hospital equipment is often needed for home care. Such equipment can be bought or rented. Or needed items can be made from home furnishings or supplies. Nurses, physical therapists, or occupational therapists help decide what is needed. They also help clients and families get the equipment or make changes in the home.

This appendix shows some equipment and devices that you may see when caring for clients. Others have been described and shown throughout the book.

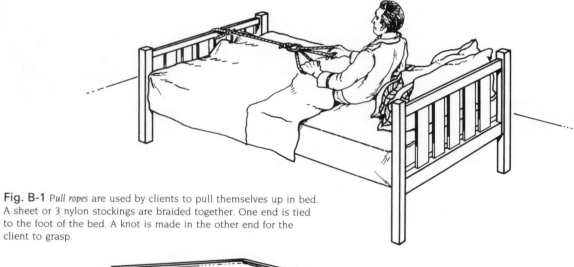

Fig. B-1 *Pull ropes* are used by clients to pull themselves up in bed. A sheet or 3 nylon stockings are braided together. One end is tied to the foot of the bed. A knot is made in the other end for the client to grasp.

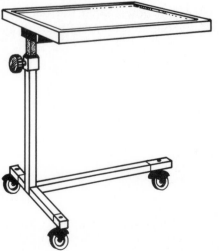

Fig. B-2 *Overbed tables* similar to the one shown can be made from household items; a cardboard box, wooden crate, or an ironing board.

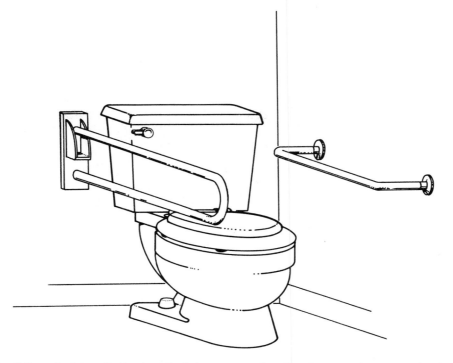

Fig. B-3 *Hand rails* installed by the toilet help promote safety. The client uses them to stand and sit.

Fig. B-4 *Raised toilet* seats are helpful for clients with mobility problems.

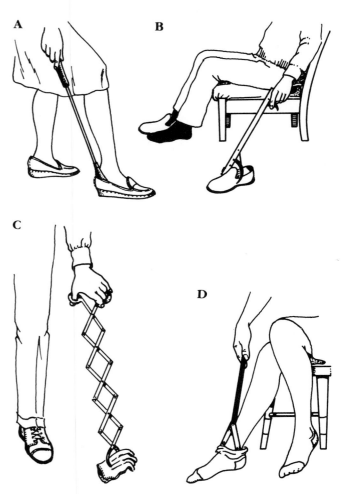

Fig. B-5 *Dressing aids.* **A,** Long-handled shoehorn. **B,** Reaching aid has jaws at the bottom. The jaws are opened and closed by a device at the top. **C,** The length of this reaching aid is adjustable. **D,** Stocking aid.

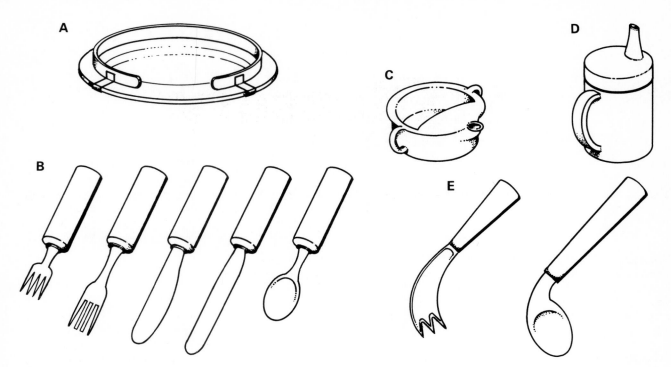

Fig. B-6 *Eating and drinking aids* are available for many types of disabilities. **A,** Plate guard. **B,** Utensils with thick handles for clients with arthritis. The thick handles are easier to hold. **C,** Feeding cup for the helpless client. **D,** Baby's feeding cup can also be used for the helpless client. **E,** Eating utensils for the client who can only use one arm. A pusher spoon and a knife and fork combined into one utensil are shown.

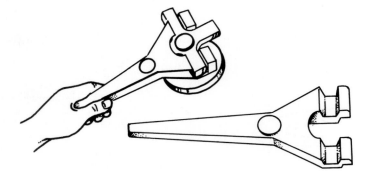

Fig. B-7 *Faucet gripper* helps wheelchair clients reach the faucet.

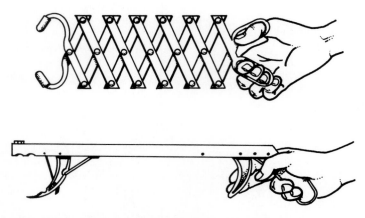

Fig. B-8 *Reaching devices* are used by clients who cannot bend or reach.

Glossary

abbreviation—A shortened word.

abdominal respirations—Abdominal muscles are used to breathe; the abdomen rises and falls rather than the chest.

abduction—Moving a body part away from the body.

Acetest—Method of testing urine for ketones or acetone.

acetone—Ketone bodies that appear in the urine due to the rapid breakdown of fat for energy.

active-assistive range of motion exercises—Exercises done by the client with the help of another person.

active range of motion exercises—Exercises done by the client.

activities of daily living—The self-care activities a person does every day.

adduction—Moving a body part toward the body.

aging—The process of growing older.

all purpose cleaner—A product used for all types of cleaning; used on walls, floors, counters, stoves, refrigerators, sinks, tubs, outside the toilet, and appliances.

allopecia—Hair loss.

alveoli—Air sacs in the lungs.

ambulation—Act of walking.

amputation—The removal of all or part of an extremity.

angina pectoris—Chest pain.

anorexia—Loss of appetite.

antiperspirant—A skin care product that reduces the amount of perspiration.

aphasia—Inability to speak.

apnea—The lack of or absence of breathing.

artery—A blood vessel that carries blood away from the heart.

arthritis—Common joint disease that involves inflammation of the joints; causes pain and swelling in the joints.

asepsis—The absence of pathogens.

aspiration—The breathing of fluid or an object into the lungs.

assault—Threatening or attempting to touch a person's body without his or her permission.

asthma—A disease in which the air passages narrow causing difficulty in breathing.

atelectasis—The collapse of a portion of the lung.

atherosclerosis—A condition in which fatty material collects on the arterial walls.

atrophy—A decrease in size or wasting away of tissue.

autopsy—The examination of the body after death.

axilla—Underarm.

axillary—Of or relating to the underarm.

base of support—Area upon which an object rests; the feet provide a base of support for the body when standing.

battery—Touching a person without his or her consent.

bed cradle—Device placed over the foot of the bed to keep top linens off the feet.

benign tumor—A tumor that grows slowly and within a localized area; benign tumors usually do not cause death.

bias—An opinion, judgment, or attitude.

binder—Cloth or elastic material that wraps around the abdomen, breast, or perineal area; used to promote comfort, prevent injury, provide support or pressure, or hold dressings in place.

bladder training—Method used to help incontinent clients regain bladder control.

bleach—Liquid or powder that removes stains and brightens fabrics; also a disinfectant.

blood and body fluid precautions—Technique used to prevent the spread of pathogens from infected body fluids.

blood pressure—The amount of force exerted against the walls of an artery by the blood.

body alignment—The way body parts are aligned with one another; posture.

body fluids—Blood, urine, feces, sputum, saliva, vomitus, semen, vaginal secretions, menstrual discharge, and respiratory secretions.

body language—Messages sent through facial expressions, gestures, and posture.

body mechanics—Using the body in an efficient and careful way.

bone marrow—The substance inside the hollow center of the bone.

bradycardia—Slow heart rate; less than 60 beats per minute.

bradypnea—Slow breathing; usually less than 10 respirations per minute.

Braille—A method of writing that uses raised dots to represent each letter of the alphabet.

brainstem—Part of the brain that controls heart rate, breathing, the size of blood vessels, swallowing, coughing, and vomiting.

bronchietasis—A disorder of the lungs; the bronchi enlarge and collect pus.

calculi—Stones.

call bell—A device used to signal for help.

calorie—The amount of energy produced when food is broken down for use.

capillary—A tiny blood vessel; food, oxygen, and other substances pass from the capillaries to the cells.

carbohydrate—A nutrient that gives the body energy and fiber for bowel elimination. One gram provides four calories.

cardiac arrest—The sudden stoppage of breathing and heart action.

cardiopulmonary resuscitation (CPR)—A procedure to help restore heart action and breathing.

care plan—A written plan that lists the client's problems and goals and activities to improve the client's condition.

cataract—A disorder of the eye; the lens becomes cloudy (opaque).

catheter—A rubber or plastic tube that drains or injects fluid through a body opening.

catheterization—The process of inserting a catheter.

cell—The basic unit of the body.

Centigrade; Celsius (C)—A scale used to measure temperature; human body temperatures range from 34°C to 42°C.

cerebellum—The part of the brain that regulates and coordinates body movements.

cerebrospinal fluid—Fluid in the brain that protects the structures of the brain and spinal cord.

cerebrovascular accident—*See* stroke.

cerebrum—The largest part of the brain that controls thought and intelligence.

chemotherapy—A type of drug therapy that kills and controls the growth of cancer cells.

Cheyne-Stokes—A breathing pattern in which respirations gradually increase in rate and depth and then become shallow and slow; breathing may stop for 10 to 20 seconds.

circumcision—The surgical removal of foreskin from the penis.

clean-catch urine specimen—Urine is collected before it is contaminated outside the body; midstream or clean-voided specimen.

clean technique—Medical asepsis.

cleanser—A product used for hard-to-clean surfaces such as sinks, tubs, and toilets.

cliche—A pat answer or common expression.

client record—The written account of a client's care.

Clinitest—A method of testing urine for sugar.

closed fracture—A fracture in which the bone is broken but the skin is intact; a simple fracture.

closed reduction—Bringing the bones back into place without opening the skin.

colostomy—An artificial opening between the colon and abdomen; feces are eliminated through the opening.

coma—A state of being completely unaware of one's surroundings.

communicable disease—A disease caused by pathogens that are spread easily; a contagious disease.

communication—The giving and receiving of information by two or more people.

compound fracture—An open fracture; the broken bone has come through the skin.

confidentiality—Keeping the information about a client private.

congestive heart failure (CHF)—A heart condition in which the heart cannot pump blood normally; blood backs up and causes congestion in the tissues.

constipation—The passage of hard, dry stool.

constrict—To narrow.

contagious disease—A communicable disease.

contamination—An object or area becomes unclean.

contracture—The abnormal shortening of a muscle.

convulsion—Violent and sudden contractions or tremors of muscles; seizure.

COPD; Chronic obstructive pulmonary disease—A group of disorders that interfere with the normal exchange of oxygen and carbon dioxide in the lungs.

coronary artery disease (CAD)—A heart disease in which the coronary arteries narrow restricting blood flow to the heart.

coroner—A public official responsible for investigating the cause of death.

culture—Values, beliefs and customs that are passed down from one generation to the next.

dangle—To sit on the side of the bed.

decubitus ulcers—An area where the skin and tissues are broken down due to a lack of blood flow to the part because of pressure; pressure sore or bedsore.

defecation—The process of excreting feces from the rectum through the anus; bowel movement.

dehydration—A decrease in the amount of water in body tissues.

deodorant—A preparation that masks and controls body odors.

dermis—The inner layer of skin that contains blood vessels, nerves, hair roots, oil glands, and sweat glands.

detergent—A cleaning agent used for laundry and dishwashing.

diabetes mellitus—A chronic disease in which the pancreas fails to secrete enough insulin; the body is prevented from using sugar for energy.

diagnostic related group (DRG)—A method of paying hospitals for the care of medicare and medicaid clients.

diarrhea—The frequent passage of liquid stools.

diastolic pressure—The pressure in the arteries when the heart is relaxing and filling with blood.

diet therapy—*See* therapeutic diet.

digestion—The process of physically and chemically breaking down food so it can be absorbed for use by the cells of the body.

dilate—To expand or open wider.

disability—Permanent loss of a physical or mental function.

discharge planner—A person who helps the client plan for care after the hospital; arranges for needed services such as home care, medical supplies, meals, counseling, and transportation.

disinfection—Process of killing pathogens.

documentation—The written account of specific activities, events, or observations; recording or charting.

dorsal recumbent position—The back-lying or supine position.

dorsiflexion—Bending backward.

dose—The amount of medication to be taken.

drainage and secretion precautions—Technique used to prevent the spread of pathogens found in wounds and wound drainage.

drawsheet—A sheet placed over the middle of the bottom sheet; protects the mattress and bottom linens or can be used to move clients in bed.

dressing—Gauze bandages that cover a wound.

dysphagia—Difficulty or discomfort in swallowing.

dyspnea—Difficult, labored, or painful breathing.

edema—Swelling of body tissues with water.

embolus—A blood clot that travels through the bloodstream until it lodges in a distant blood vessel.

emesis—Vomit.

emphysema—A respiratory disorder in which air is trapped in the enlarged alveoli; affects the normal exchange of oxygen and carbon dioxide in the lungs.

endocrine glands—Glands that secrete hormones to regulate the activities of other organs and glands in the body.

endometrium—The lining of the uterus.

enema—The introduction of fluid into the rectum and lower colon.

enteric precautions—Technique used to prevent the spread of pathogens through feces.

epidermis—The outer layer of skin.

epiglottis—A flap over the larynx that prevents food from entering the airway during swallowing.

esophagus—A long tube that carries food from the back of the throat to the stomach.

esteem—Worth and value.

ethics—Standards for behavior; deals with right and wrong.

eustachian tube—Tube that connects the middle ear and the throat.

exchanges—Groups of foods equal in nutrients and calories that are used to plan diabetic menus; foods are chosen from six categories including milk, vegetables, fruits, breads, meat foods, and fat.

exhalation—Breathing air in and out of the lungs.

extended family—The nuclear family plus grandparents, aunts, uncles, and cousins.

extension—Straightening a body part.

external rotation—Turning the joint outward.

fainting—A sudden loss of consciousness due to an inadequate blood supply to the brain.

fabric softener—A liquid or powder that takes the stiffness out of fabric and creates a feeling of freshness.

face mask—An oxygen mask that covers the nose and mouth.

Fahrenheit (F)—A scale used to measure temperature; human body temperatures range from 94°F to 104°F.

false imprisonment—Restricting a person's movements without consent.

fat—A nutrient that gives the body energy, helps the body use certain vitamins, conserves body heat, and protects body organs from injury; one gram provides nine calories.

fecal impaction—The prolonged retention and accumulation of fecal material in the rectum and lower colon.

fecal incontinence—The inability to control the passage of feces and gas through the anus; anal incontinence.

feces—The semisolid mass of waste products in the colon.

feedback—Verbal or nonverbal way to tell if the sender and receiver understand a word or idea in the same way.

first aid—Emergency care given to an ill or injured person before medical help arrives.

flatulance—The excessive formation of gas in the stomach and intestines.

flatus—Gas or air in the stomach or intestines.

flexion—Bending a body part.

Foley catheter—A catheter that is left in the urinary bladder so that urine drains continuously into a collection bag; a retention or indwelling catheter.

footdrop—Plantar flexion.

Fowler's position—A semi-sitting position; the head of the bed is raised 45 to 60 degrees.

fracture—A broken bone.

fresh-fractional urine specimen—Two urine specimens are obtained 30 minutes apart and the second sample is tested for sugar; double-voided specimen.

friction—The rubbing of one surface against another.

gait belt—A transfer belt.

gangrene—A condition in which there is death of tissue; tissues become black, cold, and shriveled.

gastrostomy tube—A feeding tube surgically inserted directly into the stomach.

glaucoma—A disease of the eye; increased pressure in the eye causing visual loss and eventual blindness.

glucosuria—Sugar in the urine.

graduate—A measuring cup or container used to measure fluids.

grand mal seizure—Contraction of all muscles at once followed by jerking movements of the body.

ground—That which carries leaking electricity to the earth away from the electrical appliance.

health maintenance organization (HMO)—A prepaid group insurance plan that provides a wide range of services to meet a client's total health care needs.

Heimlich maneuver—A procedure to relieve an obstructed airway involving abdominal thrusts.

hemiparesis—Weakness on one side of the body.

hemiplegia—Paralysis on one side of the body.

hemoglobin—The substance in red blood cells that gives blood its color; hemoglobin carries oxygen in the blood.

hemorrhage—Excessive loss of blood from a blood vessel.

hip pinning—Surgical procedure for hip fractures in which a pin is used to fix the fracture in place.

home health aide (HHA)—A health worker who provides personal care, comfort, and housekeeping services; certification or completion of a course is required in some states.

homebound—Confined to the home.

homemaker—A health care worker who provides homemaker services.

homemaker services—A program that helps families maintain the home.

hormone—A chemical substance secreted by the glands into the bloodstream.

hospice—A program for persons dying of terminal illness.

host—A place where microorganisms live and grow; a person, animal, food, water, plants, soil or other material.

hyperextension—Excessive straightening of a body part.

hypertension—Persistent blood pressure measurements above the normal systolic (150 mm Hg) or diastolic (90 mm Hg) pressures.

hyperventilation—Respirations are rapid and deep.

hypotension—A condition in which the systolic pressure is below 100 mm Hg and the diastolic pressure is below 60 mm Hg.

hypoventilation—Respirations are slow, shallow and sometimes irregular.

ileostomy—An artificial opening between the ileum (small intestine) and the abdomen.

incident—An accident or unusual occurrence.

indwelling catheter—Foley catheter or retention catheter.

infection—A disease that results when microorganisms invade and grow in the body; signs include fever, redness, increased drainage, foul odor, increased pain in the area.

inhalation—Breathing air into the lungs.

intake—The amount of fluid taken in by the body.

integumentary system—The skin, nails, and hair.

internal rotation—Turning the joint inward.

intramuscular—Into a muscle.

intravenous therapy—Fluid given through a needle into a vein; IV or IV infusion.

involved side—The side that does not function well due to weakness, paralysis or injury; impaired side, affected side, or weak side.

isolation techniques—Measures taken to prevent the spread of pathogenic microorganisms from one area to another.

Keto-Diastix—Test for sugar in the urine; a thin plastic strip has two test areas at the bottom that changes color when sugar is present.

ketone body—Acetone.

larynx—The voice box.

lateral position—The side-lying position.

living will—A statement expressing a person's desire not to have life prolonged by artificial means or heroic measures.

malignant tumor—A tumor that grows rapidly and invades other tissues; malignant tumors cause death without treatment.

mechanical ventilator—A machine that helps a person breathe.

Medicaid—A health insurance plan for the poor, elderly, blind, and disabled and for families with dependent children; sponsored by the federal and state governments.

medical asepsis—The techniques and practices used to prevent the spread of pathogens from one person or place to another person or place; clean technique.

Medicare—A federaly funded health insurance program for the elderly.

medication—A chemical substance used to treat disease; a drug.

menarche—The first menstrual period.

meninges—Protective covering over the brain and spinal cord.

menopause—When menstruation stops.

menstruation—The process in which the endometrium in the uterus breaks up and is discharged from the body through the vagina.

metabolism—The burning of food for heat and energy by the cells.

metastasis—The spread of cancer to other parts of the body.

microorganism—A small living plant or animal that cannot be seen without a microscope; a microbe.

micturation—The process of emptying the bladder; urination or voiding.

mid-stream urine specimen—Clean-catch urine specimen.

mitered corner—A way of tucking linens under the mattress to help keep the linens straight and smooth.

mobility—The ability to move about.

multiple sclerosis—A progressive disease in which the myelin sheath, the spinal cord, and white matter of the brain are destroyed.

myocardial infarction—A heart attack.

nasal cannula—A two-pronged device that delivers oxygen; the prongs are inserted a short distance into the nostrils.

need—That which is required or desirable for life and mental well-being.

negligence—The unintentional harming of another person or his or her property.

nitroglycerin—A medication that relieves the chest pain of angina pectoris; is placed under the tongue where it disolves and is absorbed into the bloodstream.

nonpathogen—A microorganism that does not usually cause an infection.

nonverbal communication—The sending of messages without using words.

nuclear family—Mother, father, and children who live together.

nutrient—A substance that is ingested, digested, absorbed, and used by the body.

nutrition—The many processes involved in eating, digesting, absorbing, and using foods and fluids.

objective recording—Charting what you see, hear, feel and smell.

obstructed airway—Chocking; blockage of the airway passages to the lungs.

open dating—Date on a food package that indicates the last day the package can be sold by a store.

open reduction—Surgical procedure in which nails, pins, screws, metal plates, or wires are used to keep the bone in place.

oral hygiene—Mouth care; keeps the mouth and teeth clean.

organ—Groups of tissues with the same function.

orthopnea—A person must sit to breath comfortably.

osteoporosis—A bone disorder in which the bones become porous and brittle.

ostomy—A surgical creation of an artificial opening.

output—The fluid lost from the body.

ovary—The female sex gland.

over-the-counter (OTC) drugs—Medications that can be bought without a doctor's order.

oxygen—A tasteless, odorless, and colorless gas.

Parkinson's Disease—A slow, progressive disease affecting the brain.

paralysis—The loss of muscle function or sensation in a body part.

paraplegic—A person who is paralyzed from the waist down.

parenteral nutrition—Intravenous feeding containing all the essential nutrients; total parrenteral nutrition (TPN) or hyperalimentation.

passive range-of-motion exercises—Another person moves the joints through their range-of-motion.

pathogen—A microorganism that is harmful and able to cause an infection.

pericare—Perineal care.

perineal care—Cleansing the genital and anal areas of the body; pericare.

peristalsis—Involuntary muscle contractions in the digestive system.

petit mal seizure—A seizure that usually lasts 20 to 30 seconds; there is a sudden loss of consciousness, twitching of the arm and face muscles, and flickering of the eyelids.

phantom limb pain—Sensation of pain in an amputated part.

pharynx—The throat.

plan of treatment—A written plan that describes the client's home care; the plan must be signed by a doctor.

plantar flexion—The foot (plantar) is bent (flexion); footdrop.

plasma—Fluid portion of the blood that carries blood cells, food, hormones, chemicals, and waste products to body cells.

platelets—Blood cells needed for blood clotting.

pneumonia—Inflammation of the lungs.

poison—A substance that can harm body tissue or cause death.

policy and procedure manual—A manual that describes how the agency operates and how procedures are to be done.

postmortem—After (post) death (mortem).

postoperative—After the surgery or operation.

posture—The way in which body parts are aligned with one another; body alignment.

prefix—A word element placed at the beginning of a word.

preoperative—Before the operation or surgery.

prepoured medications—Drugs are measured into special labeled containers with compartments by the nurse, pharmacist, or family member.

prescription drugs—Drugs that require a doctor's order; the prescription is filled by a pharmacist.

pronation—Turning downward.

prone position—Positioned on the abdomen.

prosthesis—An artificial replacement for a missing body part.

protein—Nutrient needed for tissue growth and repair; one gram provides four calories.

puberty—When reproductive organs begin to function and secondary sex characteristics appear.

pulmonary embolus—Blood clot from a vein that lodges in the lungs; may cause severe respiratory problems and death.

pulse—The beat of the heart felt at an artery; the beat is produced as a wave of blood passes through an artery.

pulse deficit—The difference between the apical pulse rate and the radial pulse rate.

pulse rate—The number of heartbeats or pulses felt in one minute.

quadriplegic—A person who is paralyzed from the neck down; function of the arms, trunk, and legs is lost.

ratiotherapy—Treatment using x-rays to kill and control the growth of cancer cells.

random urine specimen—Urine specimen that is collected whenever the person can void; routine urine.

range-of-motion—Movement of a joint to the extent possible without causing pain.

rehabilitation—The process of restoring the disabled individual to the highest level of physical, psychological, social, and economic functioning possible.

reincarnation—The belief that the spirit or soul is reborn in another human body or in another form of life.

reservoir—A place where pathogens can grow and multiply.

respiration—The process of supplying the cells with oxygen and removing carbon dioxide from them; breathing air in and out of the lungs.

respiratory arrest—Breathing stops but the heart continues to pump for several minutes.

respirtory isolation—Technique used to prevent the spread of pathogens through the air.

retina—Inner layer of the eye that contains the nerves for vision.

rheumatoid arthritis—A chronic disease that causes inflamation of the joints, heart, lungs, eyes, kidneys, and skin.

rigor mortis—The stiffness or rigidity (rigor) of skeletal muscles that occurs after death (mortis).

root—The main part of a word.

rooting reflex—A baby turns his or head in the direction of a stimulus.

rotation—Turning a joint.

routine urine specimen—Random urine specimen.

sclera—The white outer layer of the eye.

scultetus binder—An abdominal binder that is rectangular in shape with tails on each side; the tails overlap to provide support after abdominal surgery.

seizure—A convulsion.

self-esteem—When a person thinks he or she is a worthwhile and valuable person.

semi-Fowler's position—The head of the bed is raised 45 degrees and the knee portion is raised 15 degrees; or the level of the bed is elevated 30 degrees.

sex—The physical activities involving the organs of reproduction; the activities are done for pleasure or to have children.

sexuality—That which relates to one's sex; those physical, psychological, social, cultural, and spiritual factors which affect a person's feelings and attitudes about his or her sex.

shock—A condition that results when there is an inadequate blood supply to the organs and tissues of the body.

side effects—A harmful reaction to a medication.

sign—An observed change in a client's condition; something that you can see, hear, feel or smell.

Sim's position—A side-lying position; the upper leg is sharply flexed so it is not on the lower leg and the lower arm is behind the person.

sitz bath—The pelvic area is immersed in hot water for 20 minutes.

specialty cleaner—A product used for certain surfaces and cleaning problems; there are specialty cleaners for windows, laundry stains, toilet bowls, and ovens.

sphygomanometer—Instrument used to measure blood pressure.

sputum—Mucus secreted by the lungs, bronchi, and trachea during respiratory illnesses or disorders.

sterilization—The process by which all microorganisms are destroyed.

sterile—The absence of all microorganisms both pathogenic and nonpathogenic.

stethoscope—An instrument used to listen to the heart and other body sounds.

stoma—An artificial opening in the skin created by surgery.

stomatitis—Inflammation of the mouth.

stool—Feces that have been excreted.

strict isolation—Technique used to prevent the spread of communicable diseases through direct contact or air.

stroke—A cerebral vascular accident; the blood supply to a part of the brain is suddenly interrupted.

subcutaneous—Layer under the skin.

subjective recording—Charting what the client tells you.

sublingual—Under the tongue.

suffix—A word element placed at the end of a word.

suffocation—The stopping of breathing that results from a lack of oxygen.

supination—Turning upward.

supine position—The back-lying or dorsal recumbent position.

suppository—A cone-shaped solid medication that is inserted into a body opening; it melts at body temperature.

symptom—Something a person feels that you cannot see, hear, feel, or smell.

system—Organs that work together to perform special functions.

systolic pressure—The pressure in the arteries when the heart is contracting.

T-binder—A type of binder used to secure dressings in place after rectal or perineal surgery.

tachypnea—Rapid breathing; respirations are usually greater than 24 breaths per minute.

temperature—The amount of heat in the body.

terminal illness—An illness or injury from which a person is not expected to recover.

Testape—A strip of special tape used to test the urine for sugar.

testes (testicles)—Male sex glands; gonads.

therapeutic diet—A special diet ordered by the doctor because of a nutritional deficiency, disease, or to eliminate or decrease certain substances in the diet; diet therapy.

thrombus—A blood clot.

tissue—Groups of cells with the same function.

topical medication—A medication applied directly to the skin.

trachea—The windpipe.

transfer belt—A belt used to hold onto a person during a transfer or when walking; a gait belt.

Trendelenburg's position—The head of the bed is lowered and the foot is raised.

trochanter roll—Support device used to prevent the hip and leg from turning outward (external rotation).

tube feeding—A method of feeding a person through a plastic or rubber tube; the tube is inserted through the nose or a surgical opening in the abdomen; the tube extends to the stomach.

24-hour urine specimen—A collection of all urine voided over a 24 hour period.

tumor—A new growth of cells; a tumor can be benign or malignant.

tympanic membrane—The eardrum.

umbilical cord—The structure that carries blood, oxygen, and nutrients from the mother to the fetus.

uninvolved side—The side of the body that is functioning properly; the strong side.

ureter—Tube that carries urine from the kidneys to the bladder.

urethra—Tube that carries urine from the bladder to the outside of body.

urinary incontinence—The inability to control urination.

urination—The process of emptying the bladder; micturation or voiding.

unit pricing—Label that indicates the cost per weight or volume of a food product.

vein—A blood vessel that carries blood back to the heart.

verbal communication—Using words and language to communicate.

vital signs—Temperature, pulse, respirations, and blood pressure.

vitamin—Nutrient that cannot be produced by the body and must be ingested through food; needed for specific body functions.

vomiting—The act of expelling stomach contents through the mouth.

will—A legal document that states what should be done with money and property after a person's death.

wound—An area in which the skin and underlying tissues are damaged.

Index